anatomy for artists

drawing form & pose

The ultimate guide to drawing anatomy in perspective and pose with **tomfoxdraws**

3dtotal Publishing

Correspondence: **publishing@3dtotal.com**
Website: **store.3dtotal.com**

First published in the United Kingdom, 2022, by 3dtotal Publishing.

Reprinted in 2025 by 3dtotal Publishing.

Address: 3dtotal.com Ltd,
29 Foregate Street, Worcester,
WR1 1DS, United Kingdom.

Soft cover ISBN: 978-1-912843-42-8
Printed and bound in Shanghai,
China by KS Printing.

Visit **store.3dtotal.com** for a complete list of available book titles.

Managing Director: Tom Greenway
Studio Manager: Simon Morse
Lead Designer: Fiona Tarbet
Lead Editor: Jenny Fox-Proverbs
Editor: Marisa Lewis
Designer: Matthew Lewis

Cover images © Tom Fox

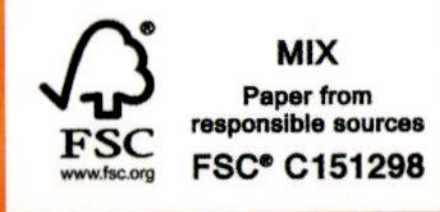

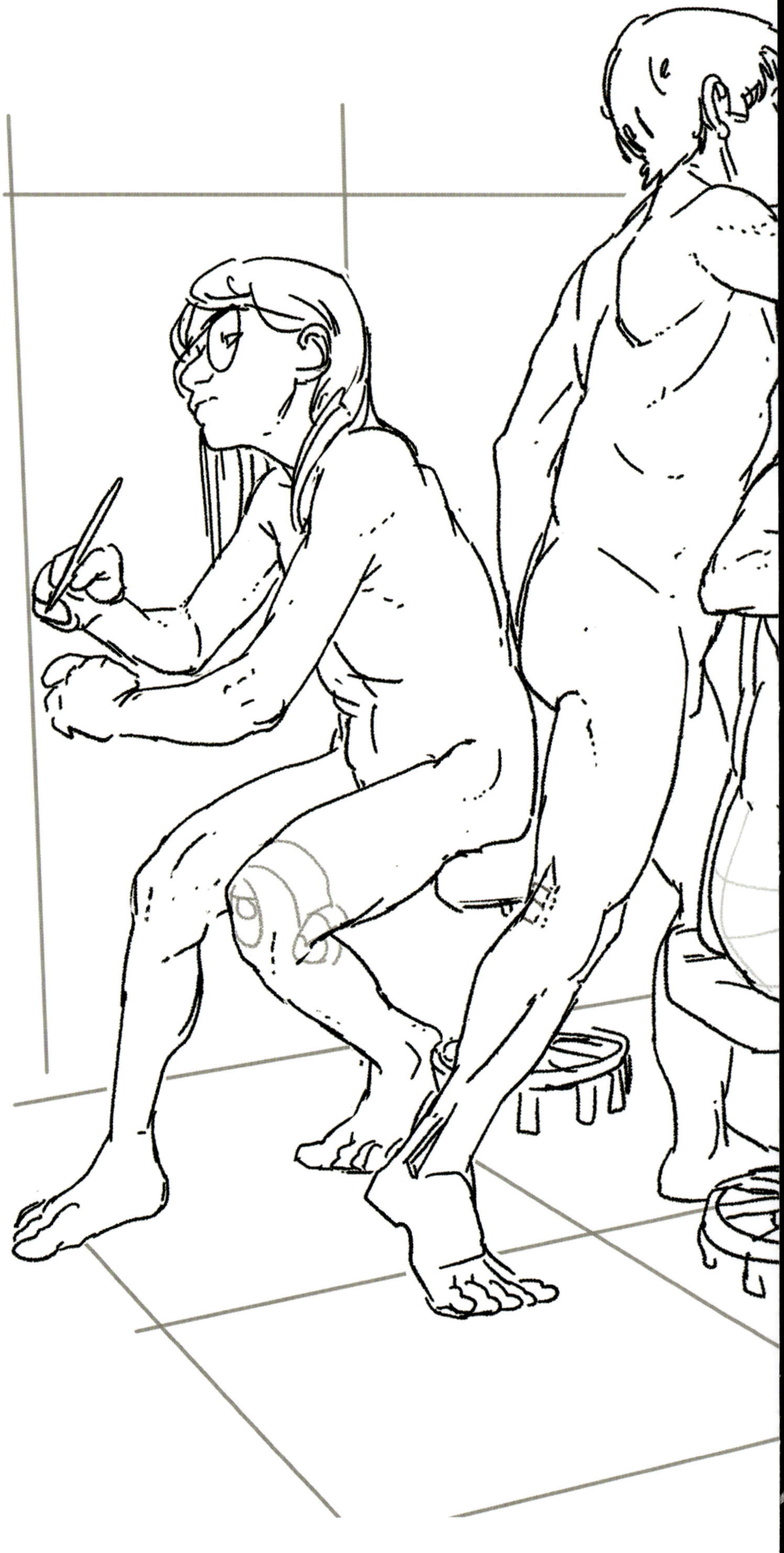

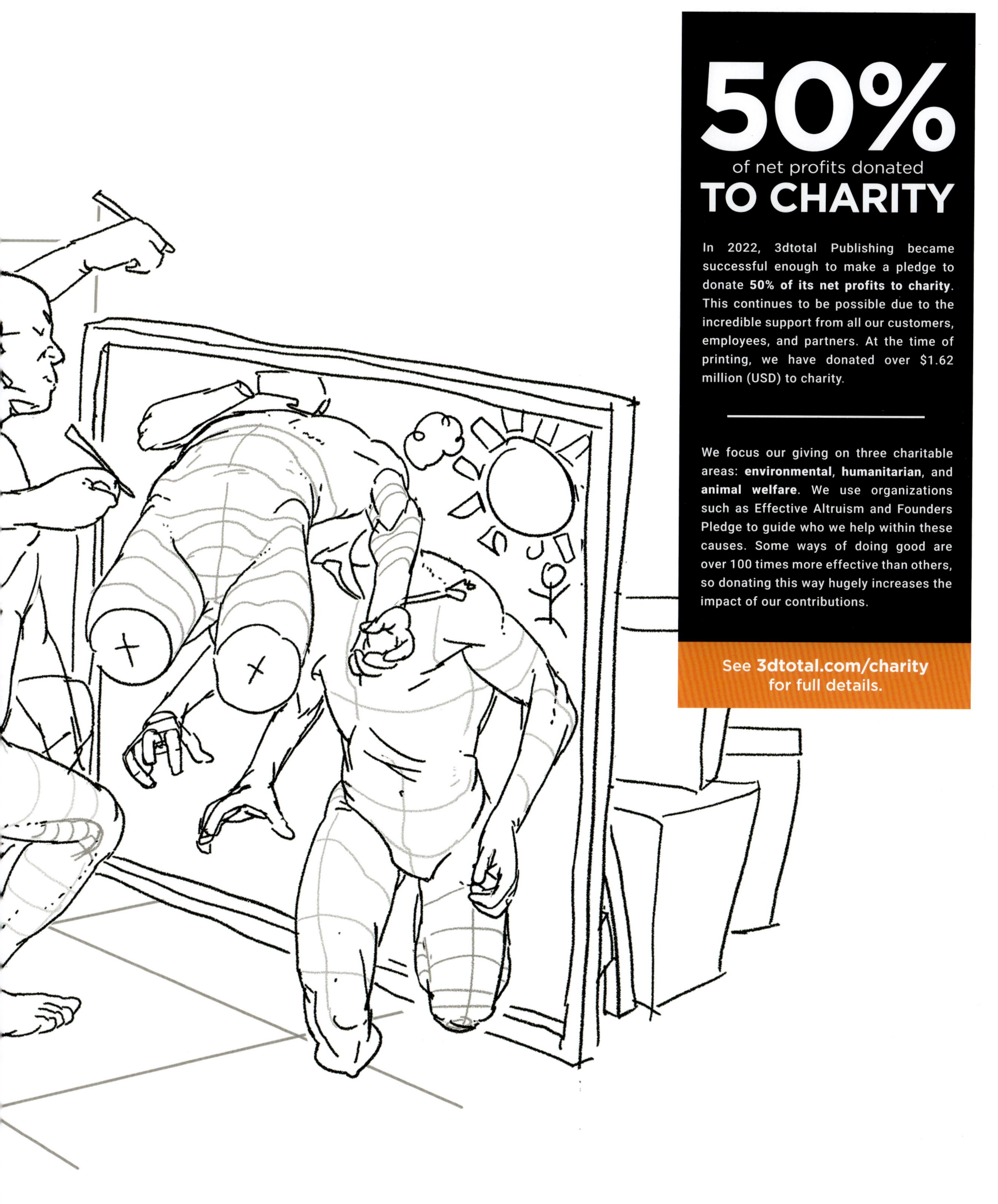
50%
of net profits donated
TO CHARITY
In 2022, 3dtotal Publishing became successful enough to make a pledge to donate 50% of its net profits to charity. This continues to be possible due to the incredible support from all our customers, employees, and partners. At the time of printing, we have donated over $1.62 million (USD) to charity.
We focus our giving on three charitable areas: environmental, humanitarian, and animal welfare. We use organizations such as Effective Altruism and Founders Pledge to guide who we help within these causes. Some ways of doing good are over 100 times more effective than others, so donating this way hugely increases the impact of our contributions.
See 3dtotal.com/charity for full details.

contents

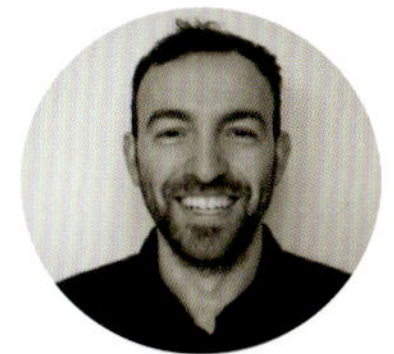

hello, i'm tom

You might know me as tomfoxdraws. I'm a figure-drawing instructor and storyboard artist who's worked in the animation industry, and now for myself, for around ten years. I believe drawing doesn't need to be complicated, and you can reduce even the most complex subjects, like perspective or anatomy, into manageable chunks to study. I focus on simplifying the form and seeing through the details to the basic building blocks underneath. I've had great feedback from students in the past about this, and it's an amazing feeling to help others progress, and even see students go on to become fantastic artists years later.

I learned almost everything I know through self-study online, by attending short courses, and by studying books. When I was at school, I never drew and had no interest in it! It wasn't that I didn't like art - I was just interested in other things at the time. I loved animals and being outdoors, so, after college, I did some traveling before going to university to study zoology. In the final term of my last year, I felt frustrated with how few practical skills I had relating to zoology.

That's when I read a book called *Outliers* by Malcolm Gladwell. It said that you had to do around 10,000 hours of study to become "international standard" at a skill. So, that same day, I wrote a list of potential skills I would be interested in learning. I considered the limiting factors, like the expense, access, and time needed. In the end, I chose drawing because it was affordable, there are many resources online, it's physically easy to practice, and I thought it could lead to multiple different career paths. That's how I began my journey to 10,000 hours of drawing.

I started drawing on that same day, 28 March 2010, and I haven't looked back. Around five years later, I was good enough to work professionally, and now over ten years later, I'm able to work for myself as a freelance artist and instructor. I've clocked up well over 20,000 hours by now, so that original goal was met a long time ago!

My work these days revolves around teaching drawing and anatomy online. When I'm not traveling with my partner, I record my studies and share time-lapses on TikTok, Instagram, and Twitter under the name tomfoxdraws. I'm fortunate and feel very grateful to do what I do for a living. I hope you enjoy reading and learning from this book as much as I enjoyed making it.

tom fox

throughout this book, images are labeled with letters to help you follow them alongside the text

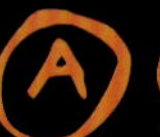

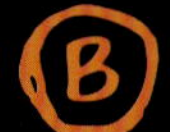

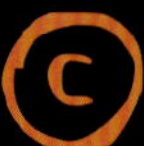

important sequences of smaller details are highlighted with numbers!

1 2 3

this book will always try to simplify and refer to forms rather than names where possible. if you're not sure, you can always check the glossary!

key skills

xyz space & form

simplification

All things can be divided into cube forms. This is the basis of understanding 3D space. No matter how complex a subject seems, it can always be simplified further. Simplification and learning to "see" these forms is a skill we are training in this book.

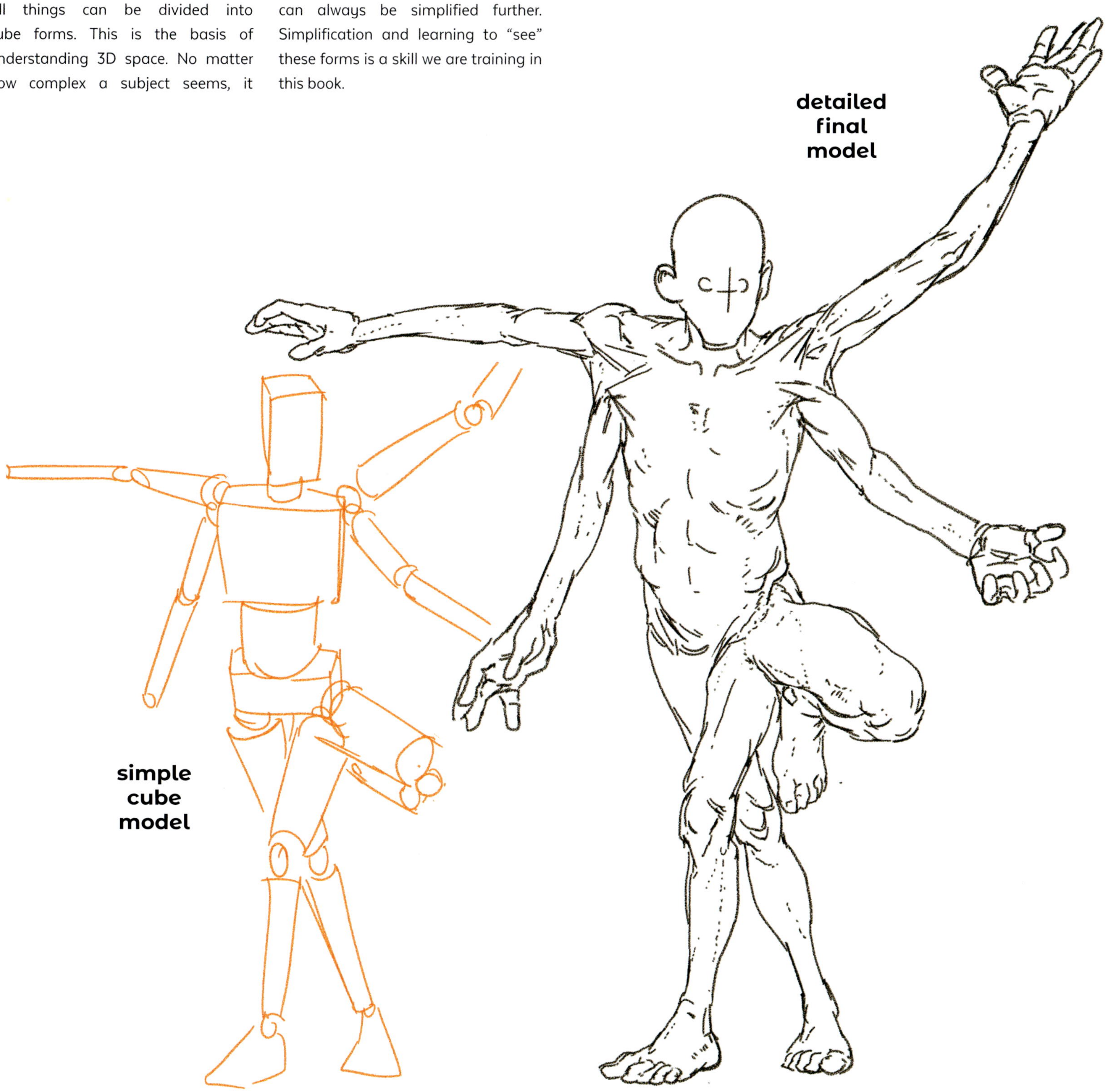

detailed final model

simple cube model

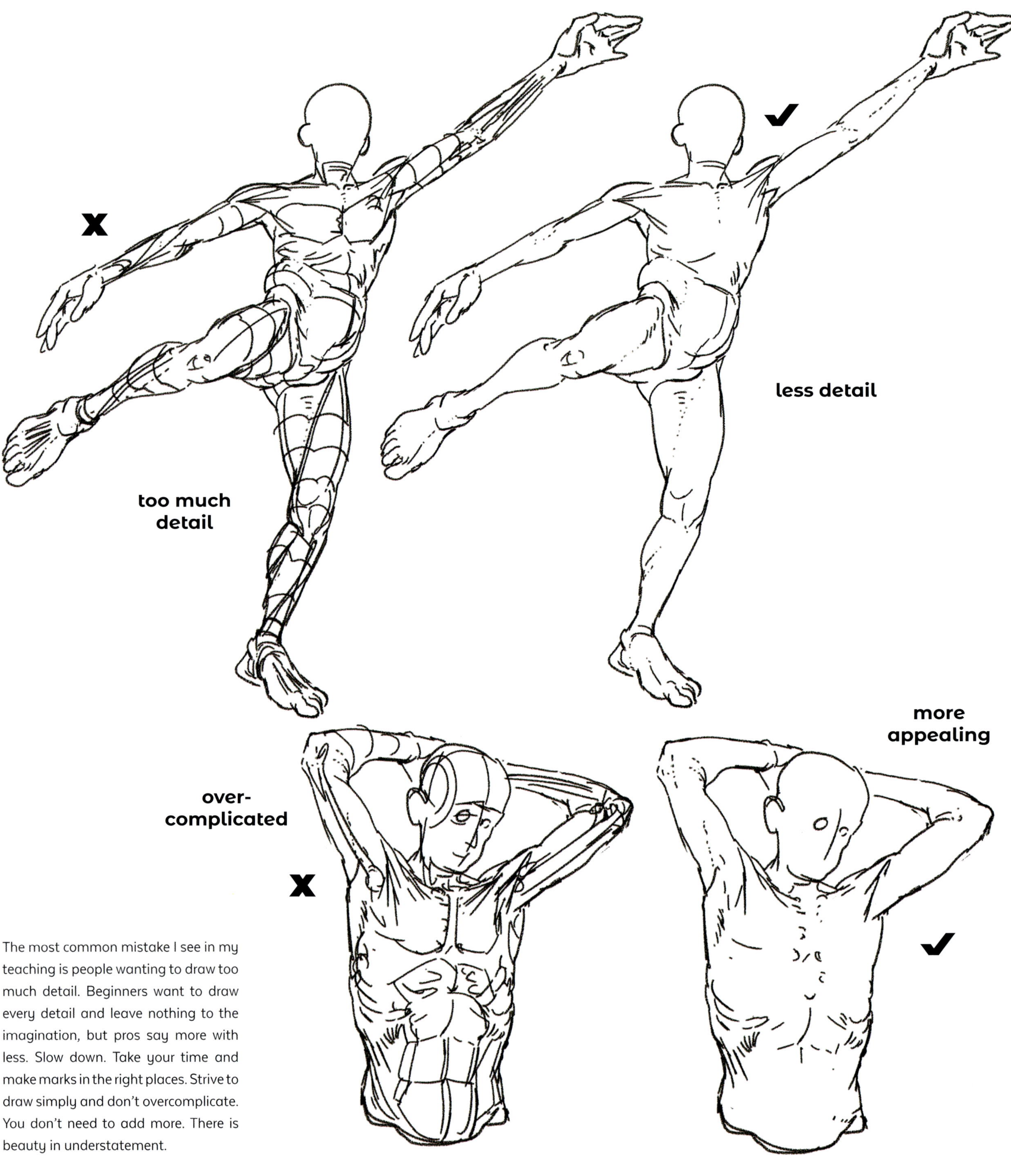

The most common mistake I see in my teaching is people wanting to draw too much detail. Beginners want to draw every detail and leave nothing to the imagination, but pros say more with less. Slow down. Take your time and make marks in the right places. Strive to draw simply and don't overcomplicate. You don't need to add more. There is beauty in understatement.

Remind yourself: More lines isn't always better. More lines doesn't mean your work has more "form." When we say "form" we mean the feeling the viewer has that the subject is physical and 3D. Beginners are unconfident in their decisions, if they're making any, and it shows in their linework, often with multiple lines without clear choices and confidence.

complex line art doesn't make a better drawing

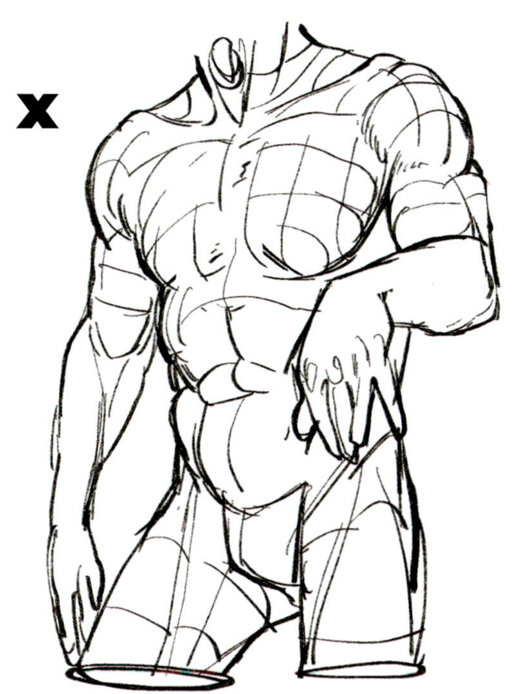

studying basic forms is more important

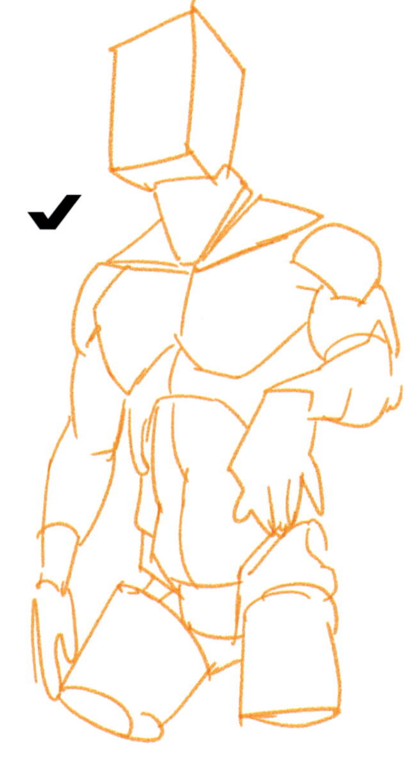

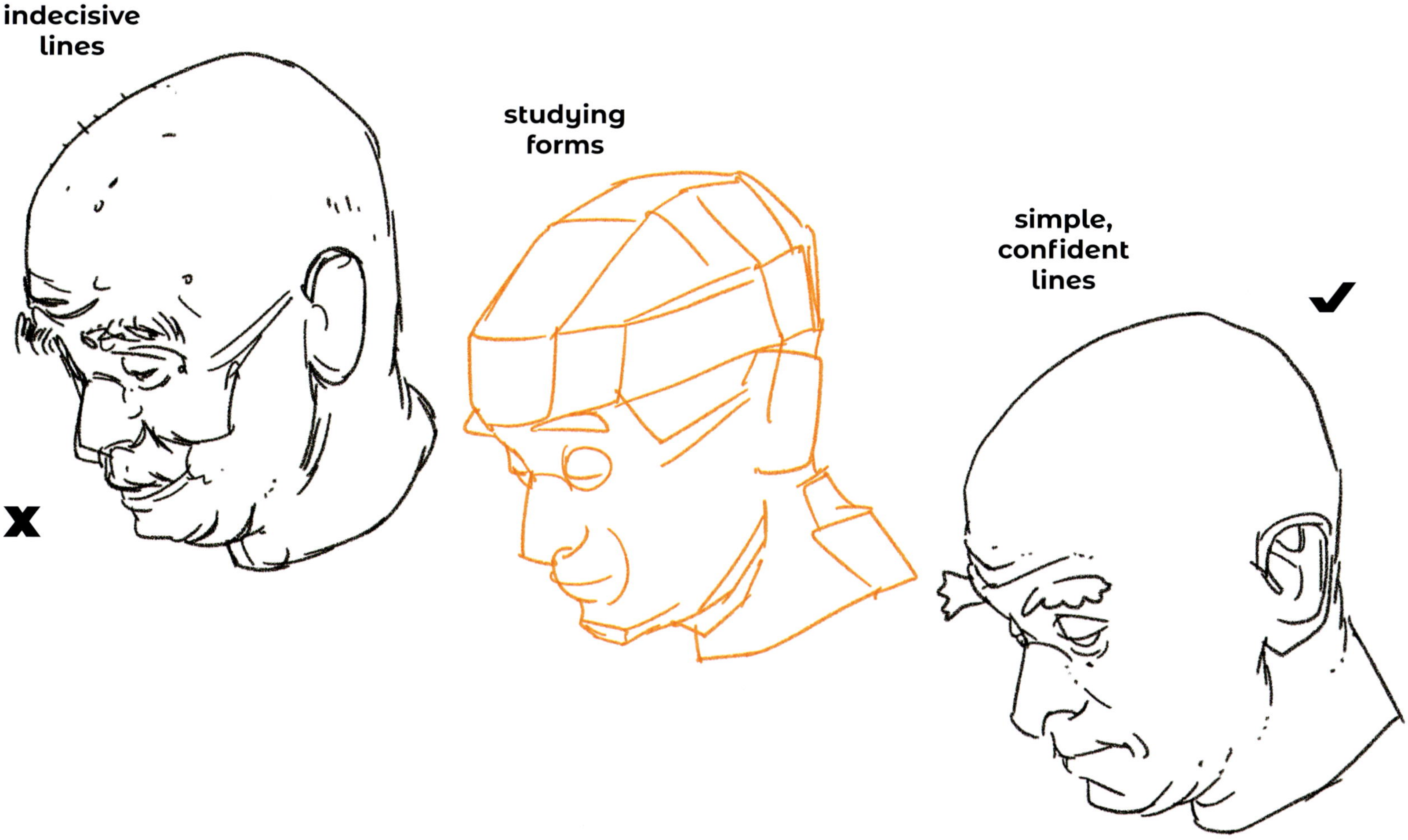

indecisive lines

studying forms

simple, confident lines

x, y & z

The world around us is a 3D space, and every object exists in it. Every object we see conforms to these three dimensions: width, height, and depth. We can call these the X, Y, and Z dimensions. This is true for simple forms as well as for something as complex as the human figure. Not only single objects, but whole scenes fit within these dimensions. Try to imagine each object sitting within its own cube form.

As a side note, you'll notice throughout this book that I draw overly large hands and feet. This is intentional, firstly because it's fun, and secondly because it's easier to learn from!

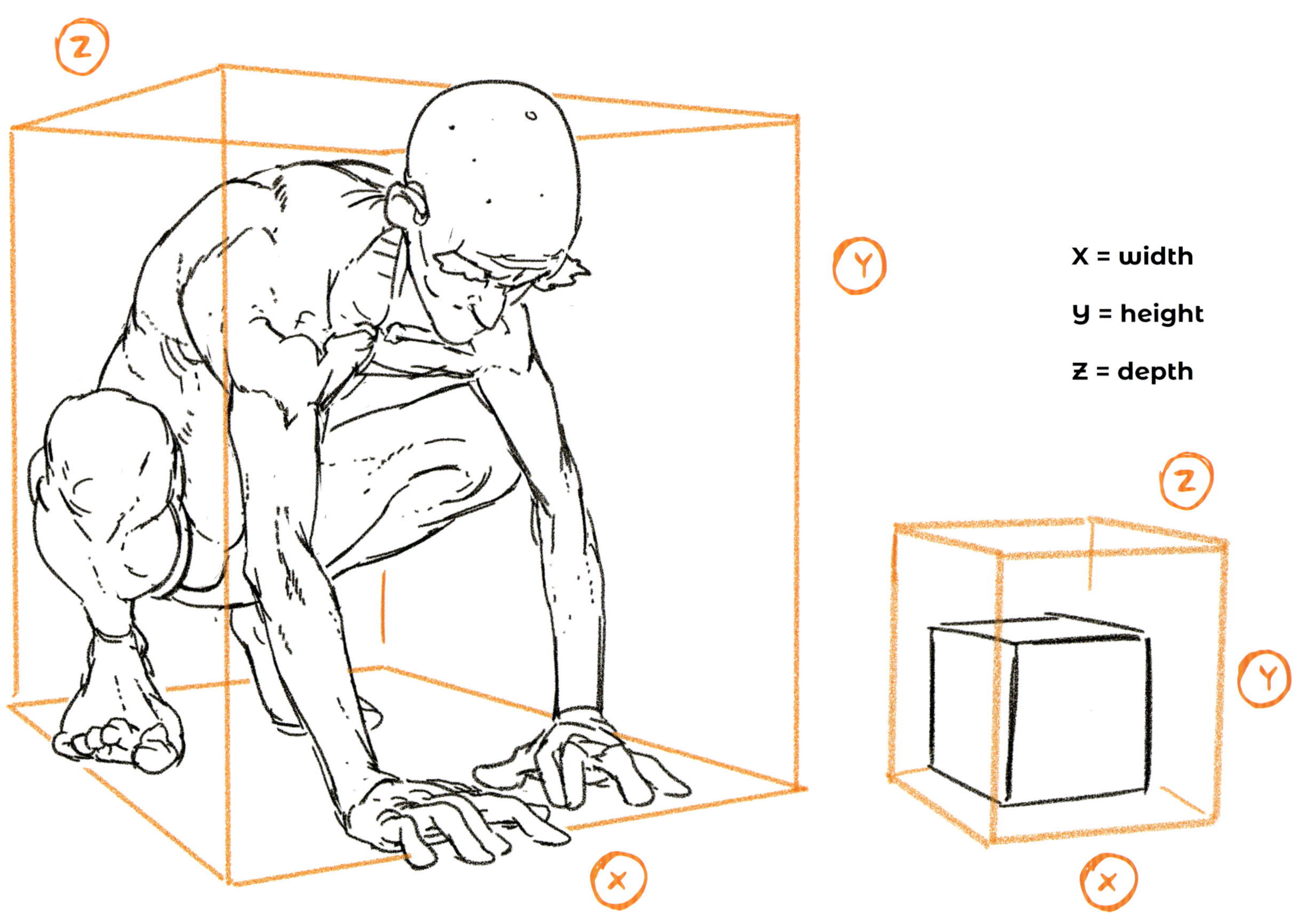

X = width

Y = height

Z = depth

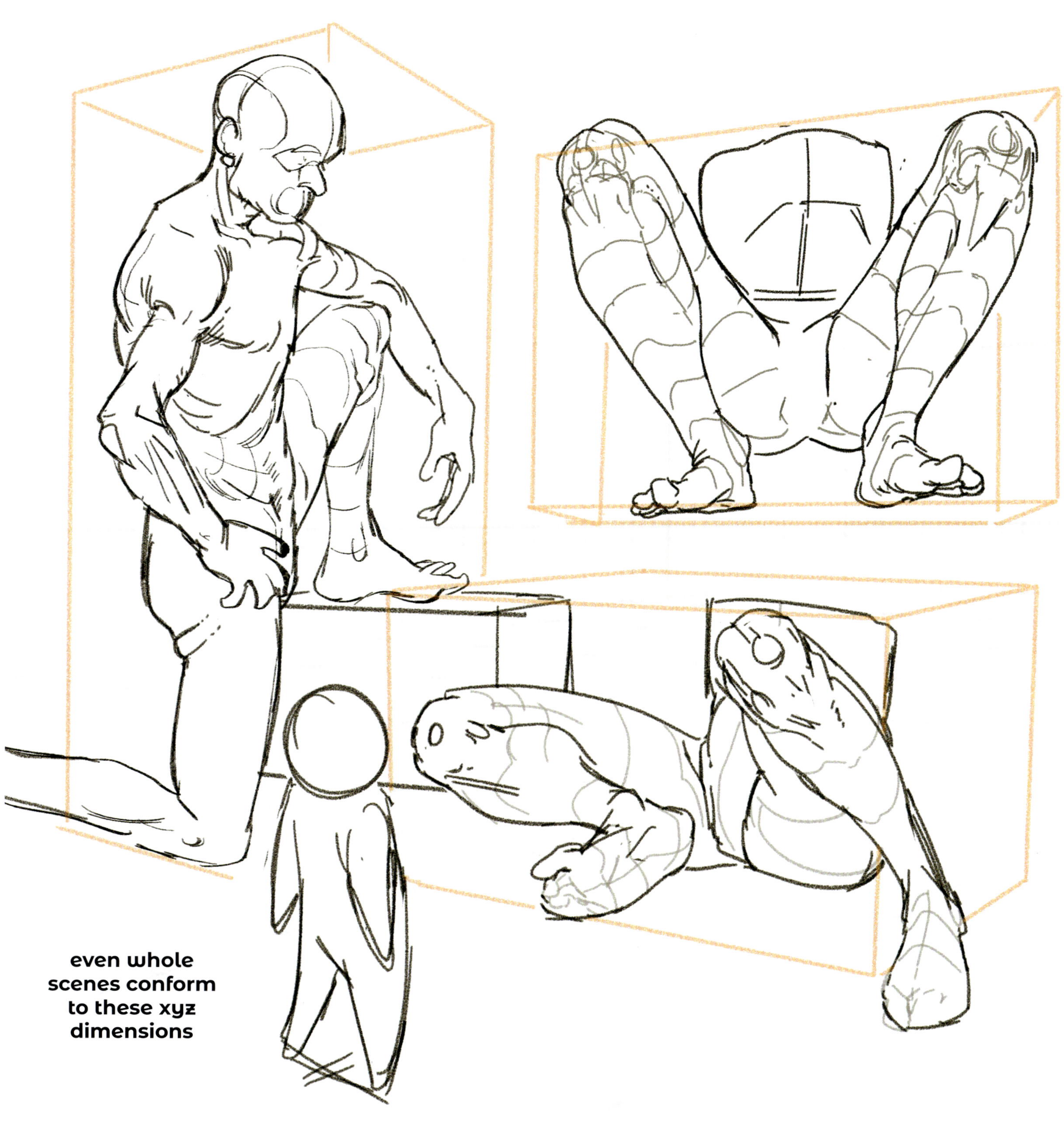

even whole
scenes conform
to these xyz
dimensions

adding form with planes

So we know that using all three dimensions is the best way to show form (A, 1–3), but how can we use this knowledge? Look at this bean shape (B). It's not clear what angle we're seeing it from. We want the viewer to feel like they're seeing these objects from a certain position.

The best way is to add "sides" or "planes" to help clarify (C). Aim for at least three planes to represent each dimension (D). Ask yourself, "Does this object have three clear sides? Does it have height, width, and depth?"

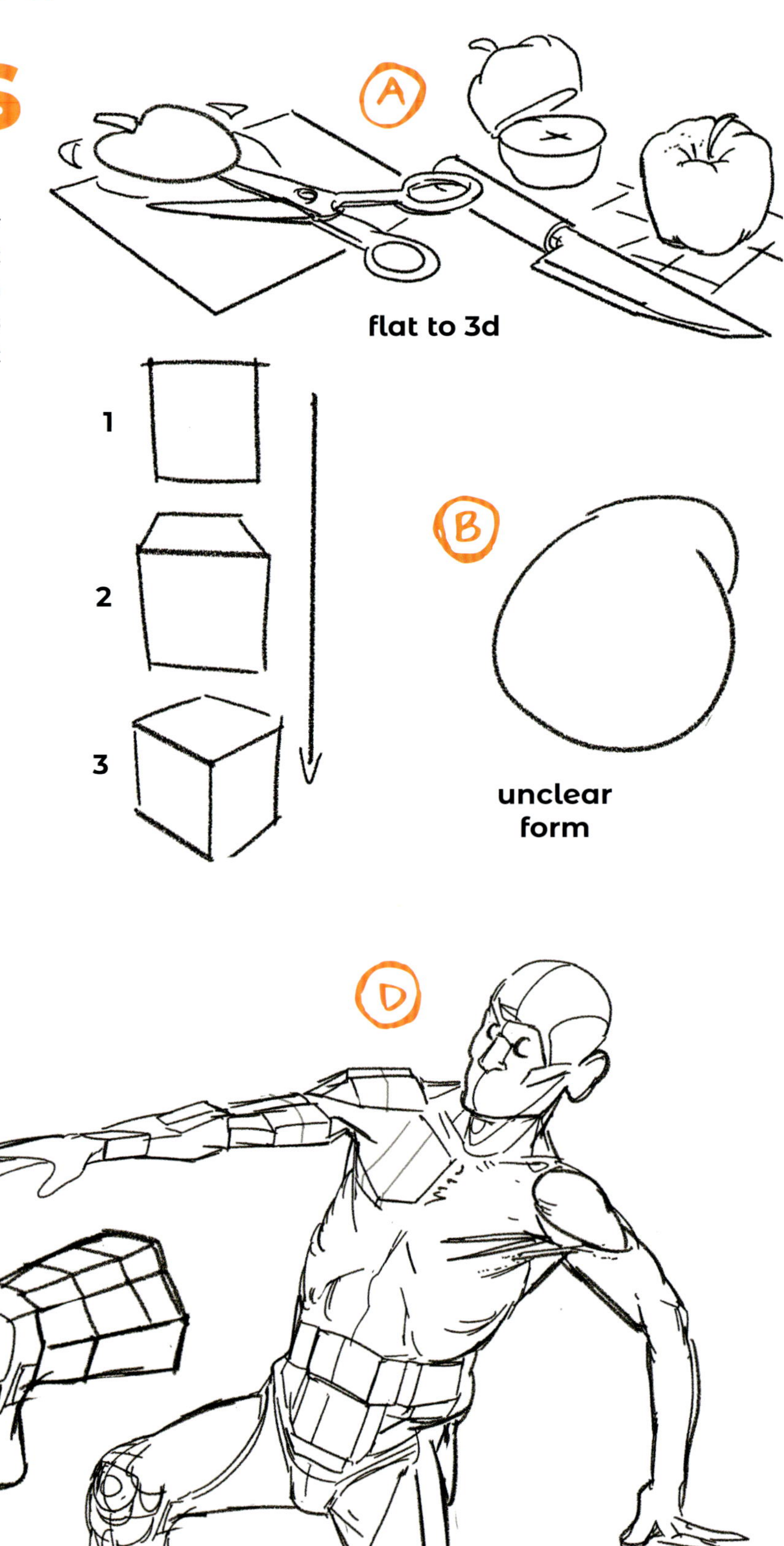

We want to include and visualize planes to help add form (E, F) – but if we draw too many planes, the results become visually confusing. We don't want to draw everything as if we're drawing a lizard's scales (G).

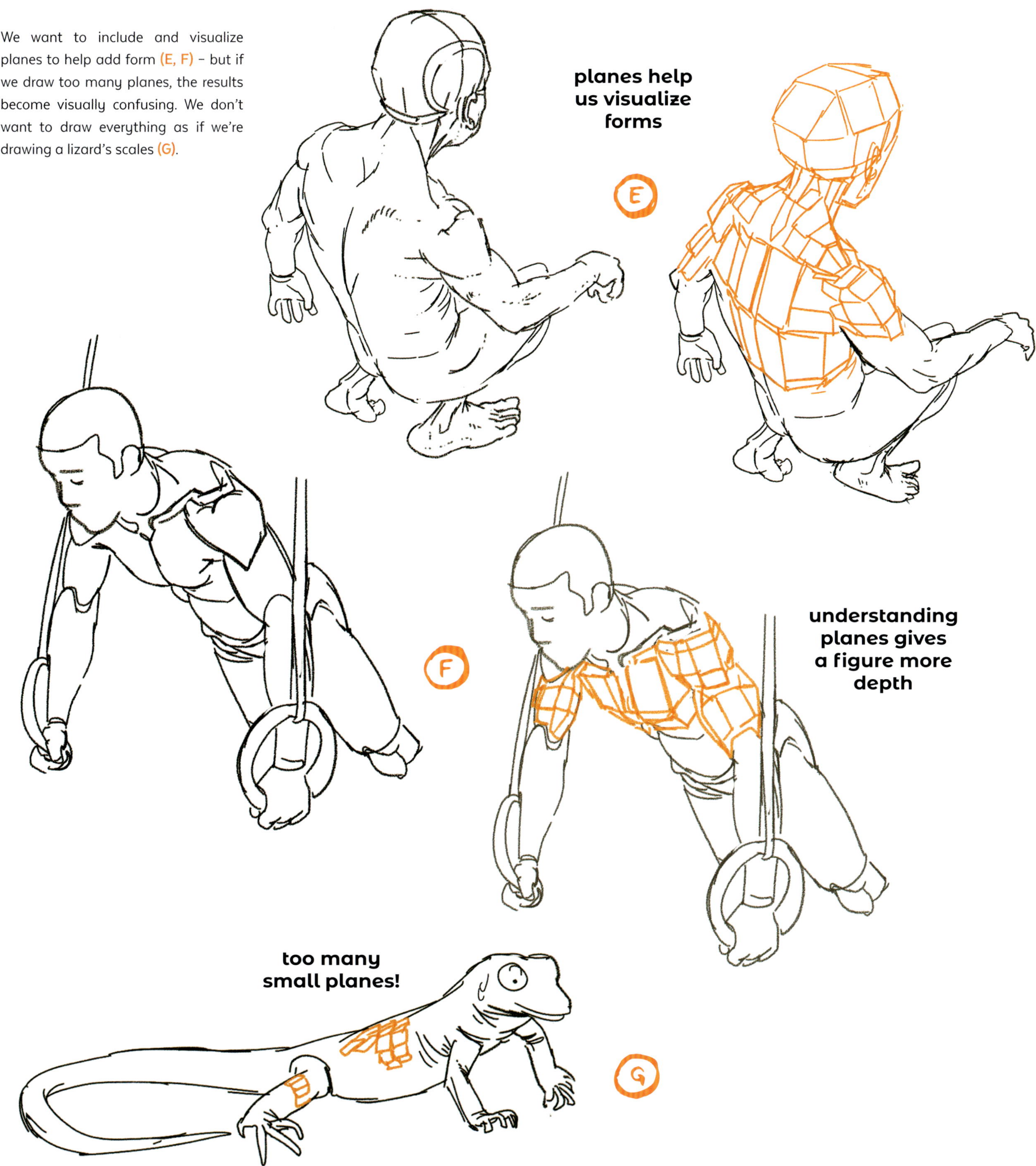

overlapping forms

We can add planes to suggest form, but another effective method is overlapping our lines. This is one of the most essential skills for conveying form clearly and successfully to the viewer. See how much more form is suggested by adding overlap (A)? Look for the regions with high levels of overlap and you'll notice they suggest the form most clearly (B).

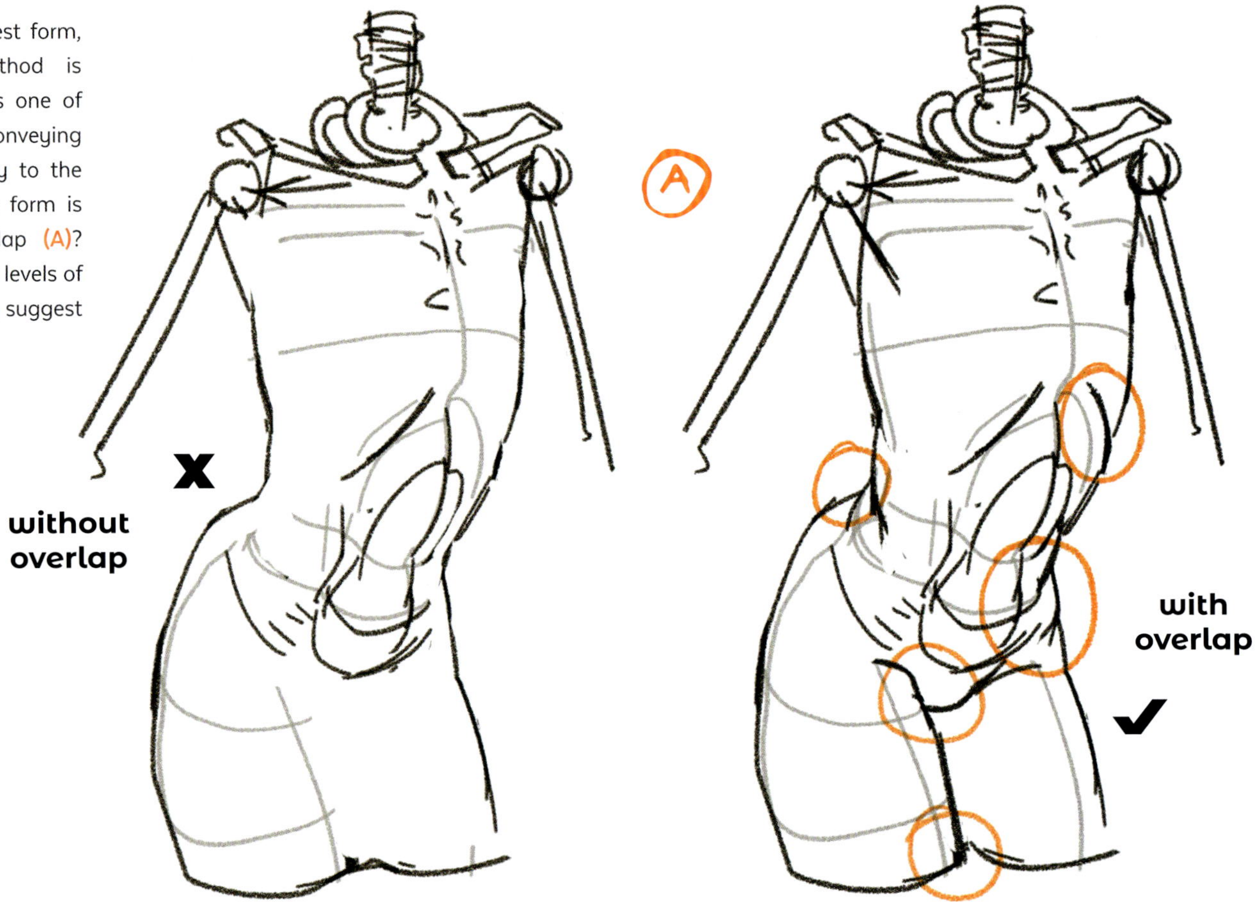

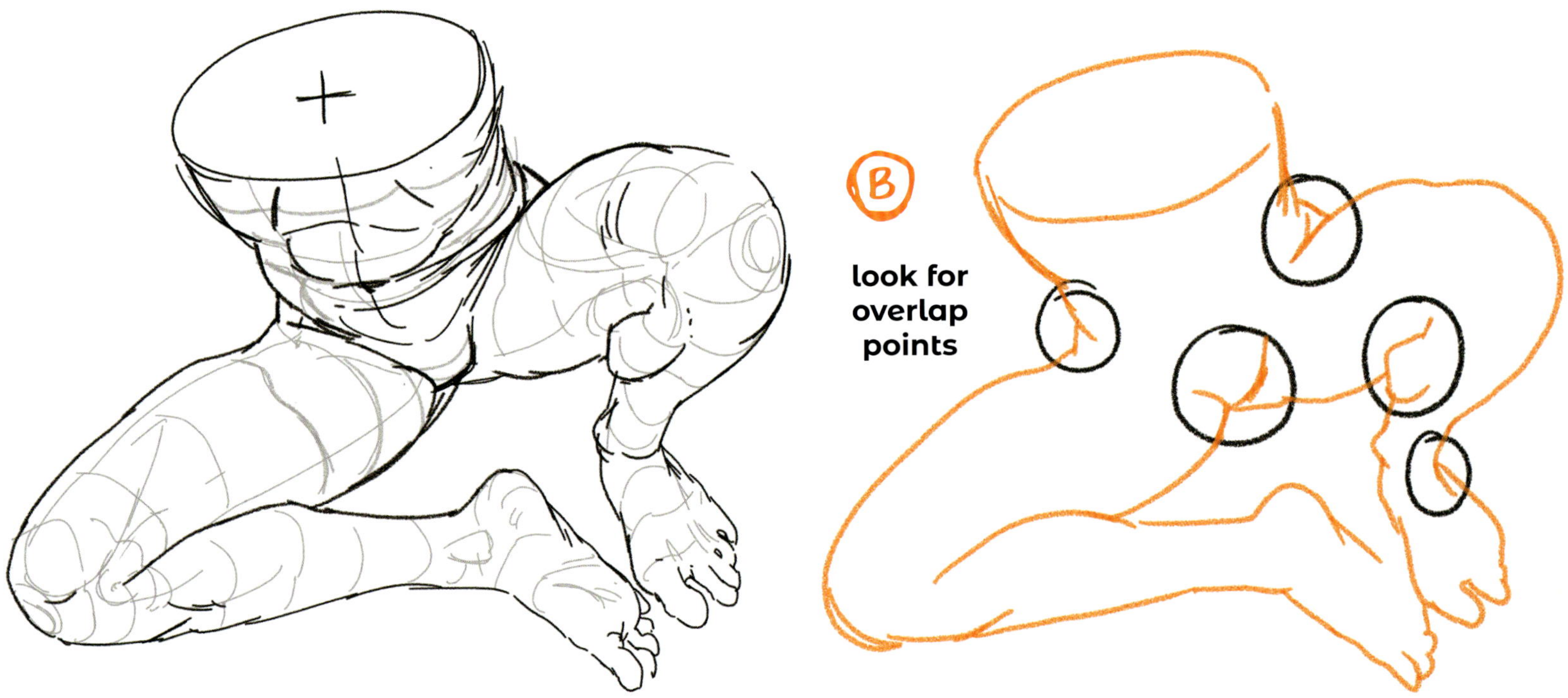

without overlap

A

with overlap

B

look for overlap points

So we know we want to add overlap, but how do we do it? The answer: Make a choice. Every line you draw will begin either above or below the previous line (C, D). Choose before you draw it.

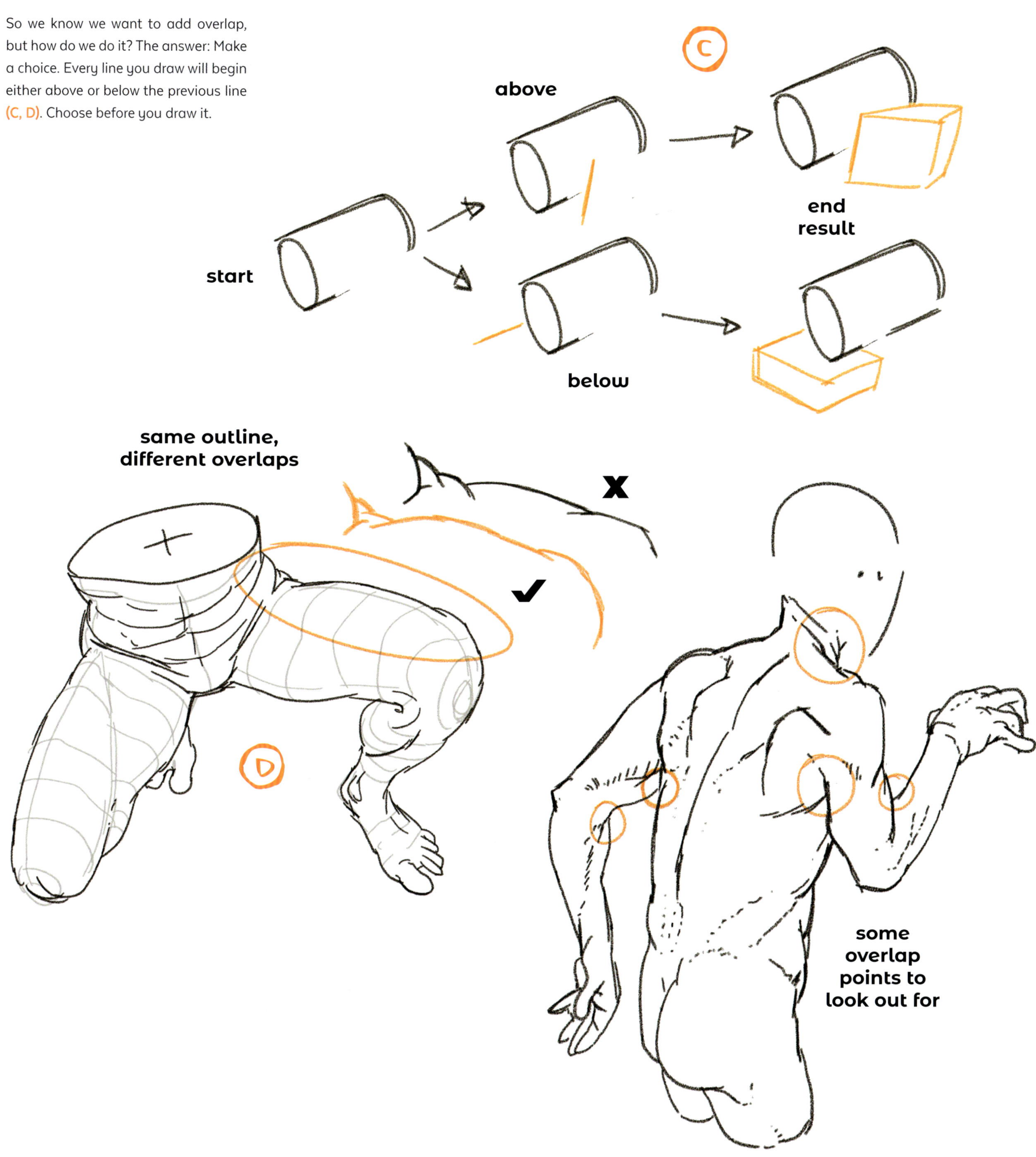

If you're not sure whether a line is in front or behind, that area needs correction. If you don't know, then another viewer will be confused as well. Compared to E, F has clearer overlap and less ambiguity. A finished drawing is the accumulation of hundreds or thousands of decisions about whether each line should go over or under another (G). Changing these decisions – of what goes over or under – changes the final result.

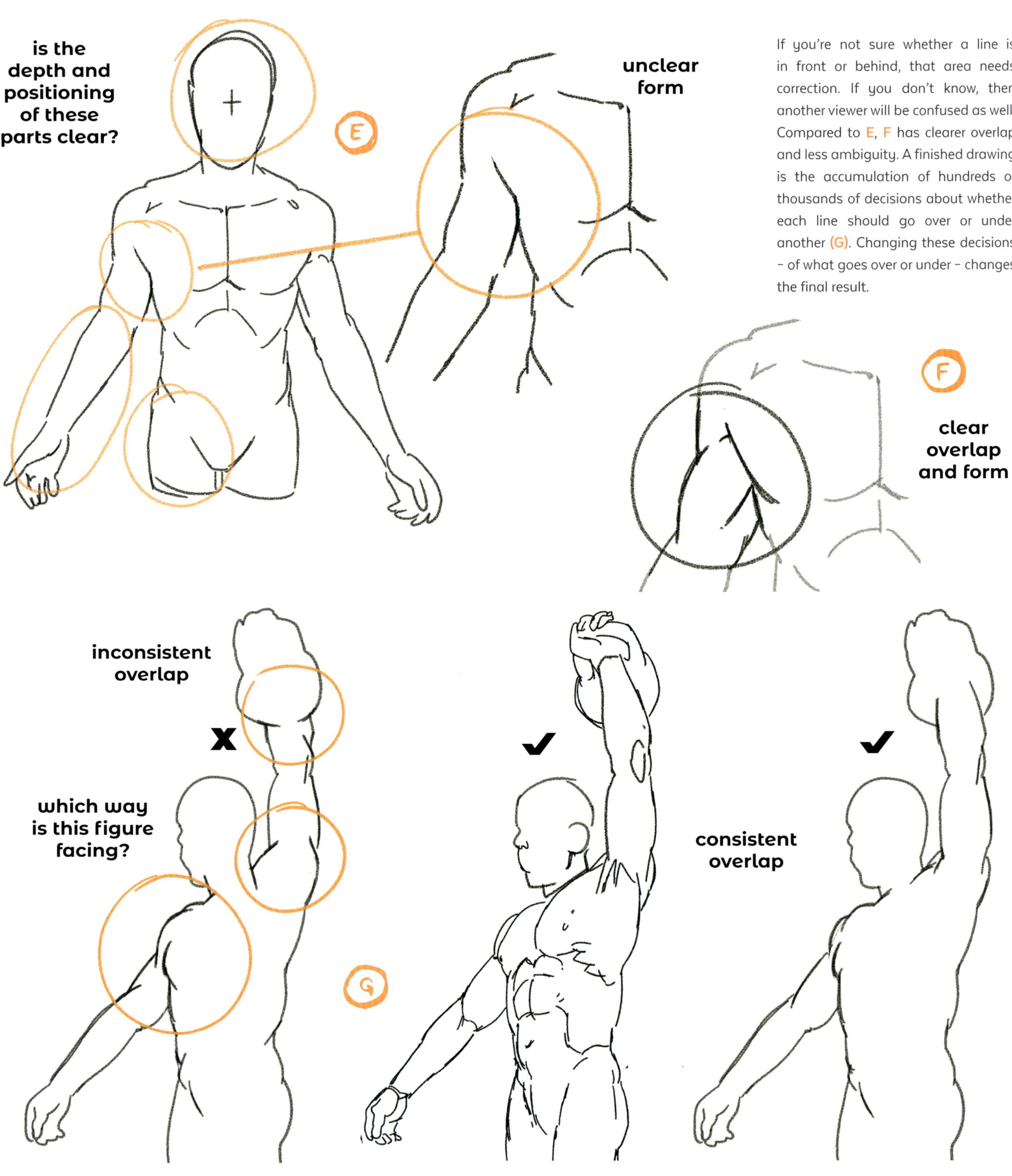

So, now we know to overlap our lines, let's think about overlapping elements. We need to think of not just each individual line, but the actual *object* we're drawing. If we're drawing a pair of cubes, before we start the second one, we need to ask, "Is this behind or in front of the previous cube?" (H, I)

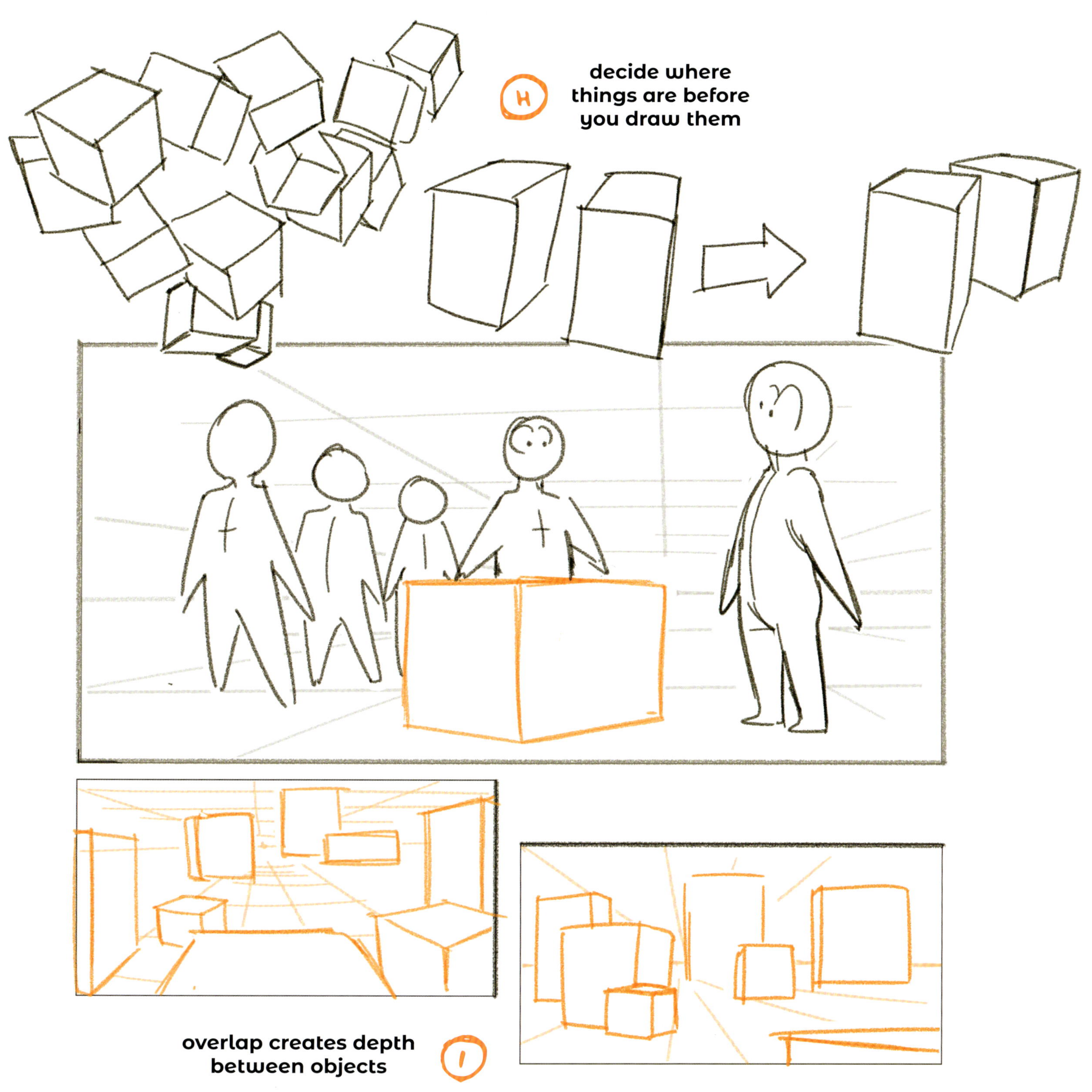

Overlapping forms are visually pleasing. They're easy for your brain to understand. Ambiguity is unsatisfying. Make sure the forms are in front of one another and you'll create something that appears solid, even if it doesn't make any sense as a subject! When we look at J, it's unclear which arm is farther forward than the other. However, in K we know that one arm is in front and the other is behind the body. Even when looking at L, we can clearly see which limbs are farther forward or back!

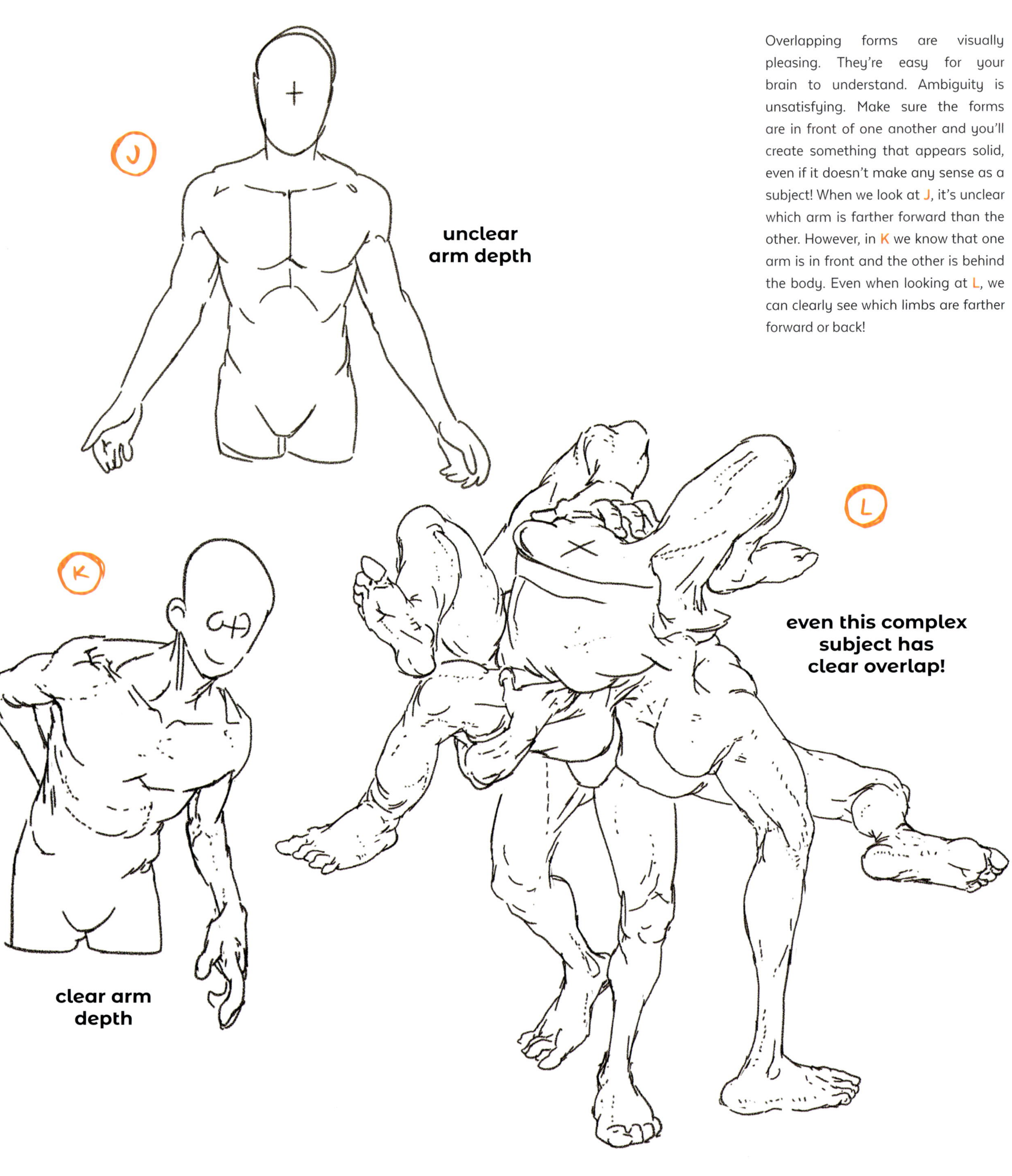

leave gaps

Let's say we're drawing several forms in front of each other. As was said earlier, this overlap will give us a more interesting image. One way to improve this feeling of depth is to make sure the lines don't actually touch. When drawing the object that's farther back, try stopping the lines just short of the nearer object, leaving a small gap. This makes the closer object stand out.

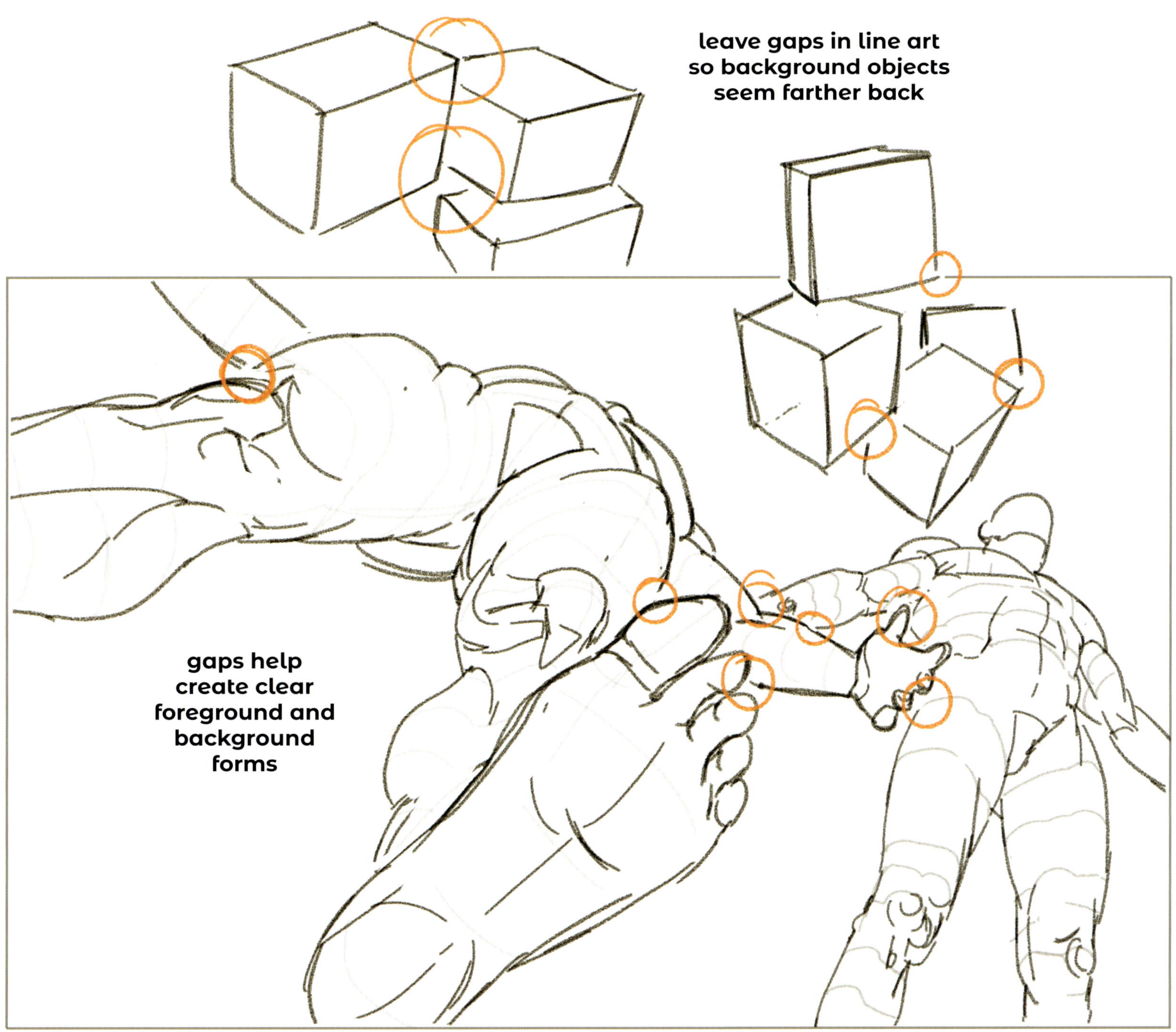

less is more

As with most things, less is more. Don't show off. Remember that you're drawing a figure, not trying to demonstrate how many muscles you know!

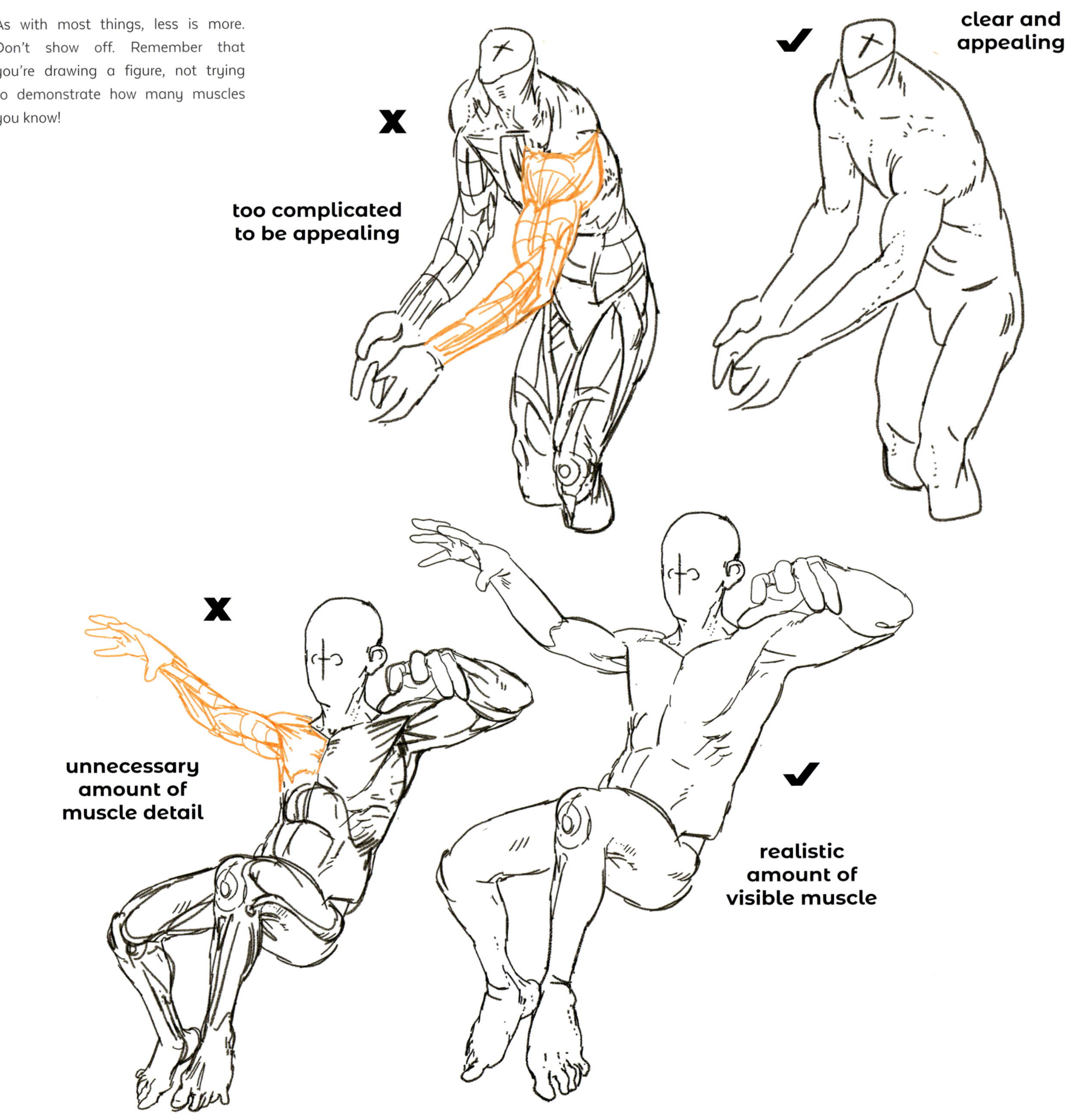

Internal lines, within the silhouette, can be helpful to describe form, but try to resist the temptation to describe everything. Remember this motto: "Indicate, don't state." Our natural tendency is to describe every small detail, like we're telling a very boring story! The viewer doesn't actually want this. They want to be challenged to do some of the work themselves!

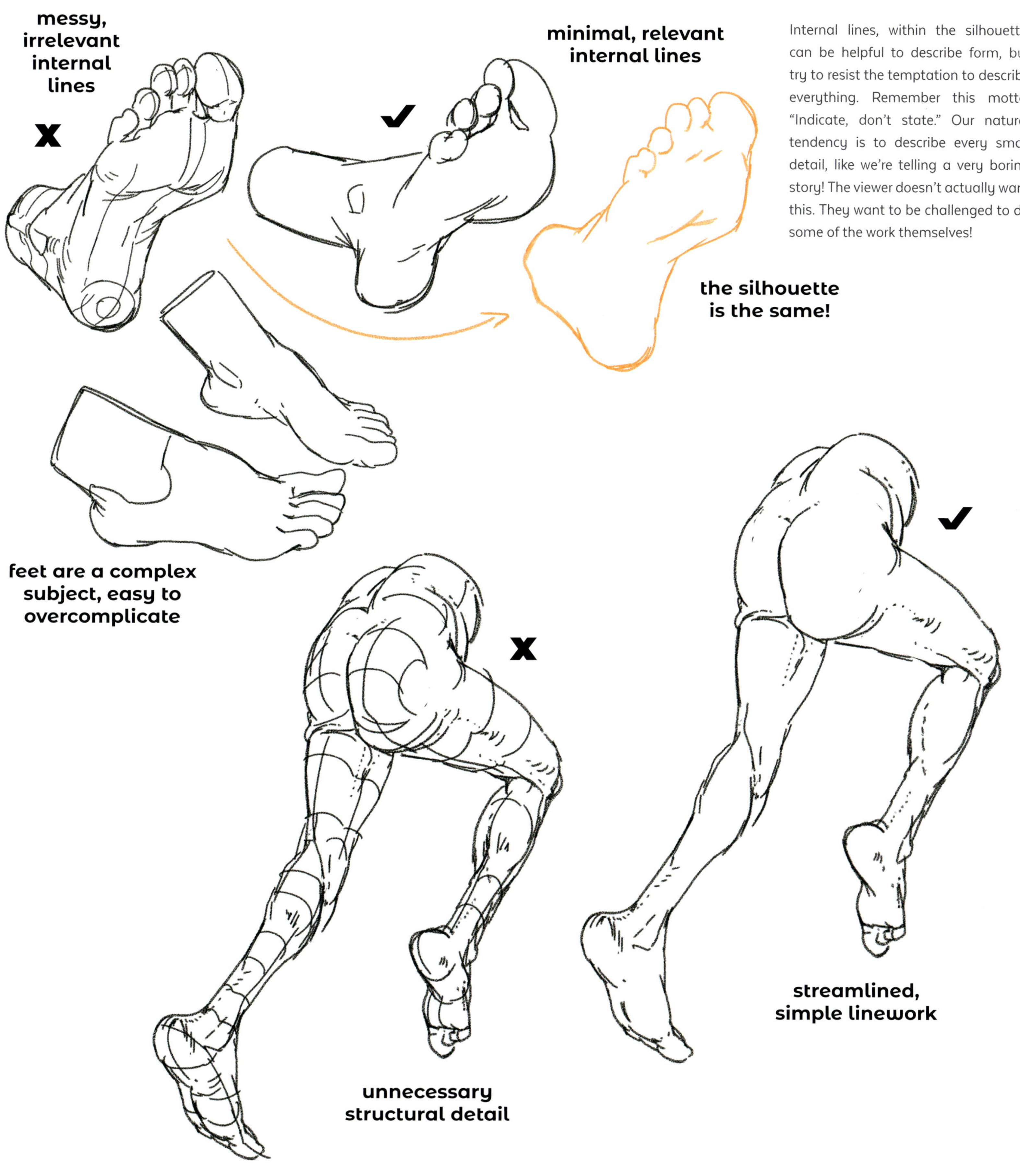

draw with care

Commit to a form. The reason I don't teach or use gestures in my own work (except for storyboarding) is because they're ambiguous. A gesture fails to define the XYZ orientation of a form, and as a result, it's very open to interpretation. If we look at A, the arm could be in various rotations and still have a similar silhouette. That's leaving an important decision until a later stage of the drawing, which is something to avoid where possible (B). You wouldn't start constructing a building and think, "I'll leave the exact measurements until later on!"

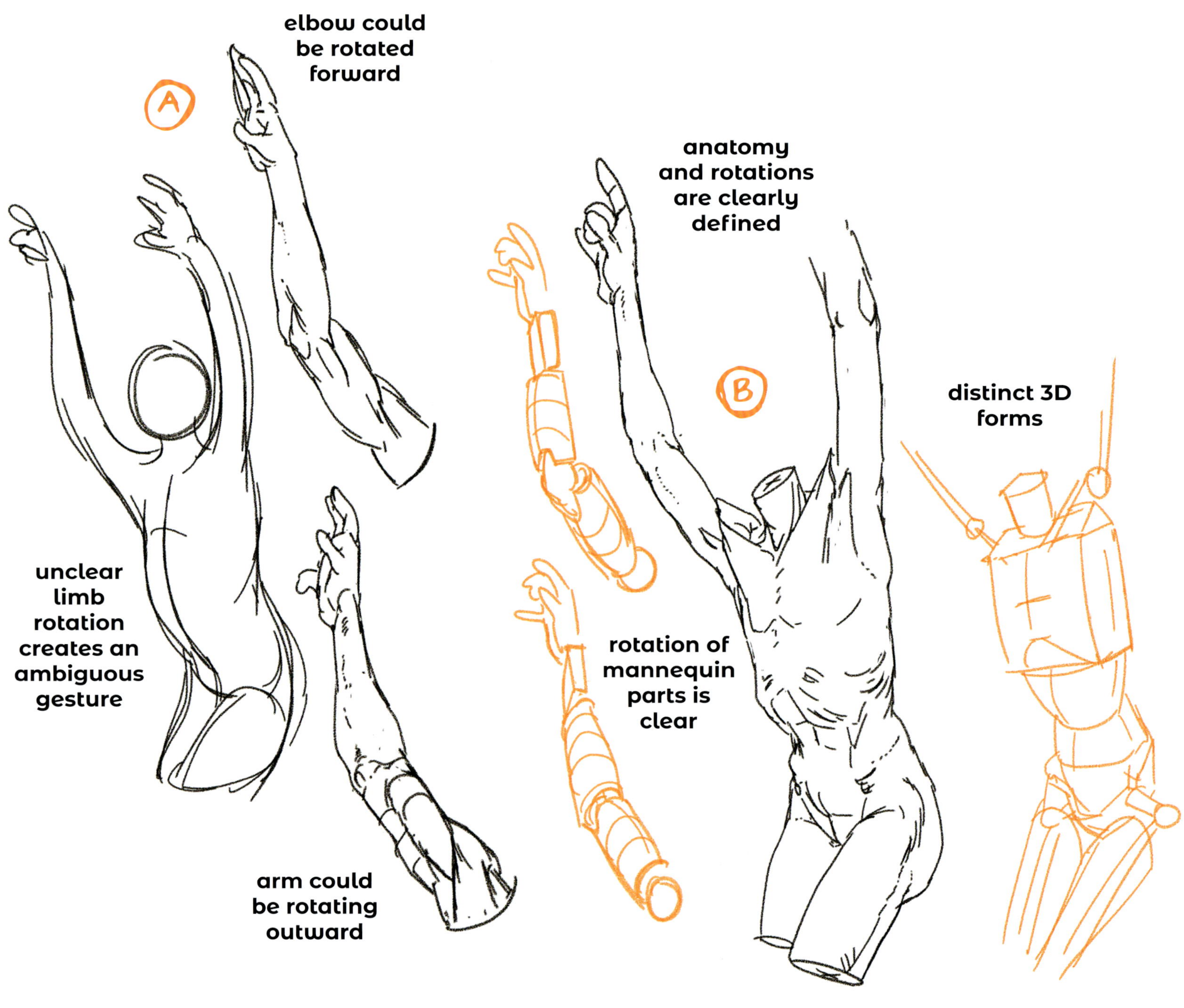

Here we can see beginner (C), intermediate (D), and advanced (E) styles of drawing. Generally, beginners focus on the lines themselves, one at a time, resulting in an image without cohesion. Everything looks disjointed! As we learn about form, things begin looking stiff and blocky, but more solid. Finally, we learn to imply construction rather than state it. For now, focus on getting the forms correct. Don't worry about making a pretty image!

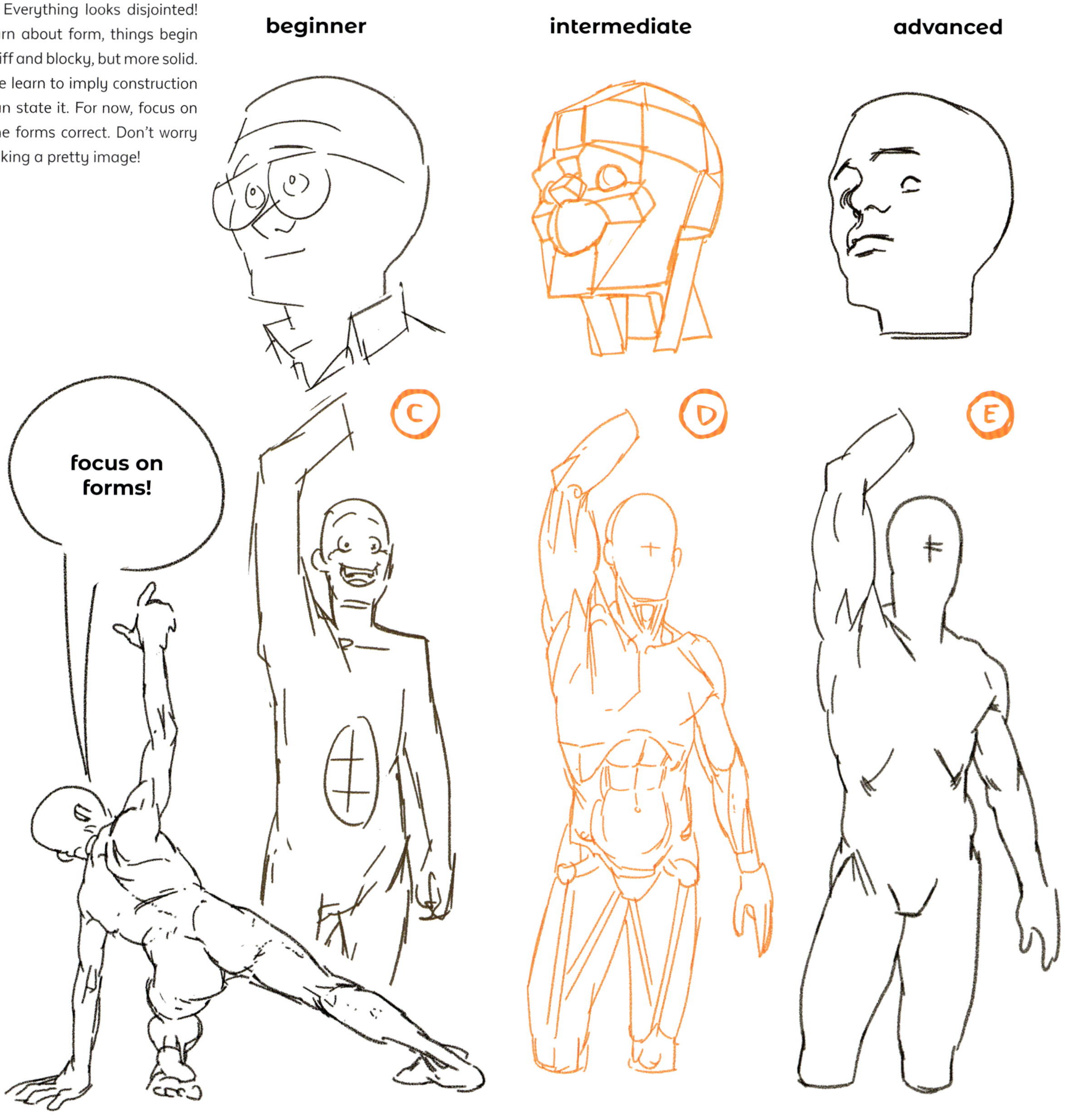

beginner **intermediate** **advanced**

C D E

focus on forms!

Slow down! Your choices are either right or wrong, and the results are cumulative. Fewer lines in the right places are better than more lines placed with less care (F). It's not a race to get the drawing done – one good, careful drawing is worth a thousand poor, unconsidered ones. Again, imagine you were building a house: You wouldn't rush the foundations (G).

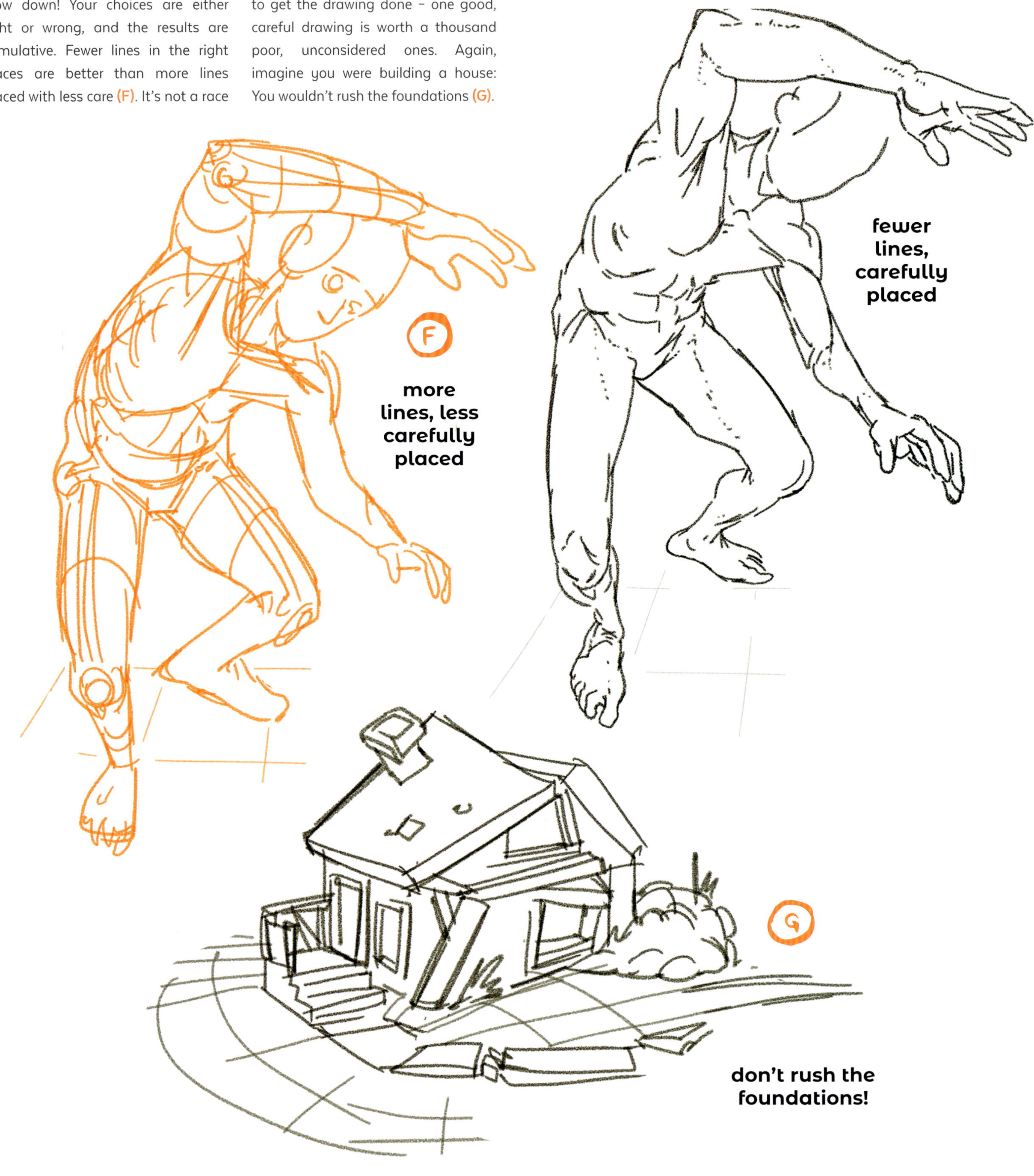

accuracy isn't everything

Make this your mantra: "Believable is better than accurate." Even though we're aiming to make "correct" choices, we're not always striving for exact realism. That would be impractical and, worse, boring! We only need to achieve something that appears to function mechanically.

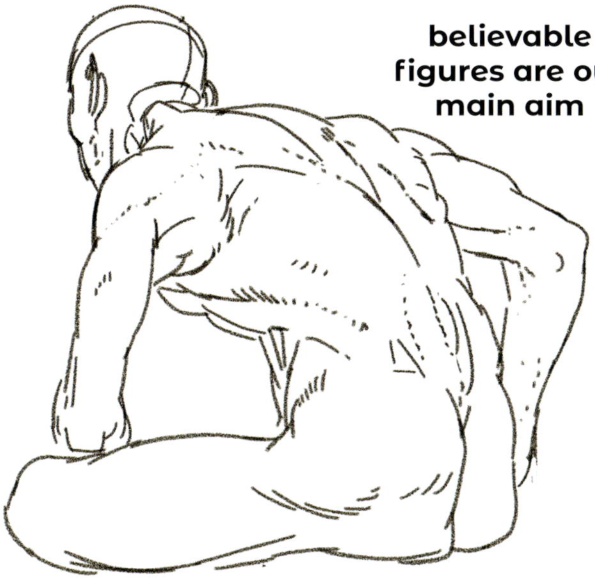

memorizing every muscle is not our goal!

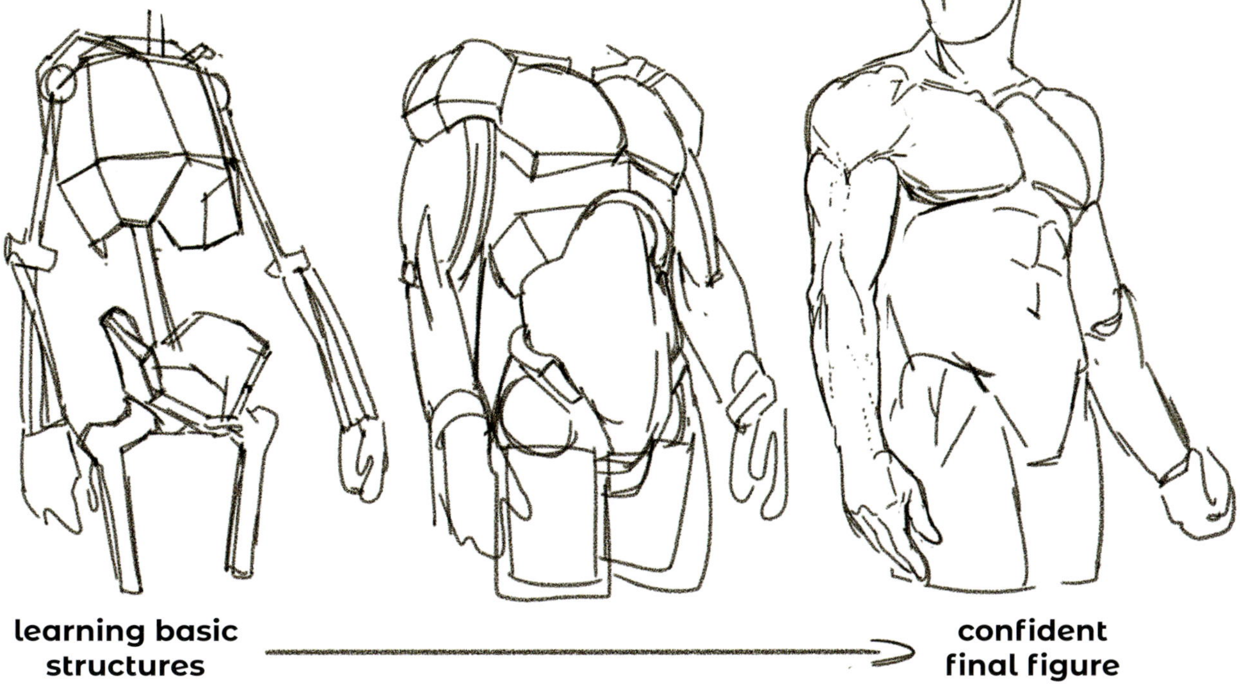

believable figures are our main aim

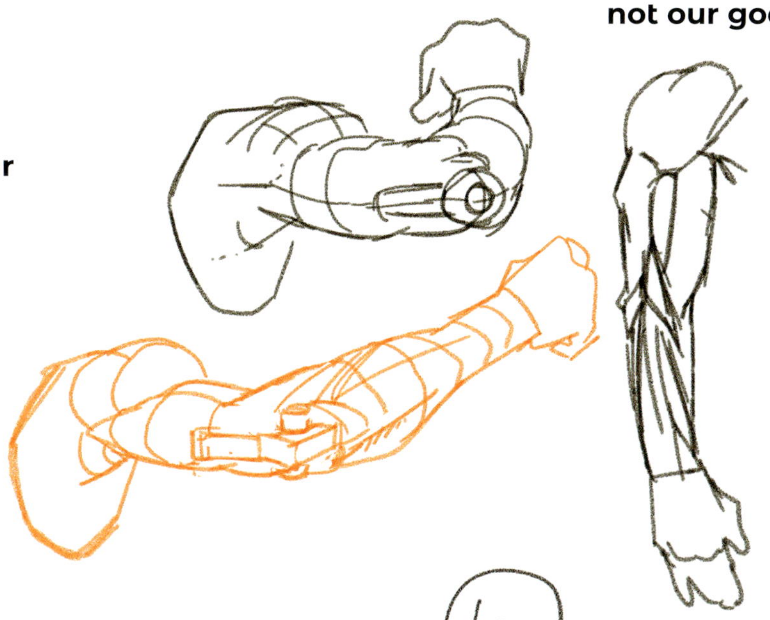

learning basic structures → **confident final figure**

wedging

"Wedging" builds on our concept of overlapping lines and elements. Think of two cube forms being pushed into each other, and see how they would wedge like two mechanical pieces (A).

Aspire to show wedging in almost everything you draw. The human body is all wedge. There are no separate pieces (B)!

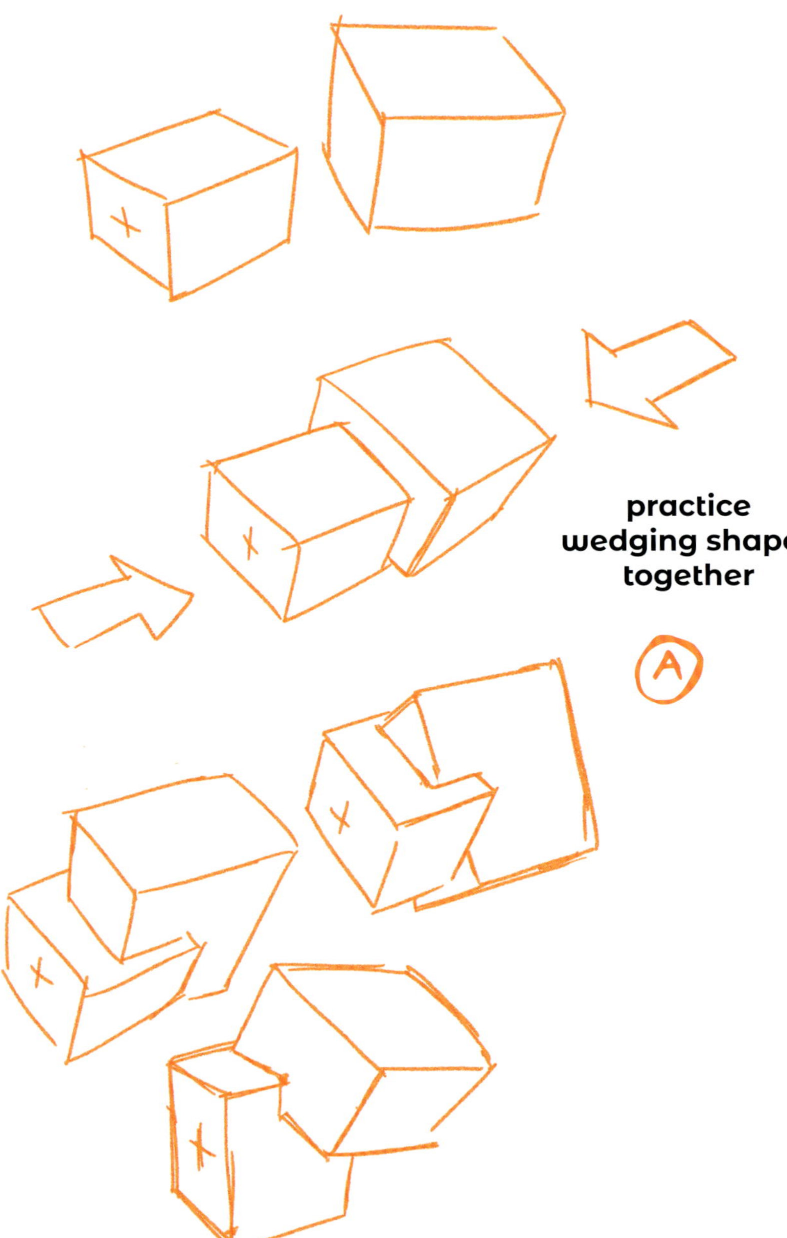

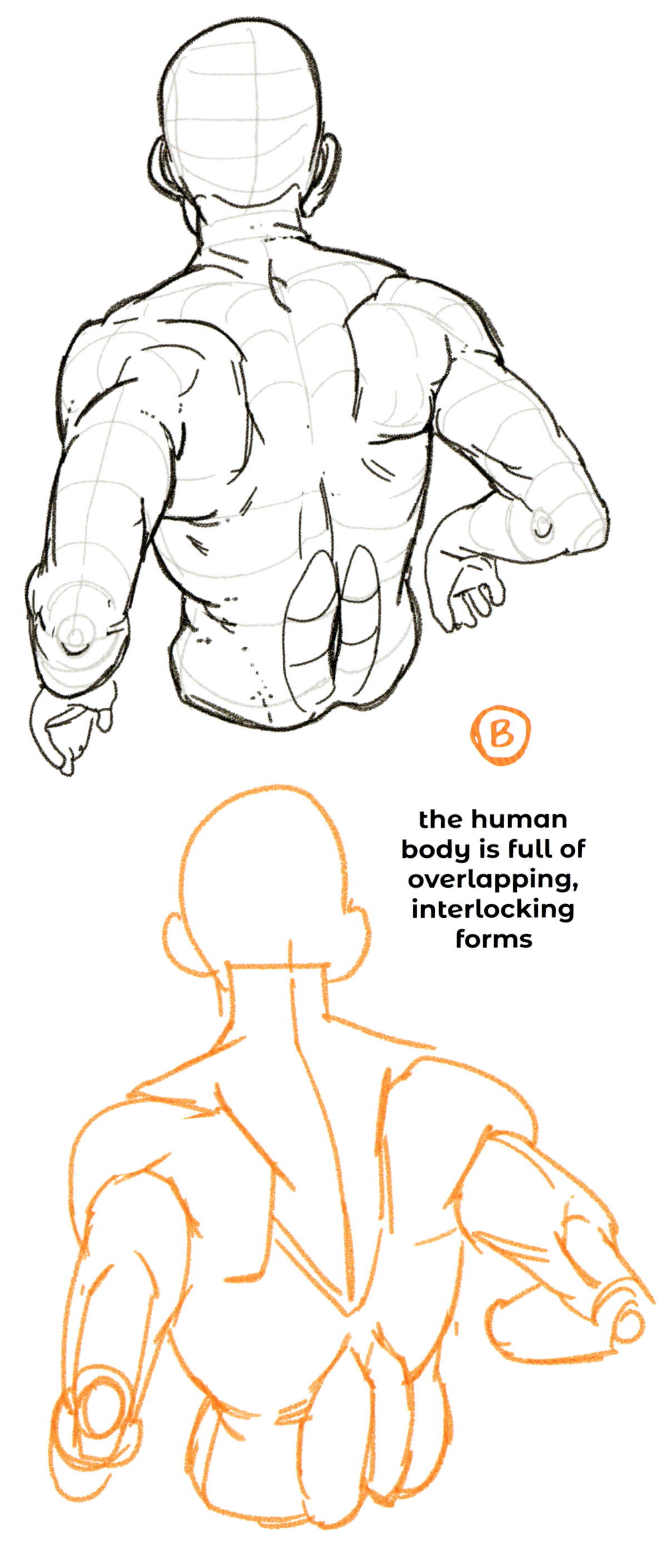

We can wedge much more than simple cube forms. Throughout this book we'll be using wedging to combine complex forms as we approach a more realistic level of anatomy. Here, C, D, and E show some examples of the direction we'll go in later.

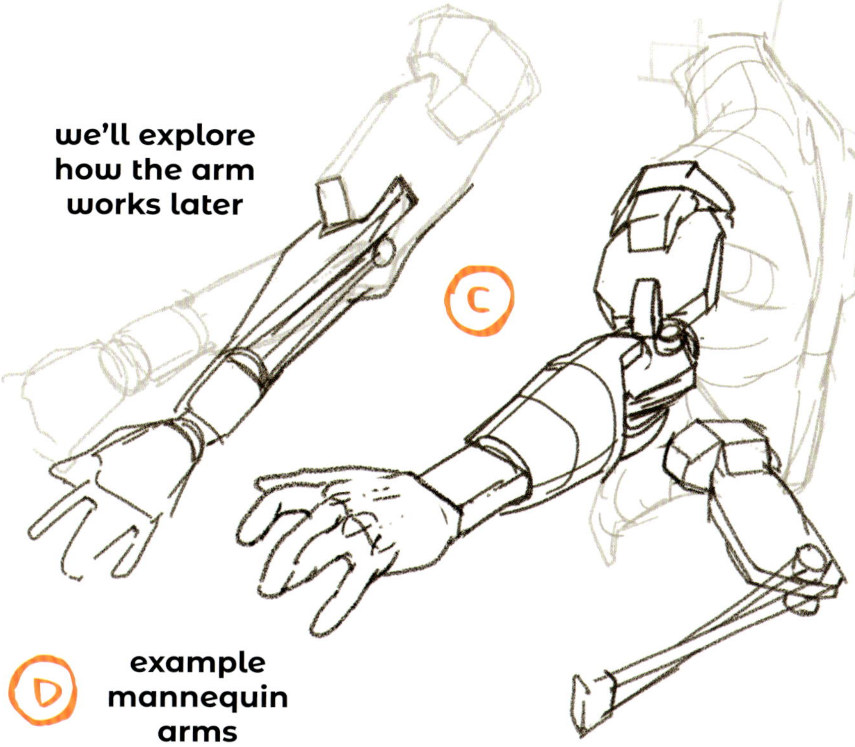

we'll explore how the arm works later

C

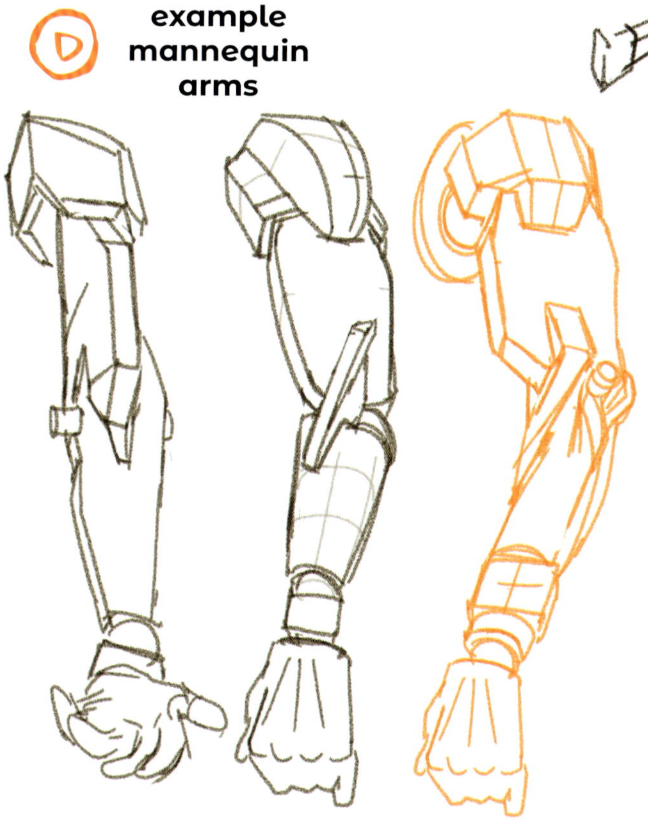

D

example mannequin arms

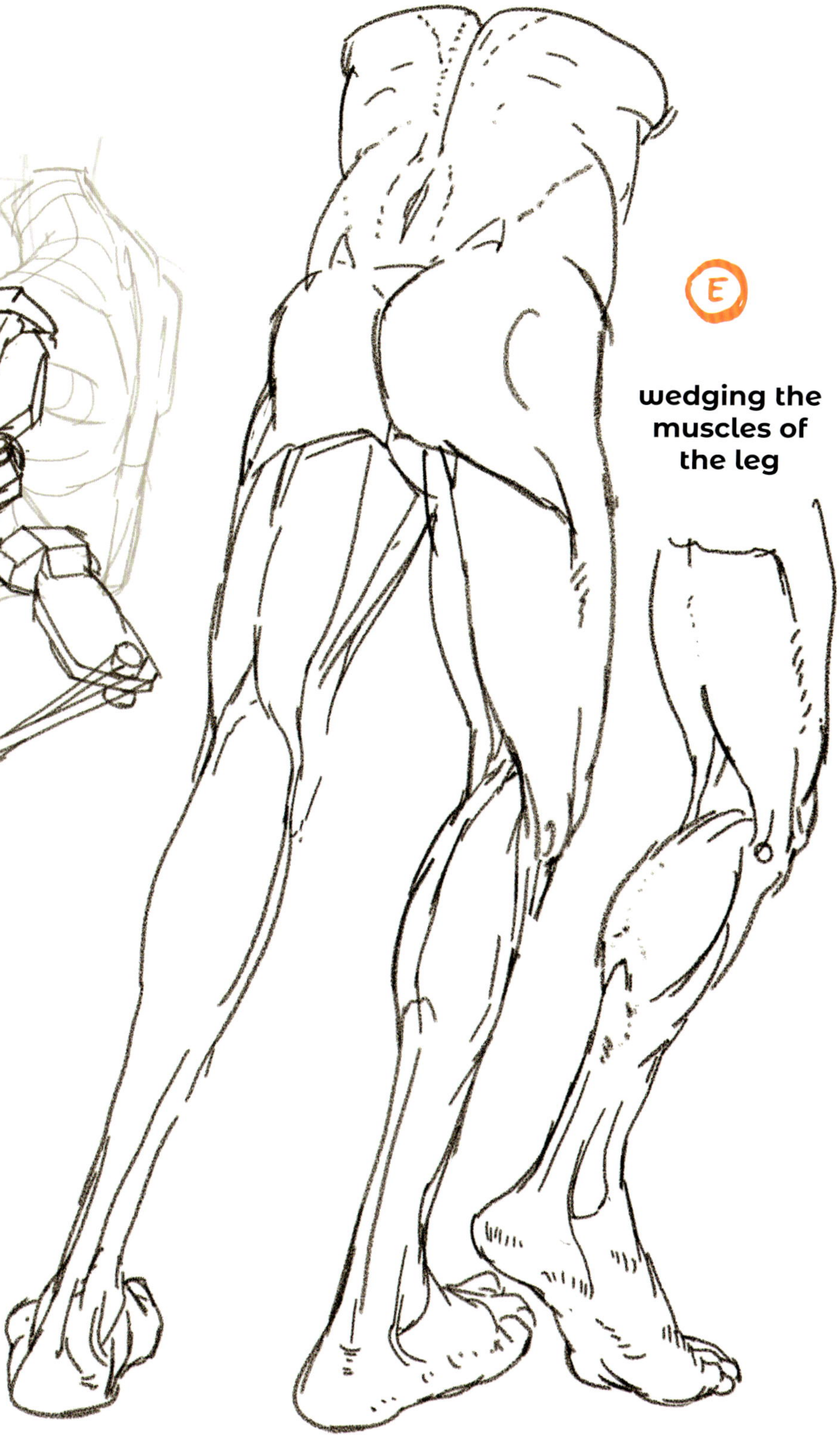

E

wedging the muscles of the leg

silhouette, contour & proportion

silhouettes & outlines

Silhouette is a powerful tool in our drawing arsenal. A clear silhouette is instantly recognizable and "readable." If we add some overlap to the contours, it becomes a 3D form. Our imaginations fill in the blanks, giving us something that's identifiable and appears to have an orientation in 3D space. Our brains are amazing.

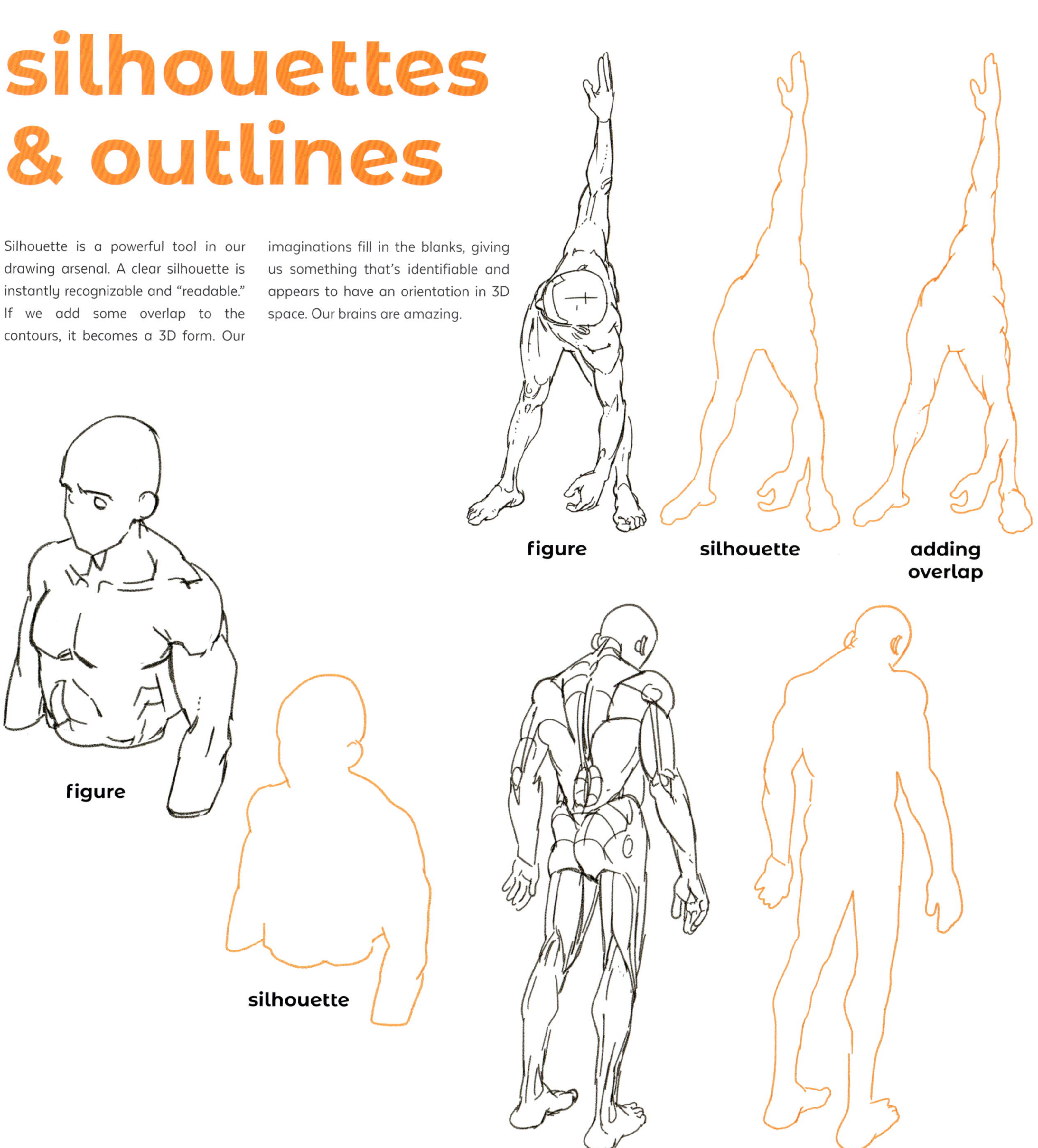

However, if a silhouette is incorrect, it won't be identifiable as an object. An incorrect silhouette is incredibly confusing for the viewer's brain. The silhouette in A doesn't read as an arm, and neither does B! Ask yourself, "Does this silhouette look correct?"

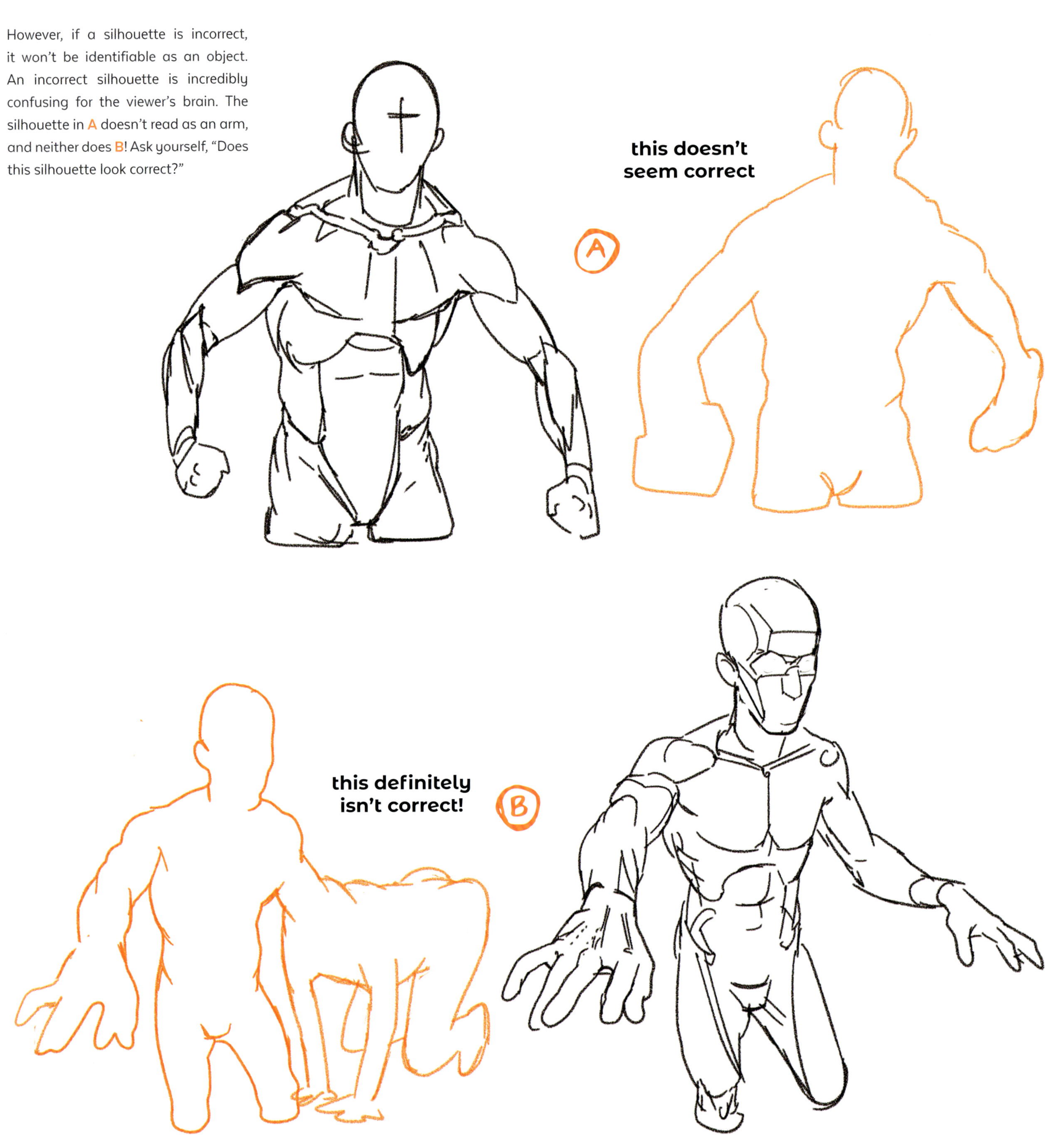

Small changes in silhouette create large changes in identification (C, D). Don't think, "Is this too small to bother changing?" It's always worth bothering! Sometimes, the difference between a successful and an unsuccessful drawing is reviewing what you've drawn, checking it, and asking, "How can I adjust this silhouette to make it more believable?" (E)

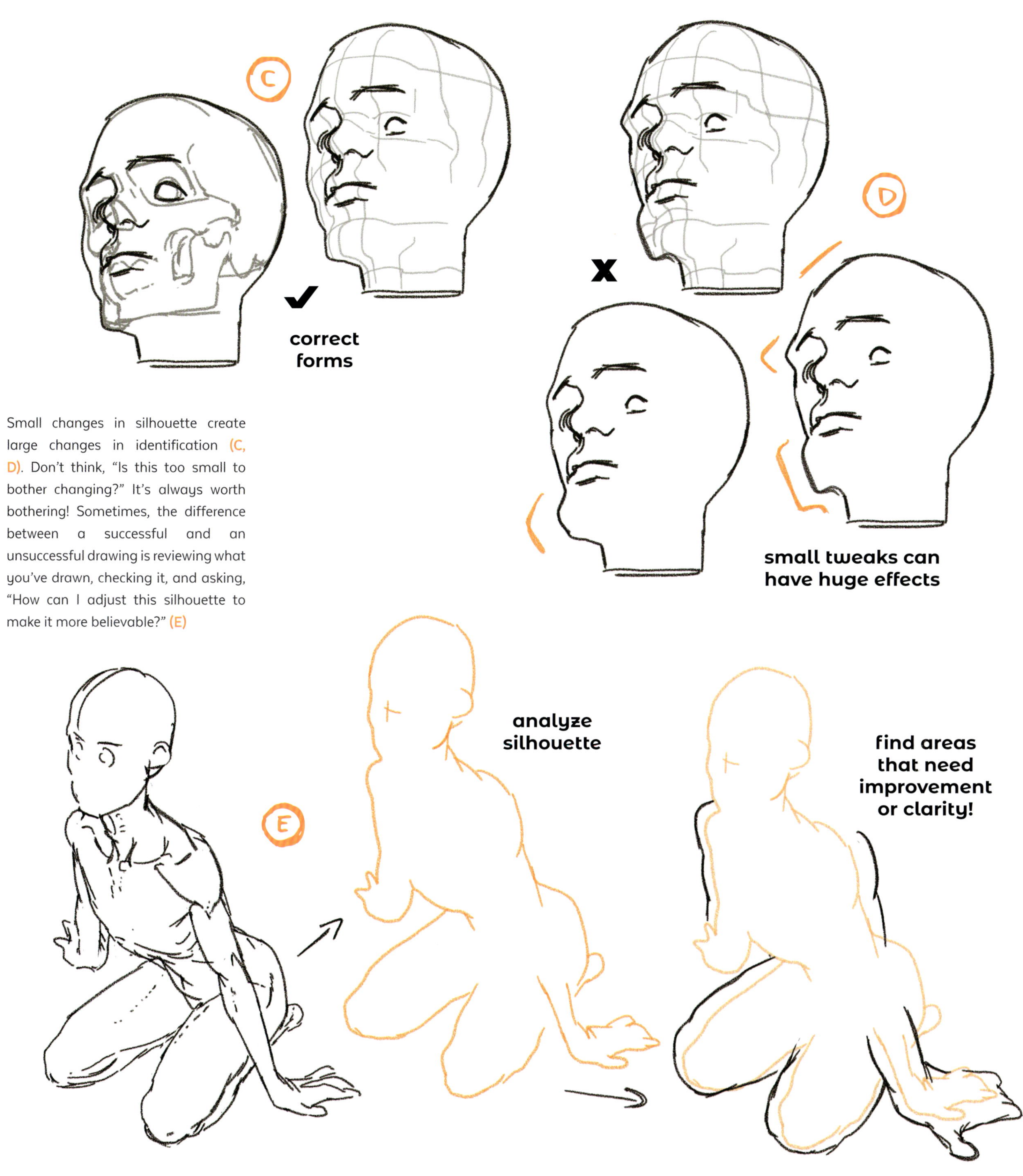

contours & forms

Contours are an essential tool for representing forms. People often talk about "cross contours" or "linear contours." They're all the same thing: lines across the subject that help describe form to the viewer. The question to ask yourself here is, "Can I draw the contours around this form?" If you can't, you don't know the form well enough yet.

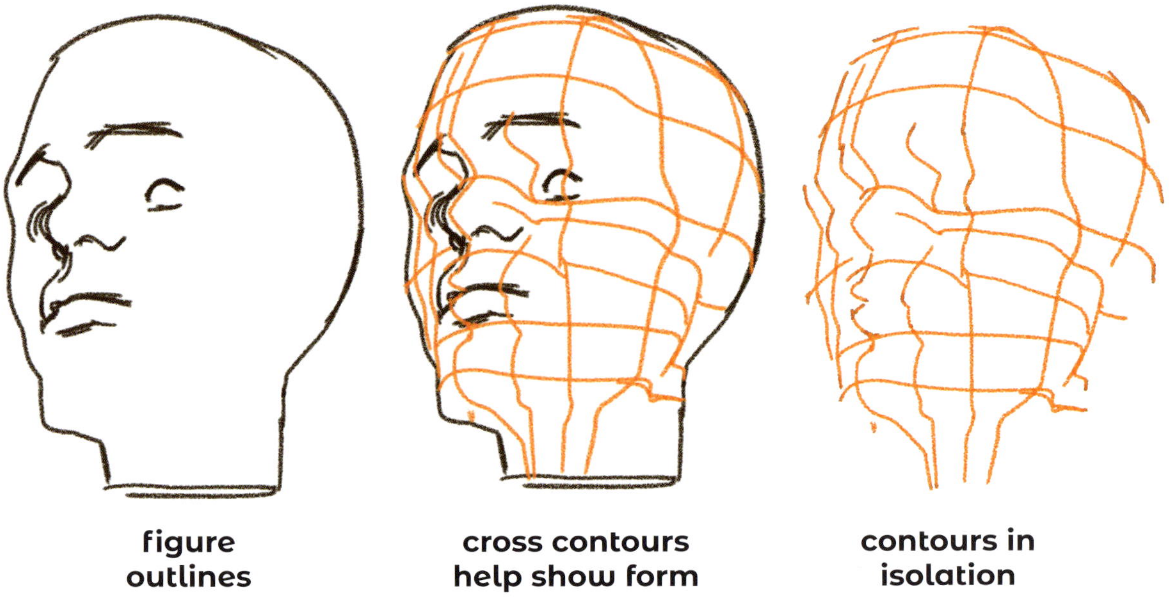

figure outlines

cross contours help show form

contours in isolation

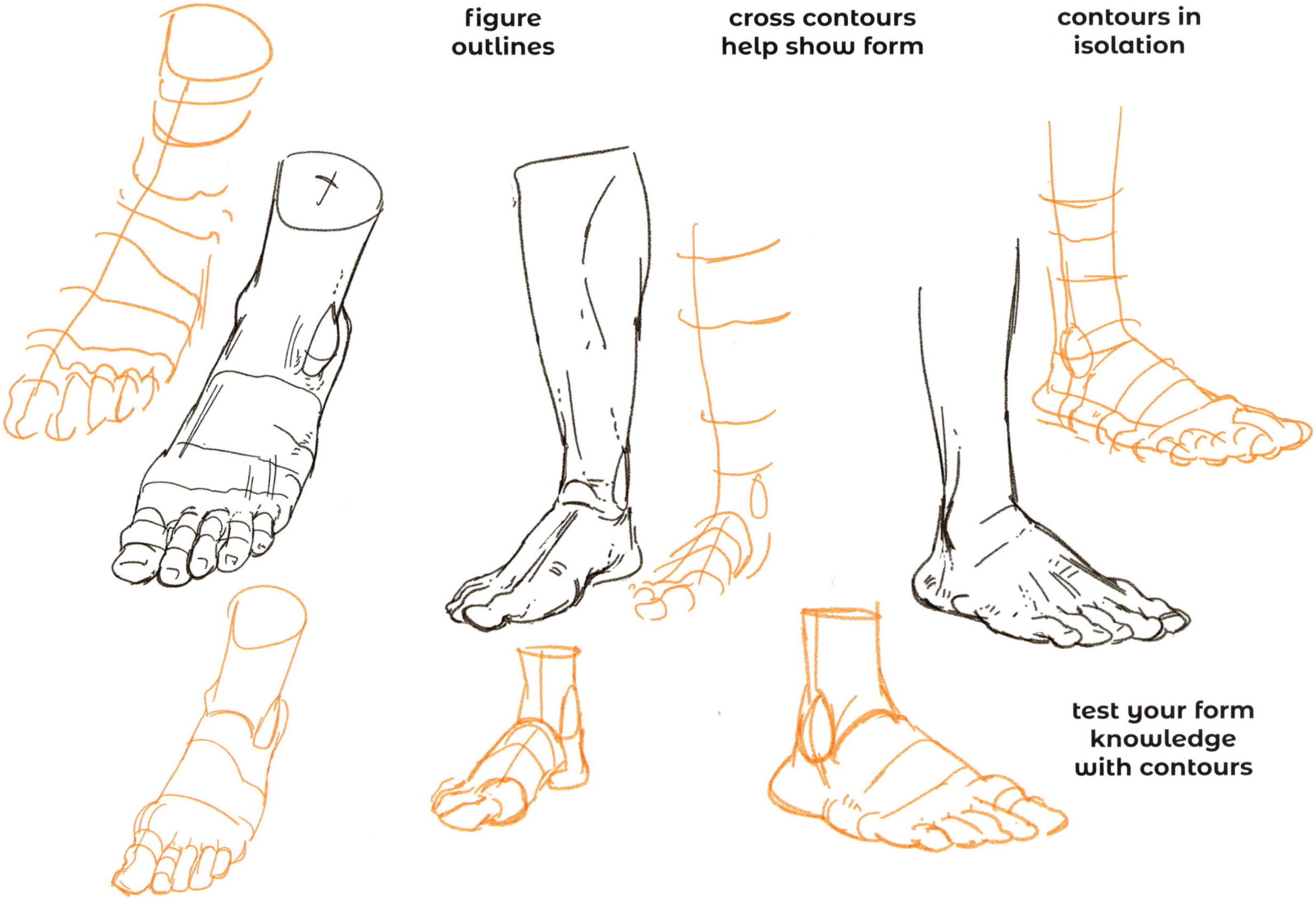

test your form knowledge with contours

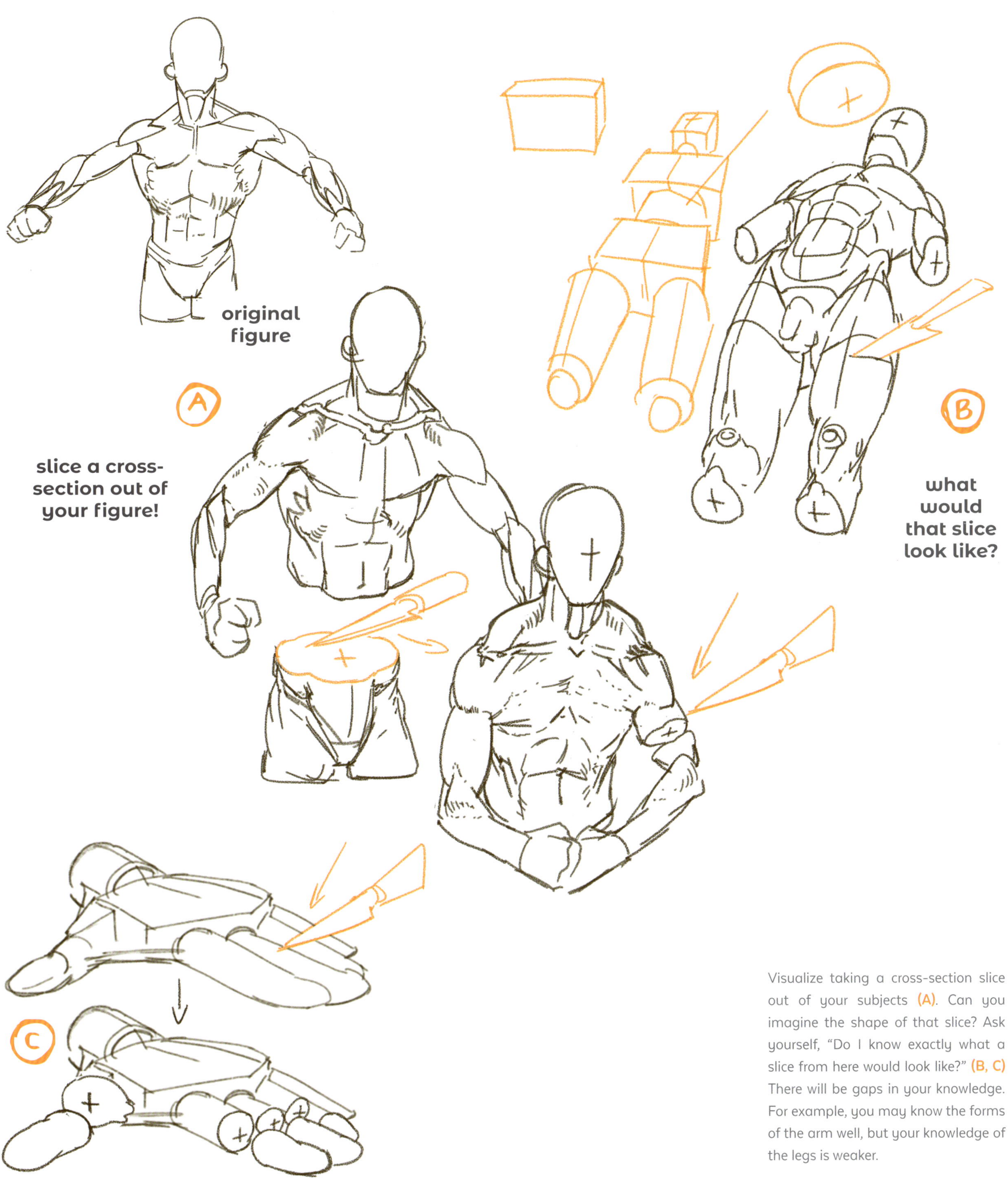

Visualize taking a cross-section slice out of your subjects (A). Can you imagine the shape of that slice? Ask yourself, "Do I know exactly what a slice from here would look like?" (B, C) There will be gaps in your knowledge. For example, you may know the forms of the arm well, but your knowledge of the legs is weaker.

So how can we use our knowledge of silhouette in our drawing process? Remember that the goal isn't to learn esoteric information about art – it's to develop skills and techniques. A great technique is to outline your figure's silhouette and look at it without internal lines (D, E). Any mistakes will be more obvious this way, and you can then adjust them accordingly (F).

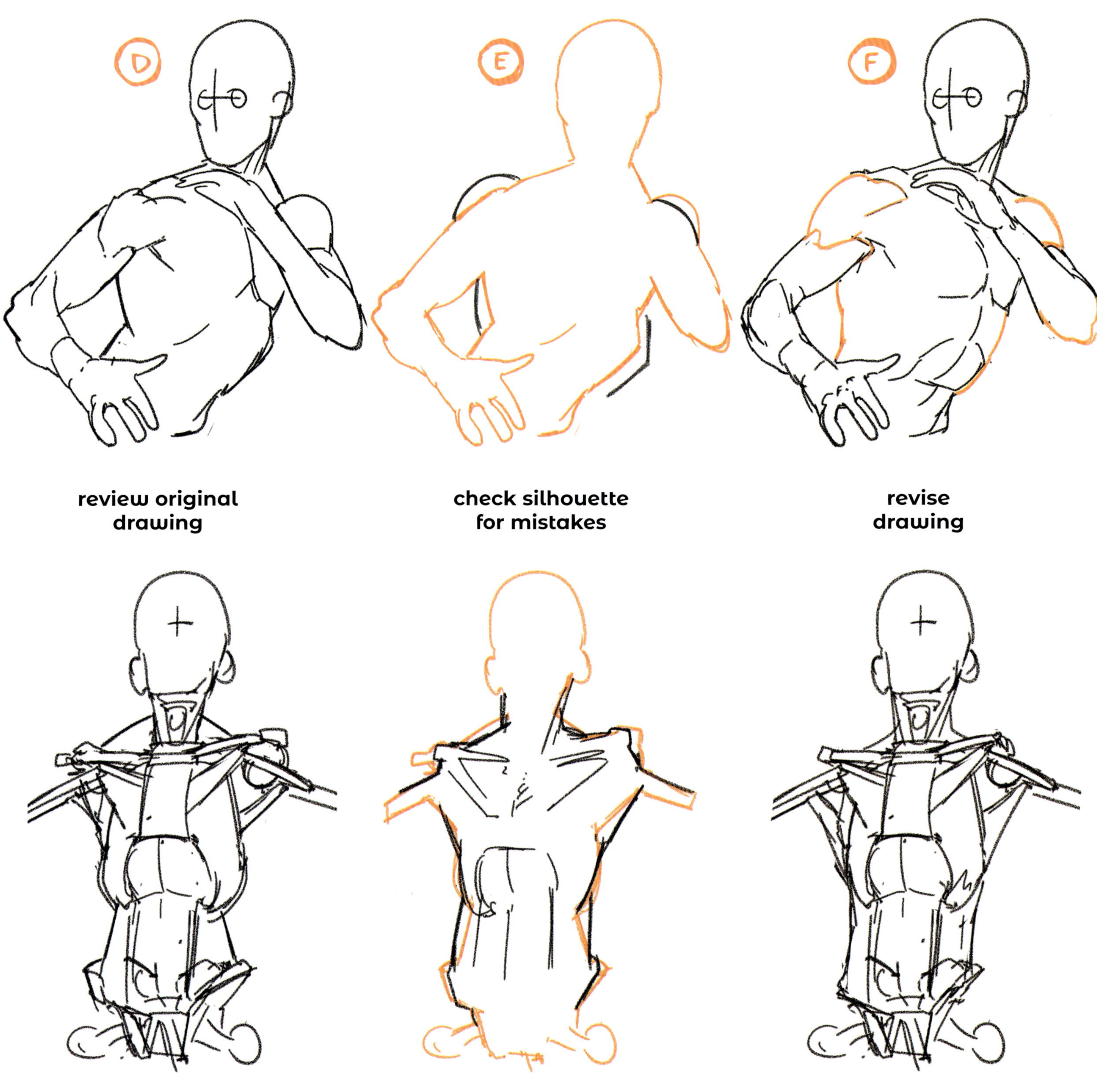

Another way to use contours for analysis is by doing a "center-line check." Draw the center line down the front or back of your model and look at it separately. Does it look correct or does anything unexpected appear? You'd be surprised how much information is included within this line. This technique allows you to look at your drawing from another perspective.

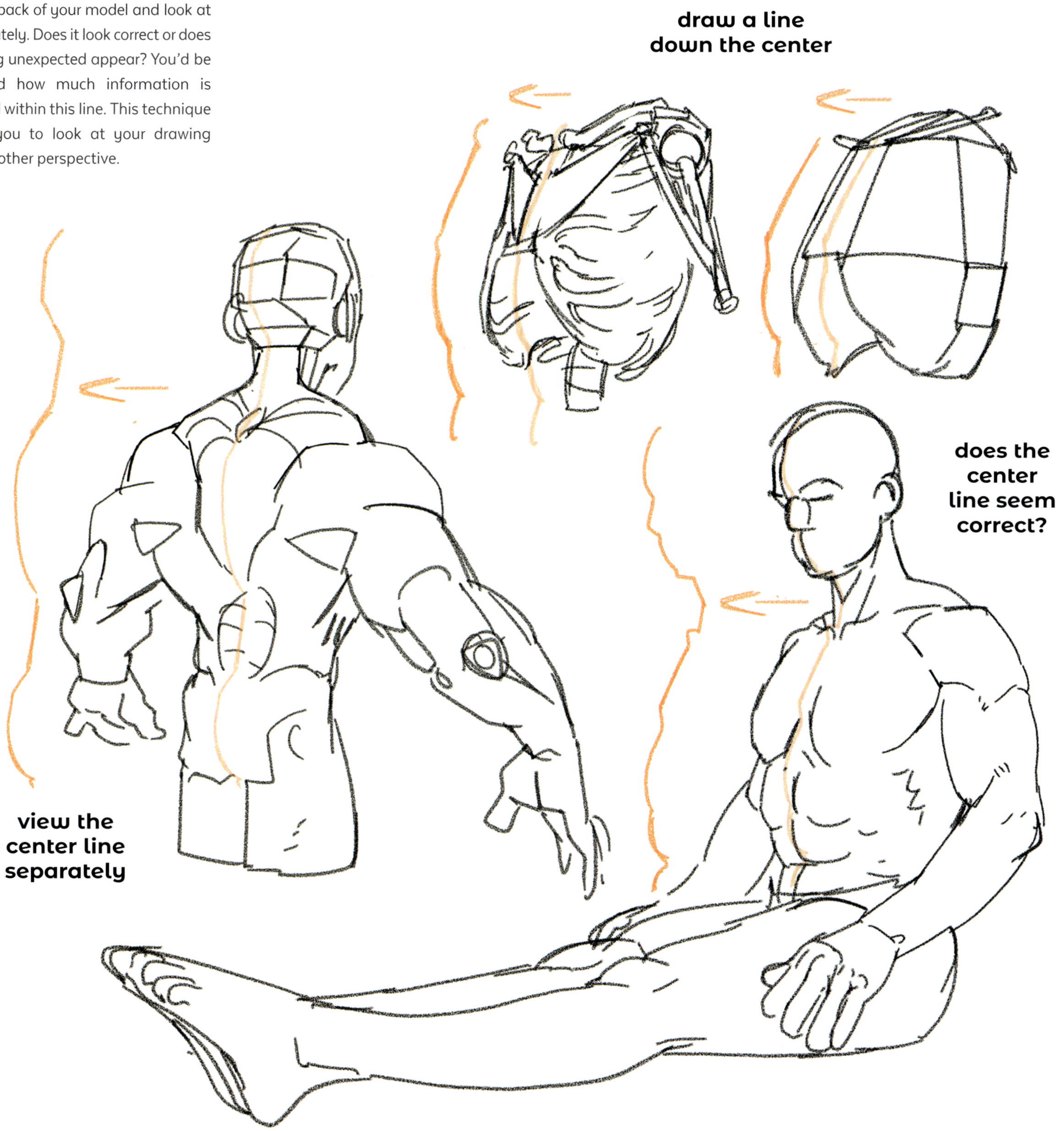

draw a line down the center

does the center line seem correct?

view the center line separately

Here's an example of that process. Here I checked the center line and decided I didn't like it because it was too ambiguous around the core **(G)**. I wanted a leaner look, so I redrew the figure's midsection **(H)** and checked again. To my eyes, the final center line describes the twist much more clearly than before **(I)**.

Are you seeing a pattern here? Figure drawing is a constant process of working forward, then looking back, then forward, then back.

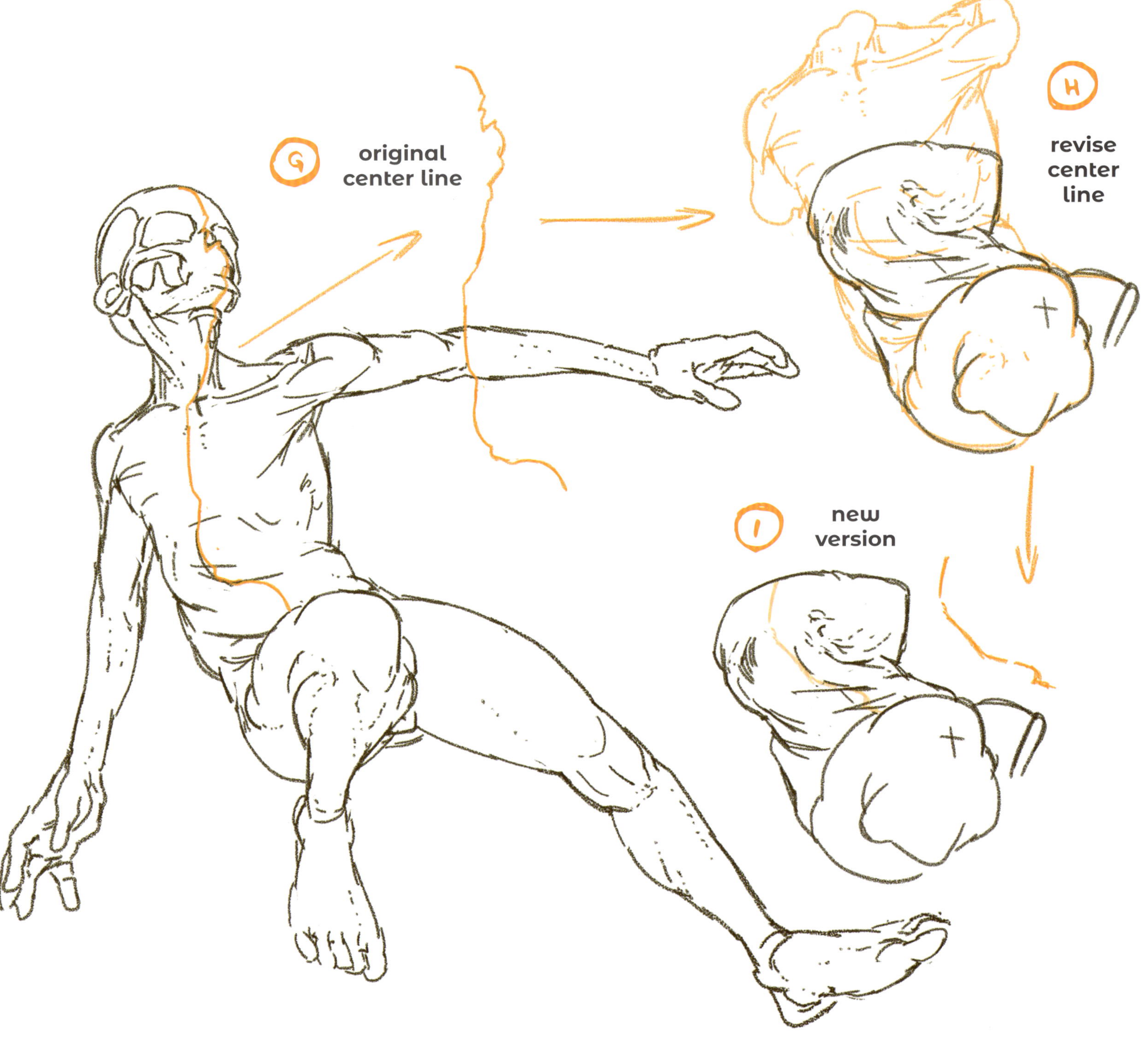

proportions

However much time you spend measuring proportions when drawing, double it. Careful measurement of the proportions and silhouette will really elevate your work. A cartoon and a figure drawing can be done with the same skill, but the results will never be similar.

Before we get obsessed with form, which is the main focus of this book, it's worth putting things into perspective. Ask yourself, "Does more form and volume mean that the drawing is more appealing?" The answer is, "No, not always." Sometimes just the shapes themselves are visually appealing because they represent the subject in the cleanest way. There is beauty in economy of line. Less is more.

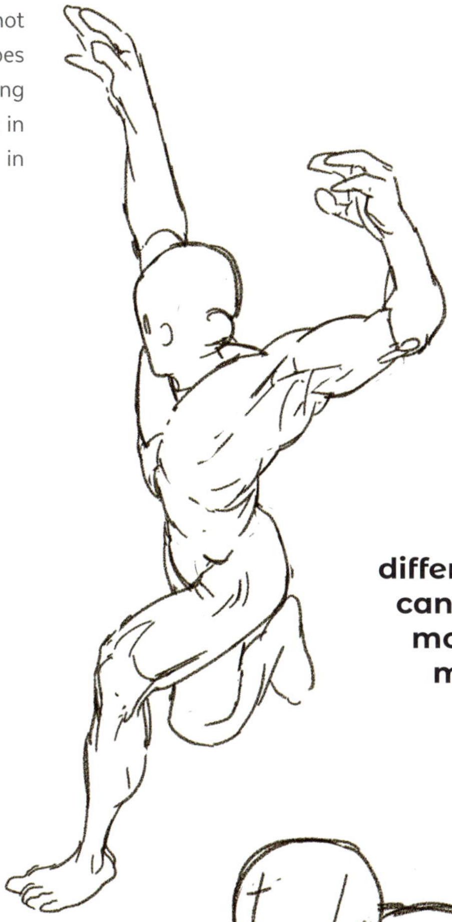

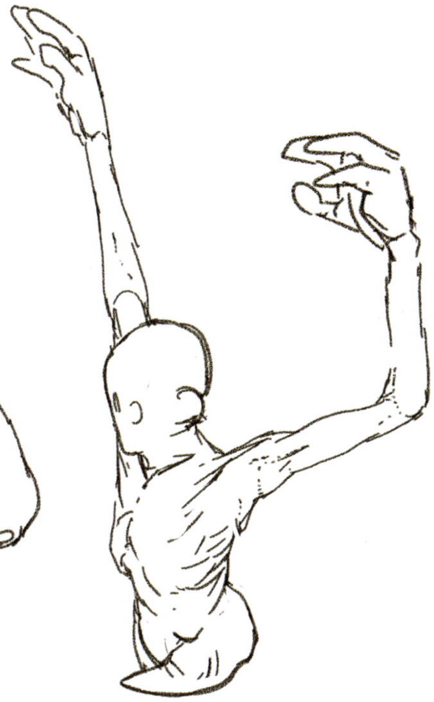

different proportions can make a figure more realistic or more stylized

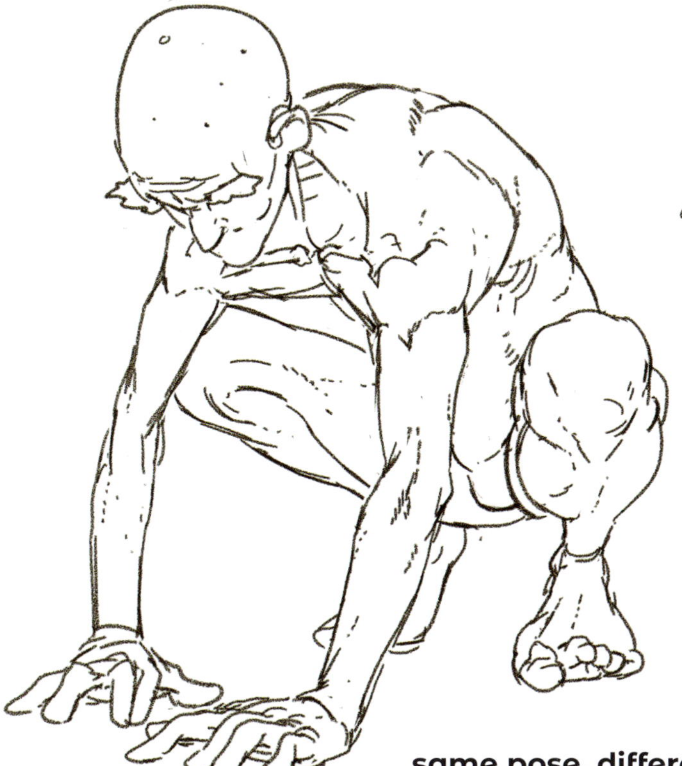

same pose, different proportions and silhouette!

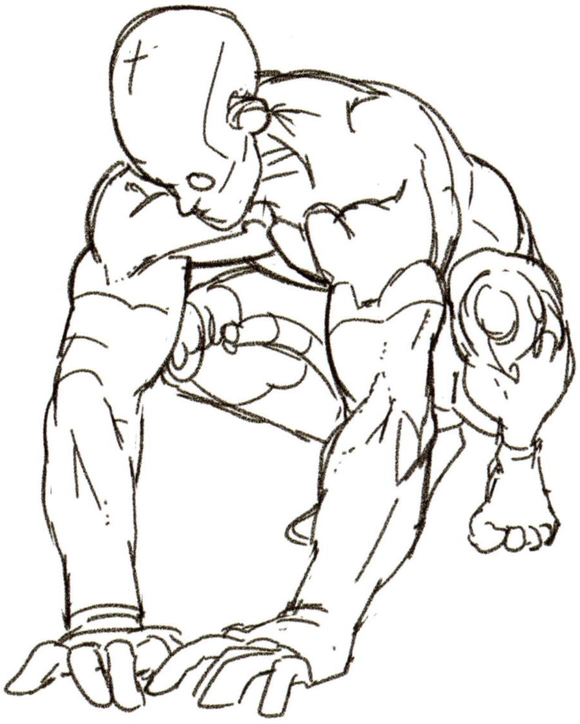

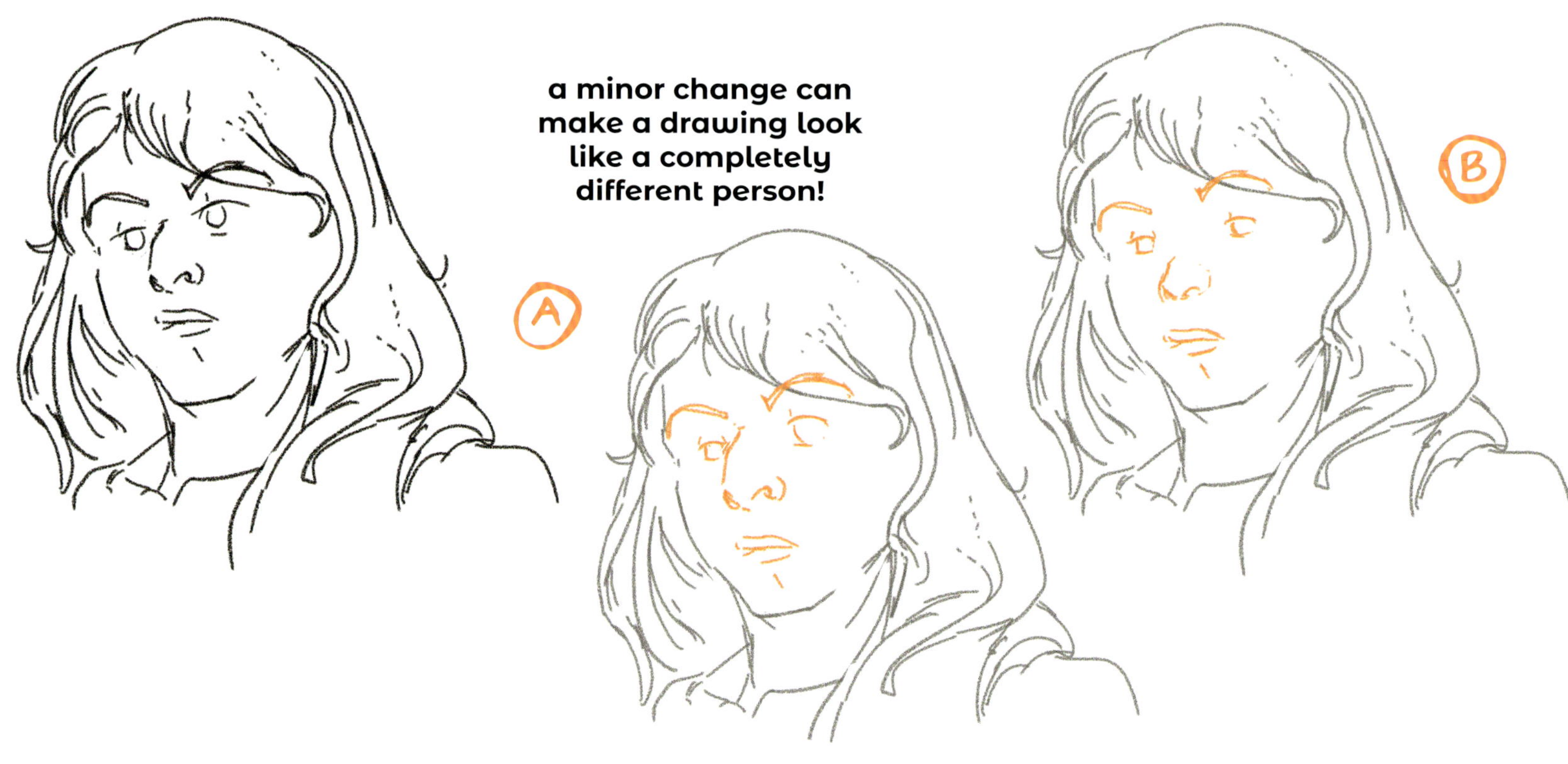

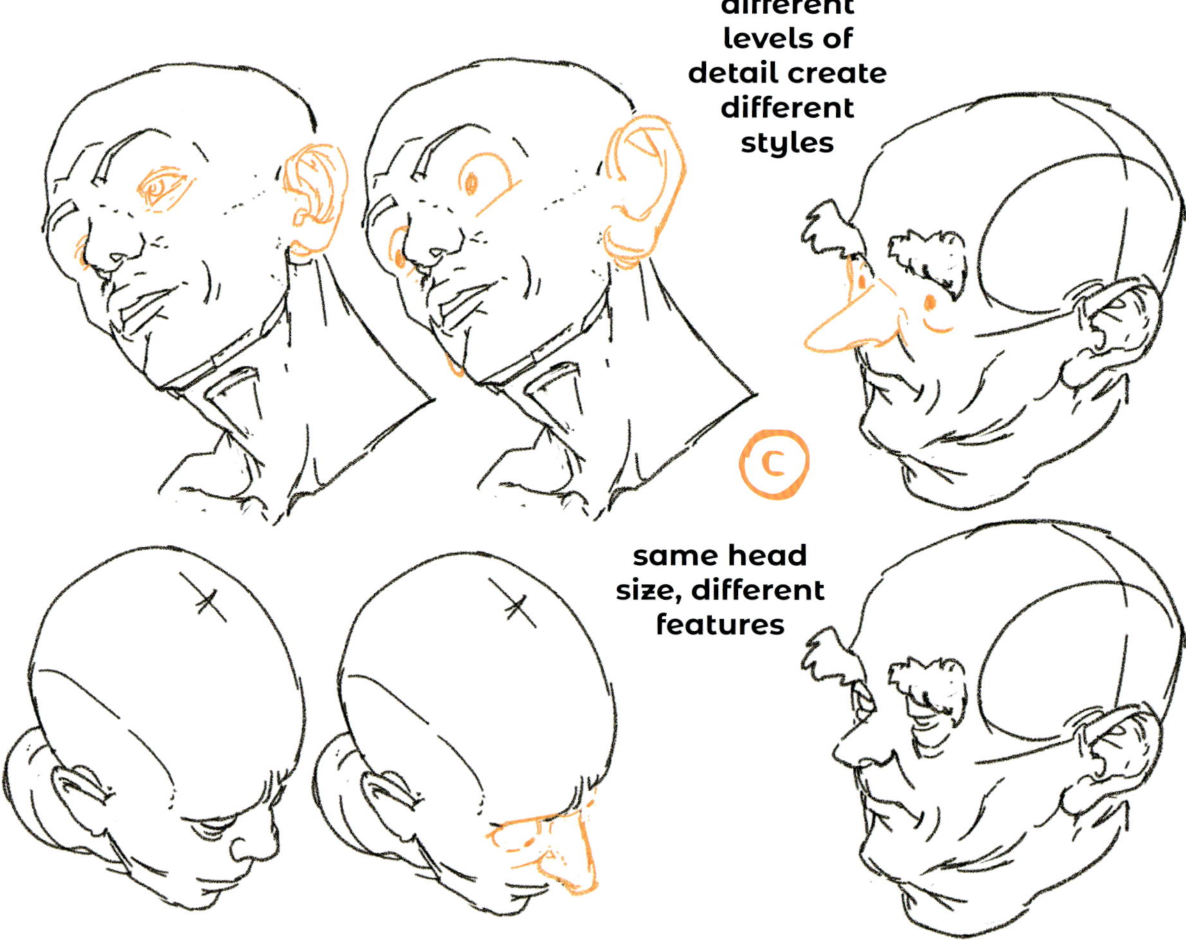

Subtle changes in proportion make a huge difference. Lengthening a nose by a millimeter doesn't seem like much, but that doesn't mean it's a small change. It's all about context. You've changed the relationship between the nose and the other features. The difference may only be a millimeter or two, but the effect is large (A). Similarly, reducing the size of features by a fraction may change the whole impression of a character (B).

By changing the size of features, level of detail, or both, you can change a head's proportions, and therefore its style. It's incredible to see the differences these changes make, even on a head of the same size (C).

We can change not only the features' sizes and levels of detail, but the distances between them. This provides very different results, even when using the same features. A larger forehead or a higher nose are significant changes!

different face placement

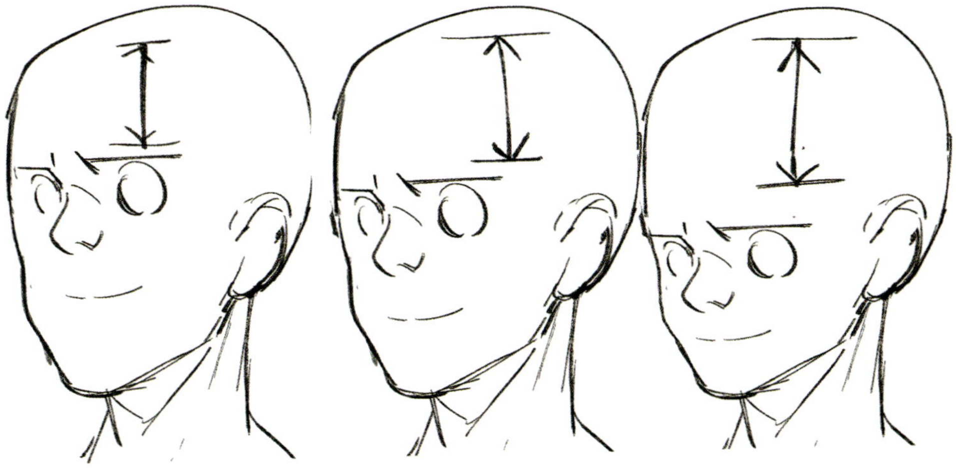

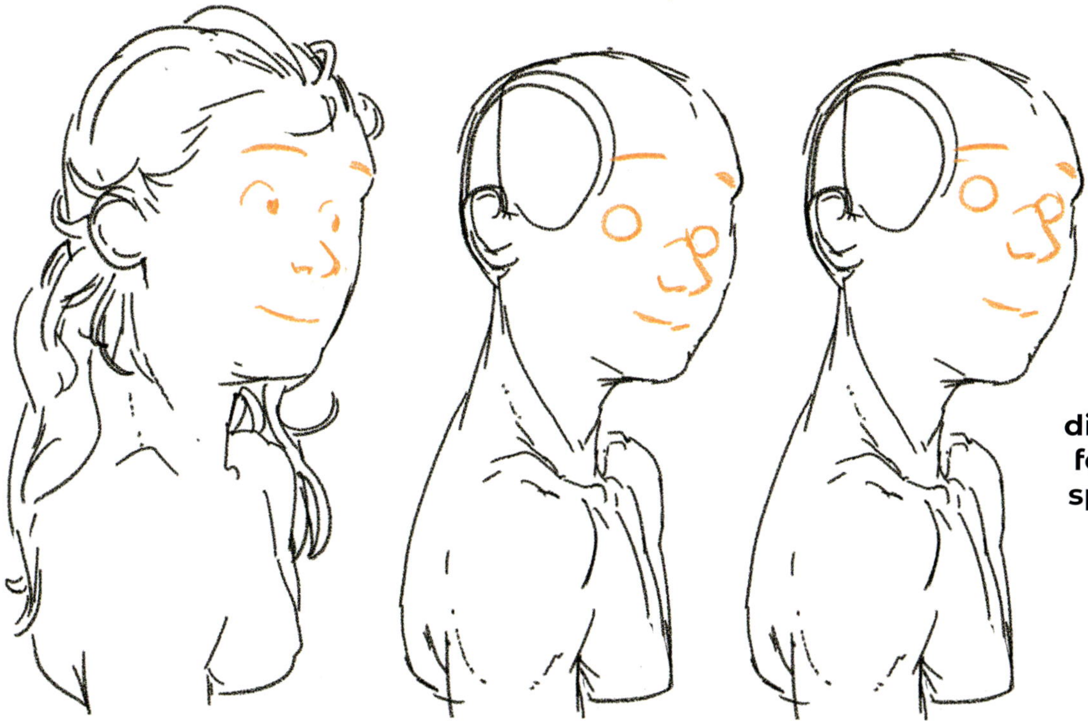

different feature spacing

different feature size

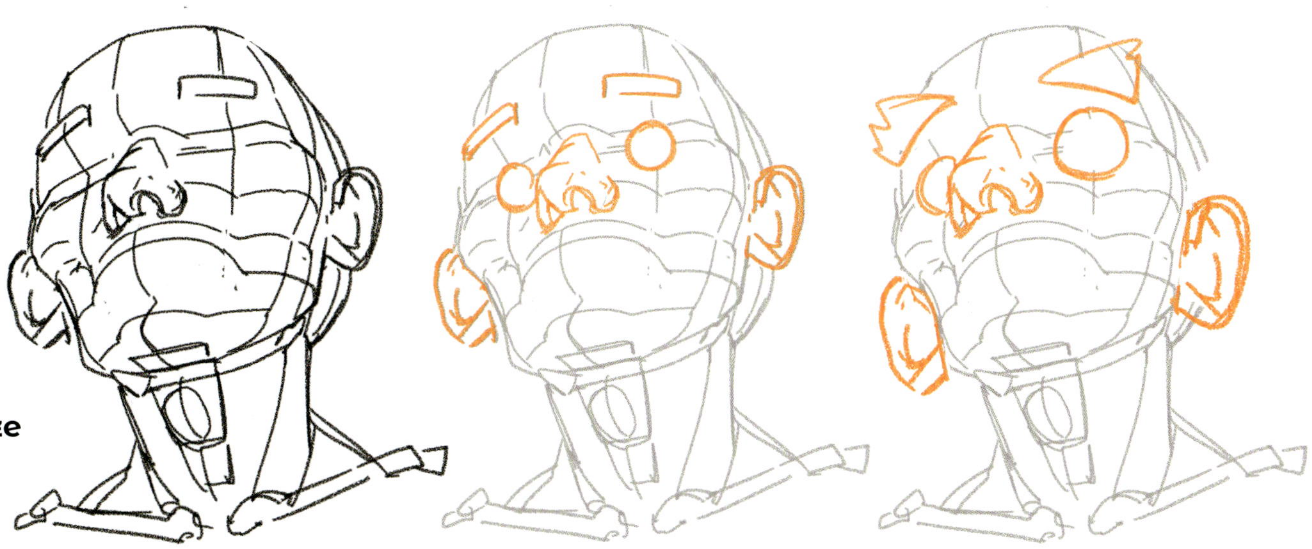

level of detail

3D variables

Every 3D object has three components: vertices, edges, and planes. In A we see that vertices are the corners, planes are the "faces" or "sides," and the edges are the edges! The more of these variables our subject has, the more complex it is in terms of detail (B). A cube has six planes, eight vertices, and twelve edges, so it's more complex than you'd think. We can break down complex subjects into planes, edges, and vertices to help us study them (C).

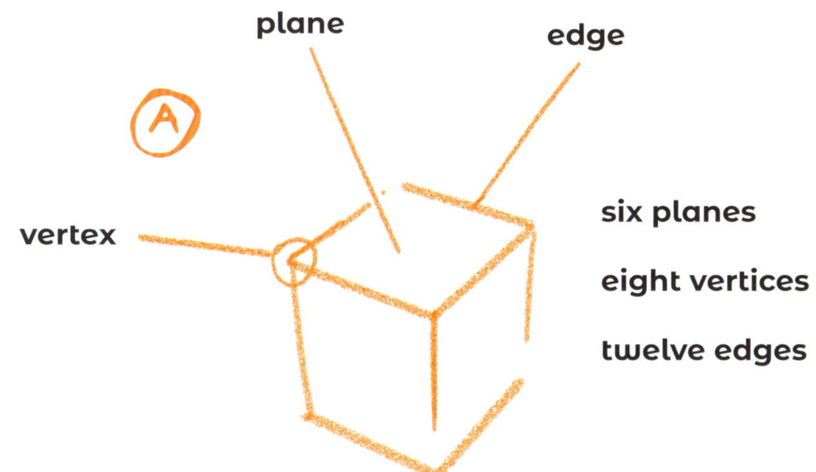

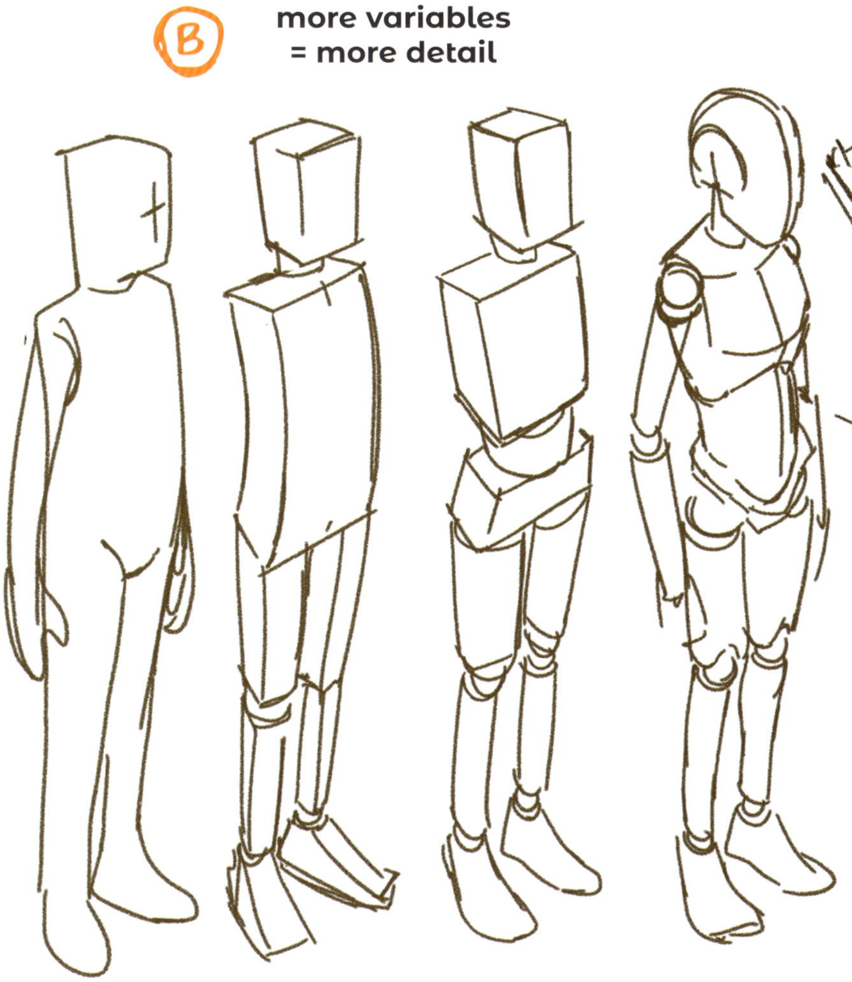

B

more variables
= more detail

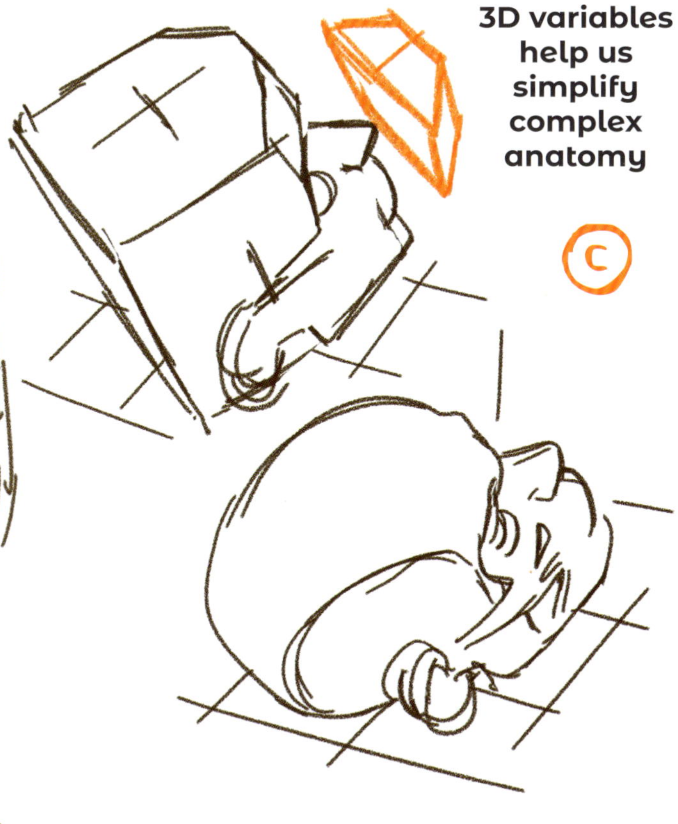

3D variables
help us
simplify
complex
anatomy

C

level of detail

When we say "level of detail" we're referring to the total amount of 3D variables (planes, edges, and vertices). As you can see in A, the same model can be drawn with different levels of detail. It's just like early video game graphics – they had to represent something with a lower level of detail because computing power was lower. See how the two skulls in B are identical in size and volume, but show a different level of detail.

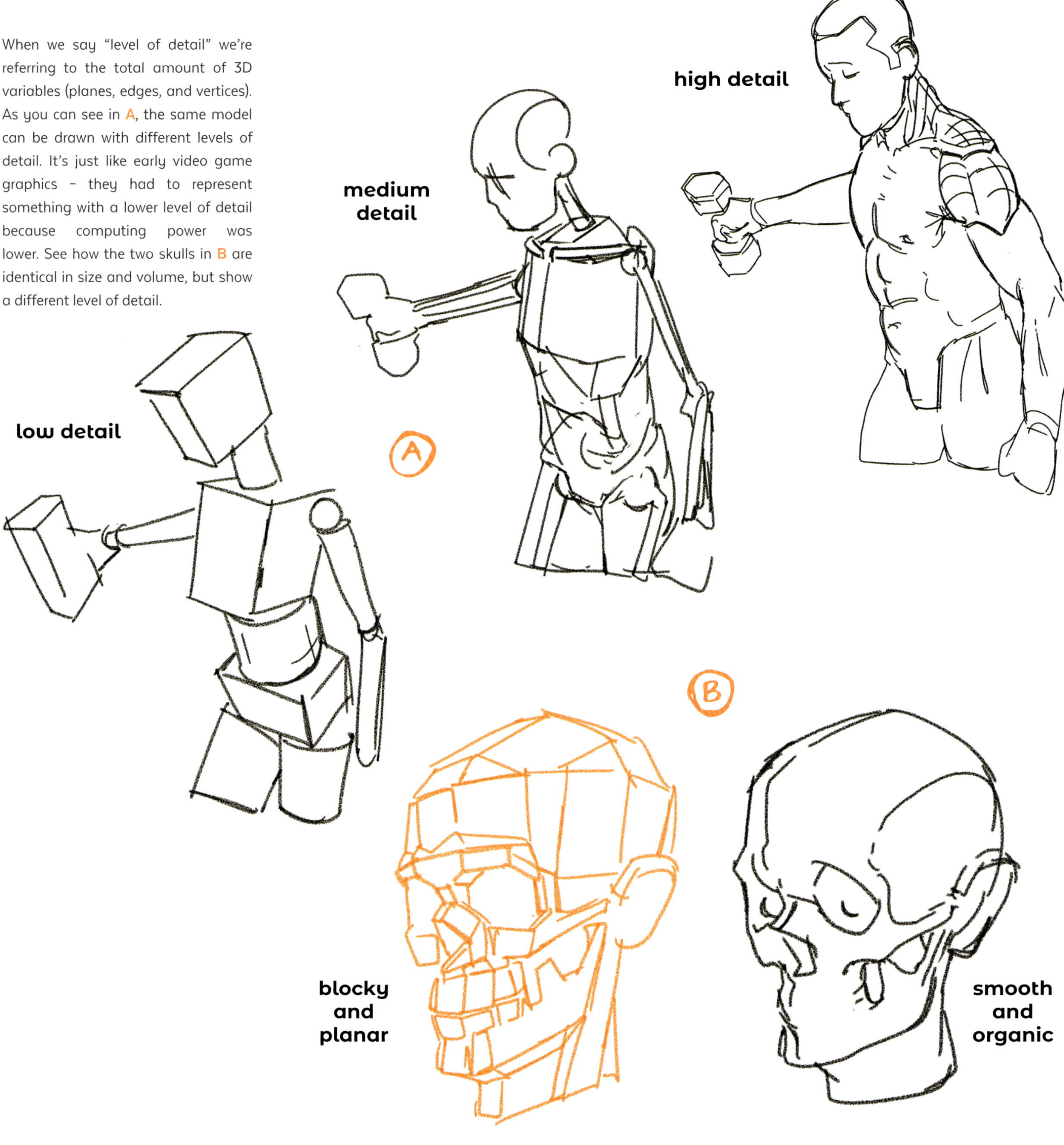

Always work at a level of detail that's appropriate for you (C). To achieve maximal growth in drawing, you want to work at a level that's just on the edge of your comfort zone, a few percent harder than you're capable of doing comfortably. This is called "the Goldilocks principle" – choosing a level that's neither too hot nor too cold!

If you're working on exercises or trying to achieve levels of detail that are just too difficult for you, the process will become frustrating and you won't learn as much. Try to access the Goldilocks zone without pushing too hard into frustration (D).

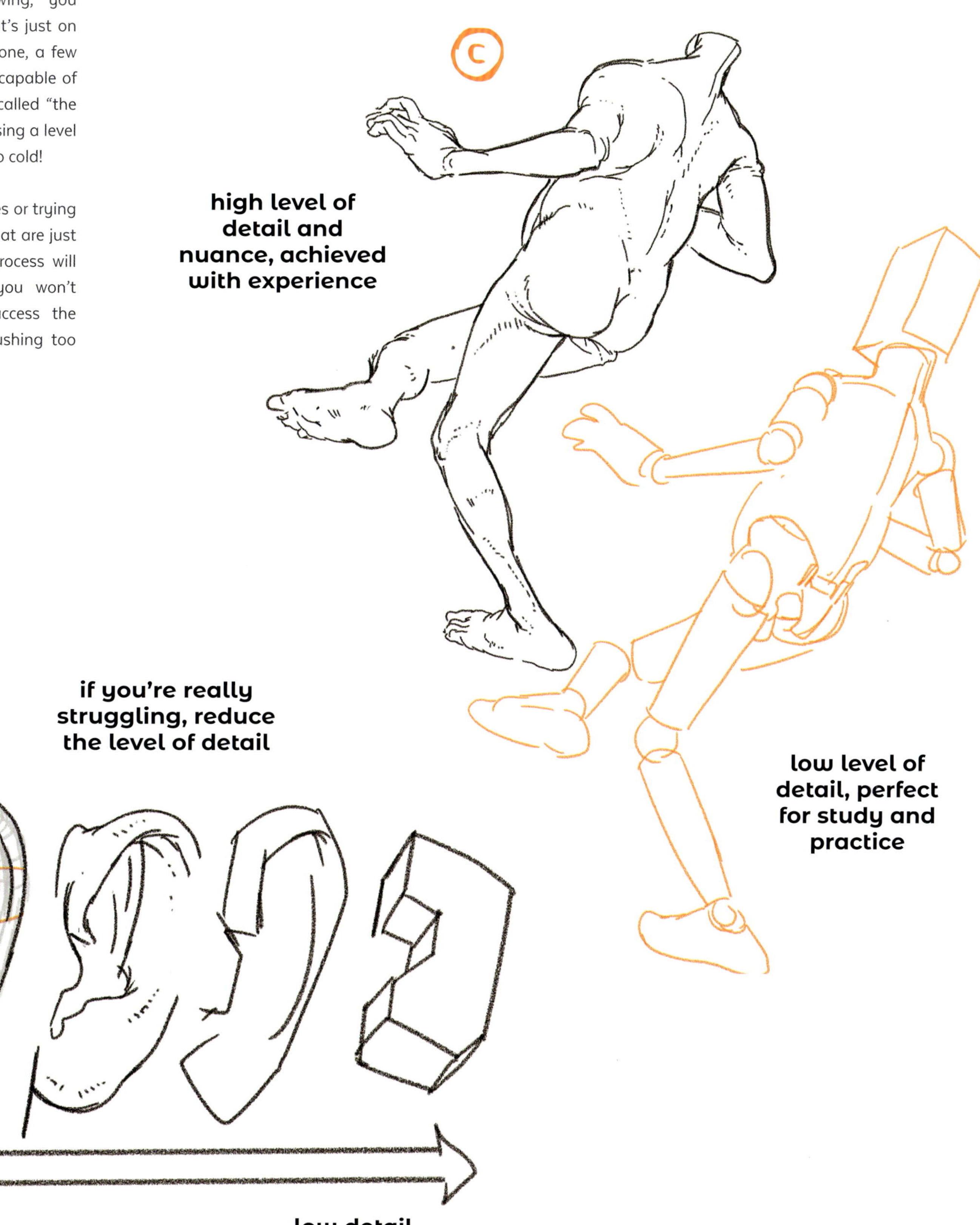

To find an appropriate level of detail, ask, "Is this too complex for me? Is this too simple?" Many people feel an urge to rush ahead in their study and try to work at a level of detail that's too complex. Different levels of detail fulfill different purposes for visualizing a figure. Is your chosen level of detail a good match for the drawing's purpose?

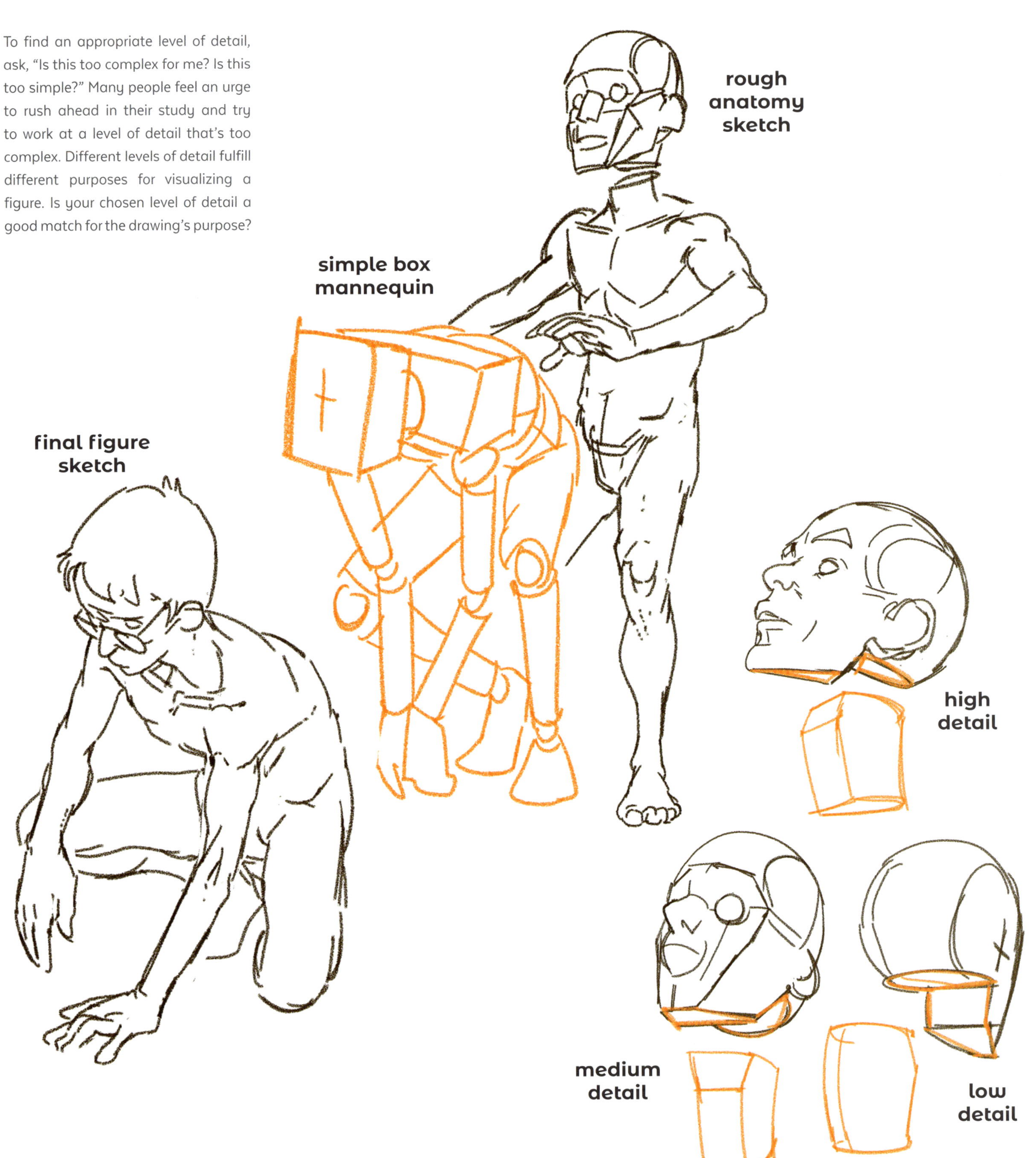

You should also ask yourself, "Can I rotate this and draw it from my mind at any angle?" (E, F) Put yourself to the test, and if you're not sure – which you probably won't be – try opting for simpler shapes and less detail!

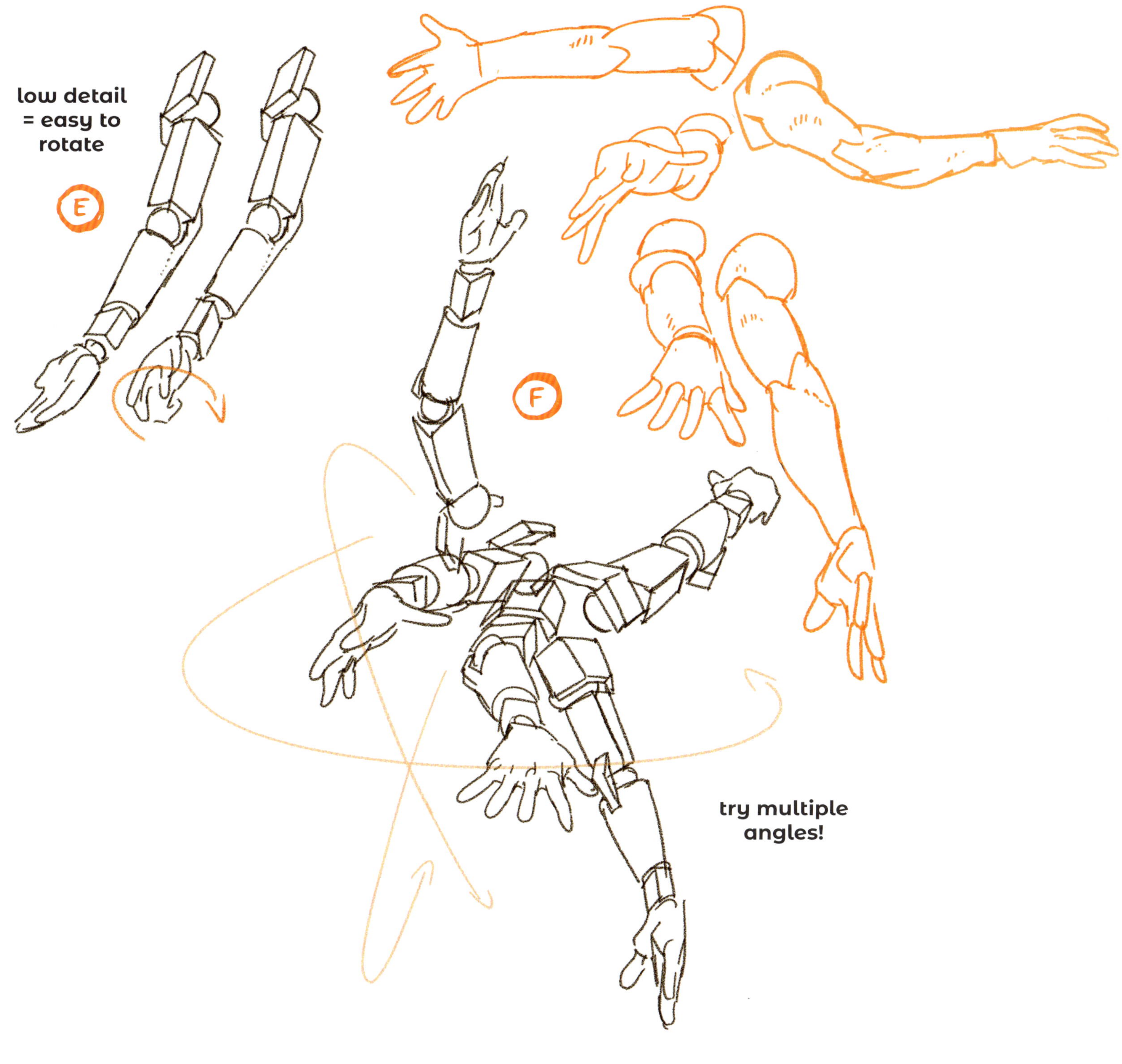

Here are a few more examples of various levels of detail (G, H), starting with blocky low-detail models and building up to a more organic, convincing figure (I). Remember, the goal is *believability*, not *realism*. If your subject looks like it could work, it will read as an appealing drawing, without diving into medical levels of detail!

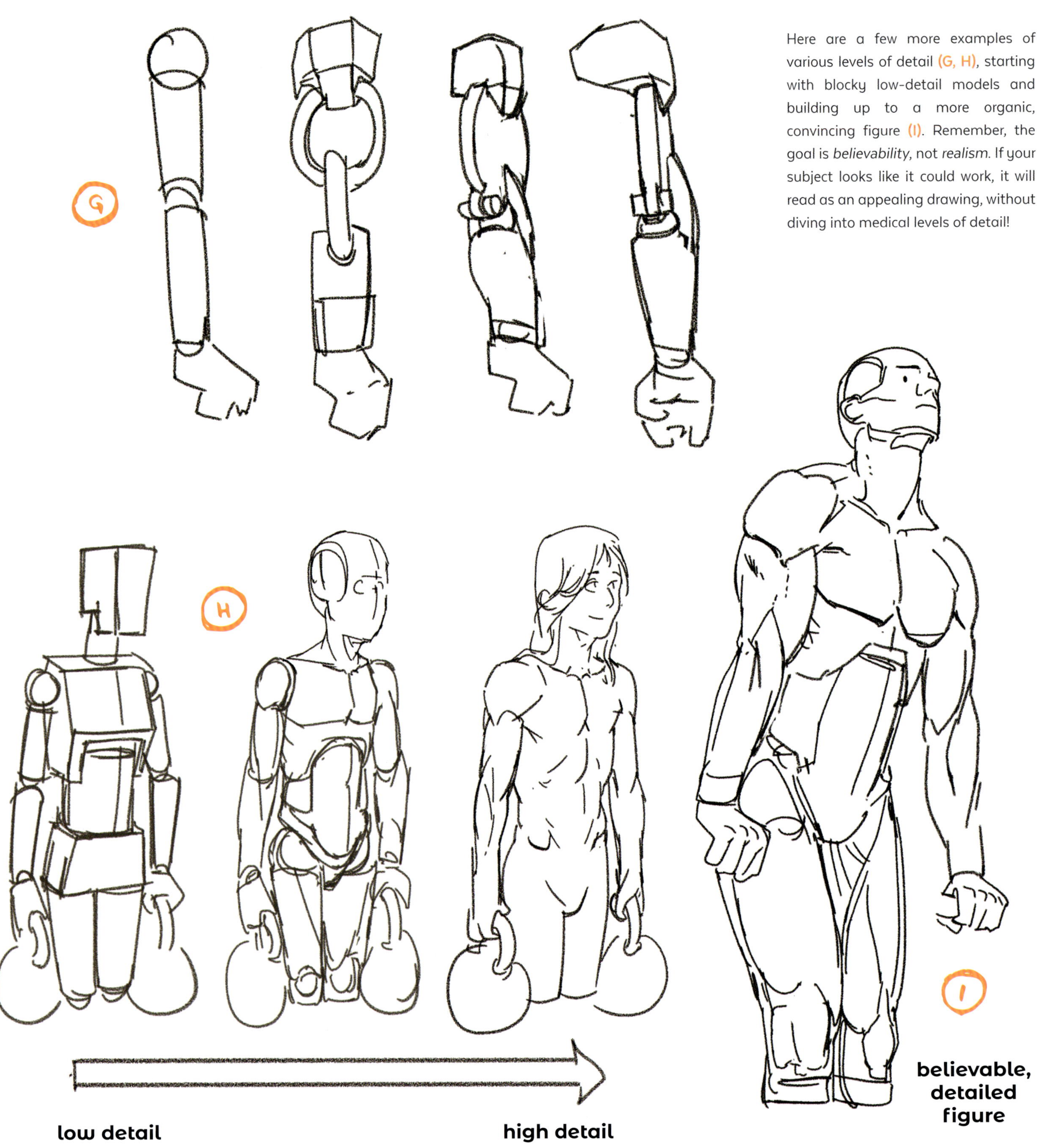

flat vs 3D forms

When you're drawing in a more cartoonish style, you can get away with using basic, symmetrical shapes to represent features, like using flat circles for eyes. However, once you depart from cartooning, you need to start thinking of everything in terms of 3D form. Ask yourself, "Are these shapes symmetrical? Was that a choice or just a habit?" Unless they are 2D shapes, symmetrical objects don't appear symmetrical when viewed from different angles.

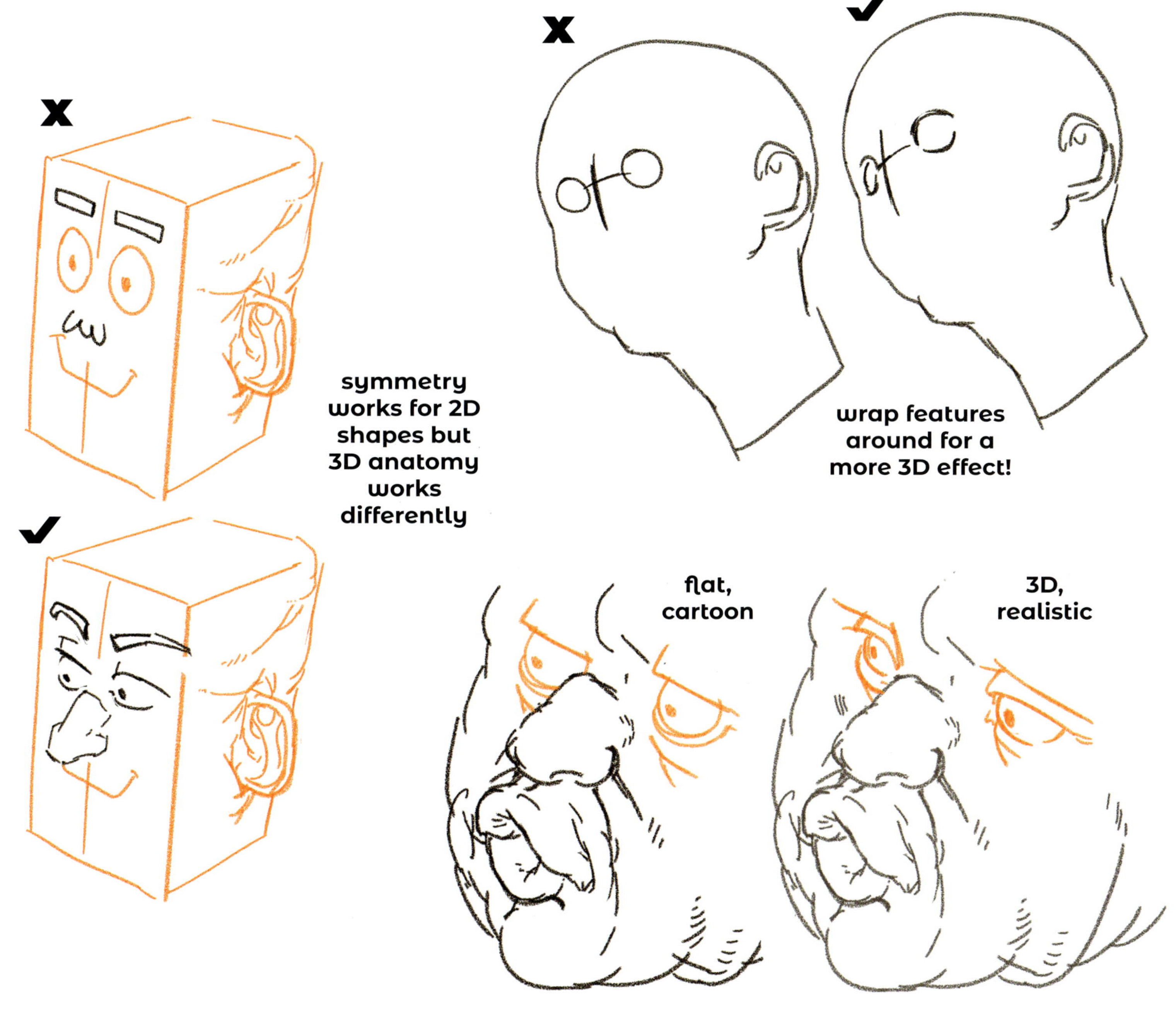

don't show off

Strive to draw representationally and faithfully to your vision. In other words, draw what you see, not what you know! The latter is just showing off your knowledge. Don't draw individual muscle fibers and striations. Focus on the silhouette and the major forms, and the rest will take care of itself.

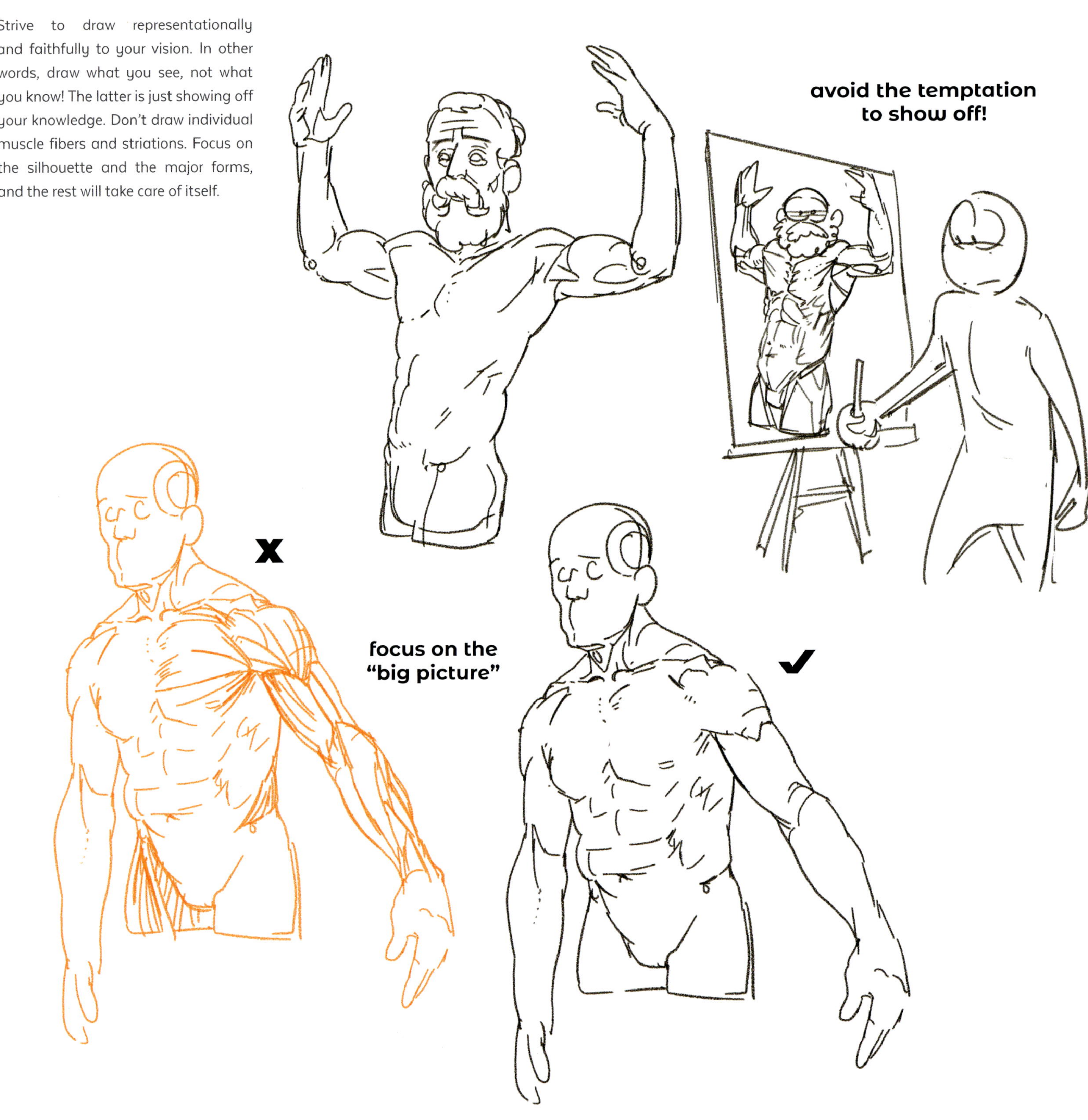

The sections of this book will be focused on leading you, region by region, through how to design models with increasing levels of detail for the anatomy of the body. We'll start with a cube form for each region and end up with something approaching a realistic human body. Along the way, you'll find a level of detail that works best for you and your art.

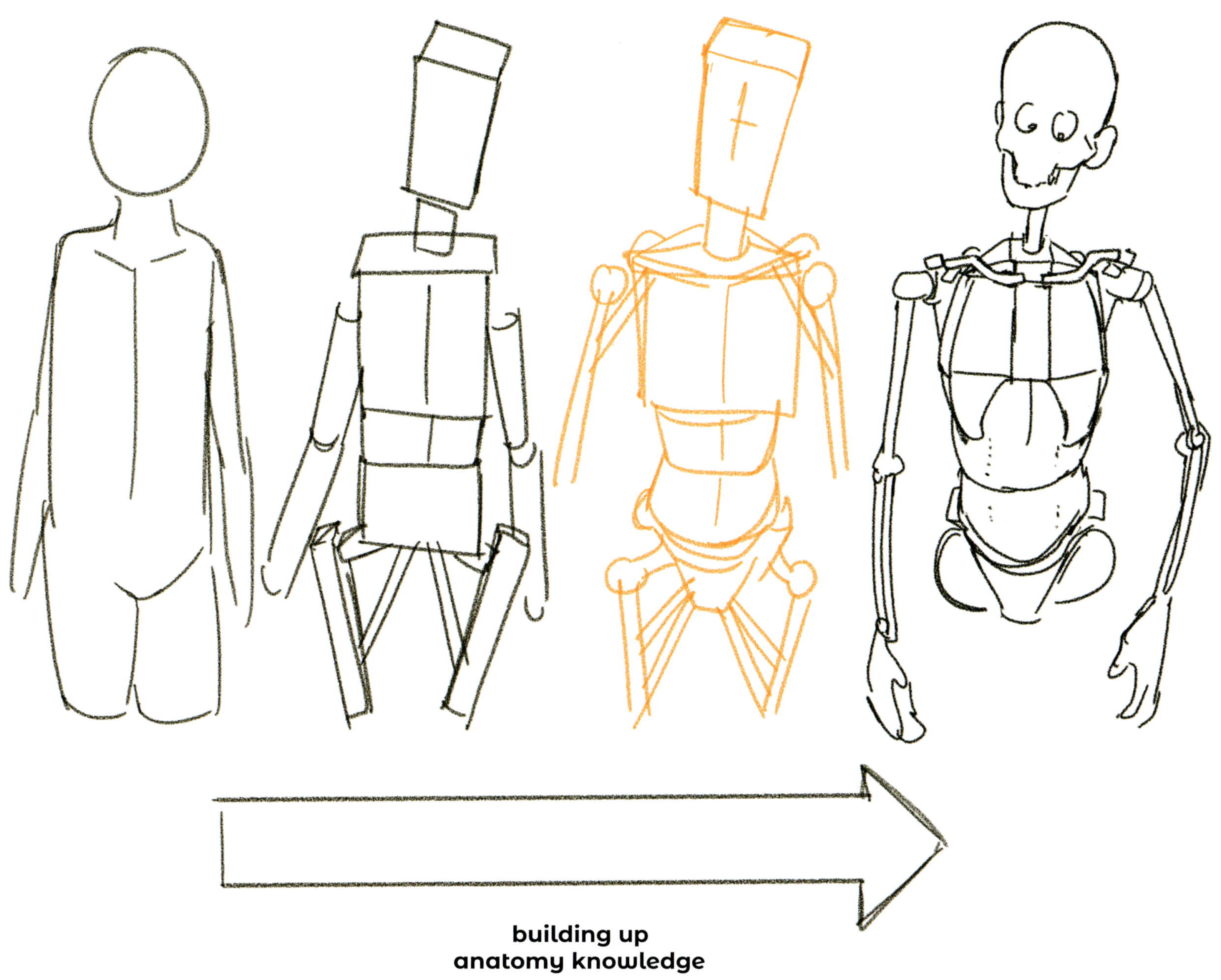

the box mannequin

mannequins

We often begin learning anatomy by using mannequins as simplified representations of the figure (A). Why? For starters, they look good! They are organic and flowing, which gives them appeal. They also seem to make intuitive sense; if our goal is to draw something organic and dynamic (B), shouldn't we start with an equally organic mannequin? Let's examine why using a hard-surface model, like a box mannequin, makes more sense for us (C).

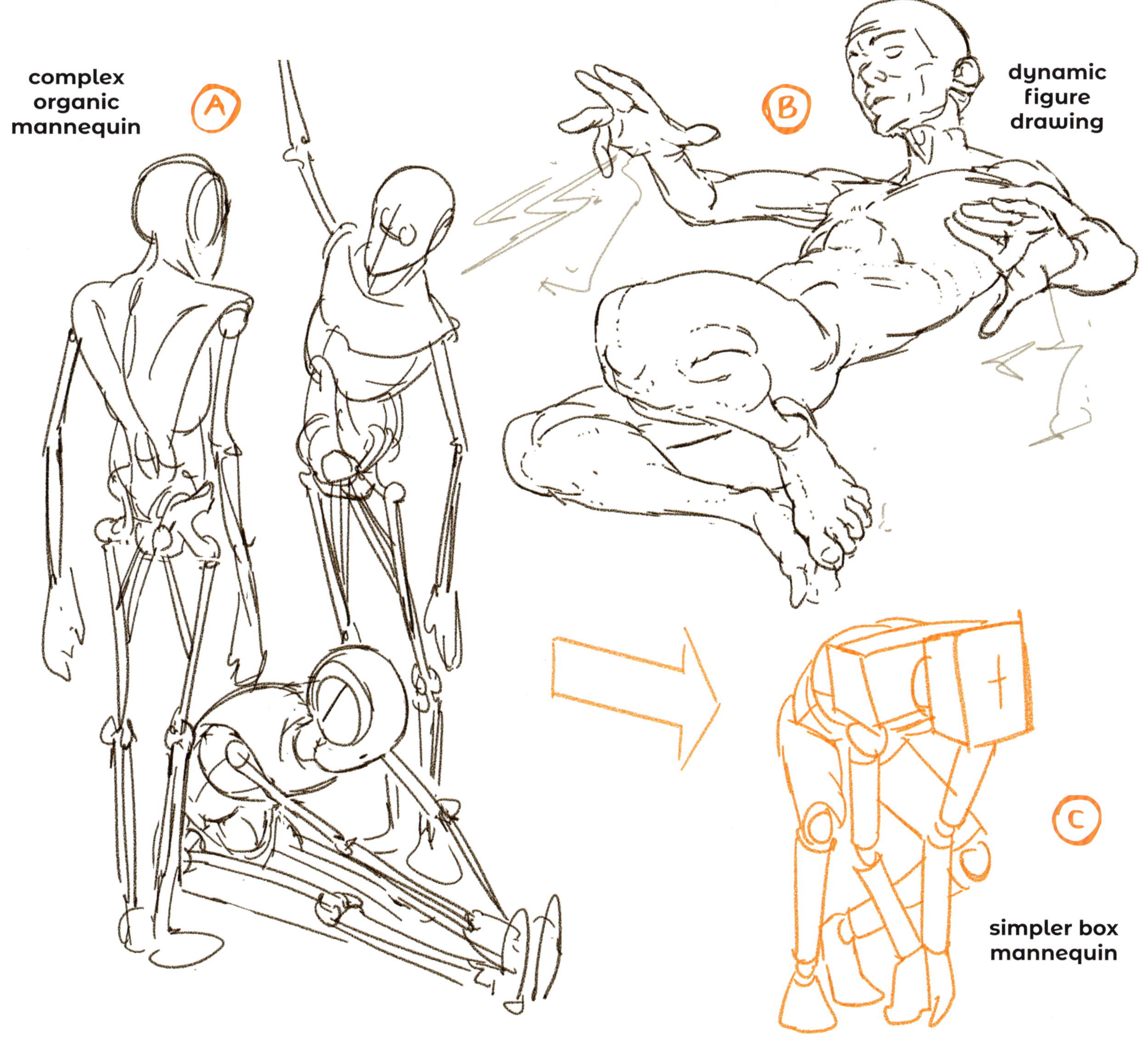

In this book, the base of our model will be the standard box mannequin. It has three basic forms: the head (1), chest (2), and pelvis (3). These are connected by cylinders to form the trunk of the body. So why would we use this (D), rather than the more appealing organic mannequin (E)? It's because the organic one looks great in simple views, but once the perspective gets more complex, things quickly become confusing for a beginner!

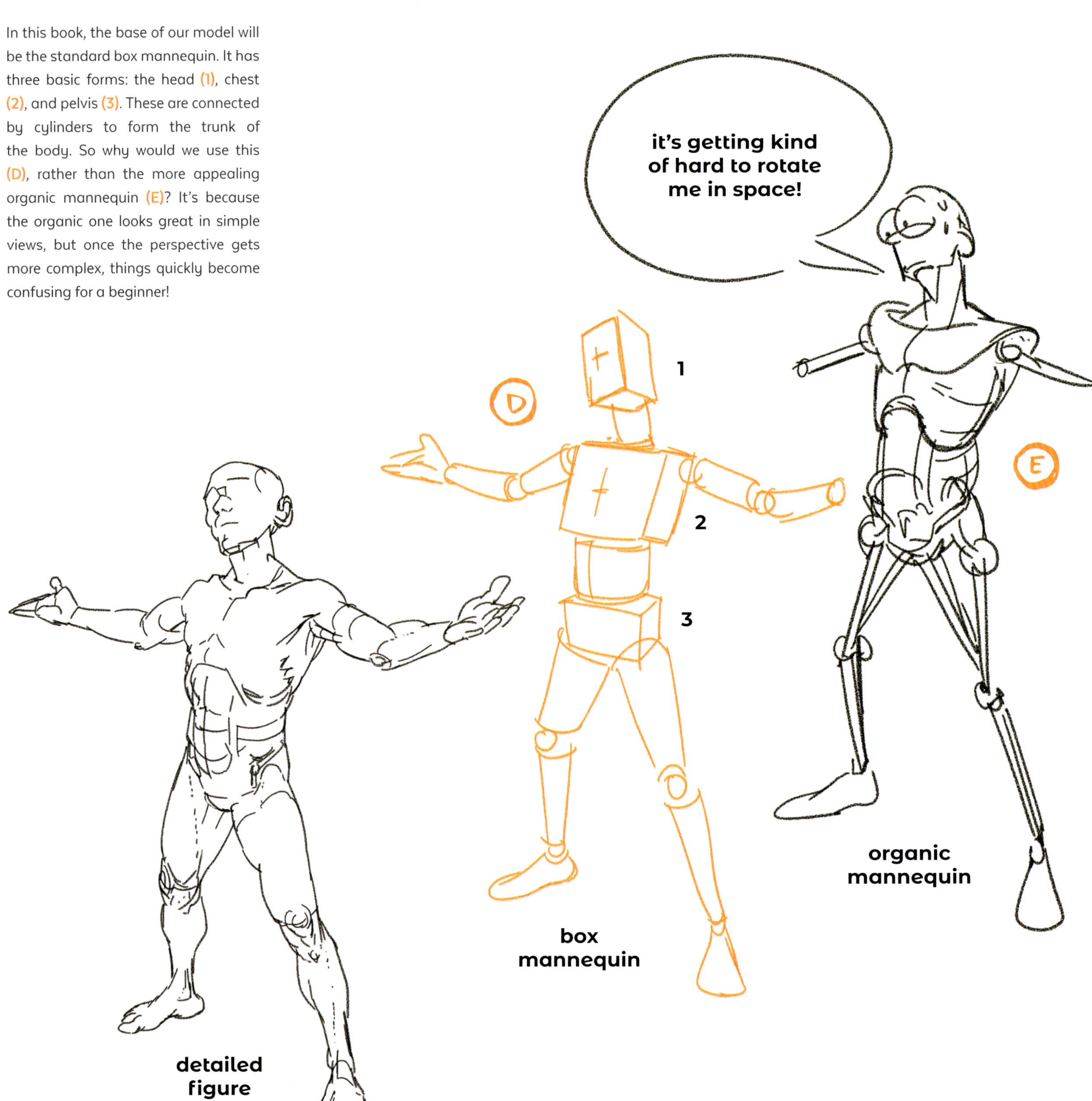

With a box mannequin, you can focus on rotating the forms in space and getting the proportions correct. The tapering of the limbs needs to be subtle and can be tougher to draw than it looks! We'll start by forgetting about the details seen in F and focusing on simpler models (G).

As we progress through this book we'll improve our knowledge and ability to raise the level of detail. Eventually we'll be able to draw complex models from all angles (H).

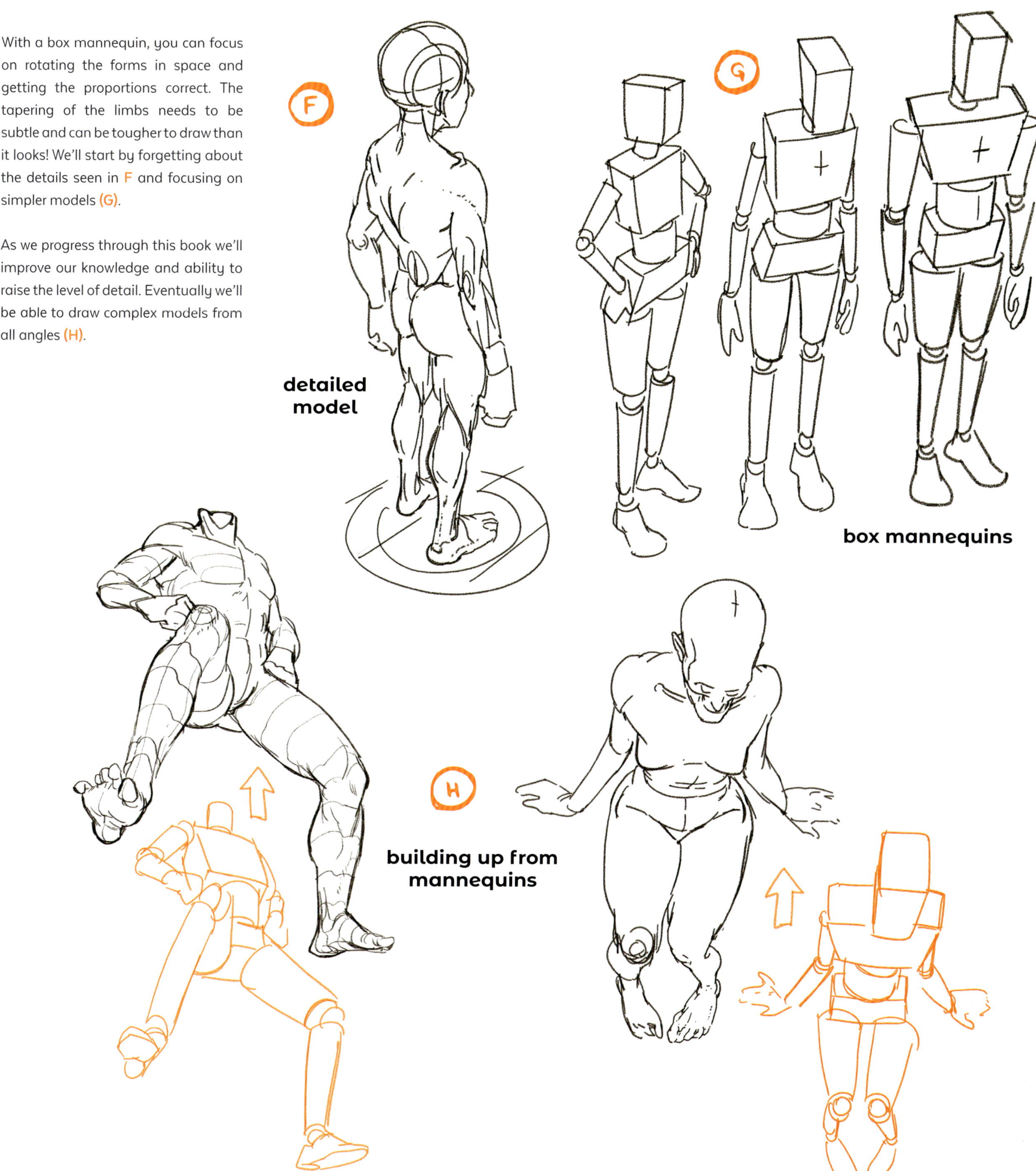

the camera & perspective

perspective

When learning about perspective, many students worry about knowing where the vanishing points are, what type of perspective they are using, and what to measure angles from.

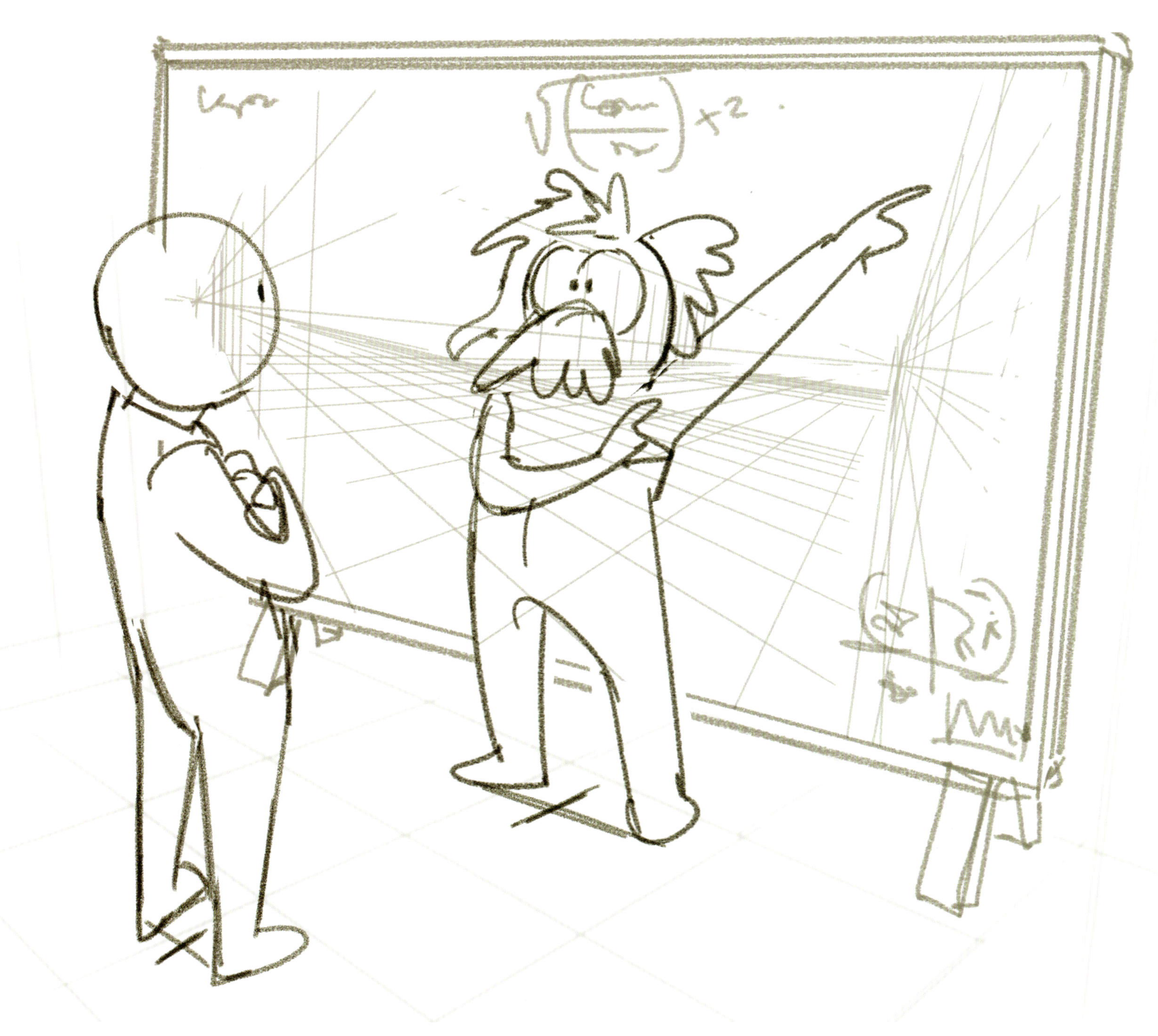

In-depth explanations of perspective are outside the scope of this anatomy book, but we can keep things simple for now and explain how to think about your view of your subject. For starters, imagine your own head is a camera.

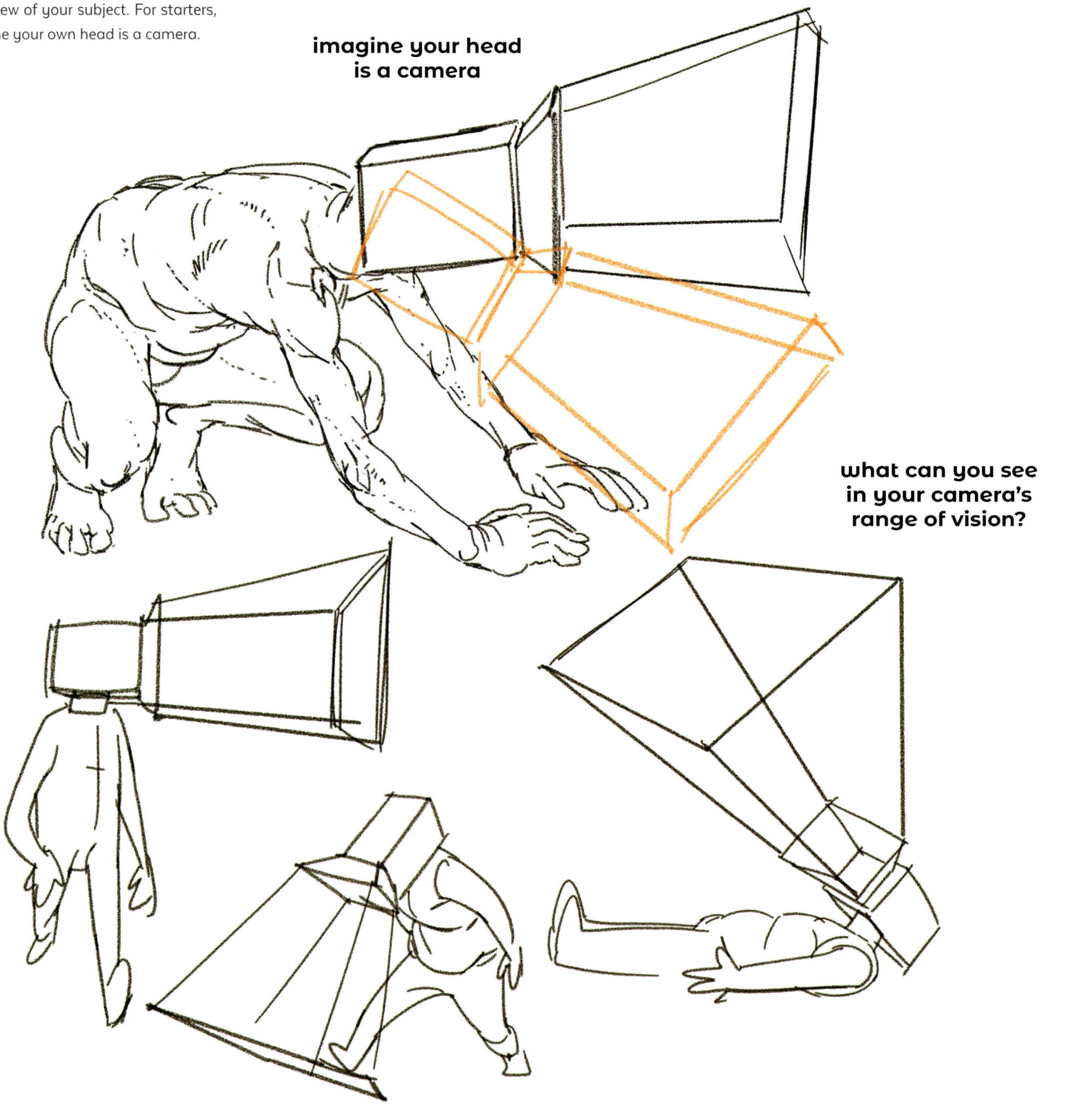

imagine your head is a camera

what can you see in your camera's range of vision?

Whatever you're drawing, try to imagine the subject existing within a scene, so it has context. Imagine yourself walking through the scene and looking around with your camera-head, observing the subject.

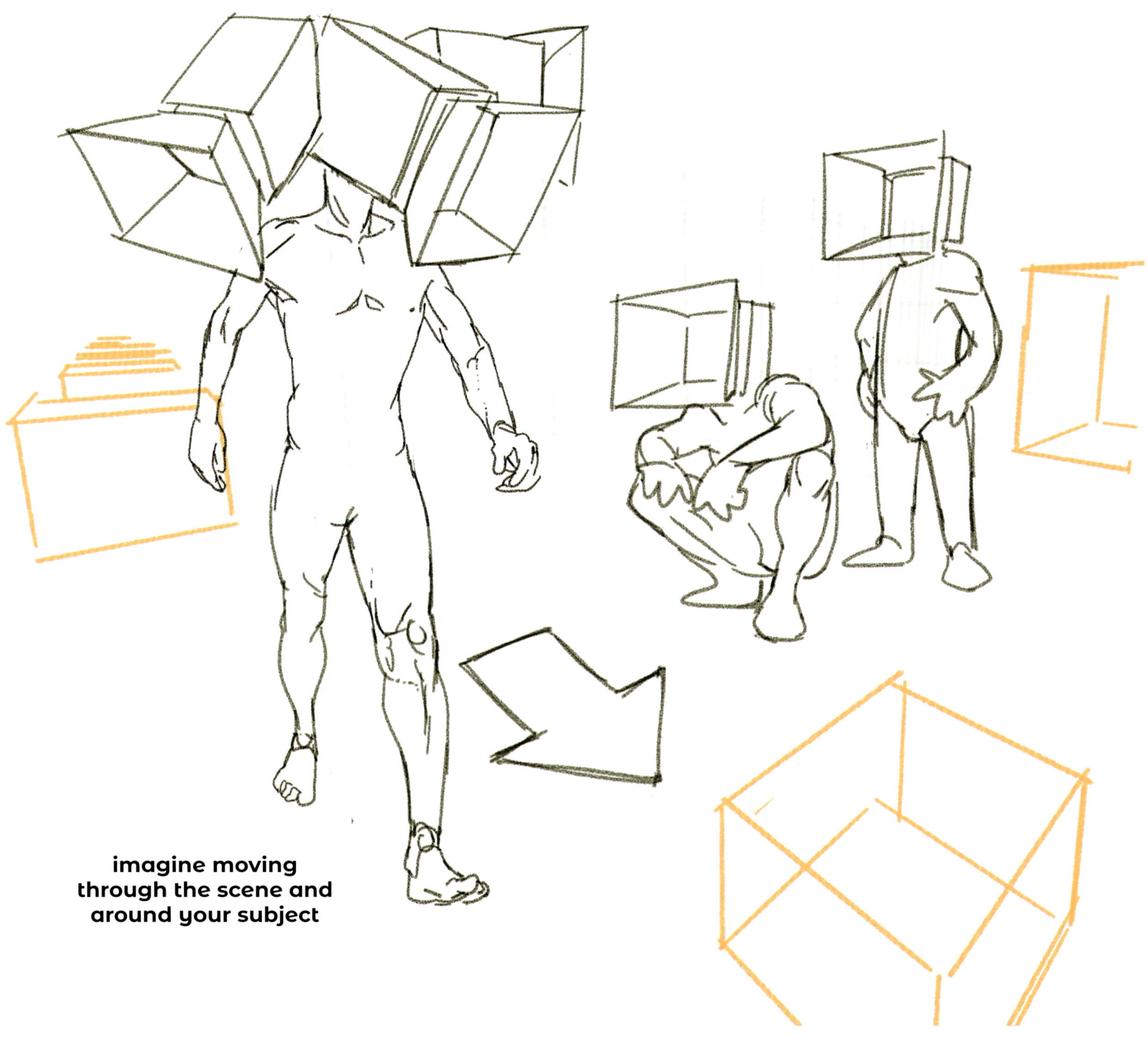

imagine moving through the scene and around your subject

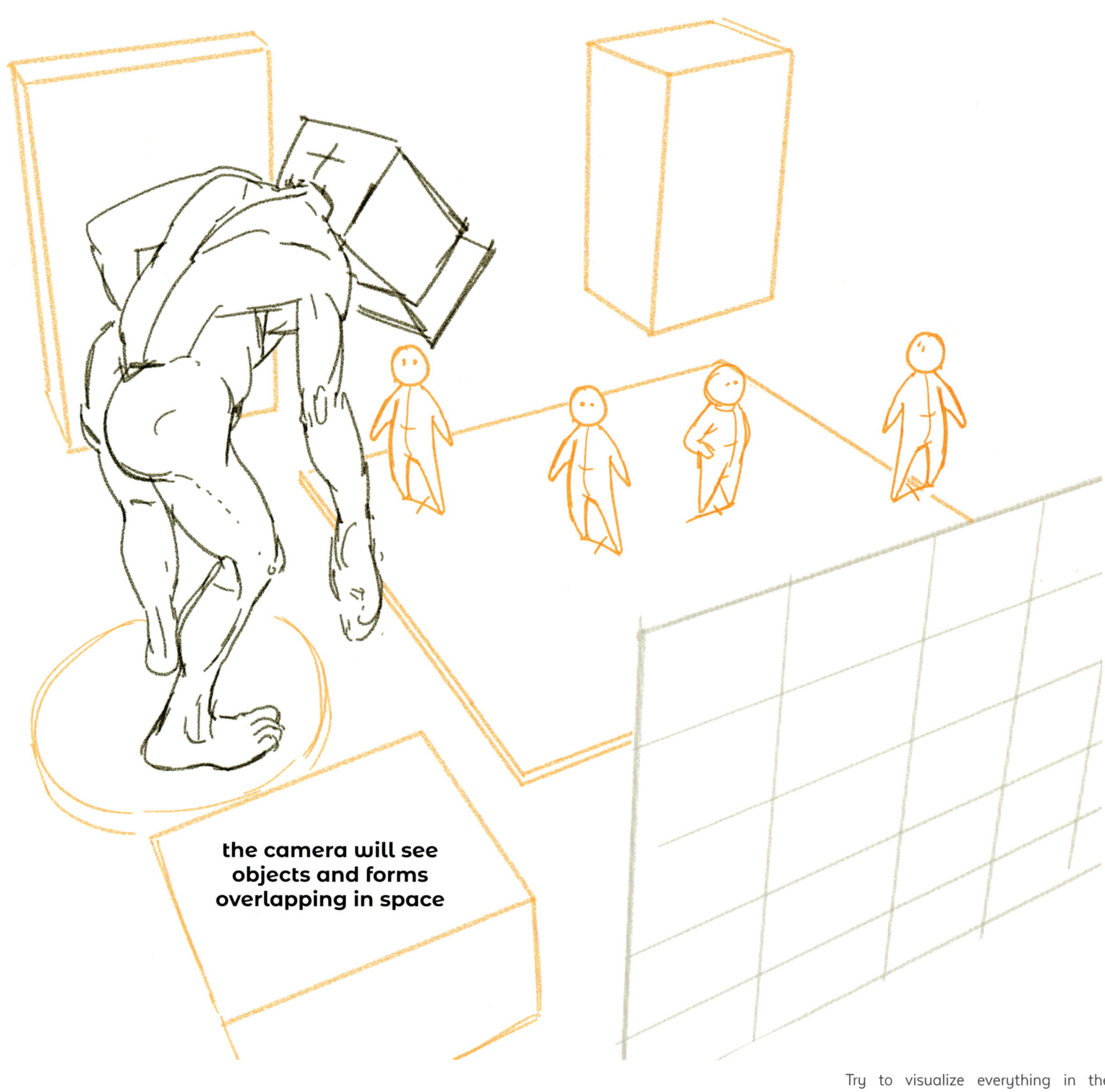

Try to visualize everything in the scene, not just what you're looking at "through the camera." This helps clarify the scene in your mind and give it context. Overlap creates depth within a scene, just as it does within objects, so don't forget to overlap elements.

Always be clear in your mind by asking yourself explicitly, "Am I looking up or down at this object?" If you're looking up, you'll probably see the bottom of it (A). If you're looking down, you'll probably see the top of it (B).

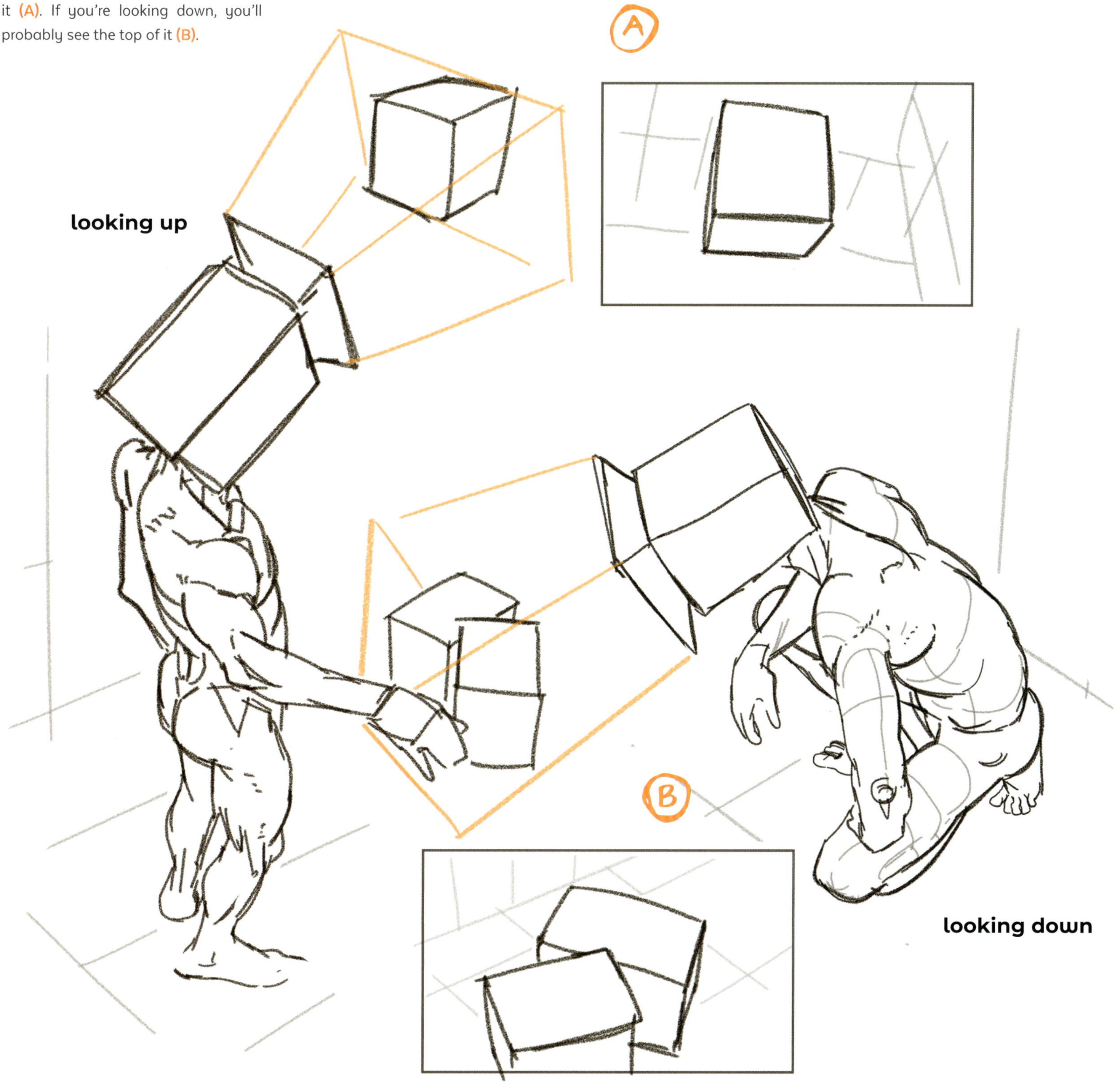

A

looking up

looking down

B

Decide the angle *before* you draw the subject. If you don't, you'll encounter inconsistencies at a later stage, where it looks like you see the tops of some parts and the bottoms of others (C). Planning ahead and sticking to an angle will help create a consistent final figure (D).

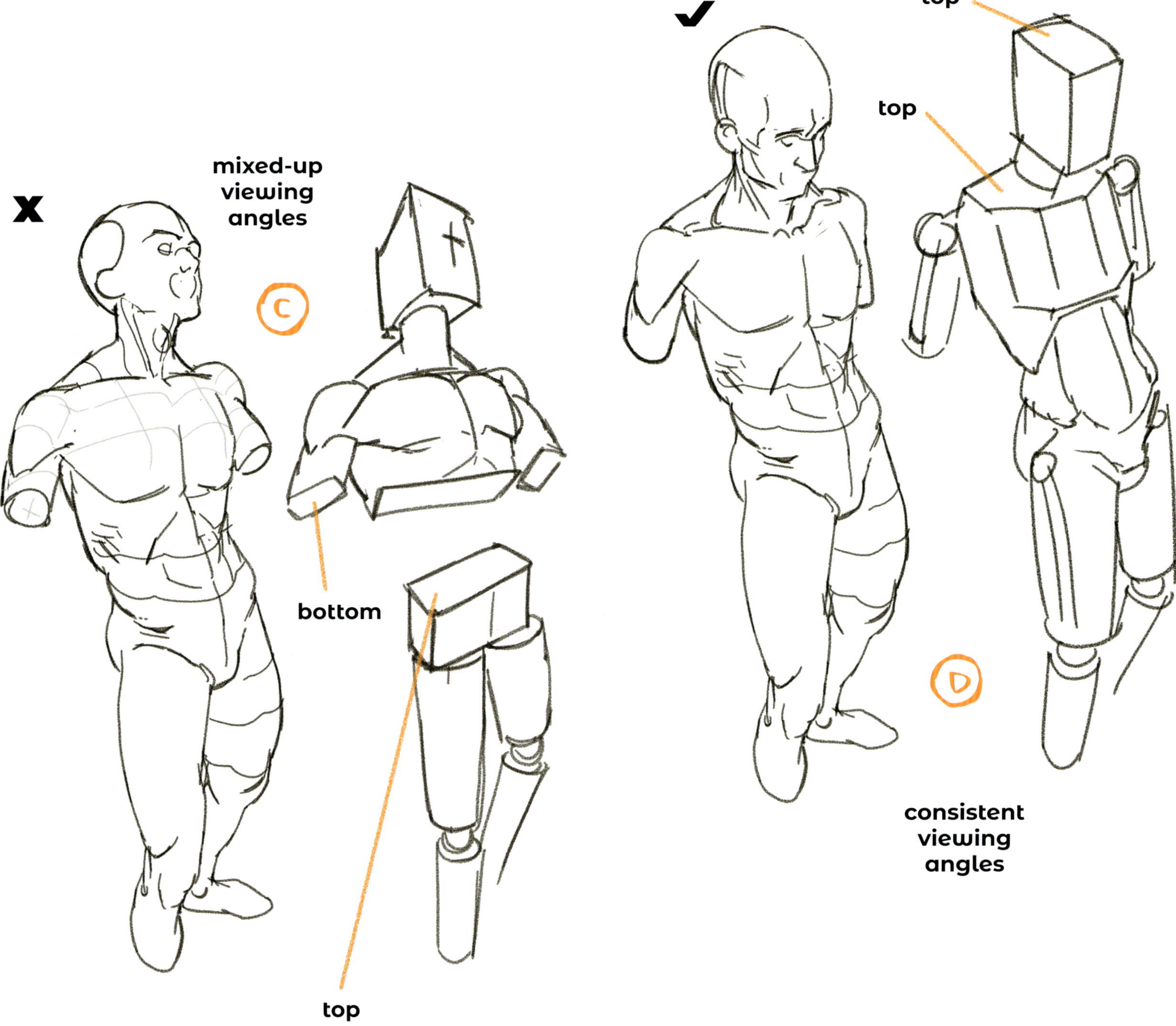

foreshortening

We create depth and perspective with foreshortening. This is the illusion of an object being rotated toward the viewer, changing the relative XYZ measurements, often giving the impression of being larger and closer to the "camera." Foreshortening is generally quite hard, but the reward is that your figure looks more dynamic and interesting to the viewer. Foreshortening hides some parts of the subject, like the upper arm in A and the lower body in B, but as we've learned, the viewer wants to do some work and figure things out, like a puzzle.

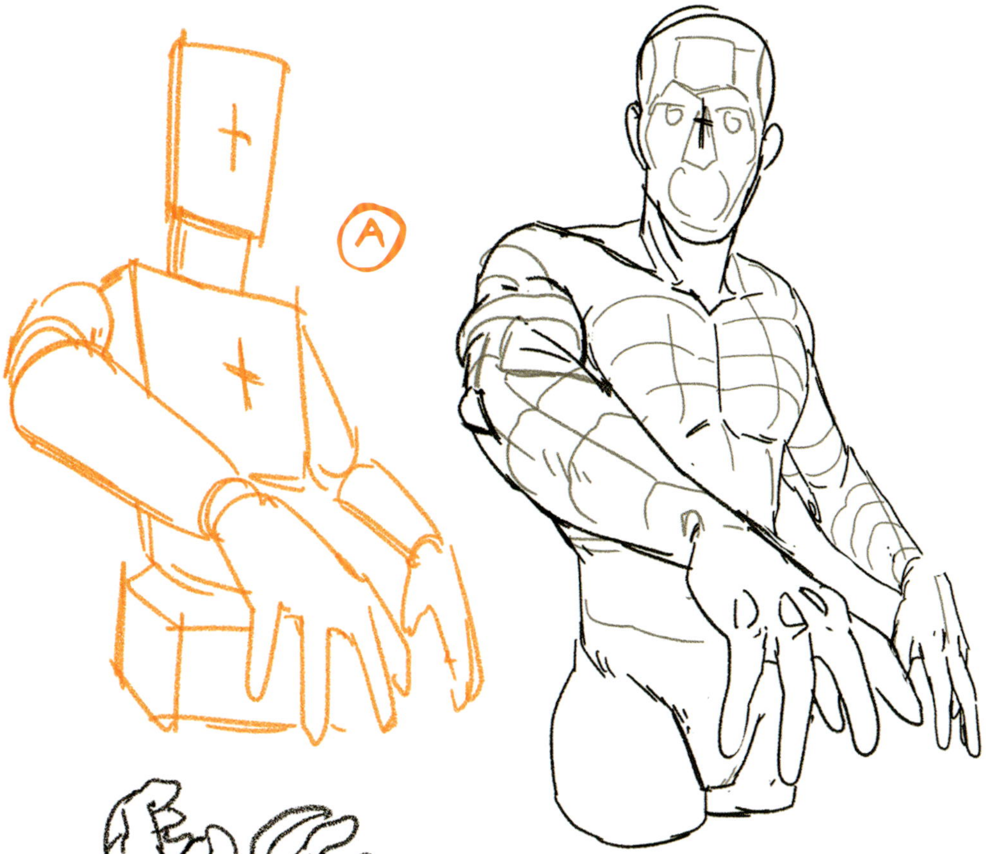

A

foreshortened parts appear closer to the viewer

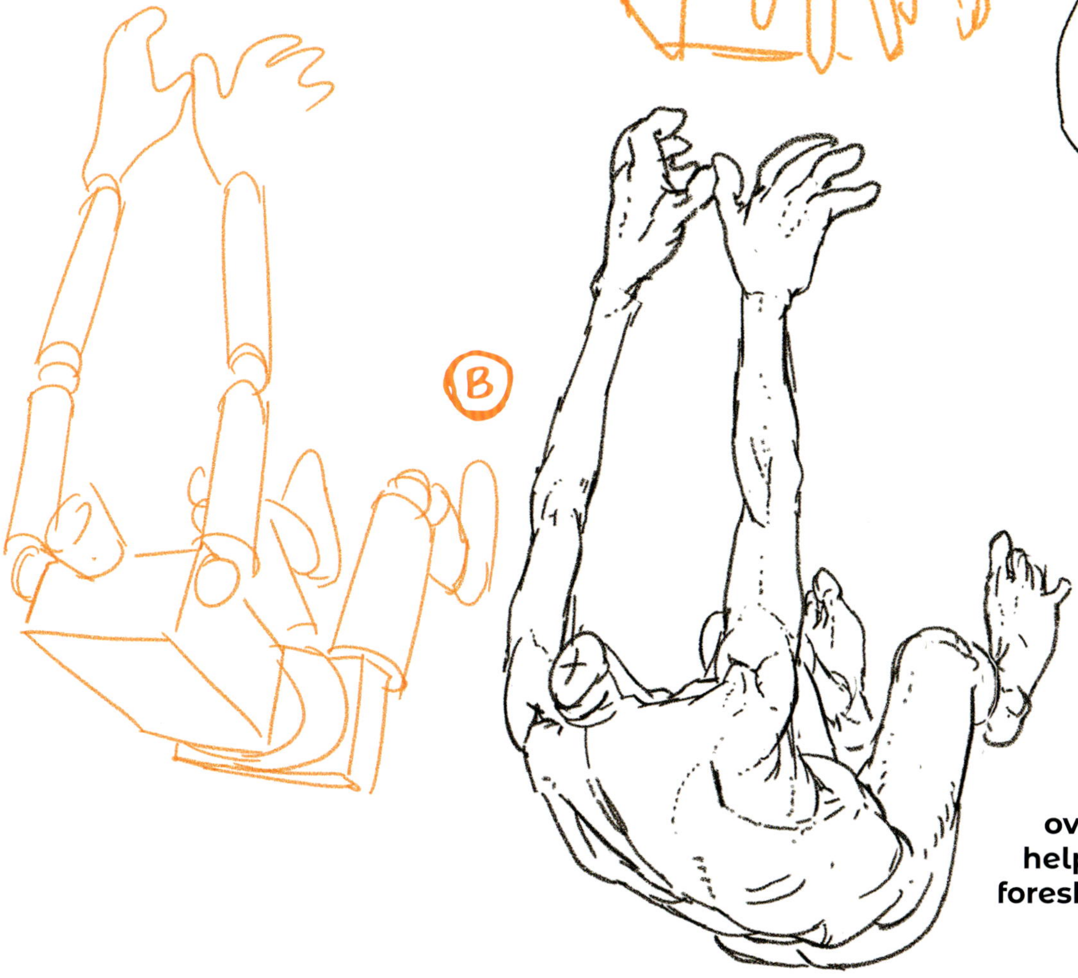

B

overlaps help create foreshortening

Dare to foreshorten. Push the foreshortening more than you'd normally feel comfortable with. Try to draw things from angles you don't often see. Sometimes I hear, "What about taking measurements?" or "I don't know the ratio of head heights to length of arms!" I don't believe in measuring your work like that, for various reasons – the main one being that your figure is constantly subject to change, depending on its distance from the camera and the camera's "lens" type. So don't worry about measurements for now!

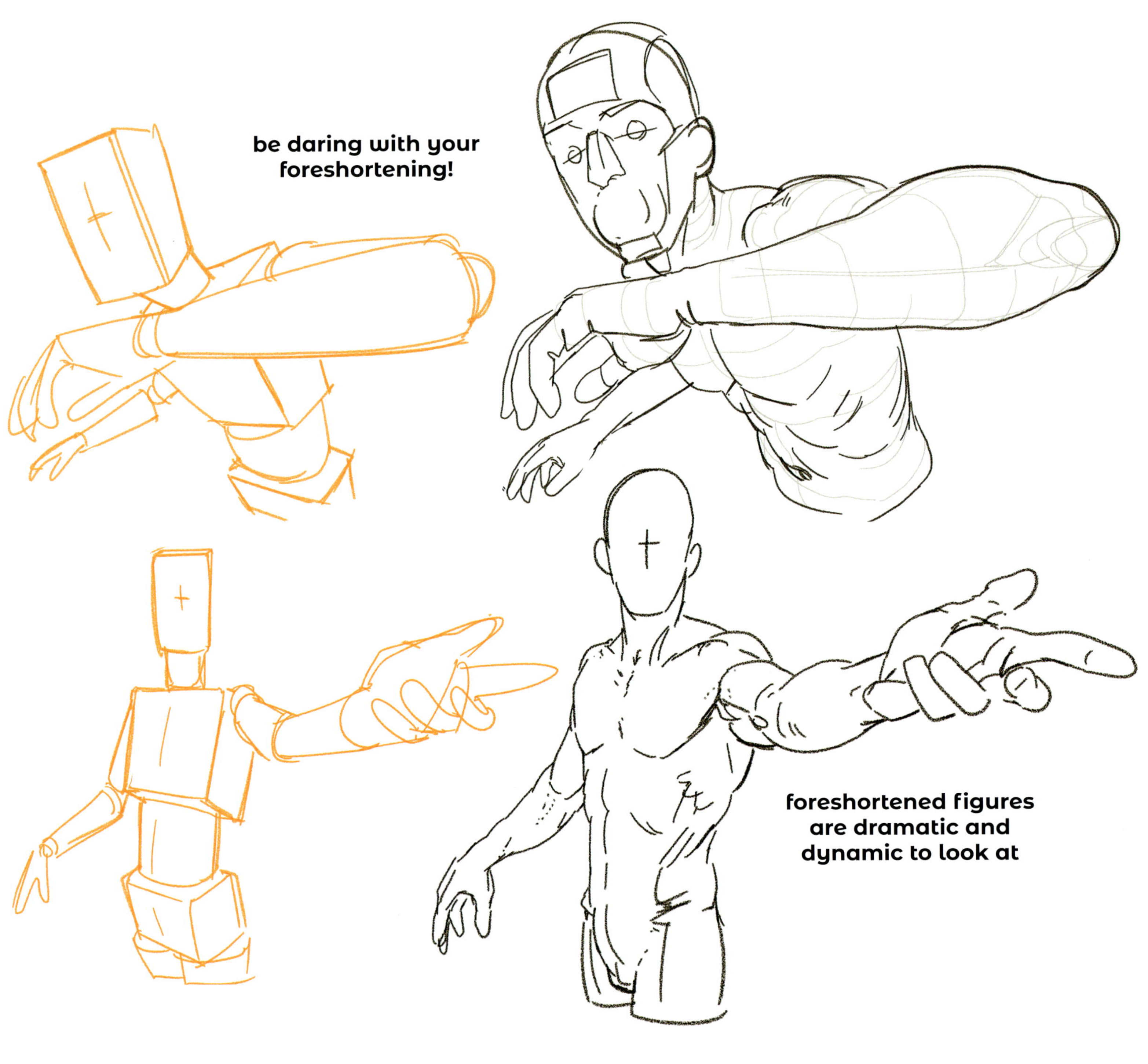

provide context

Draw things in context. When the viewer looks at your image, they should know instantly which objects are in front of which, and which ones are bigger or smaller. To check if your drawing is working, go through the elements of the image, asking yourself, "Is this in front of that? Which is bigger - this or that?" If you can't answer those questions, neither will the viewer!

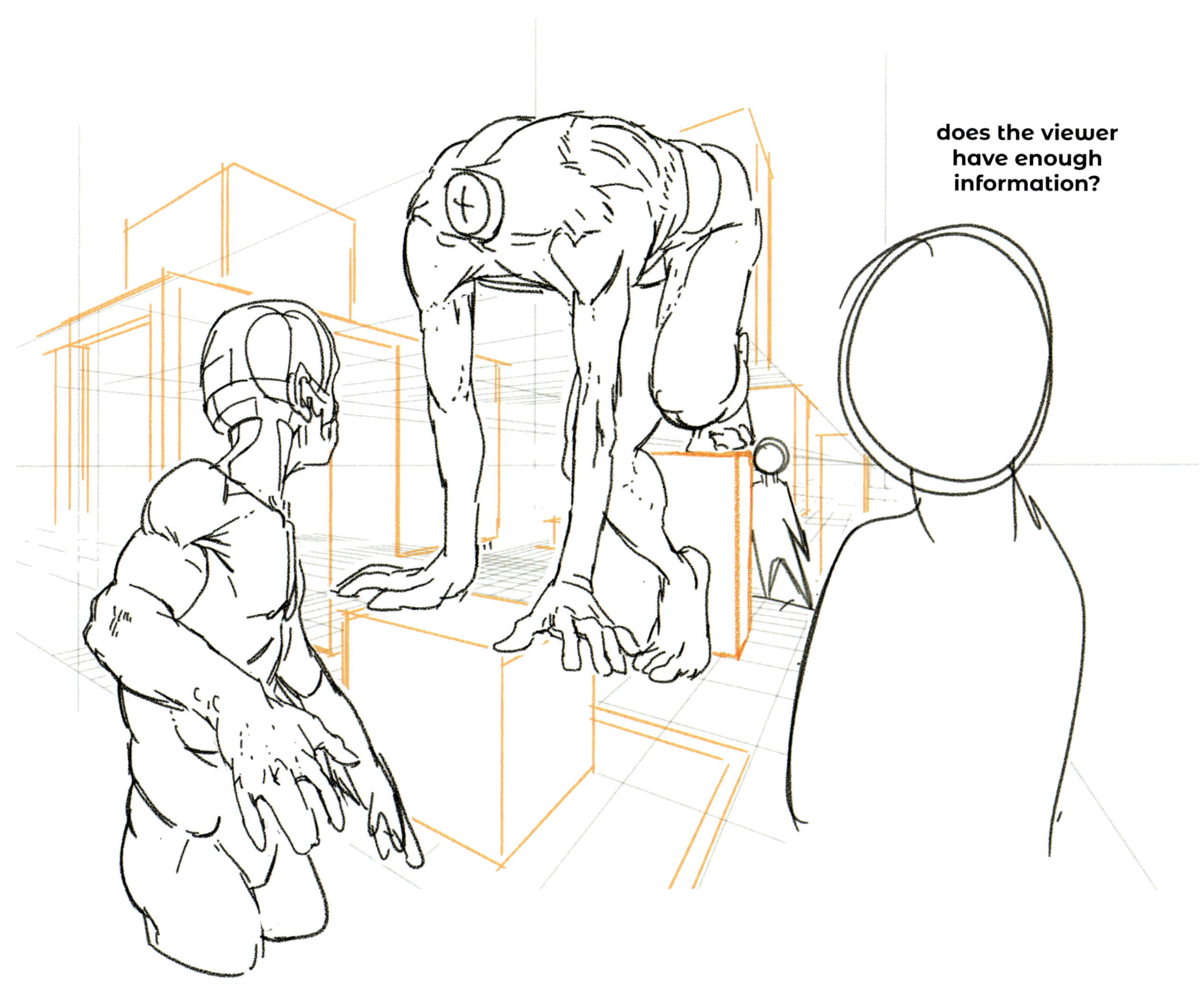

Context is everything. Clearly establish the relationship between objects in the scene before you move on to drawing the next elements. This will help the viewer to understand and navigate your world.

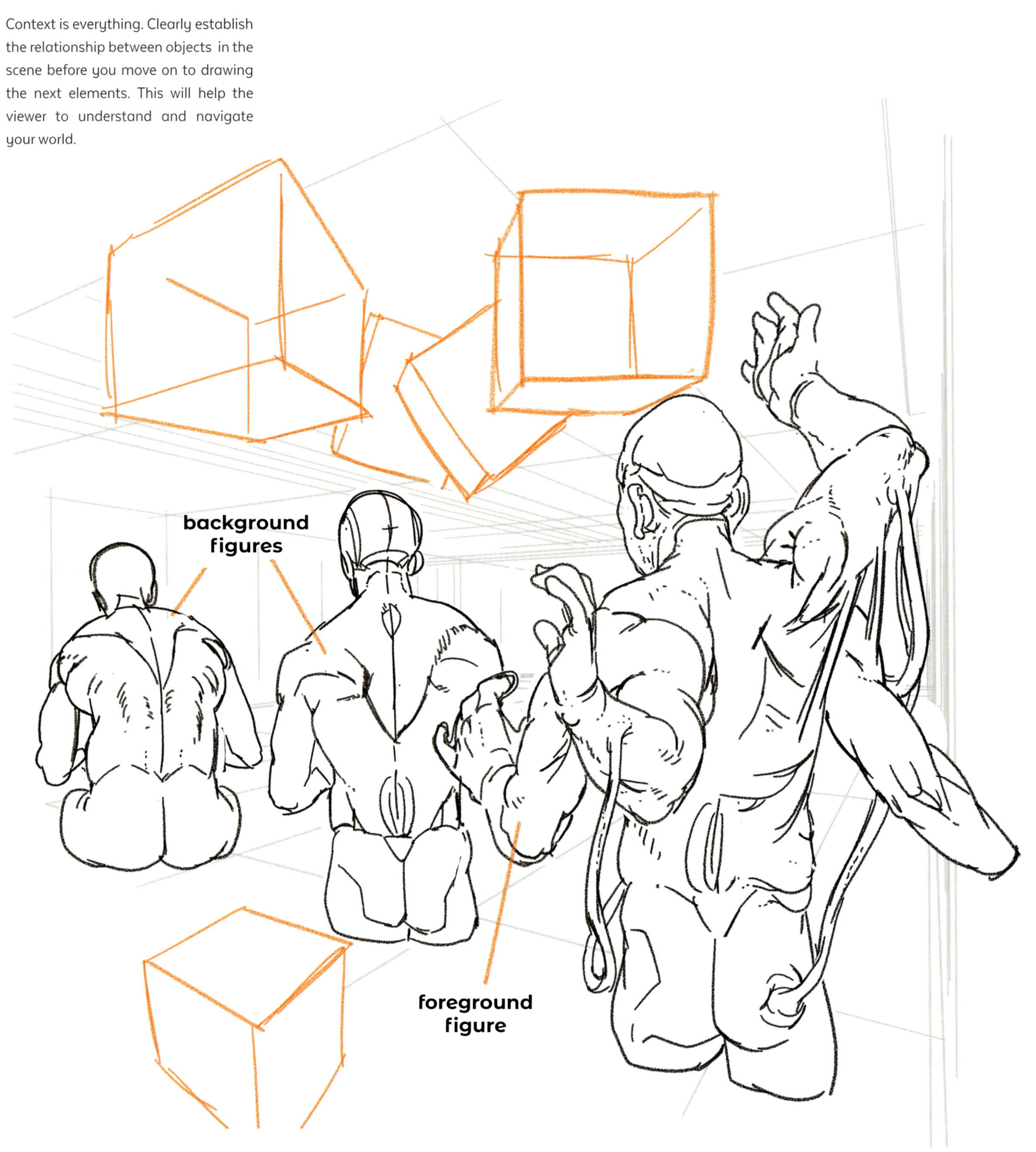

Here is one final perspective tip I can share: Objects of the same height will cross the horizon line at the same point on the body. If the people in your scene are all similar heights, the horizon line will cross through their bodies at the same places. This is powerful because it allows you to show context!

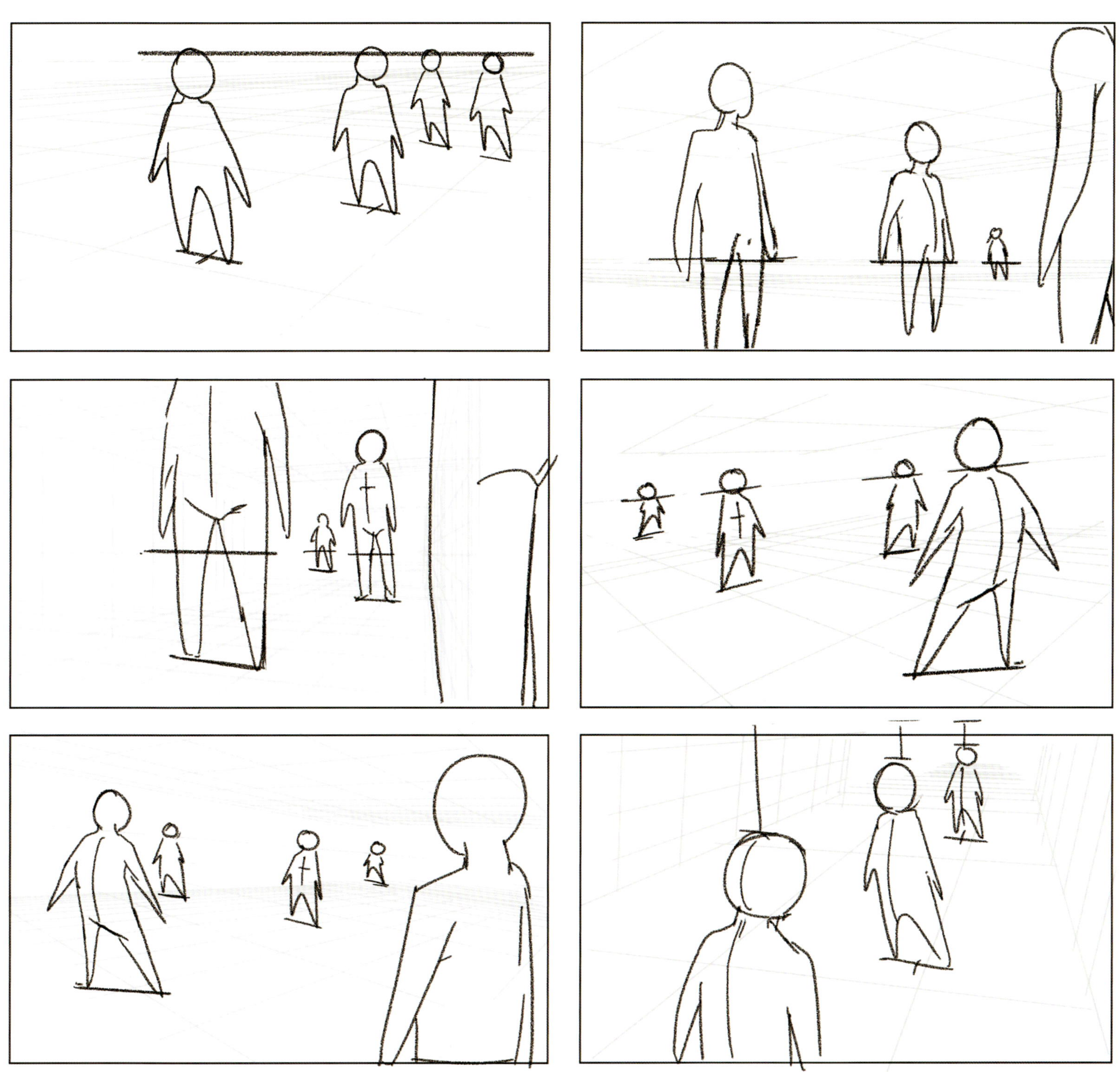

the body

lesson 1:
the head

Let's start our anatomy journey from the top: the head! We'll cover the forms of the skull, the bones and tissues of the face, and the importance of proportion for creating varied faces.

starting the head

Now we're going to look at the head. As we go along, don't forget to think in form, not line. Every line should represent a physical object, not a symbol. Imagine if you could "explode" each form, and visualize what lies beneath the surface **(A)**!

We'll start with a cube form, which clearly represents the XYZ axes in space. Take the cube and push it from the sides to give it more height than width **(B)**. Some people's heads are quite square, but generally they are taller than they are wide.

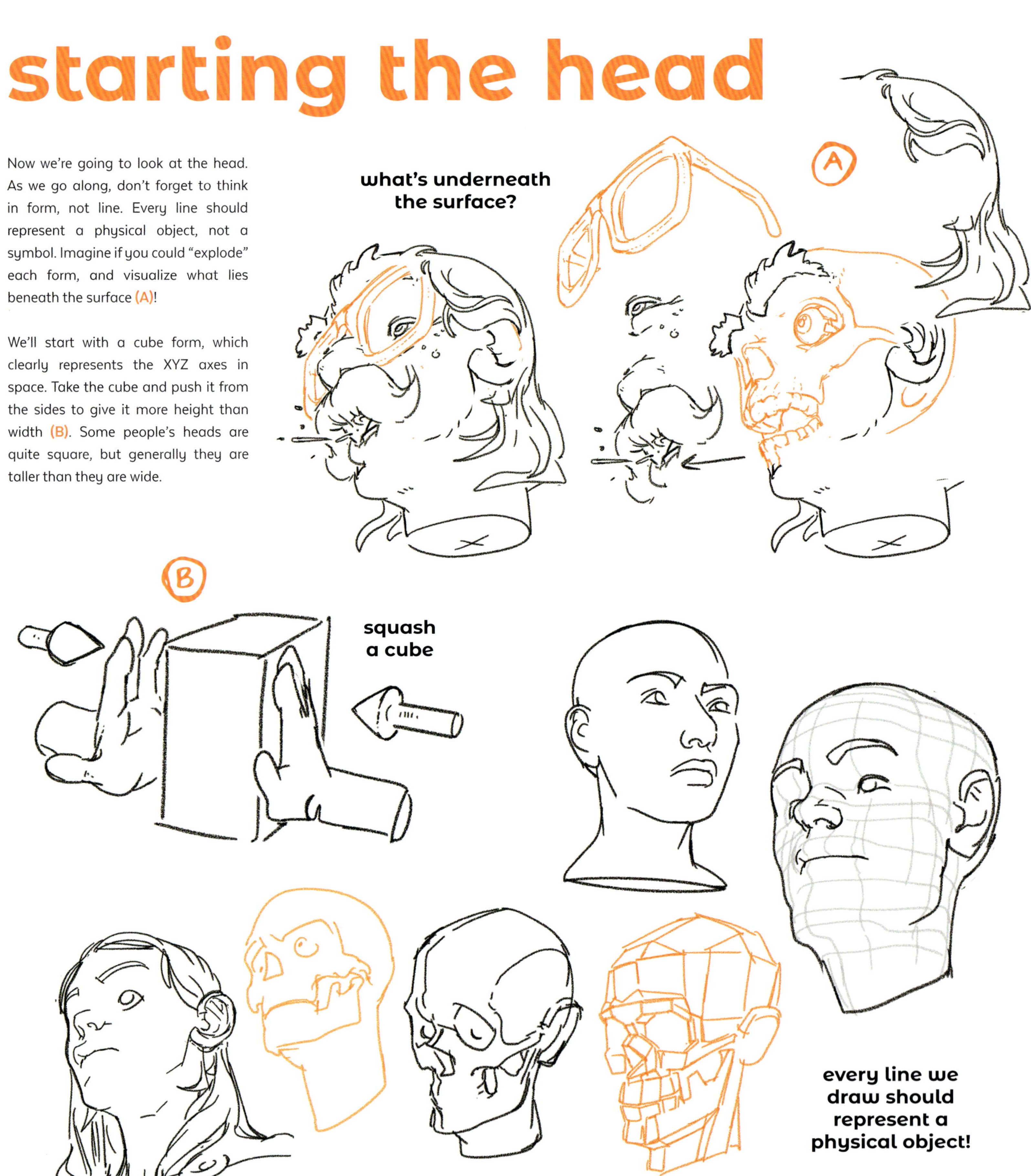

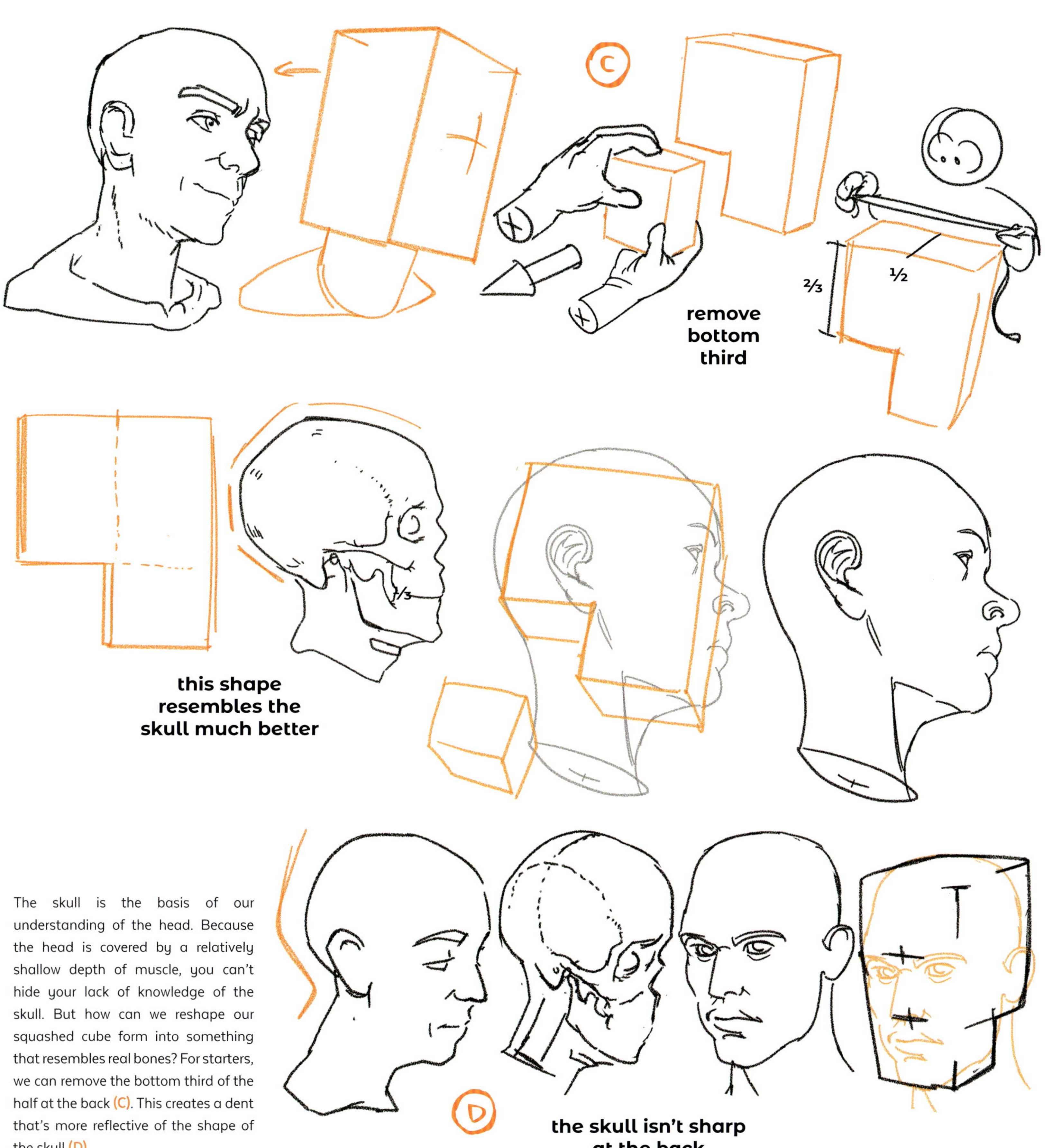

The skull is the basis of our understanding of the head. Because the head is covered by a relatively shallow depth of muscle, you can't hide your lack of knowledge of the skull. But how can we reshape our squashed cube form into something that resembles real bones? For starters, we can remove the bottom third of the half at the back (C). This creates a dent that's more reflective of the shape of the skull (D).

joining head & neck

Removing the lower rear third of the block establishes a clear relationship between the head and neck. This is an important attachment region. Without that section removed, the head would look like it's sat on the end of a stick (A). Instead, the neck wedges into the back of the head and the face sits on top of this "P" shape (B).

The neck isn't a stick. It's more tubular and flares out at the base (C). The back of the neck isn't vertical but instead leans forward (D). The volume of the neck increases when the head leans to one side, as the muscles are pulled tight, like a rope, between the skull and the shoulders (E).

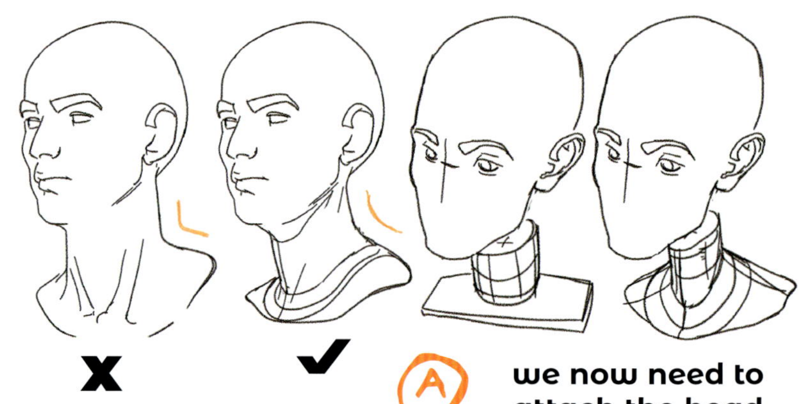

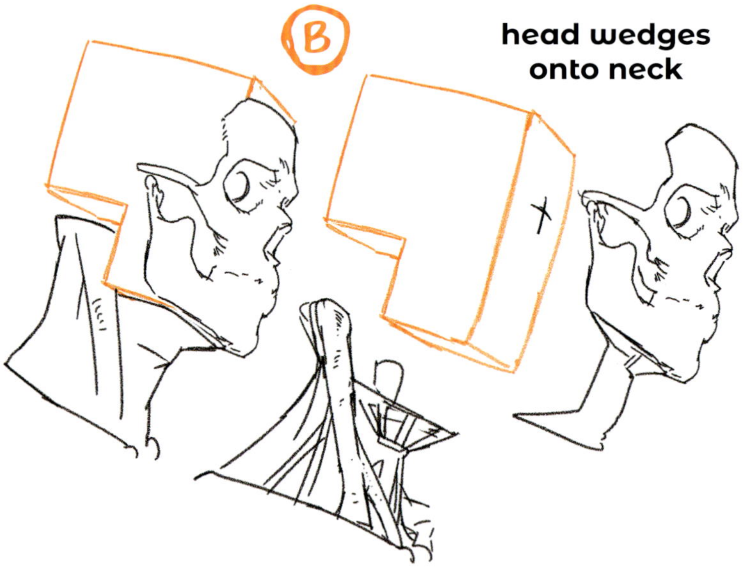

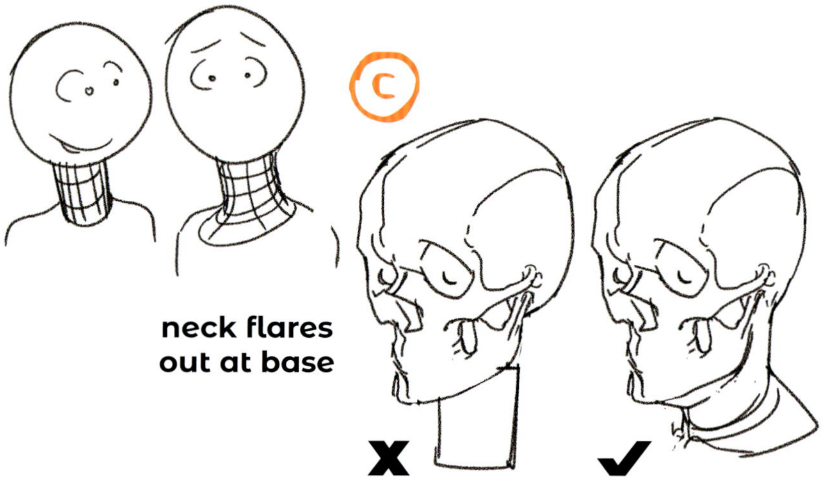

B

head wedges onto neck

C

neck flares out at base

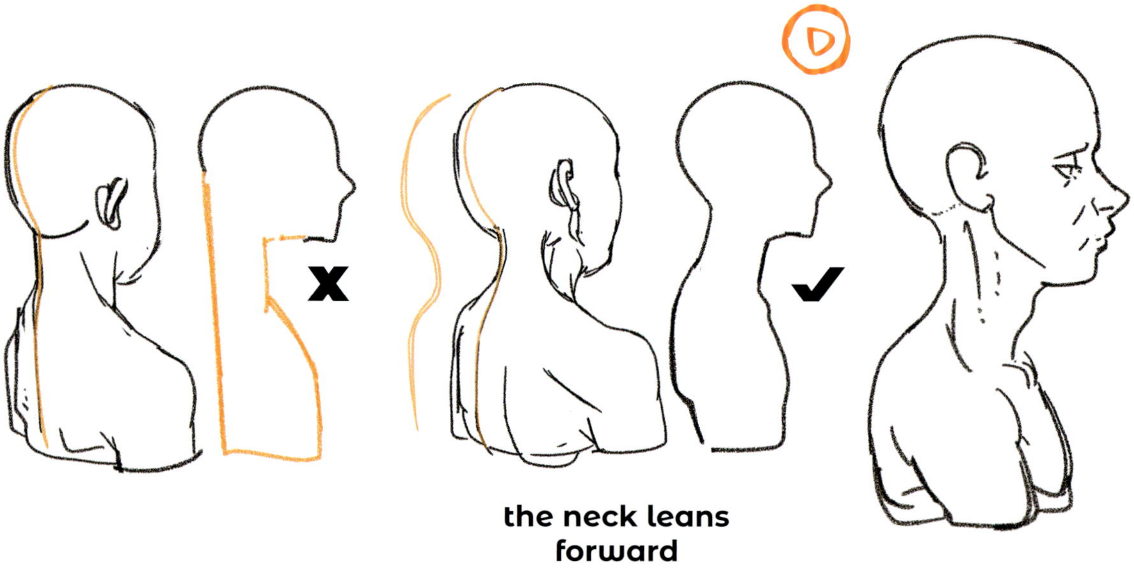

D

the neck leans forward

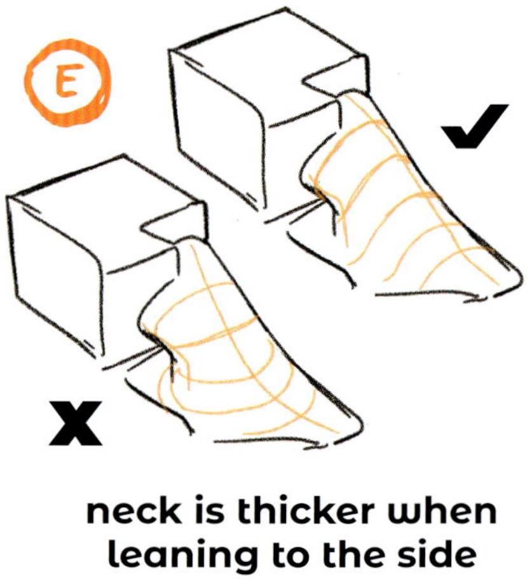

E

neck is thicker when leaning to the side

tip: how versus where

People are often more interested in *how* they are drawing things than *where* they are drawing them. This is a shame, because the *where* is much more important! For symmetrical forms, as we find on the face, it's even more important – the viewer is making unconscious measurements constantly, and will perceive even the slightest error in symmetry.

Drawing something with a different number of lines is just a style change, but drawing something in a different *place* is the difference between it "reading" as correct or not. A to B is just a different style – a change in *how* the subject is drawn. B to C is a change of *where* things are, and it ruins the drawing. In C, we see how moving a feature throws off symmetry.

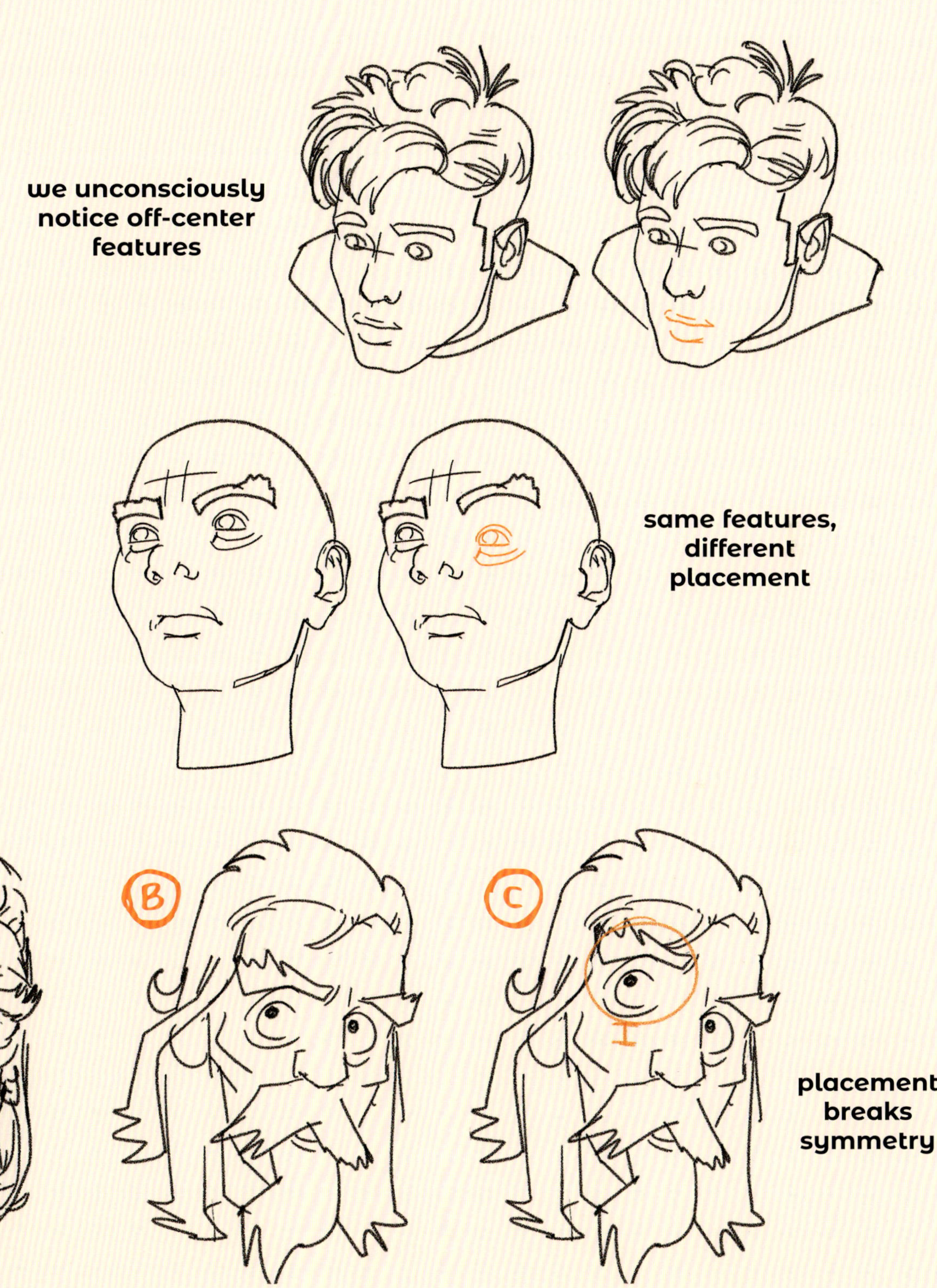

shaping the head

The head tapers from top to bottom (A). Let's slice off the sides of our squashed cube form with the rear lower third removed (B). Now the form tapers from top to bottom, and we can take off some of the hard edges (1–4). This creates a much more head-like shape (C).

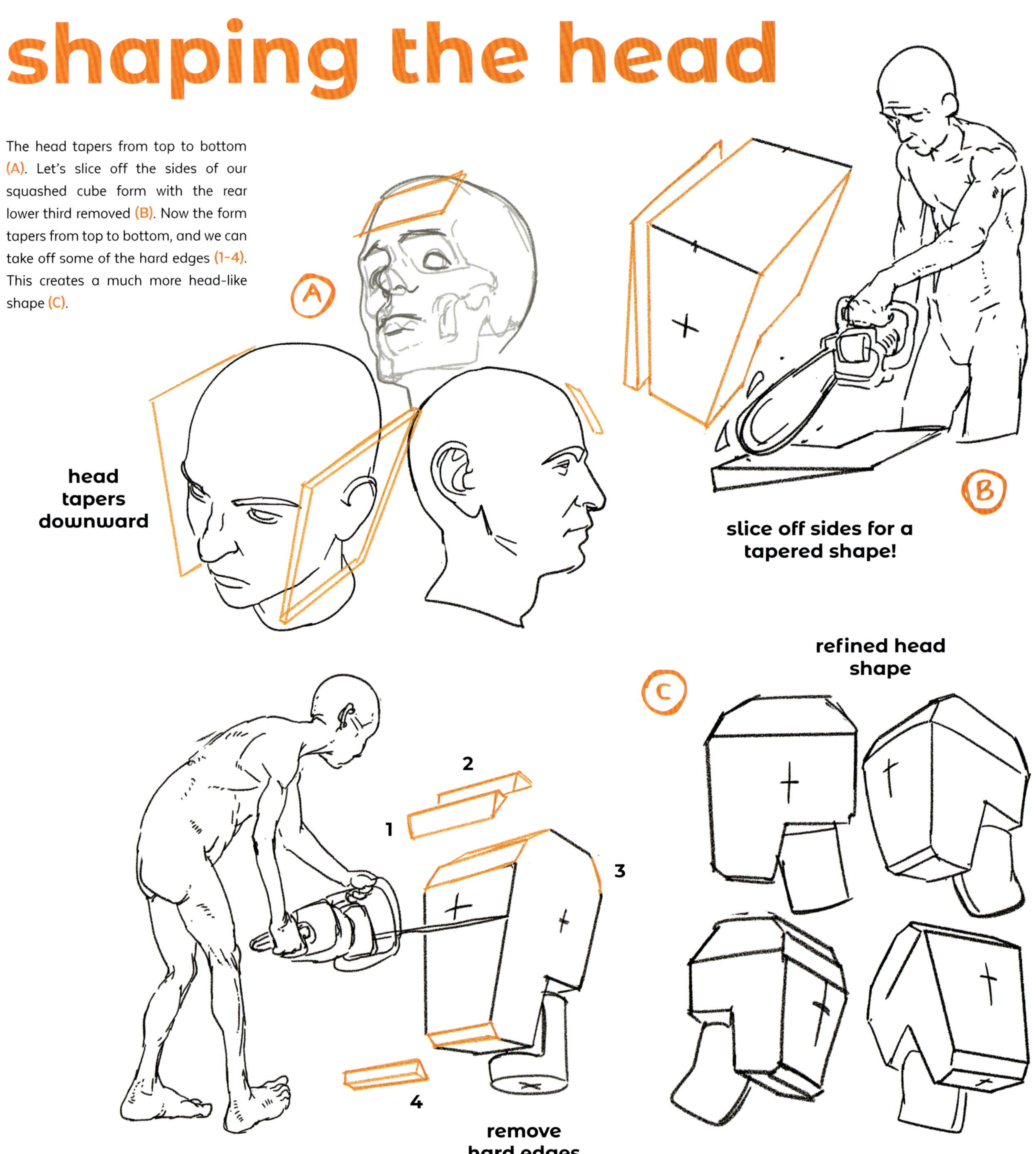

joining neck & jaw

When you think of neck muscles, you likely think of the sternocleidomastoid first – the large diagonal muscle on the side of the neck. However, let's ignore that for now so we can simplify the neck and look at its deeper structure (A). If we look "through" the muscles on the surface, we can find the function of the deeper muscle beneath. This deep muscle is the foundation that other muscles are laid on top of.

Below the jawbone (mandible) is a second smaller jaw called the hyoid bone (B). Imagine it collecting up the muscles of the neck and holding them together like a sheaf of wheat (C). The jaw and hyoid can be represented with a lower level of detail by using two identical shapes of different sizes, each with five planes that face outward (D).

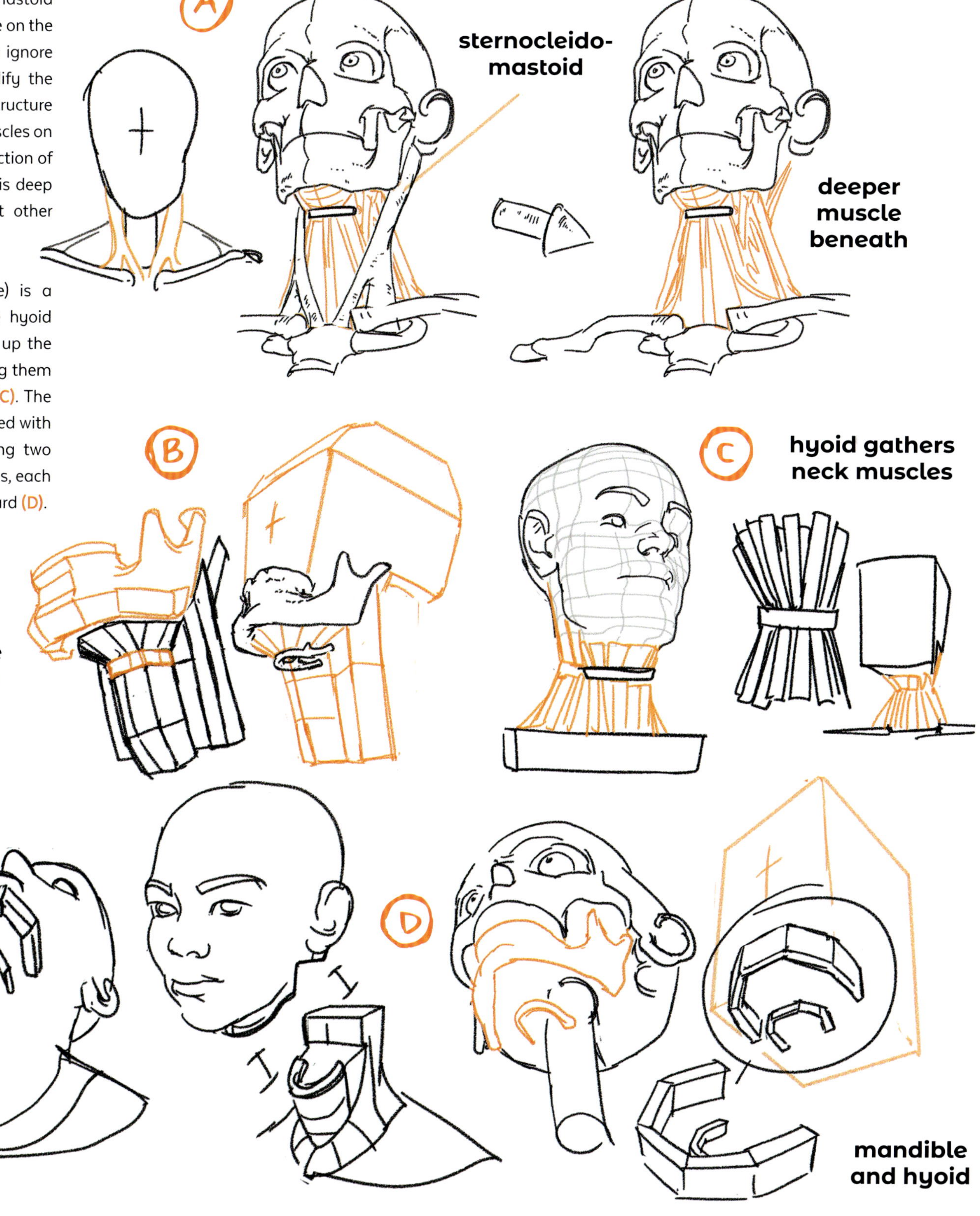

If we don't include the hyoid bone, the neck and head will look like two separate objects bumping into each other (E)! Including the hyoid allows the head to wedge into the neck, giving it real form (F).

The underside of the jaw has two surfaces. G is the muscle between the jaw and hyoid, and H is the bone of the bottom of the jaw itself. In E, the head has no relationship to the neck. In F–H we can see two forms that don't just bounce off each other, but wedge together and show clear overlap. Think of them like the parts of a puzzle! Including the hyoid and properly considering the underside of the jaw will help you build a more believable head and neck (I).

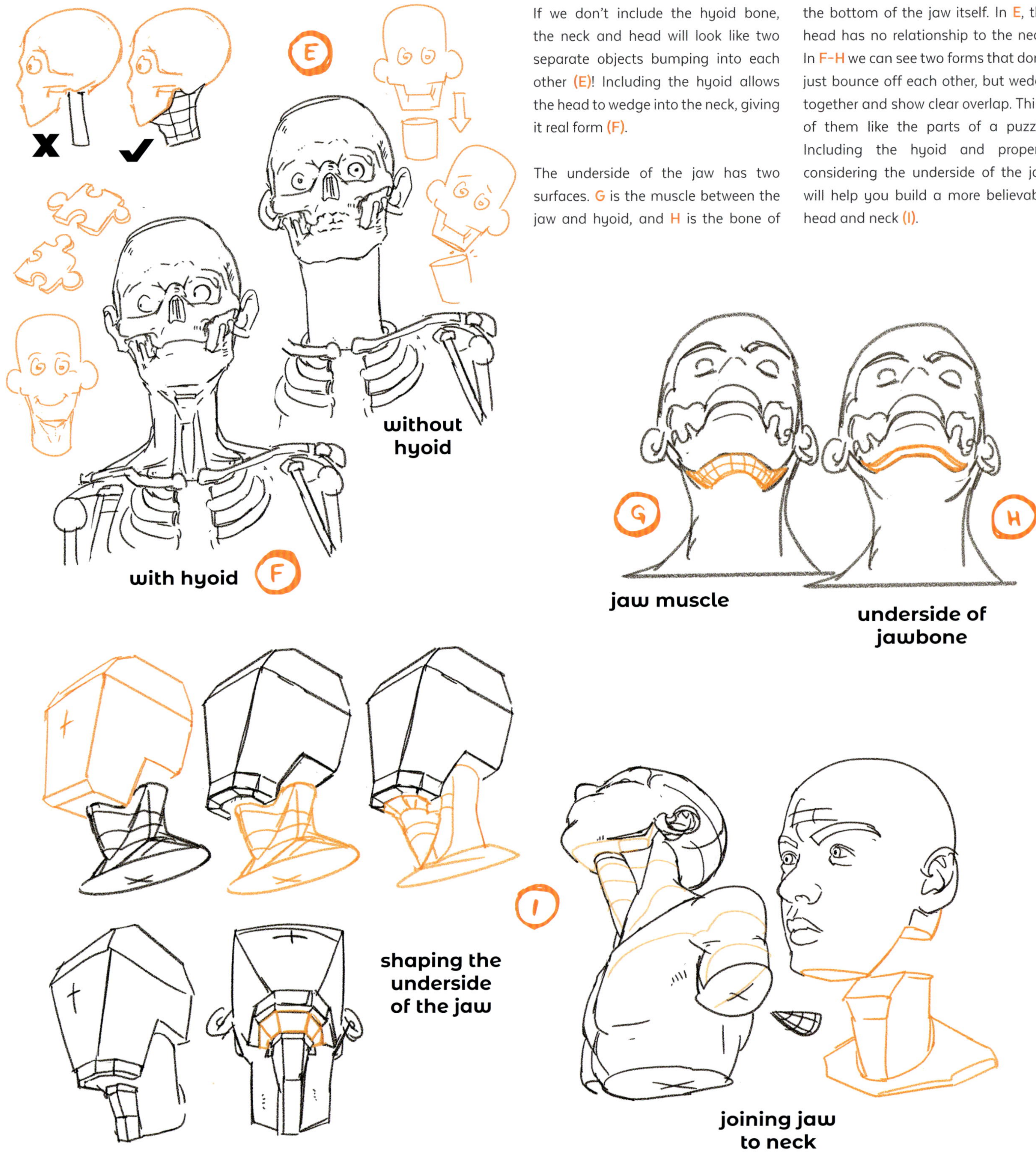

skull width

Many people draw skulls like A, but the head actually tapers from top to bottom, and the skull even more so, like B. The jawbone is much smaller than you'd imagine! We are simply used to seeing it with the volumes of the masseter muscles on the sides, which add thickness (C). We also tend to focus our attention on people's mouths, so we have a bias toward giving them more importance and size. Remember to taper the sides of the head inward to give your model a believable jawline (D).

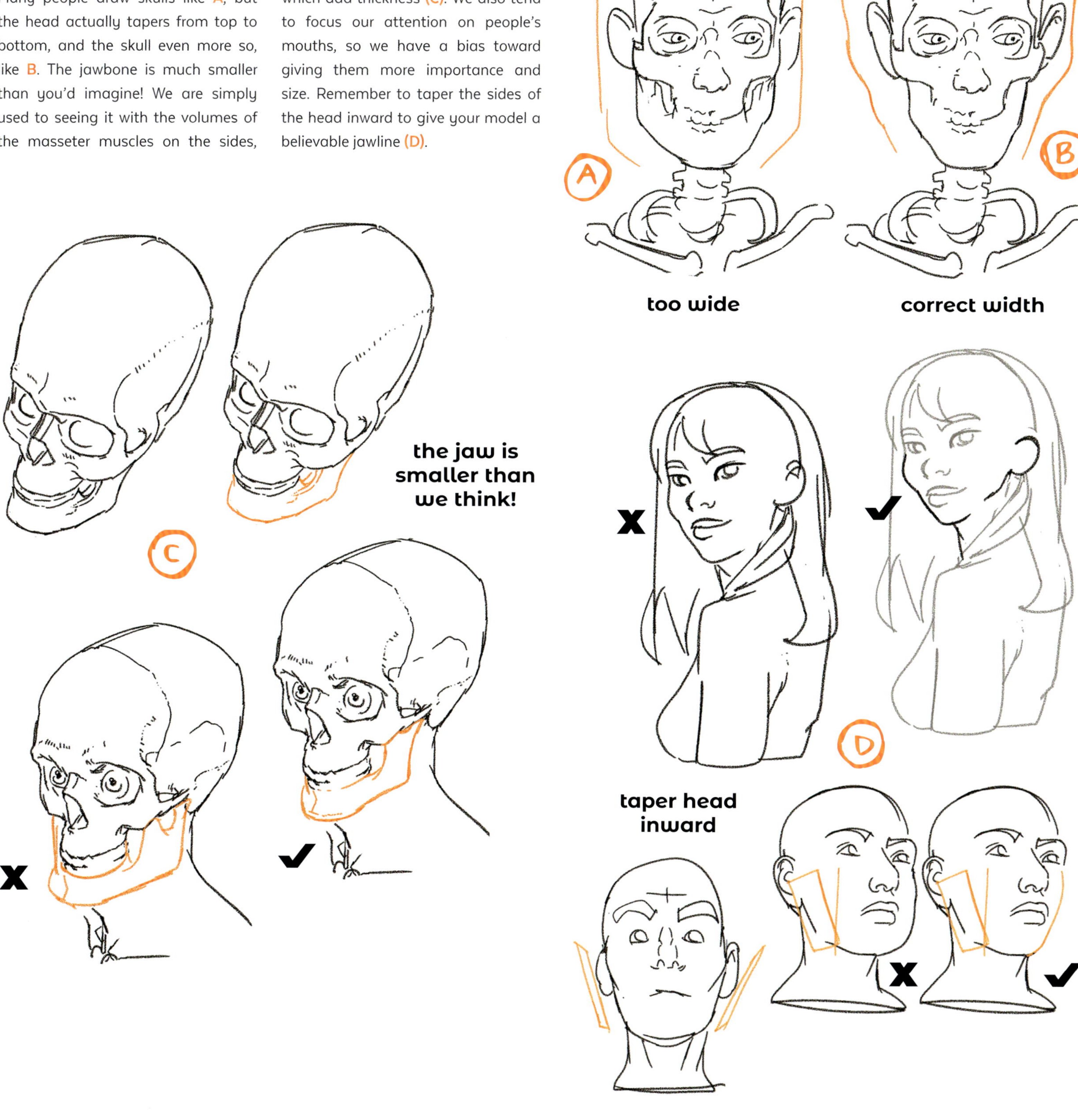

The spine attaches into the bottom of the skull, around the middle of the head – not anywhere near the back (E). Note the volume underneath the jaw – people often forget to give the area beneath the jaw enough volume.

This results in heads that look very angular and lack believability (F). When the silhouette gives more form to the hyoid and attaching muscles between the head and neck, the result looks much more natural (G).

Now that you know the structure of the neck, don't overstate it! It's natural to want to show off our understanding of form, but less is more. The less of the neck you show from above, the more believable it usually looks (H).

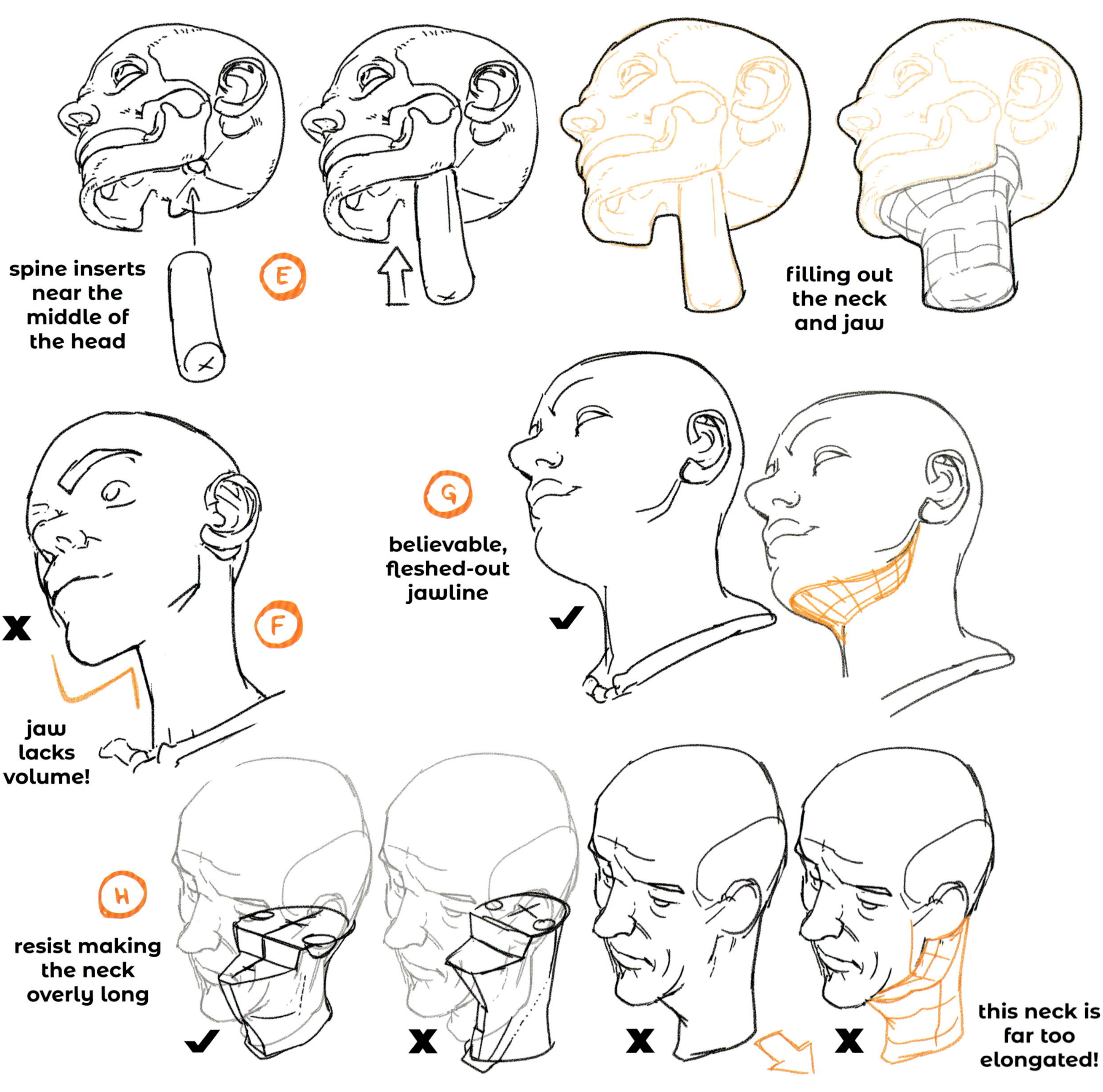

To draw the head well, it's essential to note that the face wraps around the head and isn't flat (I). Using the same model, let's add two extra planes to each side of the face to create some curvature (J).

When drawing faces from behind, we usually draw too much distance between the neck and edges of the face. This is because we underestimate how rounded the face is (K). Even from below, you can see that the head tapers toward the jaw (L).

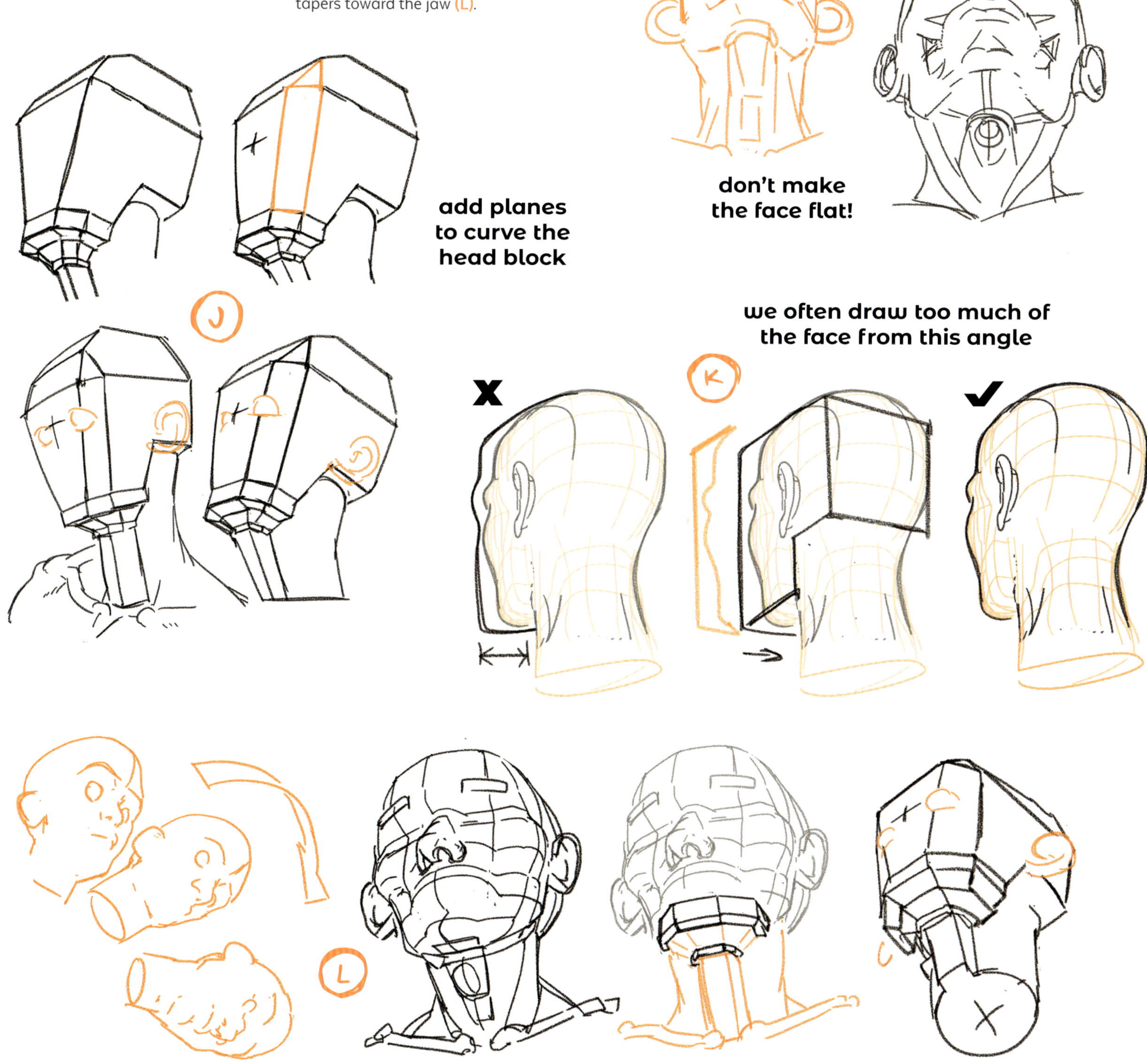

tip: useful tricks for heads & faces

When we draw the head, we can start with defined blocks and chisel away, like a sculptor. You don't need to follow my exact figures, but you can apply the same principles yourself. Here are a few more angles and example heads for you. Observe how curvature extends to almost every part of the face, wrapping it around the form of the head (A). If you're looking at some of these and thinking, "That's only subtle – I don't need to worry about including that!" – that's where the realism lies. If you are cartooning, that's fine, but to draw something approaching real life, you have to learn the subtleties (B).

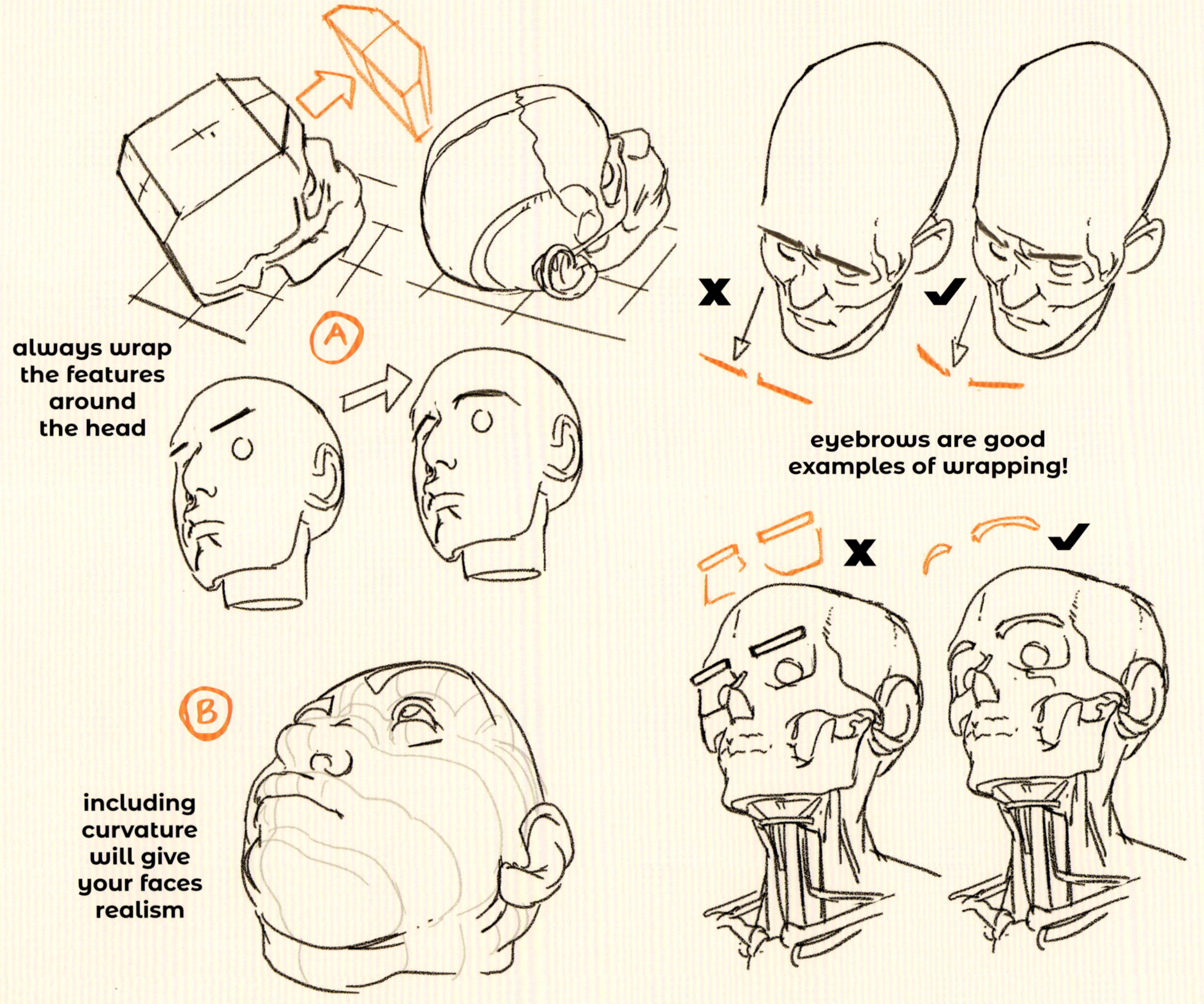

Remember the silhouette check we covered on page 31? If you're unsure how to improve your drawing, just ignore the internal lines. Draw out the silhouette and see what jumps out at you. The silhouette of the basic head forms in C already looks quite believable when we remove all the "noise" of the internal lines!

We can also lay the "mask" of the real face on top of our basic blockout to see that it fits well and curves correctly (D). If it does, that's a great sign. If you are designing your own forms, which I recommend, then use this as a check to see if your proportions look correct.

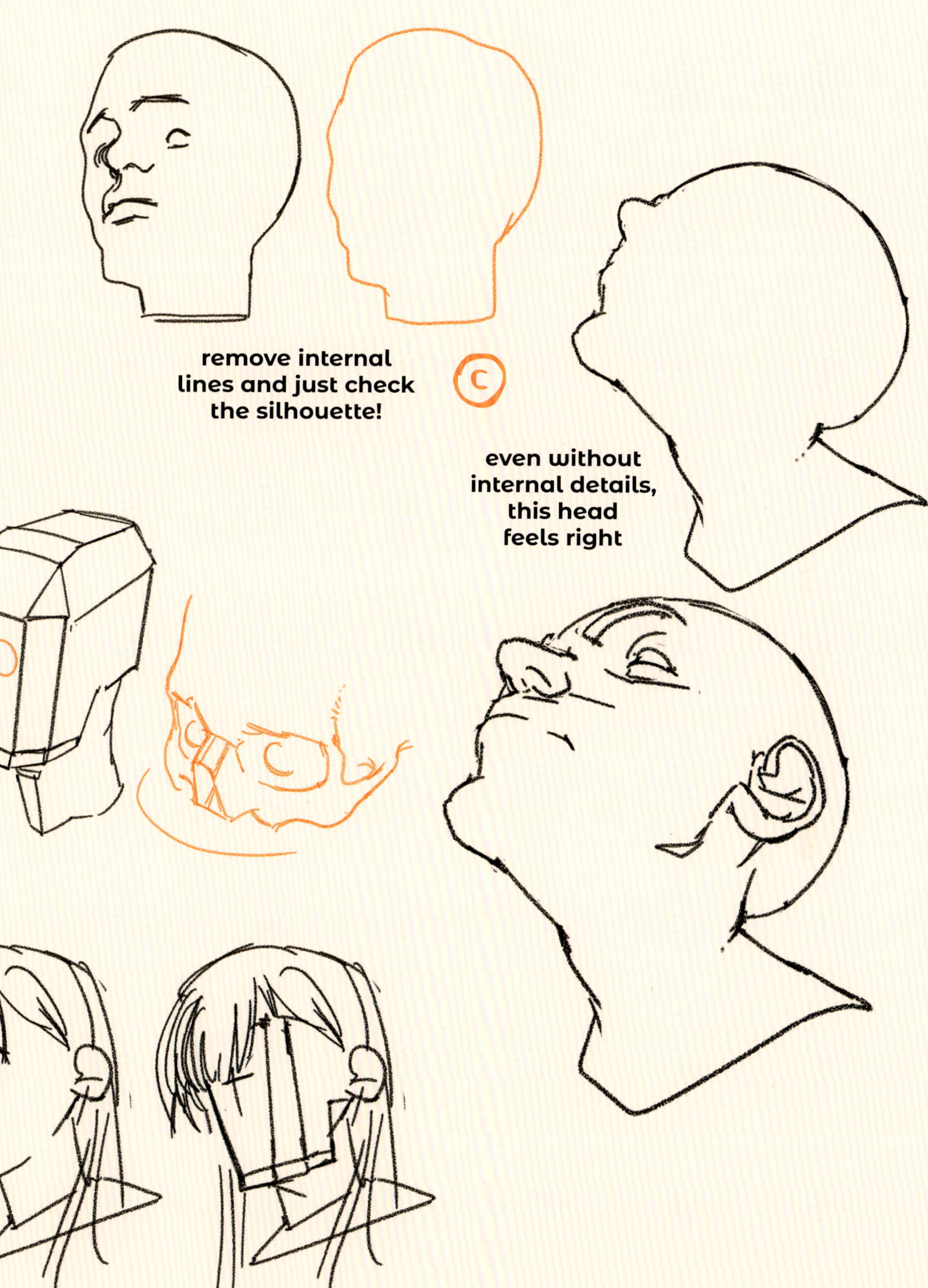

Don't worry about the style or quantity of lines you draw your heads with. As we've seen, "style" is mostly just about how many lines you use, not about where they are located! Get the *where* correct and you can adjust the style later. The E and F comparisons here all work as drawings with form and believability, even though the styles are different.

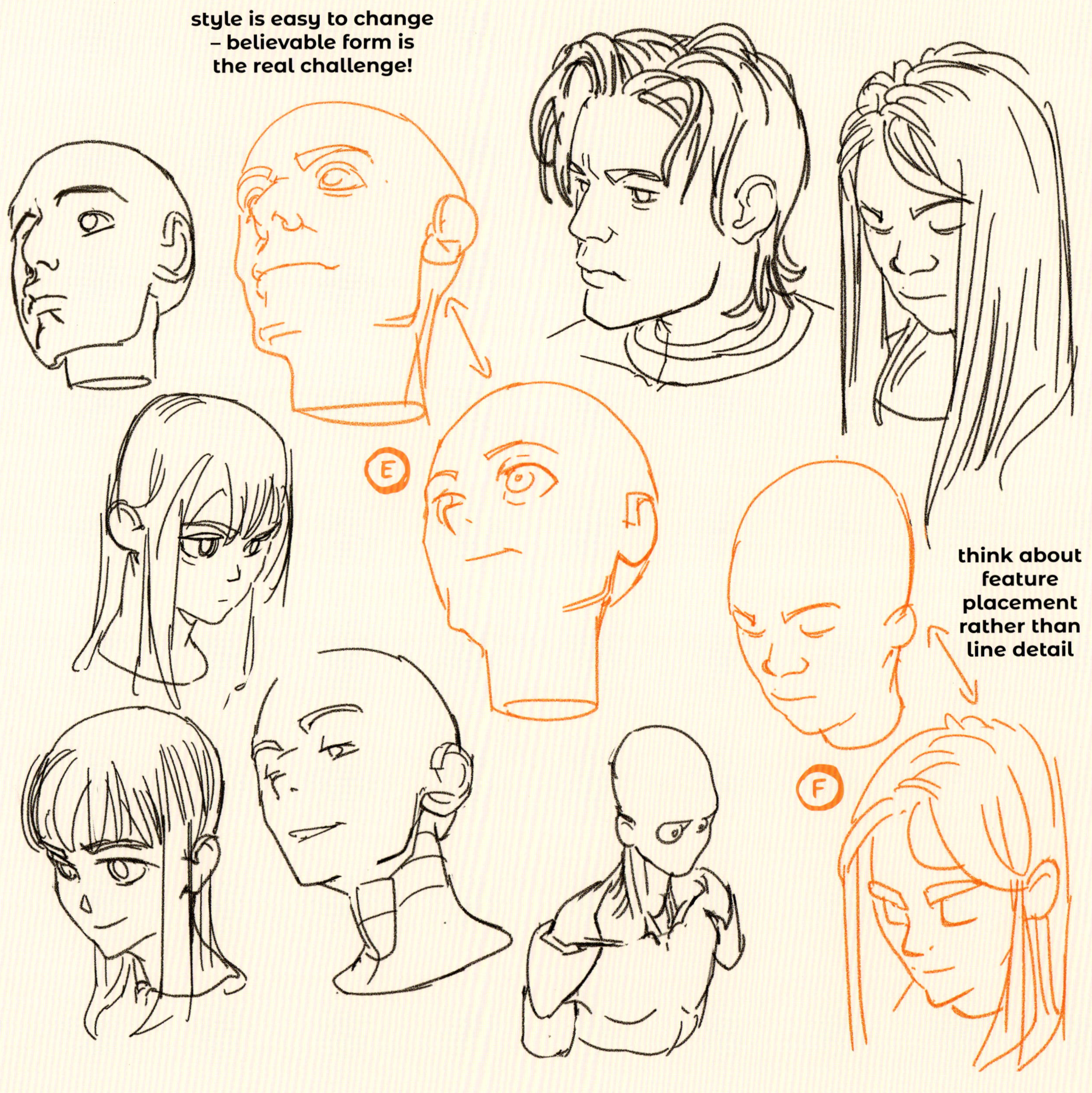

occipital bone

The head we've designed so far looks good from the front, but the rear section is still lacking. Let's compare a real profile with the one we've got so far (A). You can see that our design looks different from a real head in a few areas, particularly the back of the head and where the neck attaches to the skull. This is because we need to add the occipital bone – the bone on the bottom of the back of the skull (B).

The occipital bone has a scoop shape, almost like a trowel with a handle, and the spine runs through the hole in it. The "handle" shape isn't visible from the exterior, so let's chop that part off and fit the occipital bone to the back of our design's head (C).

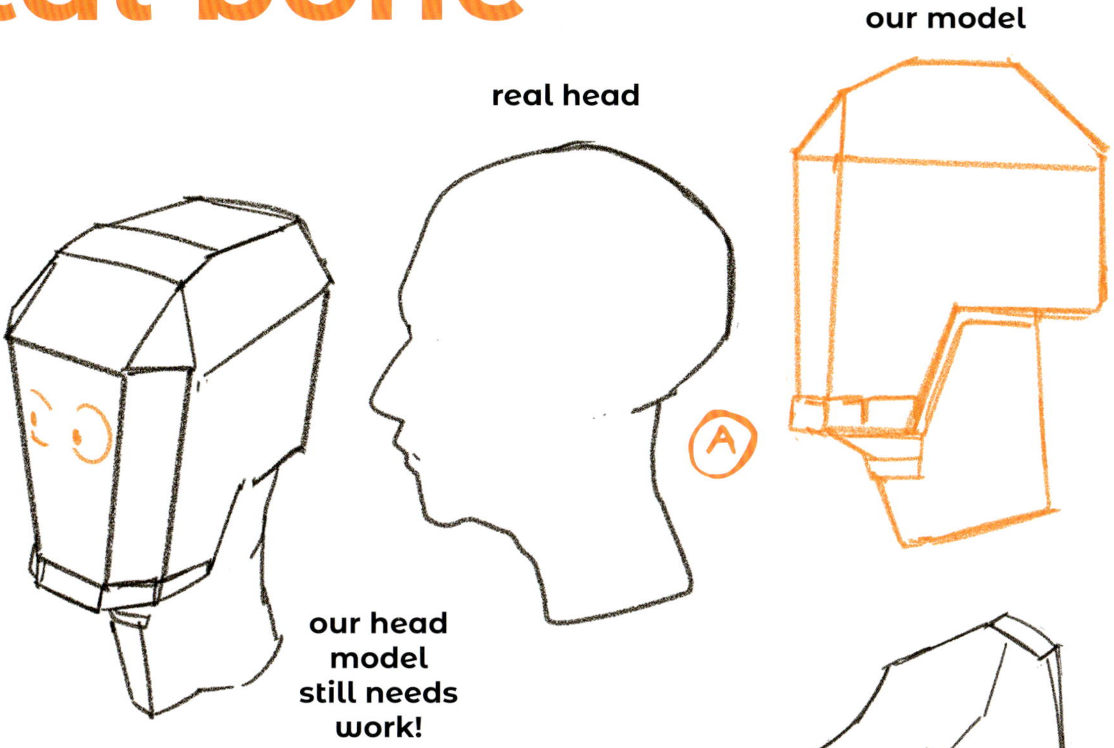

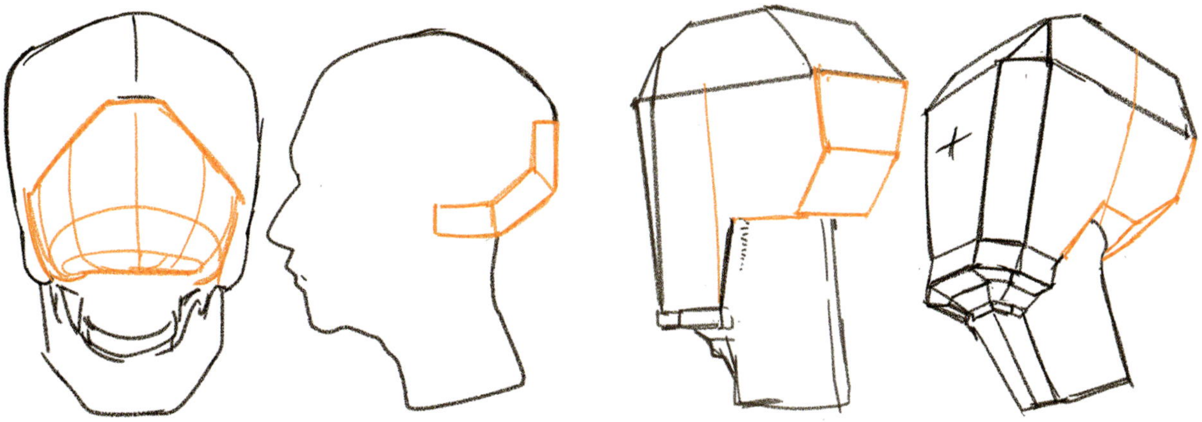

real head

our model

A

our head model still needs work!

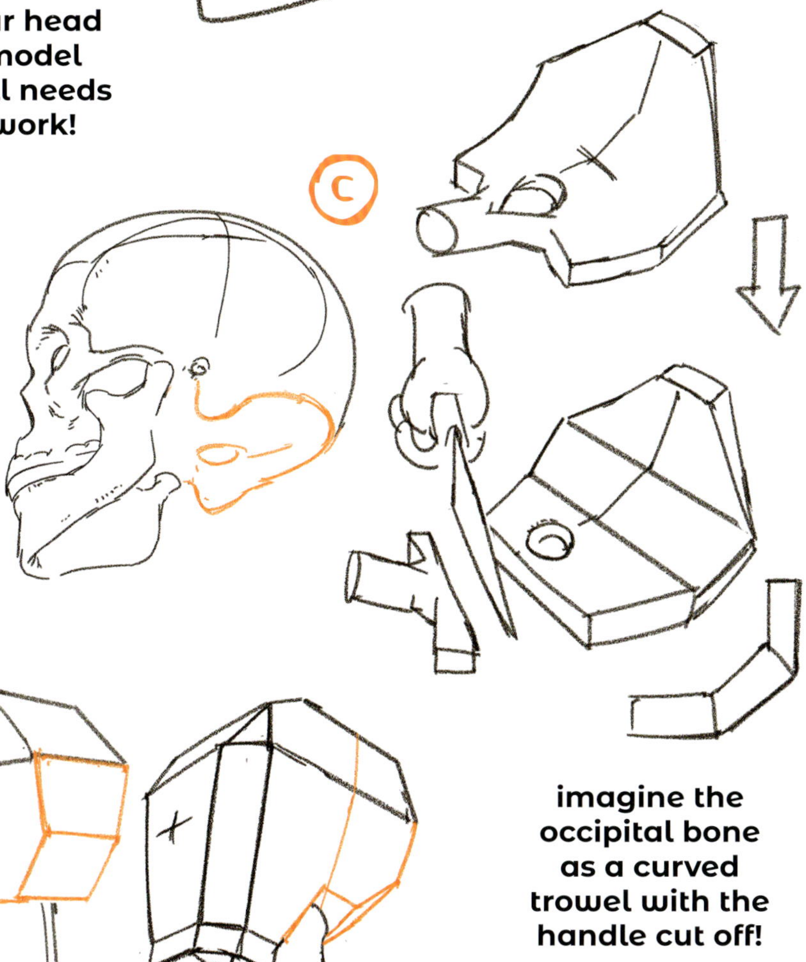

C

B

occipital bone

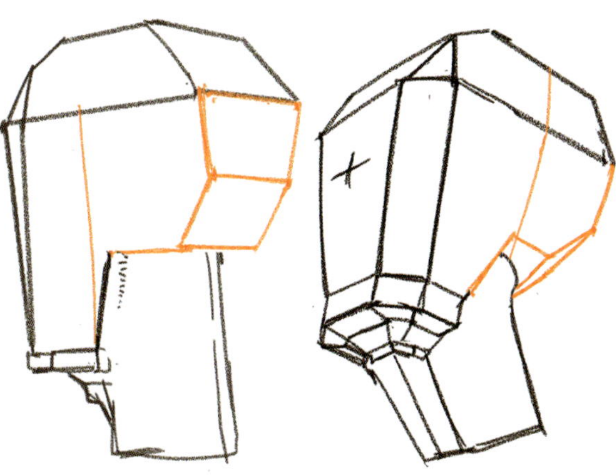

imagine the occipital bone as a curved trowel with the handle cut off!

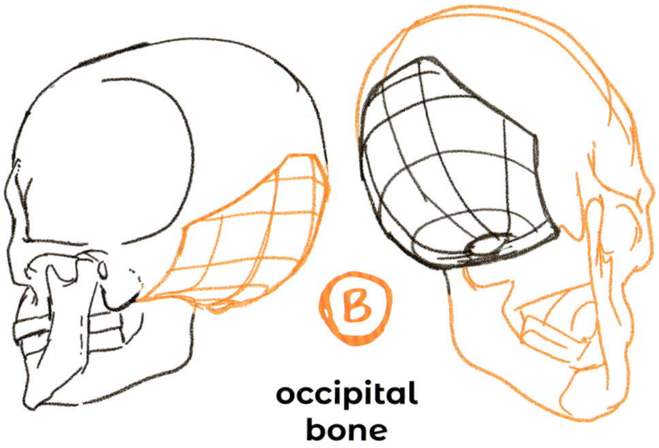

Look at D to compare the "before and after" of adding the occipital bone. The outline has barely changed when viewed from this angle, but the level of realism has hugely improved! We are looking for the subtlest of form changes to improve how we capture the human body, so don't skip small adjustments like these.

We have now converted the skull shape into something planar, which is a challenge to draw and will sharpen your skills at using the XYZ axes. Two important points are around two-thirds back from the front of the head, and around two-thirds up from bottom of the head. These are the widest and highest points of the skull (E–F). Notice how the skull tapers from top to bottom, as we learned on page 79.

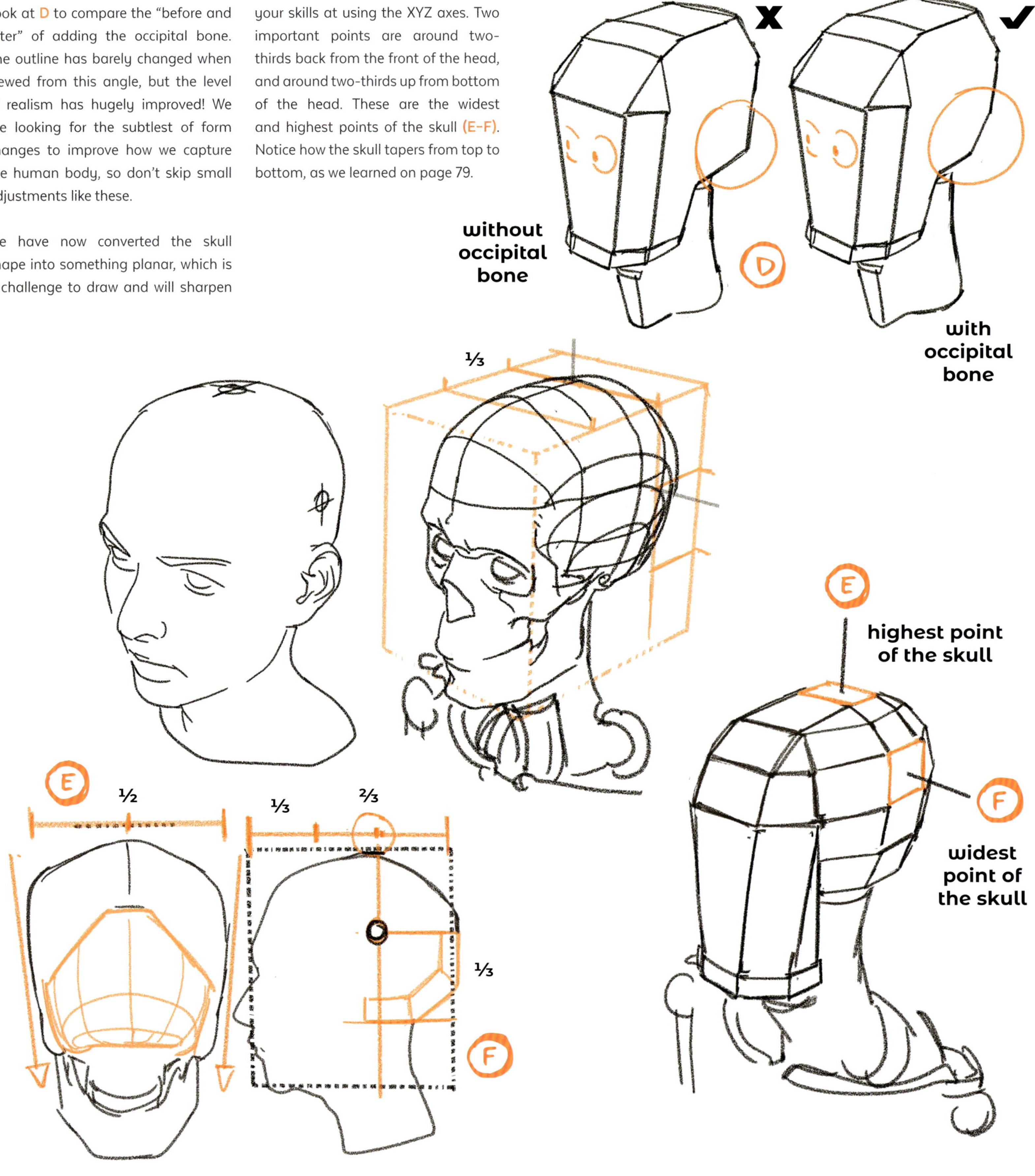

“known variables”

The head is curved on top, increasing in height up to around two-thirds of the way back. The sides of the head have a roundness, too. We can locate one key plane on top of the head that is perfectly horizontal (A) and one plane on either side that is perfectly vertical (B). These are essential as we can use them as starting points to measure the other angles of the head. I nickname them the “known variables” because I know for a fact that they are reliably horizontal and vertical across any kind of figure.

The corner of the jaw rises almost vertically to meet the edge of the eye socket (C). Again, we can test our model by laying a face onto the head shape, asking ourselves, “Does that silhouette look believable? Is that what I'd expect to see?” This one holds up well to the test.

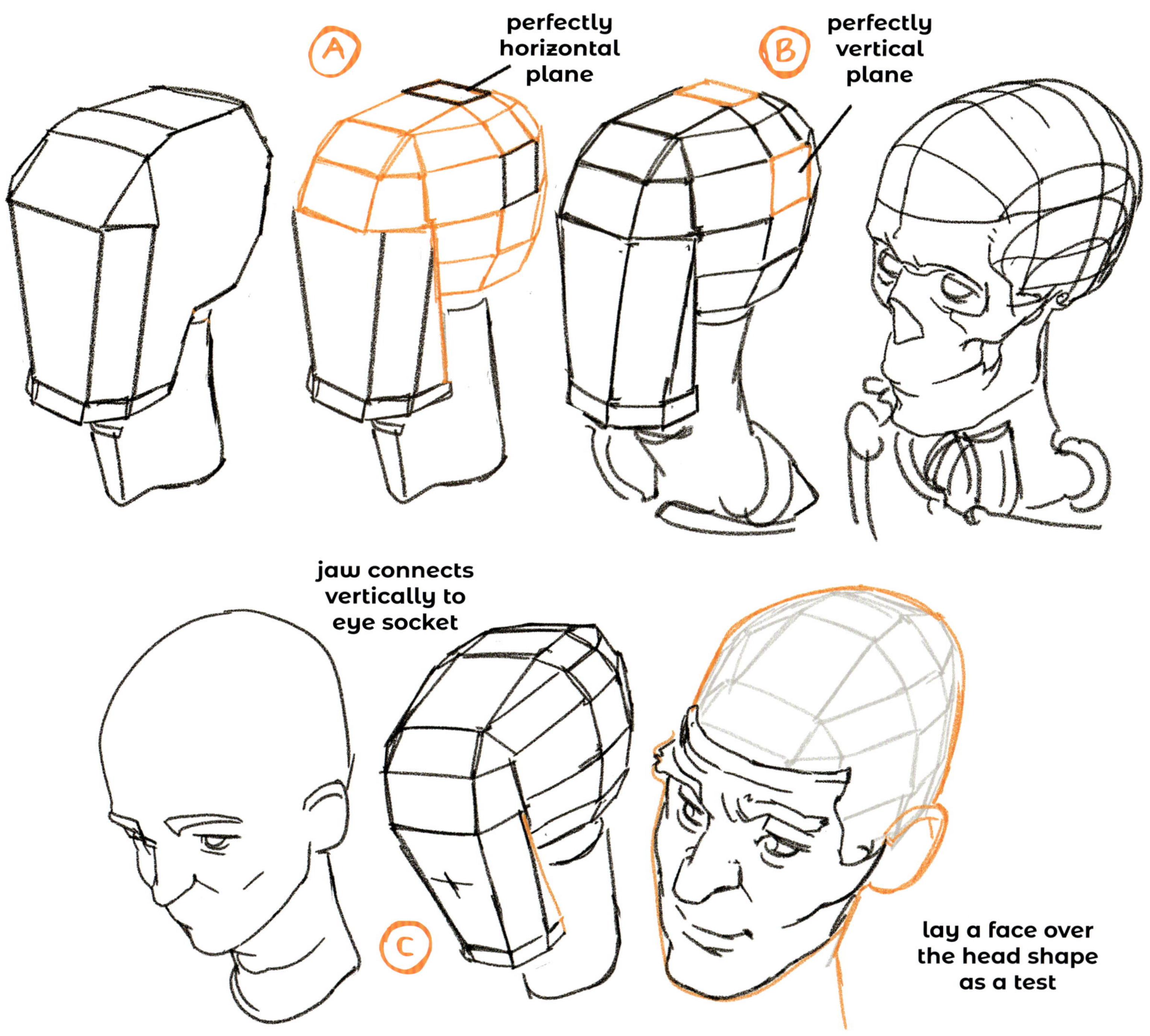

These "known variables" can also be applied to building up a whole figure or scene. At the start of a drawing, your perspective is undefined. You can choose the angle you want to see something from, and at what angle it's rotated. We can then choose to "pin" the perspective to certain lines that tell us what the perspective is for the whole object. If we start by drawing a shape like D, we can pin our perspective to that, and use it to find our X and Z axes. By the time we get to stage E, we have used other lines to establish the top of the Y axis. Now we have pinned our perspective to a few key lines. These are our known variables. We *know* these lines match up to the vertical, horizontal, and depth lines on this object (F).

For example, I begin drawing the top section of a form and establishing my known variables of XYZ (G). If I want the next form to be tilted, I use my known variables as reference points for my measurements (H). If I know those lines are vertical, then we can easily compare the other faces. Are they oriented vertically, or tilted? (I)

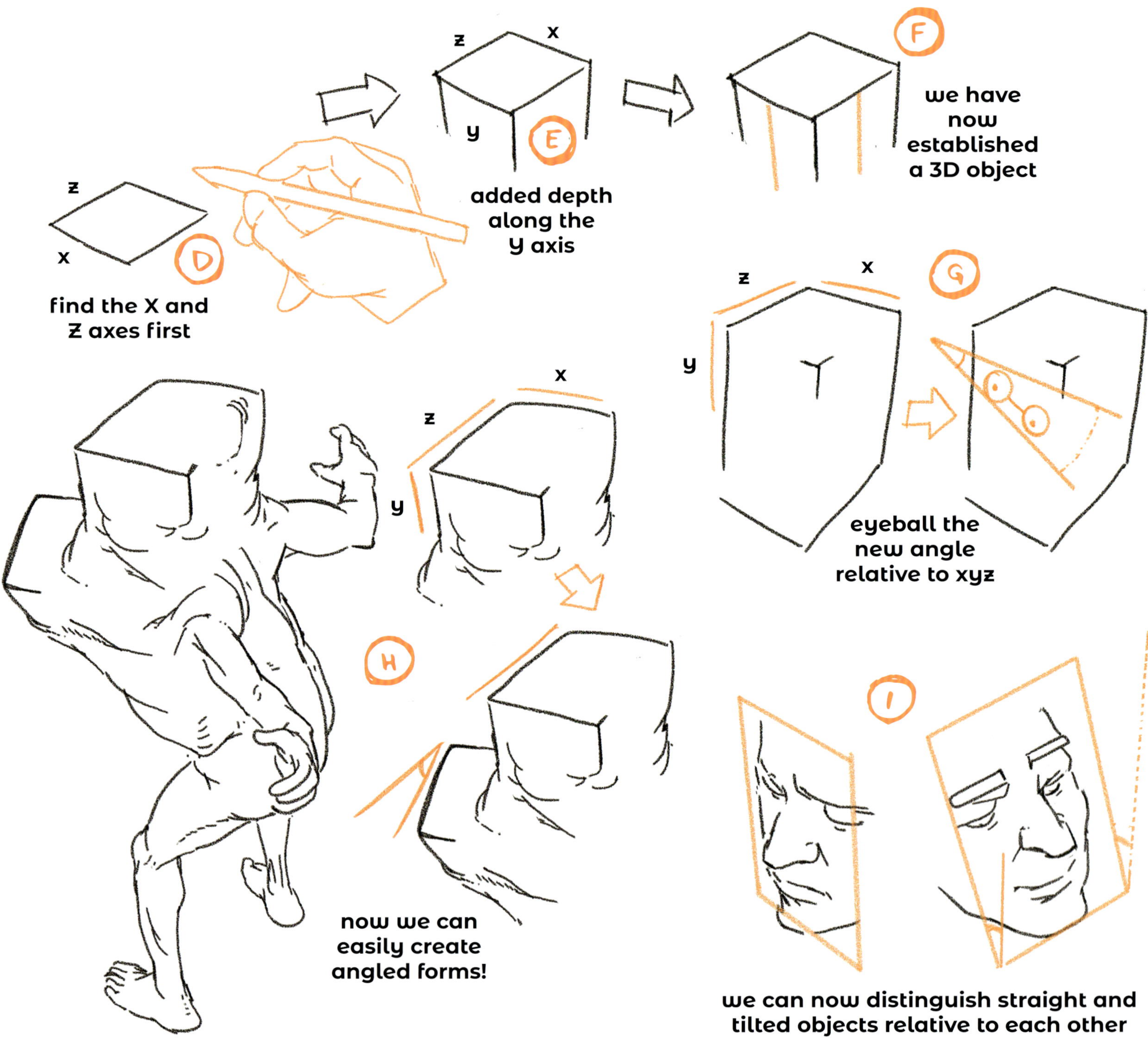

When you create or learn a new form like this, the hardest part is always memorizing it from multiple angles. A good design should be believable from every direction. Using our "known variables" technique, let's draw out a planar subject in stages.

First, we establish a box (J). Then we measure out the key points K and L, and a third (M) directly at the back of the skull. There are two L points: one on each side of the skull. We know that all of these planes are perfectly horizontal or vertical, so we can measure smaller planes tilting from them.

These points represent our XYZ axis, and we also know that they are the widest, tallest, and farthest-back parts of the head. We know that nothing will go outside of these boundaries. Then we can simply connect the dots using our knowledge that the skull has a ball-like shape (N).

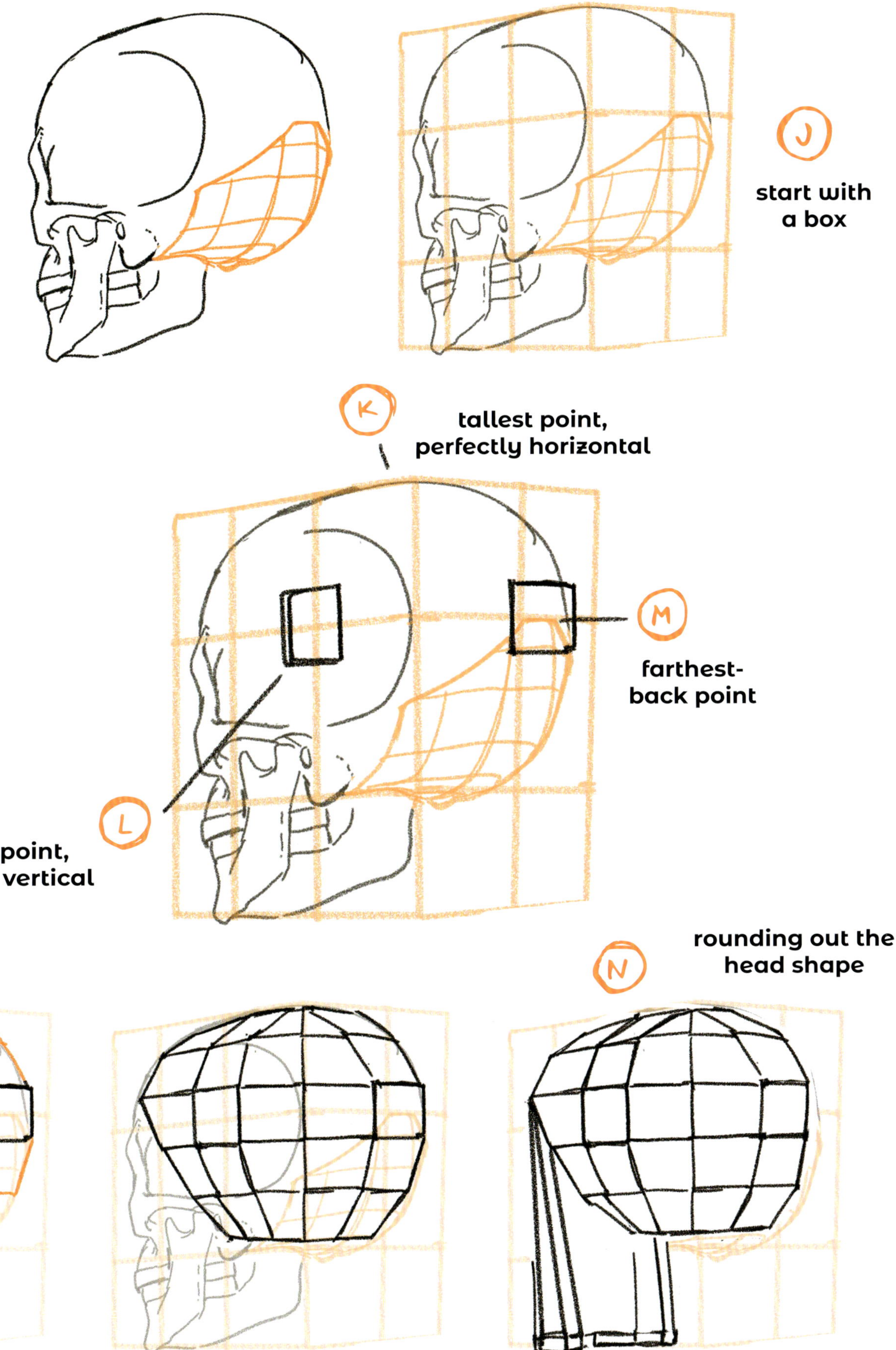

So we've established our three known variables of the skull: the highest (1), widest (2), and farthest-back (3) points. But there's another key plane at the bottom of the skull: the occipital bone (O, 4). In example P, there's a sharper curve from 1 to 2 than from 2 to 4. Note how there are only ever two planes in each direction between 1, 2, 3, and 4.

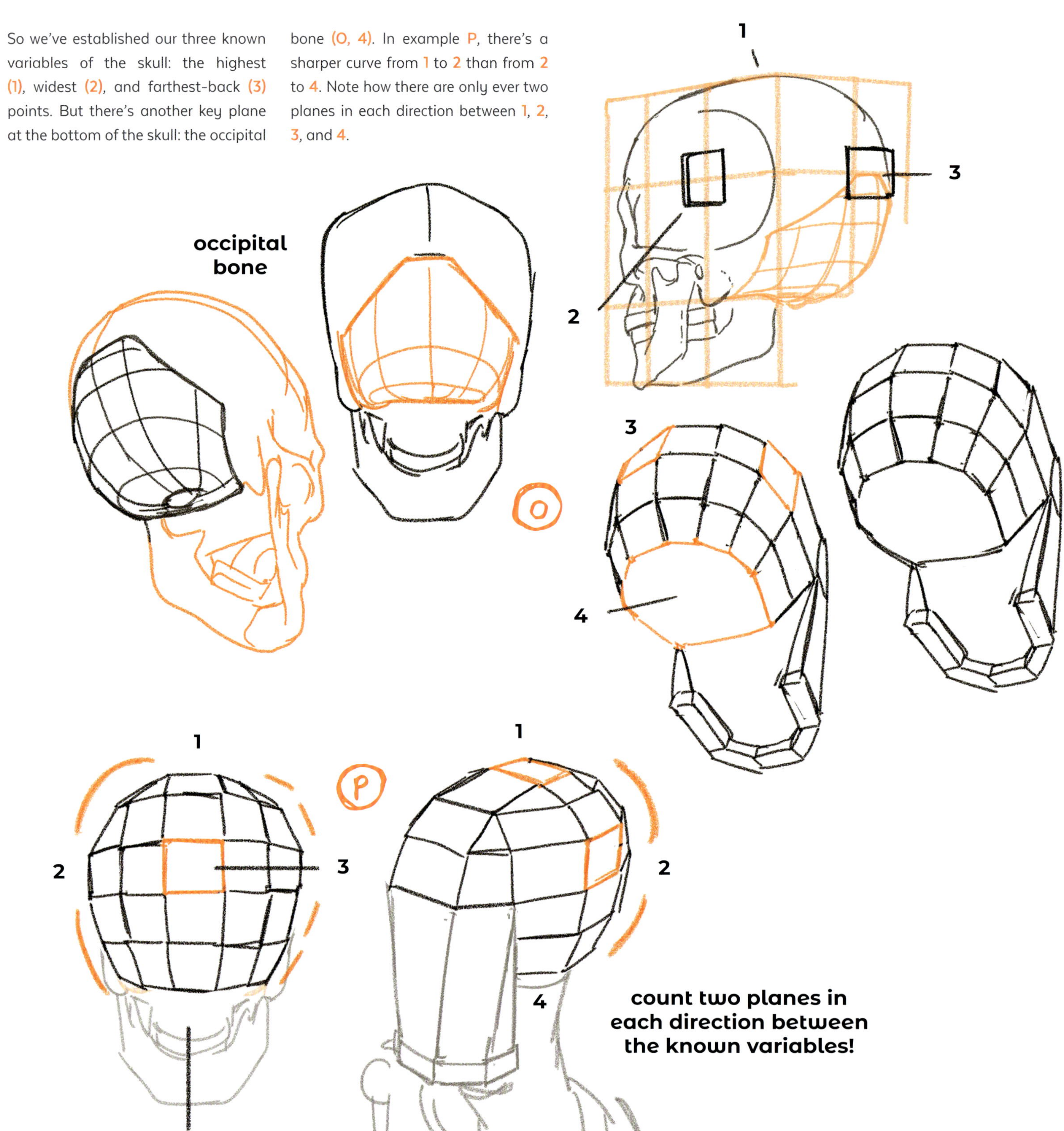

tip: silhouette ends

When finishing a portrait, people often finish off the neck in a way that flattens the head's impression of form. Progressing from A to B, we can see the impression of looking up at this head as we draw. Then, by the time we get to C, we're so pleased to have finished drawing the head that we simply draw a neck line, as if any line will do! Even when the silhouette ends, it should agree with the rest of the form.

Here's another basic head (D). The eyes give us a known variable that suggests the perspective to us. When we add the other features, we draw them from below, so that we know we're looking up (E). If you then draw a neck that looks as though you're looking down on it, it confuses the viewer, even if they aren't conscious of the reason.

As a golden rule, if you are drawing with fewer lines, pay closer attention to getting them correct. If we're looking up or down at a head or other body part, end the silhouette with a line that suggests that direction (F)!

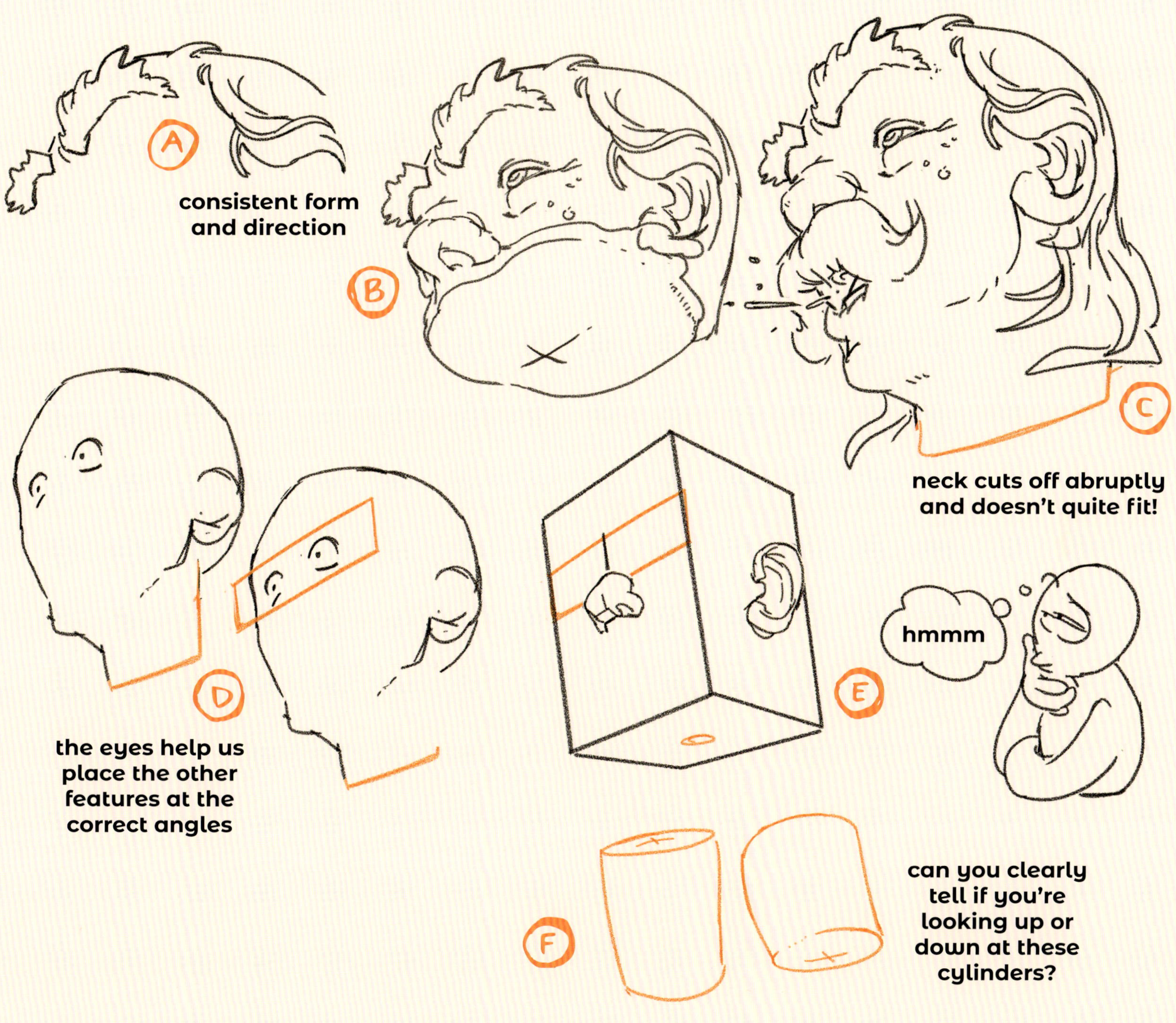

You are the artist and architect of the world you are building and sculpting in. Yes, you *could* draw shapes like G, but why would you choose to? The "silhouette ends," shown in orange, aren't visually pleasing. They don't flow with the form or match with each other. Artists usually want their work to have "appeal" and do everything in their power to achieve this. Use every trick you can! Redesign and look for silhouette ends and edges that agree with each other (H).

Why design base I when you can design base J? Strive to match these parts of the drawing with your known variables – in this case, the eye and brow sections – to improve your presentation (K).

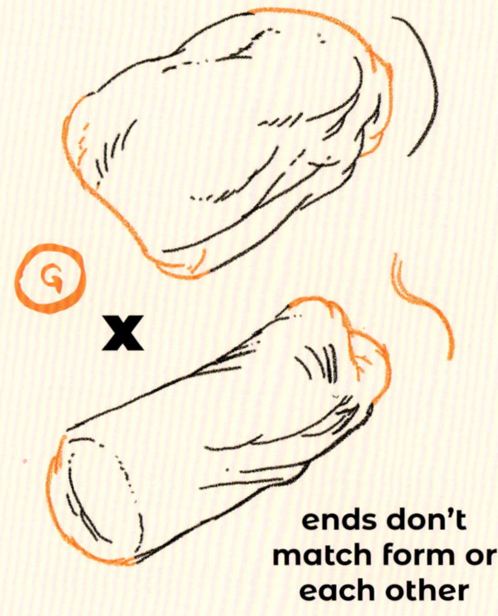

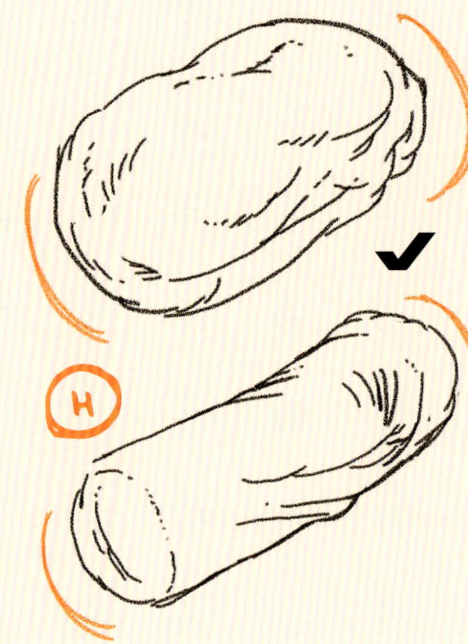

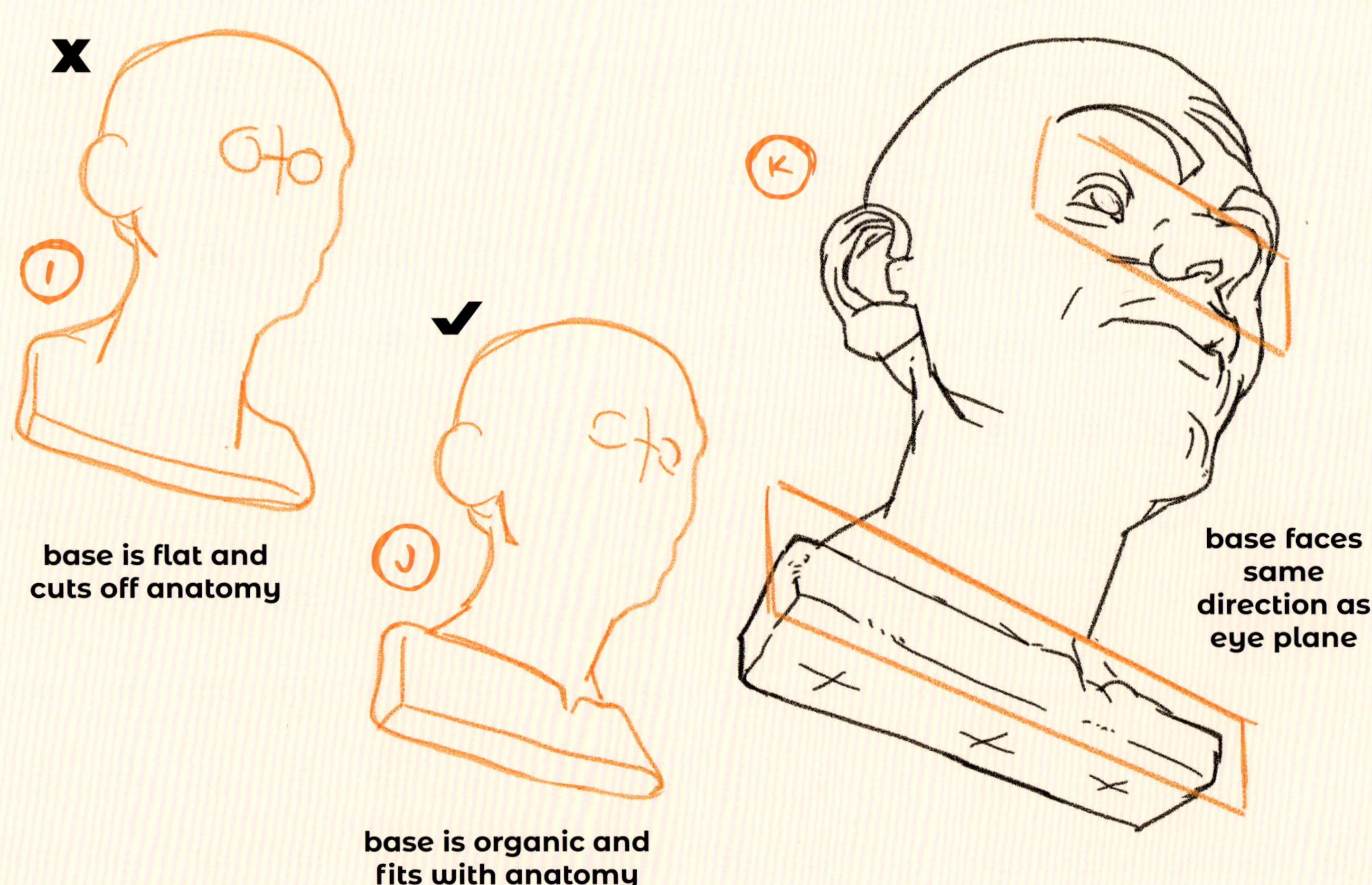

the mask

Now let's look at the face, starting with what's often called the "mask" region. This includes the frontal bone, nasal bones, maxilla (upper jaw), and zygomatic bones (cheekbones). Don't worry if these sound a bit daunting – we'll cover them in an accessible way.

People will often suggest to "draw the mask" on the front of the face, with the expectation that if you aim for a simple shape, it will be easier to draw (A). The problem with this idea is that simple shapes laid on complex forms are still difficult to draw, especially from challenging angles (B)! You're not making the form any simpler with this method – you're just trying to visualize a sticker on top of it. We need a better way to approach this area.

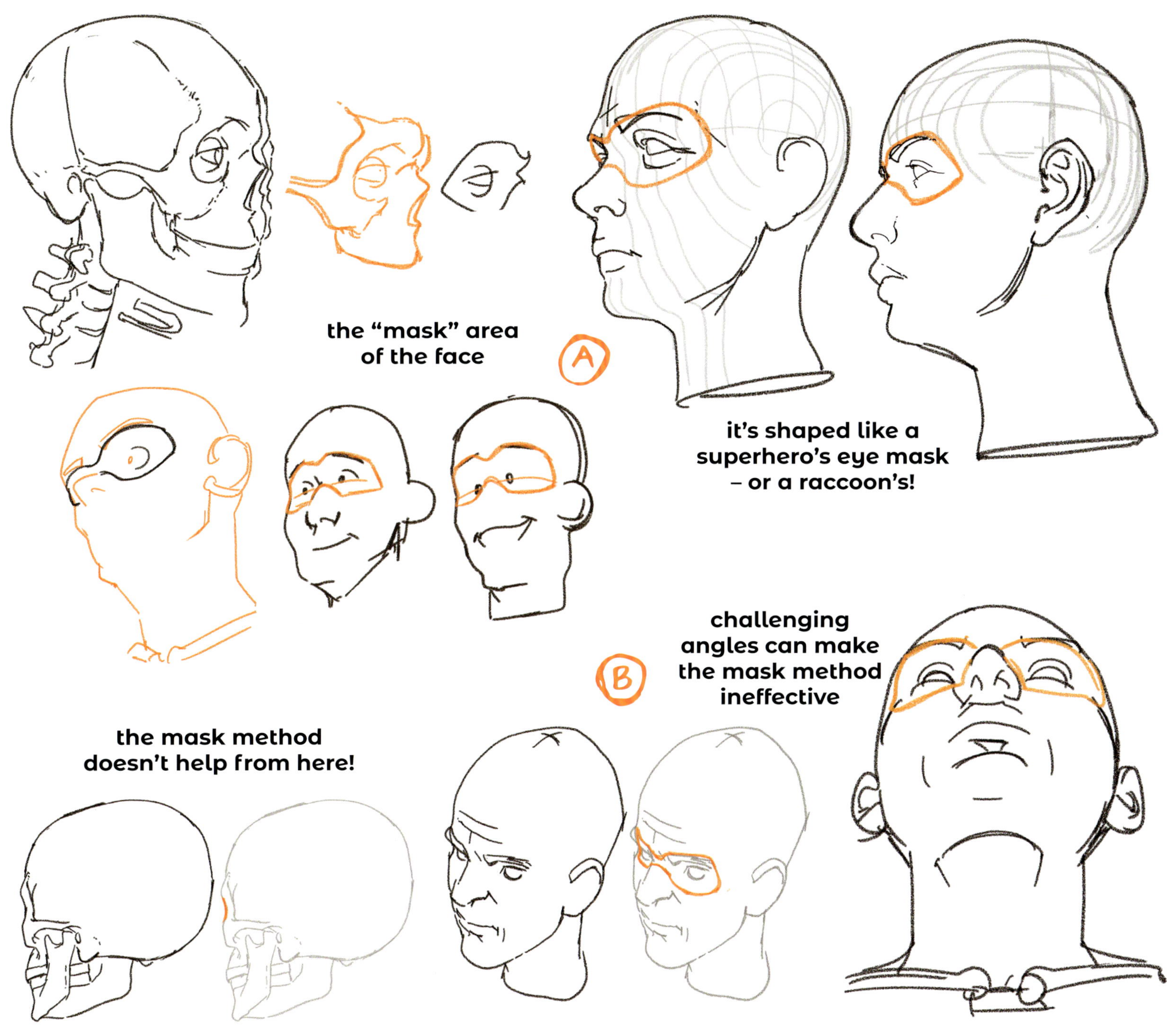

frontal bone

Let's break down the mask area by first examining the frontal bone (A). This forms the forehead and is the most important bone in the head to learn. Sadly, it's also the bone people avoid studying the most! Note how it wraps around, and also back, but has clear brow ridges that are sharper on the outside and more gently curved on the inside (B). The occipitofrontalis muscle, which connects the occipital and frontal bones, starts thick and ends thin, with muscle at the front of the skull and tendons at the back. Imagine someone has laid a piece of bacon over the top of your head (C)! The frontal bone forms the roof of the eye sockets (D). This bone has a large volume and many graceful curves, but these can be simplified down to a model approximating E, with three main sections angling upward.

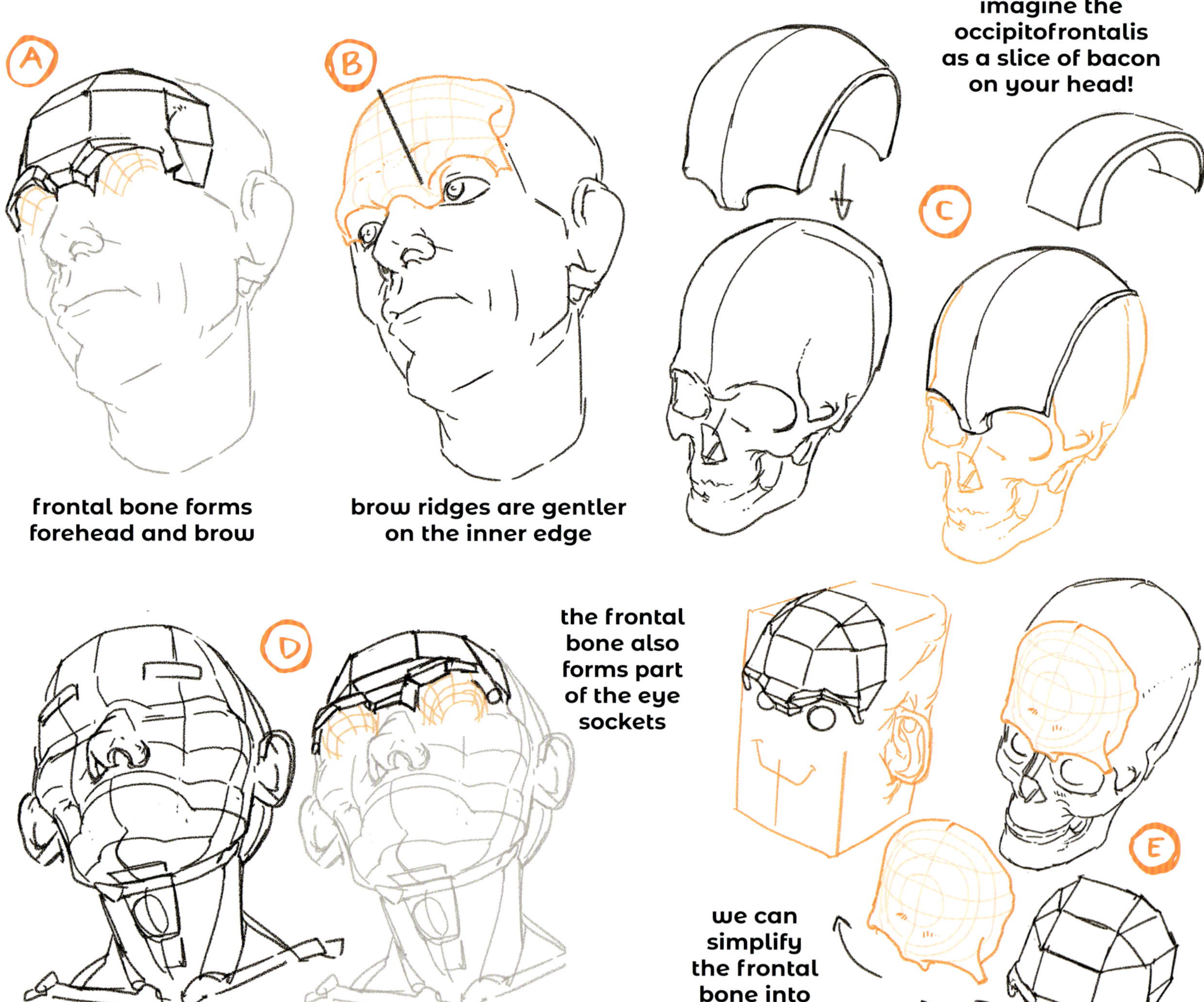

When drawing the brows, don't complete the inner-edge shapes (F). If you do that, it'll look like your skull is wearing sunglasses! That's drawing a shape, not the form. The inner eye socket has a gentle curve inward, so you don't need to draw a line there, because you'd be representing a delicate curve with a harsh edge (G).

There is a sharp edge on the lateral (outer) side of the eye socket, where the bone is very narrow (H). You can feel this on yourself quite easily. This is where the frontal bone meets the zygomatic bone below it. Remember to clearly sort your downward planes from your upward planes. There's a strong downward plane on the inner edge of the eye socket (I).

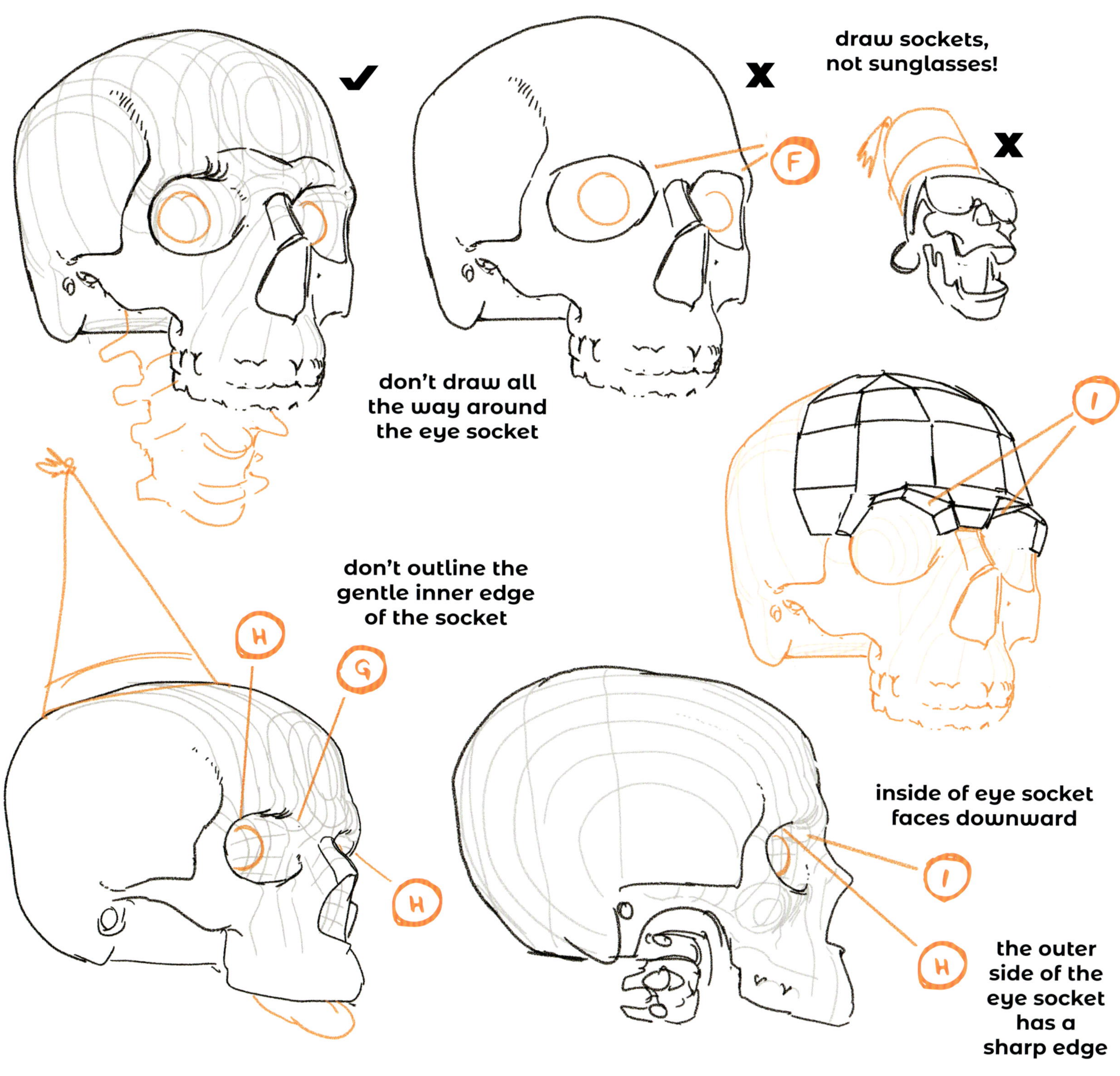

Let's move on to the region directly below the brows. Before we get into the bones, it's worth noting that the brow region tilts backward in space (J) and so does the region below it (K). If you're having difficulty judging the angles of the slopes, it can be helpful to slide a completely vertical plane into place under the brows first (L), then build the new plane out from there.

If you draw the eyes as flat shapes on this backward-tilting plane, they will look odd (M). Make sure they are represented as spheres that stick *out* from this downward plane.

Plane J represents the maxilla and zygomatic bone. Let's add the zygomatic bones first by adding these two blocky forms onto the outside of this simple "T" shape (N).

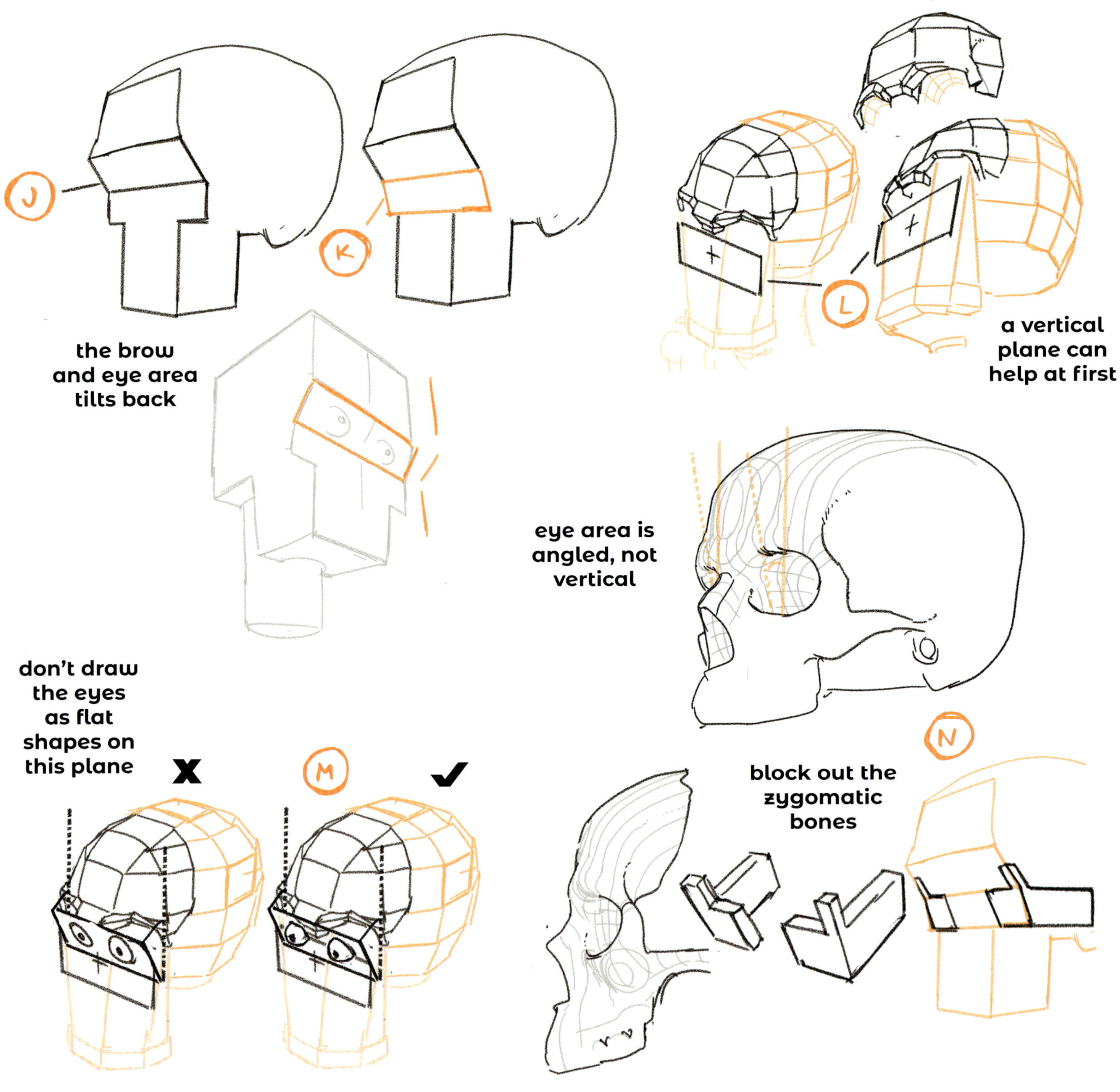

soft & hard edges

Always be on the lookout for variety in soft and hard edges. Sharp turns in form are great landmarks, while softer turns are regions where you should avoid putting too many lines (A).

Note that around the spheres of the eyes (B), there are two form changes. The inner is concave, curving inward (C), and the outer is convex, bulging out (D). There's an important upward-facing plane here, too, which is often overlooked (E).

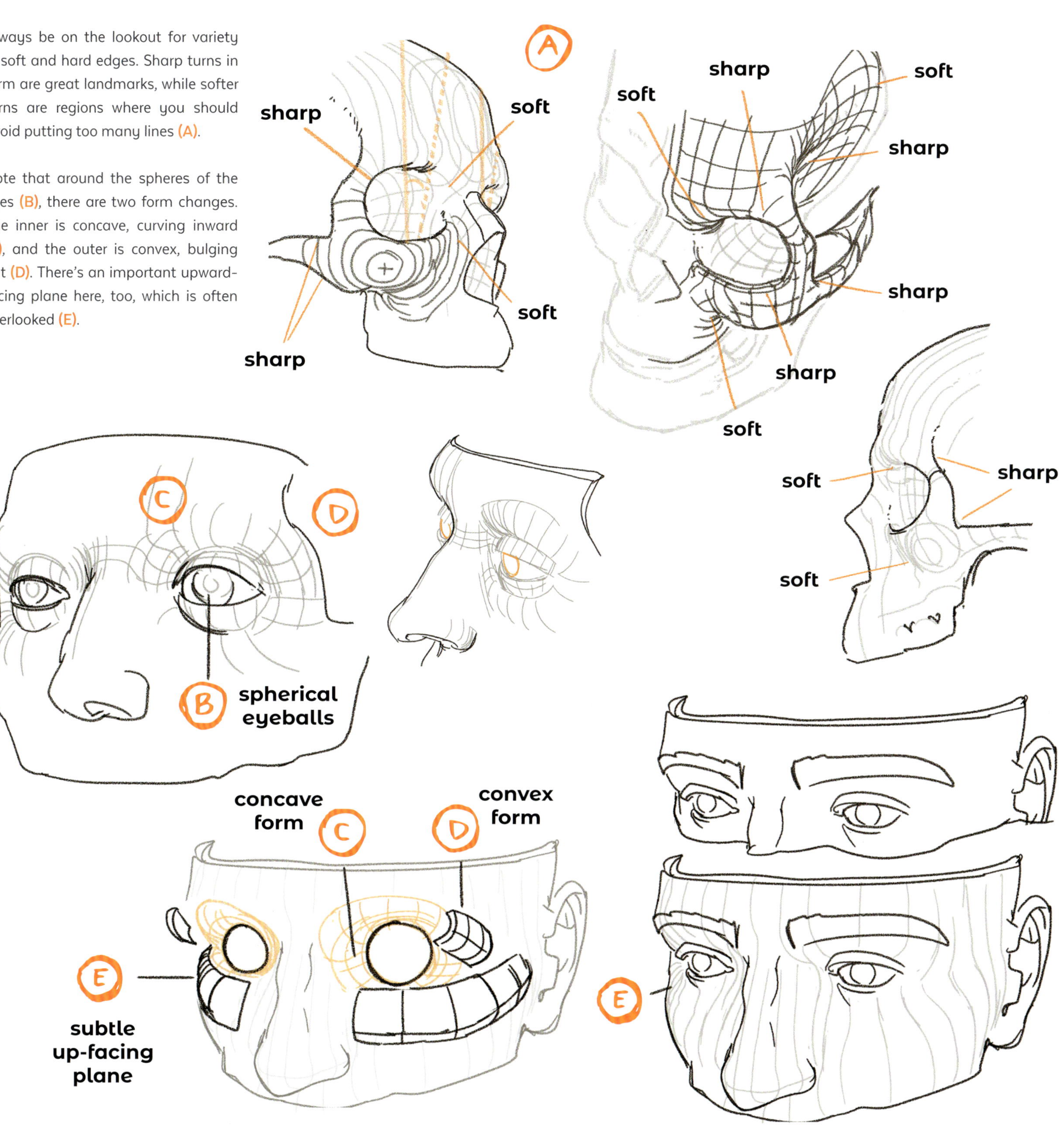

adding eyes

To draw the eyes, start with two circles on a flat plane, as if they're on a piece of card (A). Curve that card to represent the curvature of the face (B). Finally, draw spheres instead of flat eye shapes, and wrap eyelids and eyebrows over the curved surface (C).

When viewed from above, if the eyes are looking up, the line of the eyelids will appear flat, but when the lids are closed you can see how they wrap around the spheres of the eyes (D).

Imagine the eyebrows are flat stickers curving downward (E), then imagine them stuck onto a curved surface, so they wrap backward too. When looked at from above, they appear as almost straight lines (F).

In G you can see how the amount of the zygomatic bone visible from the side depends on how deeply set the eyes are. If the eye sockets are shallow, the eyes bulge out over the sides; if the sockets are deep, the opposite is true.

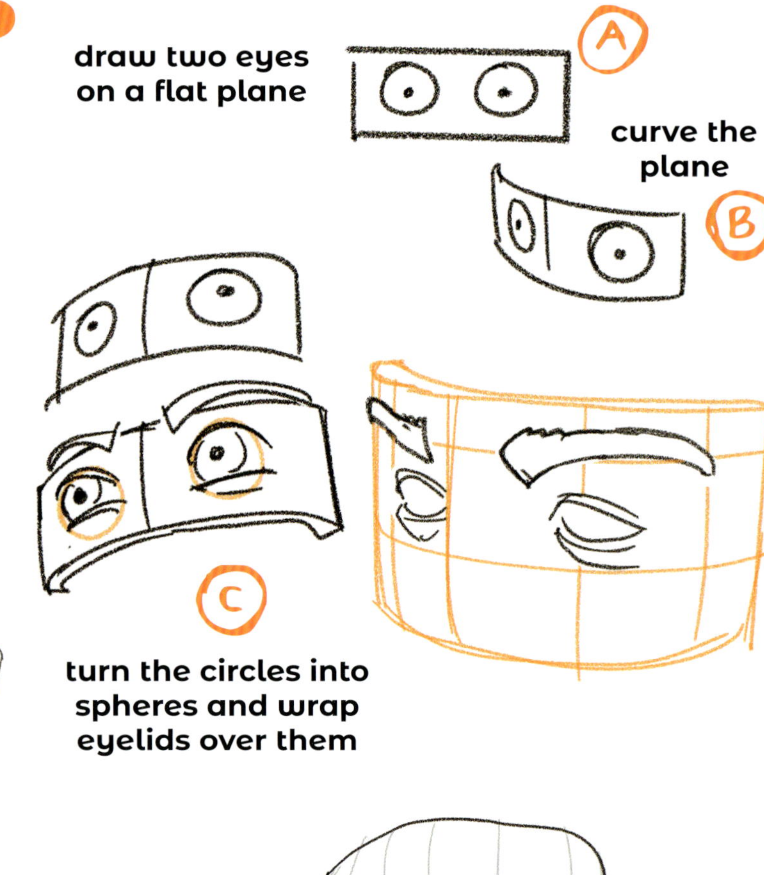

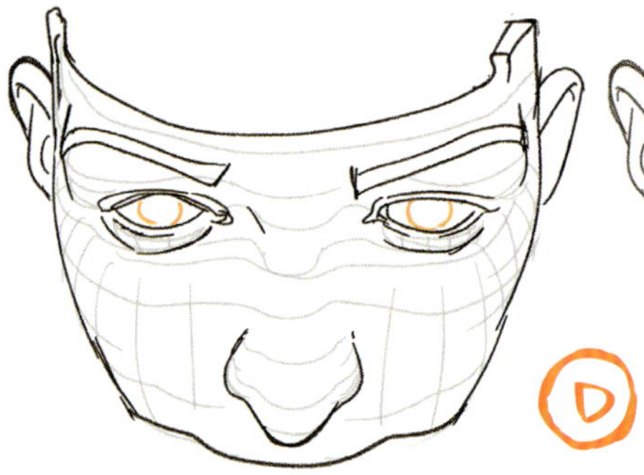

D

from above you can see how the eyelids curve

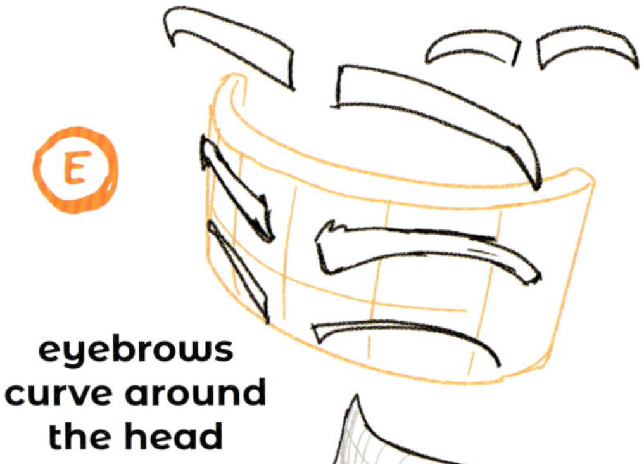

E

eyebrows curve around the head

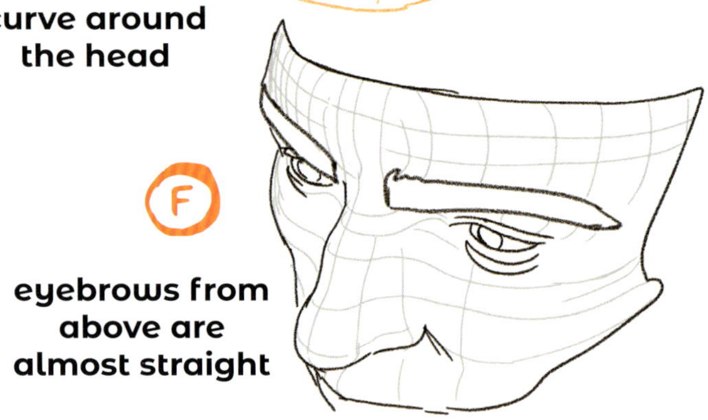

F

eyebrows from above are almost straight

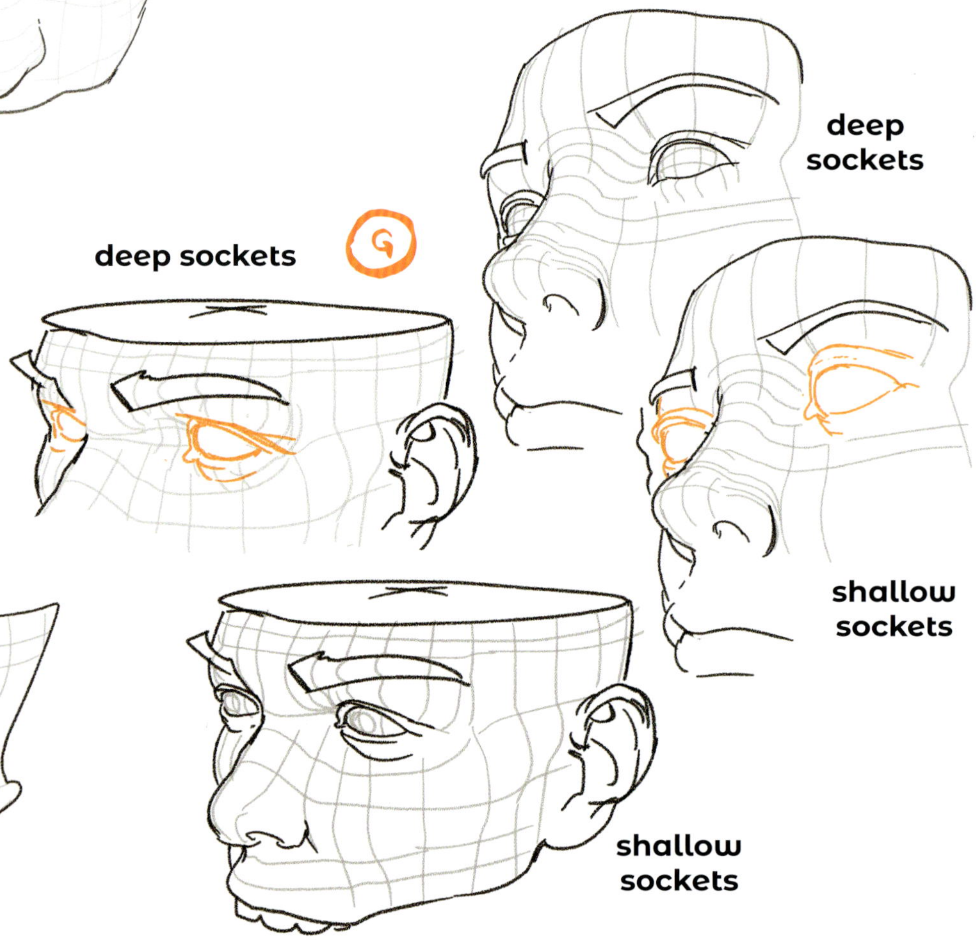

deep sockets

G

deep sockets

shallow sockets

shallow sockets

zygomatic bones

Let's increase the level of detail into something more realistic for these two zygomatic shapes that we blocked out on page 96 (A). The front section stays tilted forward, but we can curve and smooth the rest until we have more segments – a total of seven (1-7). The first segment is tilted forward at the top and gently angles back to the side (B). The whole cheekbone piece curves backward around the head, but isn't fully side-on to the front of the face (C). It generally widens to the third piece (3), then starts to curve back inward from the fourth. Note the small angled tail at the end of the shape, where the arm of the temporal bone merges into the side of the skull (D). If this seems complicated, be patient – we'll look at this whole form in more detail next!

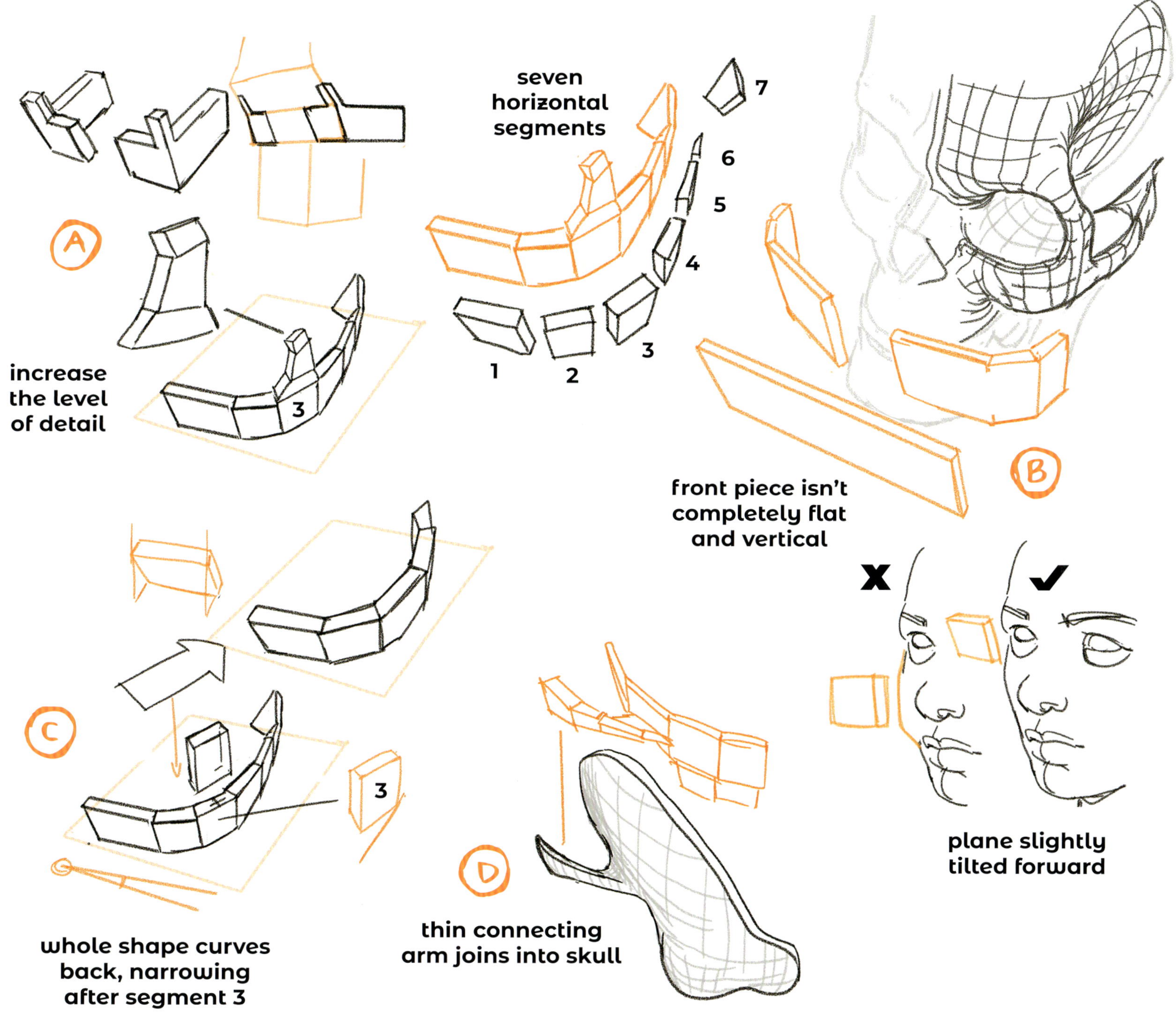

A good place to start is by drawing each of the six main sections with equal heights until you get their tilt and curvature under control (E). From there, you can progress to narrowing them as they curve around toward the bottom of the side of the skull (F). This will feel awkward to draw from below because the curve is not only wrapping around the head, but getting narrower, so you won't see as much of it as you might think (G).

You'll actually see a lot of this form wrapping around the side of the face when looking at the face from an off-center angle. Note the top-facing plane, which is only small, but appears like a small ledge (H).

By piecing together our new cheekbone section and the forehead bone we made on page 94, we can create a workable base for the top half of the head (I)!

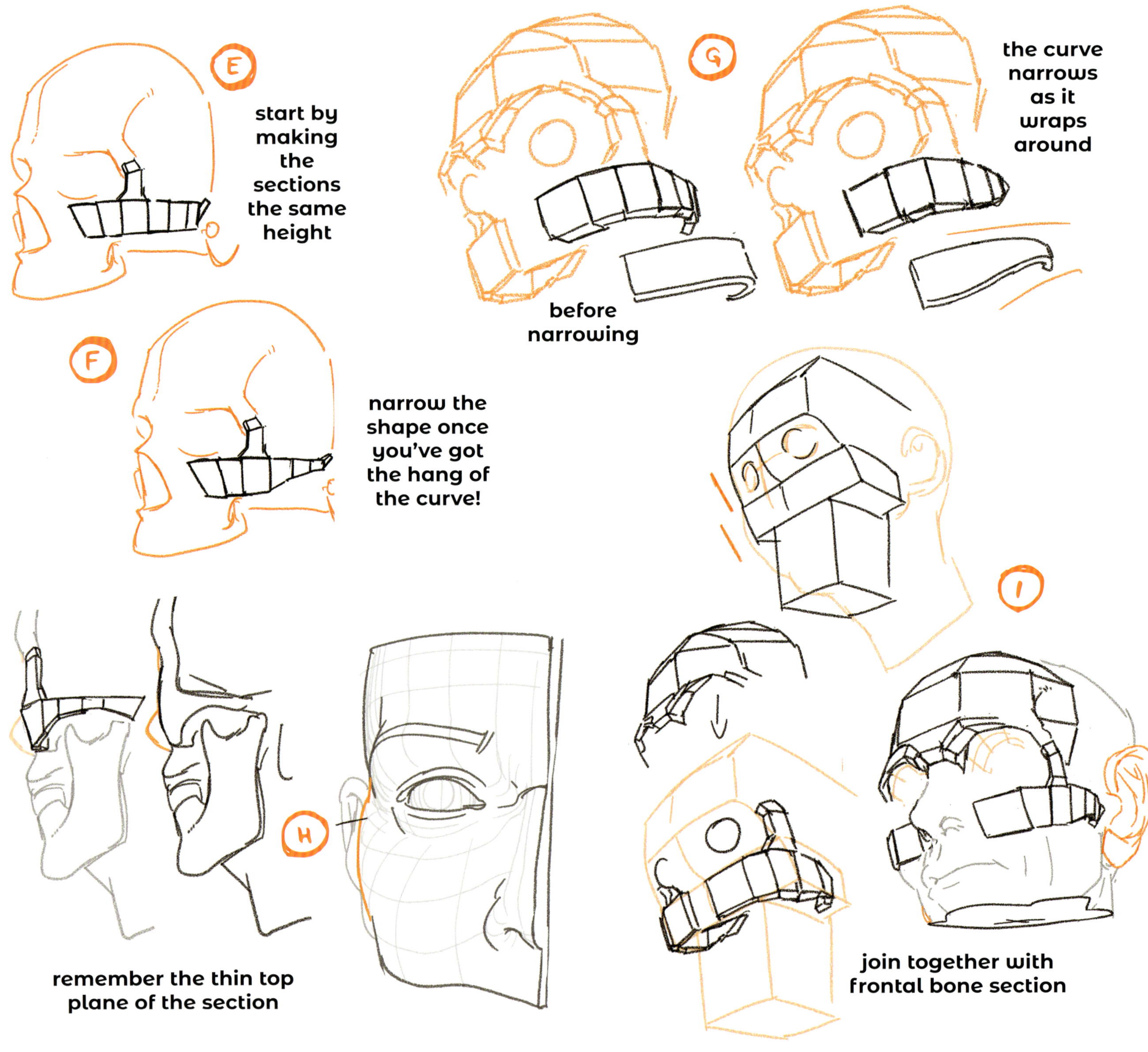

The forms representing the zygomatic bones are angled more sharply backward than the brow ridge, which you can see clearly when viewed from below. Comparing J (brow ridges) and K (cheekbones) you can see the cheeks have a more gentle and flattened curve than the brows, which are wider and project farther. Why is this? It's because our hunter-gatherer ancestors spent most of their time in a world where their food, mates, and prey were all around eye level (L). We don't have much need to be looking up, so we have a great range of vision ahead or below us, but limited vision when we turn our eyes upward (M)!

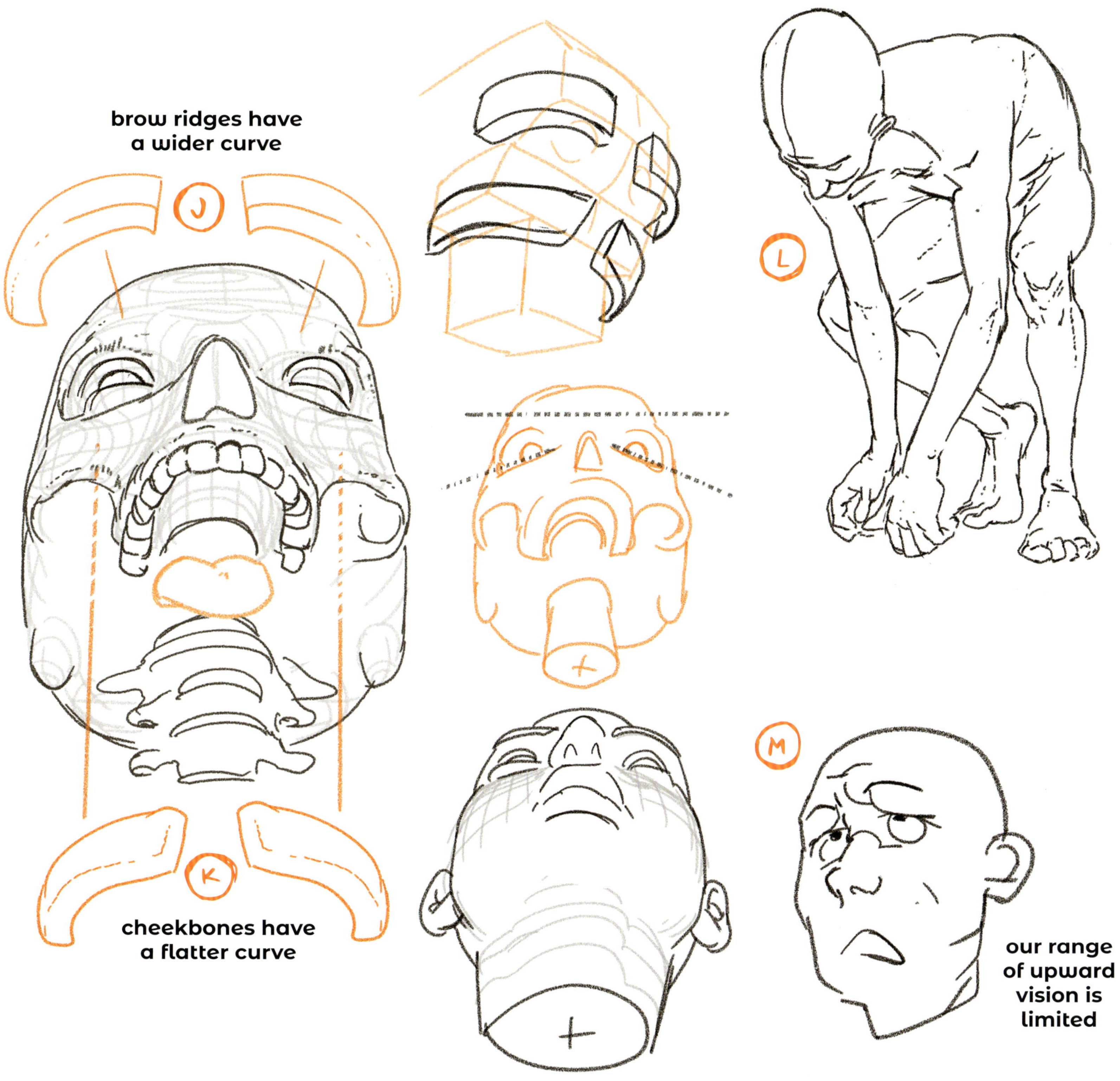

refining the eyes

When drawing the eyes themselves, be very careful where you place the pupils (A). If you rush them, a well-constructed eye can change into something formless. The eyes are tricky, and as always, it's the tricky areas that require the most attention.

Make sure the lids wrap around the spheres of the eyeballs (B). From above, you will barely see the eyes, or not at all – resist the temptation to draw them (C). Don't make the eyes symmetrical from an angle such as D – we would see much less of the farther eye as the face curves away!

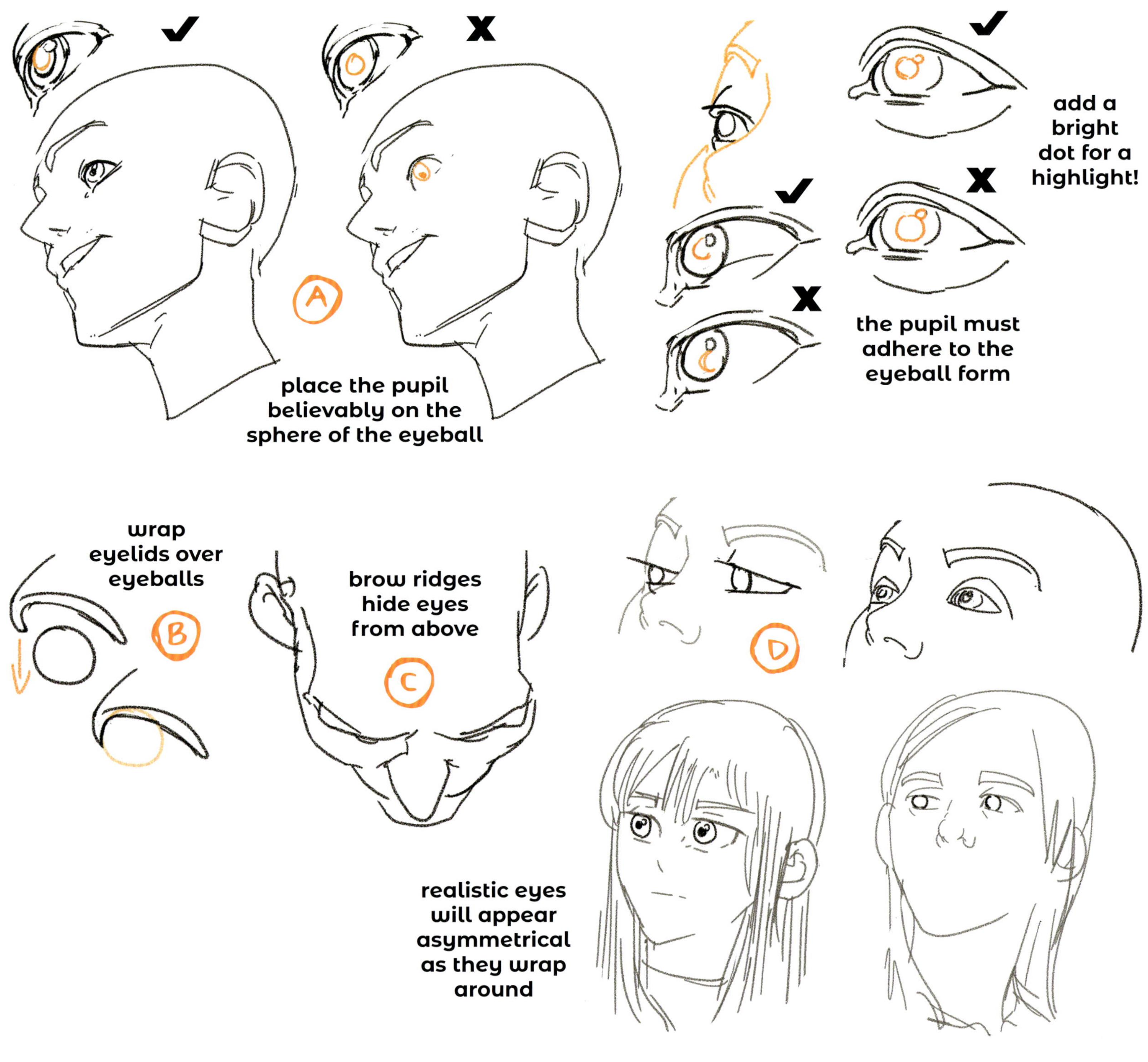

the upper jaw

Now let's look at the maxilla (A). It has a scooplike shape that can be simplified by drawing a curved form, then breaking that form into eight sections (B). On top of this we add another form that creates the arched support for the roof of the mouth (C). We're breaking this skull down into the simplest forms manageable, so let's add that roof now, even though we won't see it from most external views. Imagine it popping neatly into place in the curve we've made (D).

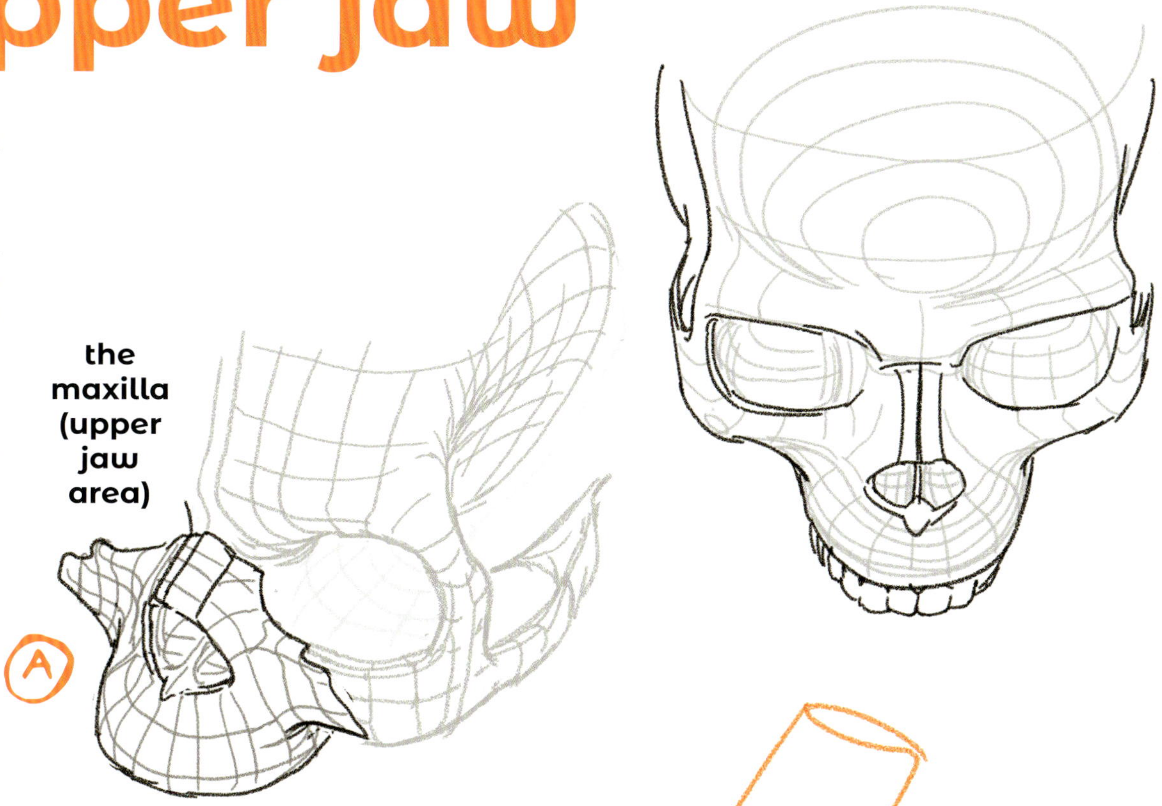

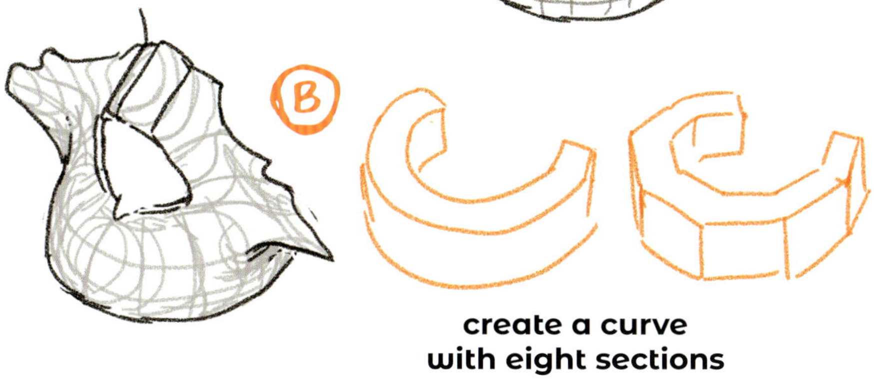

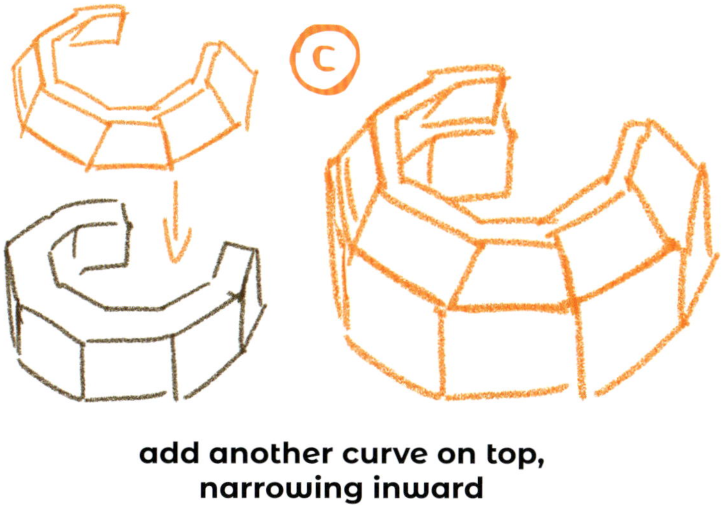

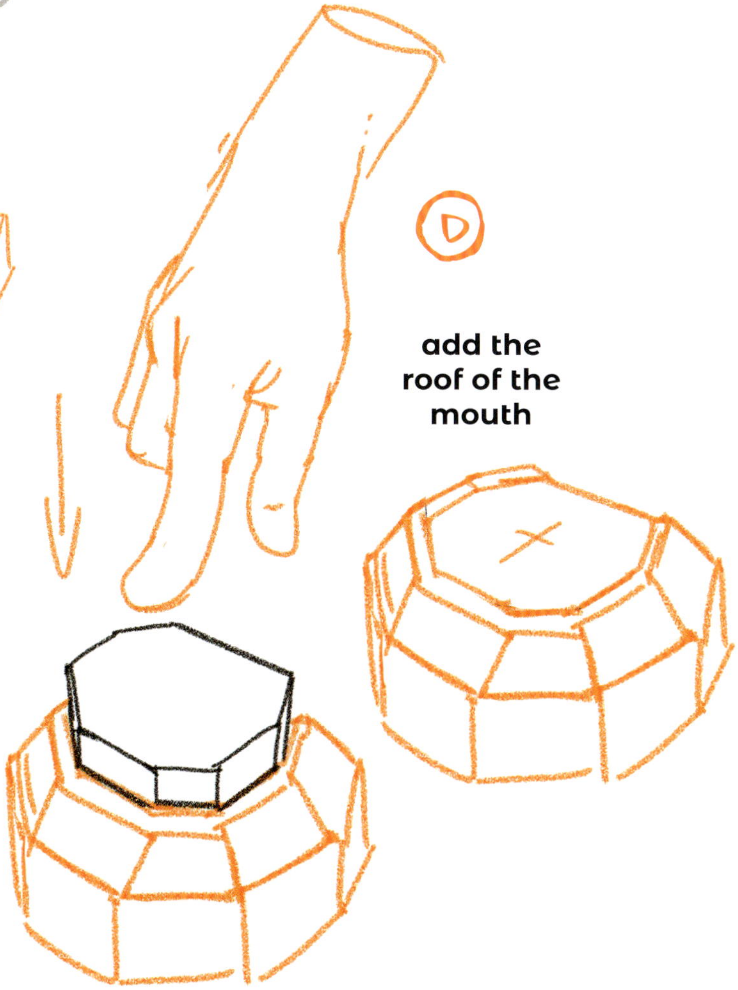

nasal bones

The maxilla encompasses not only the upper jaw, but most of the nose area (A). Let's block out the shape of the nose bones by starting with B. Chisel a section from the front, so you have a slight slope at the front of the face, then add two "wings" for where the maxilla meets the zygomatic bone. That's as simple as this area can be!

We now have our first basic nose bone, but it needs complexity (C, 1). On the top of it, you can add the two nasal bones either side of a little supporting wedge, and angle the joins of the two side wings (2). We can slot this blocked-out nose piece into the gap provided by what we've drawn so far, completing the upper head (3). If we have the foundation, the rest is a matter of adding details (D) - such as the nose, which we'll look at next!

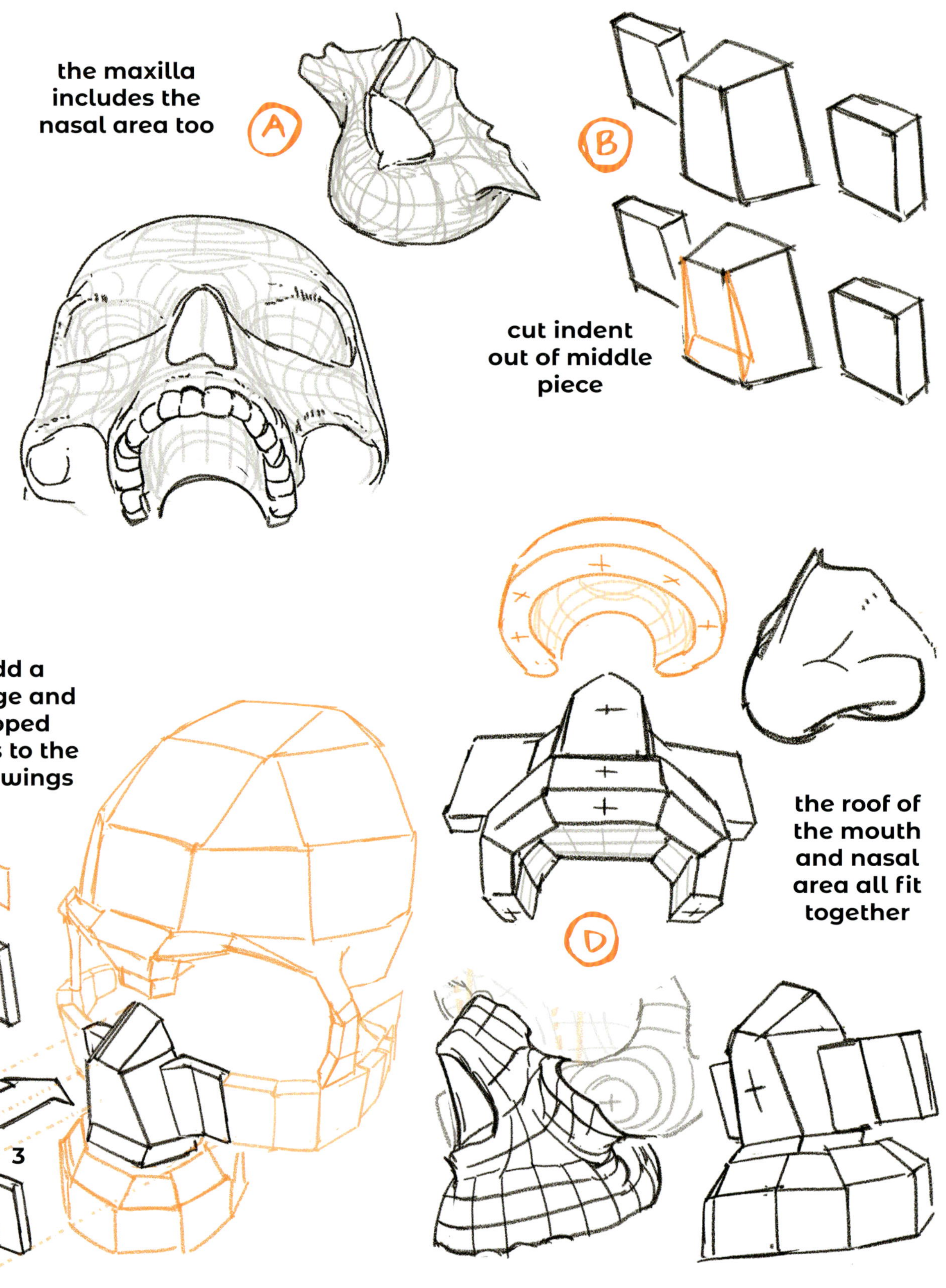

the nose

Let's move on to the nose itself, which we can attach to the maxilla base that we've just designed. The nasal cartilage divides the nose vertically in two. Take a flat block and slice off two corners, leaving a little beak (A). Slide this into the hole in the skull (B). The alar cartilage – alar meaning "winglike" in Latin – will sit on top of this foundation, as we'll see next (C, D).

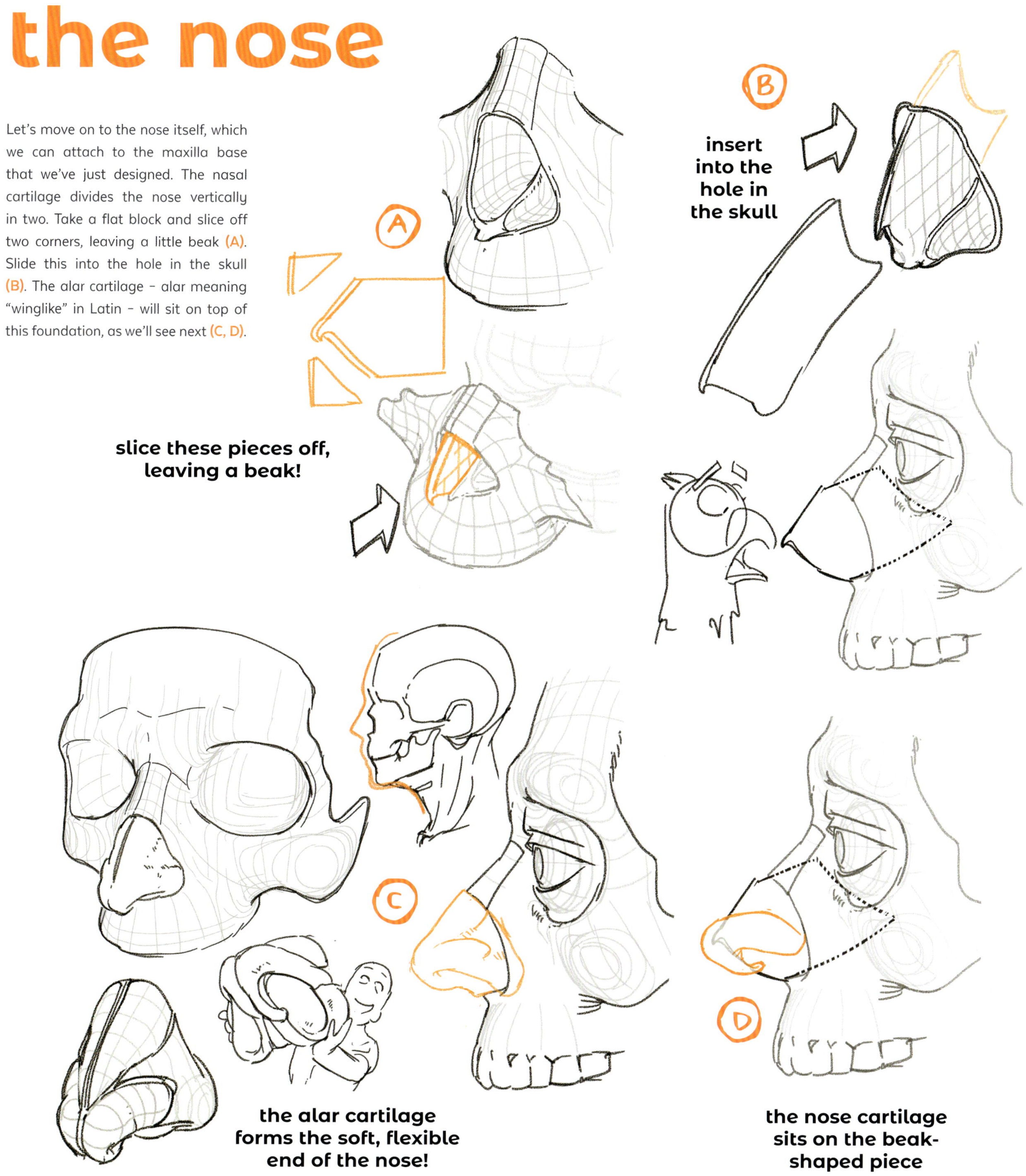

When drawing something as subtly complex as the nose, don't forget that less is more. If you learn the forms well and invest in knowledge, you won't have to draw as many lines in the future. A few well-placed marks are more believable.

The nose is much rounder than people realize (E). If you make it more bulbous, you're already halfway to success. With that in mind, let's build on our nose base by adding a little roof formed by the lateral cartilage, forming the tip and nostrils (F, 1-3).

Carefully observe the upward- and downward-facing planes in G. Once you're clear on those planes, the whole form of the nose can easily be rotated to any angle.

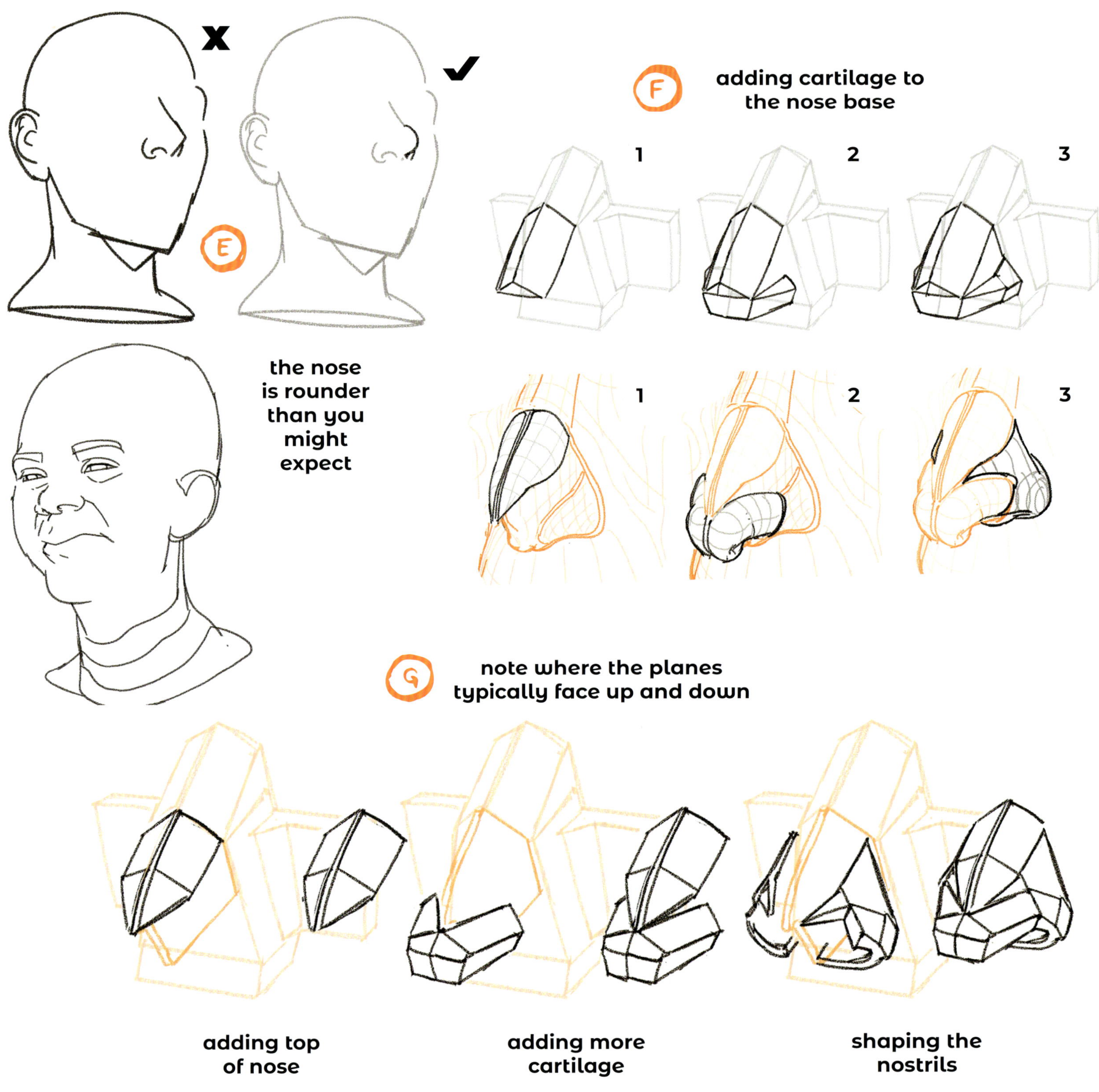

The flesh of the muzzle protrudes forward from the base of the nose, giving the mouth area thickness over the skull's profile (H) and wrapping over the curve of the maxilla (I). When viewed from a three-quarter angle, you see much less of the other side of the nostrils than you'd expect (J).

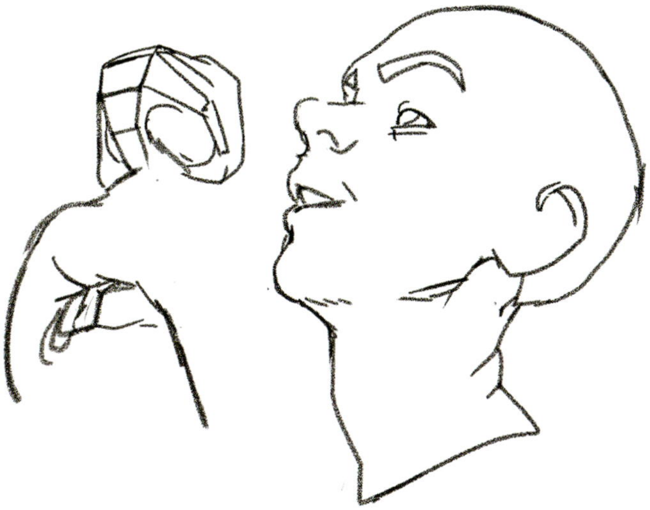

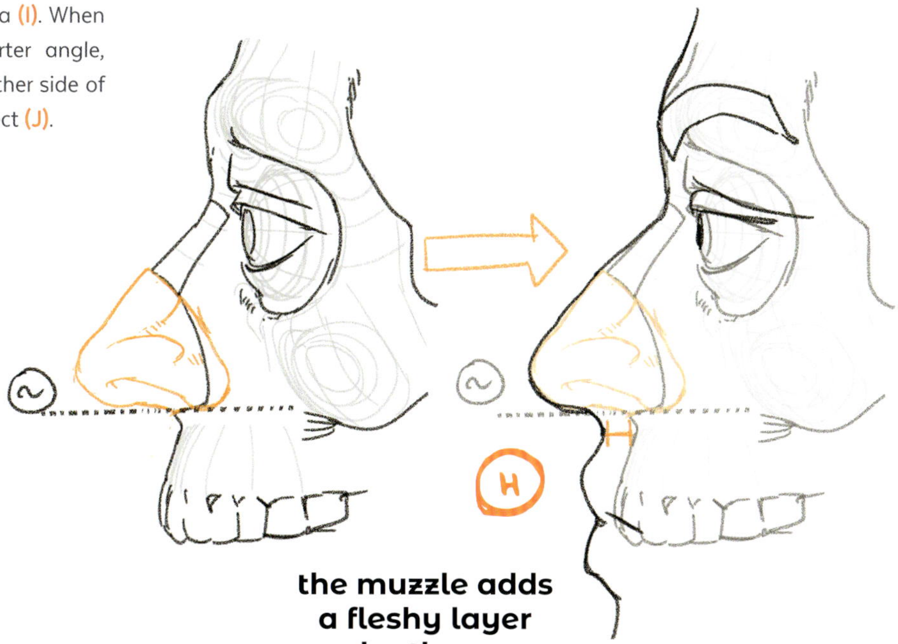

the muzzle adds a fleshy layer under the nose

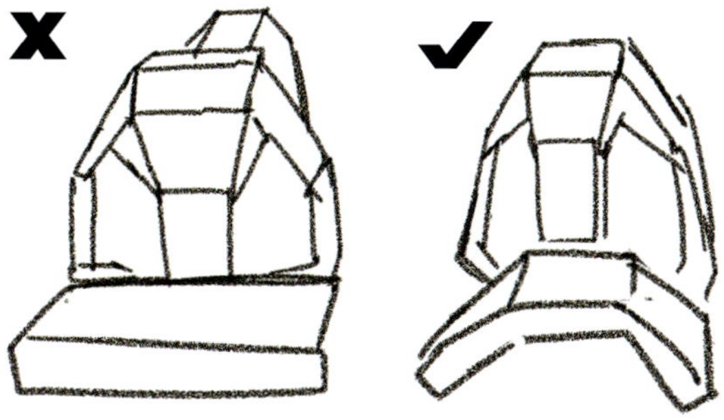

(I) note how the muzzle wraps in a curve

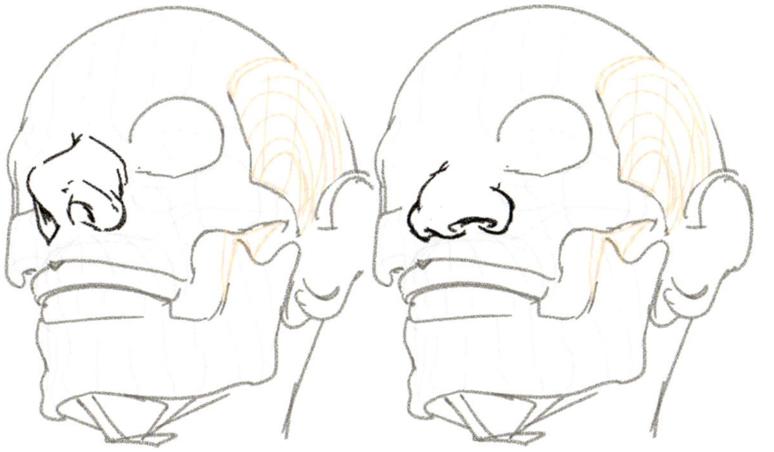

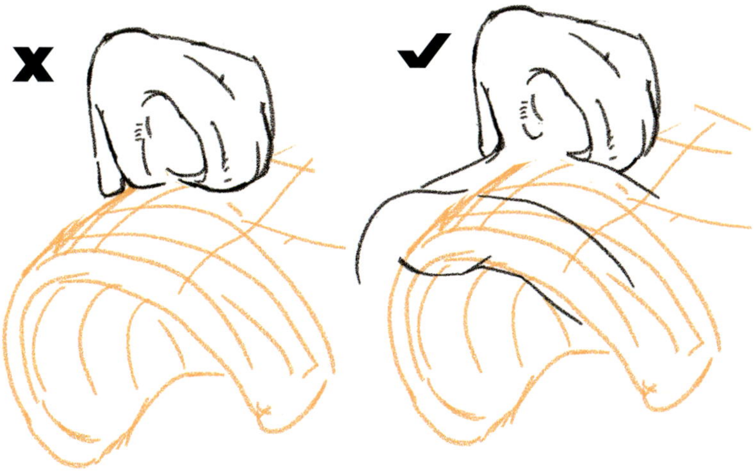

(J) from this angle, you can't see much of the other nostril

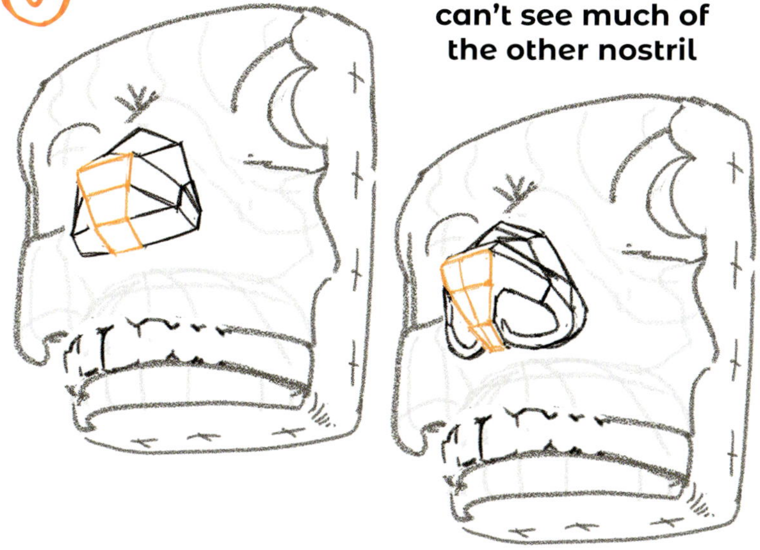

tip: indicate, don't state

While it's true that less is more, if you are unsure whether you'd see something, then show a tiny fragment (A). This is visually interesting to the viewer by suggesting forms they can't fully see, as if the forms they are looking at are turning in space and continue out of sight. Avoid these commonly added lines that usually detract from a good portrait (B). For a simple way to make a face appear younger, change the proportions. Keep the head size similar but shorten the length of the jaw and nose. You don't need to do much more than that to create a younger model (C).

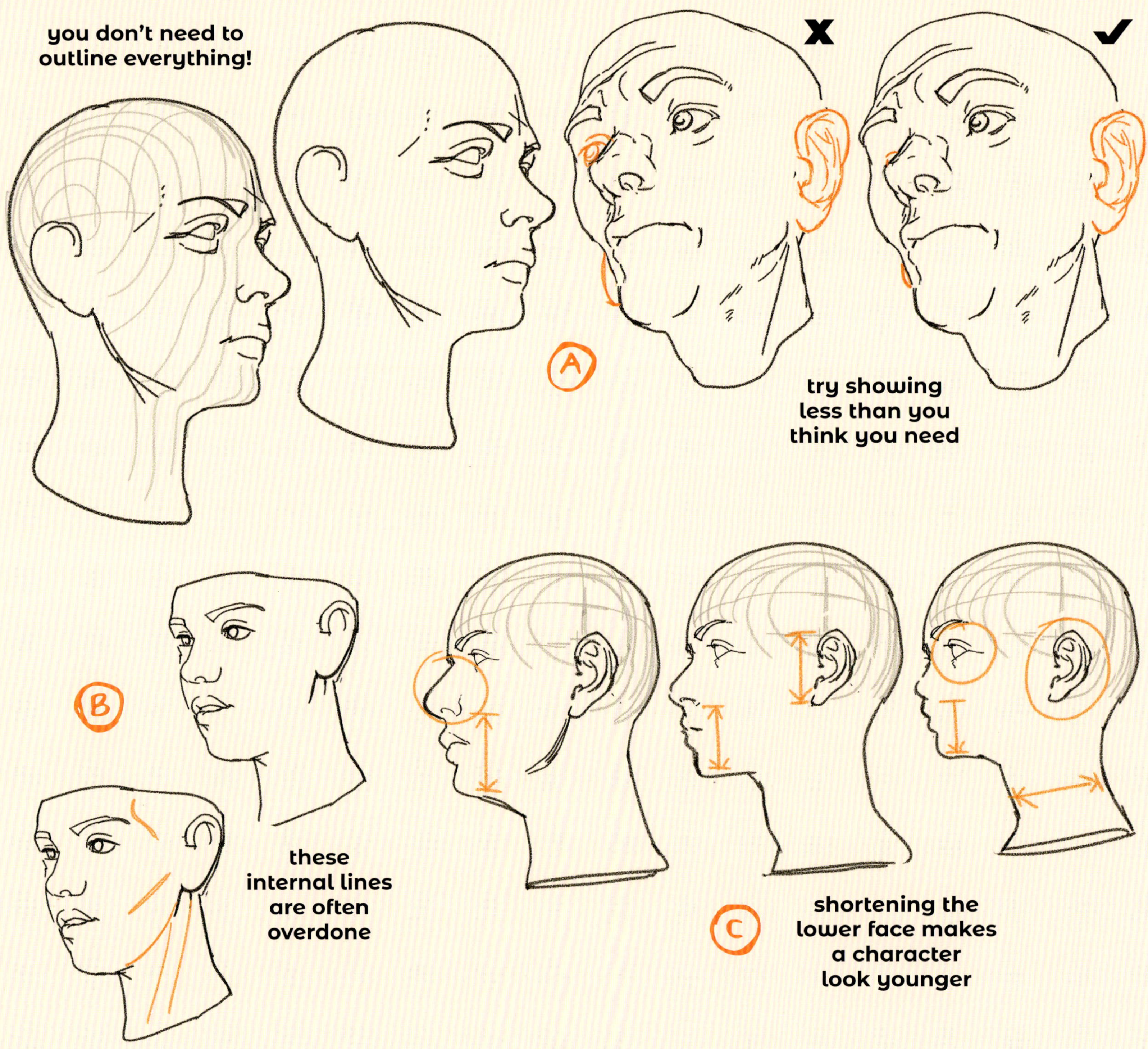

lower jaw

To draw the lower jaw (mandible), start with a blocky form for the section holding the teeth, then add two panels to the back (A). These panels flare up and widen toward the back. From here, we can chisel the blocky section into a rounded piece like the maxilla, and add a notch to the two panels (B). The temporalis muscle attaches to the side of the skull and to the very front of the "arms" of the mandible (C). It pulls up and assists with closing the mouth and chewing. To draw a more typically masculine model, you can flare the jaw out at the back corners (D). This width gives a more powerful look to the head. A more typically feminine jaw would be the opposite.

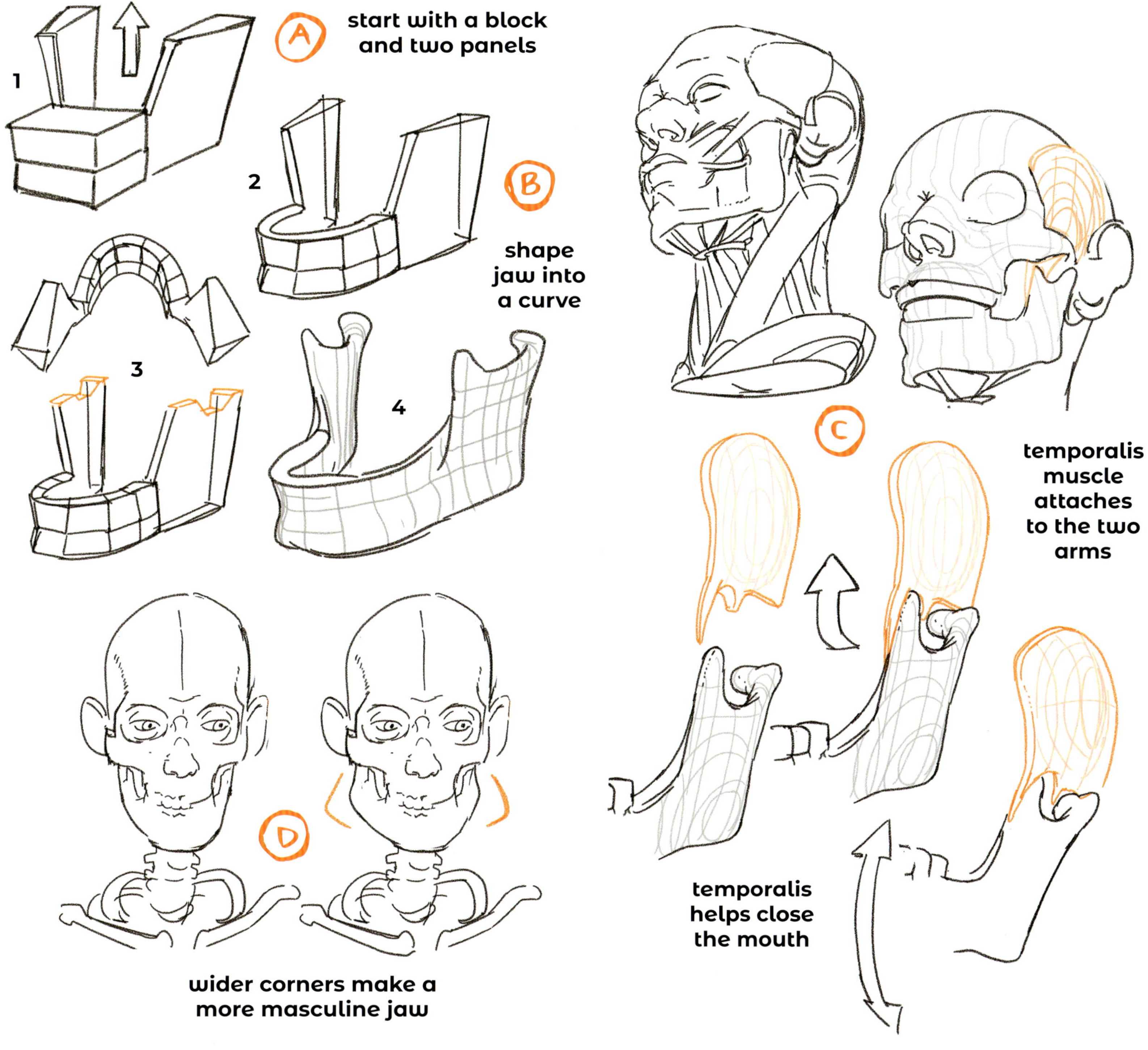

When drawing the chin, make sure to include the roundness of its curve in both directions. It doesn't just wrap around horizontally (E), but also wraps from top to bottom (F). Forgetting to include this dimension will result in an unrealistically sharp chin (G).

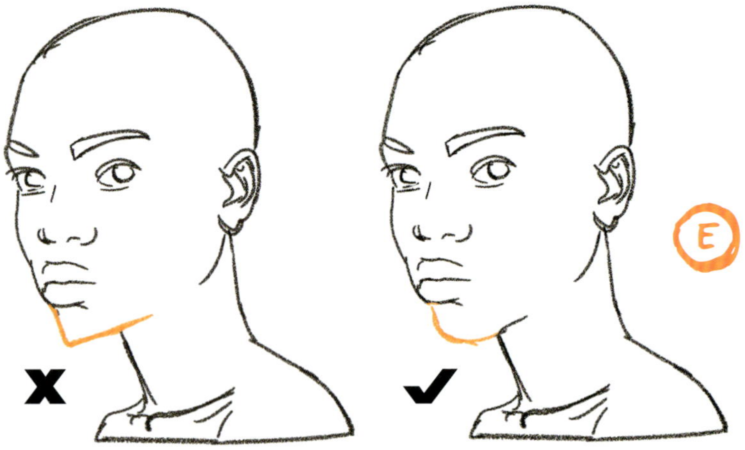

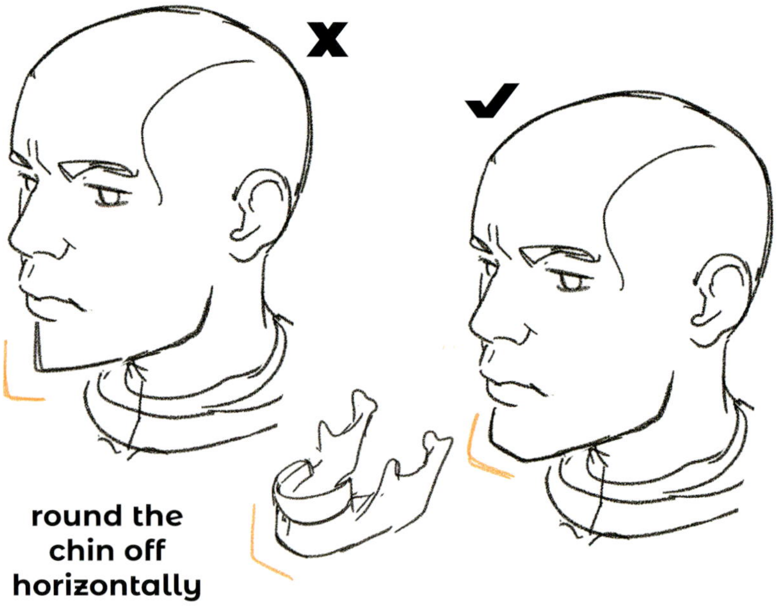

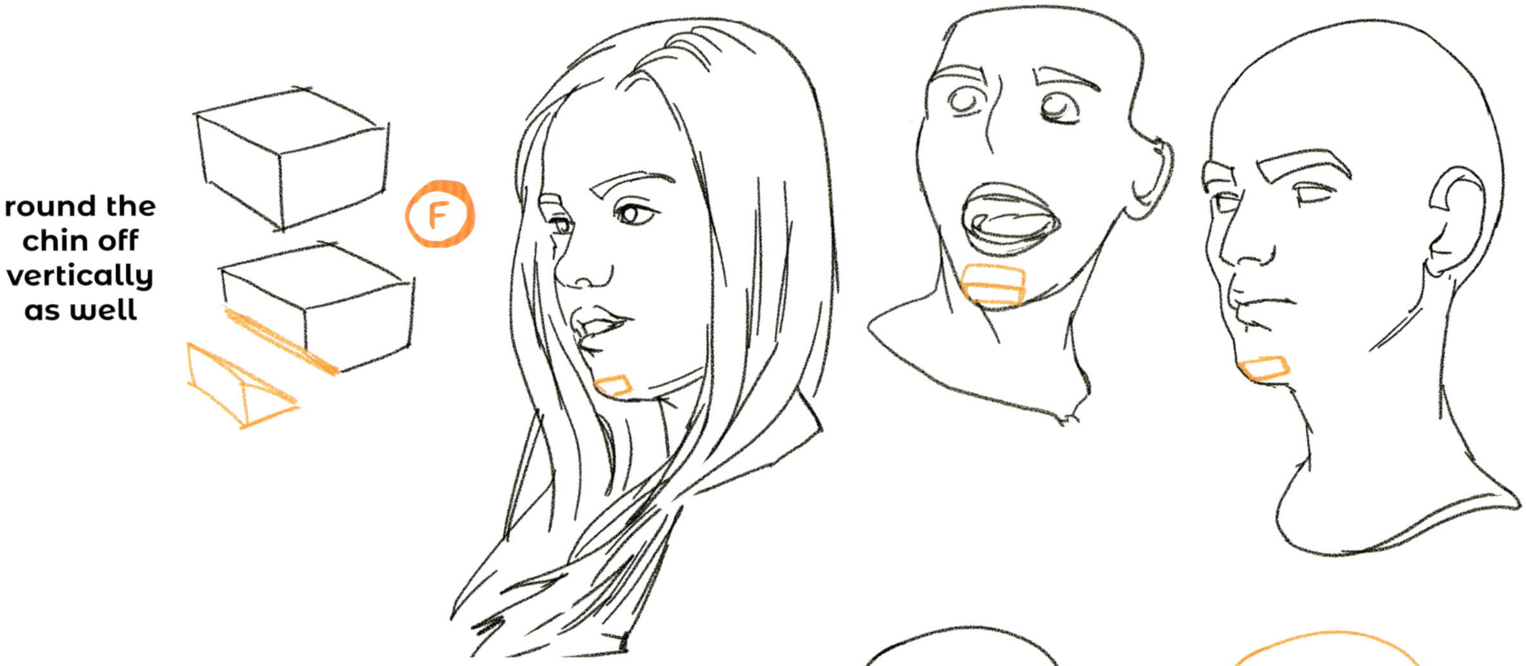

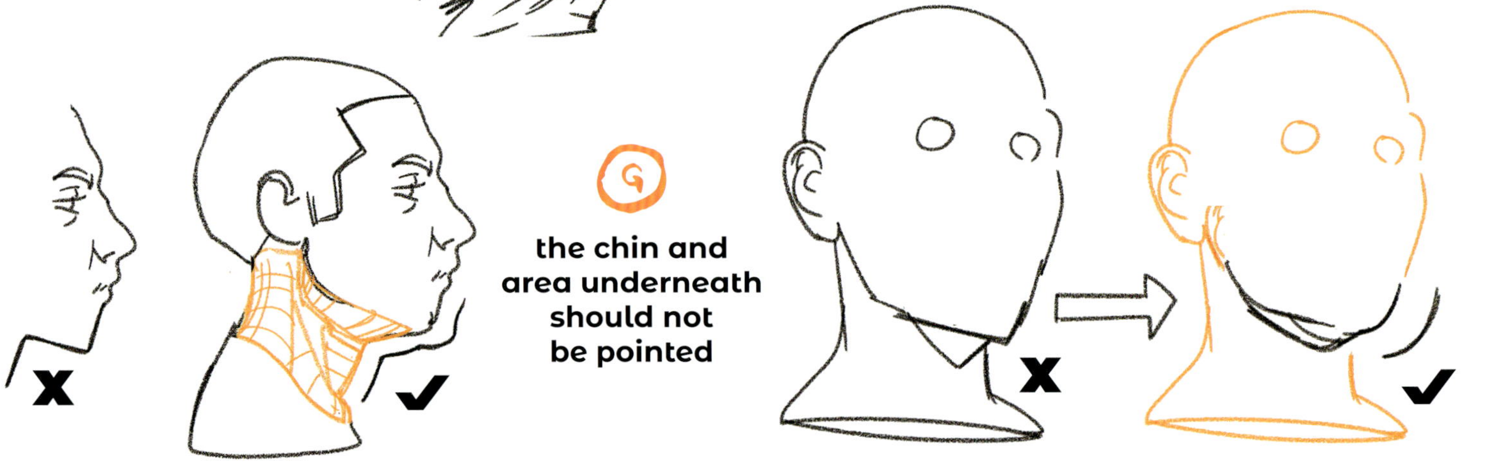

Note how the mandible flares upward (H) while also being angled at the back (I). An indented curve also runs around the width of it (J). When the mouth opens, the jaw doesn't drop down vertically, but instead swings down and backward with the help of the masseter and temporalis muscles that attach to its sides (K).

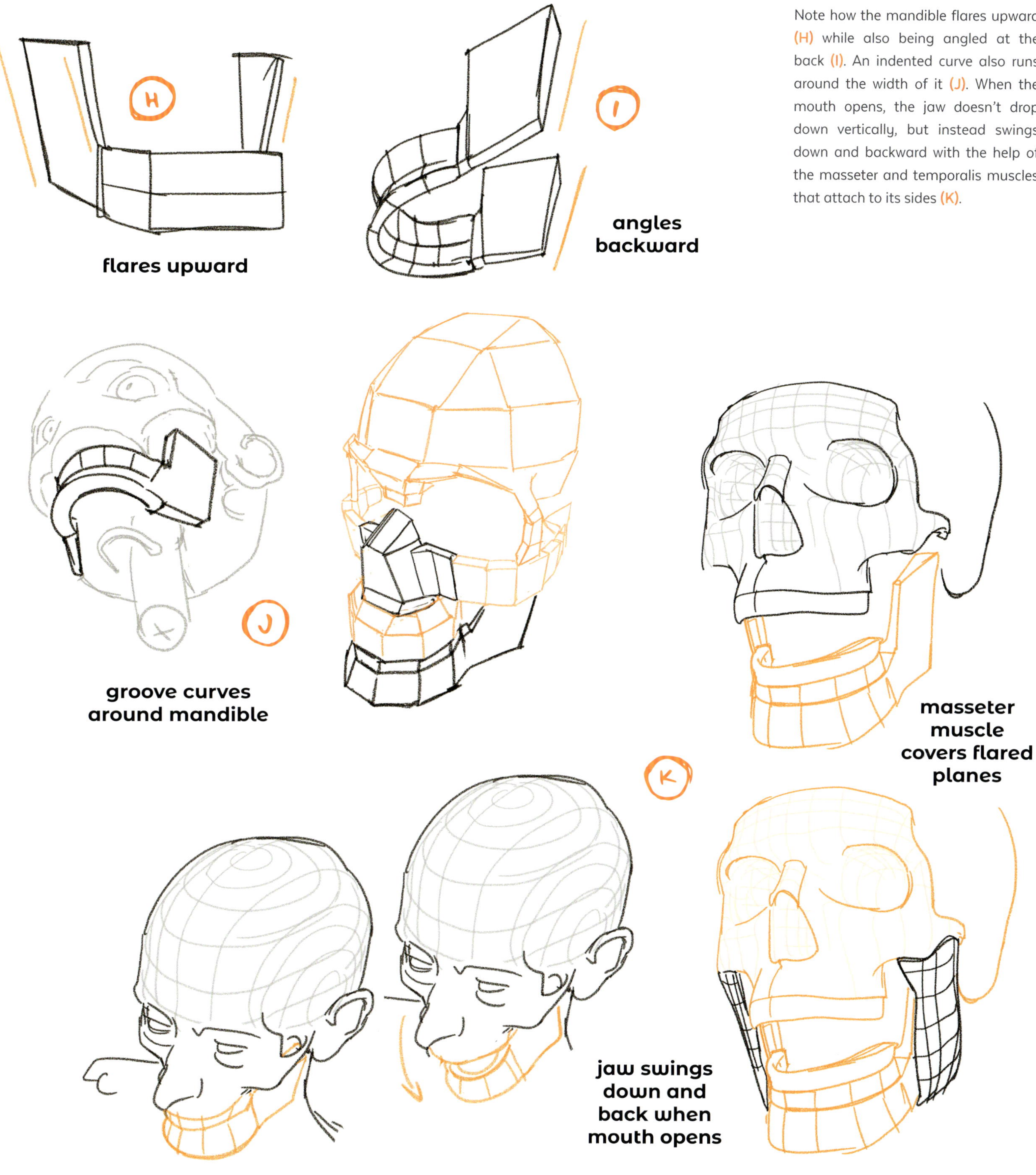

Here you can more clearly see that the rear section of the jaw, where it meets the temporal bone, detaches from the skull and moves separately (L). The details of the teeth aren't important to learn for figure drawing, but you should know that the front six of each jaw are generally sharp (for cutting and tearing) and the rear teeth are blocklike for chewing (M).

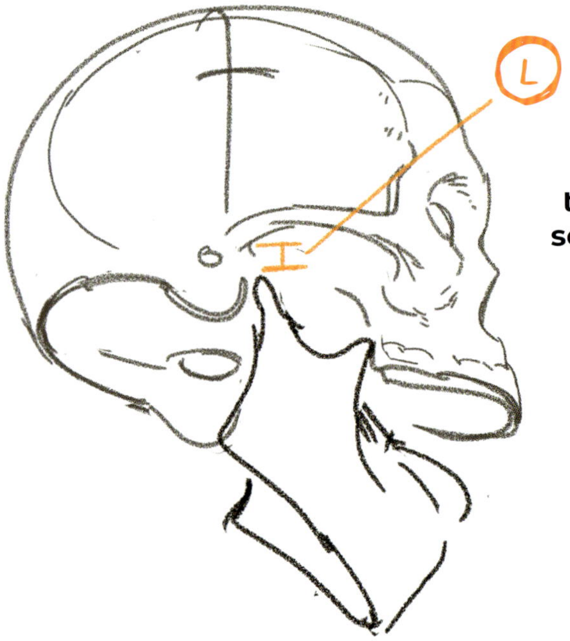

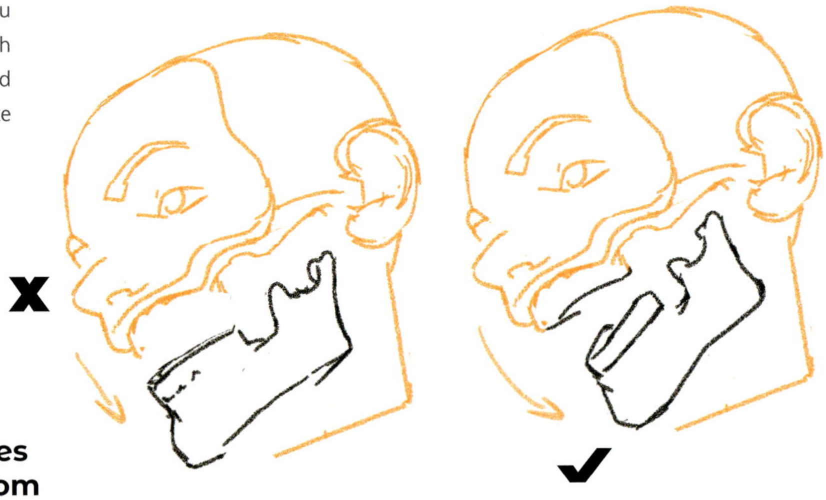

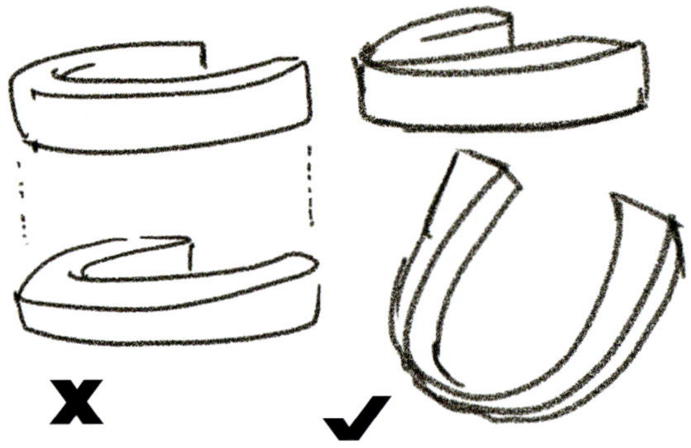

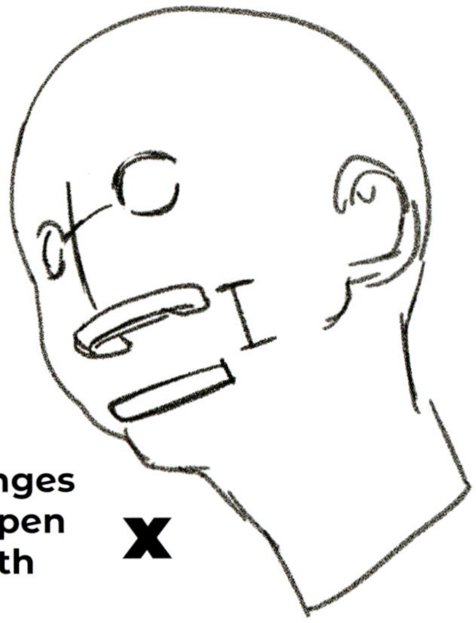

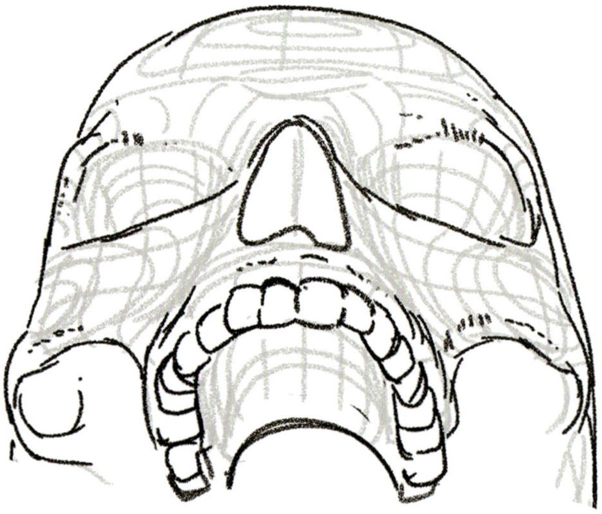

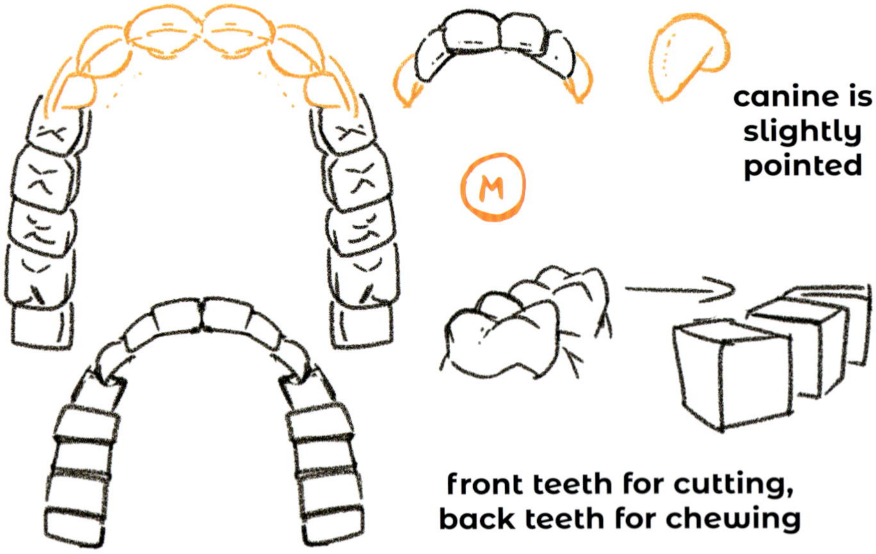

mouth & lips

When drawing the lips, remember that the mouth has to open in all directions. It's like a muzzle laid over the front of the face, with muscles expanding out in all directions (A).

However, there is a small gap without muscle, beneath the zygomatic bone (B), which stands out as a small depression on muscular faces with a lower percentage of body fat (C).

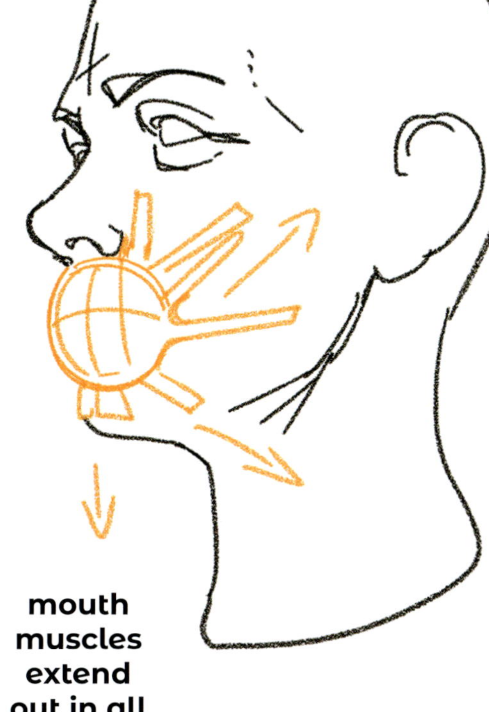

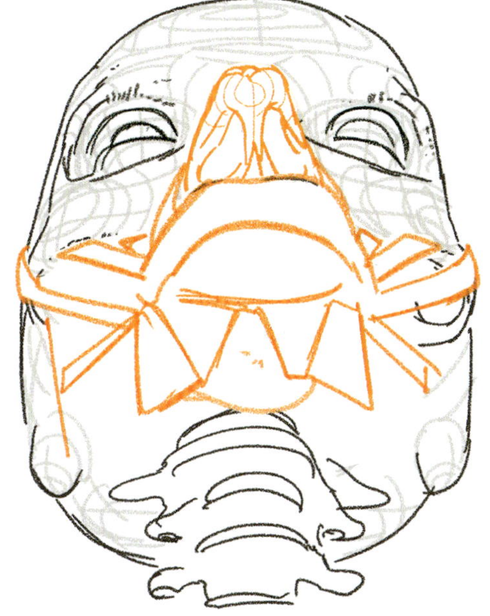

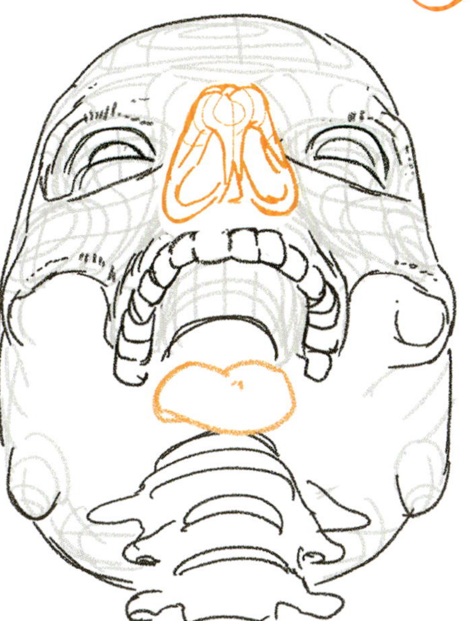

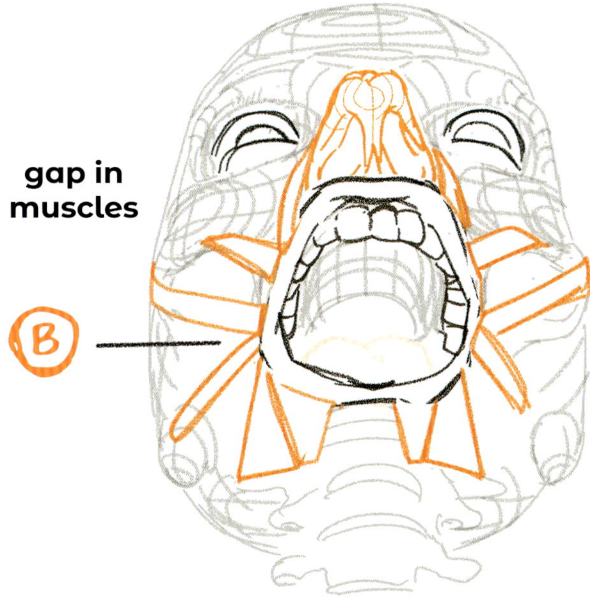

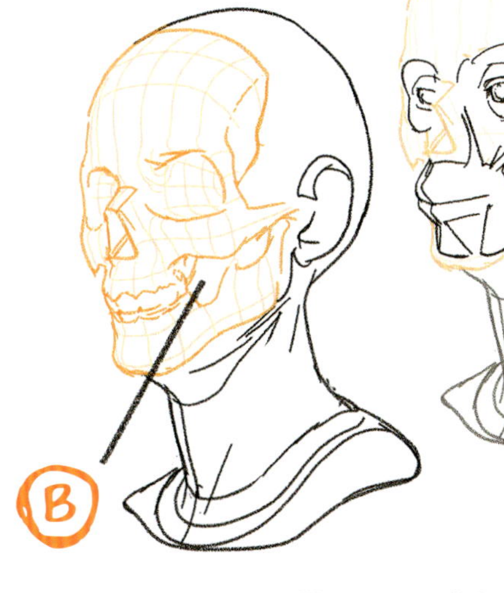

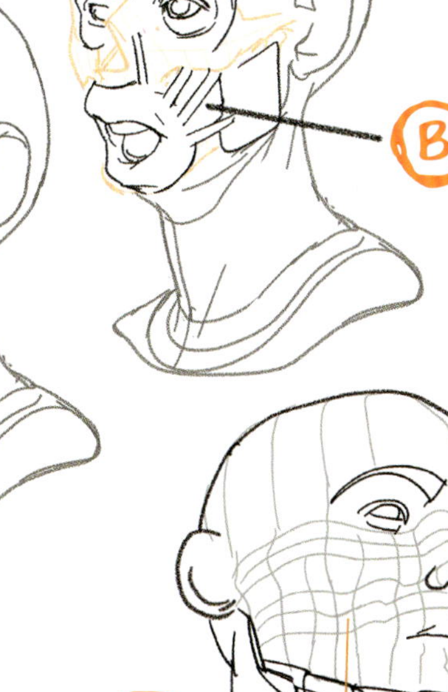

The corners of the mouth affect expression, so position them carefully. Notice the difference between the examples in D and E – when we're happy, the corners of the mouth lift up, but if we're at the dentist, the corners remain lower. When the corners of the mouth pull back, the curvature of the teeth is revealed, which we can indicate by adding shadows to this region (F).

The line dividing the teeth is rarely positioned exactly across the center of the mouth. You'll usually see much more of the top row of teeth (G). The lips and surrounding muscles have a lot of thickness, so make sure they project out in front of the teeth to show volume (H).

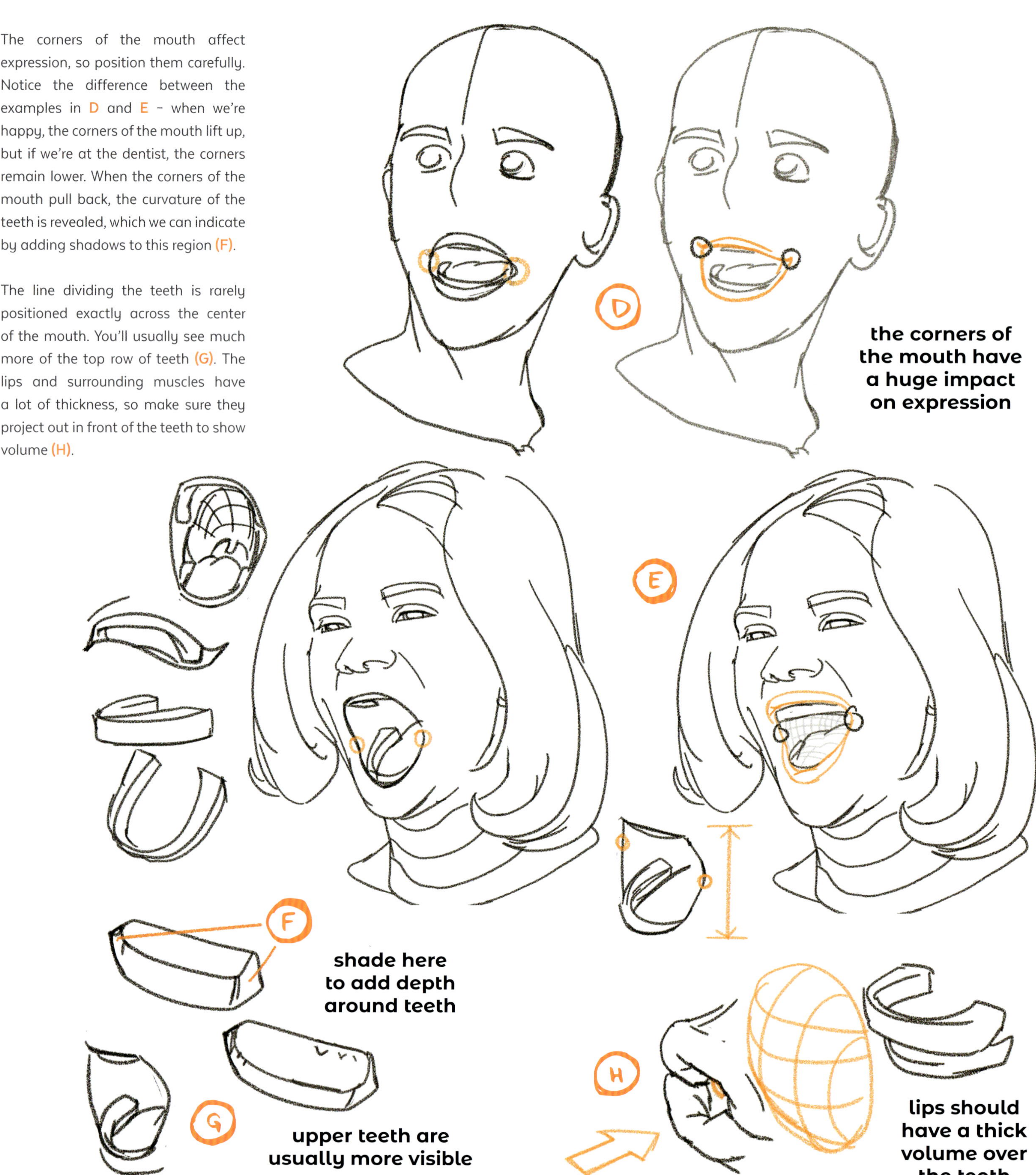

forms, not symbols

When seeing how appealing mouth shapes can be in cartoons, we may be tempted to draw symbols rather than forms. That can be the most efficient way to communicate an expression quickly in storyboards or cartoons, but symbols lack form (A). Instead, give the muzzle area volume and roundness in all directions. The mouth wraps around this rounded form, leaving some space between the teeth and the outside of the lips (B). That breathing room between the teeth and front of the lips is key to conveying the form and muscle of that area (C).

However, in expressions like D, with the mouth wide open in shock or to shout, the lips appear narrower because they are wrapped and stretched around the teeth.

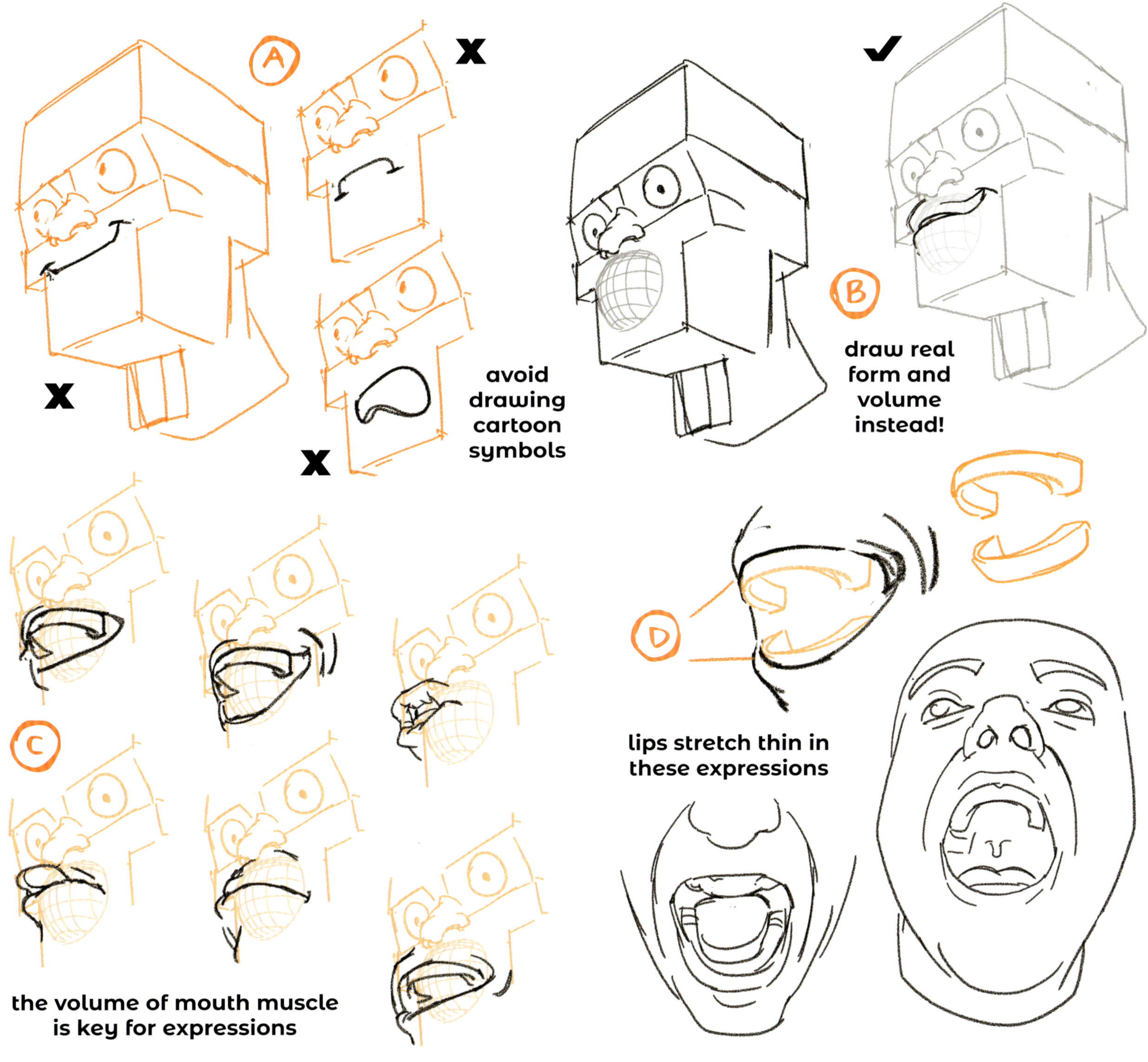

adding hair

When adding hair to the head, I have two main tips. First, you must be able to simplify the hairstyle into a few simple forms, rather than trying to draw every strand **(A)**. Second, you must know how far from the skull those simple forms are sitting – the "volume" of the hair **(B)**. Much of the "style" of a haircut comes from changing the variety in distance between the skull and the outer edge of the hair. Treat drawing hair like you would a helmet. It sounds simplistic, but it's the only way to approach such a complex form **(C)**. Ask yourself, "Am I totally clear on the shape of the skull?" Struggling to draw hair is usually a sign that you're not sure what is beneath it.

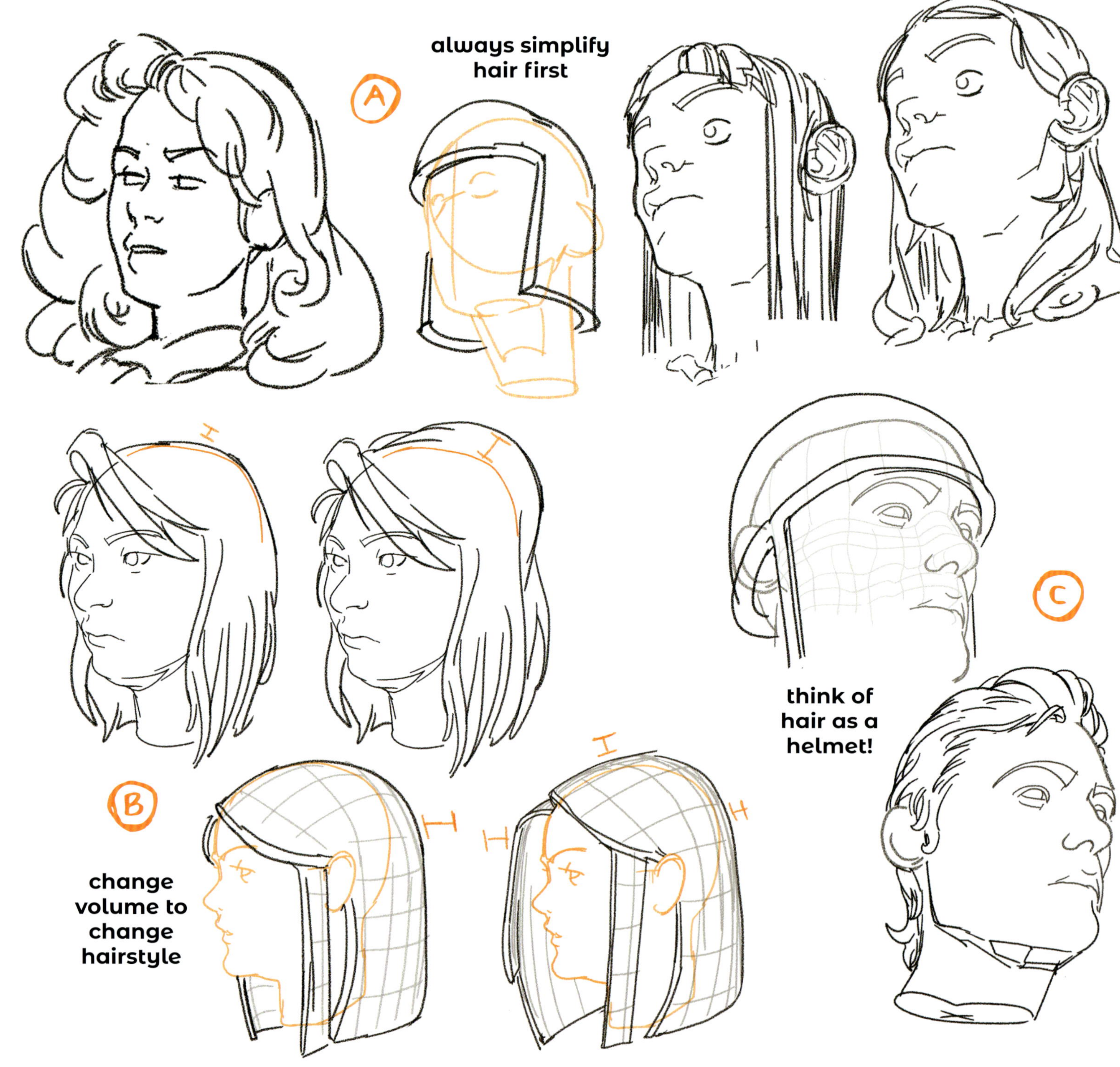

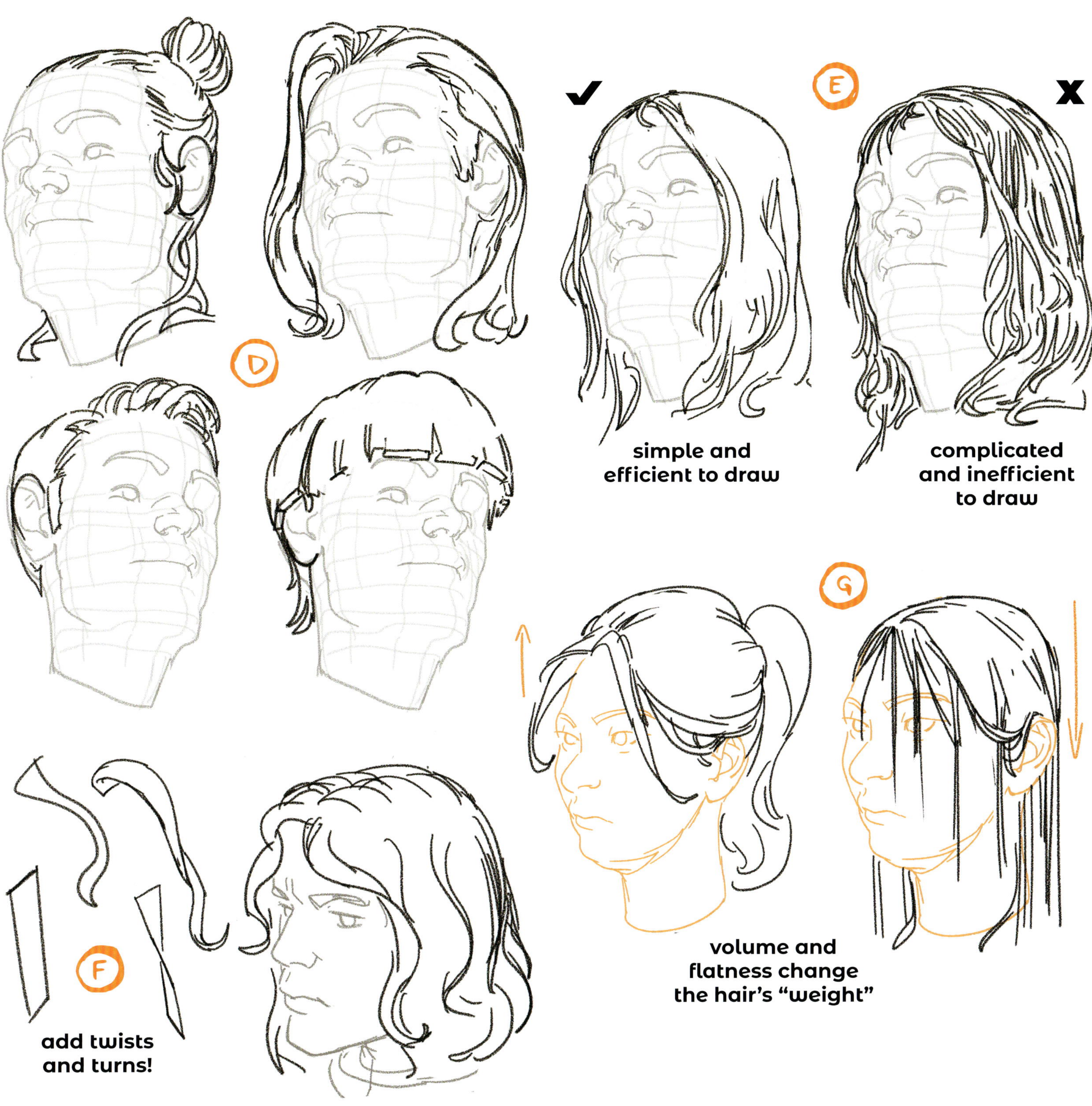

Avoid the temptation to draw every hair – it's not practical. The examples in D are restrained and believable, while E shows the overcomplicated "noodle hair" effect that we're trying to avoid. Simplify those details! Include plenty of twist in your hair forms (F). Hair masses rarely fall flat against the head, as the hair itself has a form of its own. Play around with the "weight" of the hair by suggesting more or less volume (G).

the head from behind

Experiment with drawing features from behind – it's great practice to solidify your understanding of planes. There's a plane at the back of the jaw, just below the ear (A), as well as an upward-facing plane (B) and downward-facing plane (C) that form a depression in the cheek (D). That hollow is very evident from a three-quarter rear view, and allows us to see a surprising amount of the lips.

The chin has an upward plane on the front edge (E), but this flattens out and angles inward as we move around from 1 to 3. The hair doesn't start right behind the ear, so make sure you leave a gap (F). Finally, as we covered earlier in this section, remember that the head narrows downward (G).

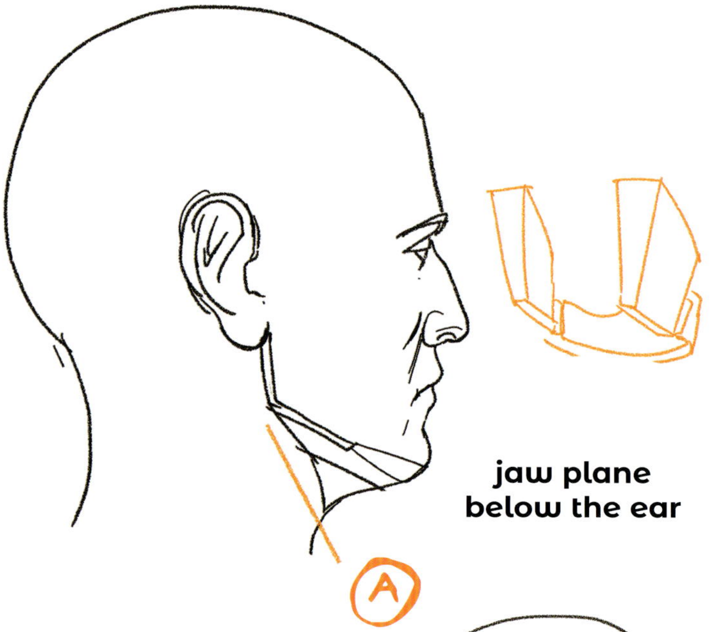

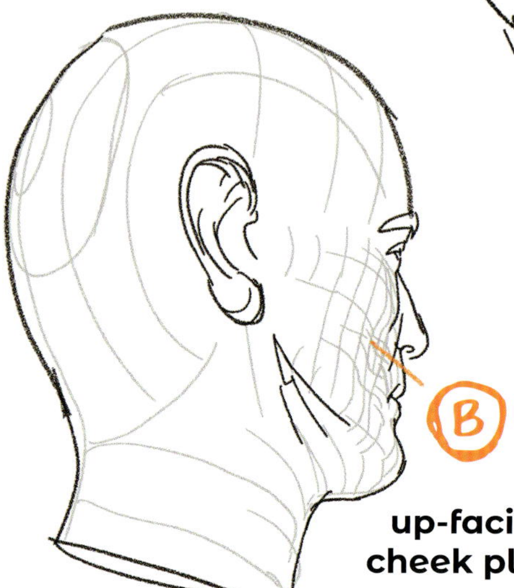

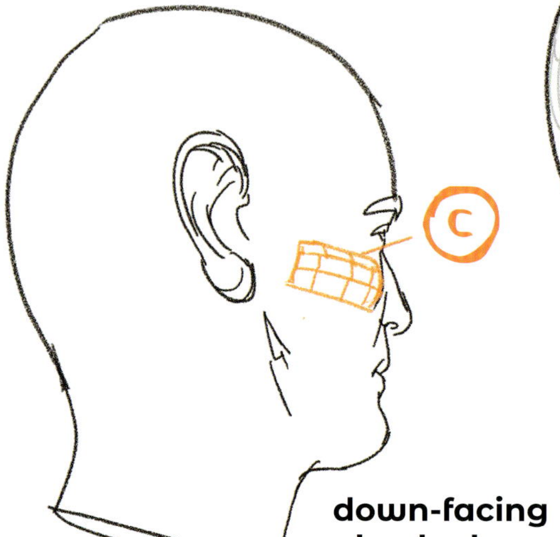

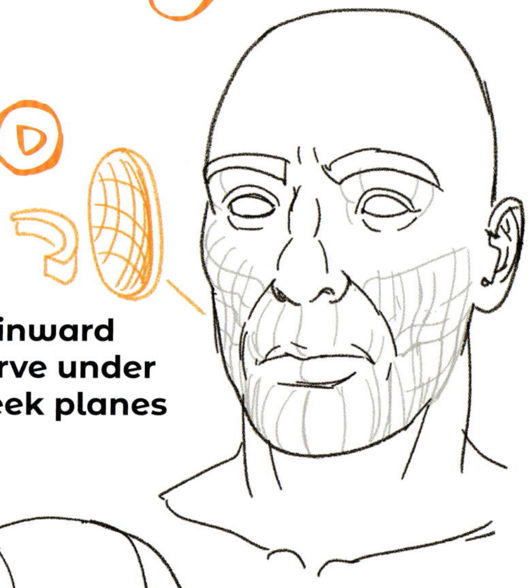

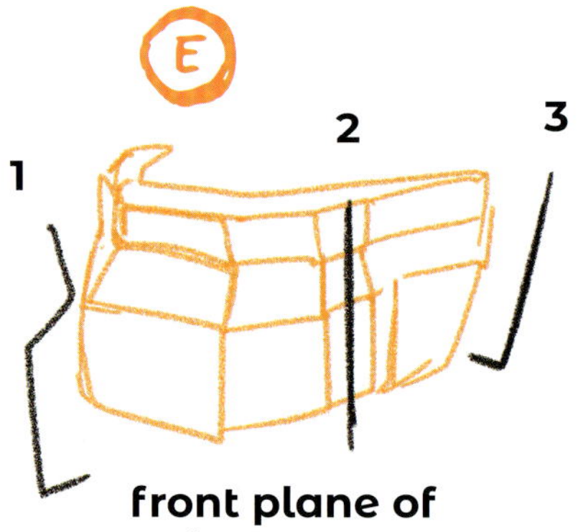

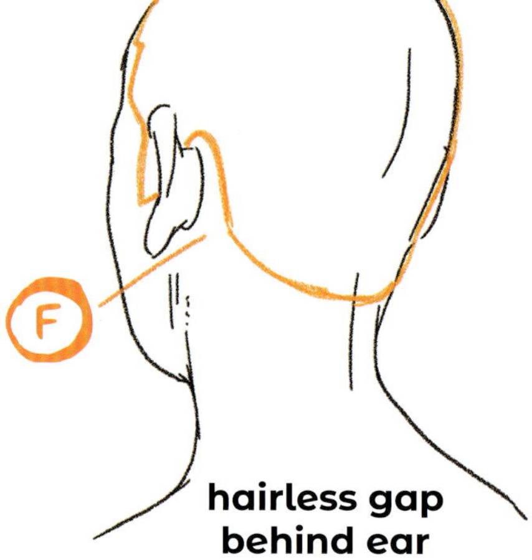

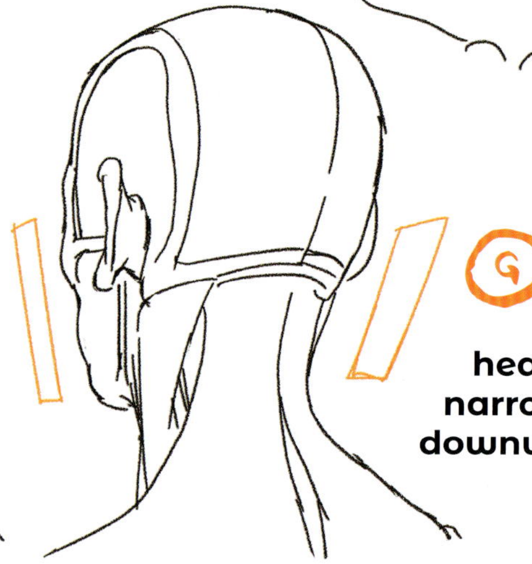

adding ears

Most people draw the ears last, as an afterthought, but the ears' placement and angle are important. Changing the rotation and placement of the ear just slightly can appear to rotate the whole head (A)!

We don't want to draw the ear flat against the side of the head – it needs to angle both slightly out and slightly back (B). To do this, angle the whole ear mass backward, so it sits at a slight diagonal on the head, then swing it out like a barn door! This can be tricky to visualize at first, but very effective once you grasp it (C).

As the head tilts back, the height of the ears is compressed and foreshortened; remember to flatten the ears even more as the head tilts farther back (D).

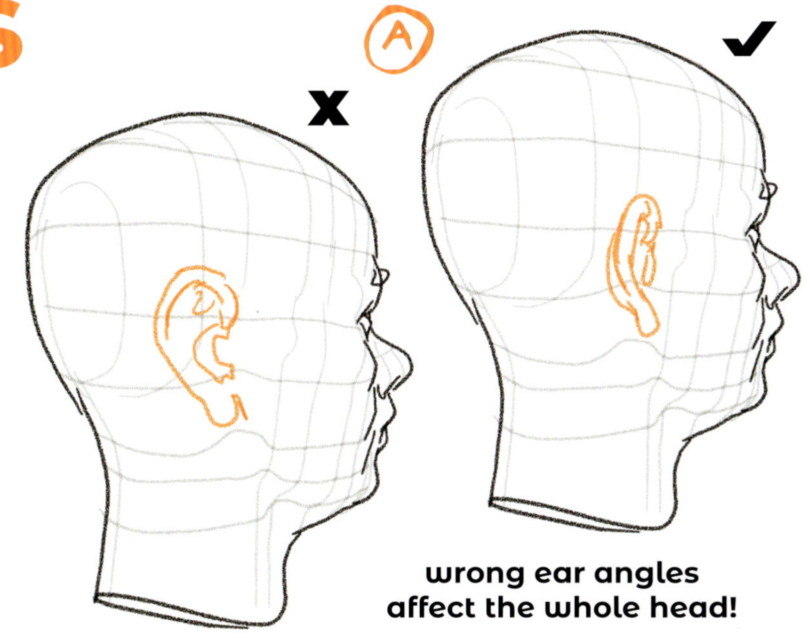

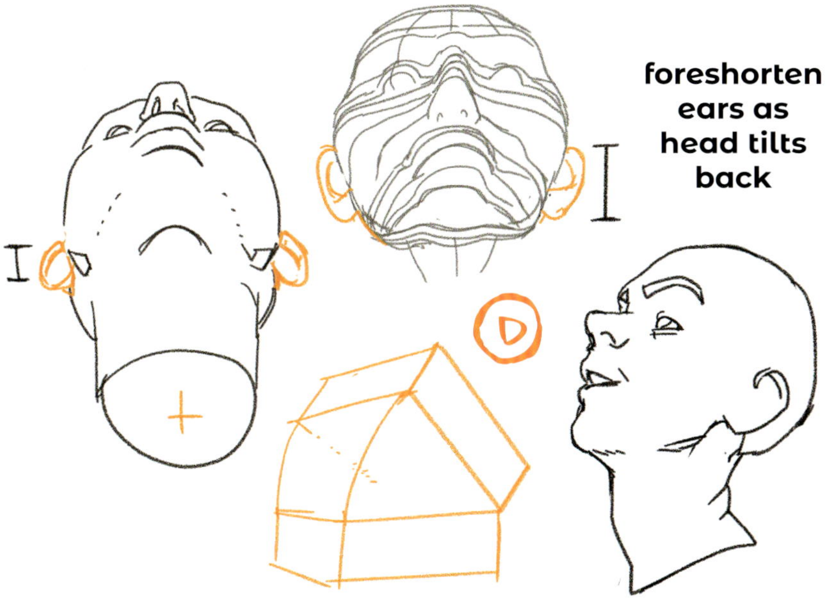

wrong ear angles affect the whole head!

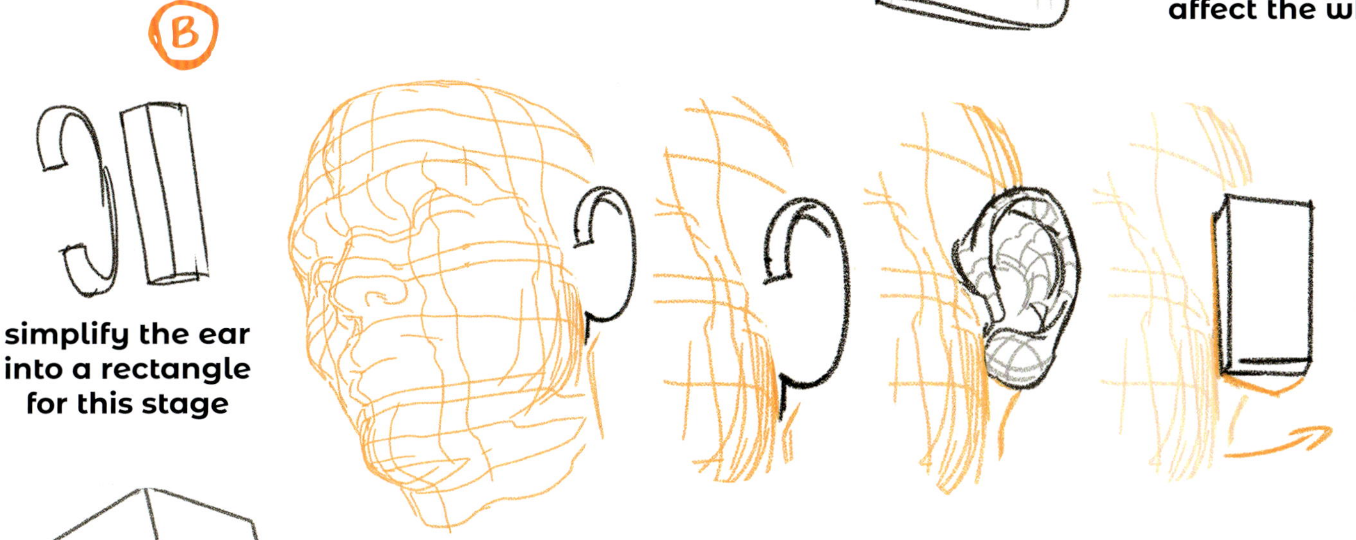

B

simplify the ear into a rectangle for this stage

the ear doesn't sit flat against the head

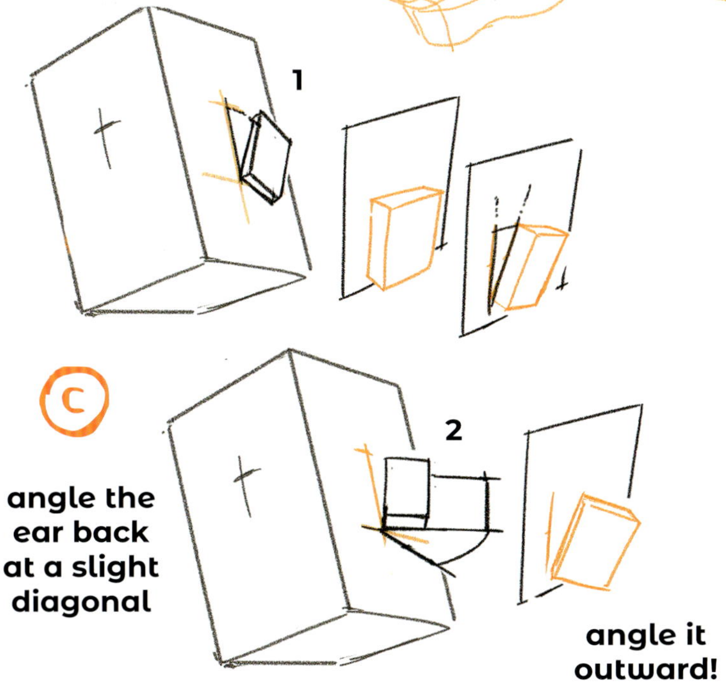

1

C

angle the ear back at a slight diagonal

2

angle it outward!

foreshorten ears as head tilts back

D

The tube-shaped ear canal angles down and into the skull through the temporal bone, just behind where the jaw attaches. Though we can't see the ear canal externally, knowing this attachment point helps us locate exactly where to base the ear (E).

The whole ear is a bit like the wheel of a car (F). The top section (the helix) angles out as we move back, and is basically a horseshoe shape. Closer inspection reveals it has a roundness like a bike tire, which helps us catch sound waves (G).

Give the earlobe region more volume than you'd expect (H). Earlobes have some mass to them, but you don't tend to see it because it's most clearly visible from below.

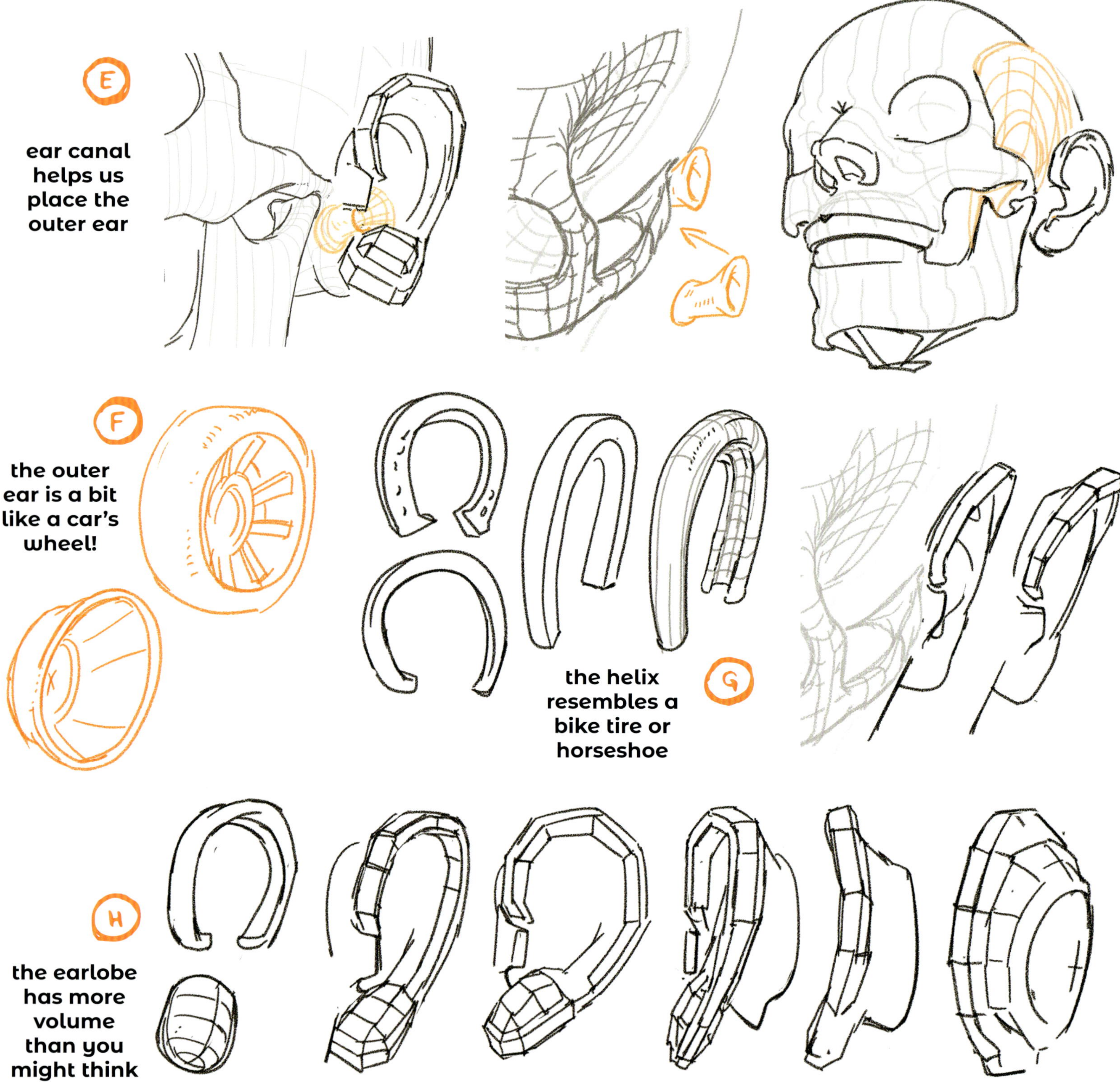

The external ear (I) consists of the earlobe, helix, tragus, and antihelix, which is so named because it runs in the opposite direction to the helix. The angle and rotation of the earlobe varies hugely from person to person, but I like to draw it as almost a jewel shape (J). Avoid drawing the antihelix as a couple of lines. Either represent the form or leave it out, because it doesn't add much to the overall rotation of the ear (K).

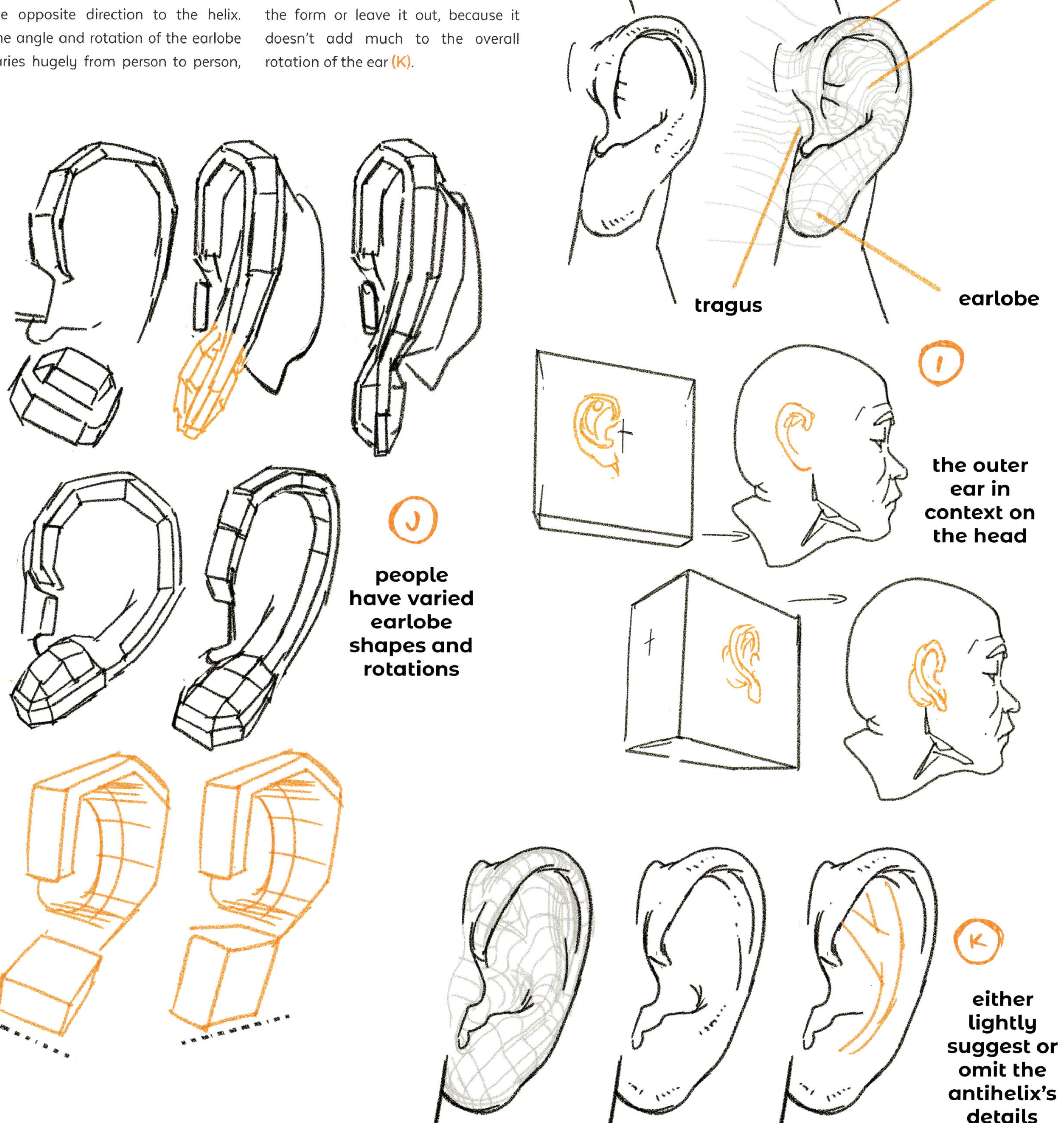

lesson 2:

upper torso

Now that we have covered the head, let's progress downward through the body, starting with the bones and muscles of the upper torso.

upper torso & yoke

Our box mannequin (A) now has a believable head, but we need to learn the shapes of the bones surrounding it. We're going to cover the thoracic cage (rib cage) (B), and what I like to call the "yoke" area around the neck and shoulders (C). Through a combination of box mannequins and anatomy knowledge, we'll be able to create believable poses for our figure (D).

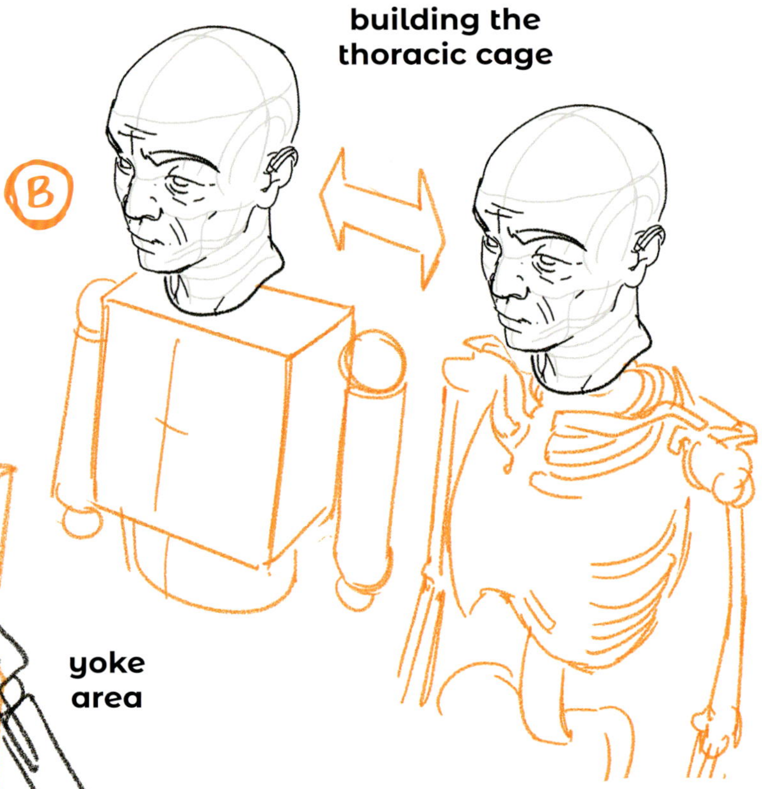

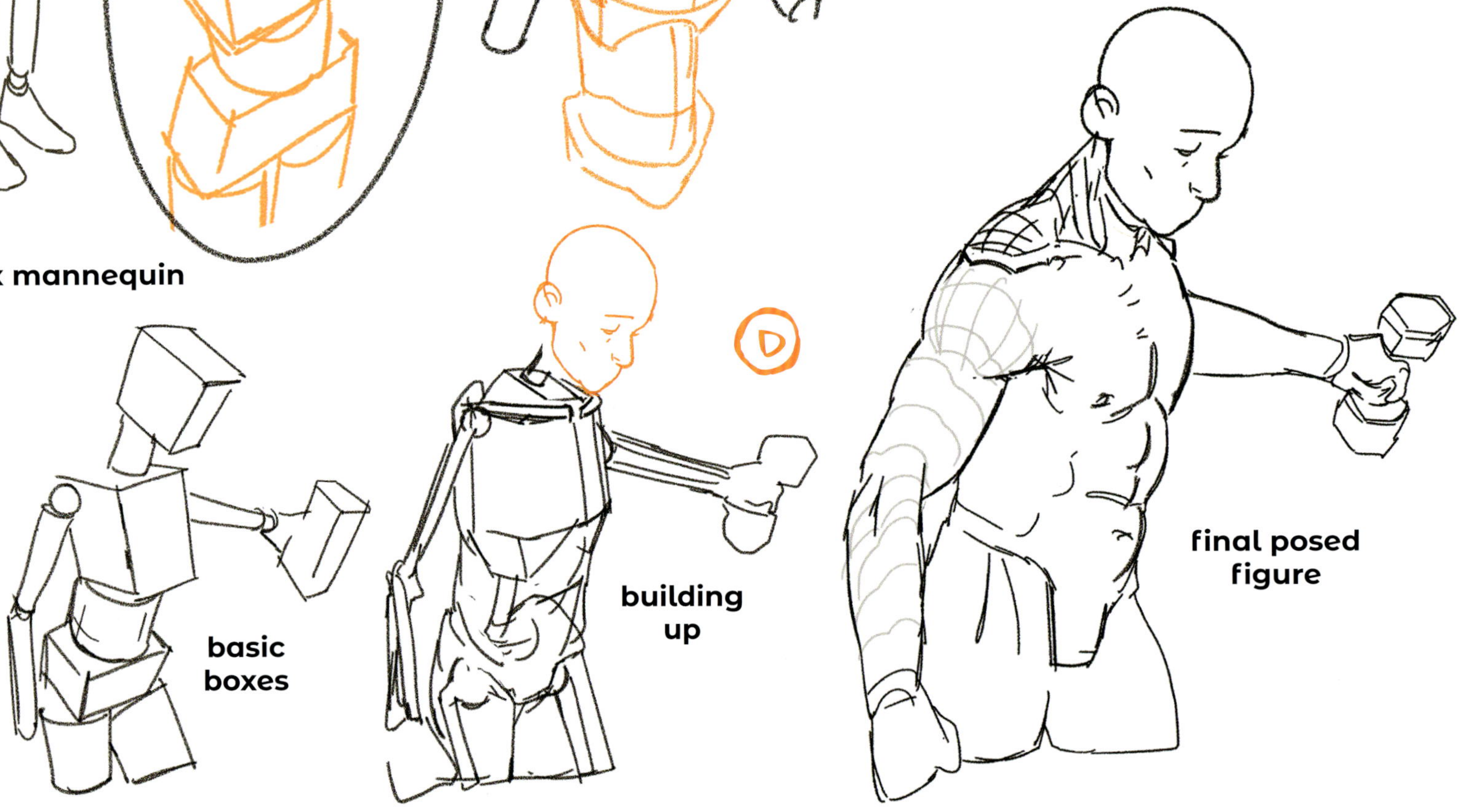

building the thoracic cage

B

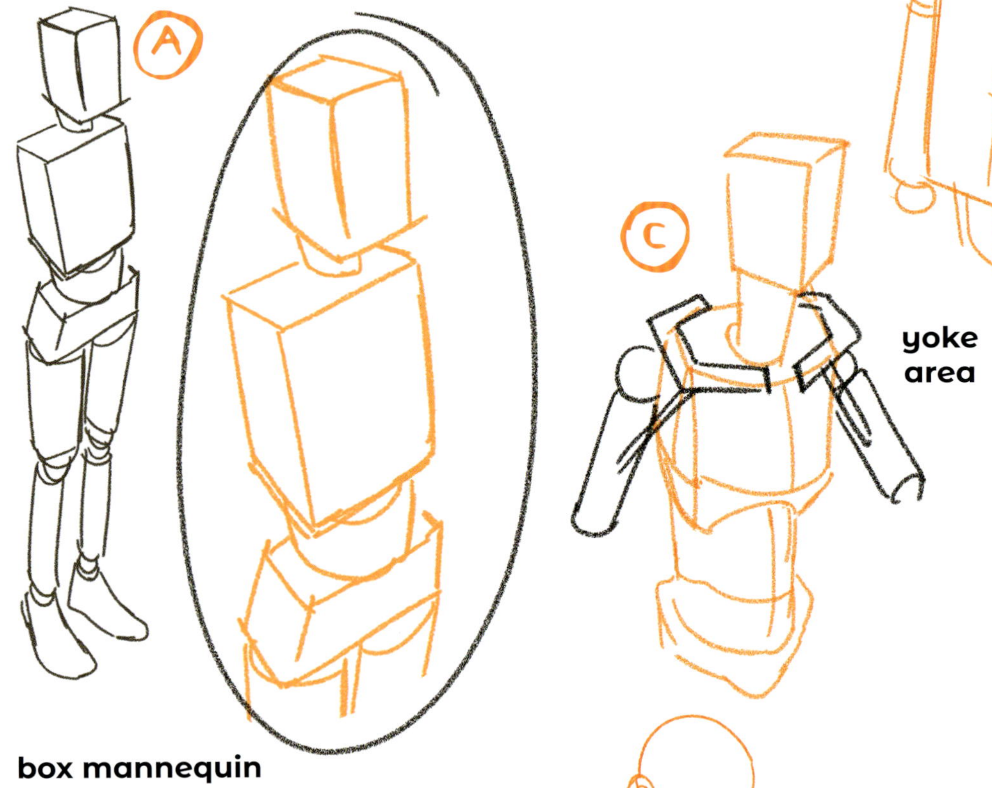

A

C

yoke area

box mannequin

D

basic boxes

building up

final posed figure

rib cage

It's difficult to memorize forms without understanding what they need to achieve. Start by asking yourself, "What do these forms need to be able to do? What do these muscles or bones need to achieve?"

The torso must allow for expansion in body fat and muscle mass, but must also be able to bend in multiple directions. We need to be able to bend forward without our bodies pinching (A), and also have scope for the body to "bulge" out with muscle and fat (B). For this reason, the rib cage is higher at the center. The shapes in C allow the body to bend forward without pinching the organs, but where would the soft mass of the torso go? The answer is D, which allows bulging.

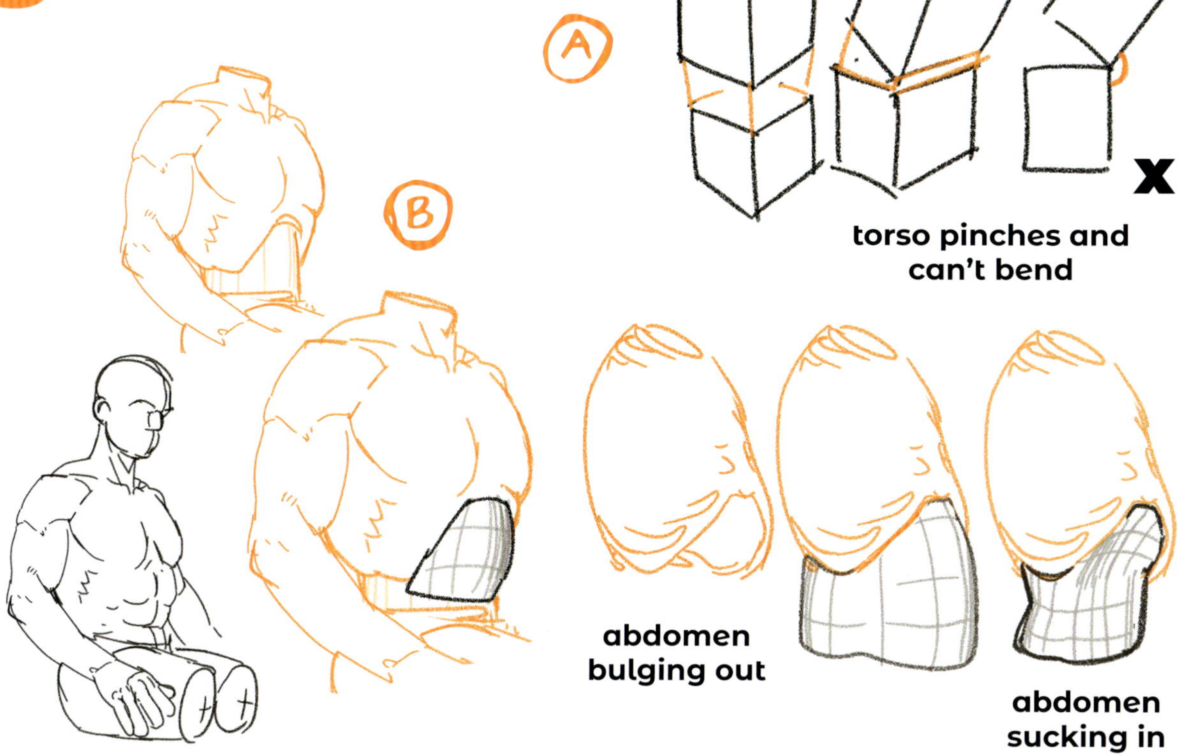

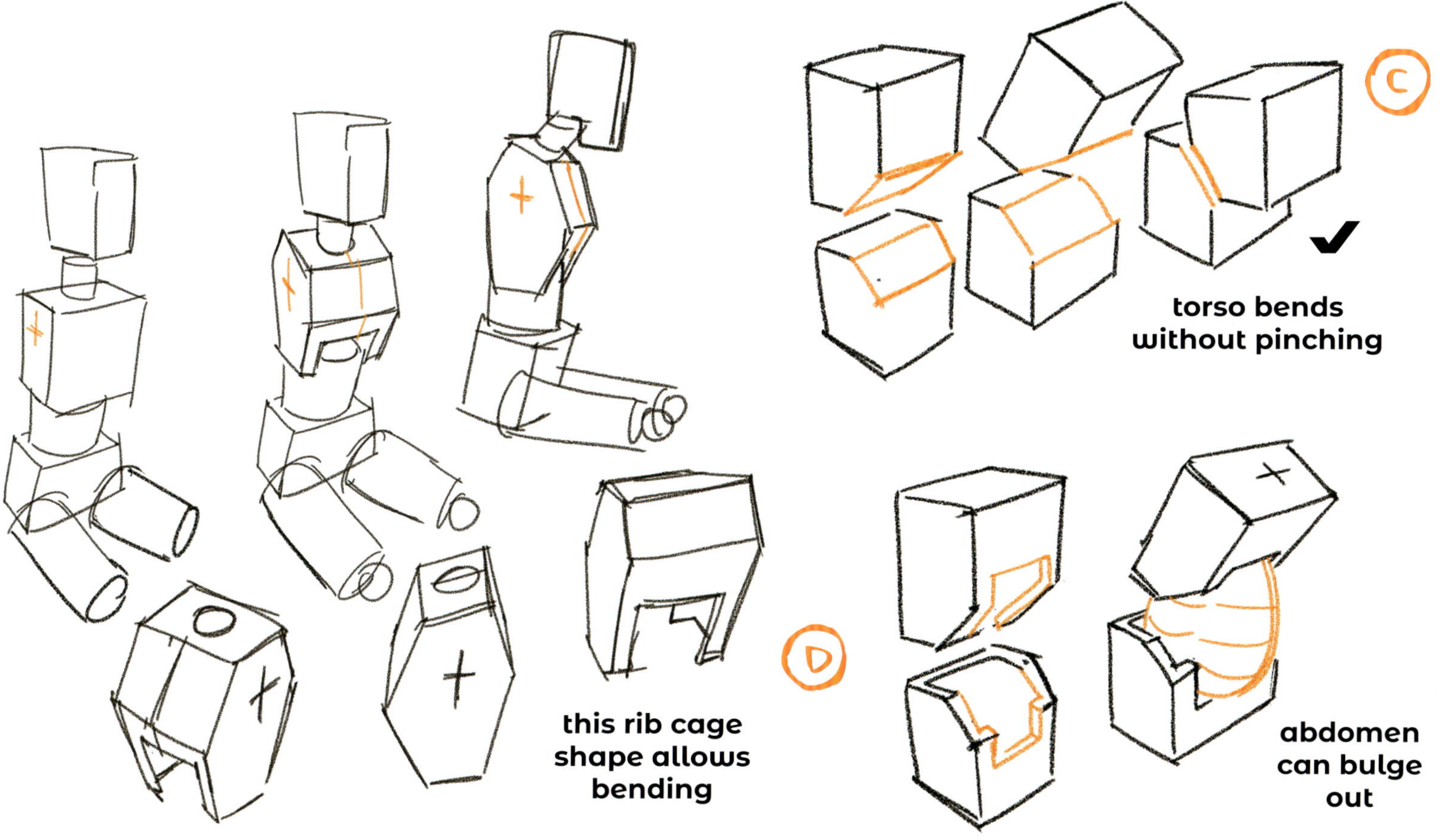

We can think of the rib cage as a container that protects the lungs and heart. Start with E and take slices off the front to create three planes, numbered 1, 2, and 3. The top plane is the longest and represents the sternum (breastbone).

Observe in F the change in the planes' direction through 1, 2, and 3. The rib cage also flares out at the bottom while being narrower at the top (G). Some people's rib cages flare out even more toward the bottom (H), so allow for some variation in your figures.

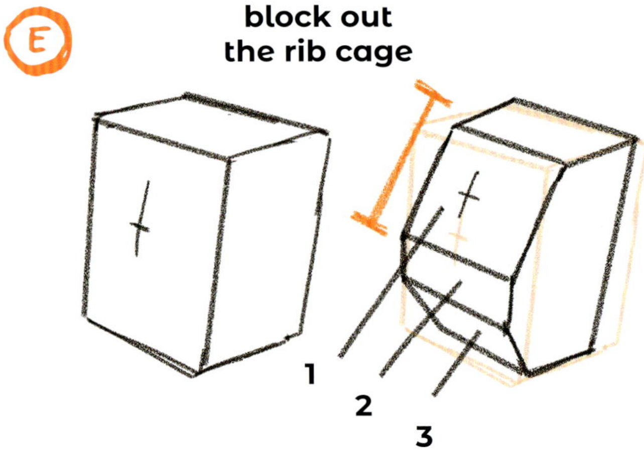

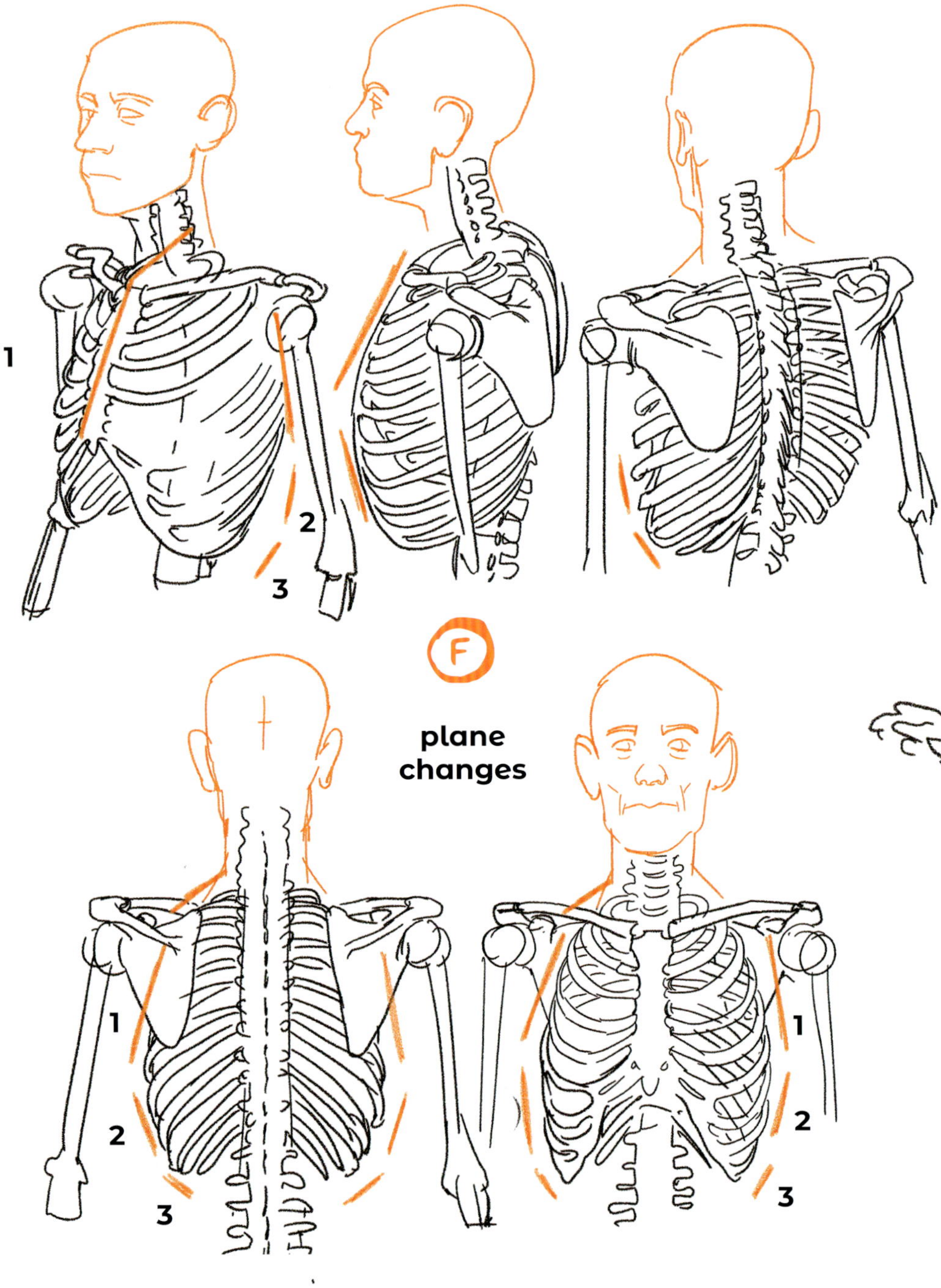

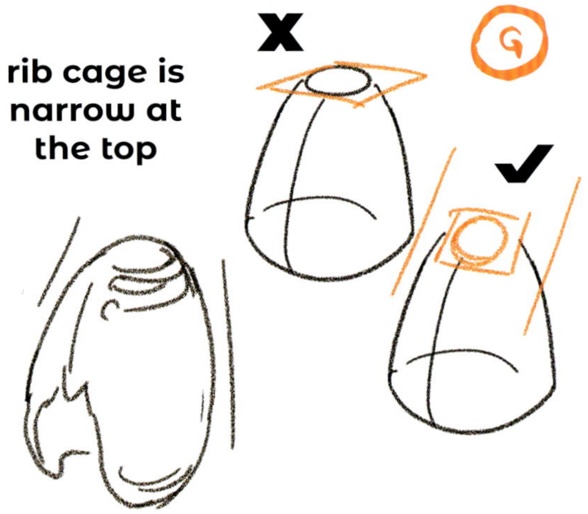

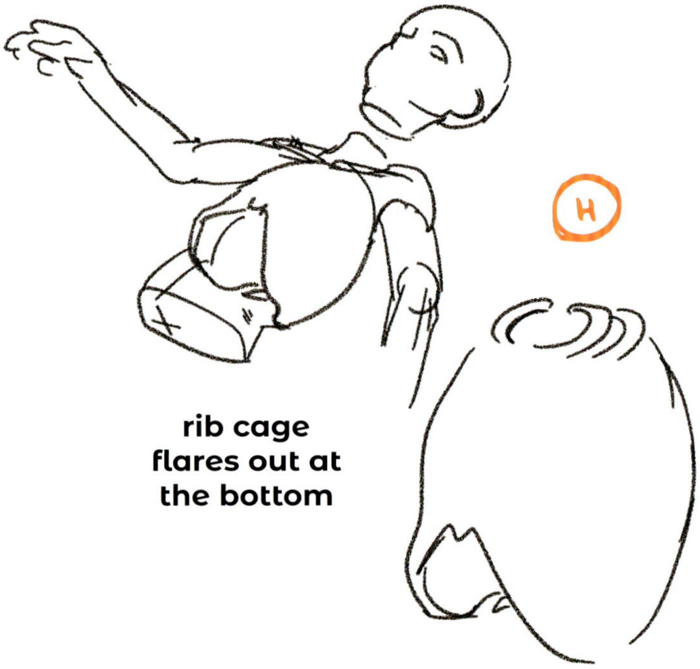

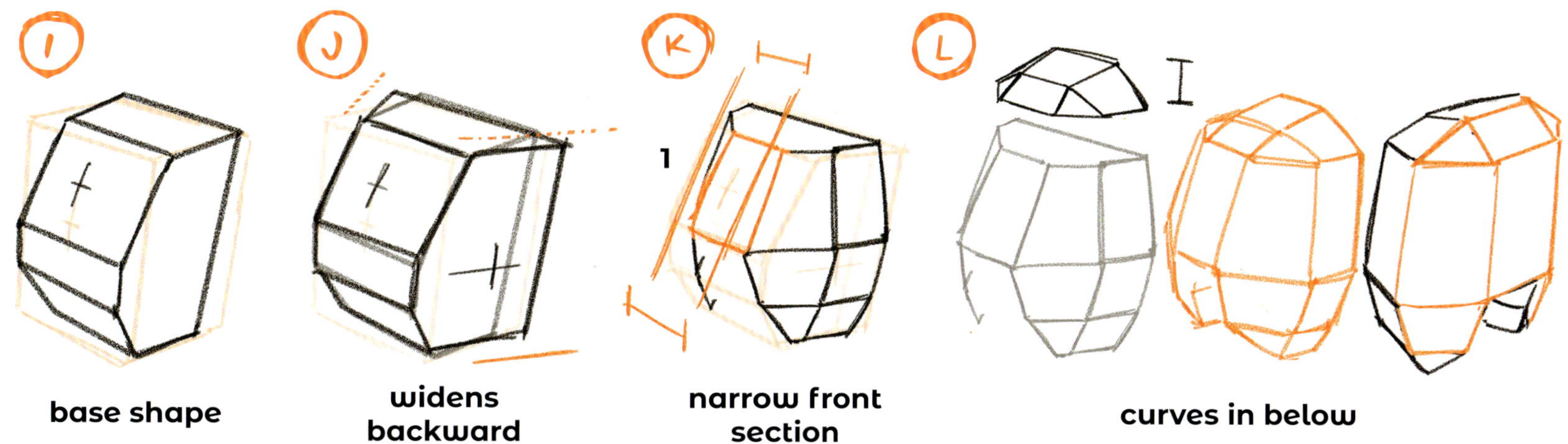

Let's refine our rib cage (I). As well as widening toward the bottom, it gets wider toward the back (J). Reflecting this in our current model looks odd, so let's narrow down plane 1 to more closely resemble the sternum (K). The rib cage also curves back in at the bottom, so let's add some planes on the sides to show that. Now the form has taper as well as flaring. Let's add a top surface to reflect the angle of the upper ribs (L). Throughout this process, keep in mind that we're aiming for a rib cage that will fit above a softer lower torso that bulges out (M).

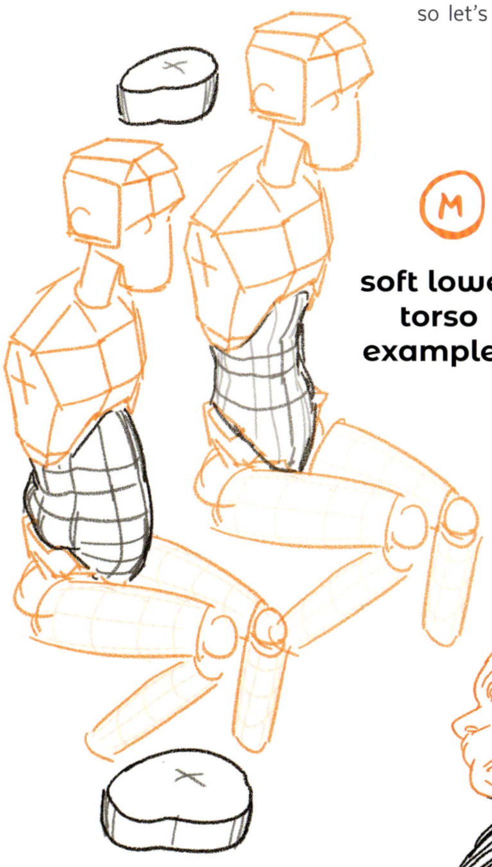

M

soft lower torso examples

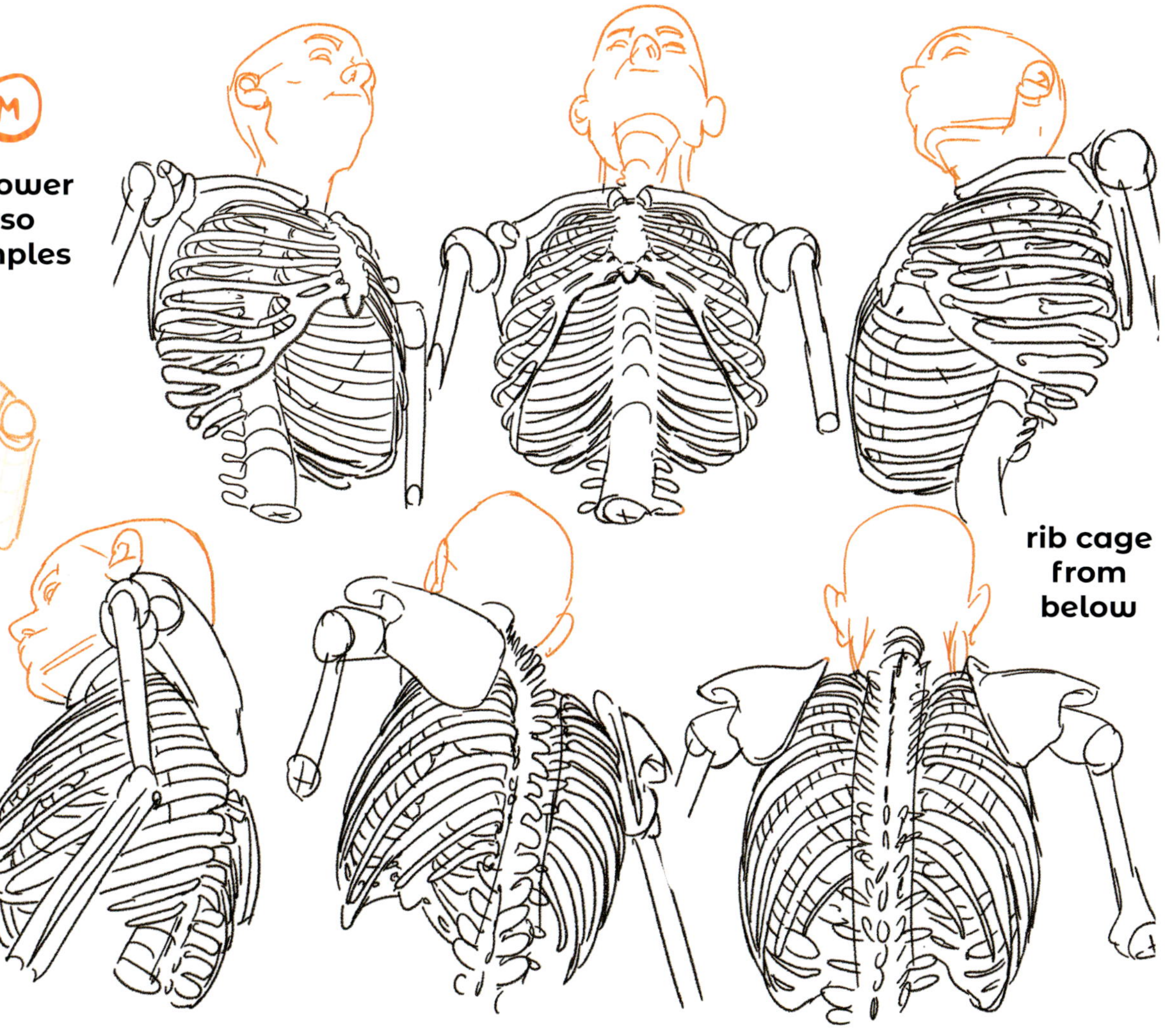

rib cage from below

The rib cage flares toward the back to accommodate the requirements of our movement (N). We need to be able to bend forward and put our chest between our legs. If our chest was as wide at the front as it was at the back, we'd struggle to do that (O).

The spine's range of movement is unequal. We can manage around 90 degrees of flexion (forward) (P) and 40 degrees of extension (backward) (Q, R).

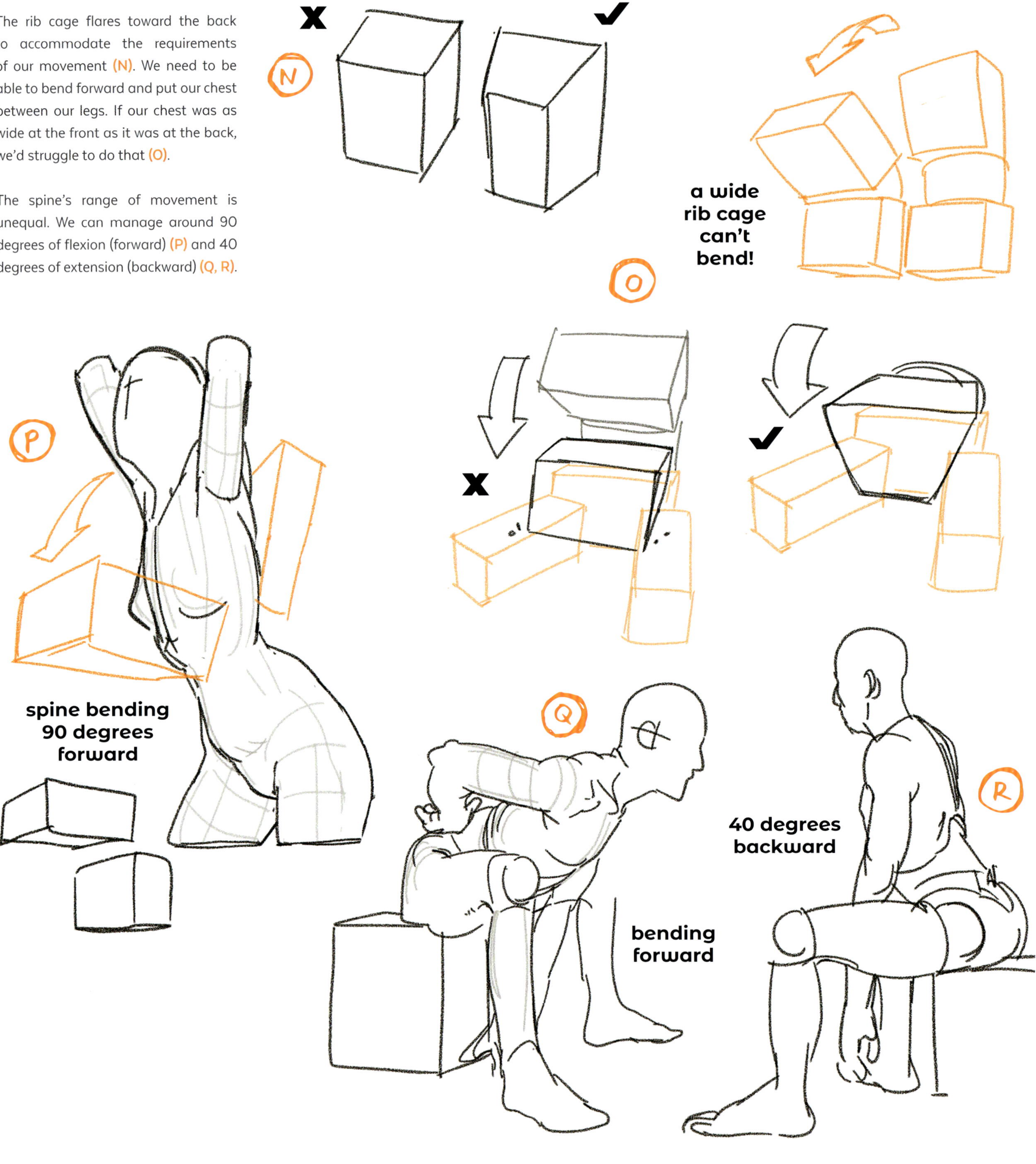

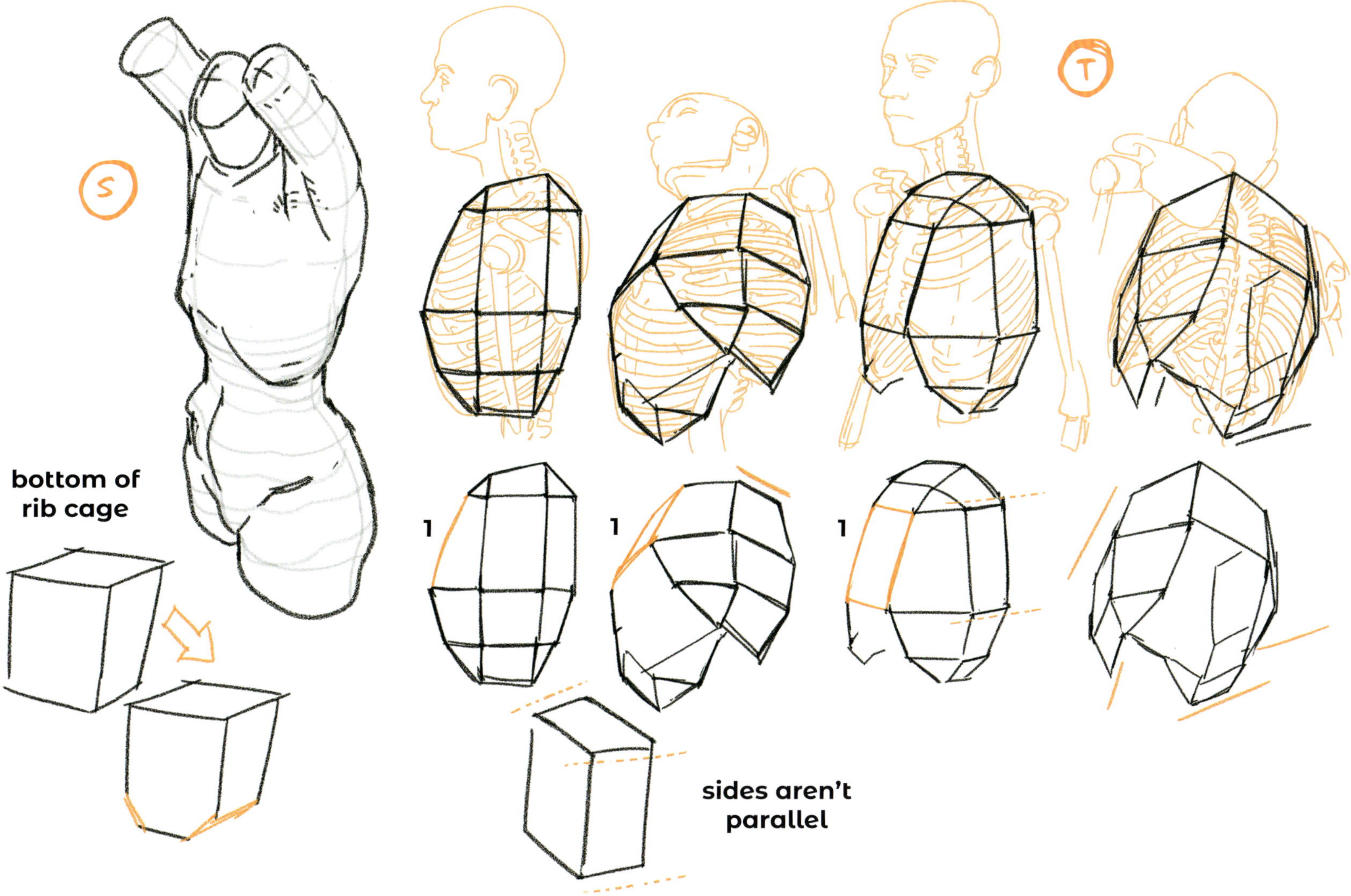

bottom of rib cage

sides aren't parallel

Don't rush the rib cage. It's difficult to draw and doesn't have obvious corners, and if you draw it incorrectly it will usually be noticeable. The bottom of the rib cage is tricky, as it widens toward the back but also curves in toward the spine (S). Plane 1 now has a slight curve and taper to it. The sides of the rib cage aren't parallel, as you can see in T and U. When you bend forward, the bottom of the rib cage rotates into the mass of the abdomen, hiding the downward-facing bottom plane (V).

plane rotates into abdomen

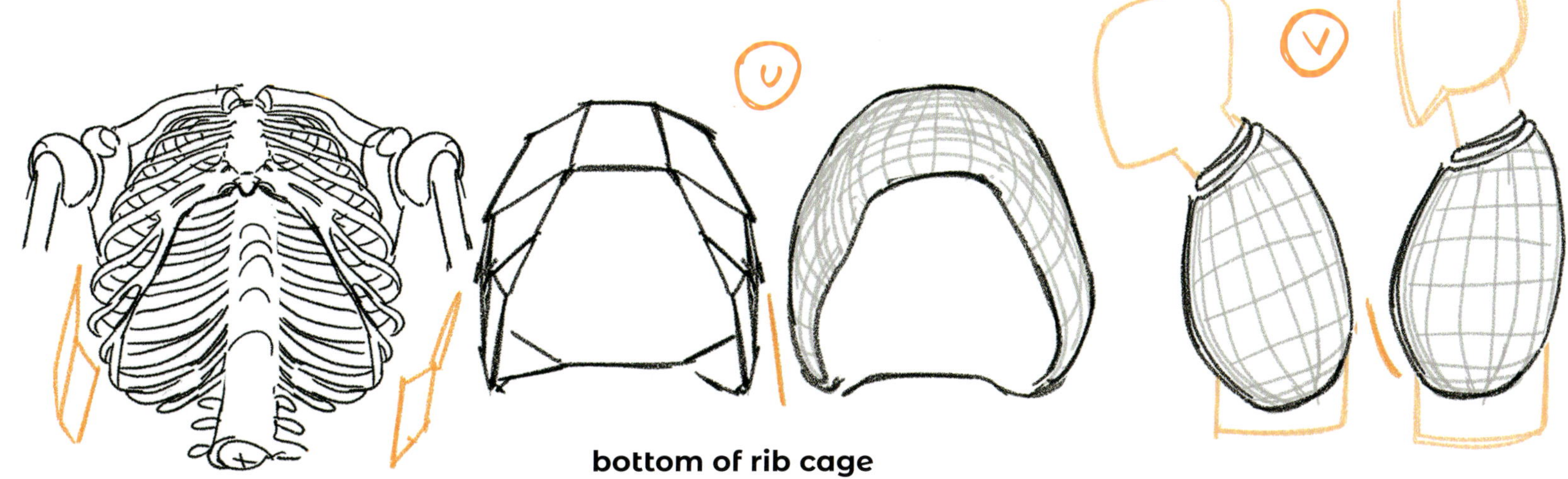

torso shape & motion

There's a strong backward angle to the whole rib cage (A). The ribs themselves slant up and back. A few at the bottom of the sternum drop down first, but they will still swoop around and up again toward the spine. There is variation in how flared the ribs are, but if you stick with this general shape, the results will look realistic. For example, the rib cage shapes in B are slightly different but all correct.

Practice drawing the rib cage from different angles, with the narrow top and sternum widening toward the back and bottom (C). But now that we've learned about the shape of the rib cage, how do we begin building form and muscle on top of it (D)?

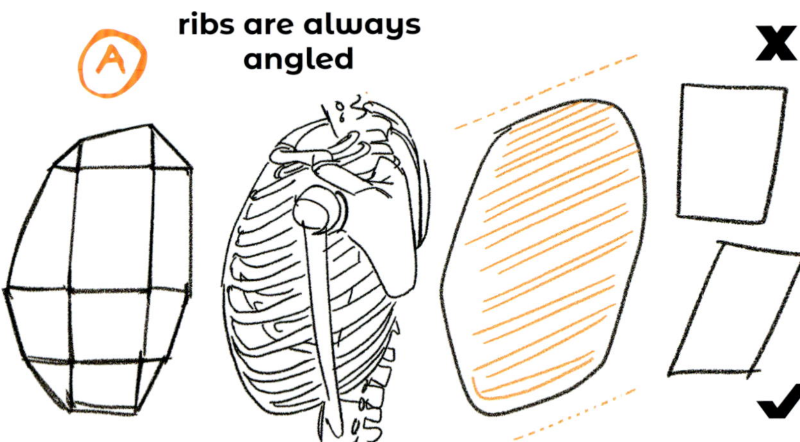

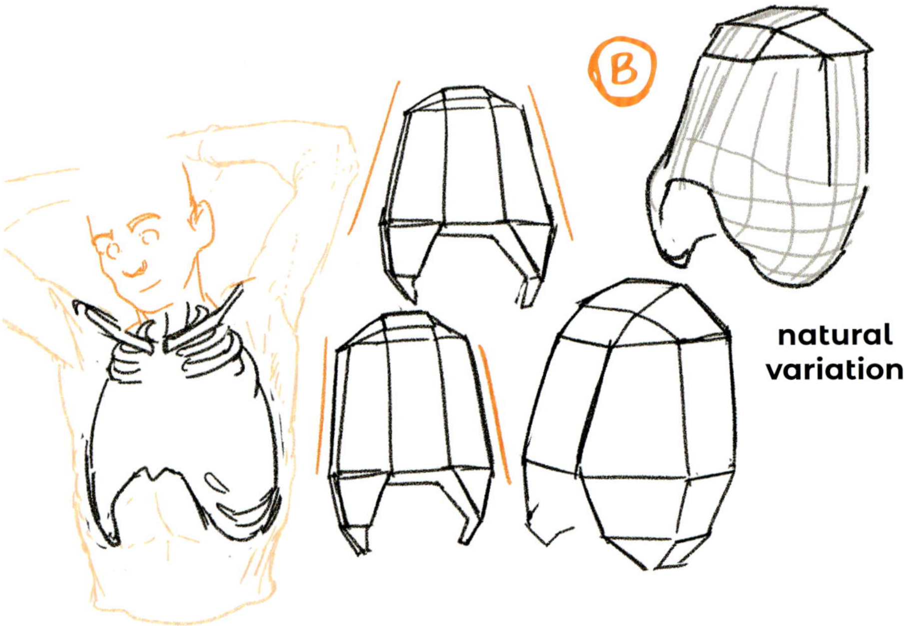

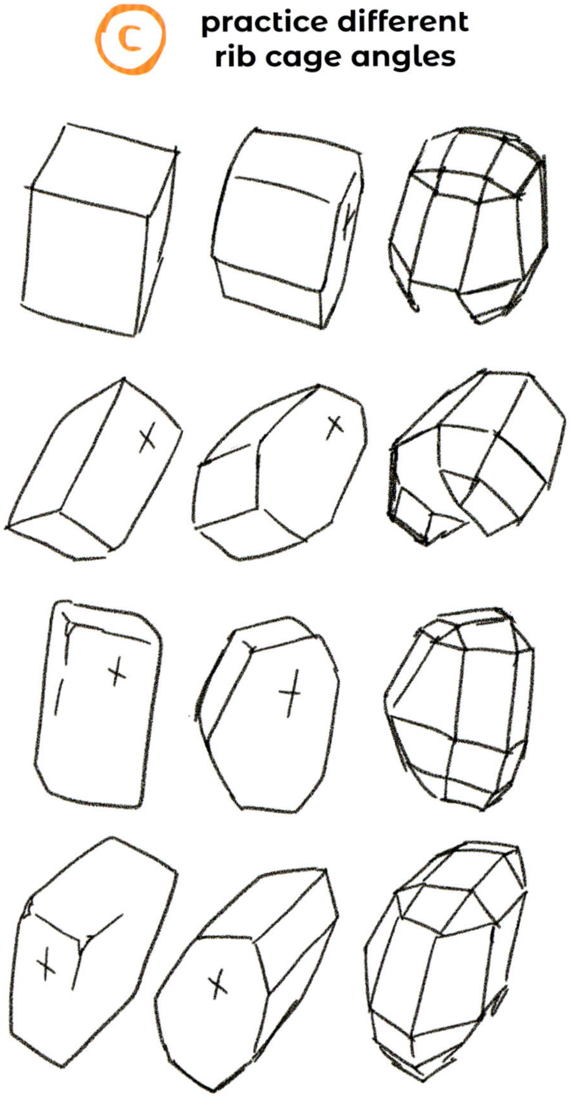

B

natural variation

C

practice different rib cage angles

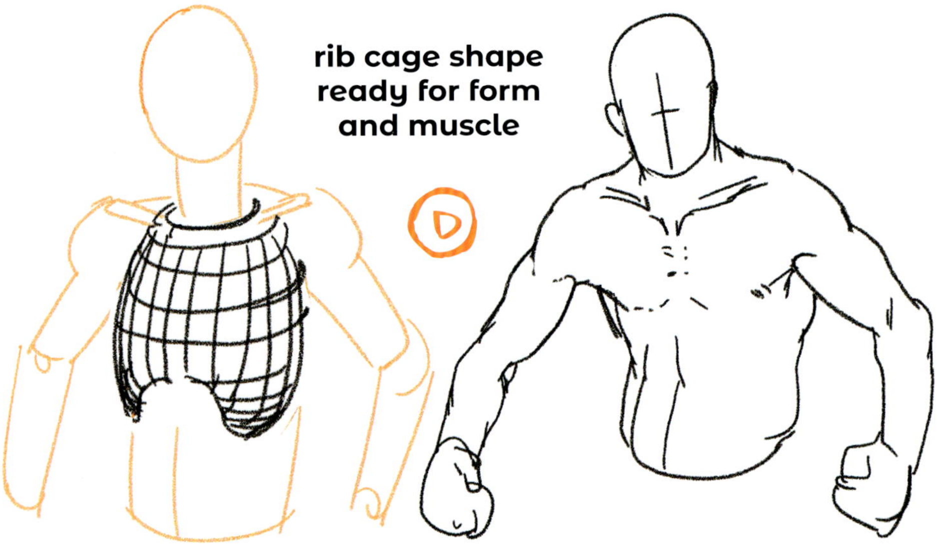

rib cage shape ready for form and muscle

D

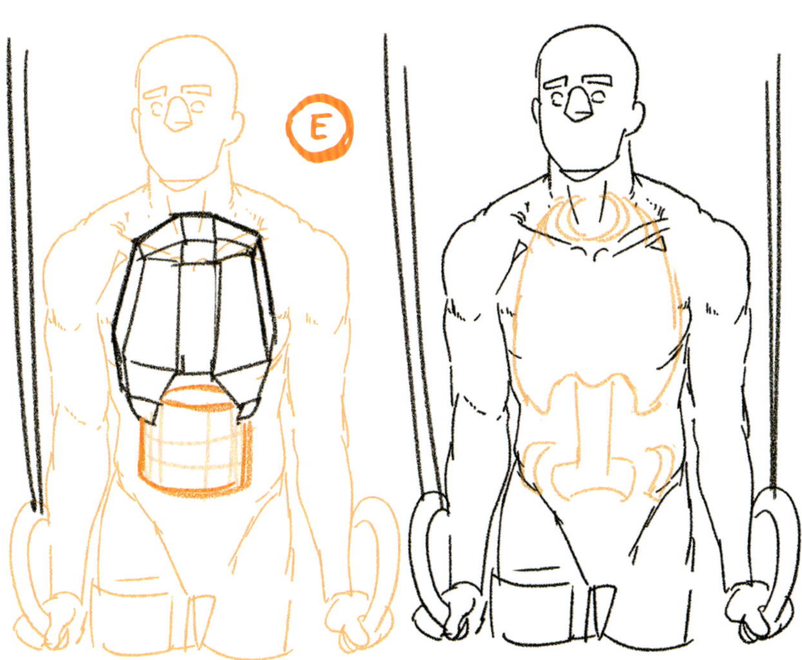

G

limited sideways motion

bottom corners of ribs are hidden

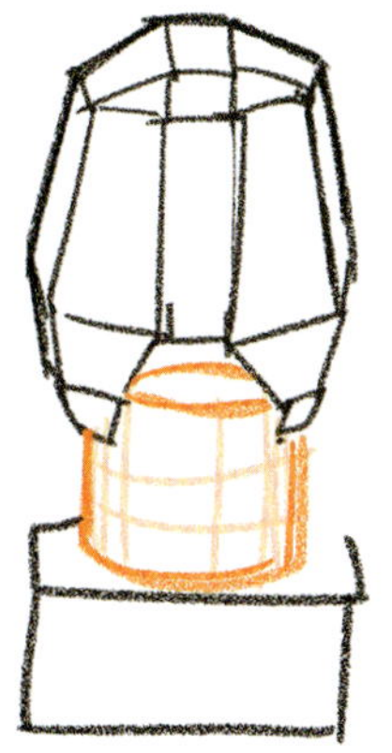

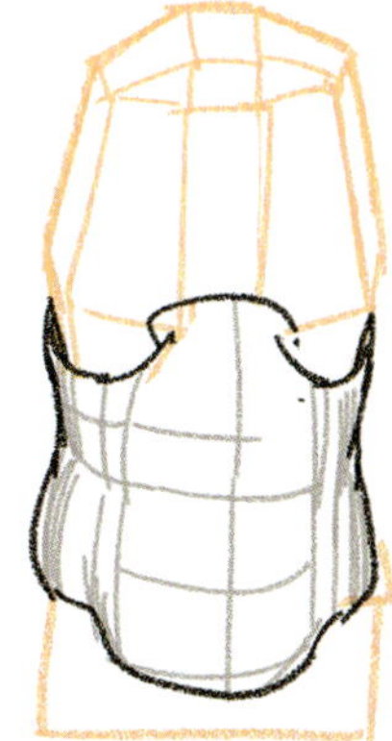

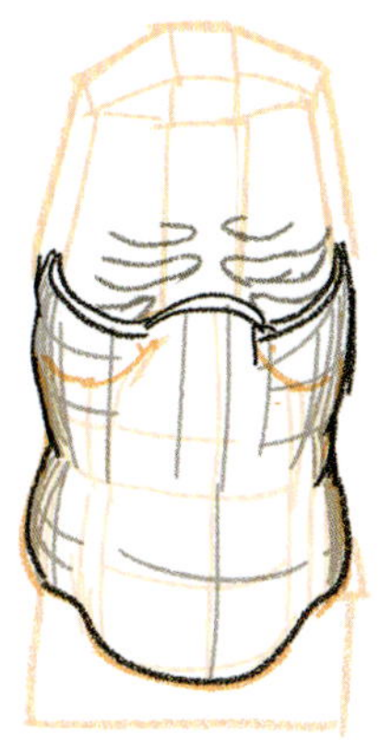

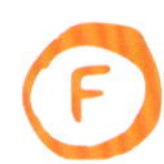

obliques form a "corset" joining rib cage to pelvis

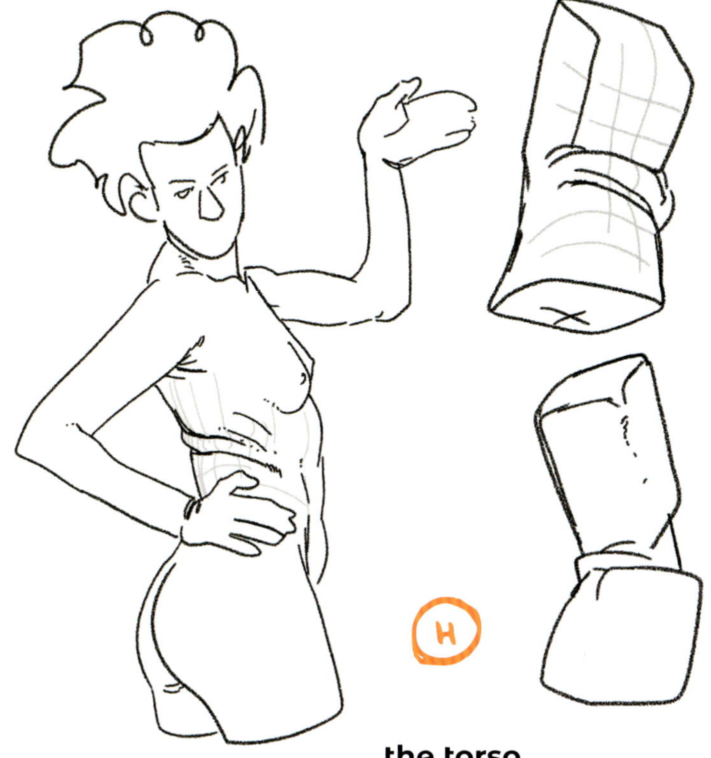

the torso can twist!

When drawing the mannequin, we will typically draw the abdomen sitting inside the volume of the rib cage, with the bottom of the ribs exposed. In reality, we will almost never see the bottom corners of the ribs (E).

The major muscle groups of the internal and external obliques sit on top of the ribs, providing the "joint" that wedges the pelvis and ribs together. Think of the obliques like a corset connecting the chest and hip regions (F).

The pelvis is highest at the sides. The rib cage is lowest at the sides. Therefore our range of motion is limited when bending to the sides (G). To increase this range of motion, the pelvis flares out at the top and the bottom ribs taper inward. We can increase the range of motion further by twisting (H)!

tip: camera b

When we focus on individual muscles, we must also keep the whole figure in mind. After all, the whole figure is our ultimate goal, not learning every muscle and attachment! Always visualize forms from another angle – let's call it "camera B." This will help us visualize the folds formed in the skin and body fat.

Body fat is an important part of the figure – without it, all of the people we draw will look like bodybuilders or anatomical diagrams. The folds in A are there because I visualized the model from "camera B" and realized that a bend in the major forms would cause creases in the skin (B).

We'll cover the clavicles (collarbones) shortly but, for now, know that we rarely see much of them from the surface. Suggesting them, rather than stating them, is much more powerful (C). Like parts of the rib cage, they become hidden as we build our figure.

When it comes to fat, skin folds, and soft tissue, make a habit of thinking what "camera B" might see from a slightly different view (D).

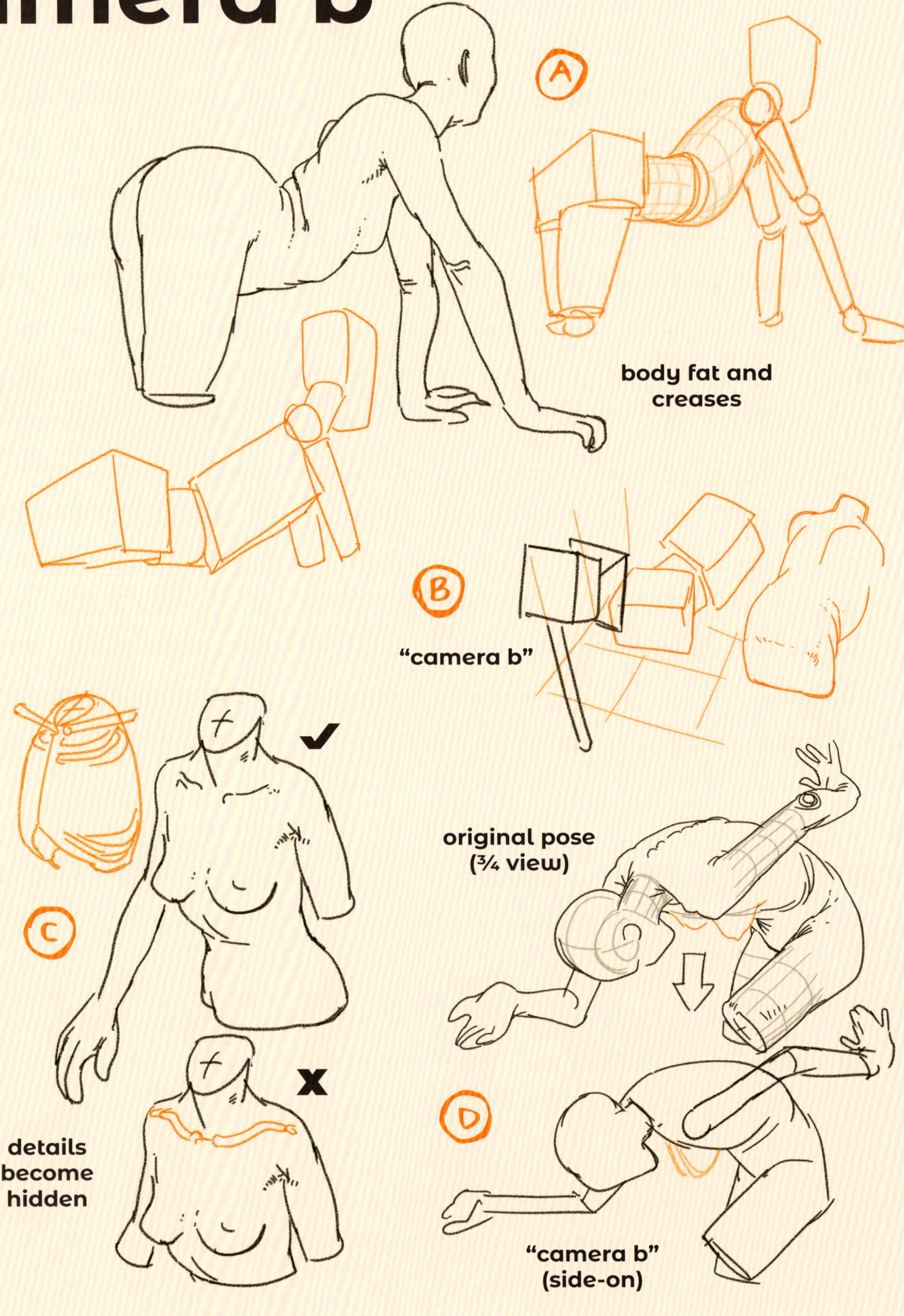

the spine

It isn't necessary to know every detail of the spine, but it's useful to understand its role and basic structure. Don't draw the spine as a cylindrical tube stuck to the back (A). It sits within a groove in our rib cage, so make sure you embed it into the body.

The spine is a form with planes, so it's easier to visualize its bend and twist when we use edges and corners. Start with the two ends of the form and join them together, starting from the corners (B).

Each piece of the spine, or vertebra, is connected by muscles and ligaments. Start each vertebra as a cube form, then hollow out the inside (C). The hollow spinal column exists to support and protect the delicate spinal cord that runs through it. Attached to each hollow vertebra are three projections that are joined by connective tissue (D). These give strength to and act as flexible anchors for the muscles of the spinal column. Without these spikes, we wouldn't be able to extend our backs at all!

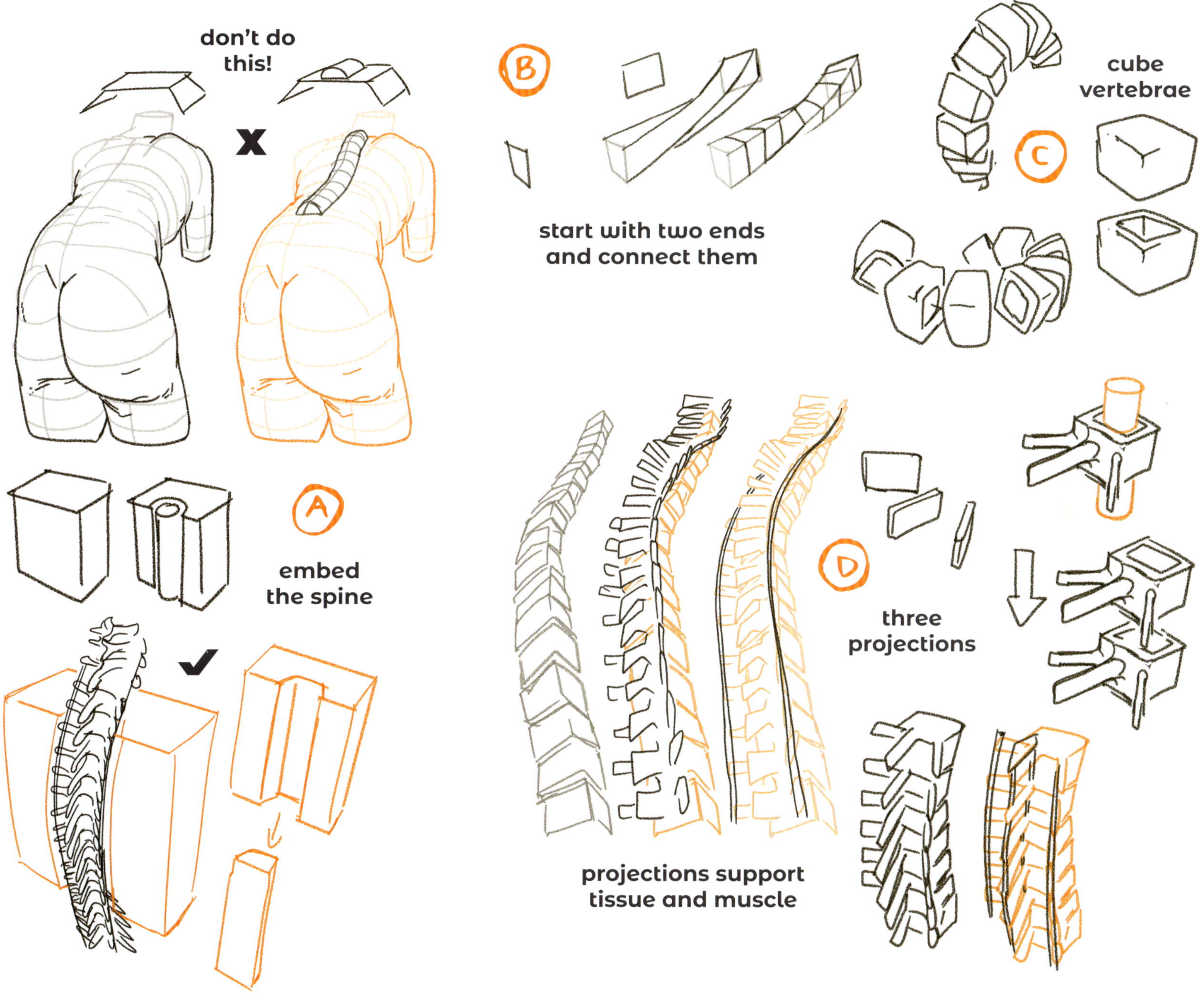

So what role do these three projections from each vertebra fulfill? To simplify, think of these spikes forming three ridges along the spine (E). Small connective muscles join the two outer ridges to the rib cage (F), which anchors the spine and ensures that any twist in the spine is transferred to the rib cage.

As we move down the spine, the vertebrae become wider. The sides of the ridges move from 90 degrees to 45 degrees and back again by the time we get to the lumbar region (the region between the ribs and pelvis) (G).

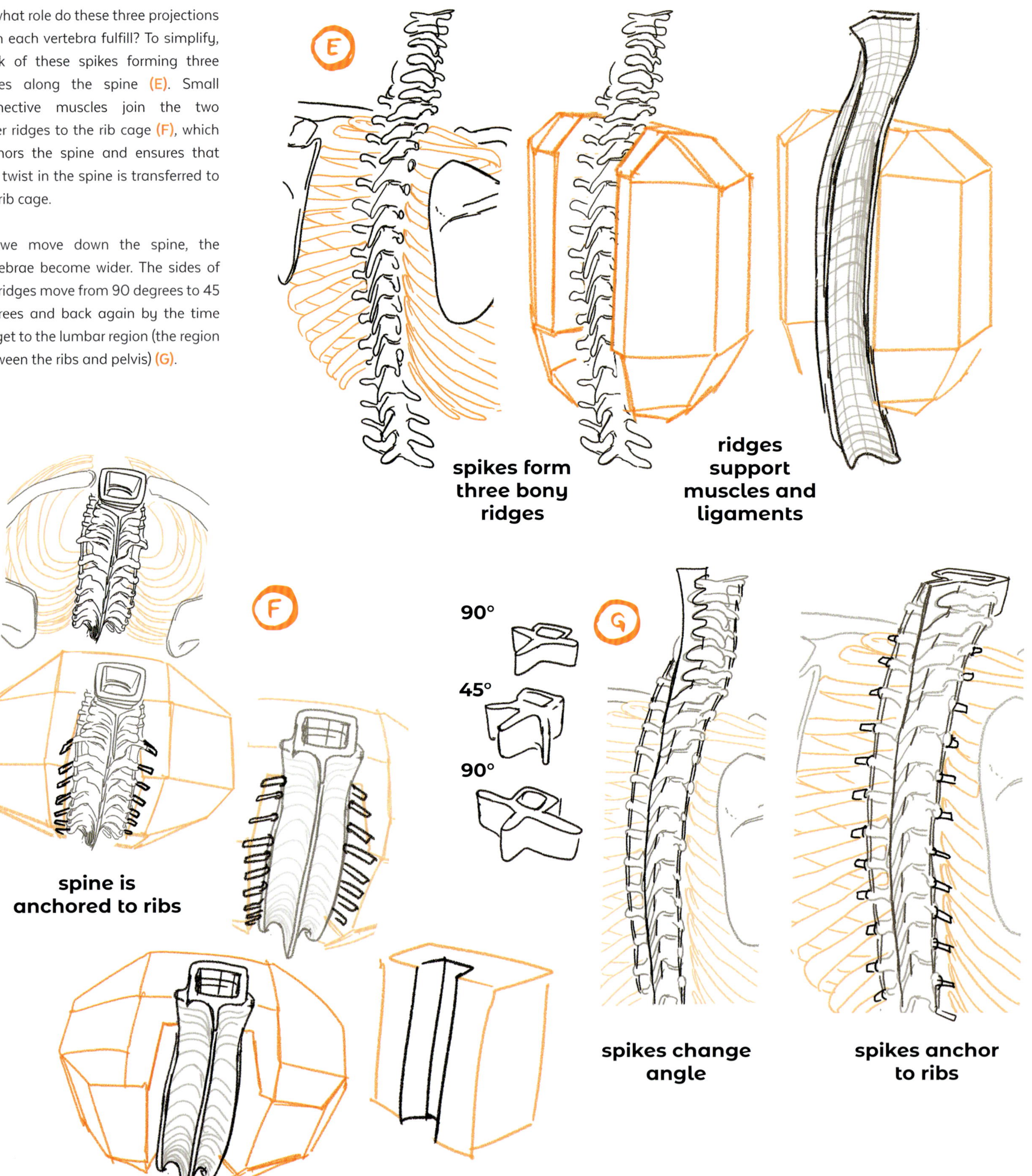

shoulders

The "yoke," or shoulder girdle, is comprised of the scapulae (shoulder blades) and the clavicles (collarbones). We need these to rotate our figure's arms and raise or lower them relative to the rib cage. Let's start with our simplified rib cage shape and two arms (A).

If we attached the arms directly to the rib cage (B), we'd only be able to move our arms a little. We'd be able to pull our arms in toward us, but we wouldn't be able to raise them! For that, we must add an extra attachment point for the muscles (C). This provides an anchor to pull against to raise the arms. It also gives us an anchor to pull down or up, relative to the head, if we want to raise or lower the whole arm (D).

A common mistake is drawing the arms too close to the rib cage. The arms have a lot of muscle attachment points to accommodate, so the humerus (upper arm bone) needs room to move around before we add the muscles in (E).

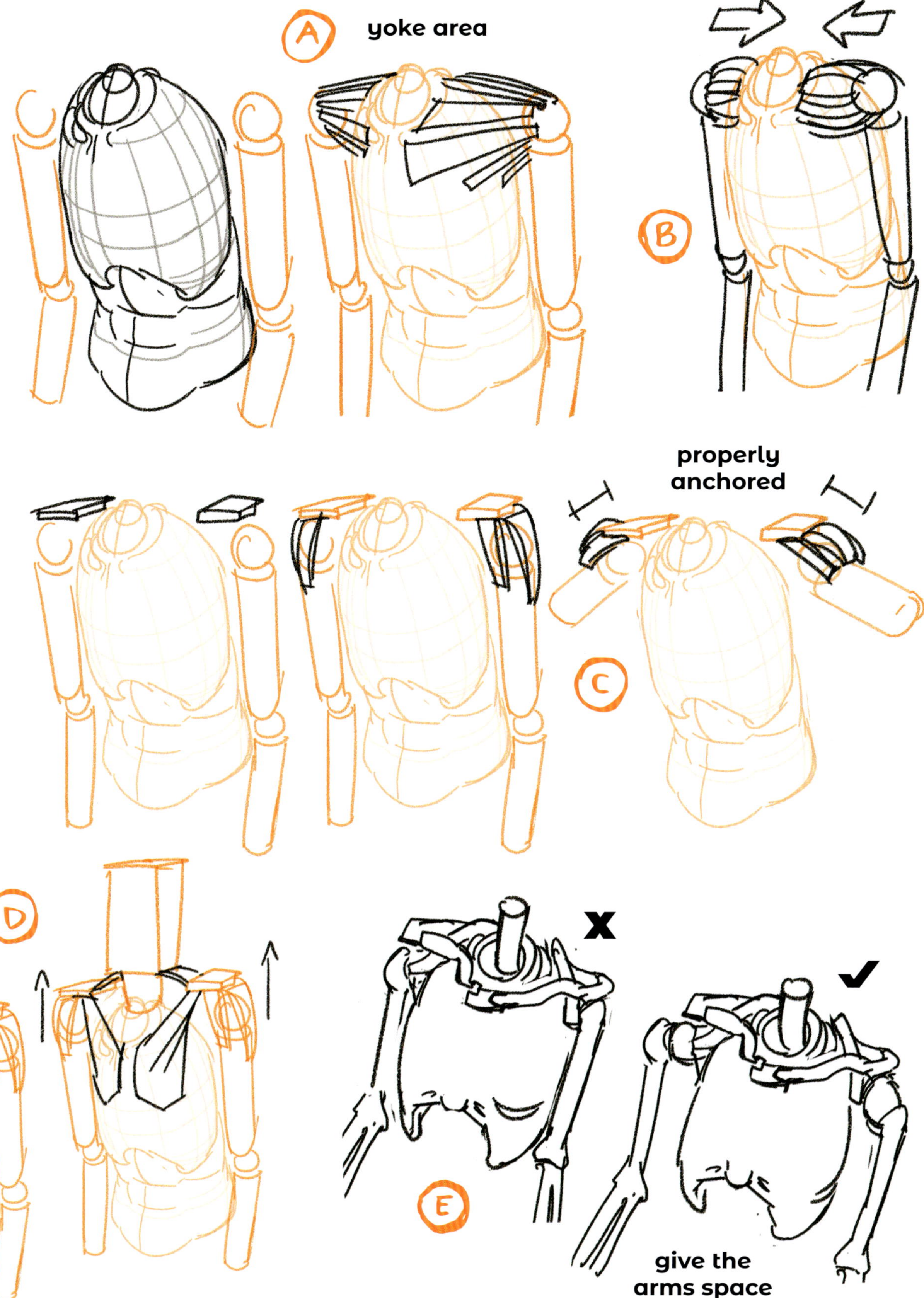

The arms can move both fully independently and in perfect coordination, so we must join all the following parts together. To give the arms stability, we connect them at the front with the two flexible poles of the clavicles (collarbones) (F). These can't stretch, but their attachments to the rib cage allow plenty of movement (G).

The scapulae (shoulder blades) at the rear of the rib cage create anchors for us to pull our arms down (H). They also allow us to bring our arms together behind our rib cage, allowing for all sorts of pulling movements (I). They don't sit flat against the back but curve with the form of the rib cage (J).

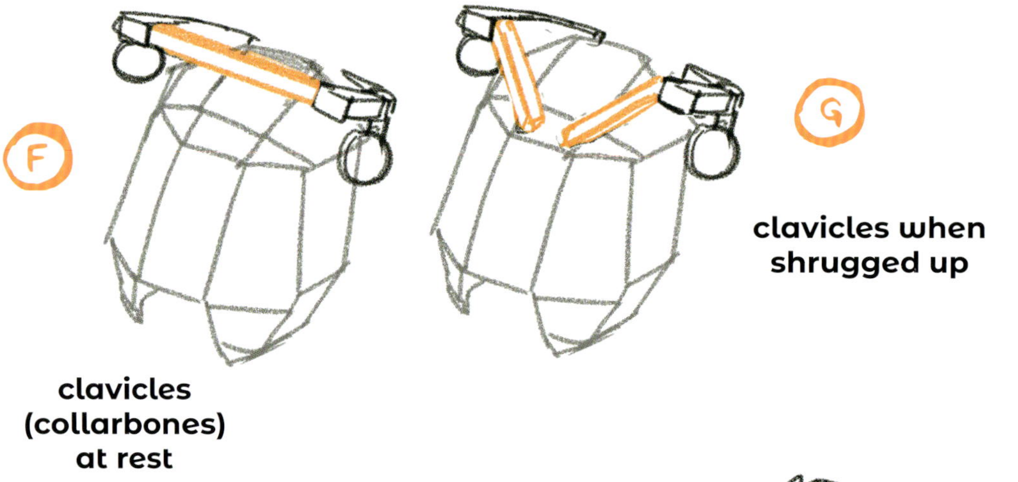

F

G

clavicles when shrugged up

clavicles (collarbones) at rest

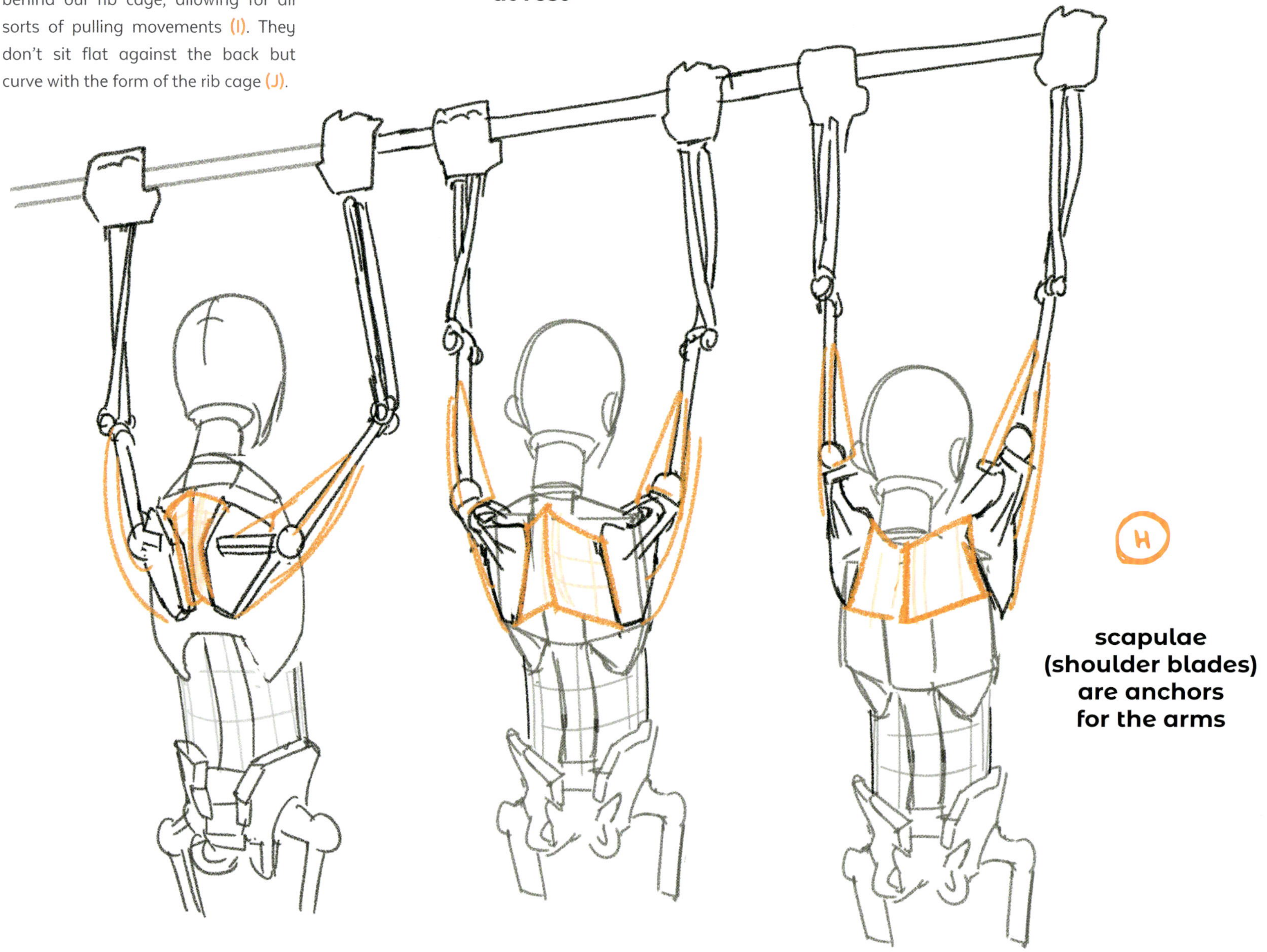

H

scapulae (shoulder blades) are anchors for the arms

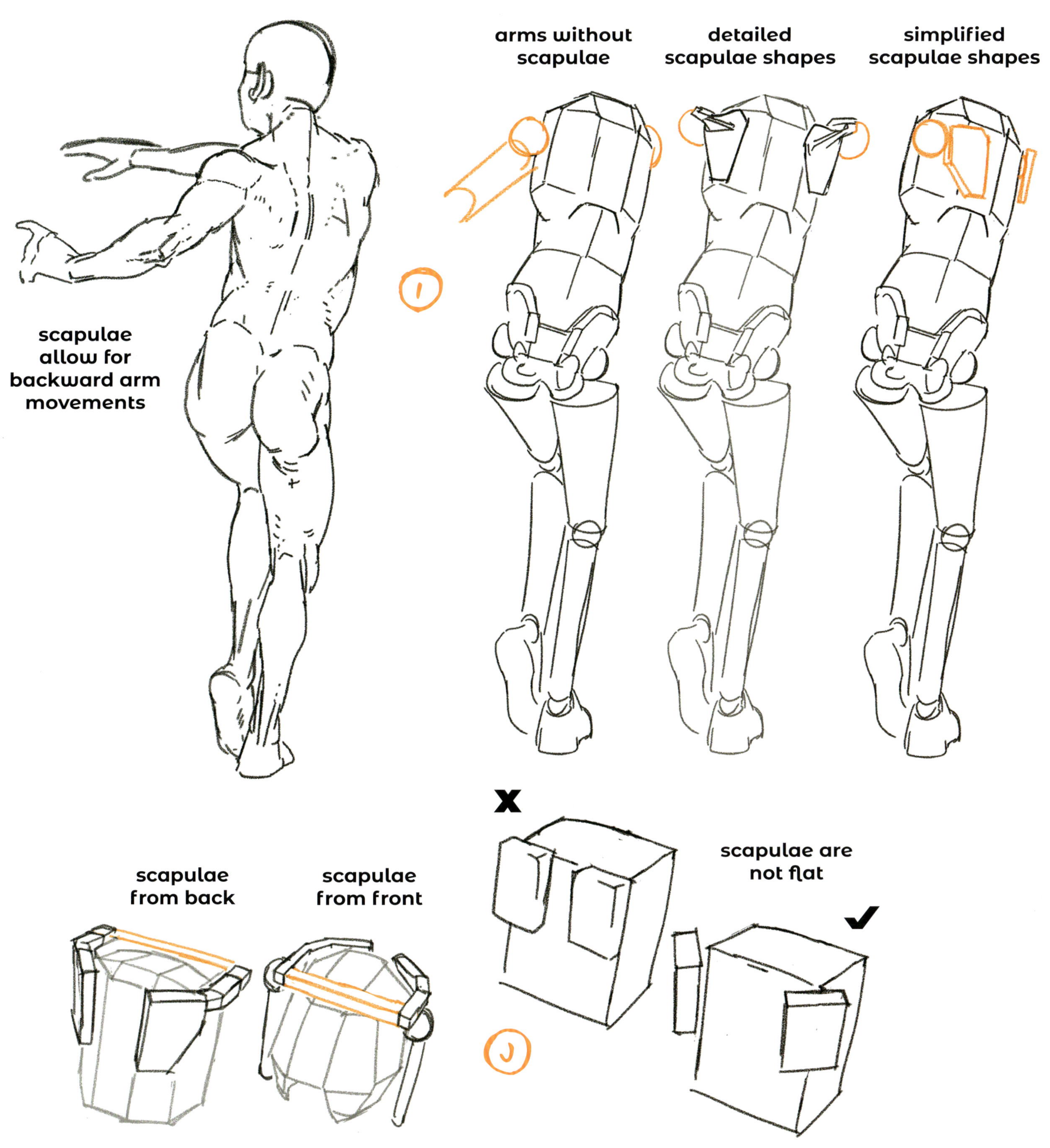
arms without scapulae
detailed scapulae shapes
simplified scapulae shapes
scapulae allow for backward arm movements
scapulae from back
scapulae from front
scapulae are not flat

building the yoke

Let's build the yoke area using simple geometry as a base (A). Add simple, flattened cuboid forms for each scapula. Two thin cylinders will do for the clavicles, for now, with a ball at each end for the glenohumeral joint (shoulder joint). Note that the clavicles aren't flat, but angled back and slightly upward in most poses (B).

Let's chop off the top inner and bottom outer corners of the scapulae cubes to create a more winglike shape (C). From above, note how the yoke shape is almost a diamond. These parts are all linked, providing enormous strength and flexibility to the arms and shoulders through the muscle and tendon attachments (D).

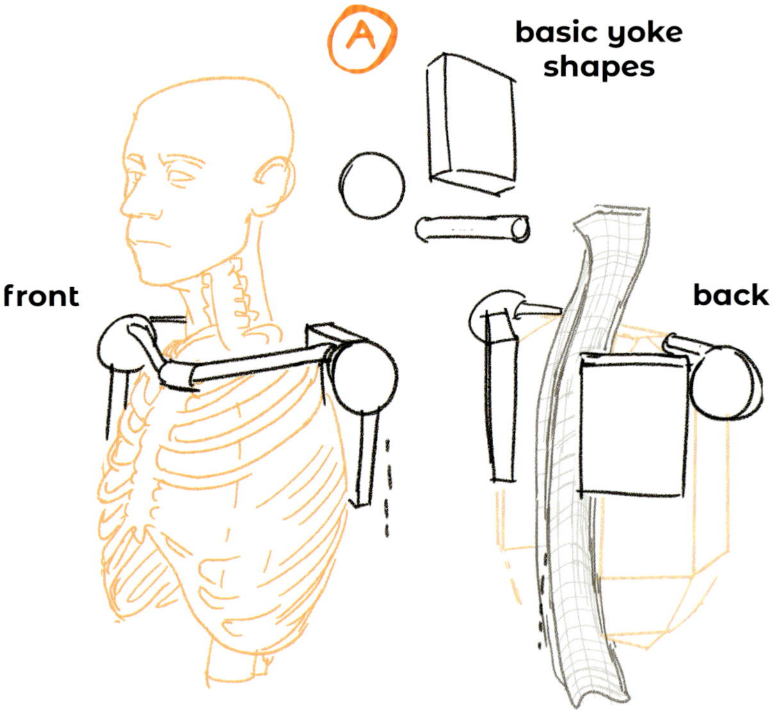

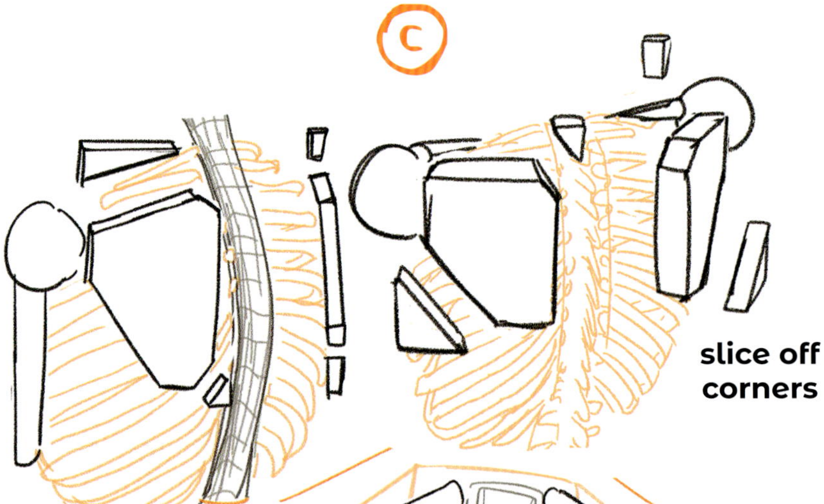

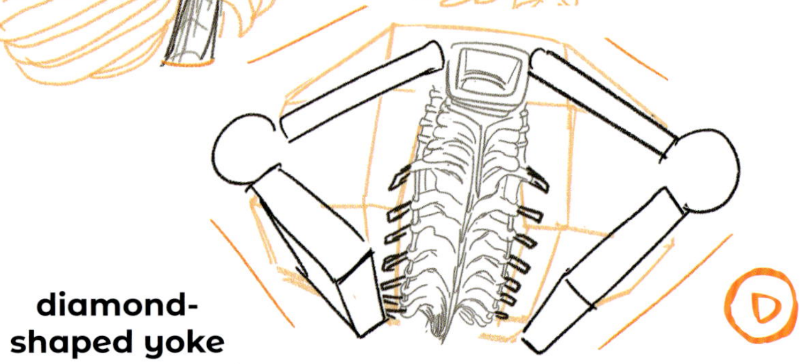

A

basic yoke shapes

front

back

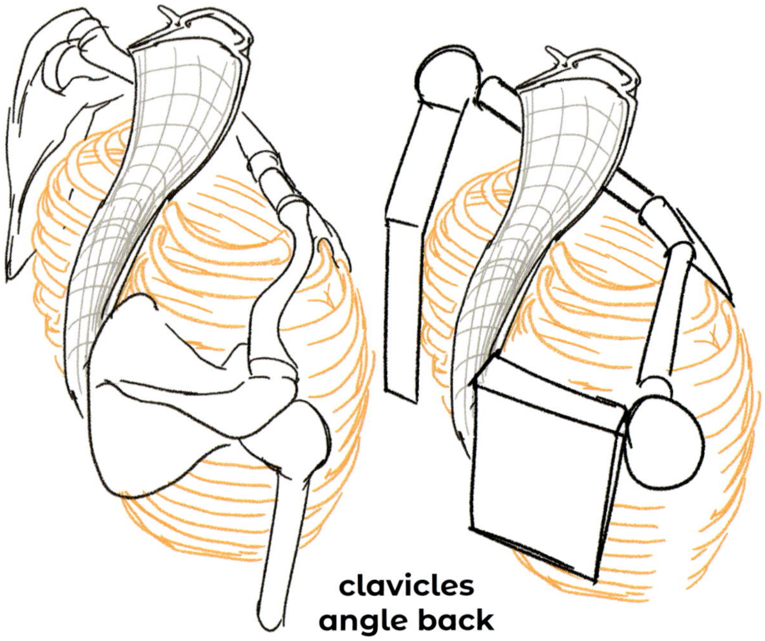

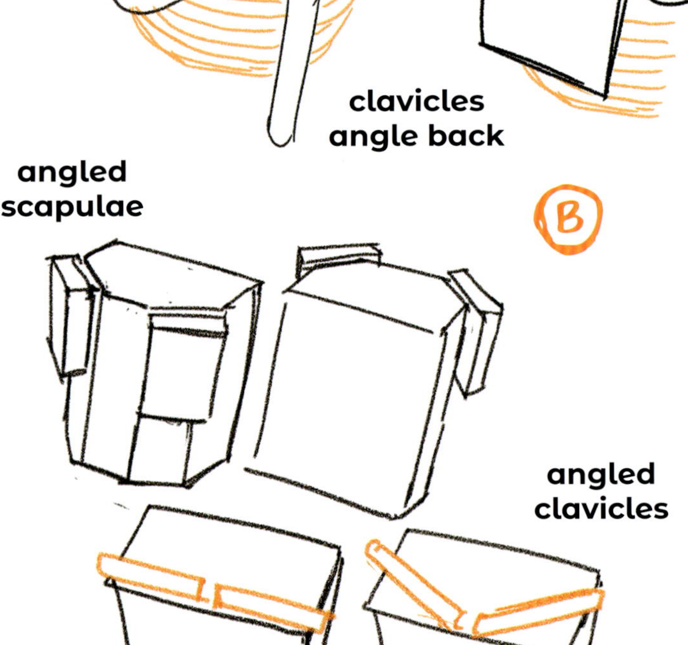

C

slice off corners

diamond-shaped yoke

D

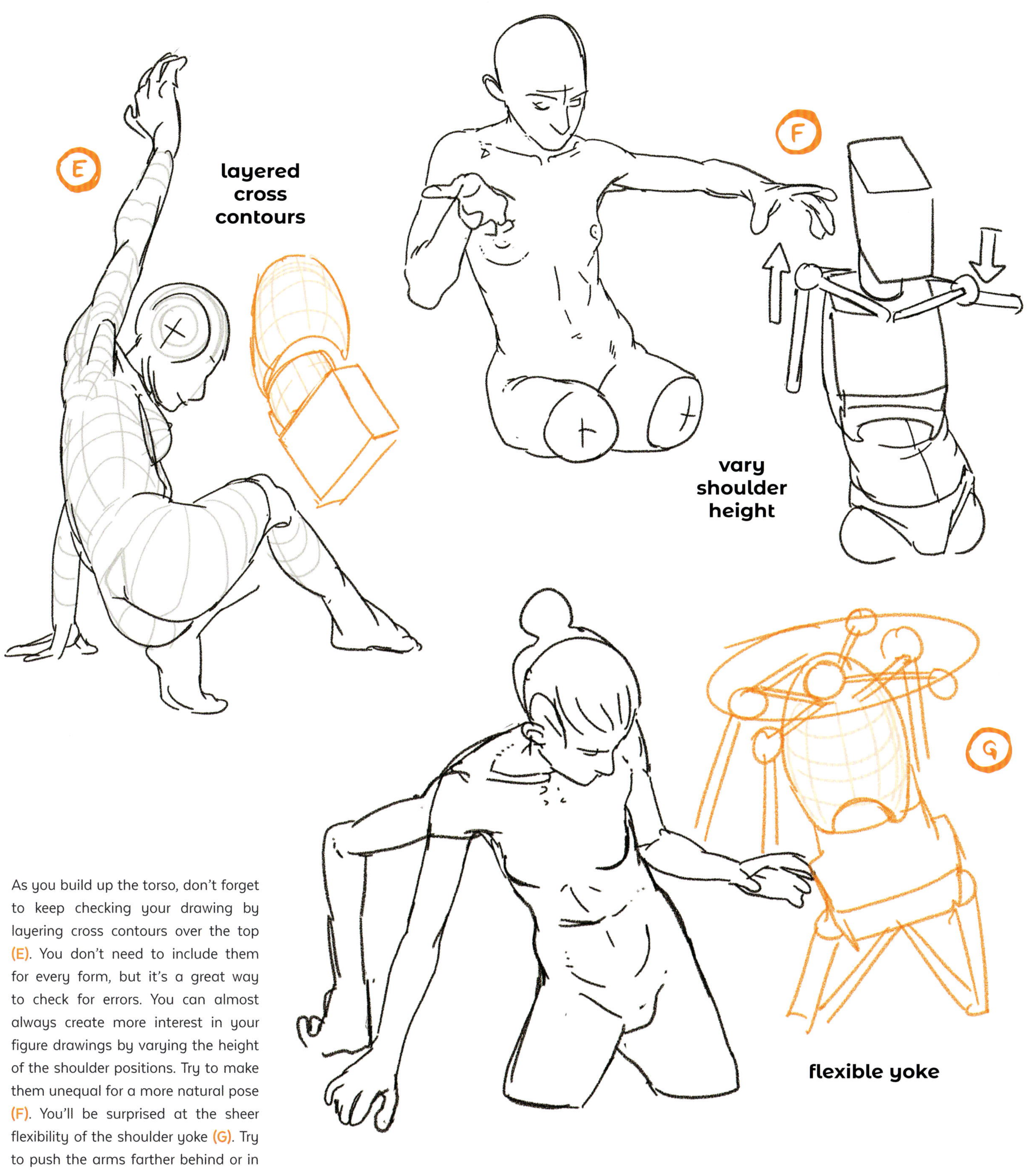

As you build up the torso, don't forget to keep checking your drawing by layering cross contours over the top (E). You don't need to include them for every form, but it's a great way to check for errors. You can almost always create more interest in your figure drawings by varying the height of the shoulder positions. Try to make them unequal for a more natural pose (F). You'll be surprised at the sheer flexibility of the shoulder yoke (G). Try to push the arms farther behind or in front than you'd usually draw them!

refining the yoke area

To refine our scapula shape, let's taper it from the outside in. It's thicker by the shoulder joint and becomes thinner near the spine (A). Next we add the coracoid process – basically a little finger at the front of the scapula, which points forward and outward, away from the center of the body (B). On top of this we add the acromion process, which is shaped like a buffalo horn (C). It attaches to the flat section at the back of the scapula and wraps around and forward. The end curls inward and is connect to the clavicle by a small, flexible joint (C). To this, we can add a couple of angled planes, just to connect it to the scapula more solidly (D). This whole shape forms the "spine of the scapula," the prominent ridge found on each shoulder blade.

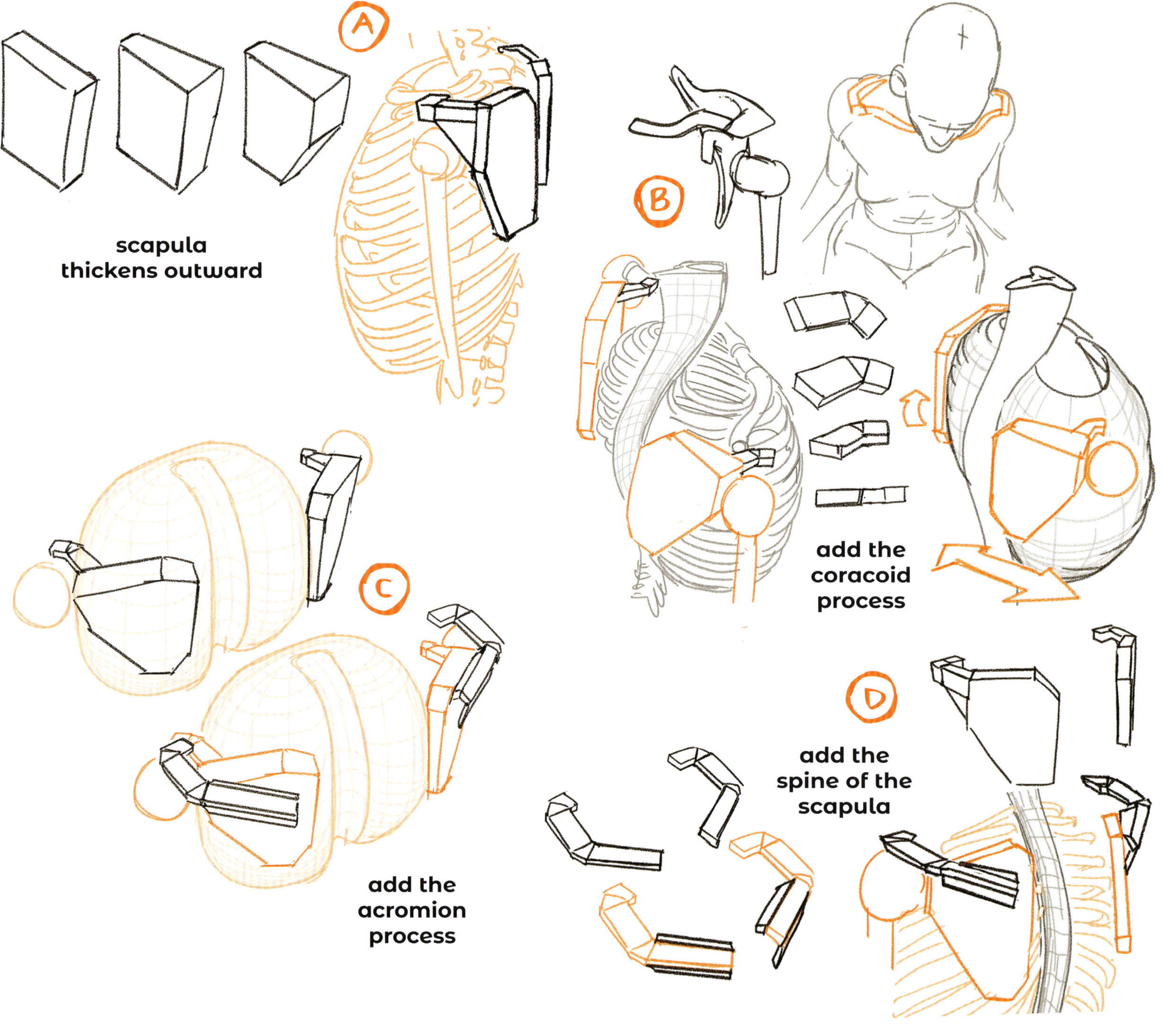

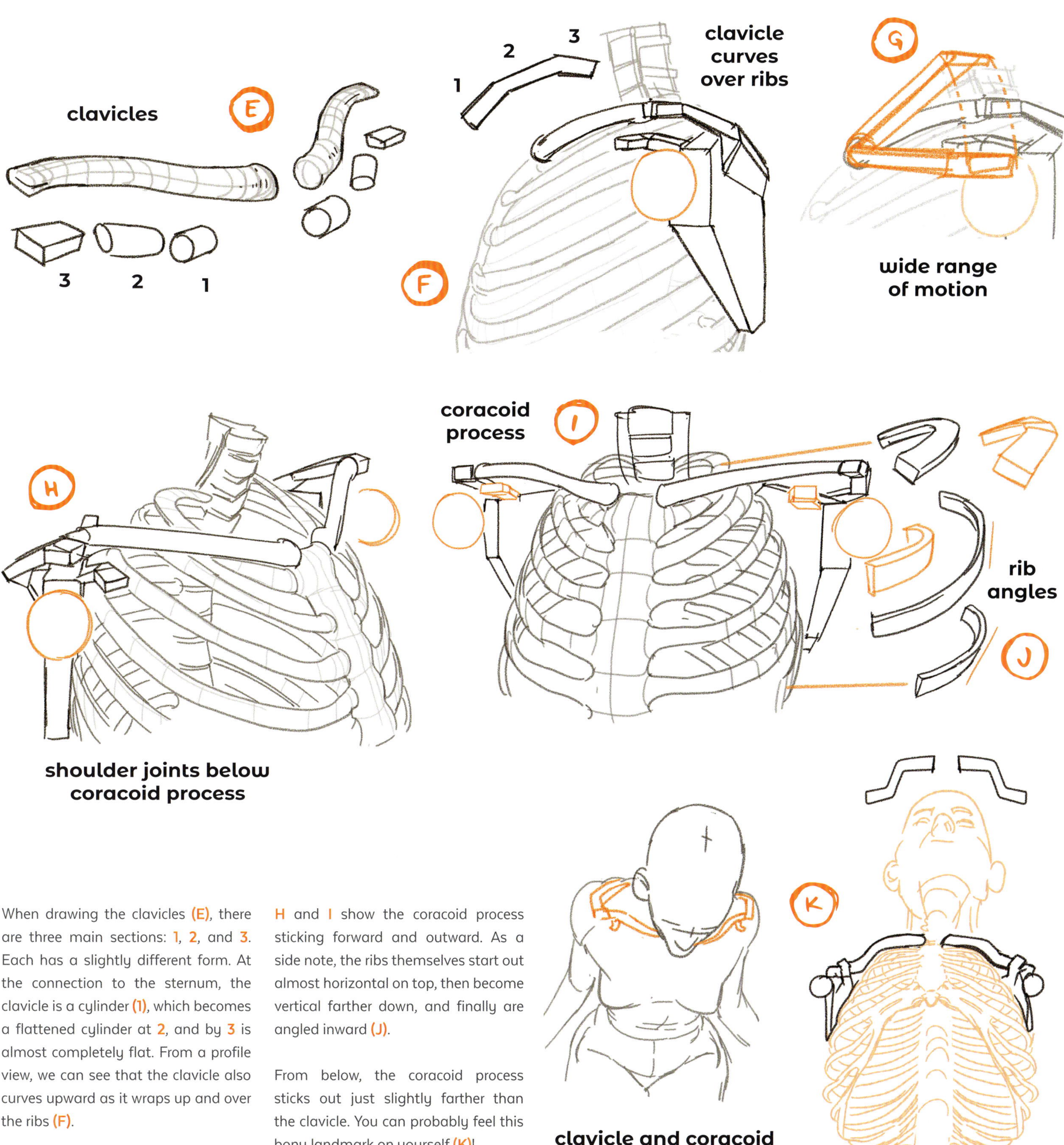

When drawing the clavicles (E), there are three main sections: 1, 2, and 3. Each has a slightly different form. At the connection to the sternum, the clavicle is a cylinder (1), which becomes a flattened cylinder at 2, and by 3 is almost completely flat. From a profile view, we can see that the clavicle also curves upward as it wraps up and over the ribs (F).

The clavicles have a large range of motion up and down (G). Note how H and I show the coracoid process sticking forward and outward. As a side note, the ribs themselves start out almost horizontal on top, then become vertical farther down, and finally are angled inward (J).

From below, the coracoid process sticks out just slightly farther than the clavicle. You can probably feel this bony landmark on yourself (K)!

pectoralis minor & serratus anterior

Let's begin adding torso muscles, starting with the pectoralis minor and serratus anterior.

Minor means "lesser" and pectoralis means "relating to the breast." The pectoralis minor attaches to the front of the rib cage and the coracoid process **(A, 1)**. Several large muscle groups attach to the coracoid process, so it's worth remembering it! The pectoralis minor pulls directly on the coracoid process of the scapula – not the arm, like the pectoralis major does, as we'll see on the next page.

The serratus, meaning "sawlike," has teethlike projections that form little triangles **(B, 2)**. You don't see them this sharply in reality; instead, they are just indicated as volumes.

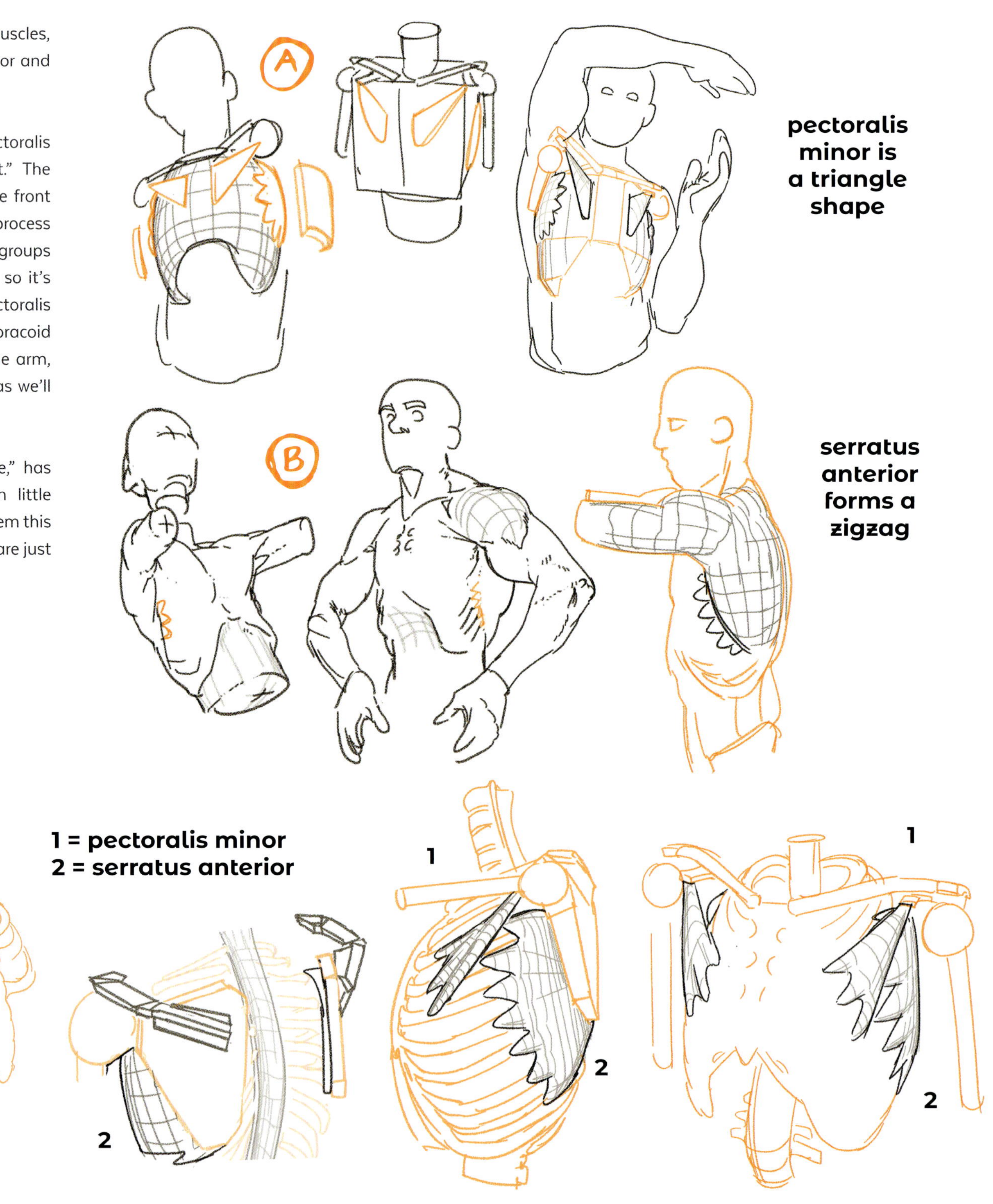

pectoralis major

On top of the pectoralis minor, we'll add the pectoralis major muscles. Major here means "greater" – this muscle is larger. It connects the sternum and ribs to the exterior of the humerus (upper arm bone) (A). It pulls the arm itself inward, rather than pulling the front of the scapula. It fully covers the pectoralis minor and attaches to the outside of the humerus, meaning that it rotates the arms internally (toward the center of the body) (B).

The pectoralis major attaches in a rounded way to the sternum. It doesn't run straight down the middle (C). It also wraps around the rib cage, which is itself rounded. When viewed from a three-quarter angle, we usually don't see much of it because it's wrapping around out of sight (D).

When the arms are brought together, the distinction between these "pecs" and deltoid muscles is lost and they become one mass (E). Don't try to separate them.

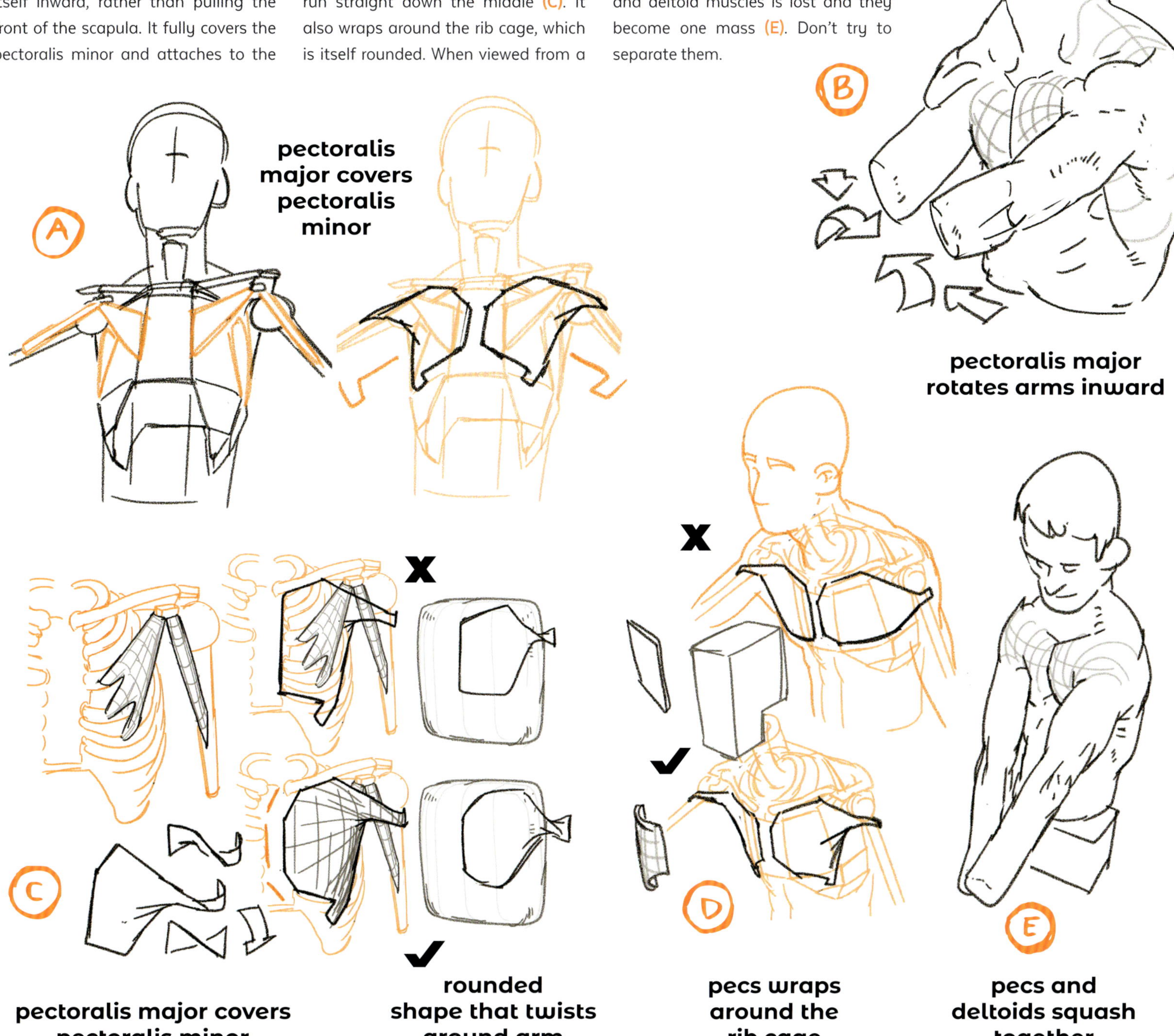

The pectoralis major is very flat where it attaches to the sternum, and slowly builds in volume as it approaches the humerus. For this reason, draw it more tubular at the intersection of the arms, while underplaying the volume around the inner chest (F).

The pectoralis major is also attached closely to the sternum, but at the humerus end there is less attachment. This allows it a range of movement. When the arms are extended, we may see a gap beneath it (G), between the muscles of the back and the pecs.

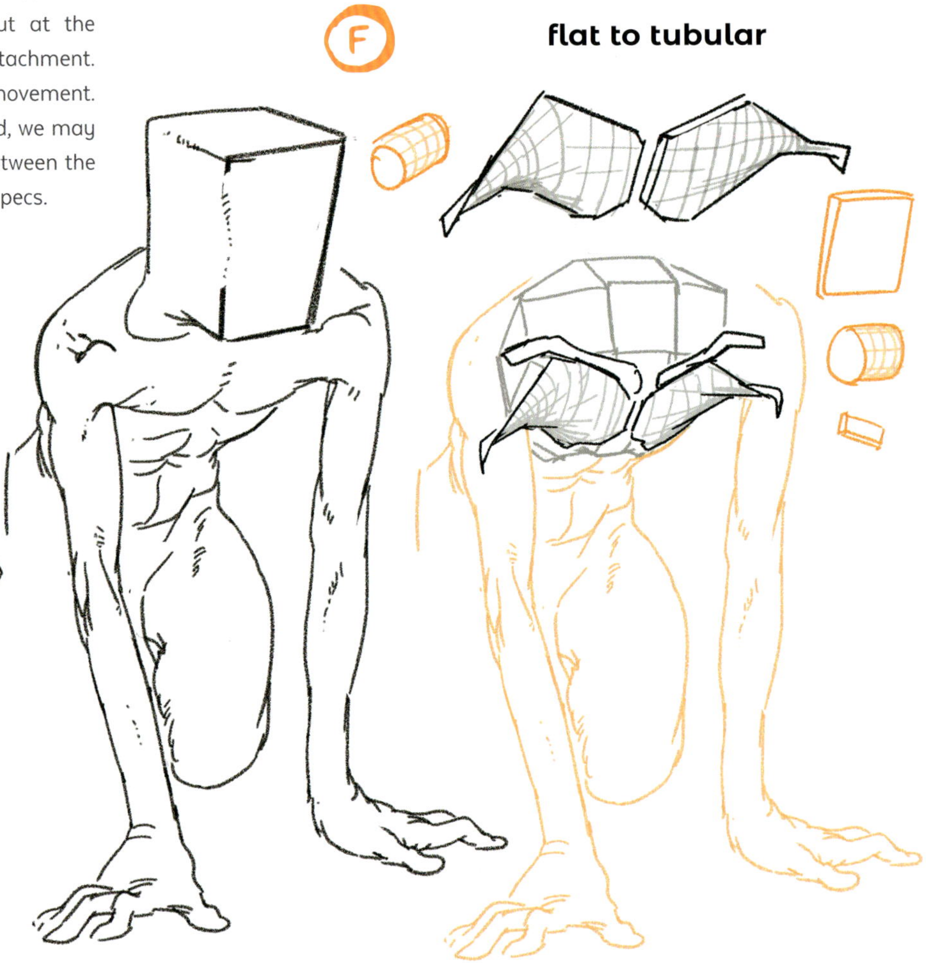

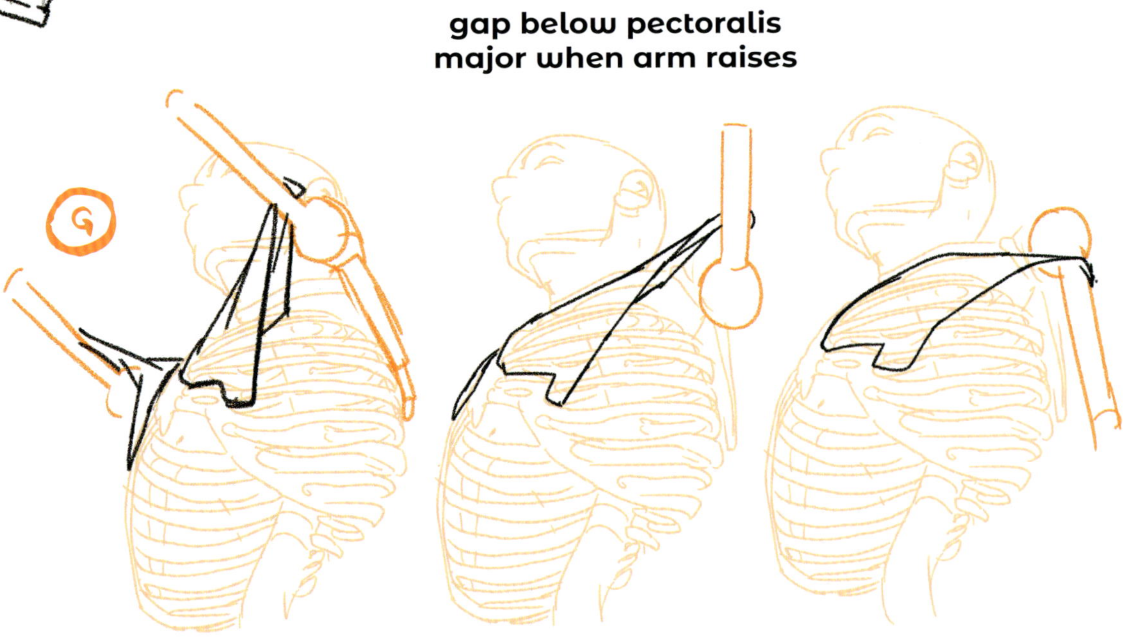

F

flat to tubular

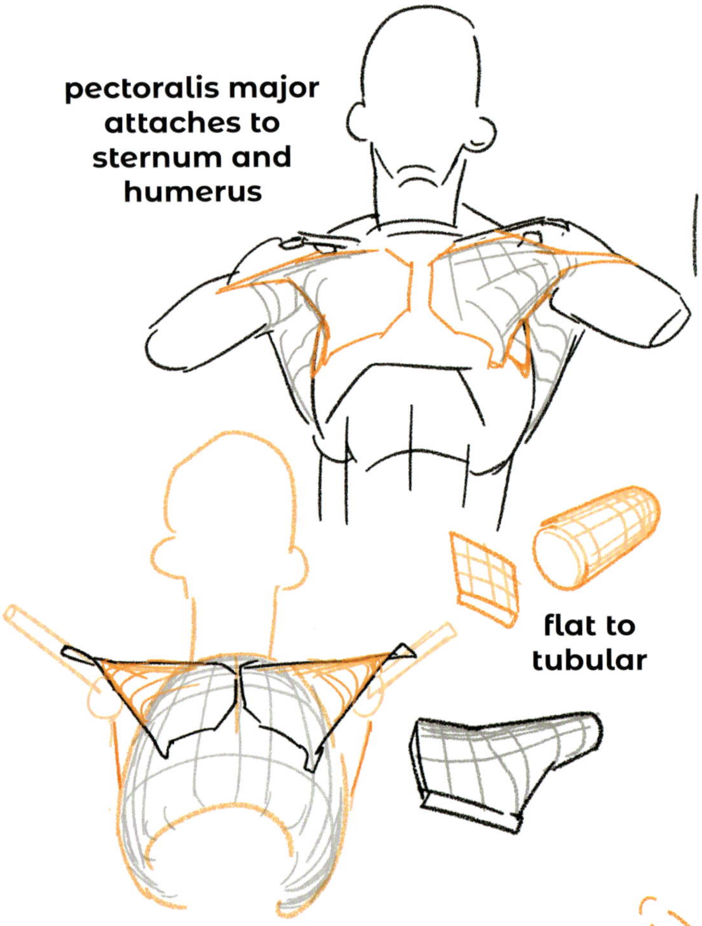

pectoralis major attaches to sternum and humerus

flat to tubular

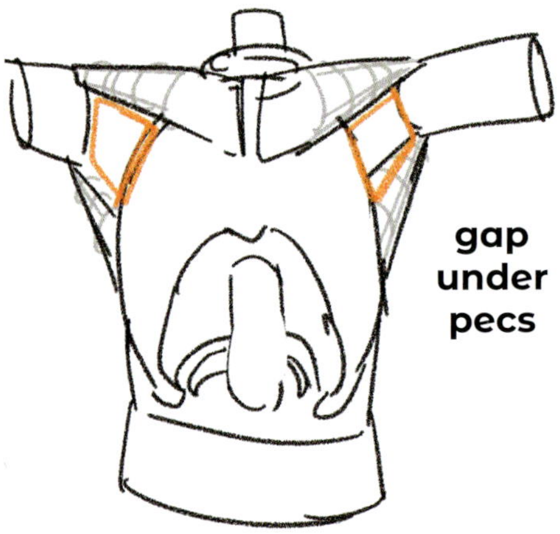

gap below pectoralis major when arm raises

G

gap under pecs

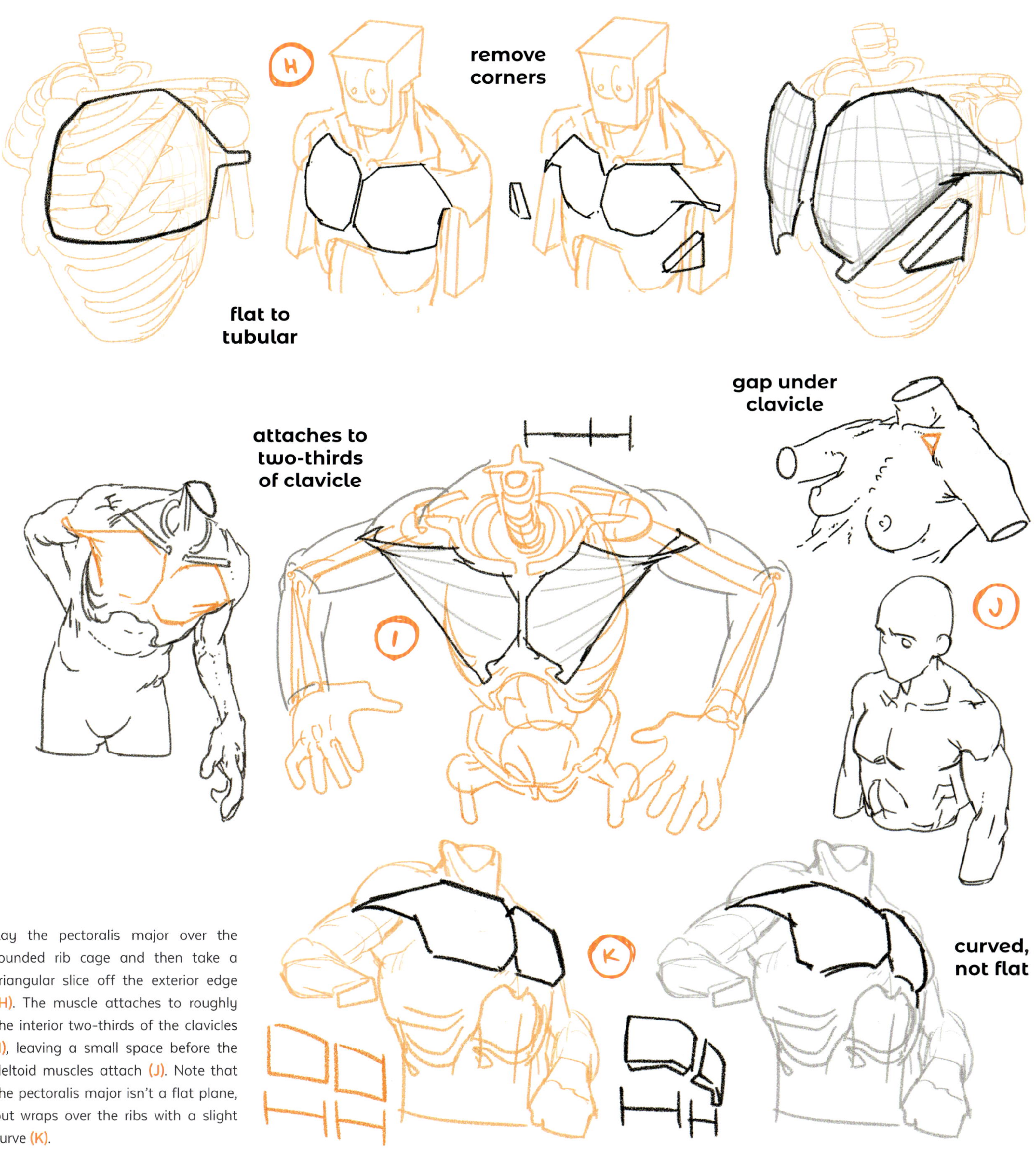

Lay the pectoralis major over the rounded rib cage and then take a triangular slice off the exterior edge (H). The muscle attaches to roughly the interior two-thirds of the clavicles (I), leaving a small space before the deltoid muscles attach (J). Note that the pectoralis major isn't a flat plane, but wraps over the ribs with a slight curve (K).

tip: keep your distance

When drawing anatomy studies, try to study at all "distances." What does this mean? Well, we tend to begin anatomy drawing quite loosely, and get more detail-oriented the more we study. When looking at a drawing like A, you will tend to lose sight of the big picture. Like in the saying, "You can't see the wood for the trees," you aren't drawing a figure any more, but a collection of muscles! B is another example of this. It's believable as a form, but it doesn't look like a real person. Our goal is to acquire the skills needed to draw a relatively realistic person! A good way to practice is to learn to draw the muscles themselves, but, every few hours, to also draw some looser figures where you aren't detailing the individual muscles (C).

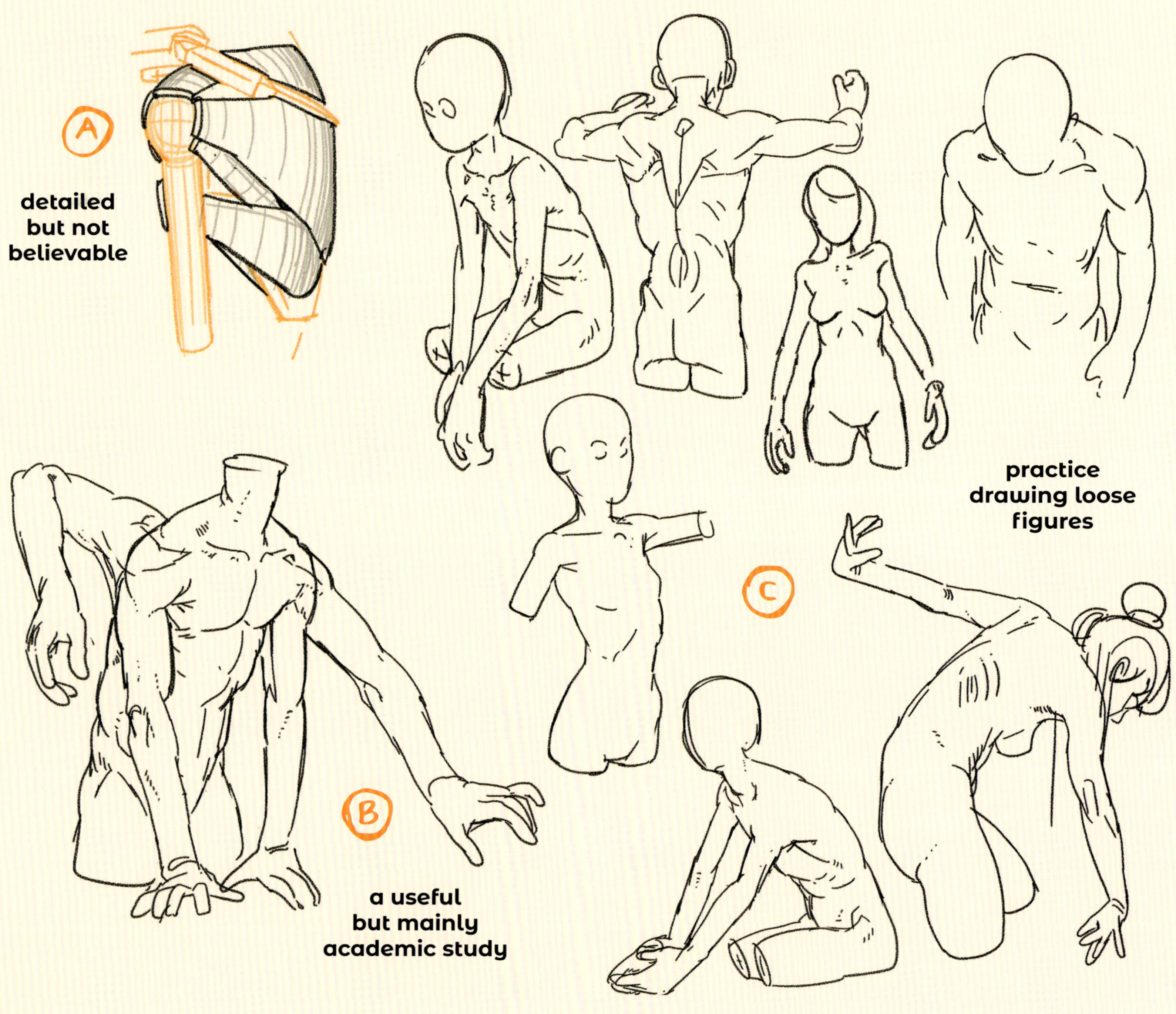

scapular muscles

Let's examine the muscles of the scapulae and their roles (A). These muscles stabilize the shoulders and play an important role in resisting the internal rotation of the pectoralis major and latissimus dorsi muscles (B). The scapular muscles are powerful, and without them, our shoulders would be strongly rounded inward (C). In D we can see them numbered. Muscle 1 is the supraspinatus (supra meaning "above" and spinatus meaning "spine"). Muscle 2 is the infraspinatus (infra meaning "below"). Muscles 3 and 4 are the teres minor and teres major, respectively. The most important thing to note here is that the teres major, the bottom muscle, attaches to the interior of the humerus. The rest attach externally or on top.

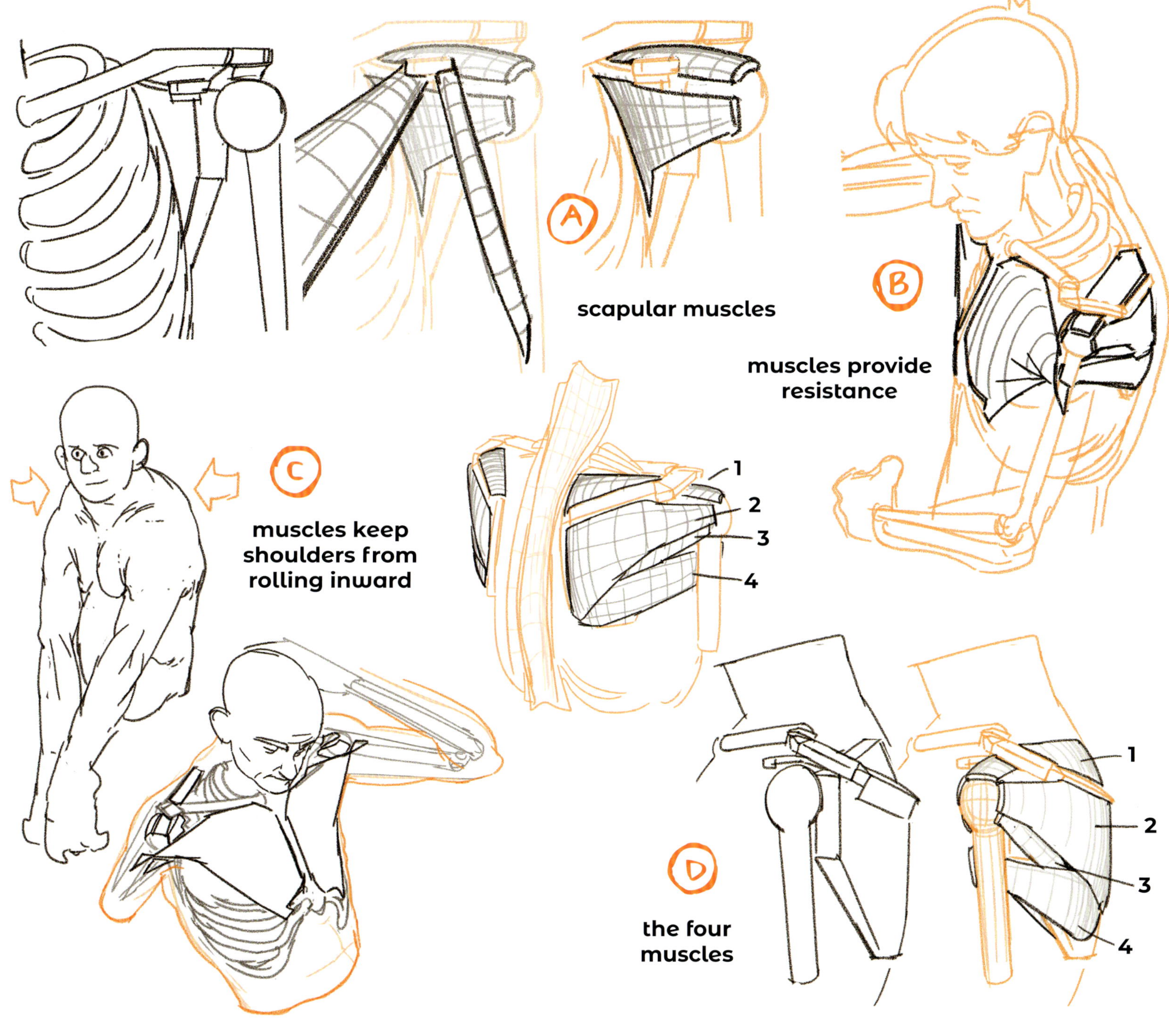

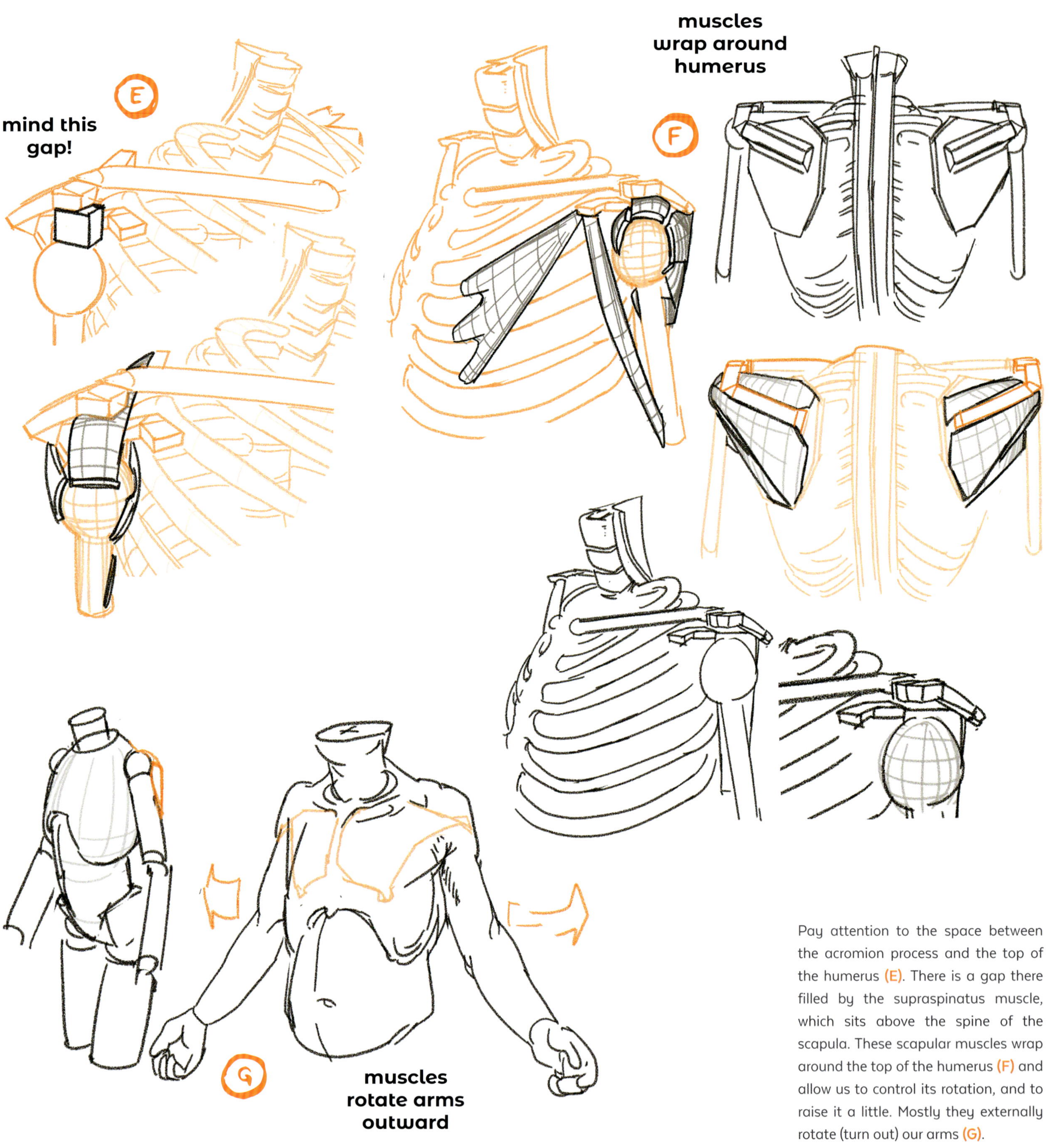

Pay attention to the space between the acromion process and the top of the humerus (E). There is a gap there filled by the supraspinatus muscle, which sits above the spine of the scapula. These scapular muscles wrap around the top of the humerus (F) and allow us to control its rotation, and to raise it a little. Mostly they externally rotate (turn out) our arms (G).

From below, the function of the scapular muscles is clearer (H). They attach to the back edge of the humerus and allow the external rotation of the arms. The teres major is the only one that internally rotates the arm (turning inward). These muscles have a lot of mass in stronger individuals, so don't forget to show them clearly (I, J).

H

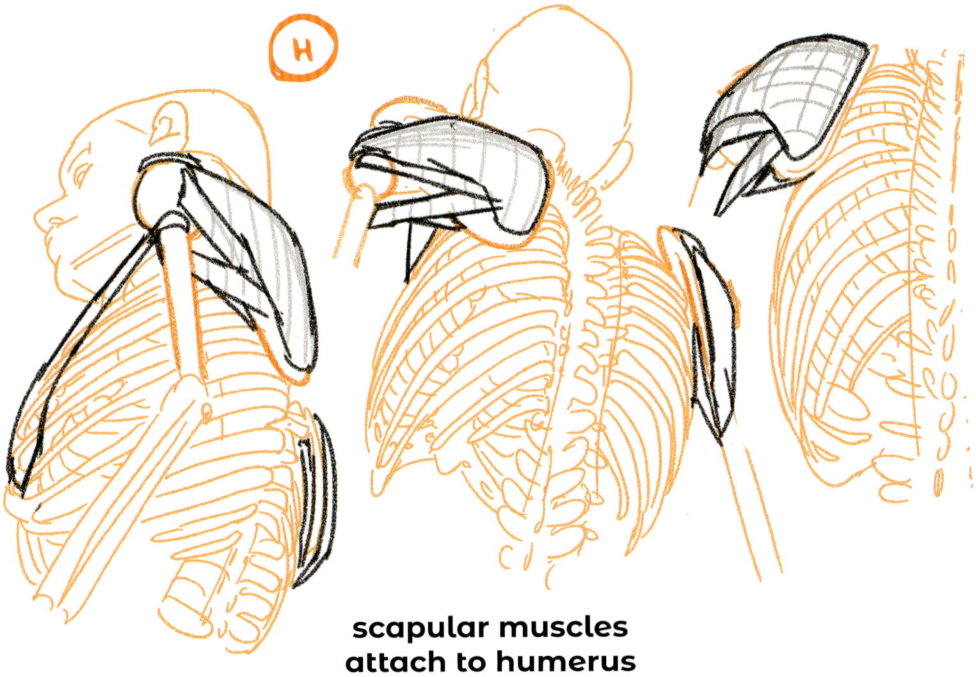

scapular muscles attach to humerus

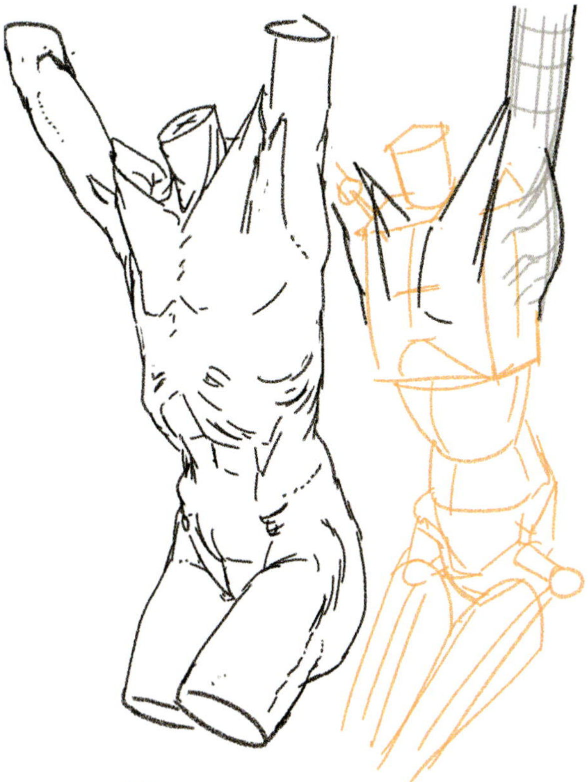

J

muscles have prominent mass on some figures

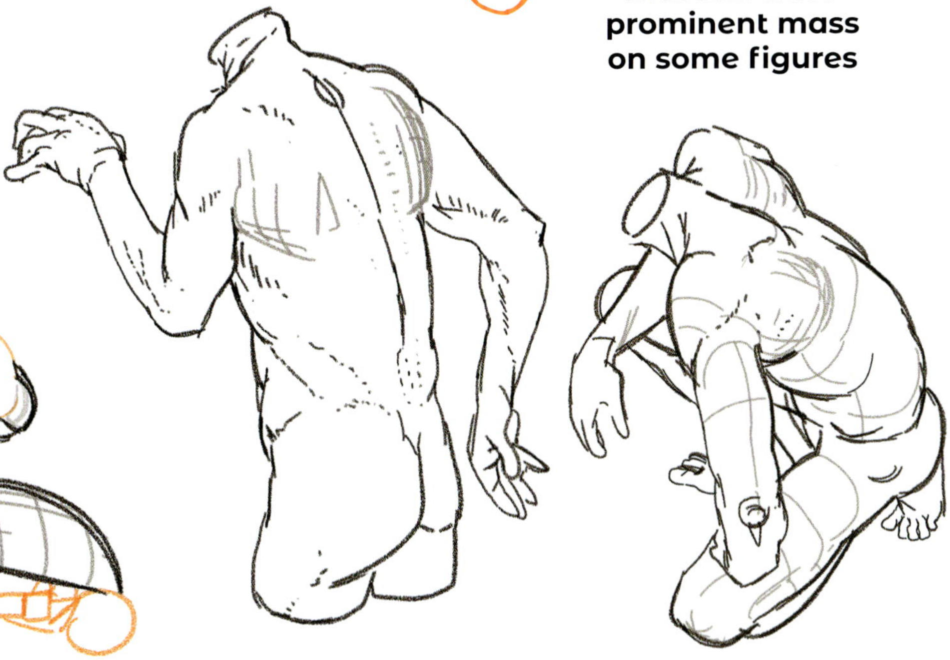

I

typical scapular muscles

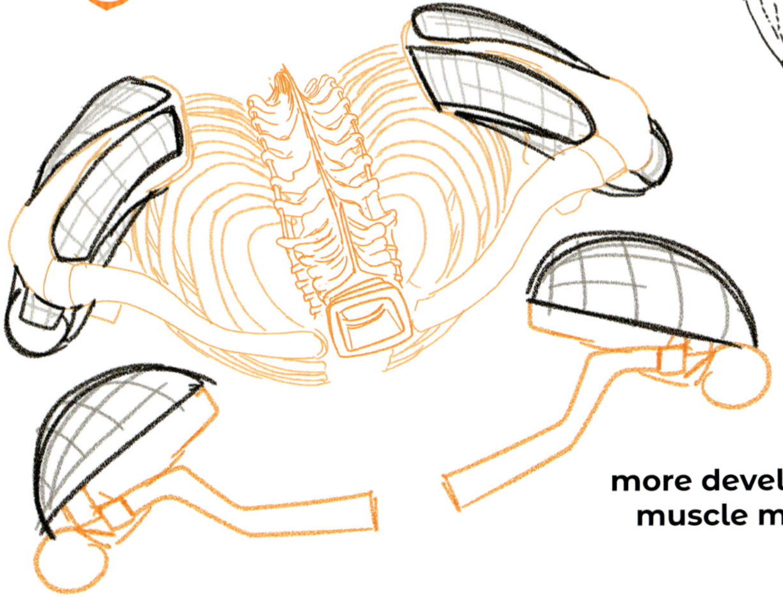

more developed muscle mass

trapezius

The trapezius muscle connects the bottom of the skull to the back and scapulae. Its diamond shape provides great stability to the back by connecting the head to the yoke and spine (A).

Note the strong curvature of the attachment to the head (B). There are three planes on the back of the trapezius where it attaches to the head – it's not a vertical line.

When the shoulders are raised, the trapezius (or "traps") bunches up, creating the illusion of more mass (C).

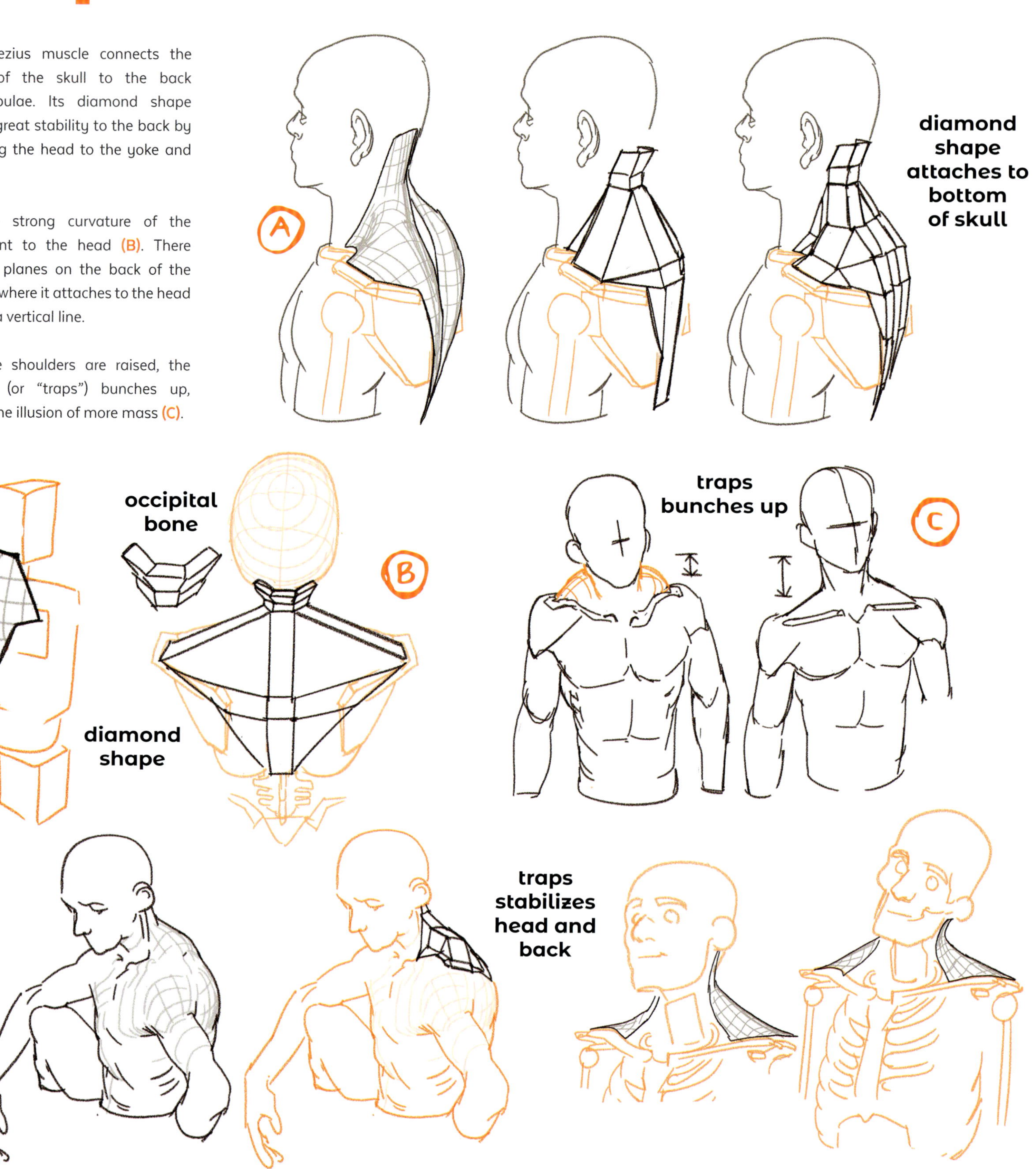

Because the trapezius covers the top of the scapulae, and it angles from front to back (D), we don't see much of it from below. People tend to draw two "triangles" connecting the shoulders to the head, regardless – even for poses and angles where those forms wouldn't be visible (E). As always, make sure you consider the angle from which you are viewing the subject.

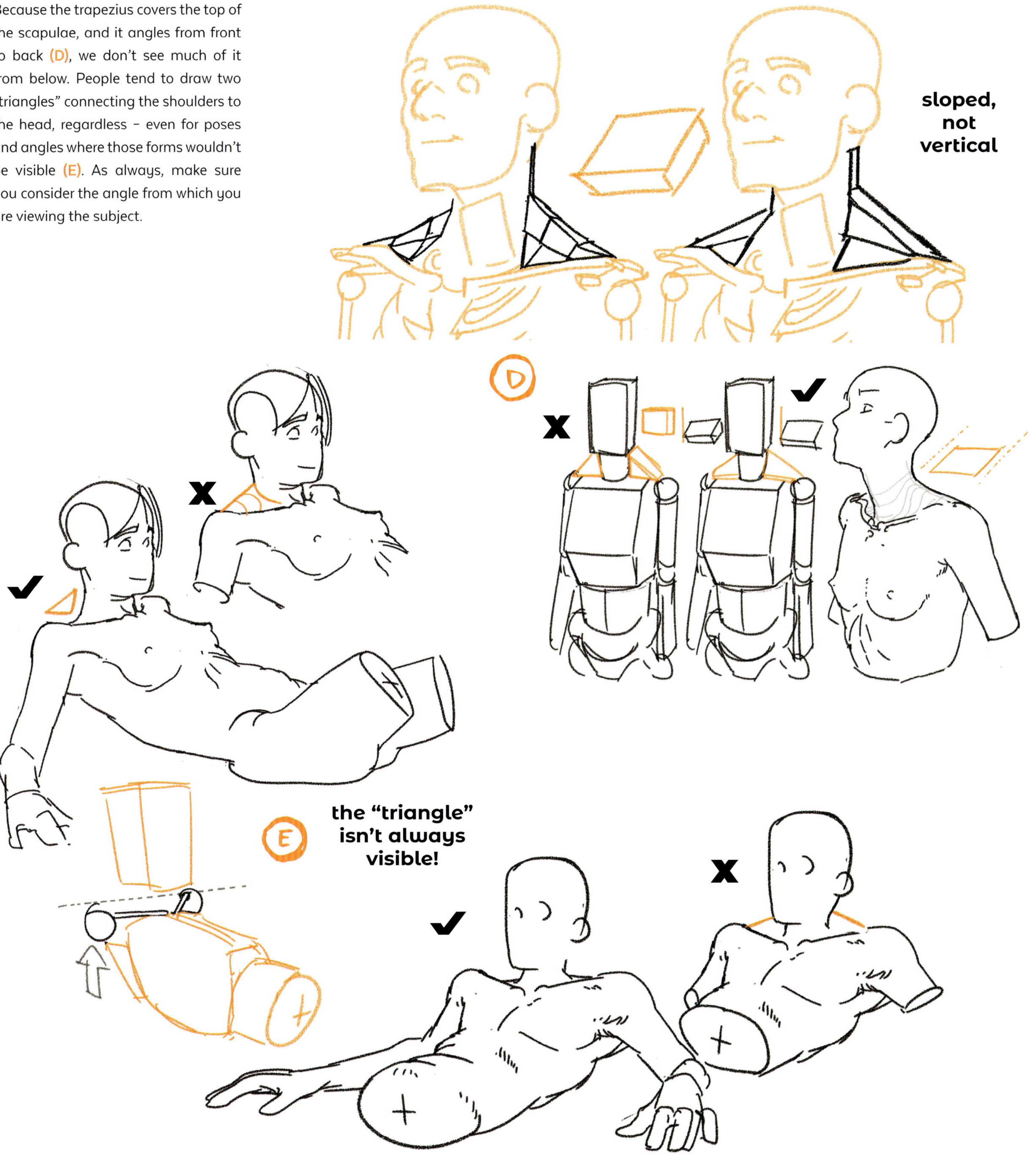

We have our diamond shape (F), so let's now carve a ridge down the center, giving us the gap where the trapezius attaches to the spine. The result is a diamond that's divided vertically (G). Next we add complexity by showing that the attachments to the acromion process (the shoulders) are flatter and have less volume than the central sections (H).

Now let's imagine taking two paddles and pushing in those sections surrounding the spine, around halfway down (I). The trapezius is more tightly bunched here, between the volumes of the scapulae and all its covering muscles. The curvature of this whole area matches the curvature of the rib cage, shown by the planes 1, 2, and 3.

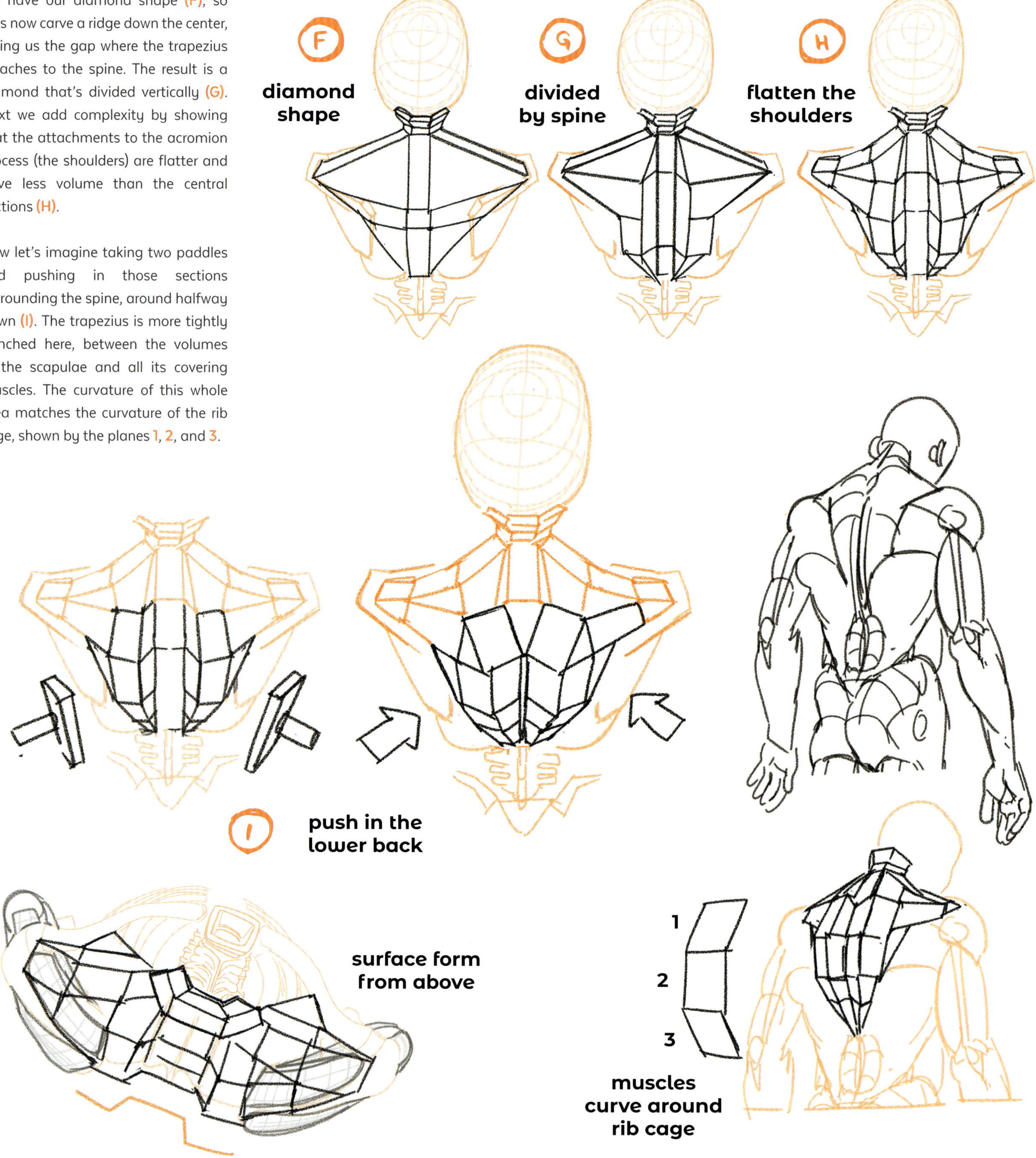

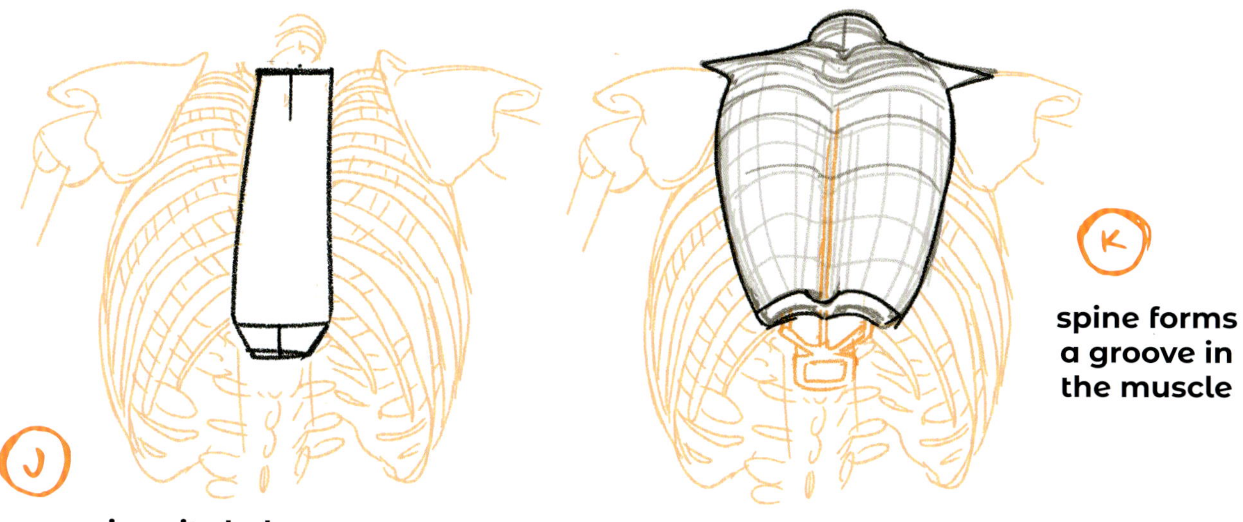

L

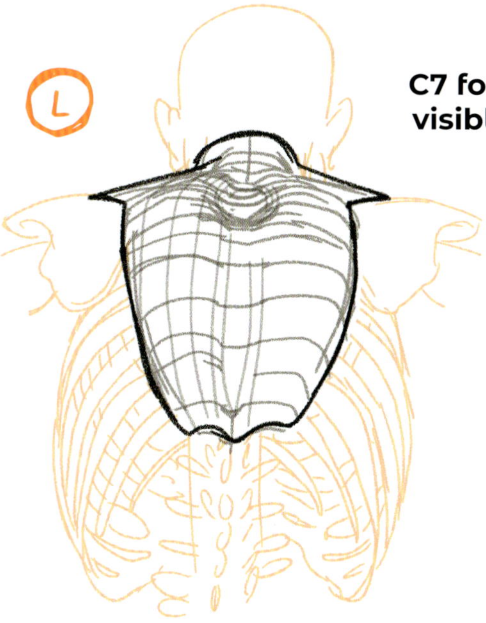

C7 forms a visible dip

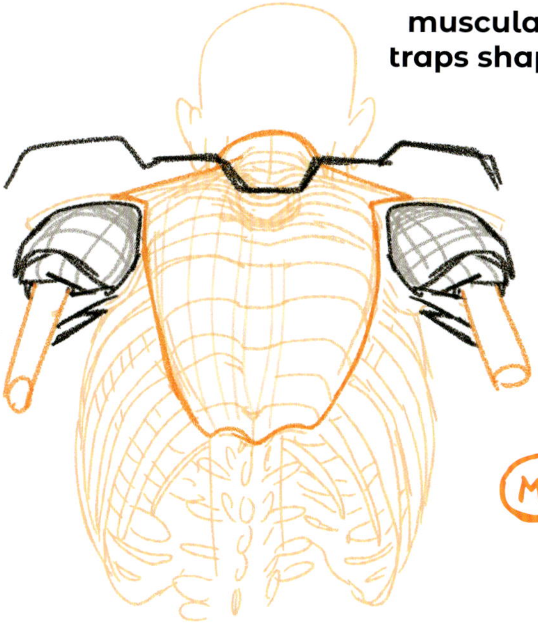

muscular traps shape

M

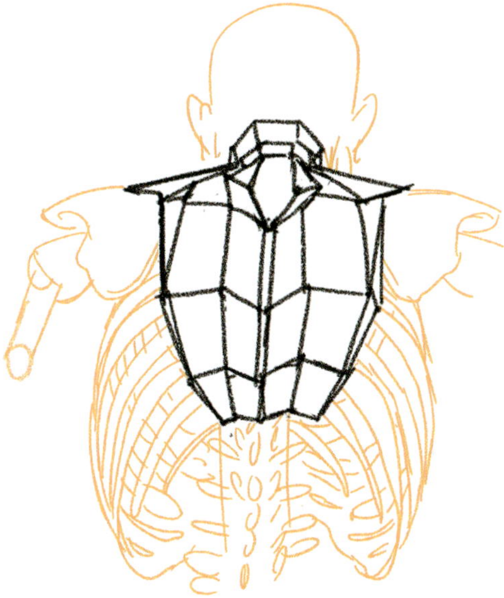

N

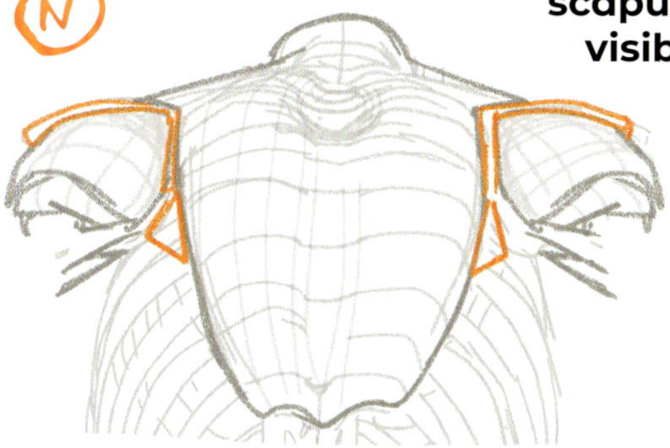

spine of the scapula is visible

When simplifying the trapezius, remember that the spine is a wedge occupying the space between the ribs at the back (J). We know from page 133 that the spine also has three ridges. When we lay the trapezius over it, the largest central ridge ends up as a groove due to the thick muscles covering it (K). This happens often throughout the body – bony projections become dips in the layers of muscle.

In L, you can see a depression in the thickness of the trapezius. This occurs around the seventh cervical vertebrae or "C7." The C7 is the largest vertebra at the bottom of the neck, but all you really need to know is that it's just above the scapulae!

In M we see the cross-section of the back when at rest in a muscular individual. More athletic people tend to have more developed scapular muscles, which can become very prominent. Note the double step down toward the spine. We will also usually see the spine of the scapula (N), as it has no muscle directly covering it.

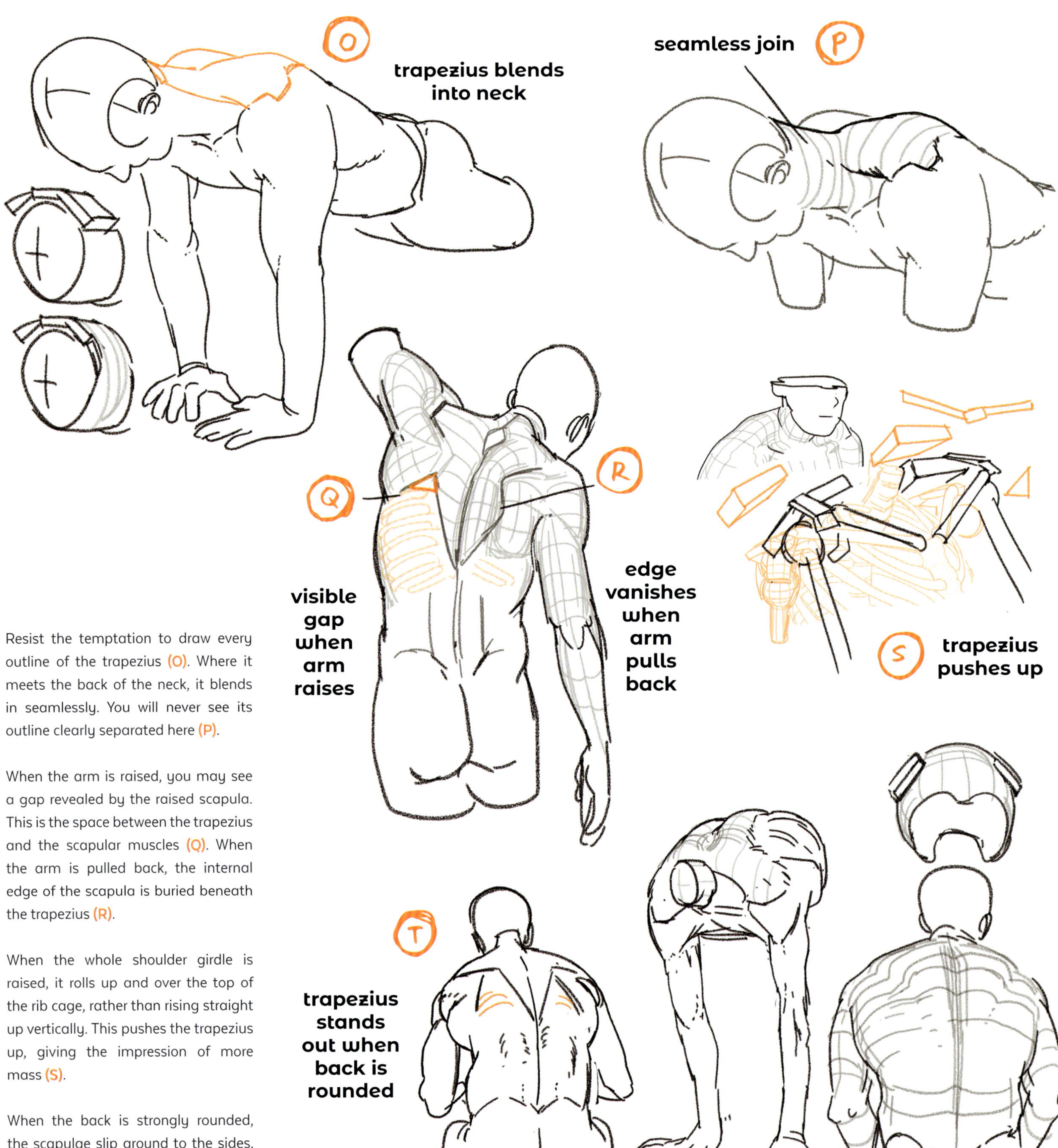

Resist the temptation to draw every outline of the trapezius (O). Where it meets the back of the neck, it blends in seamlessly. You will never see its outline clearly separated here (P).

When the arm is raised, you may see a gap revealed by the raised scapula. This is the space between the trapezius and the scapular muscles (Q). When the arm is pulled back, the internal edge of the scapula is buried beneath the trapezius (R).

When the whole shoulder girdle is raised, it rolls up and over the top of the rib cage, rather than rising straight up vertically. This pushes the trapezius up, giving the impression of more mass (S).

When the back is strongly rounded, the scapulae slip around to the sides, leaving a space between the trapezius and the scapulae (T).

The scapulae rise and rotate forward when the back is in such a rounded pose (U). You can see how the raised scapulae push the mass of the trapezius up, creating a clear form on top (V). When this happens, we should round out the top of the trapezius, eliminating the sloped triangular angles we saw earlier (W).

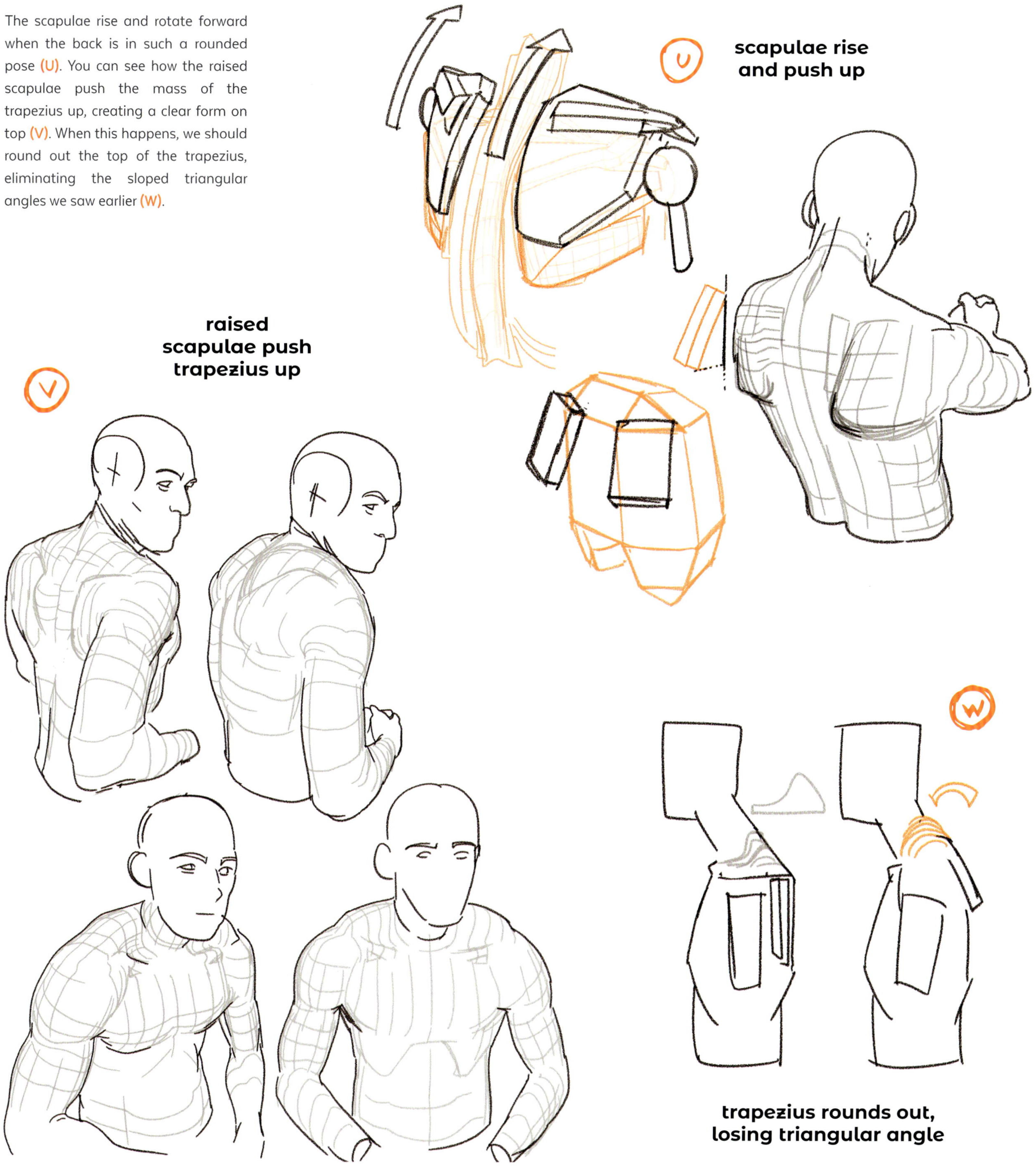

drawing breasts

When drawing breasts, clearly visualize the rib cage's shape beneath. Avoid drawing "car headlight" breasts that both face directly forward (A). The rib cage is rounded, so we should instead aim to separate the breasts out, making them point away from the sternum (B). Next, apply the weight of gravity to pull their forms downward (C). The greater the mass of the breasts, the more obviously they will be affected by gravity. As they are such rounded forms, we will usually see very little in terms of edges, so just like when drawing the jaw, less is always more. In steps 1 to 3, we first draw the rib cage and body, then add cross contours (taking gravity into consideration). Finally, we erase the cross contours so we are left with minimal lines.

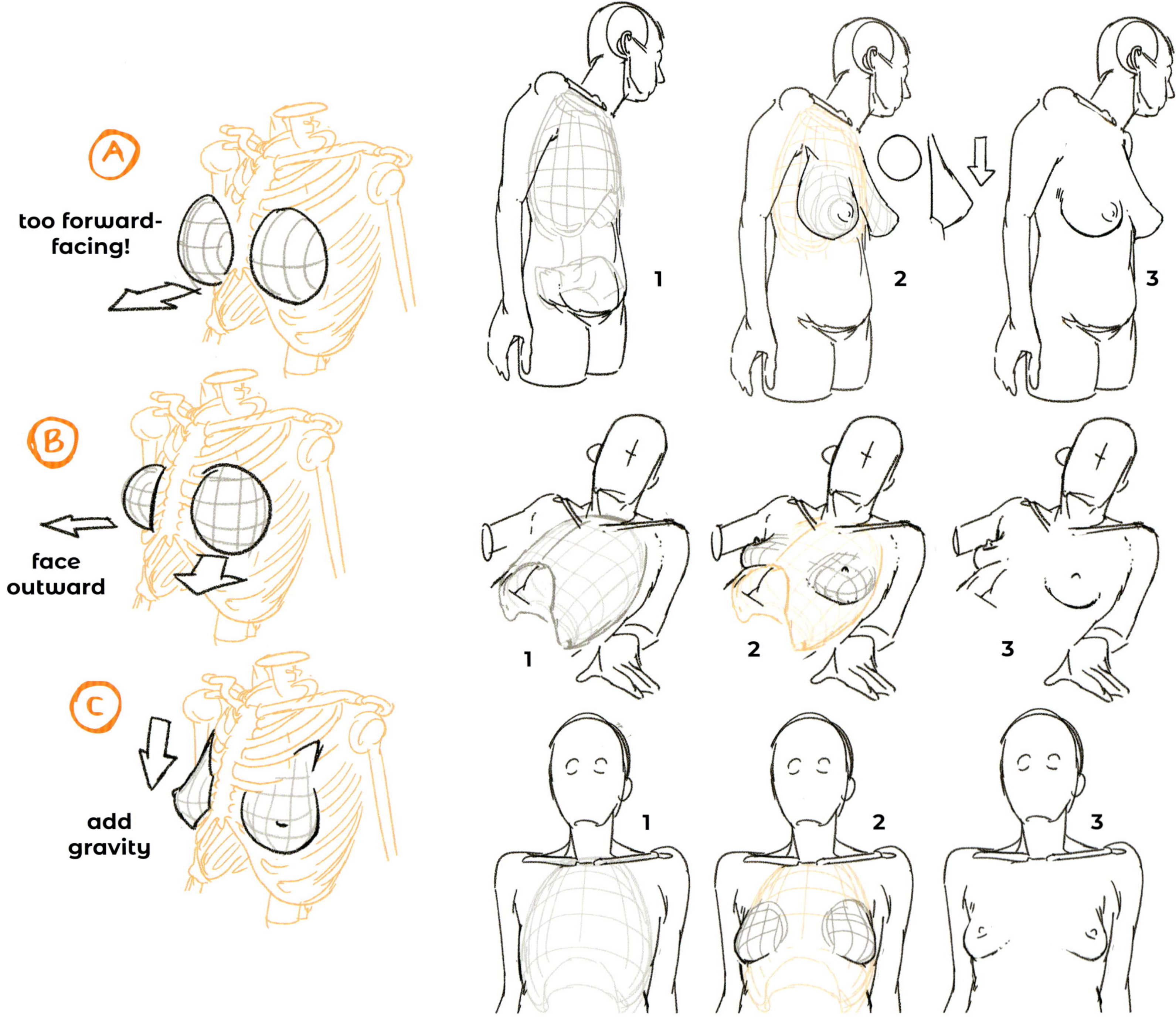

tip: fat & muscle

To repeat once more: Don't draw out all the muscles and muscle striations individually (A)! Give your figures a believable amount of fat around the kidney area and your drawings will look much more believable (B).

When aiming for a successful figure drawing, the most important thing is that the forms look believable as physical elements interacting. If they look real, they will "work" for the viewer, even if the anatomy isn't one hundred percent accurate (C)!

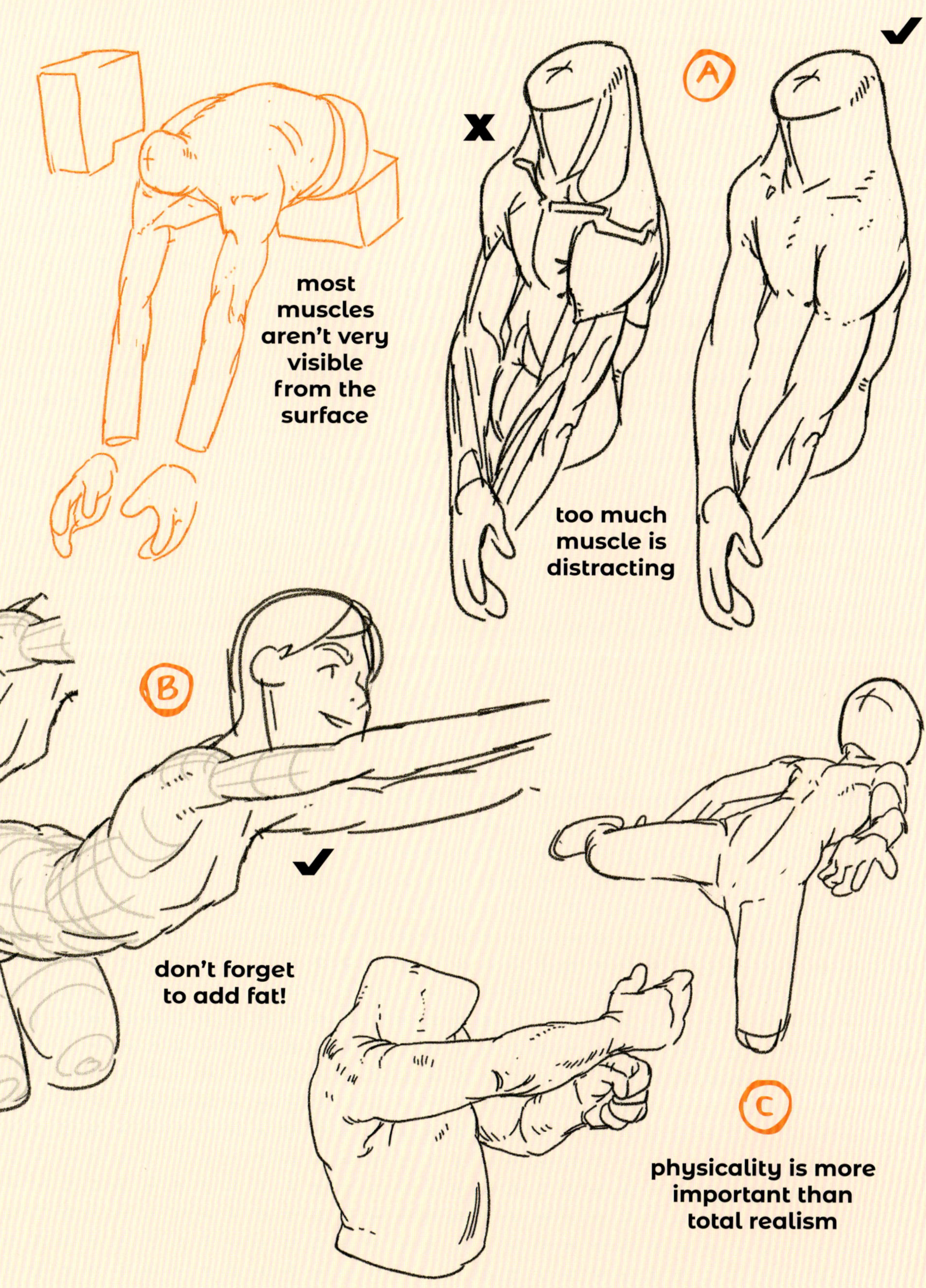

latissimus dorsi

The latissimus dorsi (the "lats") is a large back muscle that attaches to the interior of the humerus, about a third of the distance from the top. It runs down the back and into the top of the pelvis (A, B). It attaches to the spine centrally. The two loose ends attach to the arms. These ends are highly flexible and elastic (C, D).

The latissimus dorsi lies over the bottom section of the scapulae (E). On some people – but not all – it is attached to the scapulae, too.

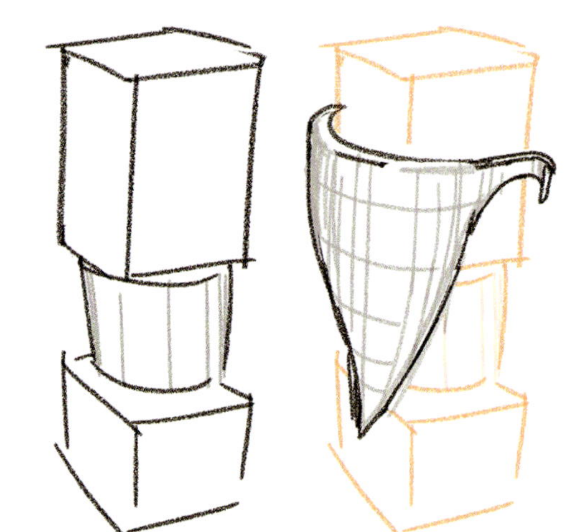

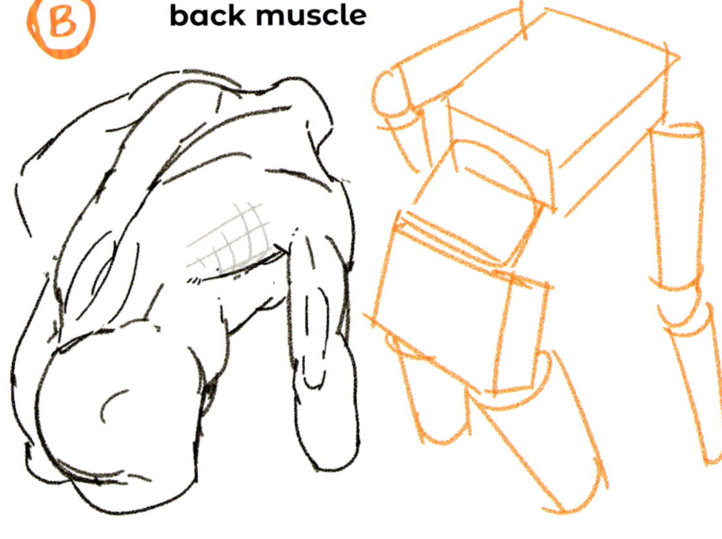

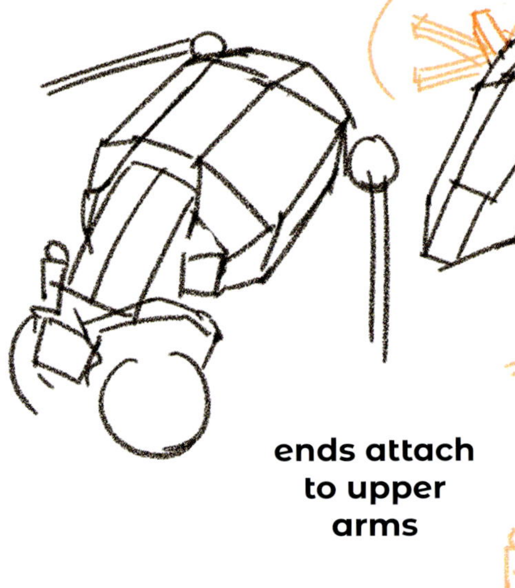

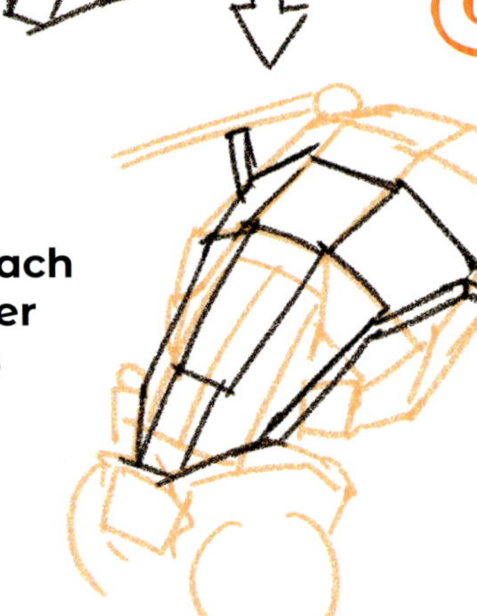

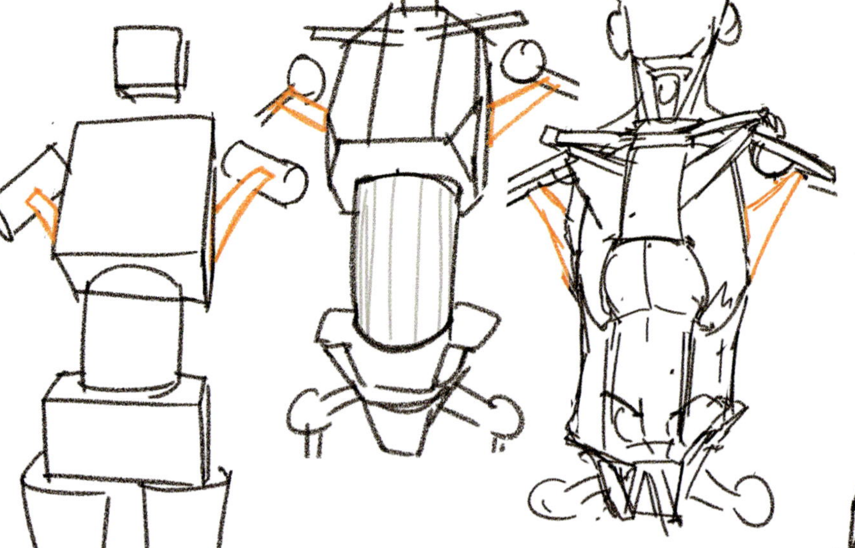

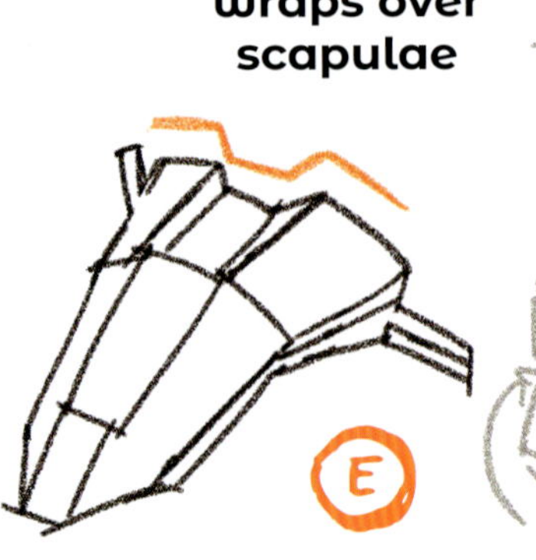

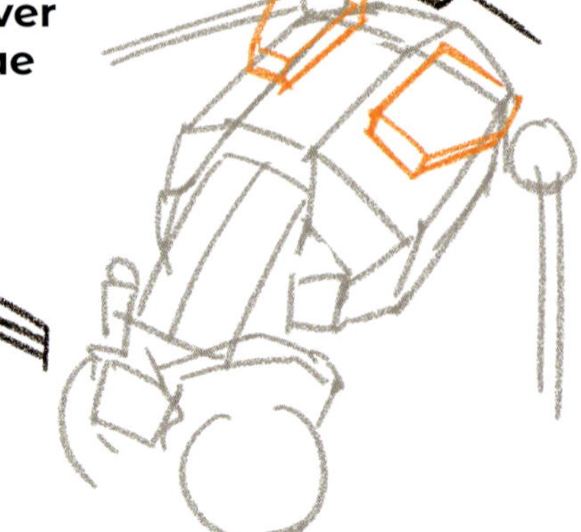

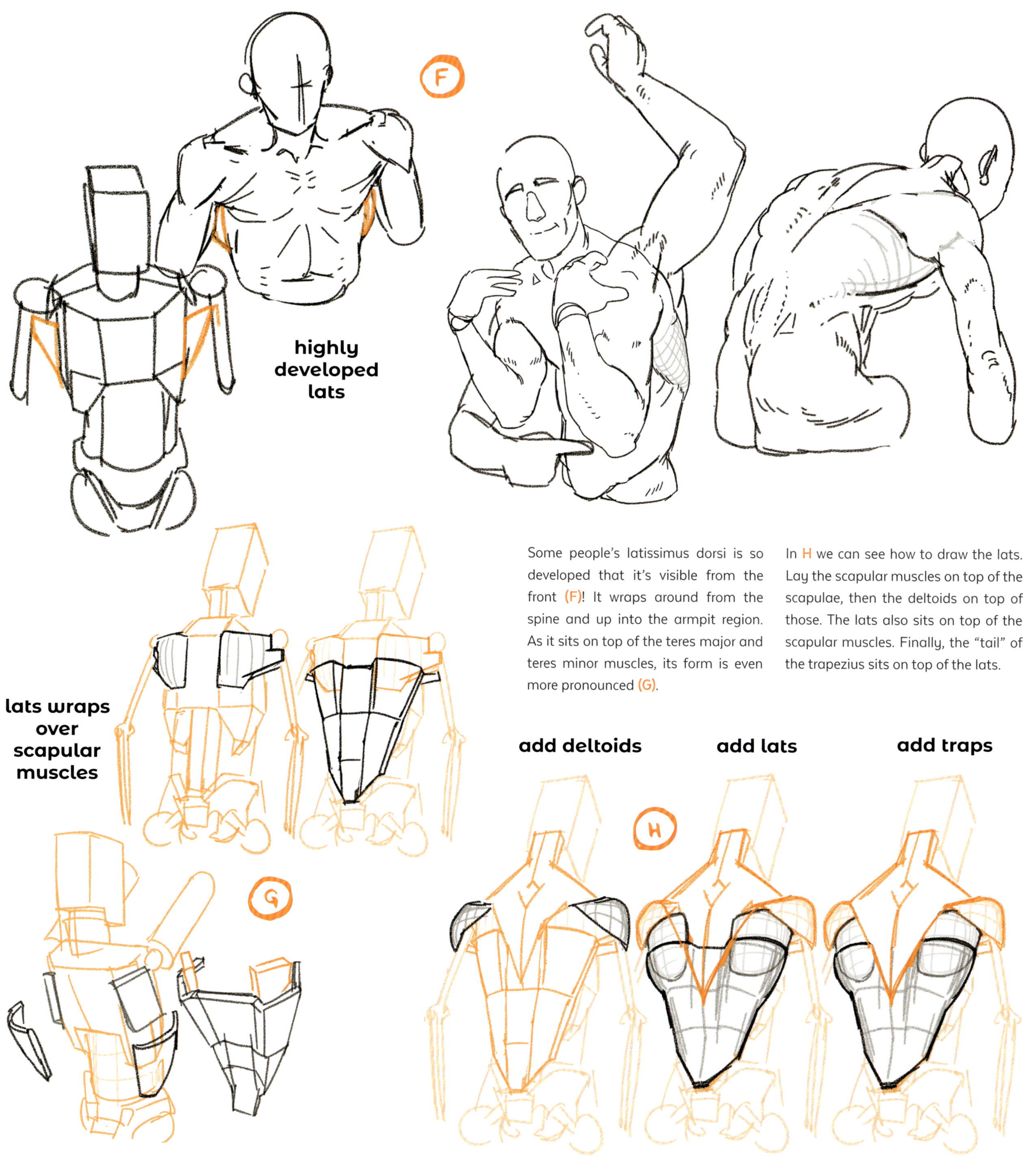

Some people's latissimus dorsi is so developed that it's visible from the front (F)! It wraps around from the spine and up into the armpit region. As it sits on top of the teres major and teres minor muscles, its form is even more pronounced (G).

In H we can see how to draw the lats. Lay the scapular muscles on top of the scapulae, then the deltoids on top of those. The lats also sits on top of the scapular muscles. Finally, the "tail" of the trapezius sits on top of the lats.

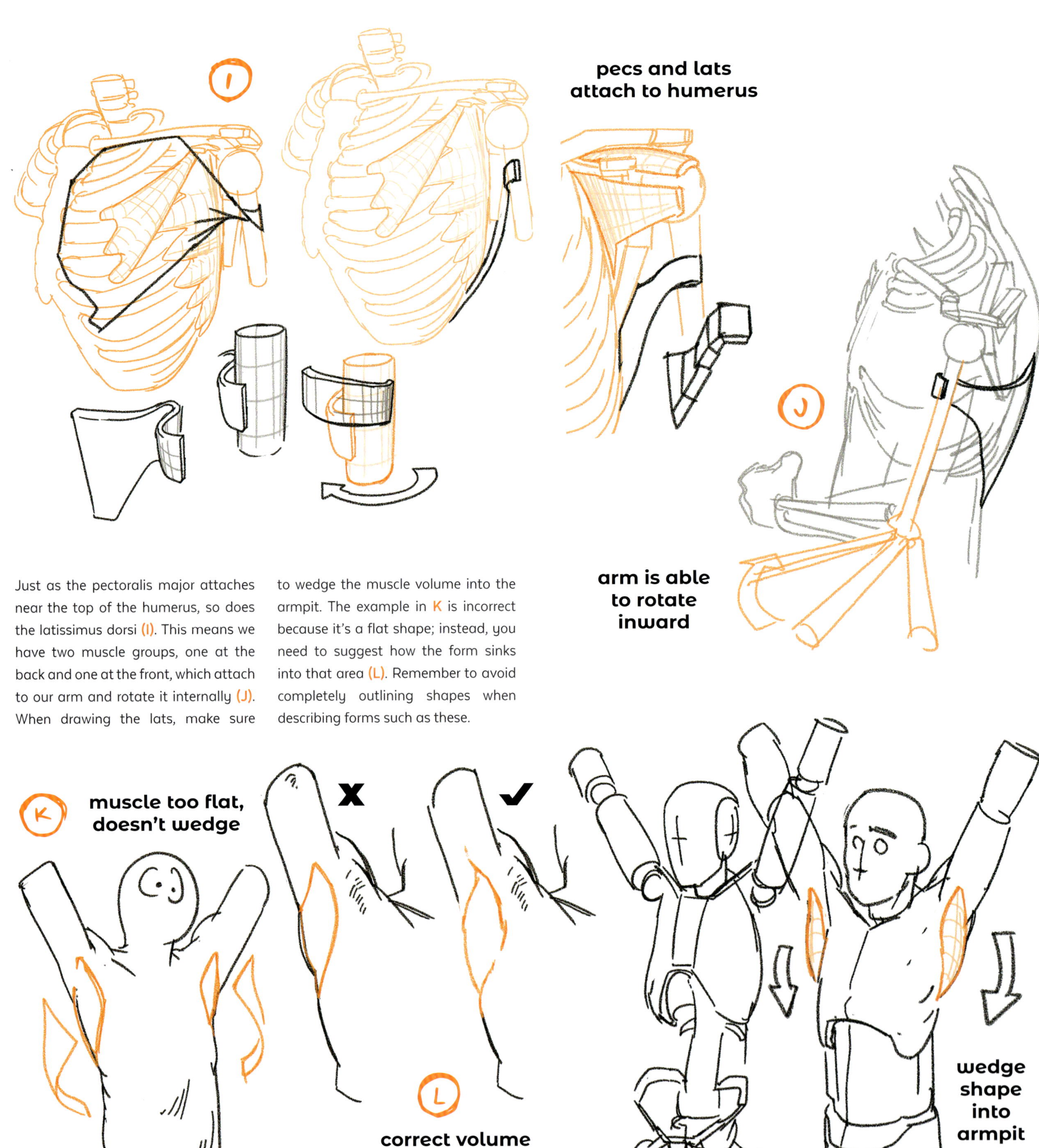

Just as the pectoralis major attaches near the top of the humerus, so does the latissimus dorsi (I). This means we have two muscle groups, one at the back and one at the front, which attach to our arm and rotate it internally (J). When drawing the lats, make sure to wedge the muscle volume into the armpit. The example in K is incorrect because it's a flat shape; instead, you need to suggest how the form sinks into that area (L). Remember to avoid completely outlining shapes when describing forms such as these.

shoulder joint

The position of the shoulder joint (glenohumeral joint) is the most important thing to consider when drawing the upper torso. If you can visualize how high, low, forward, or backward this joint is, you can work out the position of the scapular bones. If you know where those bones are, you can draw the volume of the muscles on top (A)! When the arm is raised, the shoulder joint is higher, causing the scapulae to rotate around the rib cage (B). This causes the lats and scapular muscles to form a bulge visible from the side and front (C).

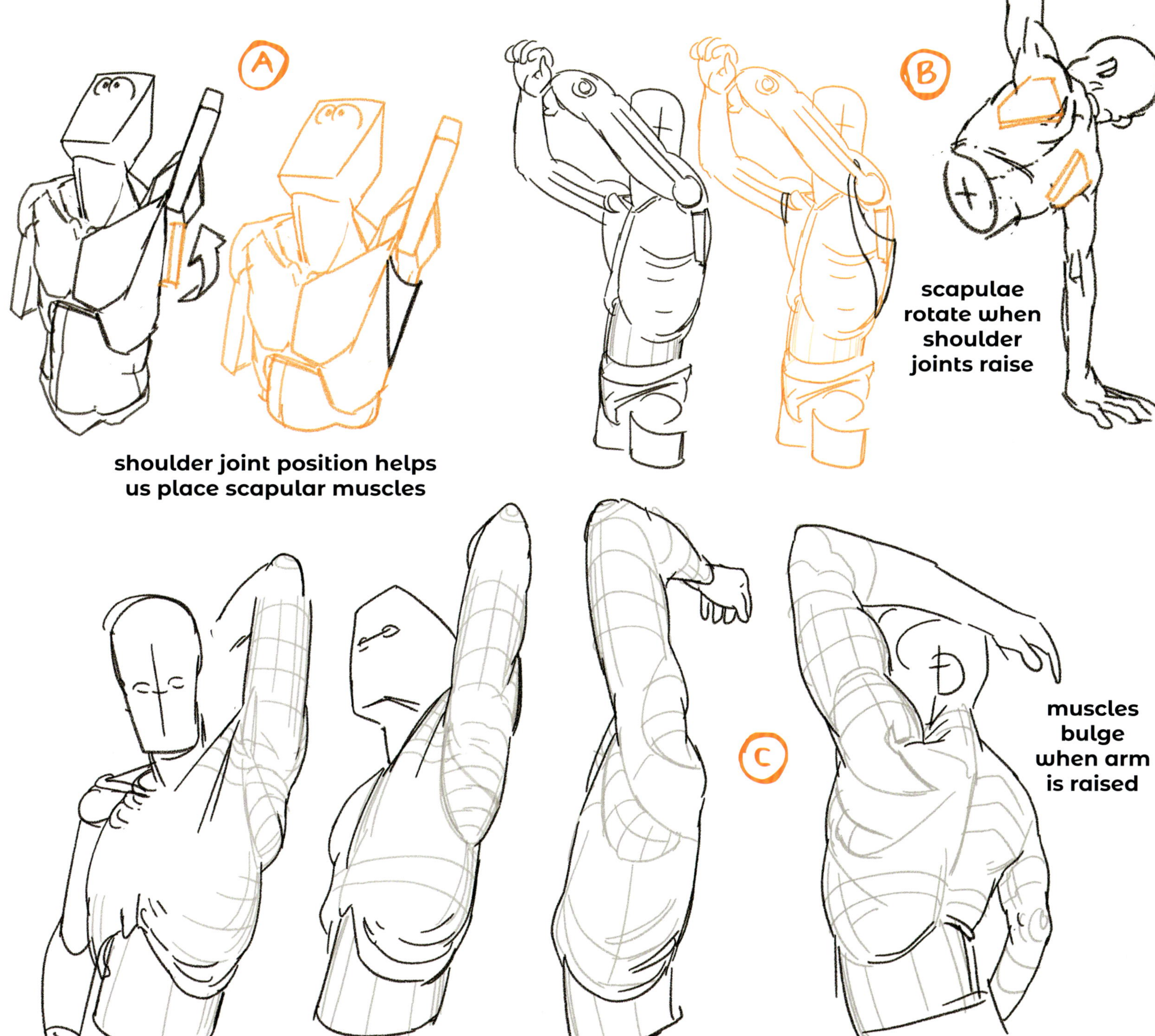

rhomboids

The rhomboid muscles form an upside-down V in the middle of the back and connect the spine to the internal edges of the scapulae (A). The levator scapulae (levator meaning "to raise") attaches to the spine just below the skull and raises the scapulae (B). Both these muscle groups are rarely seen because they're covered by the trapezius, but it's important to know that they're there because of the roles they play. The rhomboids pull our scapulae together. When we retract (pull back) our arms, the trapezius bulges (C), giving the impression that it's doing the pulling. It's doing some of the work, but most of the power actually comes from the rhomboids!

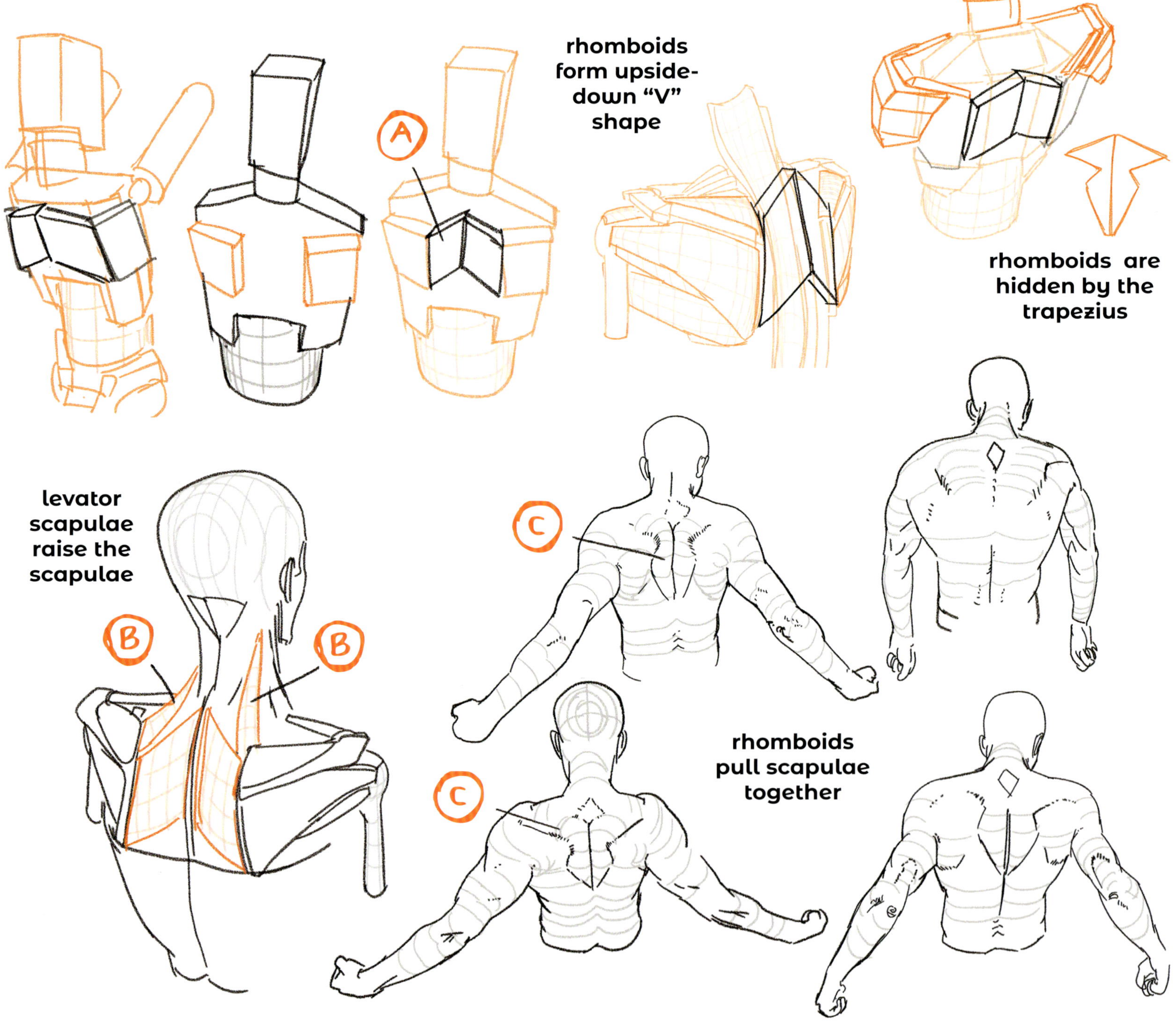

deltoids

The deltoid muscle forms the biggest mass of the shoulder. When simplified, it has three sides from front to back (A). These are angled, sloping down from front to back; they are attached to the acromion process on the scapula, which is also angled backward (B). The result is a sloped, caplike shape that wraps around our shoulder (C).

A common mistake is making the shoulders the widest part of the arm, but they naturally look more like D. Here, the scapular muscles push against the mass of the arm, causing a bulge that's wider than the shoulder. This is very common in people with less-developed shoulder muscles or more-developed backs.

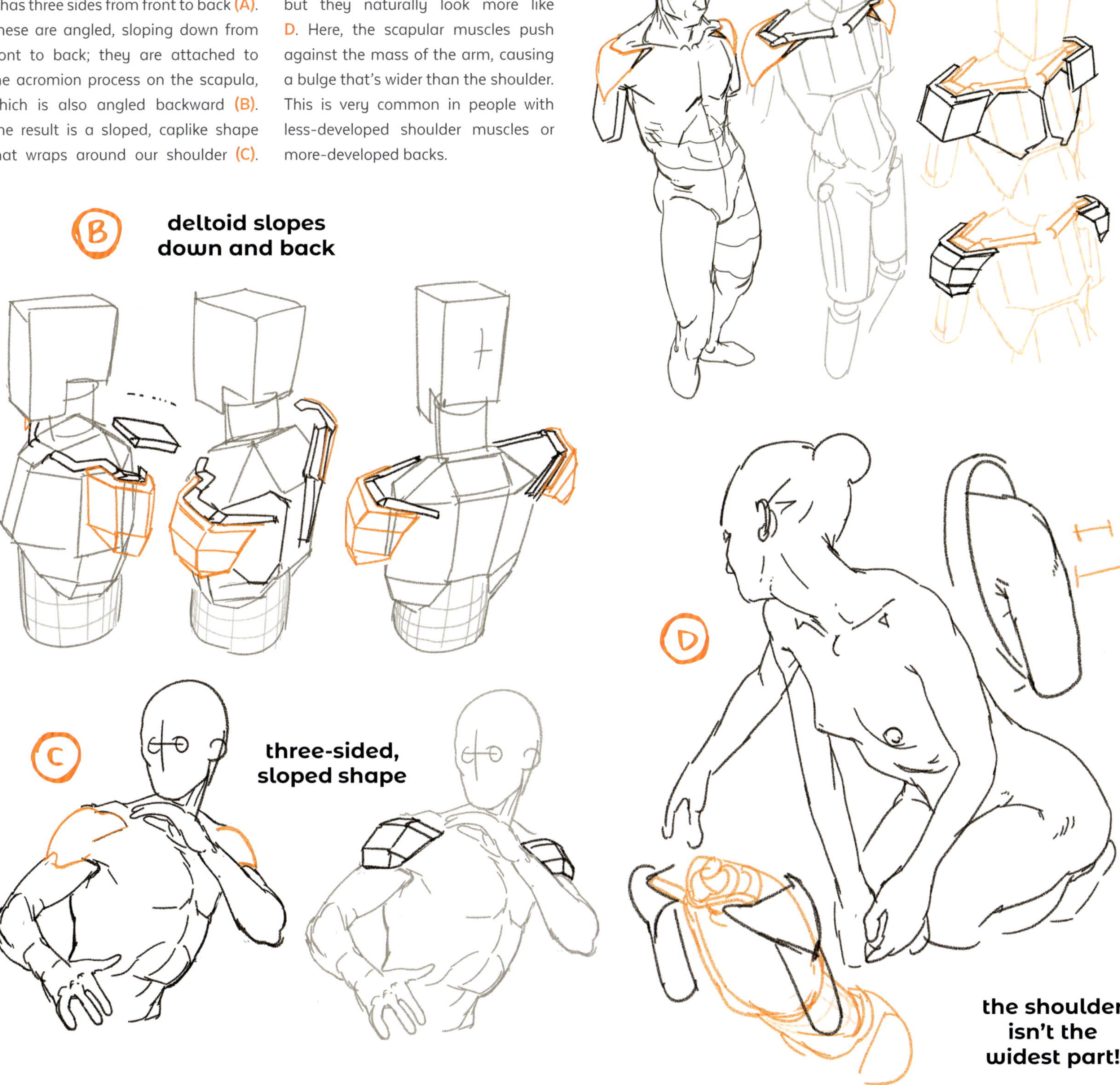

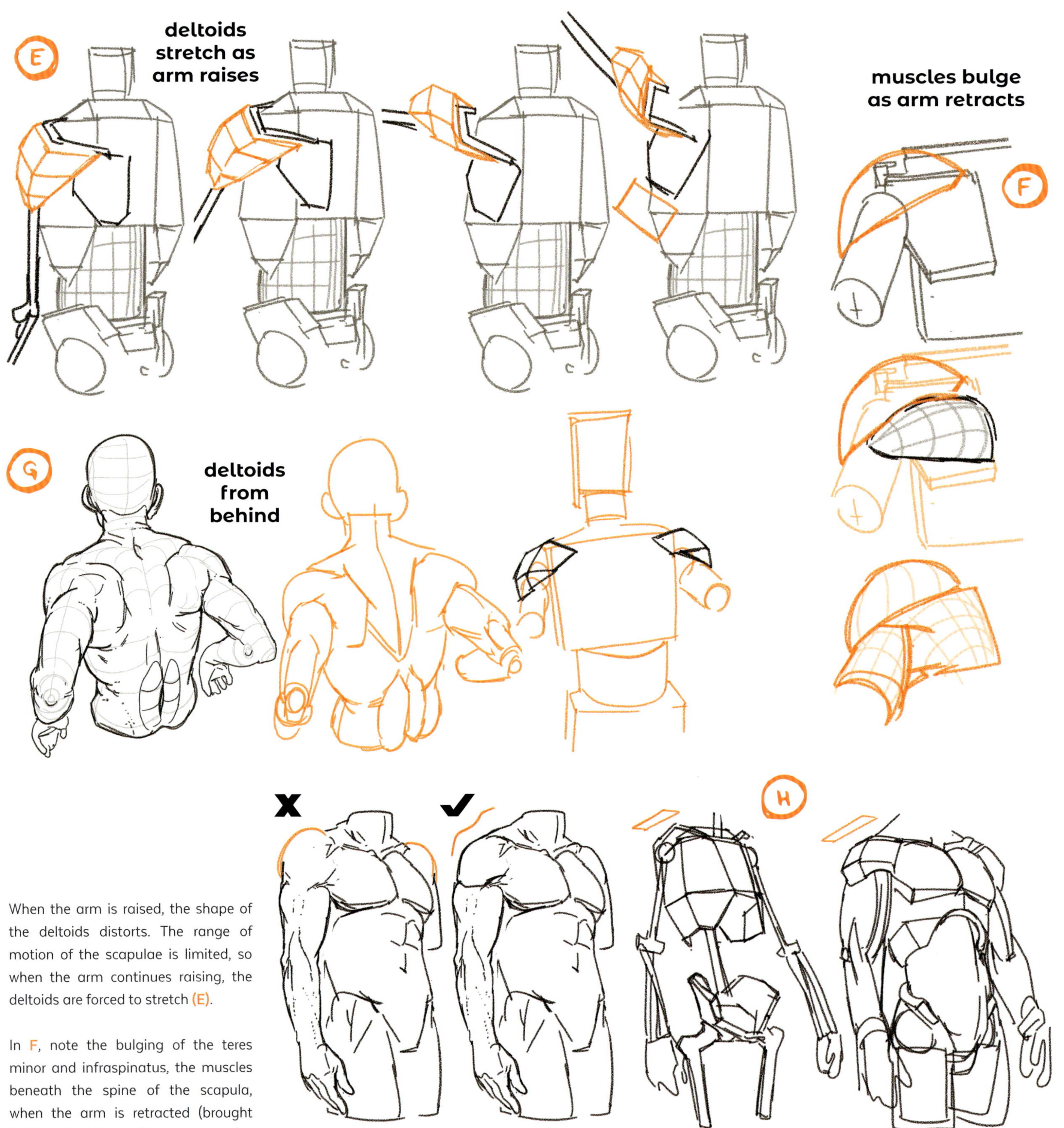

When the arm is raised, the shape of the deltoids distorts. The range of motion of the scapulae is limited, so when the arm continues raising, the deltoids are forced to stretch (E).

In F, note the bulging of the teres minor and infraspinatus, the muscles beneath the spine of the scapula, when the arm is retracted (brought backward). In G and H you can see the front and back view of the deltoid as it wraps over the shoulder.

joining the torso & arm

We'll move on to the upper arm shortly, but for now, let's just imagine that the upper arm itself is a flattened cylinder (A). This shape is a great tool for us, as it allows us to explore the arm's rotation more clearly. The deltoid attaches to the outer third of the clavicle, and then there's a gap between its attachment and that of the pectoralis major. We often see a small groove or triangle in this space (B). The muscles of the shoulder form a cap-like shape over the upper arm (C).

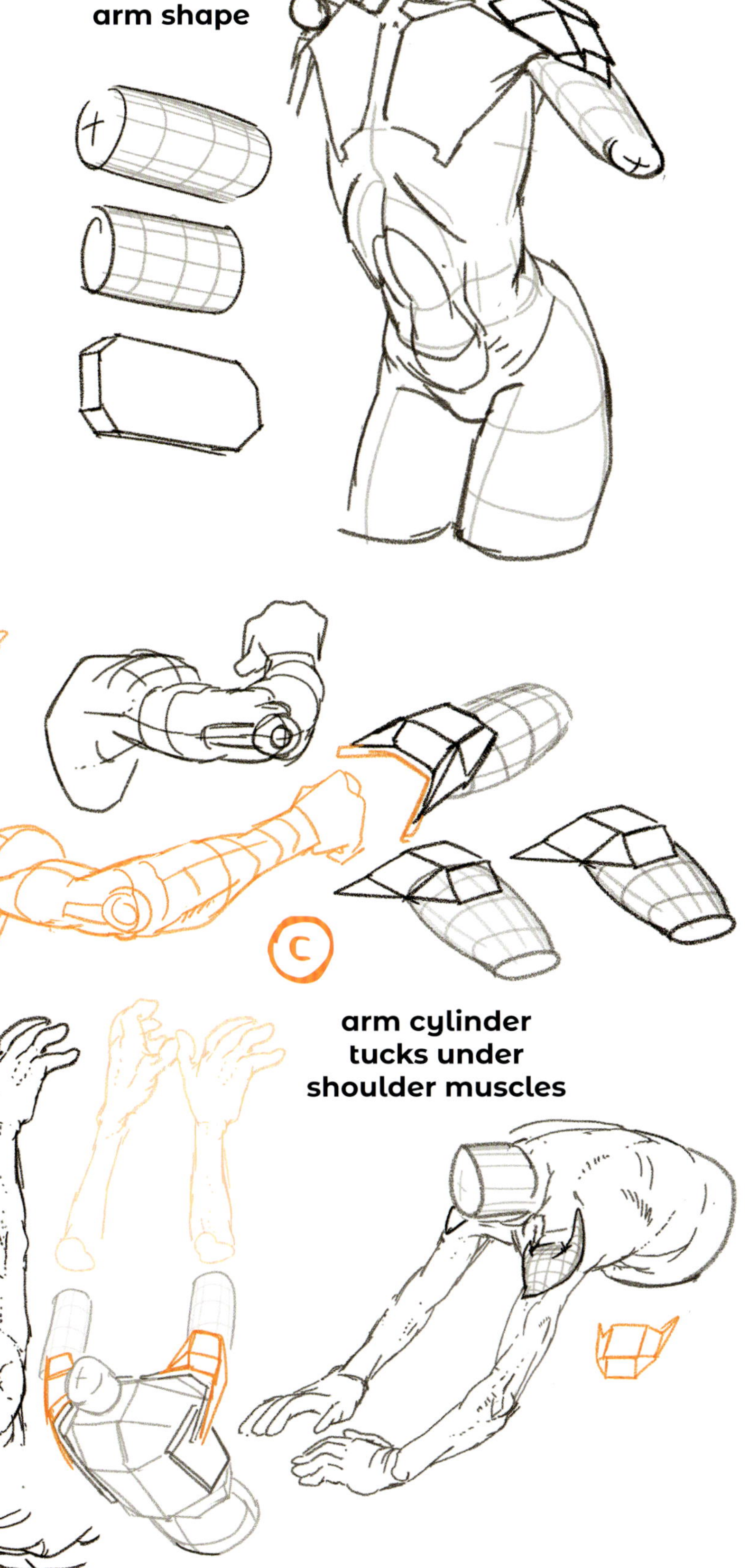

visible groove between muscles

B

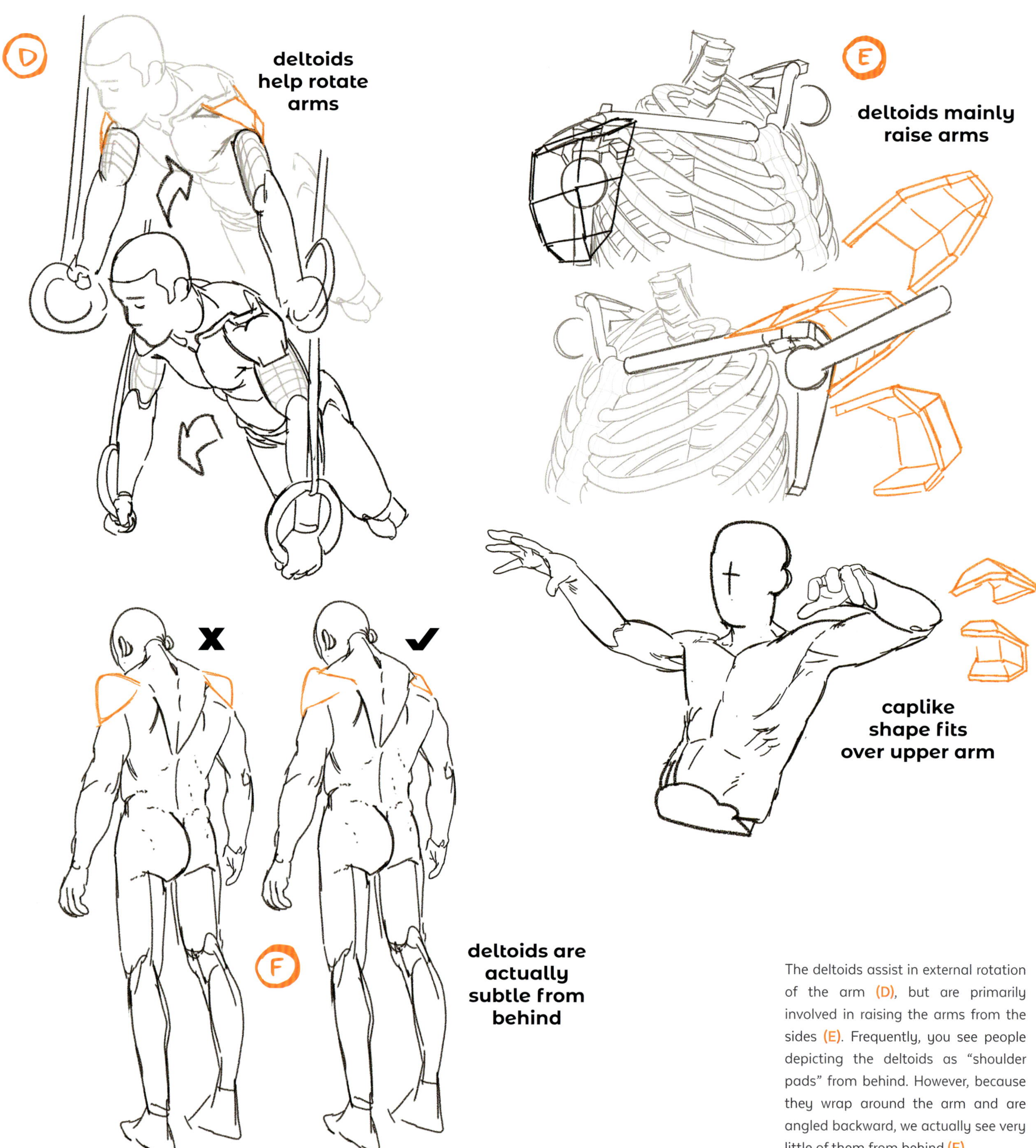

The deltoids assist in external rotation of the arm (D), but are primarily involved in raising the arms from the sides (E). Frequently, you see people depicting the deltoids as "shoulder pads" from behind. However, because they wrap around the arm and are angled backward, we actually see very little of them from behind (F).

When drawing the bottom of the rib cage, consider the level of body fat. For slimmer people, the abdominal section tends to be relatively flattened (C), as there isn't much fat around the kidneys (at the back, either side of the spine). Adding more body fat, the abdominal section becomes rounder, bulging out more at the back in a graceful curve (D). The higher the percentage of body fat, the more the bottom of the ribs is covered (E).

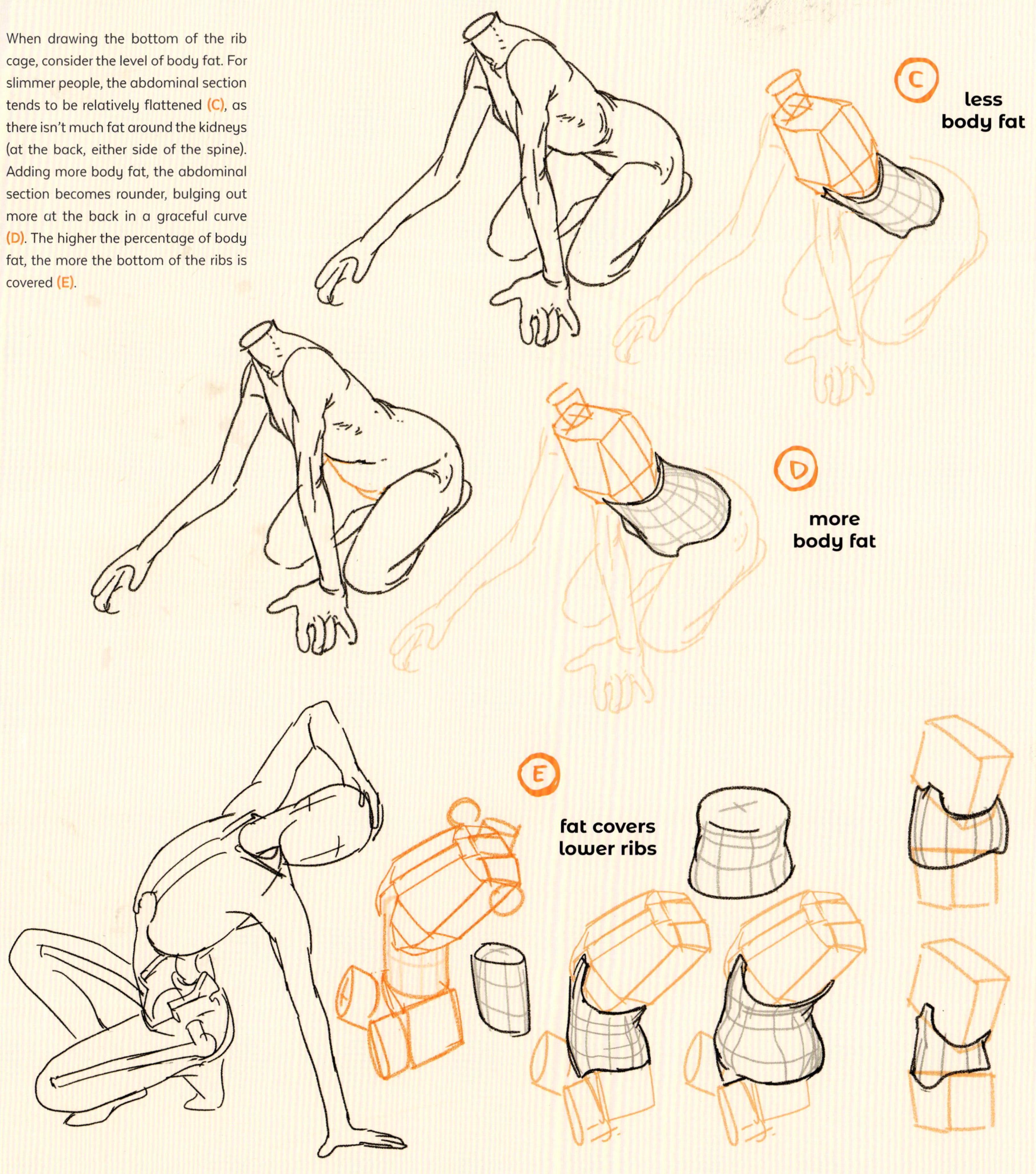

Even if you can visualize the rib cage accurately, it's better not to draw it explicitly. It's more believable to imply the volume, as we see in everyday life. Because our torsos are required to twist and stretch, we have looser skin located around the sides and bottom of the rib cage. This loose skin allows us greater flexibility (F). Use these folds to help describe the bend and stretch in your poses (G). On slimmer people, we often see the ribs at the sides, but you will almost never see them under the arm area (H), where the muscles of the scapula and back wrap around to cover them.

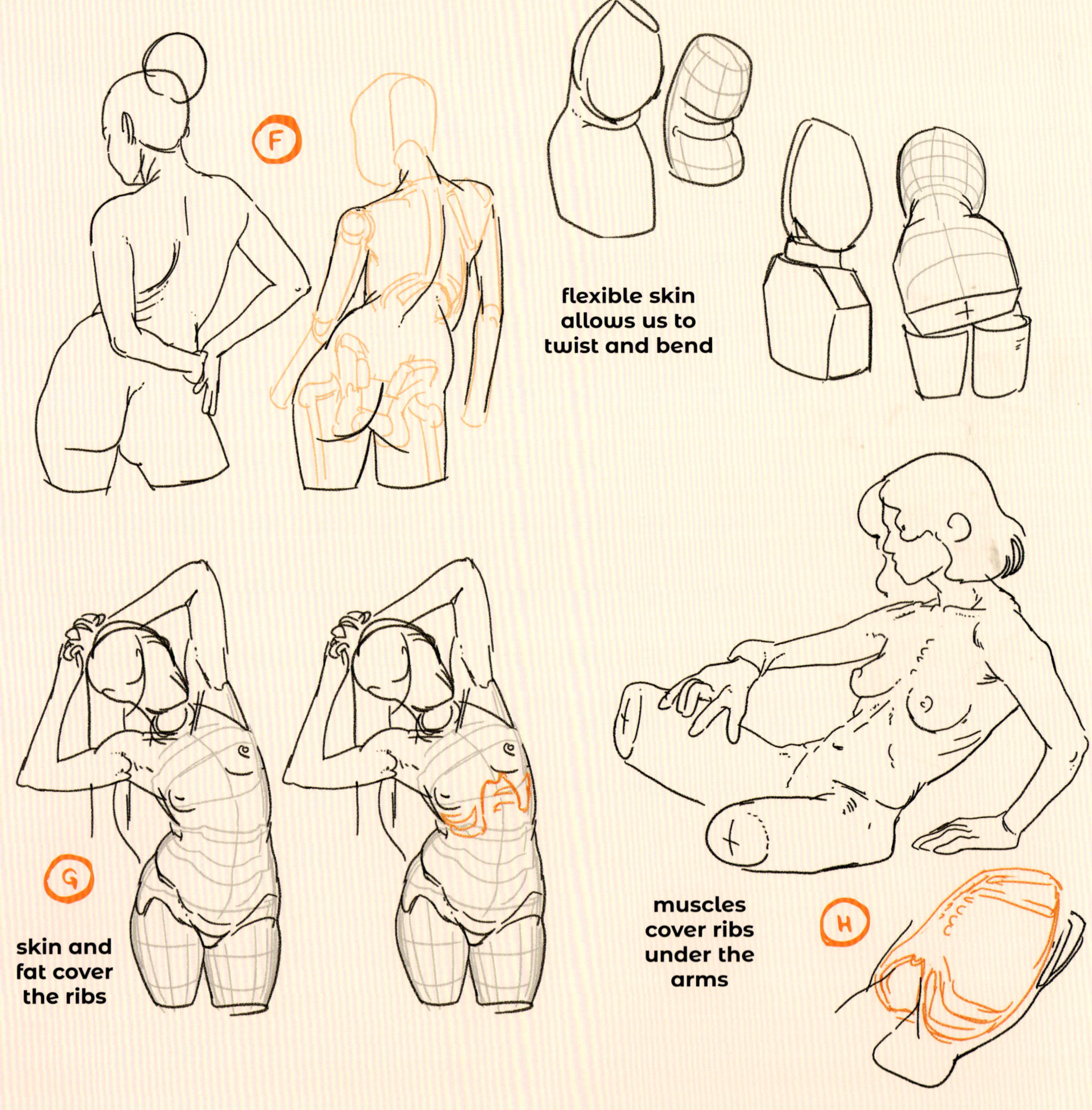

upper torso summary

Let's review the level-of-detail changes to the upper torso so far, and recap the key areas and muscles we've learned. We began with a simple box with spheres for the shoulder joints and cylinders for the arms **(A)**. We then established the rib cage's major planes, angling them out and then back inward **(B)**. We added the yoke of the clavicle and scapulae to create anchors for the arms to pull against **(C)**. We added the pectoralis muscle group to the rib cage, attaching it to the inner two-thirds of the clavicle **(D)**.

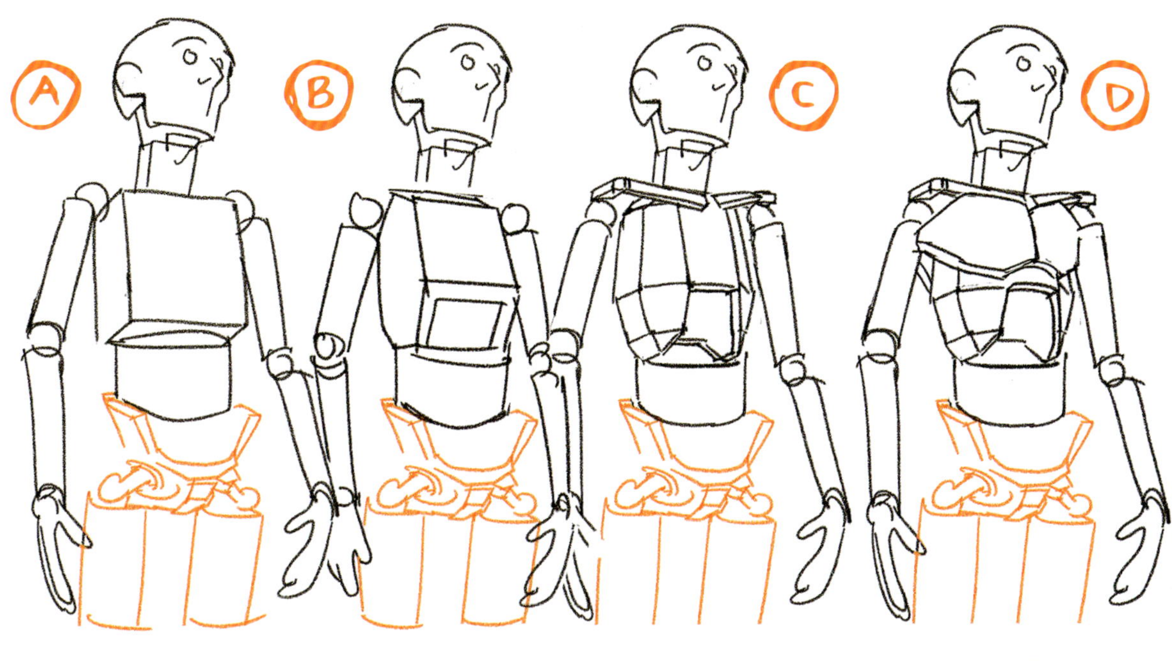

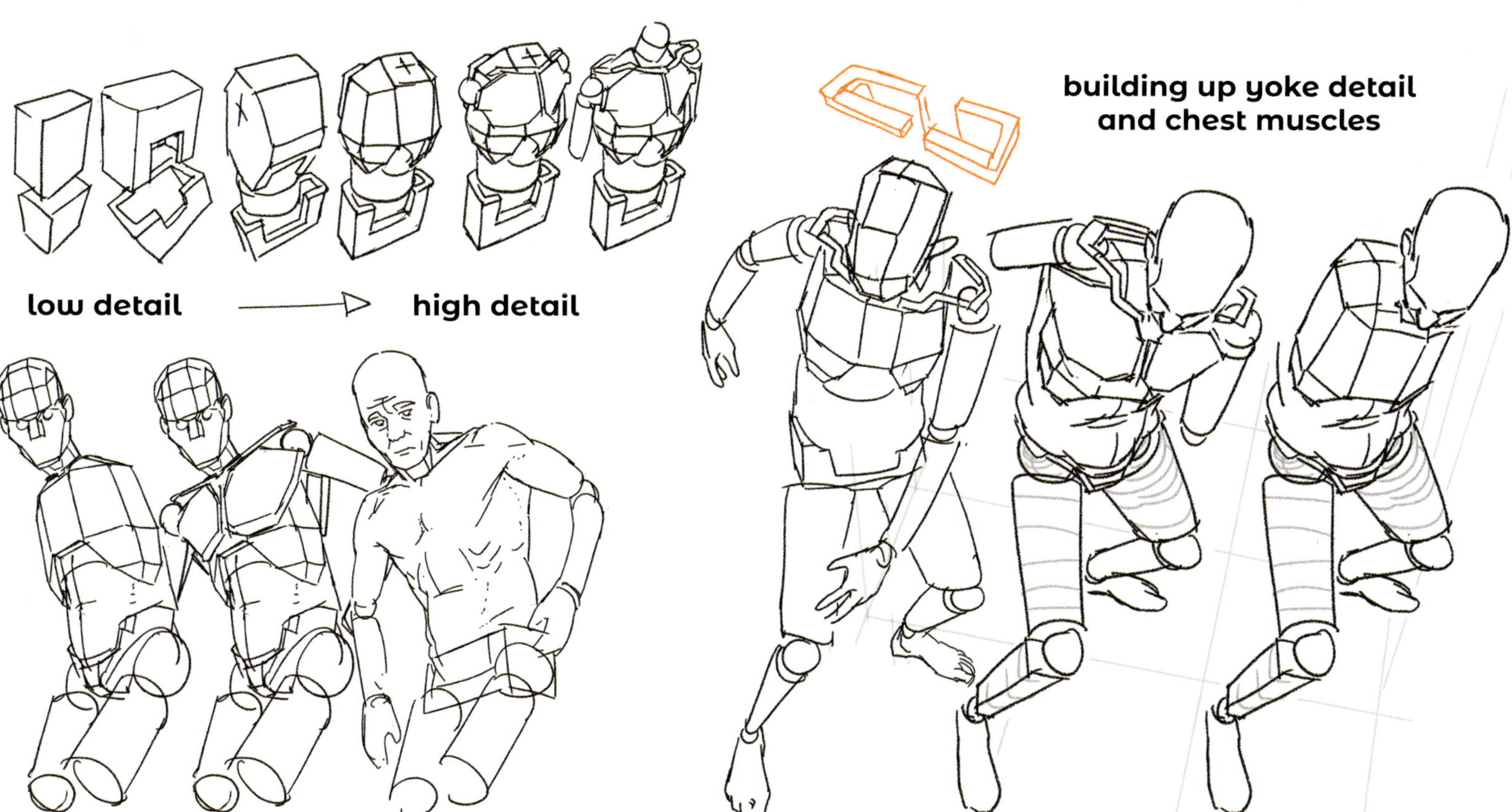

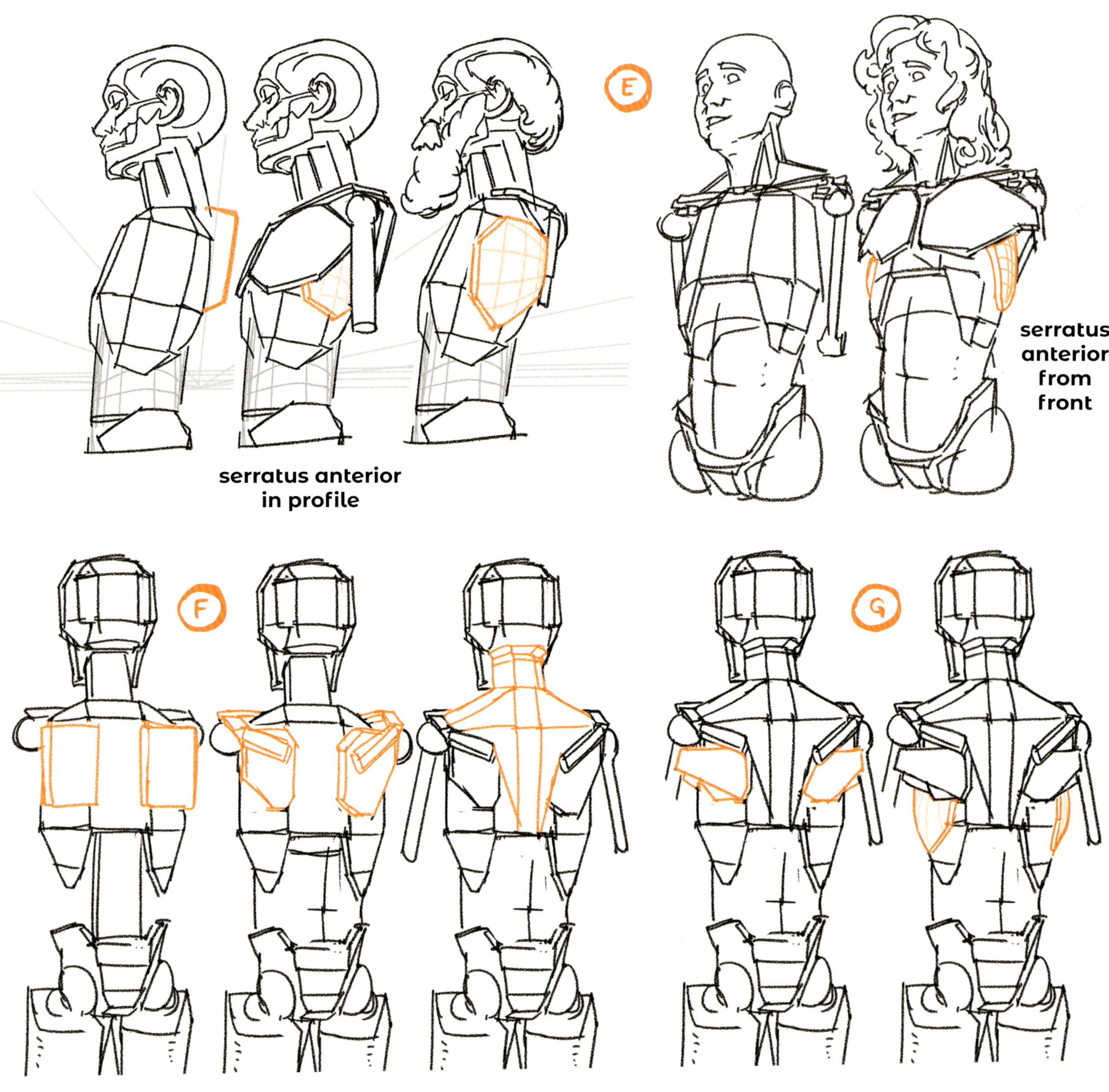

Next, we added the mass of the serratus anterior muscle to the sides of our rib cage form (E). We added the forms of the scapulae to the rear (F).

We covered various levels of detail for the scapulae and saw how the muscles attached to them and wrapped around the head of the humerus (G).

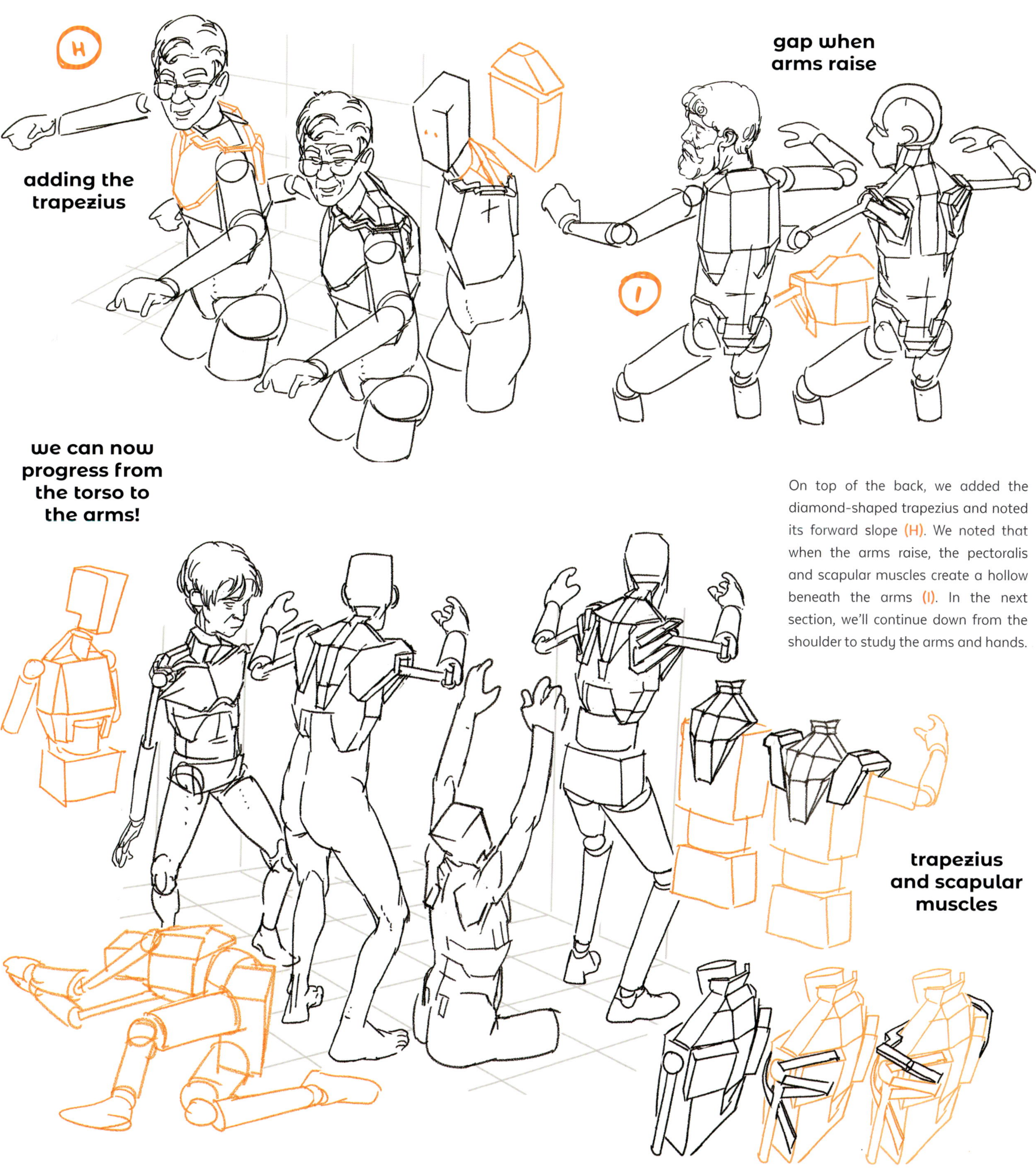

On top of the back, we added the diamond-shaped trapezius and noted its forward slope (H). We noted that when the arms raise, the pectoralis and scapular muscles create a hollow beneath the arms (I). In the next section, we'll continue down from the shoulder to study the arms and hands.

lesson 3:

arms & hands

The arms and hands are intricate mechanisms capable of complex movement, even just for everyday actions! Luckily, like everything else so far, we can break them down into very simple parts for study.

arm bones

Now let's examine the arms and hands. For now, we have two tubes for the arms (A). These actually consist of three bones (B). The top half of the arm is one bone: the humerus (1). The lower arm consists of the radius (2), which attaches directly into the humerus, and the ulna (3). The ulna hinges and the radius twists. To simplify, you can draw them as one shape – a flexible forked shape like C.

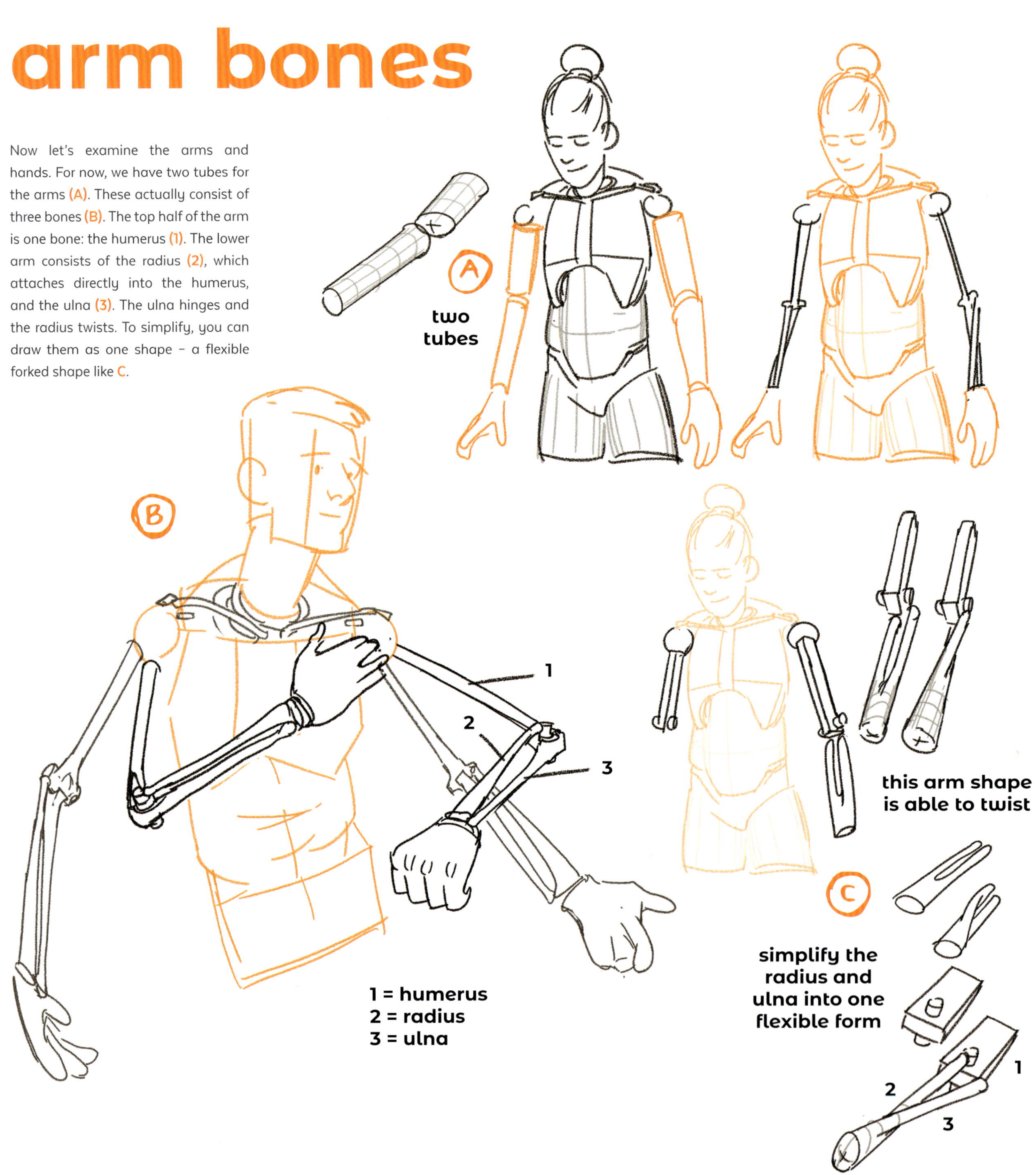

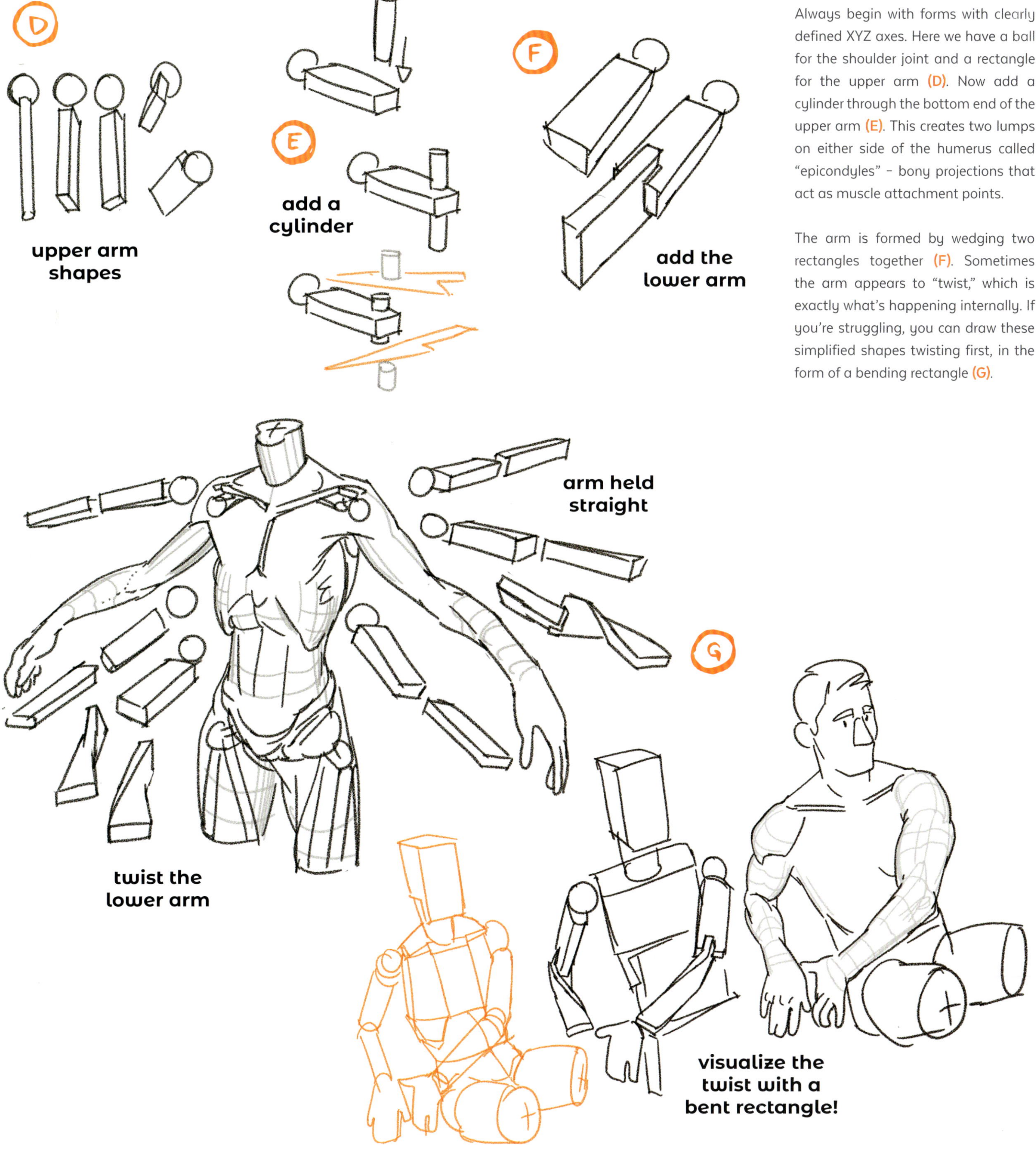

Always begin with forms with clearly defined XYZ axes. Here we have a ball for the shoulder joint and a rectangle for the upper arm **(D)**. Now add a cylinder through the bottom end of the upper arm **(E)**. This creates two lumps on either side of the humerus called "epicondyles" – bony projections that act as muscle attachment points.

The arm is formed by wedging two rectangles together **(F)**. Sometimes the arm appears to "twist," which is exactly what's happening internally. If you're struggling, you can draw these simplified shapes twisting first, in the form of a bending rectangle **(G)**.

The radius attaches to the lateral (meaning "outer") epicondyle. The ulna *doesn't* attach to the medial (meaning "inner") epicondyle. This is important to remember (H).

If you're struggling to draw the twist, try drawing from "point to point." Draw the end of the humerus first, then block in the hand, and then fill in the gaps. This technique makes it easier to visualize the intermediate forms (I). The radius is narrow at the epicondyle and widens toward the hand, while the ulna does the opposite. They are around the same width somewhere in the middle of the lower arm (J).

Imagine the humerus as a rectangle with a sphere on top. The shoulder is a ball-and-socket joint, which makes it highly flexible. The cylinder we added at the distal end (the end farthest from the center of the body) allows the ulna to hinge around it (K). The ulna grips around the humerus like a wrench, hinging up and down with almost no lateral (sideways) movement (L).

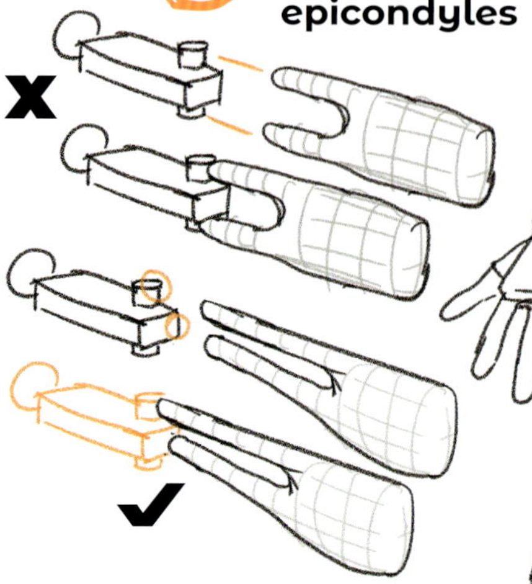

H

don't attach ulna to epicondyles

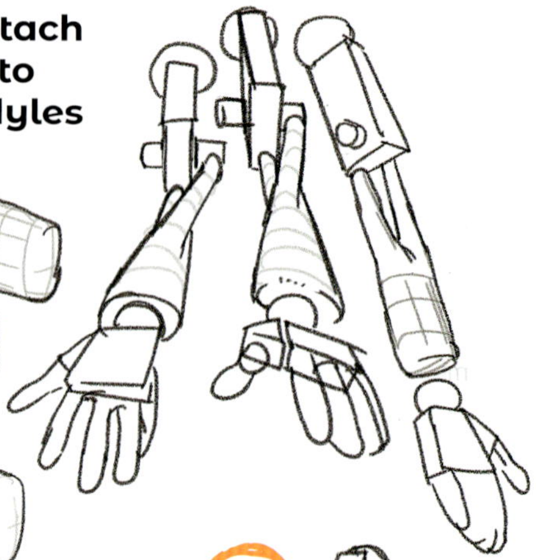

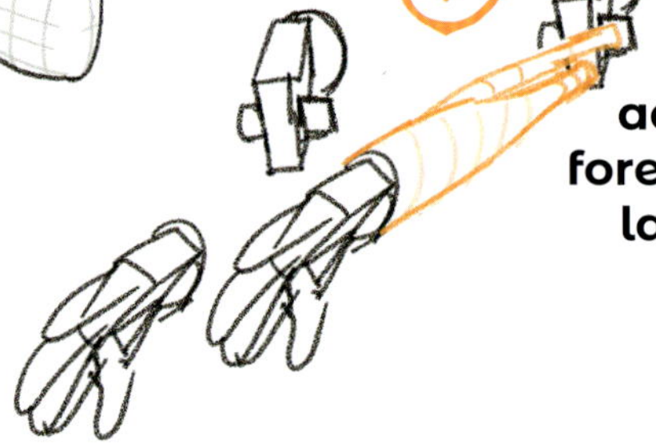

I

add forearm last

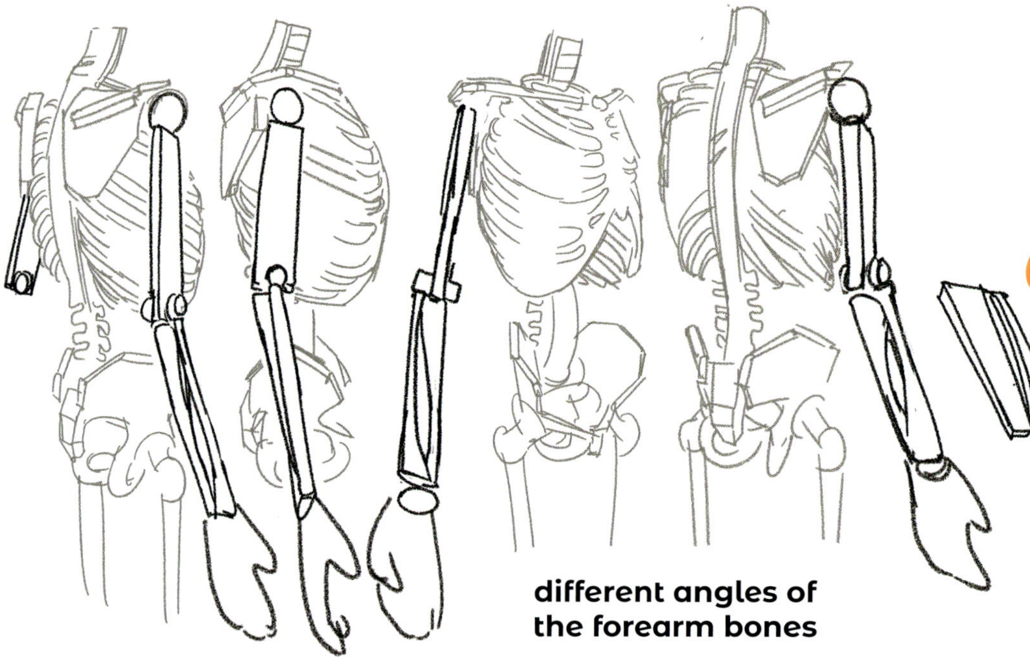

different angles of the forearm bones

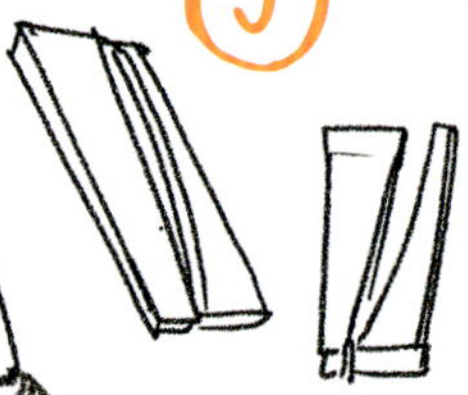

J

the radius is wide at the wrist and the ulna is wide at the elbow

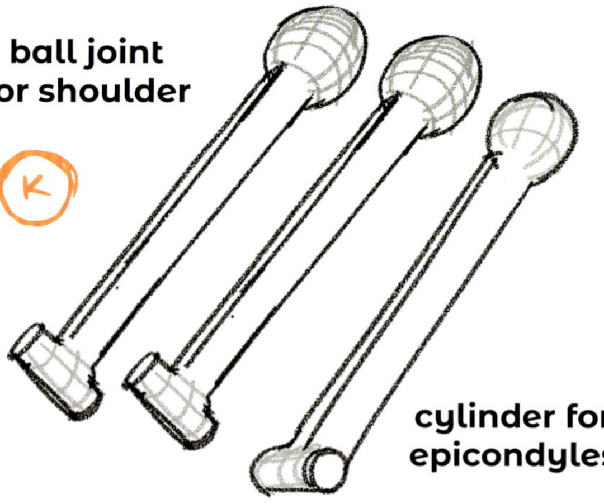

ball joint for shoulder

K

cylinder for epicondyles

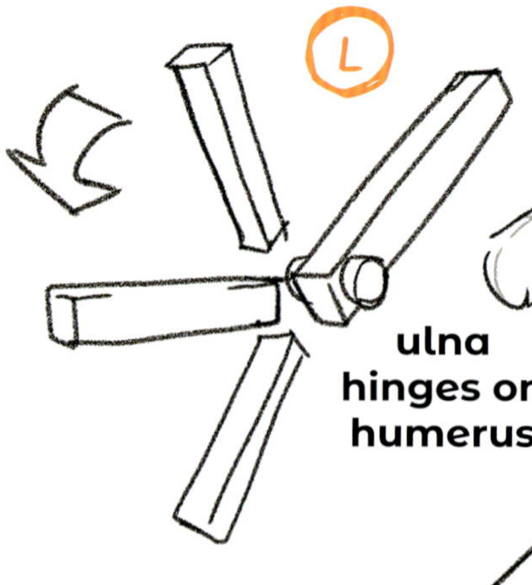

L

ulna hinges on humerus

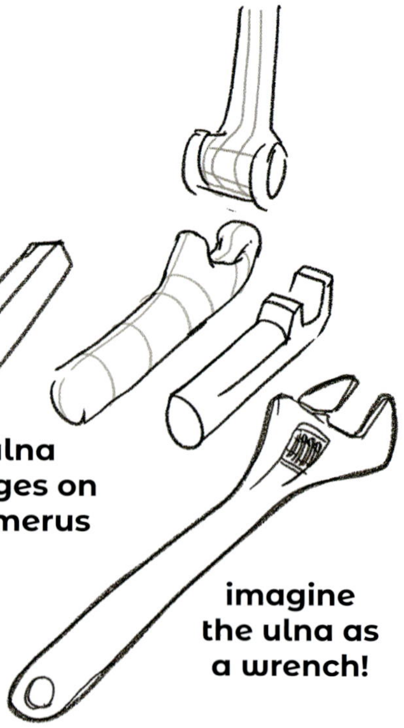

imagine the ulna as a wrench!

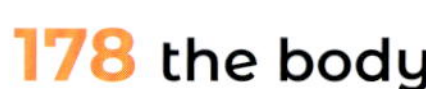

moving the arm

When adding the cylinder (for the epicondyles) to the end of the humerus, note that it doesn't attach right in the middle of the block, but forward of the center (A). Add two triangular supports on either side of the cylinder to strengthen it (B). Take a notch from the back of the humerus to allow the wrenchlike shape to fully straighten (C). Without this notch, the arm wouldn't be able to fully extend!

When the hand is turned outward (palm up), it's called "supination" (D). When turned inward (palm down), it's "pronation" (E). When pronated, the radius wraps up and over the ulna. The radius always ends on the thumb side of the wrist, while the ulna always ends on the little finger side.

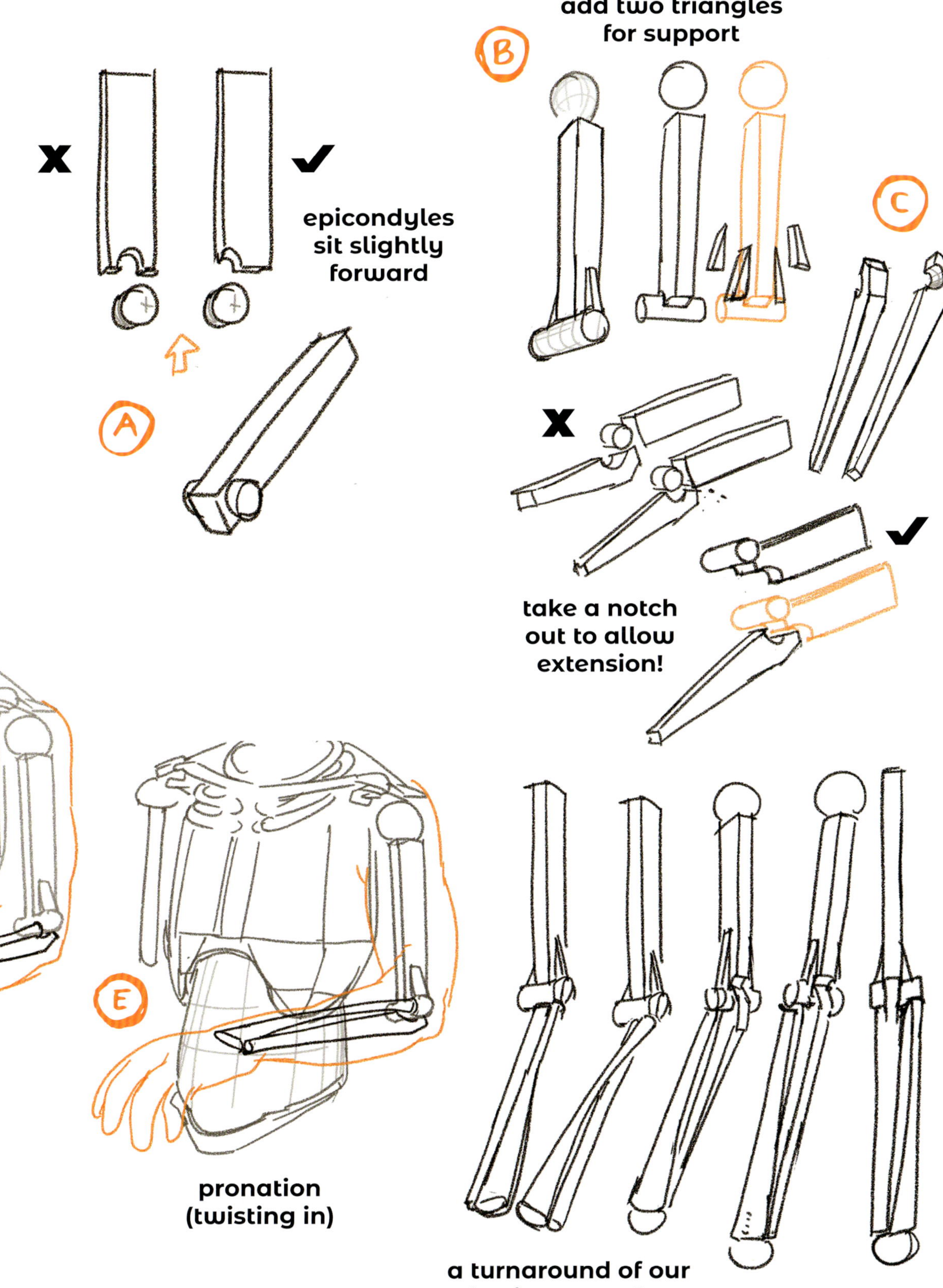

When the radius wraps over the ulna, it pushes the muscles above it (the extensors) upward. This causes a visible rise on the top of the forearm (F). This is an important part of the silhouette to adjust, as without this rise the forearm won't look convincing. When pronating, the ulna remains in the same position and the radius rotates around it. They don't switch position. One moves (G). The radius isn't as long as the ulna. The ulna continues past the end of the humerus, but the radius stops at the bony lump of the lateral (outer) epicondyle (H).

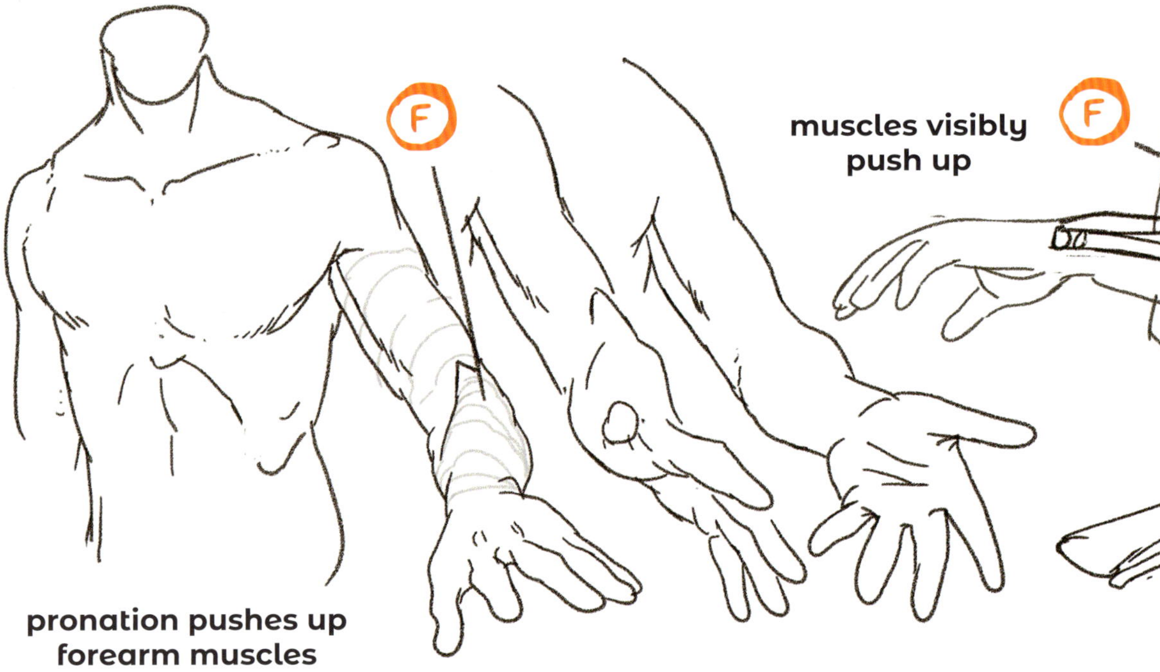

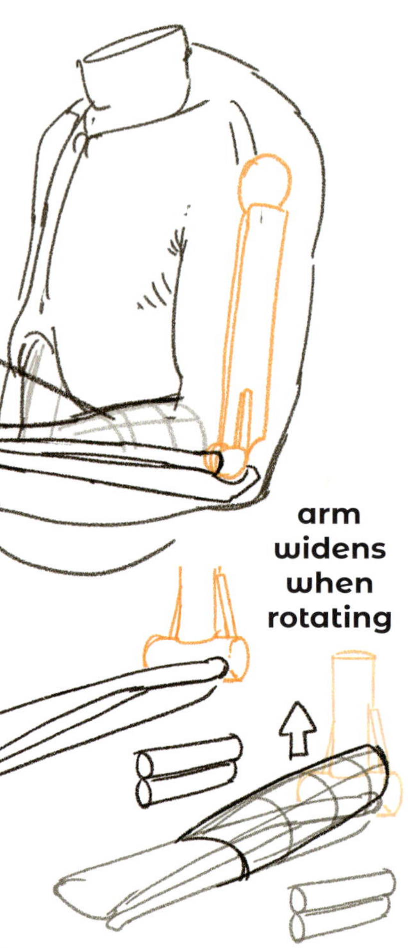

F

pronation pushes up forearm muscles

muscles visibly push up

arm widens when rotating

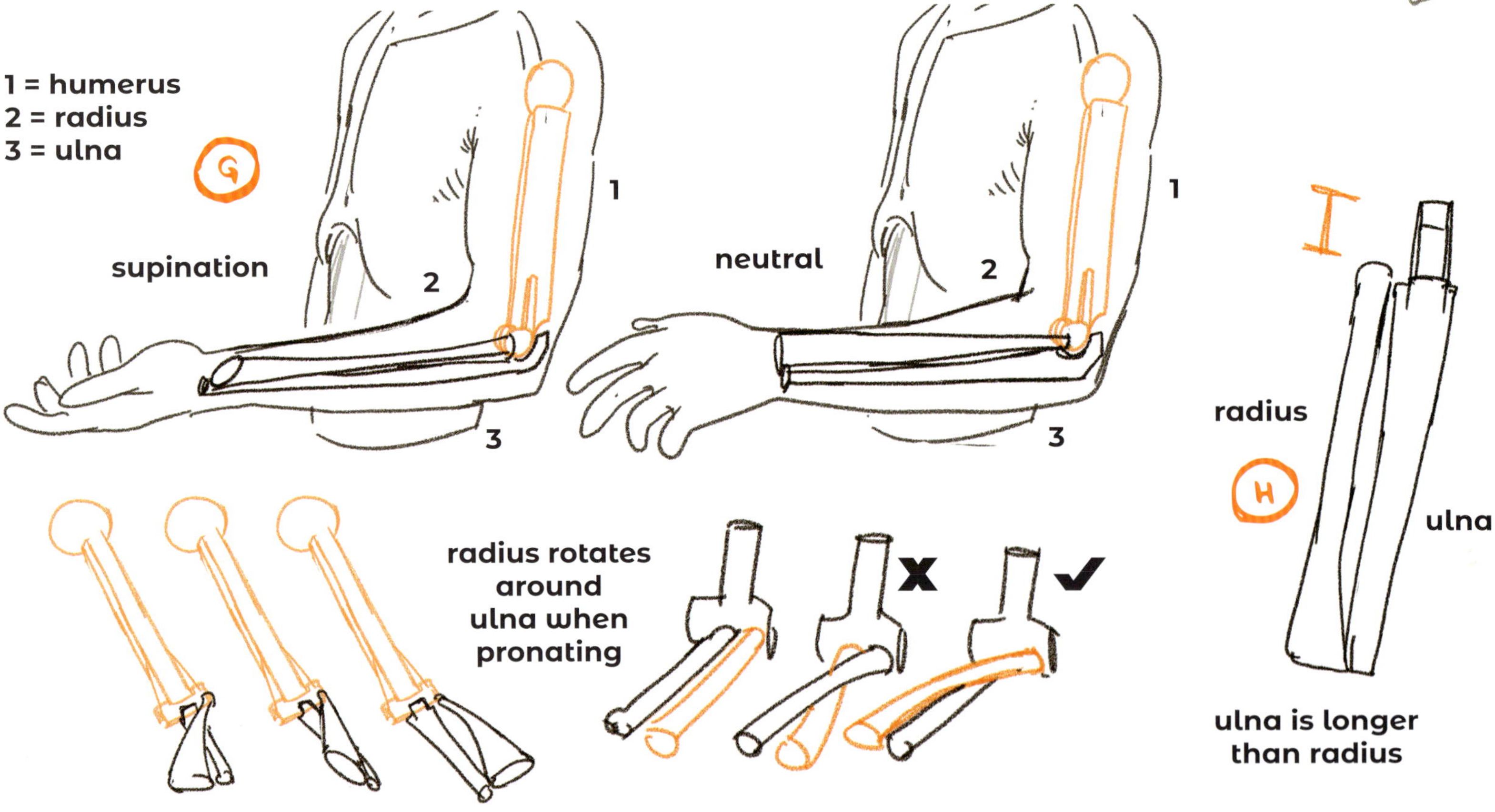

1 = humerus
2 = radius
3 = ulna

G

supination

neutral

radius rotates around ulna when pronating

H

radius

ulna

ulna is longer than radius

designing the arm

Design basic forms to emulate the shapes of the bones and muscles, creating a shorthand version of the arm to use. This will improve your understanding of the arm. Ask yourself what functions the parts need to perform. The whole arm must be able to rotate within the shoulder socket, as well as bending at the elbow (A).

B looks like a good potential design for the arm, but there's something wrong with it – it doesn't reflect the arm movements we need. The tip of the elbow (the olecranon process, which is the end of the ulna) doesn't rotate around a ball like this.

C is a better design for the arm. The ulna fits into the notch we made at the back of the humerus. The elbow always faces in the same direction as the upper arm, so parts 1 and 2 must always be aligned (D).

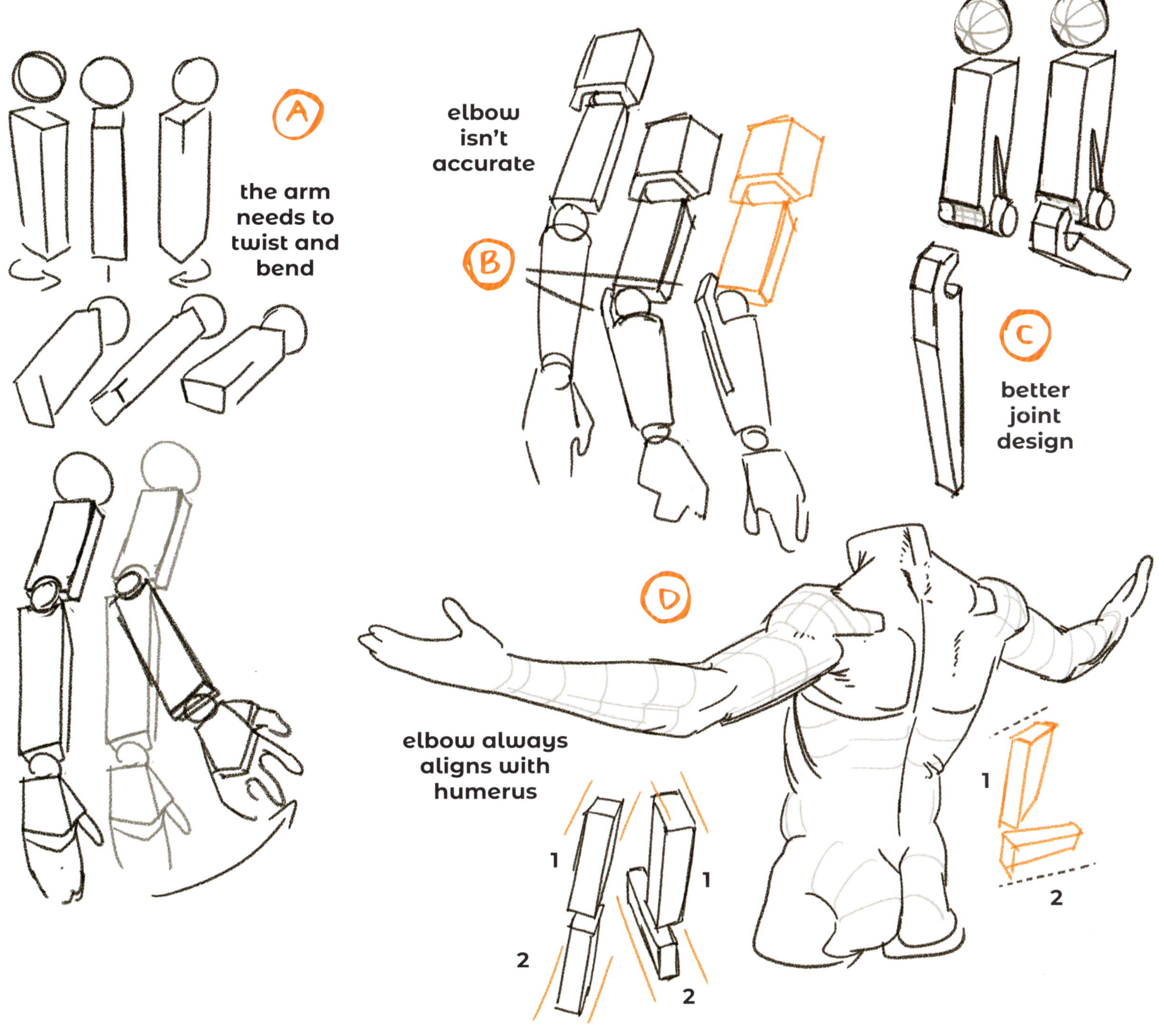

The arms in E are relatively accurate, but they're difficult to rotate from imagination because of the lack of clear edges, planes, and corners.

The design in F fails our function test because the epicondyles are attached to the lower arm. The epicondyles are part of the humerus, the upper arm, so they wouldn't rotate like this. What does work well about this design is that the wrist can rotate (G). This is a good addition to take forward.

This leads us to the functional shape that I personally favor. To create this base for the whole upper arm, we elongate the flattened rectangle of the humerus (H), take a round notch out of the back, snip the corner off the front, and attach the epicondyles directly to it (I). The pieces we remove allow the ulna to attach and have a range of movement.

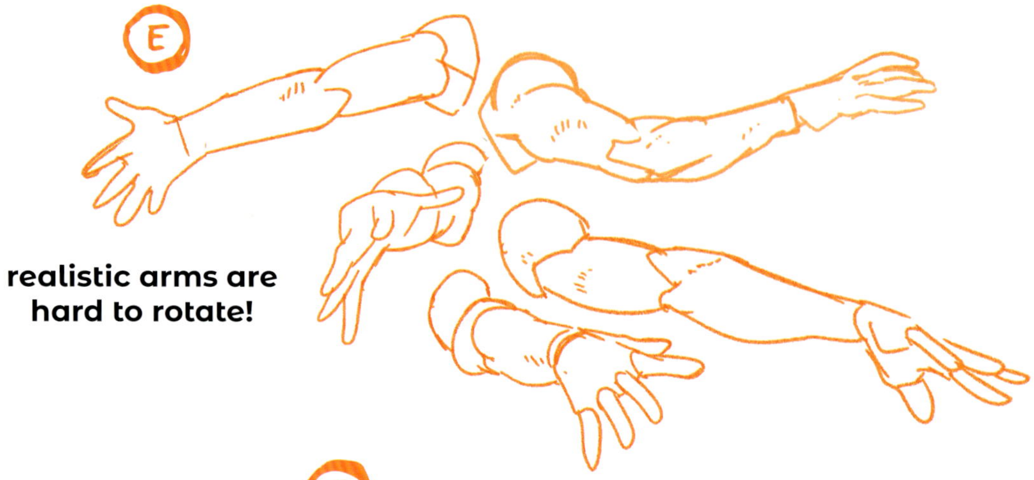

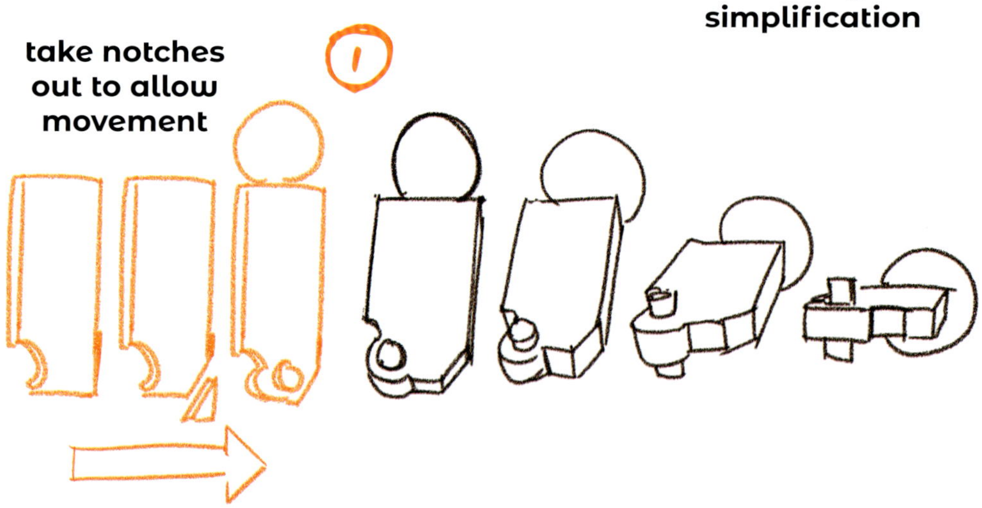

realistic arms are hard to rotate!

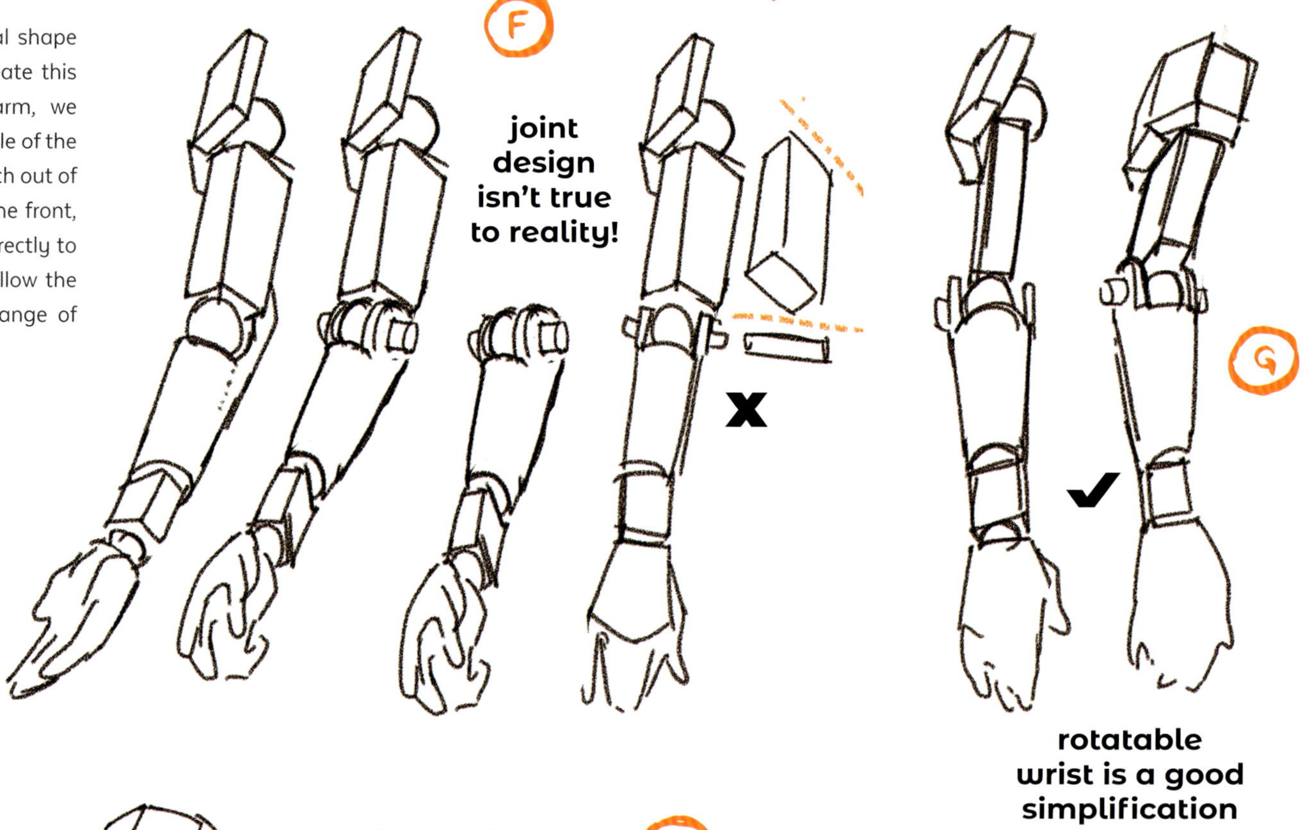

joint design isn't true to reality!

rotatable wrist is a good simplification

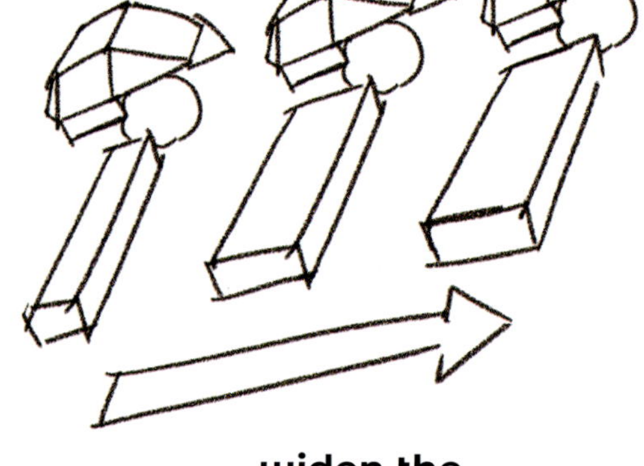

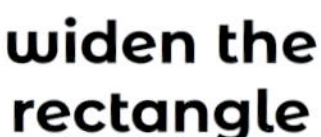

take notches out to allow movement

Try to design your own forms for the arms. True understanding comes from your own investigation and thought. I'm describing the thought process more than suggesting you use exactly these models! Experiment with different simple forms: cylinders, rectangles, or triangles. Whatever you use, the design should always be informed by function. Constantly check that your parts can pronate, supinate, and be drawn easily from different angles. If your design is too complex, it defeats the purpose of making a box mannequin!

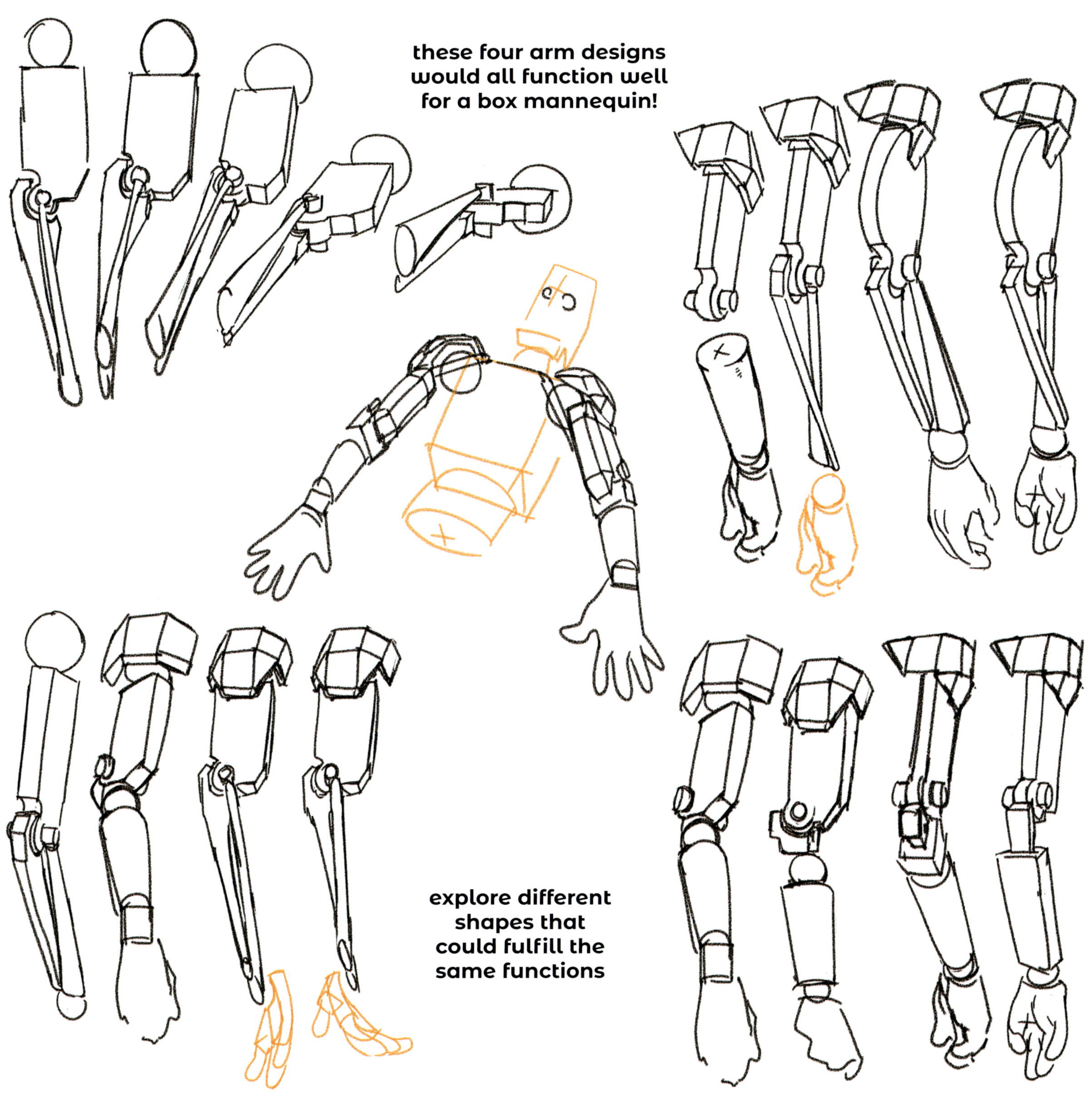

triceps

There are two major muscle groups in the upper arm: the triceps that straighten the arm (extension) and the biceps and brachialis that bend it (flexion). Let's start with the triceps at the back of the upper arm. "Tri" means "three" and "ceps" means "head." The "head" of a muscle is its origin point, where the muscle attaches to a fixed point, like an anchor. From this anchor, the muscle usually pulls and moves another bone. So the triceps muscle has three heads: one attached to the back of the humerus, one to the lateral (outer) edge of the scapula **(A)**, and the third buried under the other two **(B)**. The triceps attaches into the end of the ulna (the olecranon process) **(C)**. The flattened section at the back is the triceps tendon **(D)**. It's often drawn flat, but it bulges out because it lies on top of the third head of the triceps. The more we bend the arm, the less visible the triceps tendon will be **(E)**.

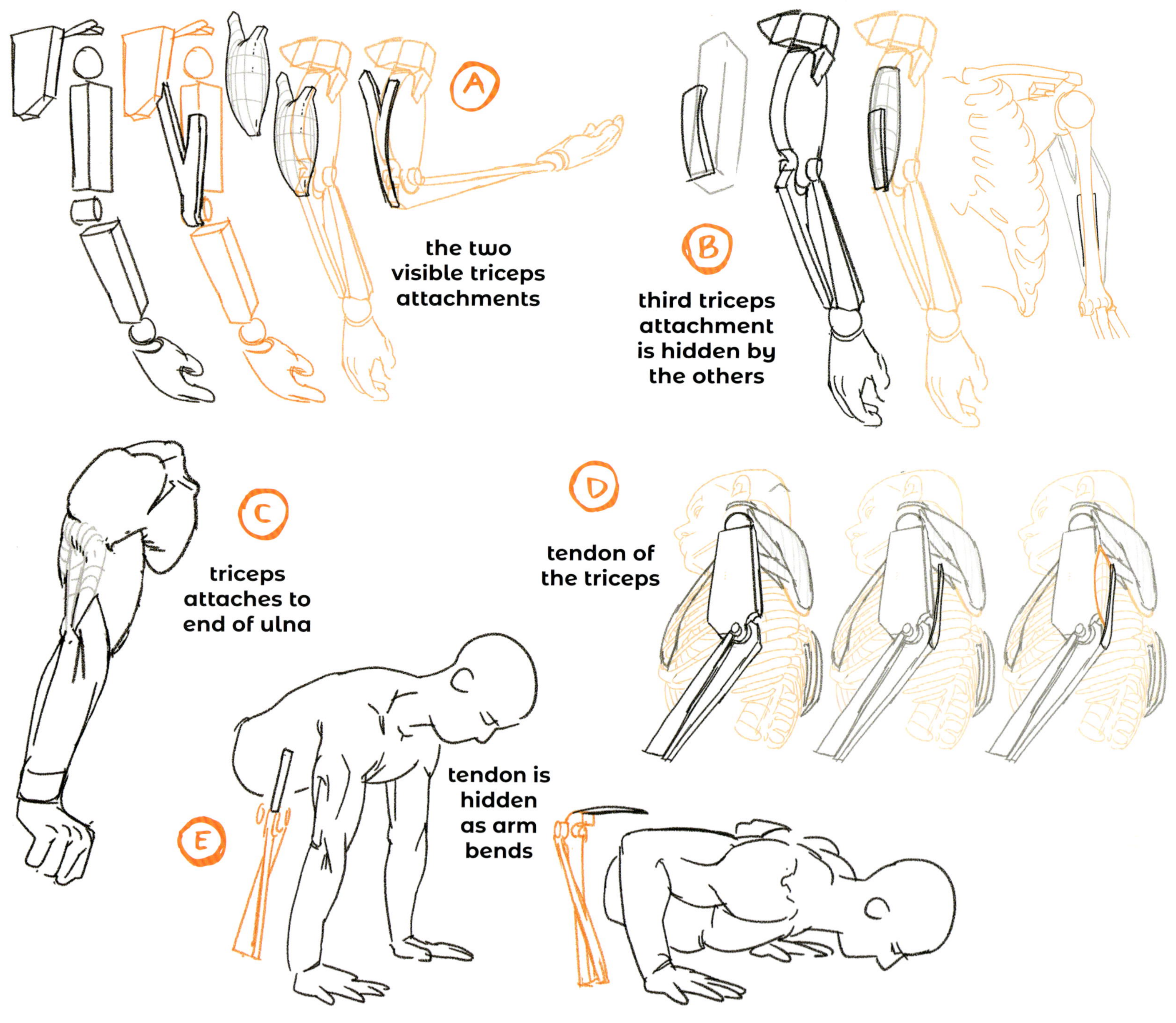

If you want to make three objects work together, you need something to connect them. For oxen, we would use a yoke to harness the animals into working together. The shoulder girdle or "yoke" area we learned about on page 135 serves this purpose with our arms (F). With the yoke providing an anchor for the arms to pull against, we can not only bend the arms (G), but raise them in different directions (H).

The biceps and triceps both have one direct connection to the yoke, enabling the biceps to bend and raise the arm forward and the triceps to do the same backward. When the arms are raised, you can clearly see that they widen toward the back (I).

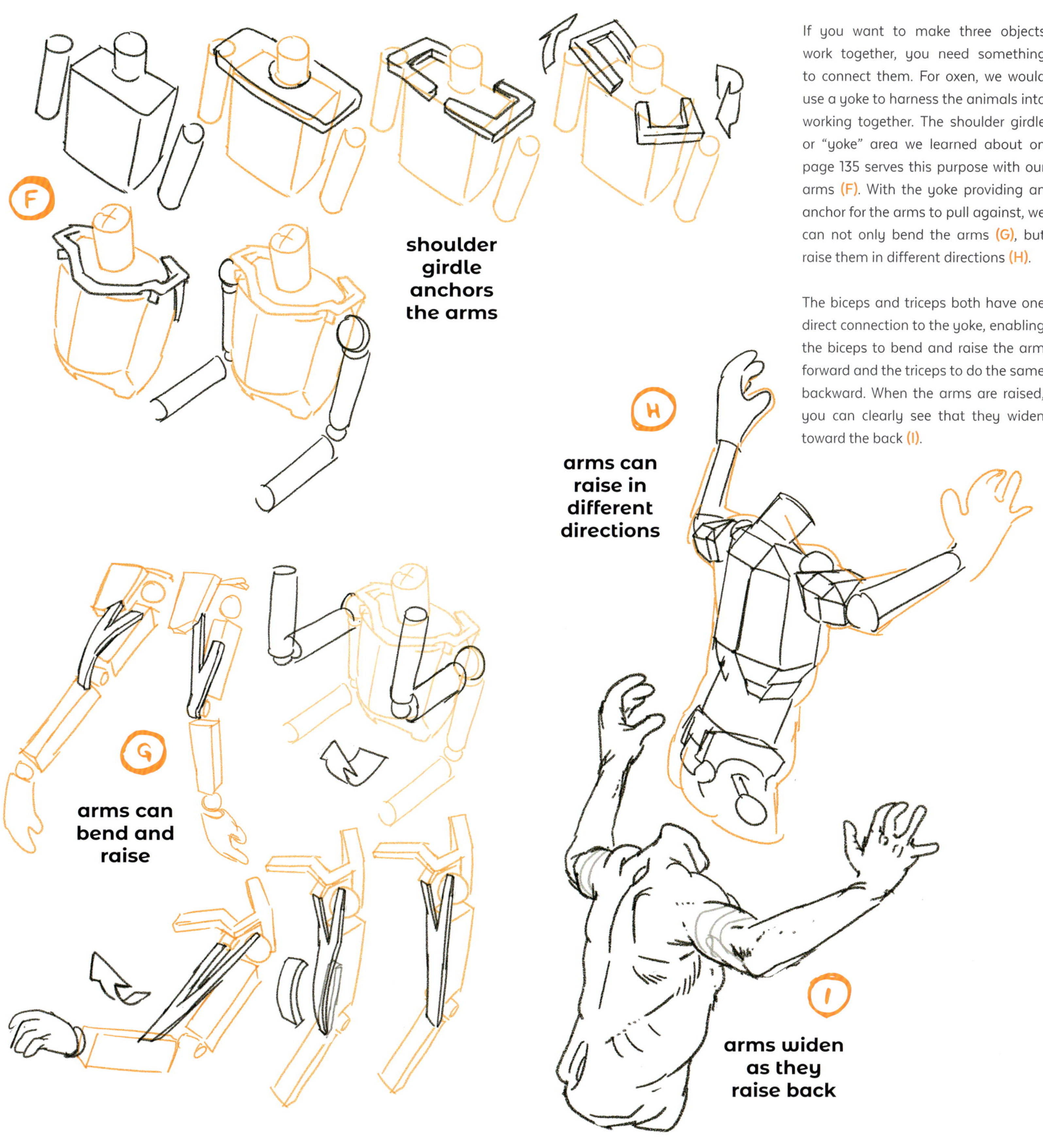

The arm is often represented as a chain, which is a good way to visualize the wedging of the forms (J). The side of the rib cage isn't flat, but tapers backward and is rounded. This has an effect on the forms of the arm, making them wider at the back and curved on the inner edge (K).

The upper arm is rounded at the rear and increases in width as we move higher and approach the connection to the scapula and chest. The interior head of the triceps wedges into the scapula and chest (L). It doesn't just extend your arm, but also assists in pulling the whole arm back toward the scapula. Note the three planes on the back of the triceps (M). We can lay this angular shape over our basic design to form quite a convincing model of the upper arm (N).

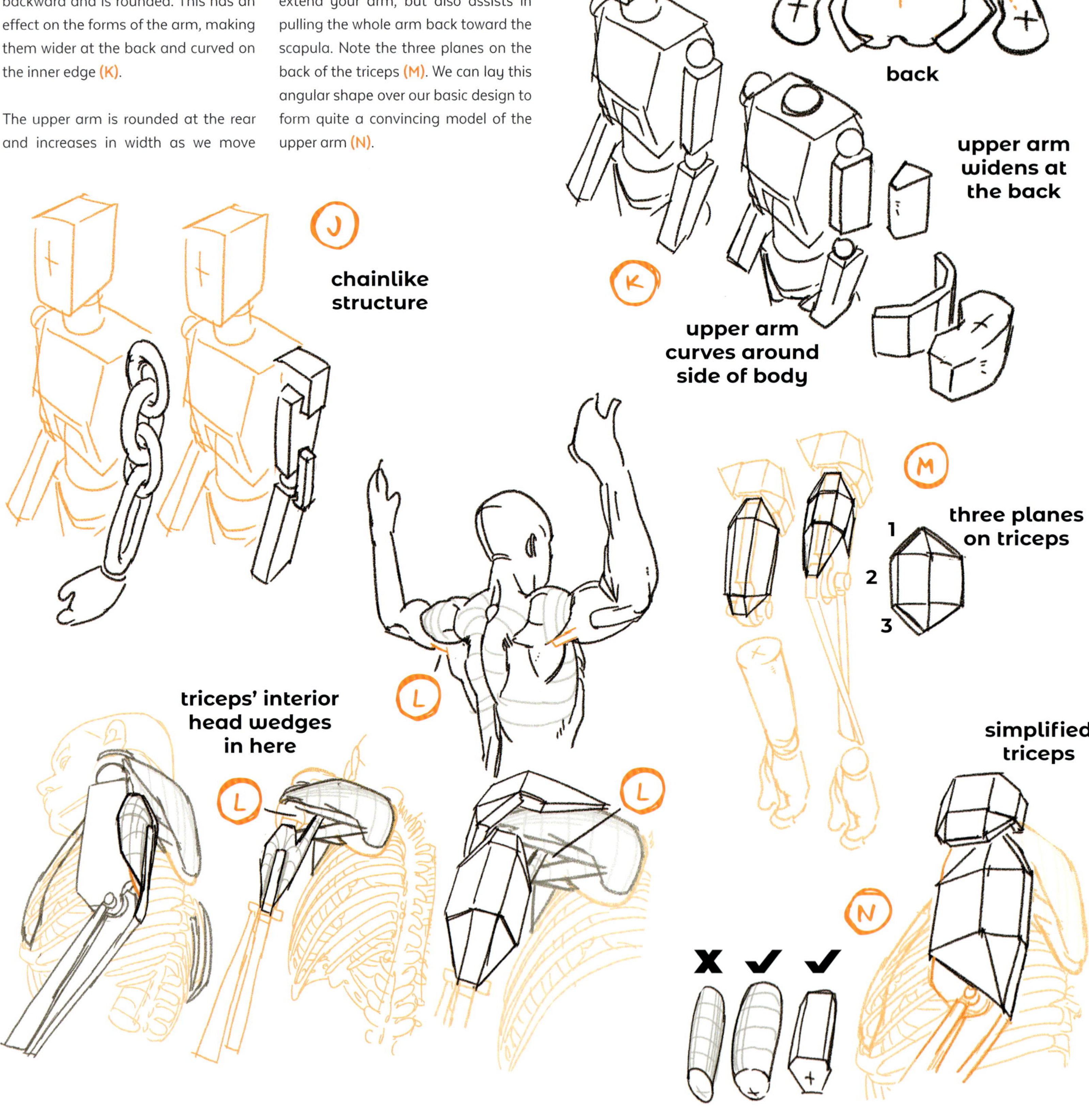

biceps & brachialis

When stretched, the biceps ("bi" meaning "two") becomes thinner, as with all muscles. It has the same volume, but stretched over a larger area, so it appears smaller (A). One head attaches to the coracoid process on the scapula and the other wraps up and over the top of the humerus (B).

The biceps inserts into the radius, not the ulna. The brachialis muscle (meaning "relating to the arm") sits beneath it and attaches to the ulna. So we have two large upper-arm muscles that each pulls on one of the two lower arm bones (C).

All these muscles may seem complex in form, but I prefer to simply think of the upper arm as having an octagonal gem shape (D).

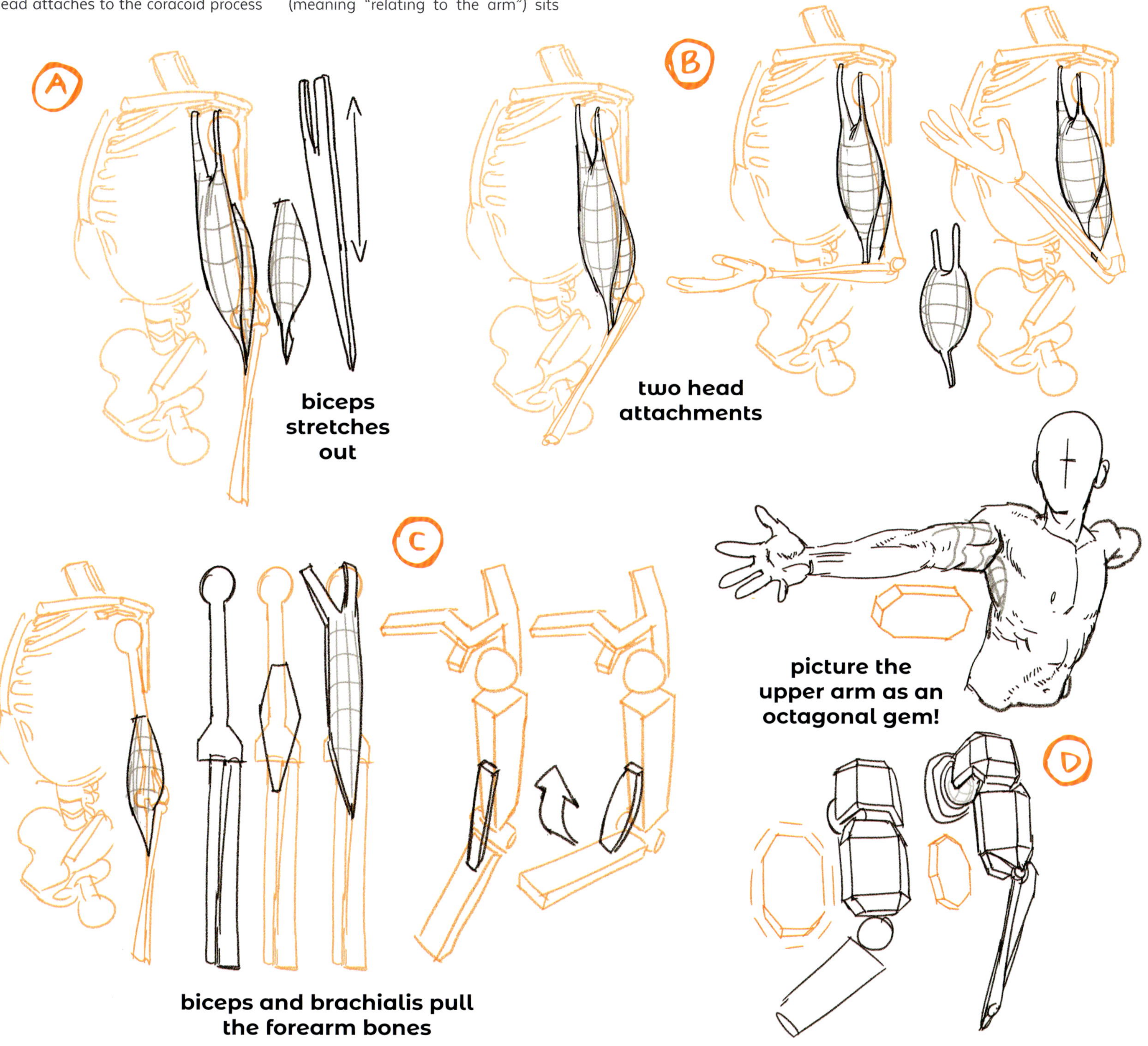

the elbow

As we associate the elbow with the end of the ulna, we tend to exaggerate its point. Sometimes the elbow does appear like A, but often the olecranon process will be hidden within the silhouette of the arm, more like B. The elbow is formed of a triangle of the three major attachment points (C): the olecranon process of the ulna and the two epicondyles to either side of it. Always think of this triangle when drawing the elbow. Sometimes you'll see all three points; sometimes you'll just see one as the others are buried.

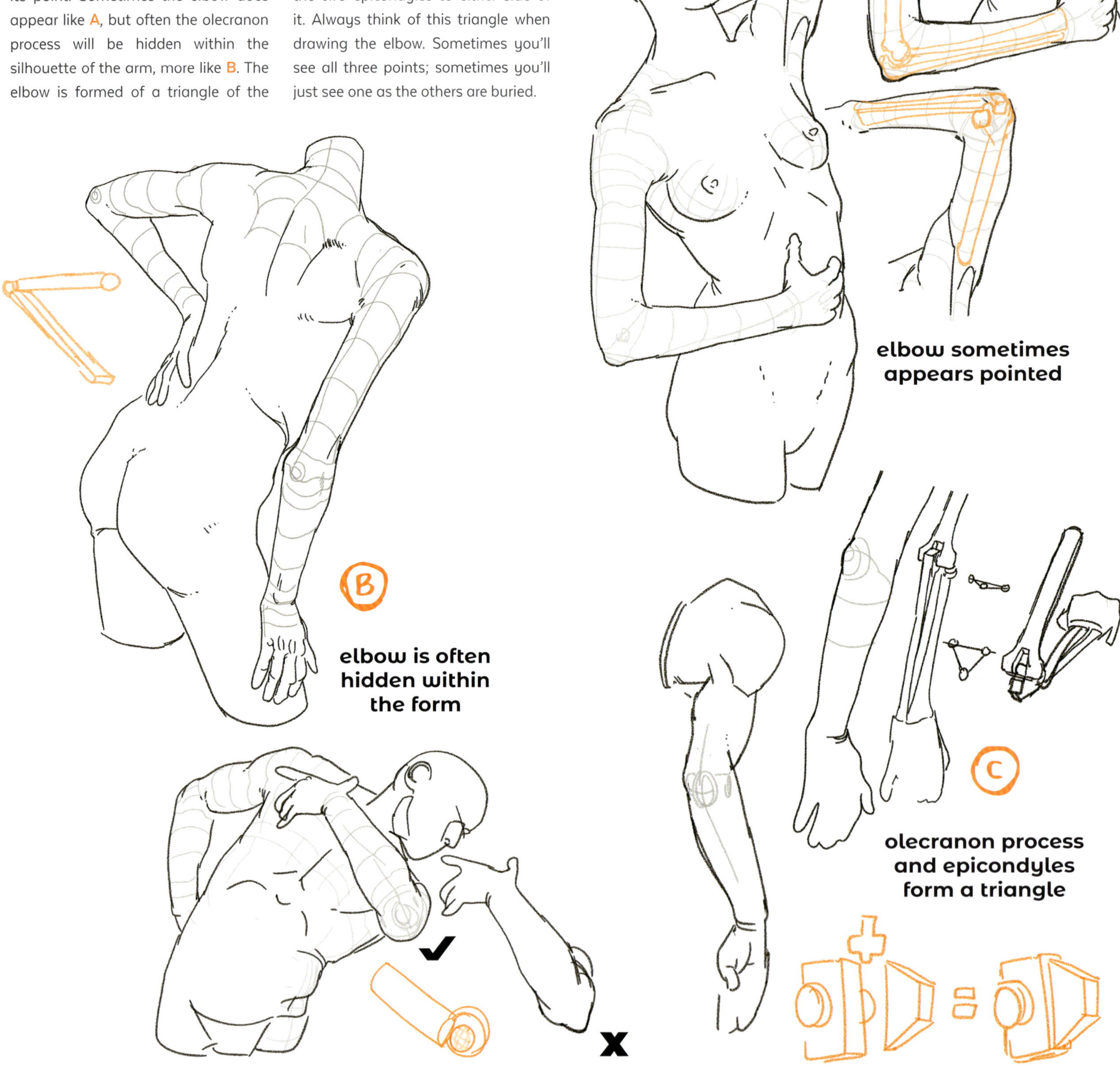

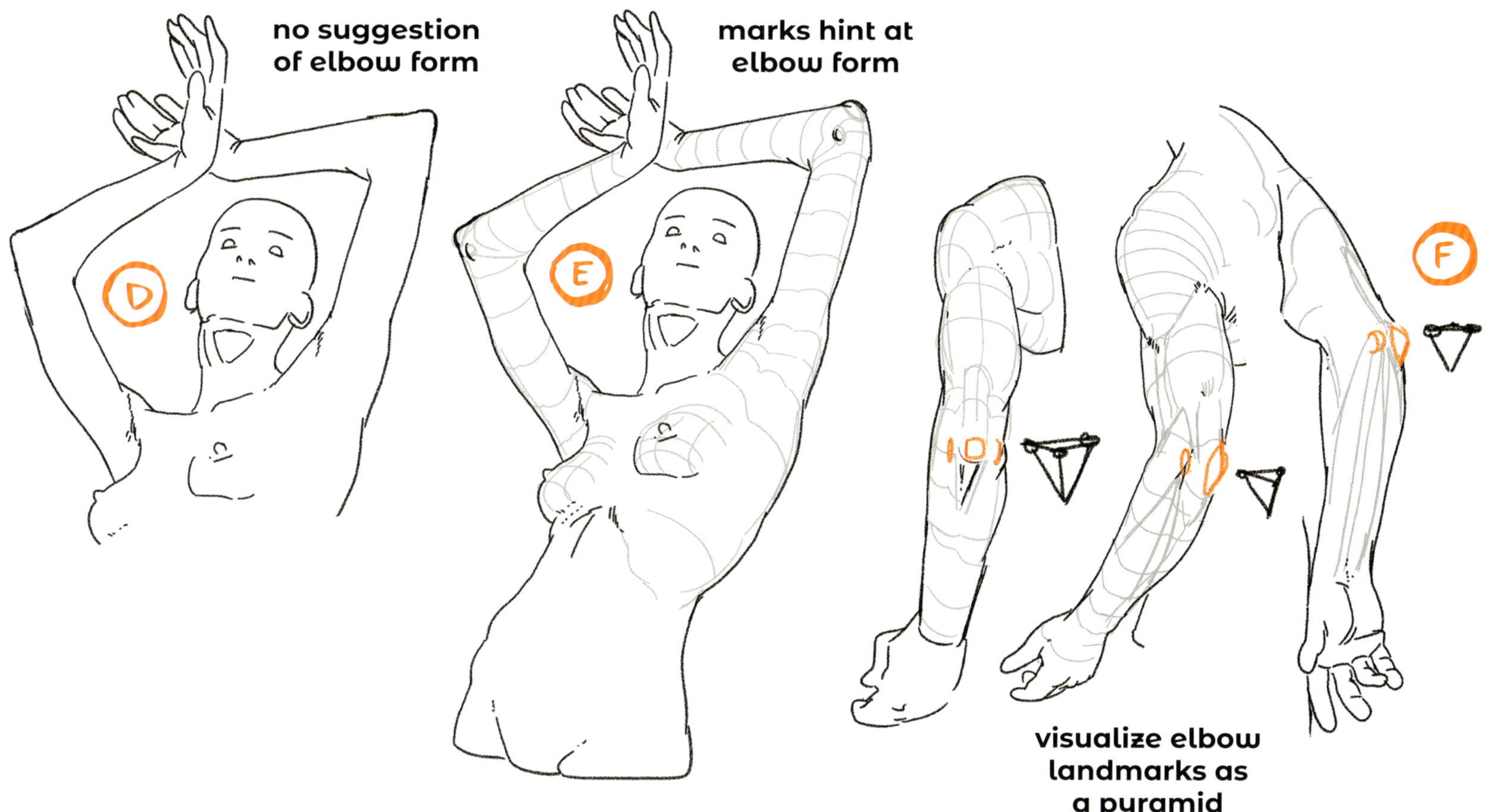

Include just a suggestion of the elbow's structure. In D we see no hint at all and the silhouette struggles to convey the elbow's form. In E we see a slight mark, which is enough to help the viewer. Our visual library is vast, so we need only the subtlest of hints to recognize anatomical structures. Recall and recognition are very different skills, and despite not being able to "recall" the structure of the arm, most people will recognize it instantly without any training at all.

It can be helpful to draw out the triangular elbow landmarks as a 3D pyramid shape, to check the relative heights and positions of those three major attachment points (F). However, as mentioned, remember that we won't always see all three points of the elbow. Learn their form, but have the confidence to deliberately leave one out if the pose or angle calls for it (G).

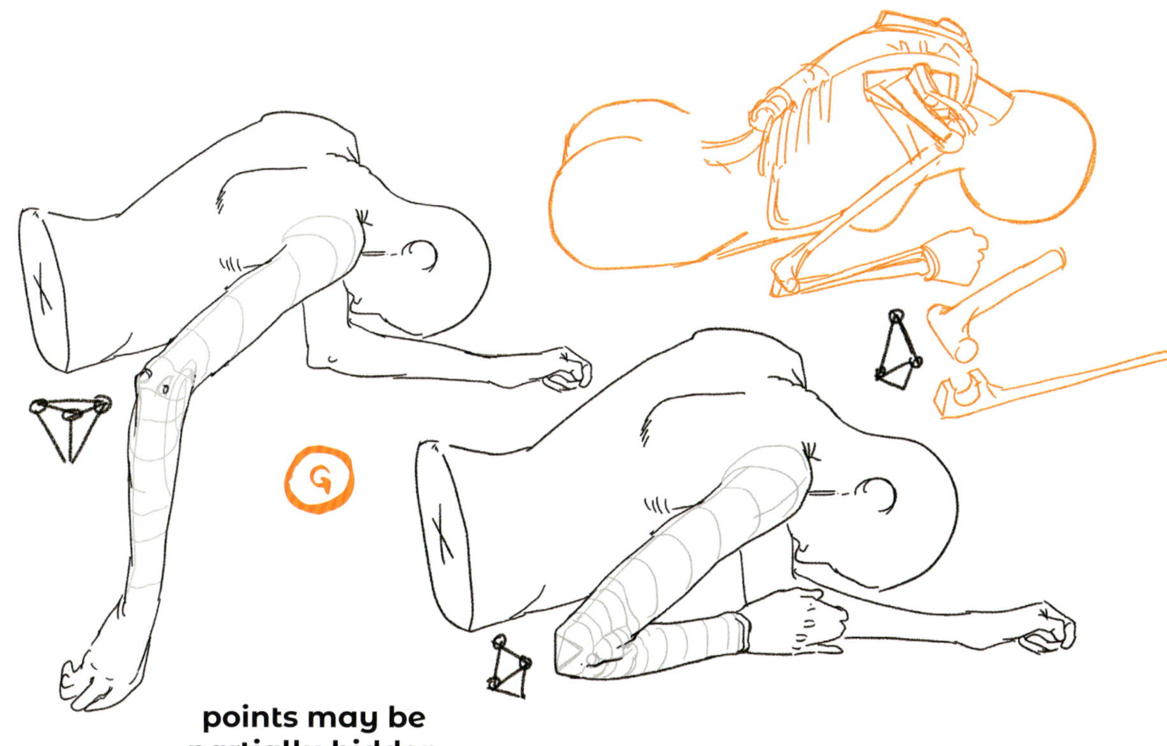

tip: arm muscles & forms

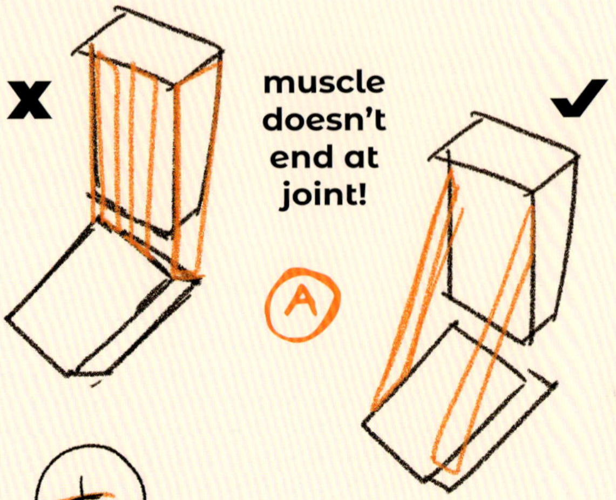

Muscles don't begin and end at joints. That's a common misunderstanding. Muscles wouldn't serve their function if they ended exactly at a joint (A)! Instead, they overlap and wrap around the joints more than you'd expect. If you're not sure where a muscle attaches, ask yourself, "Where would it best attach to fulfill its purpose?"

If we see a concave curve on one side, we'll often see the opposing curve on the other side of the form (B). This interlocking is a useful trick if you need to draw a figure but have no clue about the anatomy! Take a guess at the opposing curve and you're likely to be correct (C).

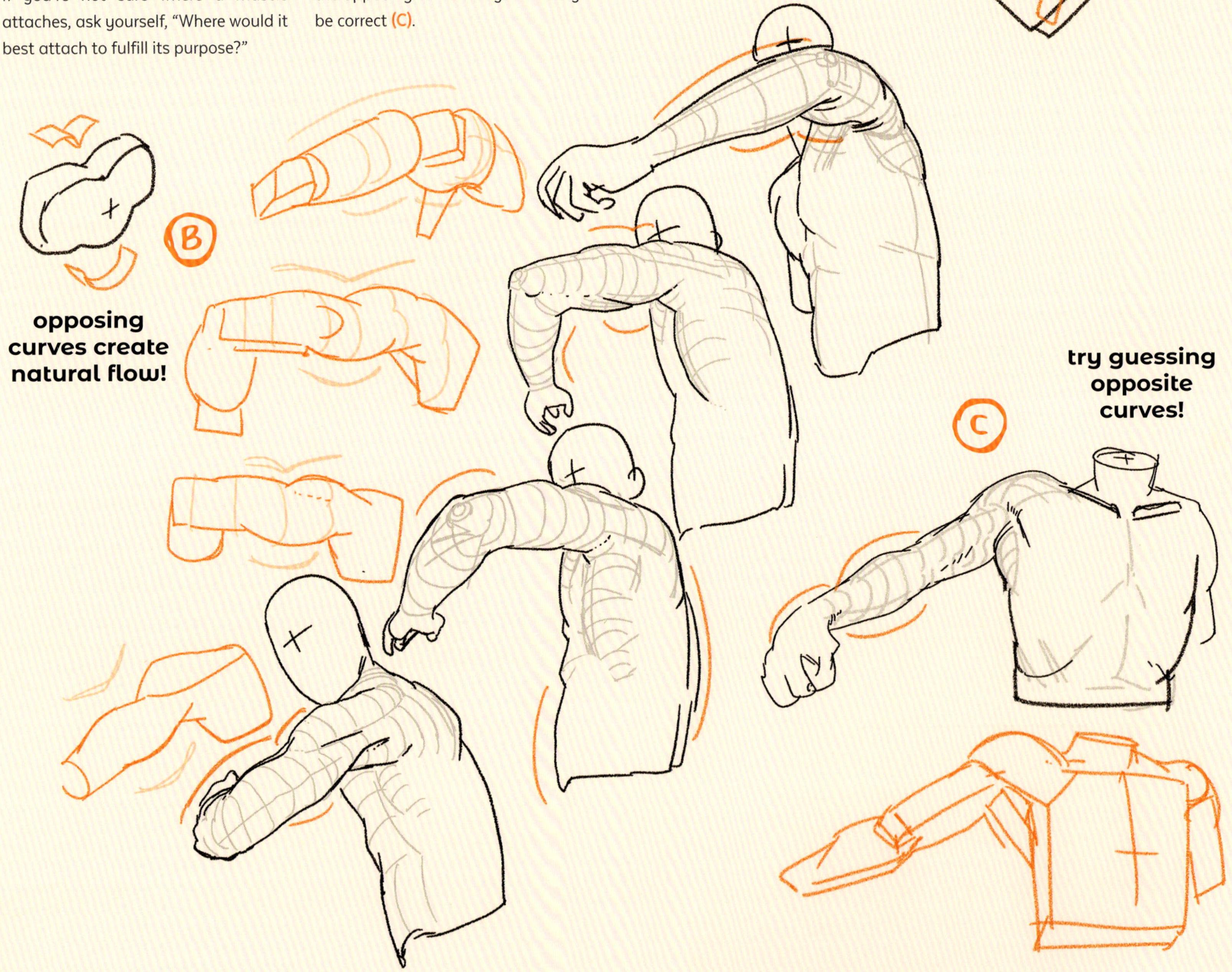

Here's a study tip. Breaking down photos is a fantastic method to improve your knowledge. The best reference to use is yourself, as you can control the angle and pose exactly! Draw the silhouette out, then challenge yourself to two methods: either draw the muscles on or draw the cross contours.

Are there any gaps in the silhouette where you're unsure what muscle is within that space? See if you can "fill" the whole silhouette with muscles. Once you've filled the whole silhouette, cover it up and draw just the silhouette again. This time, try to draw the cross contours without drawing the muscles in. If you get stuck, you can refer to the muscle version.

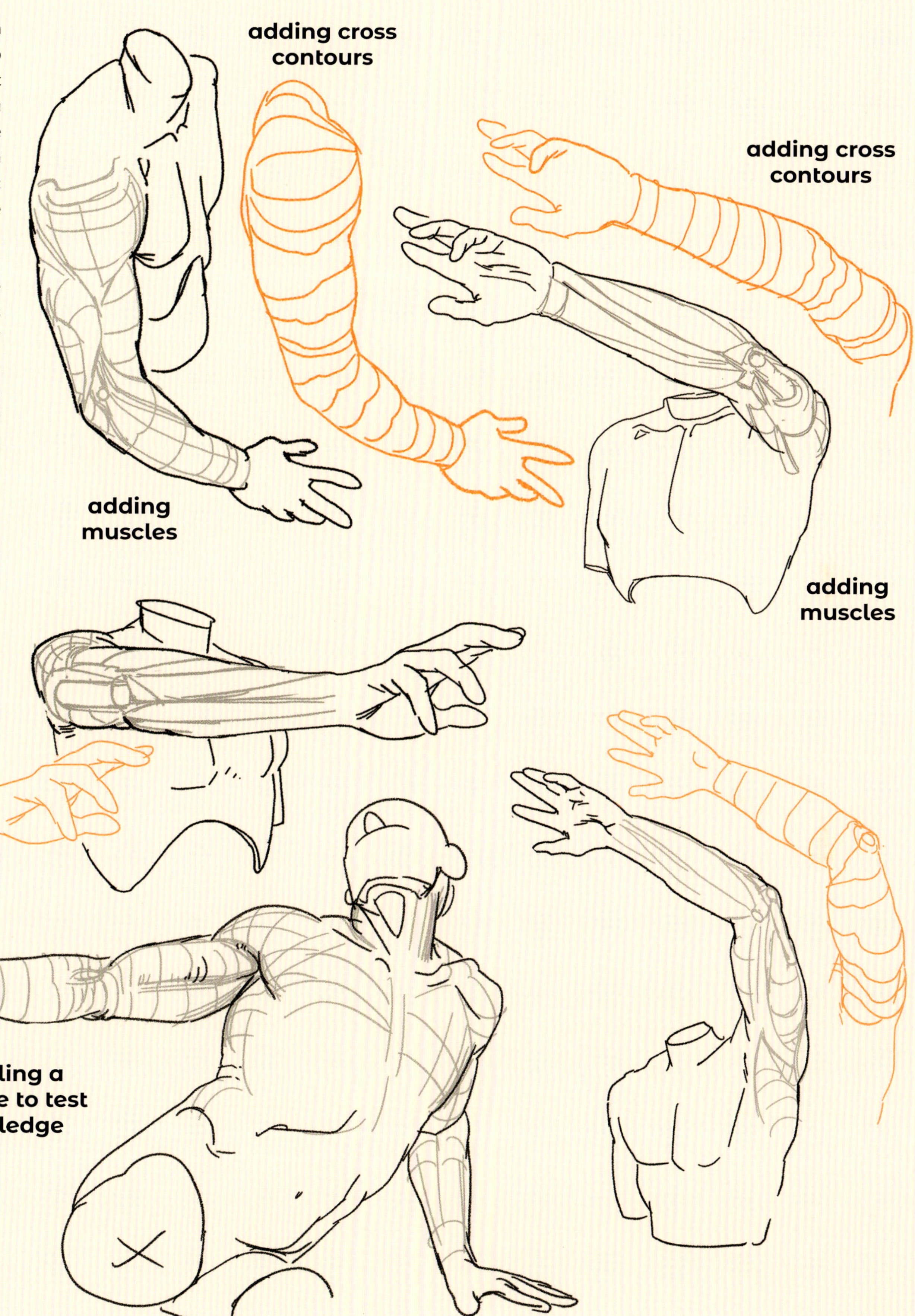

The arm has a hollow interior shape, as we saw on page 186, so you can frequently see the triceps when viewing the arm from the front. It's visible from most angles (D). The triceps wedges in beneath the deltoids and narrows to a point between them, with the latissimus dorsi and scapular muscles below it (E).

The arm basically has three layers: flexing muscles at the front (1), deep muscle in the middle (2), and extending muscles at the rear (3). They form a wedge and widen toward the back.

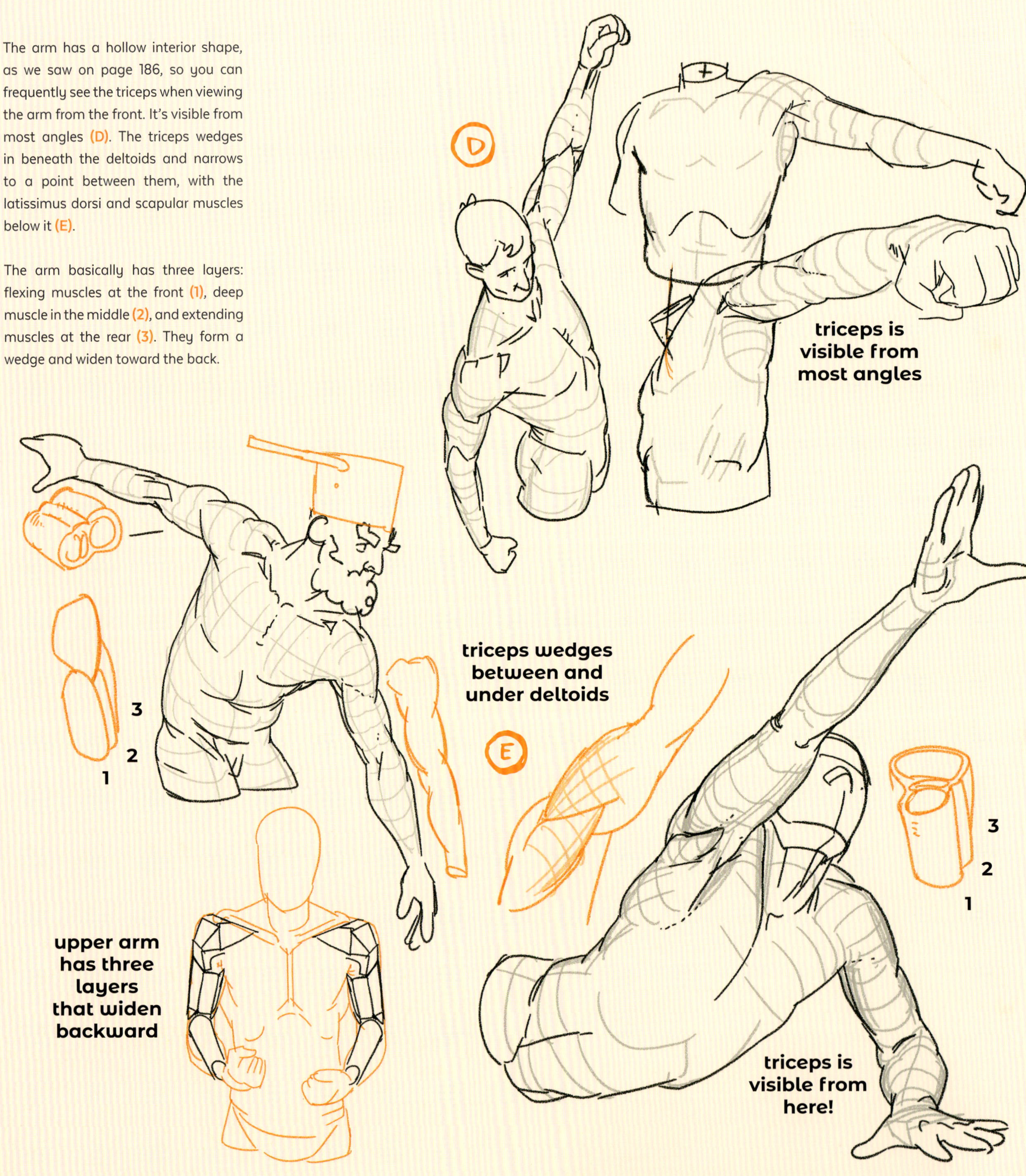

Don't think that you can just add a few indents and the arm will have form! Adding marks that aren't correct will confuse the viewer (F). When we draw the arm, we want to be absolutely sure which parts are the extensors, the triceps, and the flexors (G). These guide the marks and indents we place.

When the arm is supinated or pronated, it is almost never straight (H). The scapular muscles and latissimus dorsi push the arm's whole angle outward slightly, so the forearm doesn't just hang vertically.

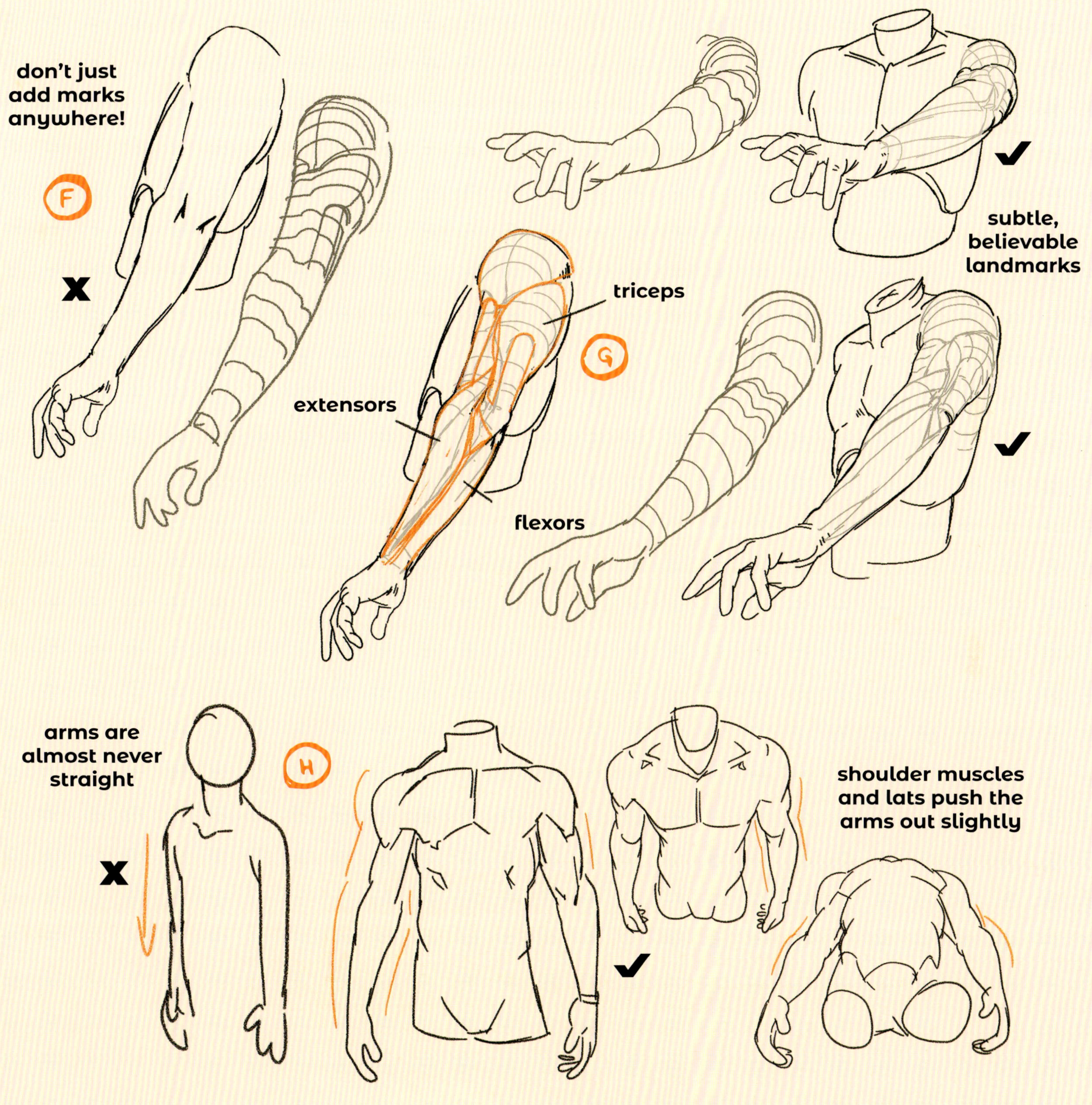

flexors & extensors

The extensors originate at the back of the lateral (outer) epicondyle (A). Their role is to pull on the back of the hand to raise it, and to generate the pull to open the fingers (B). Alongside the extensors lies another muscle, the brachioradialis, which attaches to the end of the humerus and flexes the lower arm (C). It's not technically a true extensor, but it's easier to group it with them (D)!

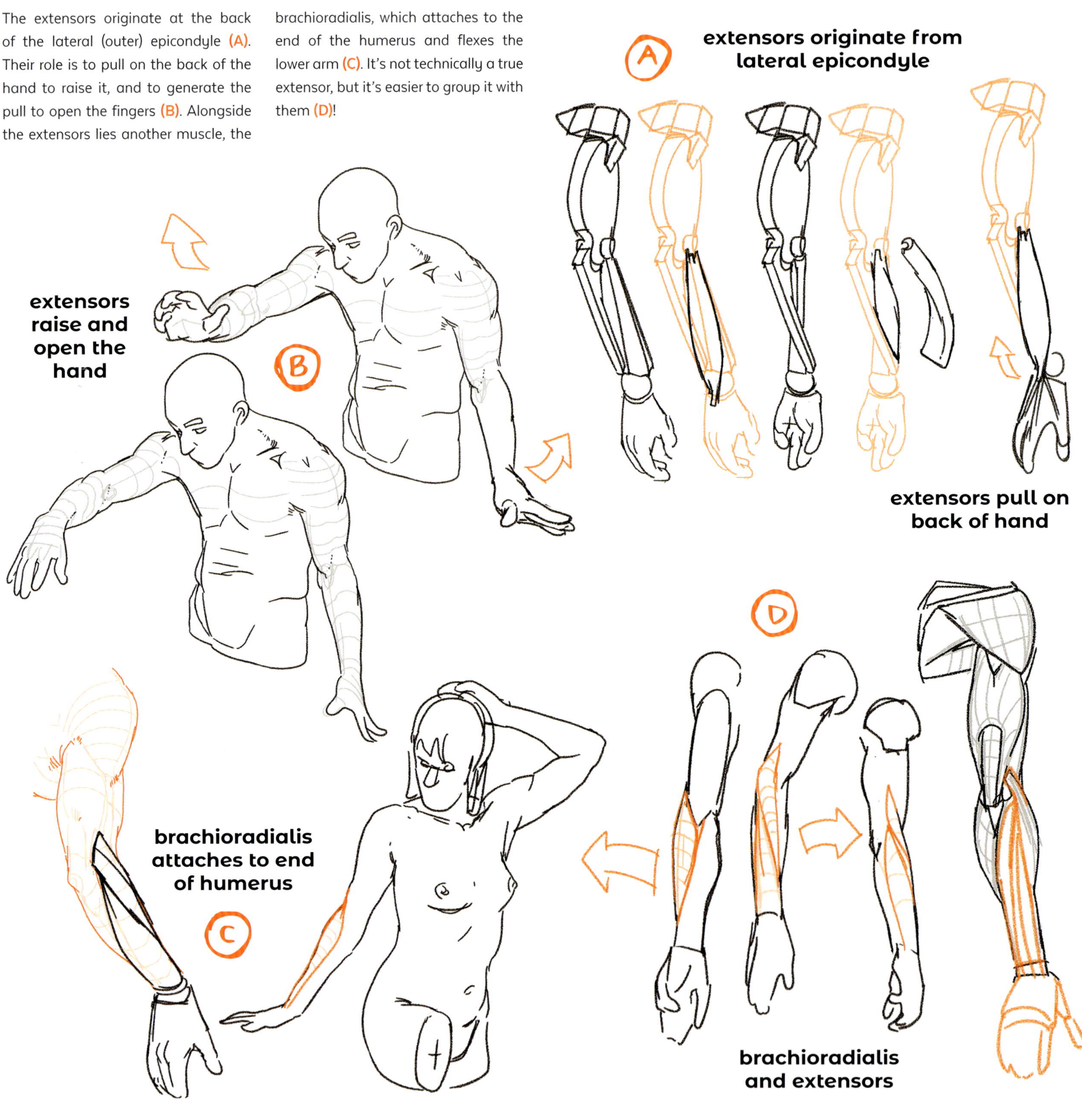

Note the difference in height between the extensor and flexor groups (E). The extensors connect the outside of the arm (the back-of-the-hand side) to the lateral epicondyle and the bottom section of the humerus. They start higher up the arm.

Most of the extensors attach to the lateral epicondyle (F), but the largest extensor attaches directly to the upper arm instead. The brachioradialis is the biggest muscle in this area, but as we learned already, it flexes the arm rather than raising the hand. When we bend our arms, the extensors bury the lateral epicondyle (G).

When the arm faces us, the extensors form a prominent bulge on top (H).

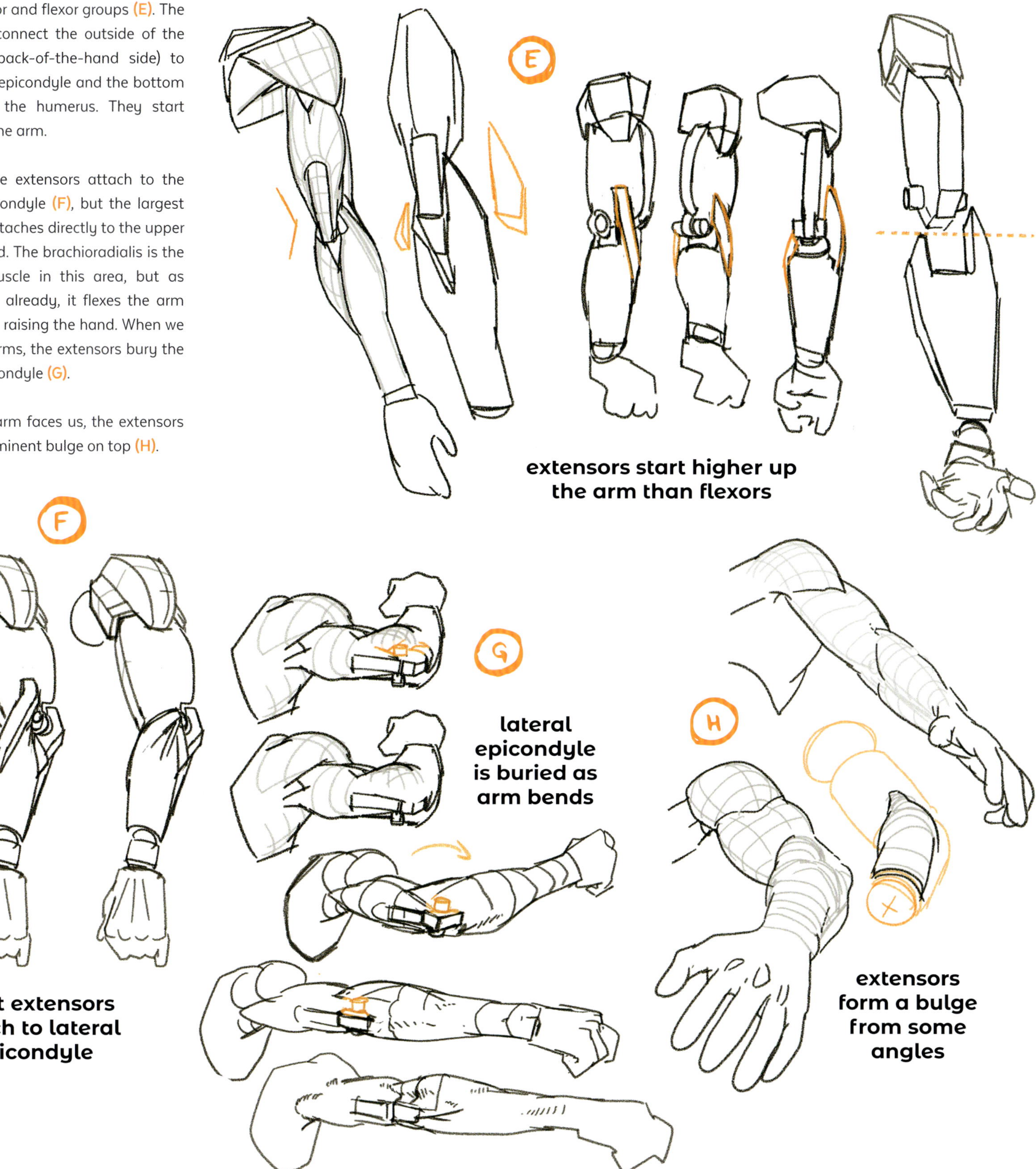

The medial (inner) epicondyle is less covered by muscle. The flexors, which attach lower than the extensors, begin at the medial epicondyle and run to the inside of the hand. They bring the hand up (I).

From behind, the triceps tendon doesn't cover the medial epicondyle (J). The back of the epicondyle is uncovered and you can feel it on your own arm quite easily. Don't draw the triceps running parallel along both sides of the tendon – instead, it narrows rapidly (K).

The inner, hidden head of the triceps is wider and peeks out from behind the outer tendon (L).

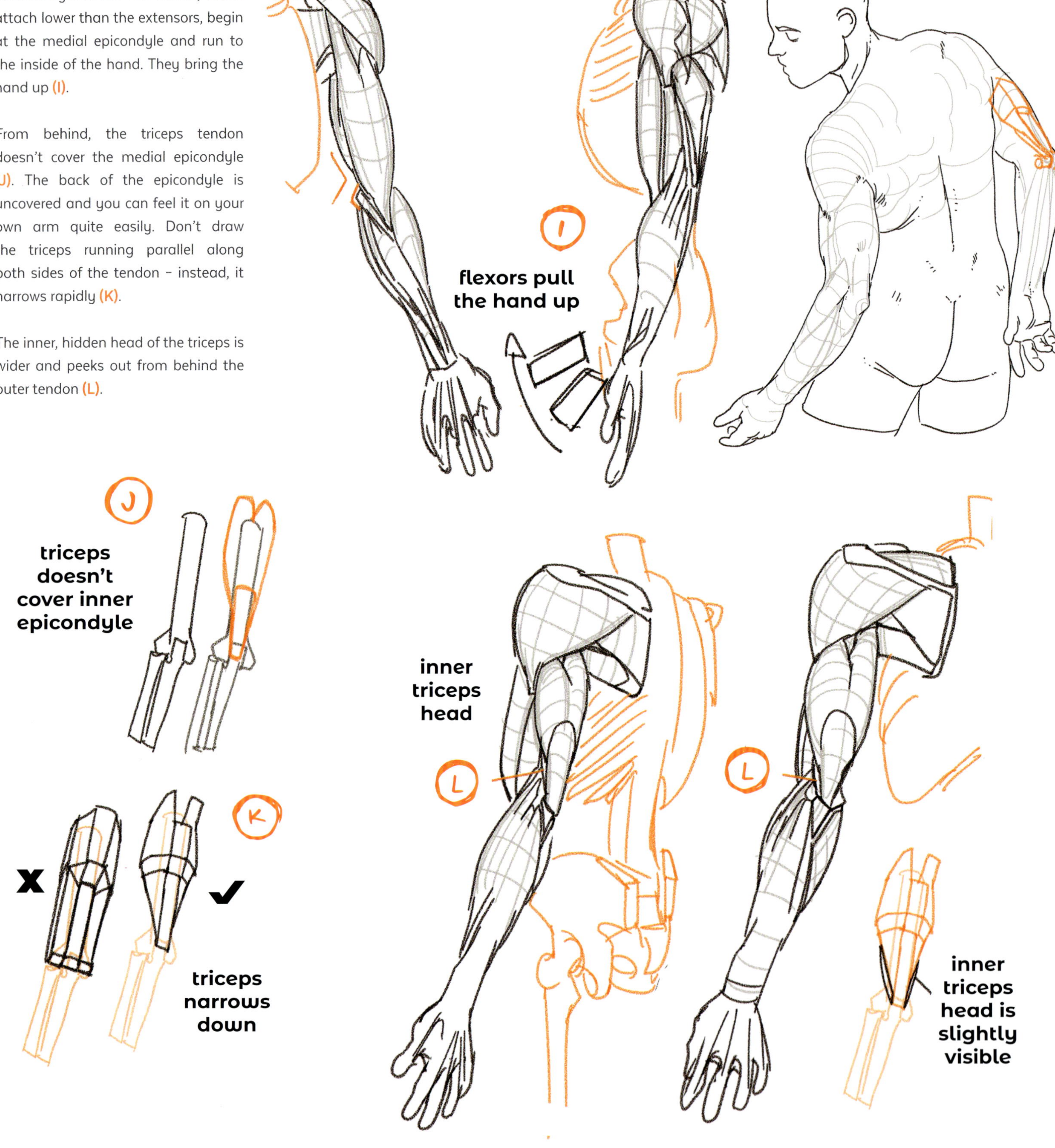

Even though they are evenly placed either side of the elbow tip, the outer and inner epicondyles appear to shift position when bending the arm (M). This is due to how the triceps, normally rounded at the back, becomes more pointed when raising the arm as the heads are stretched lengthways (N). The majority of the mass protrudes on the other side, not internally (O).

Usually the wrist section remains angled outward, instead of facing directly ahead, when the arm is raised (P). We struggle to rotate our hand and arm fully inward. When we straighten the arm, we create a depression between the end of the biceps and the place where the extensors and flexors meet (Q).

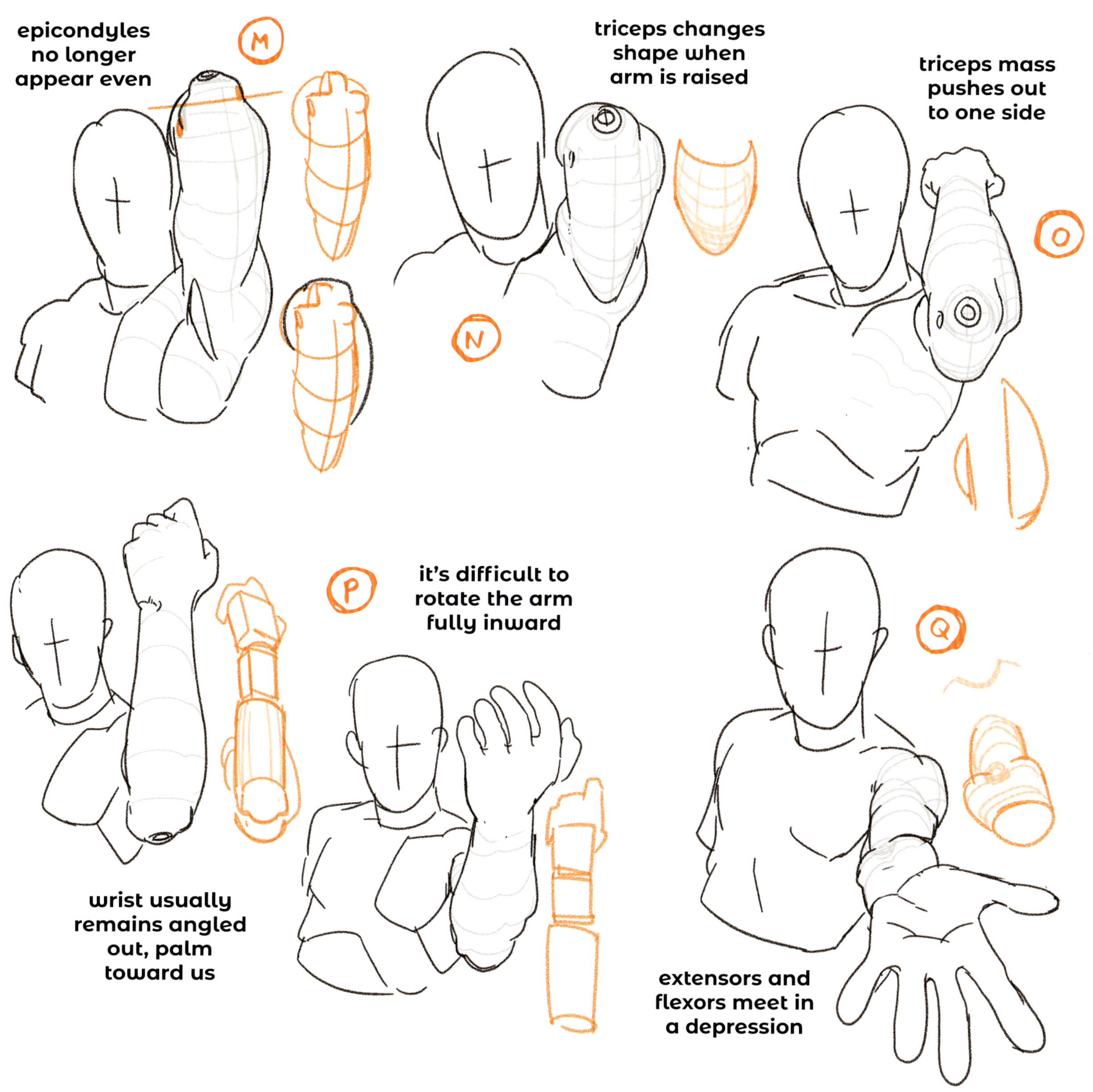

tip: stack your knowledge

Sometimes anatomy requires a bit of reverse engineering. If you start with a basic drawing of an arm and aren't sure where the muscles are located, you can look for marks that indicate the bone positions (A). Then you can draw out the bones to give you the anchor points. Now you know the attachment points to build the arm!

For maximum efficiency, "stack" your knowledge. For example, memorizing the brachioradialis is easy when we know the locations of the biceps and triceps. It just sits between them (B). If you only have half an hour, learn one muscle really well, rather than five that you'll soon forget. That one muscle then provides context for the rest (C)!

Constantly ask, "What muscles are on either side of this muscle?" Once you've identified the muscle locations, you can remove details until you find the minimum amount of marks needed to suggest accurate anatomy (D). For example, the deltoid always faces the lateral epicondyle. If you have an indent for the epicondyle, you have the direction for the deltoid, too!

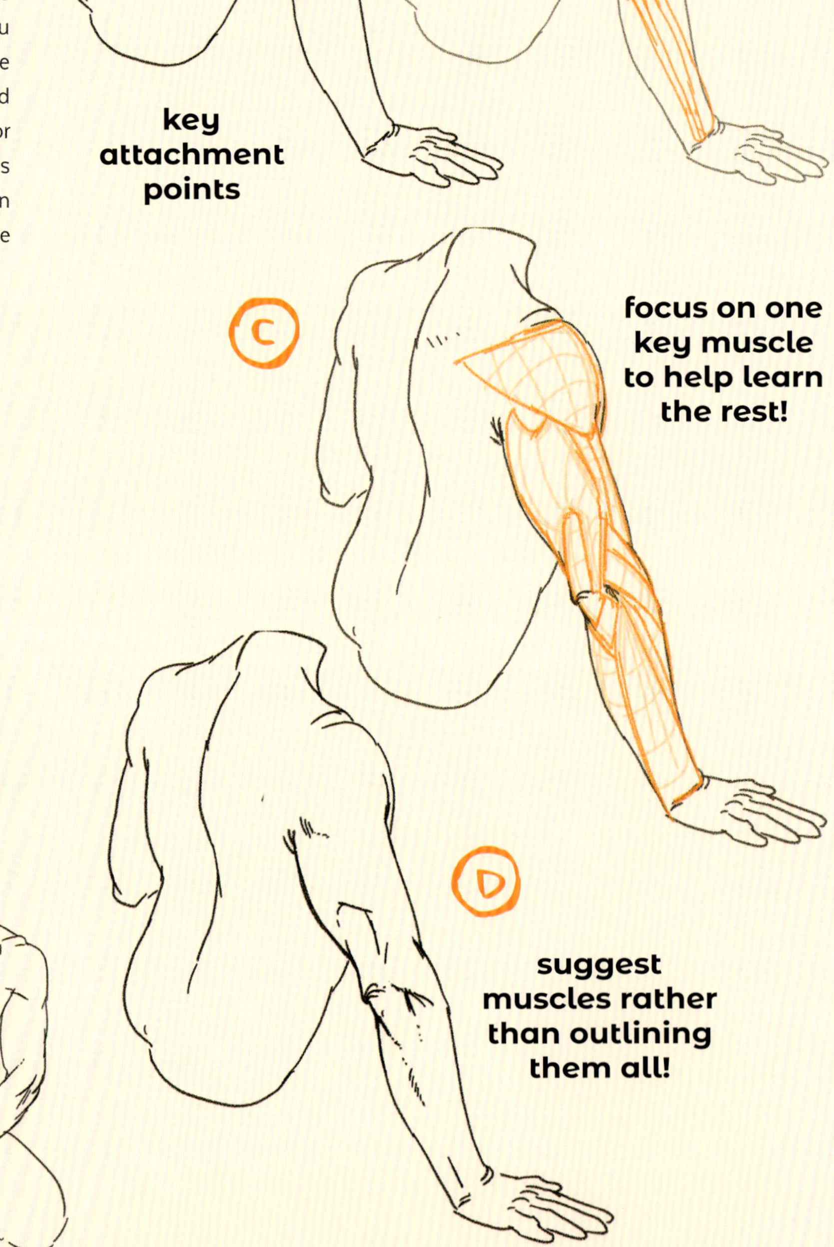

B

brachioradialis sits between biceps and triceps

pronation & supination

Silhouette is everything when drawing the arms. They are the anatomical region we see most after the head, so we tend to pick up on mistakes. When pronating the forearm (rotating it inward), there's a limited range of motion. Past a certain point, we must rotate our upper arm too, in order to achieve the twist (A). In supination (twisting outward), we see a bulge on the back of the forearm caused by the extensor muscles lying flat against the bones (B). In pronation, we see a bulge below as the flexors hang down – I always think of this as being shaped like a rhino's stomach (1)! Above it we can see two steps up as the lower extensors meet the upper ones (2, 3).

Where we draw overlaps, remember to keep them subtle. The arms have many subtle bumps but, overall, are basically tubes. If we draw too many interior lines, the arms will begin to look mechanical (C).

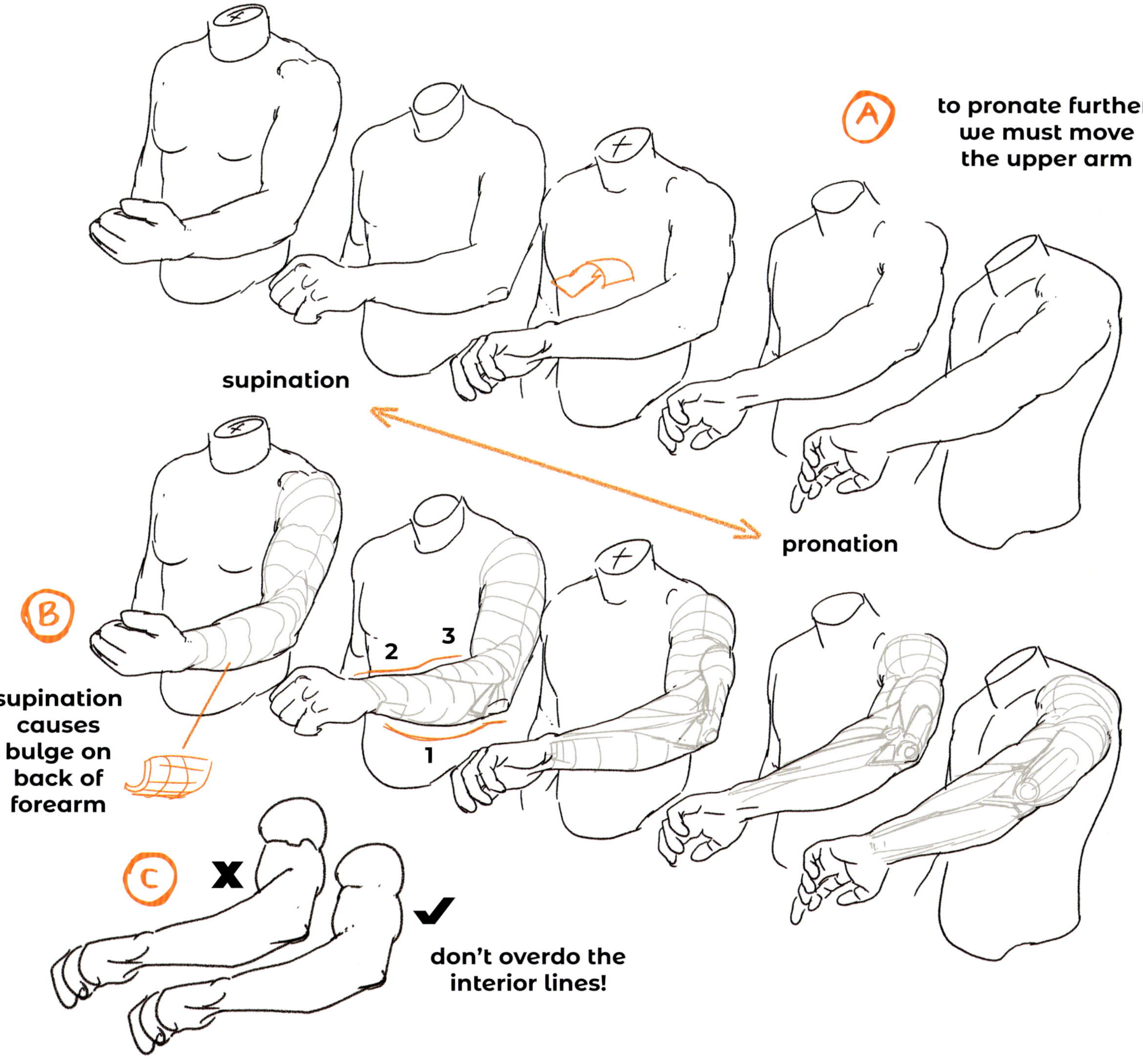

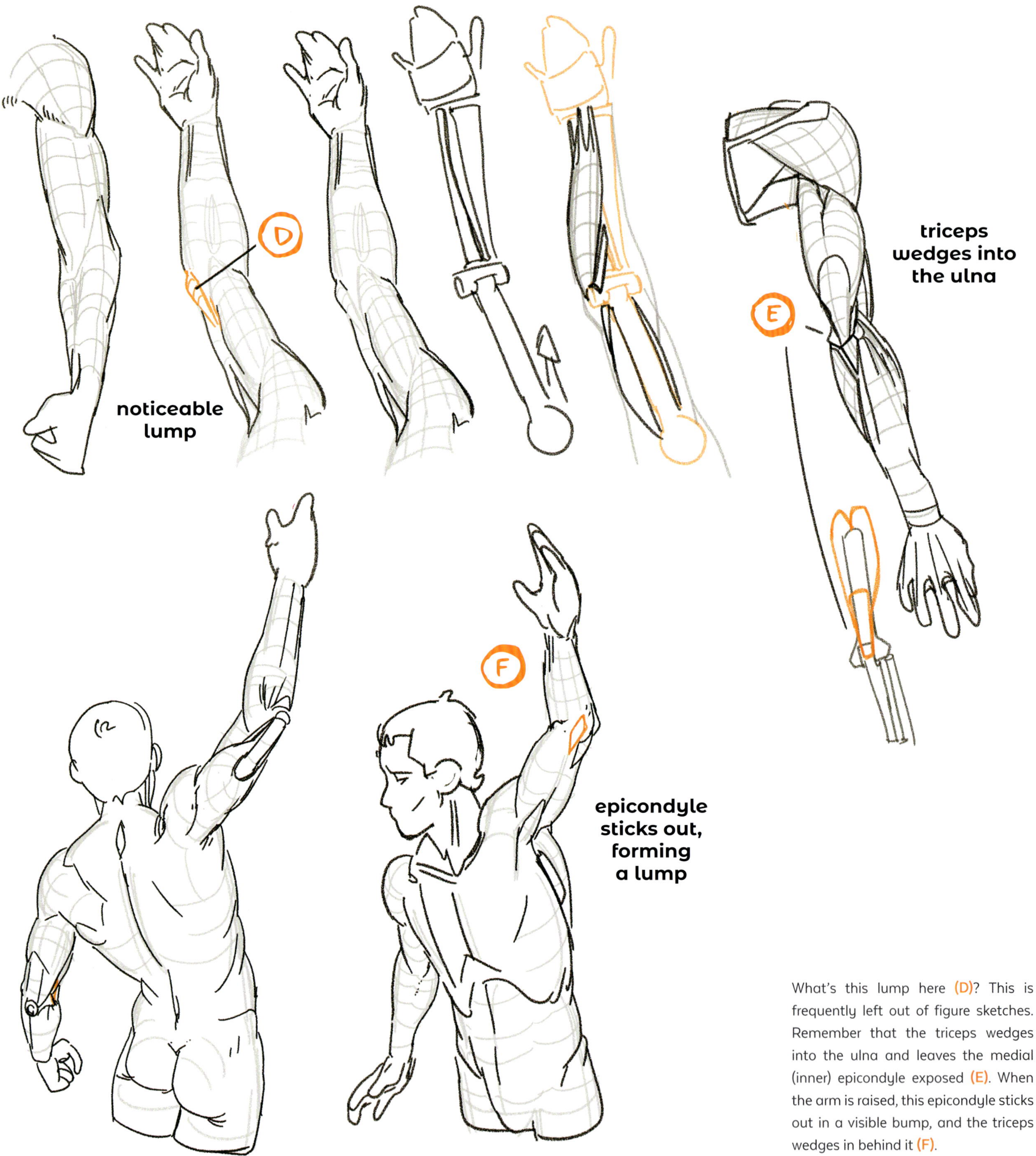

What's this lump here (D)? This is frequently left out of figure sketches. Remember that the triceps wedges into the ulna and leaves the medial (inner) epicondyle exposed (E). When the arm is raised, this epicondyle sticks out in a visible bump, and the triceps wedges in behind it (F).

It's a common mistake, when the arms are bent, to draw an equal fold crossing the form (G). When supinated, the arm is actually higher on the outside. When we pronate, this is exaggerated further (H). Keep this angle in mind when drawing the arm even slightly bent.

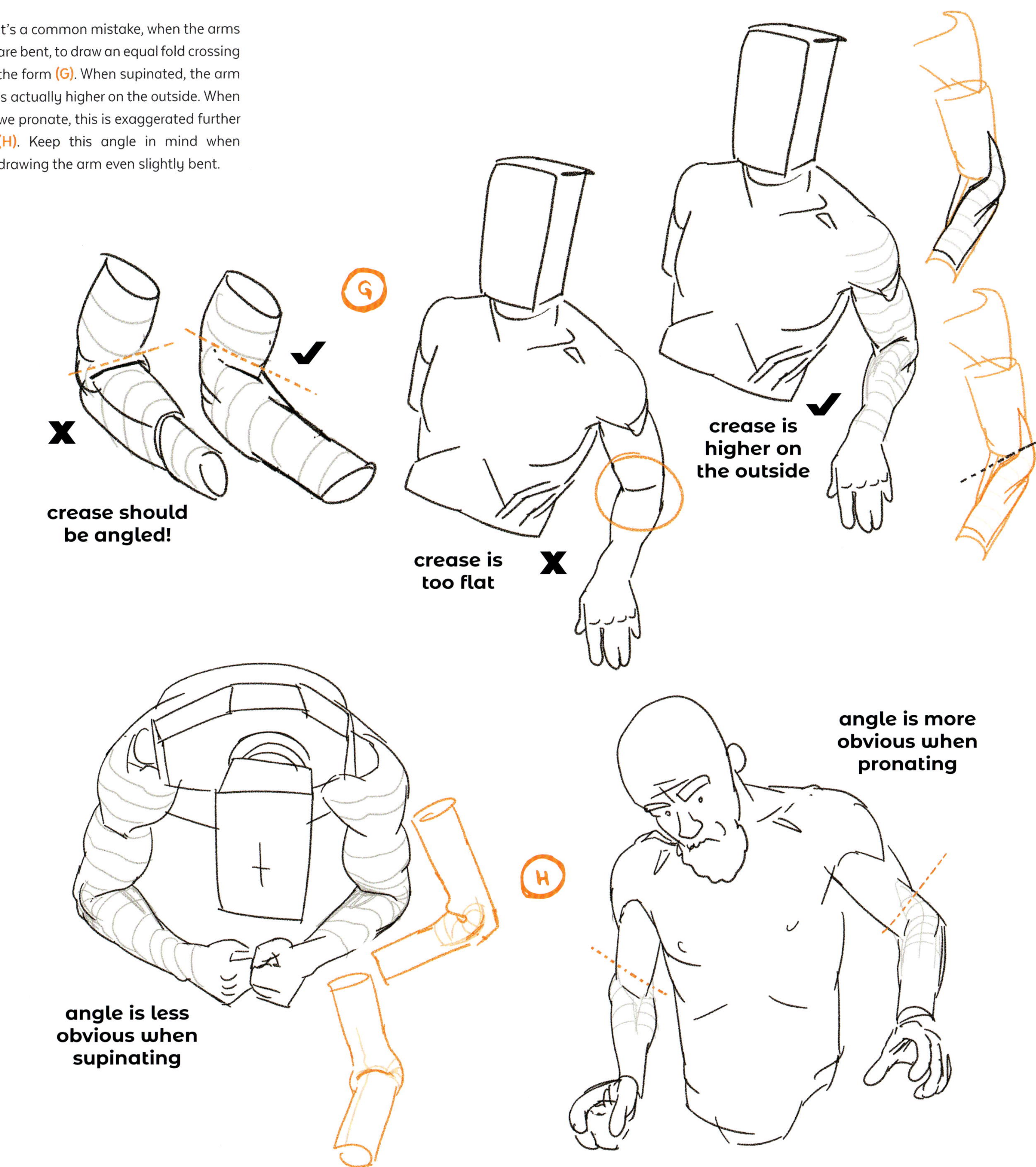

What are these small marks (I)? They're an indication that the biceps isn't flat at the bottom, but instead angles inward because the brachioradialis and extensors push it over toward the medial (inner) side of the arm (J).

When the arms are supinated in muscular individuals, we see some of the extensors fold over themselves, creating this line (K).

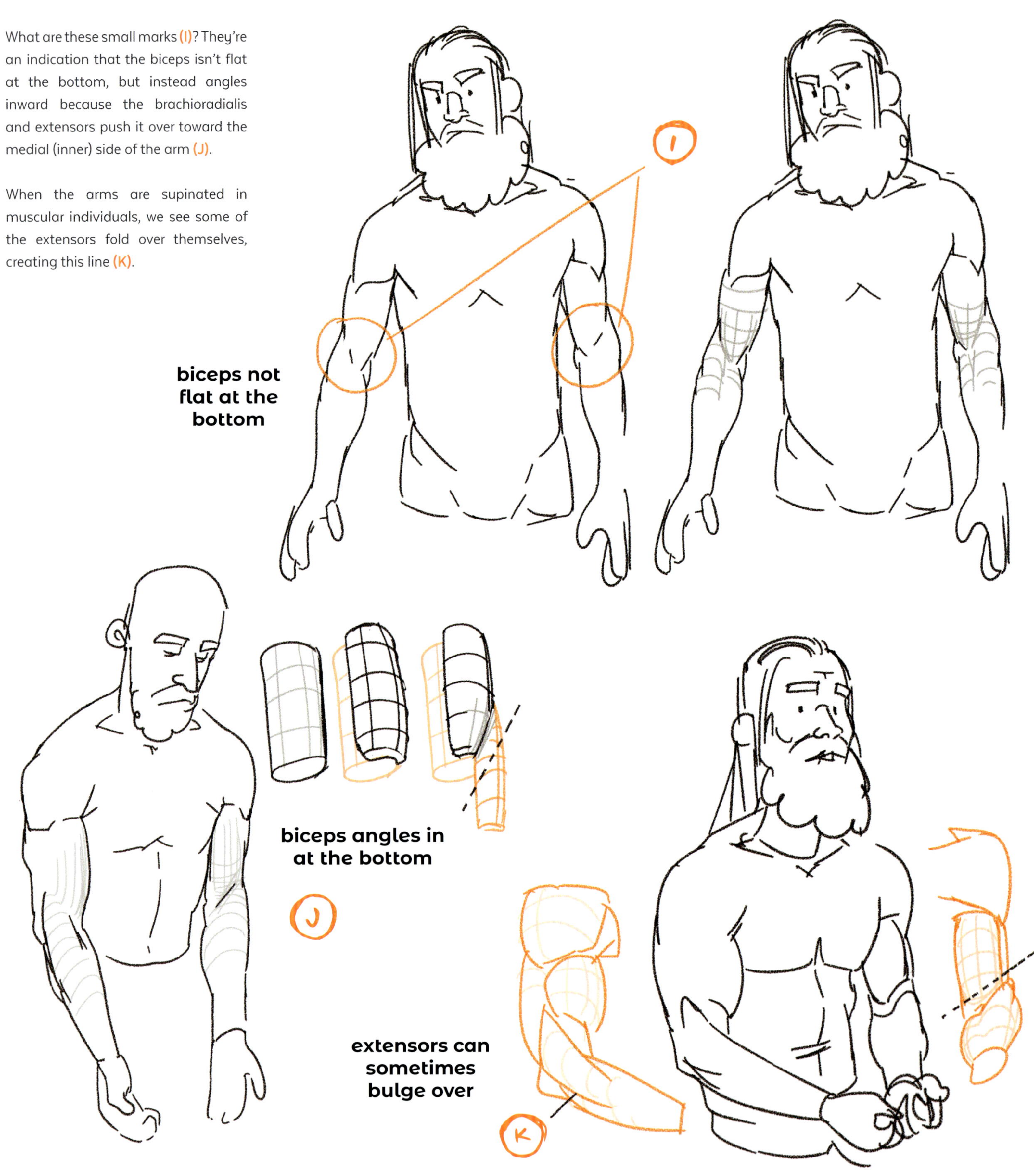

Even for people with extremely large biceps, when the arm is bent, the biceps almost never touches the muscle of the lower arm (L). The biceps contracts and shortens in length as it flexes the lower arm. As the arm raises, so does the biceps (M).

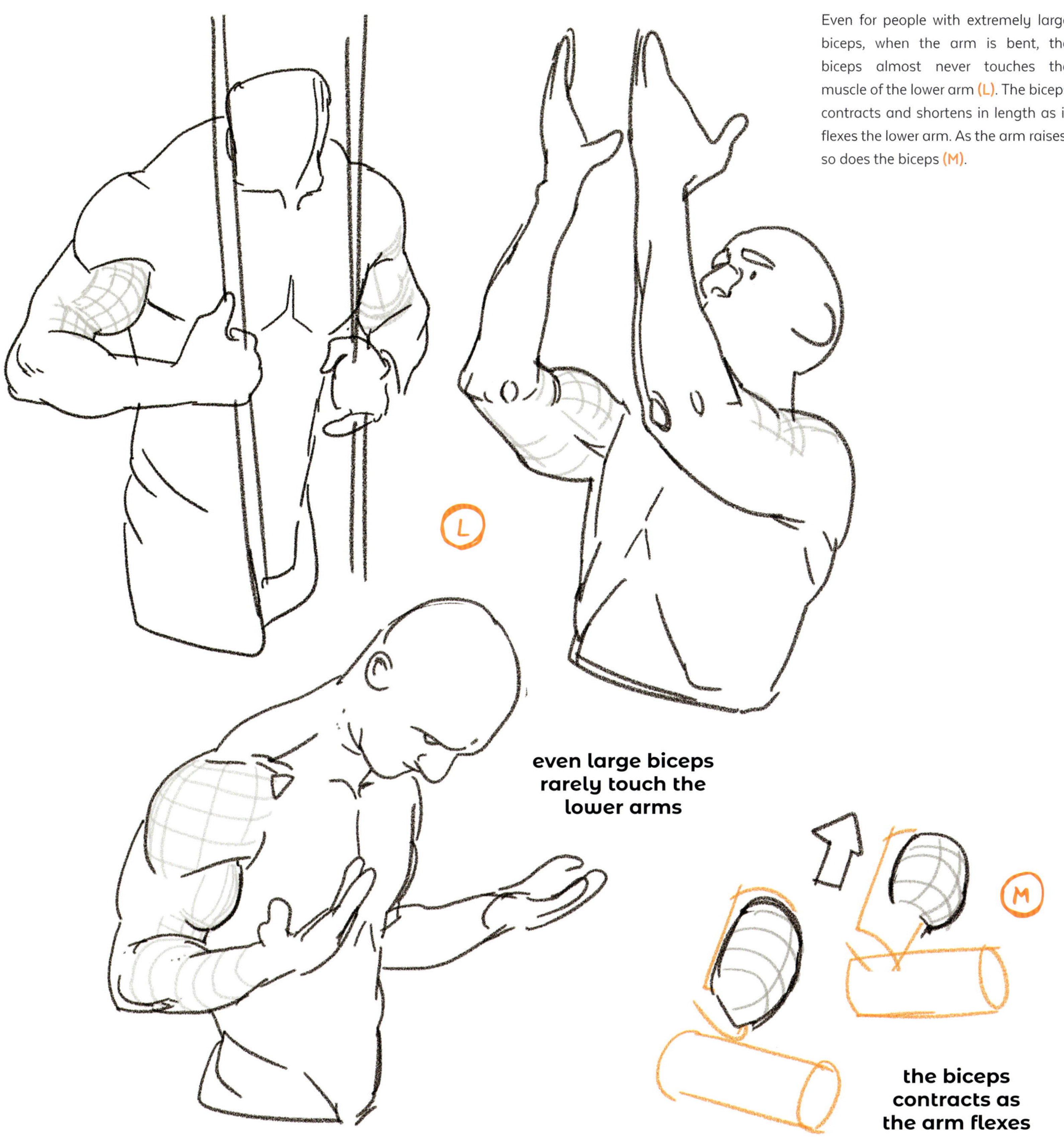

carpals

The bones of the hand can be intimidating, as they look complex, but let's break them down as simply as possible. Attached to the end of the lower arm bones (the radius and ulna), we have the carpals (A). You don't need to memorize each carpal bone – instead, we can imagine them as a small ball that gives us flexibility (B), supporting hand movement (C). The other hand bones will be attached to this ball-shaped mass (D).

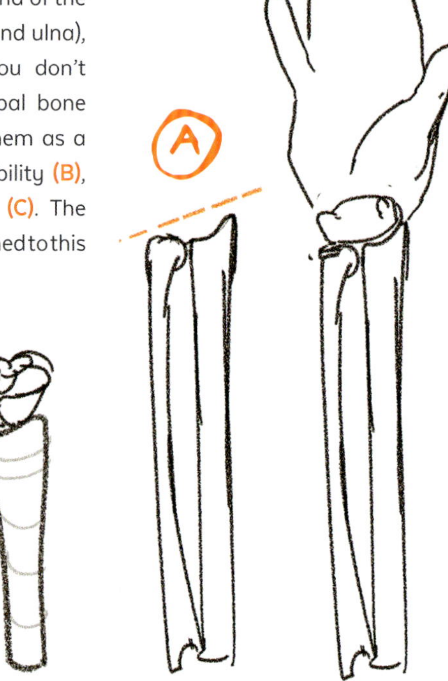

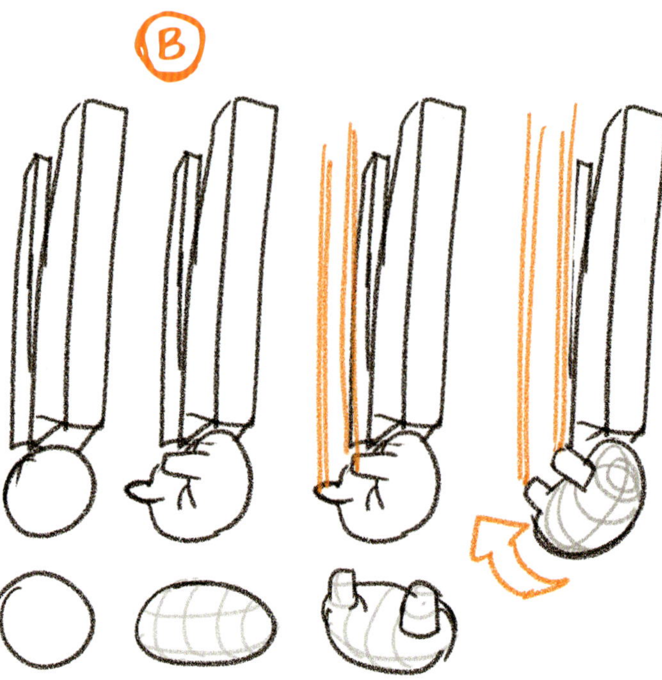

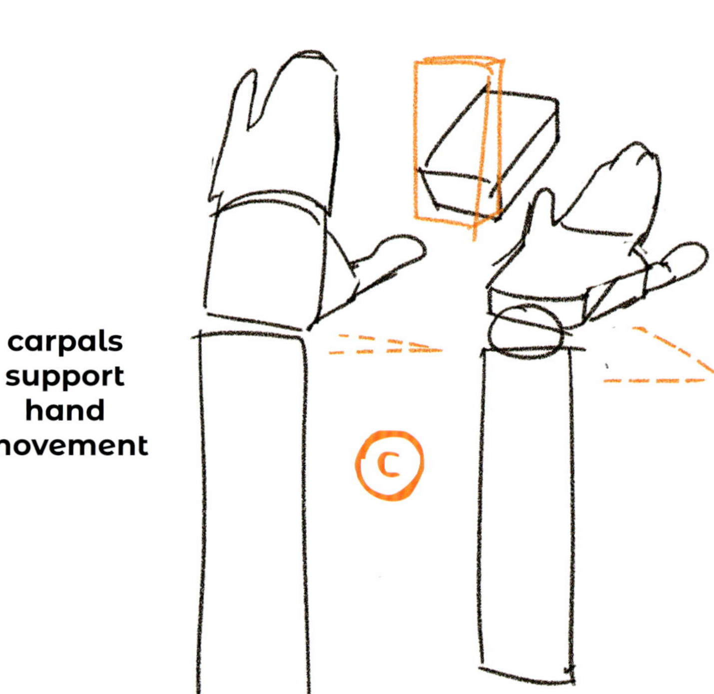

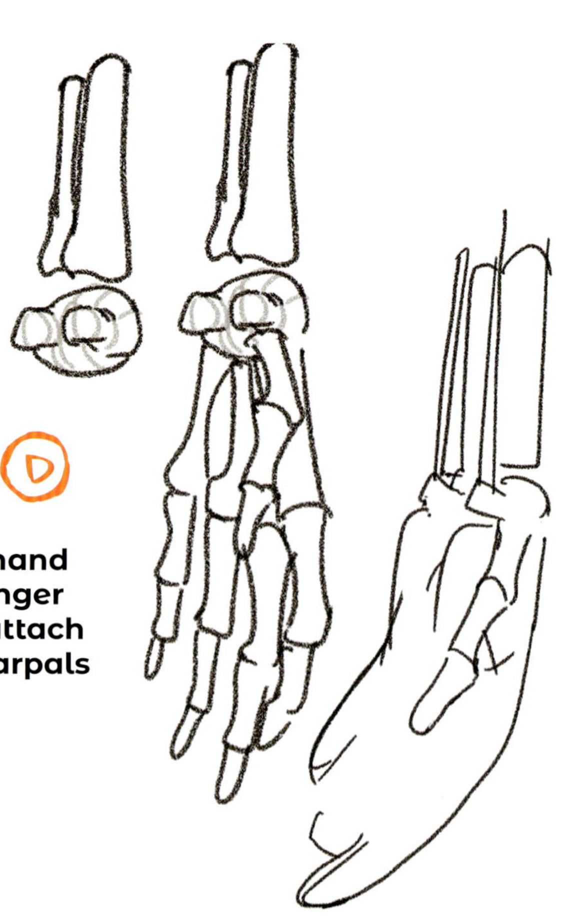

fingers

The fingers themselves aren't parallel. They expand outward from the carpals (A). We can form the palm of the hand by curving a block, and then chopping the corners off, because the fingers wrap and don't begin in a straight line (B). The same is true of the knuckles' position on the back of the hand. The metacarpals (meta means "after," so literally "after the carpals") form the mass of the hand itself, and attach directly to the fingers (C). The finger has three segments called phalanges, while the thumb only has two (D). The first phalange of the finger is the same length as the second and third together. Not only do the fingers radiate outward, they also form a scoop shape and rarely lie flat unless held in a tense pose (E).

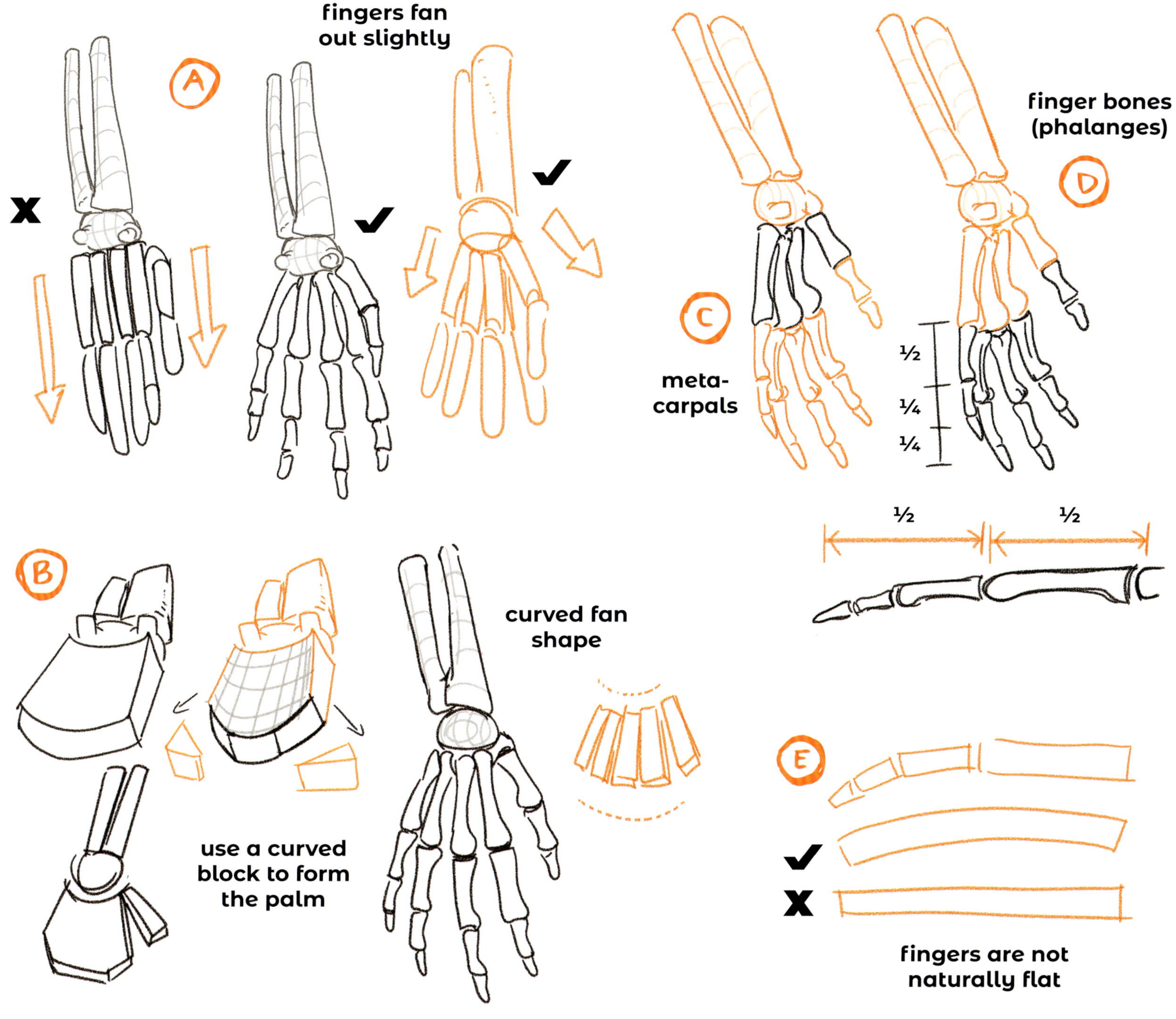

The metacarpals aren't just tubes – they're each shaped like a rectangle with a bulbous end. Those ends are rounded and covered in cartilage so the phalanges can bend around them, allowing our fingers to curl in.

To draw a metacarpal, take a rectangular block and add a ball on the end (F). Take two slices out of the block's sides, so that the form tapers in the middle like an hourglass. This allows space for the muscle and connective tissue to attach in between and hold the fingers together (G).

Finally, remove a slice from the bottom of the block, so the metacarpal forms a sort of arch (H). The phalanges mirror this shape exactly, except for the final phalange (the fingertip), which has a pointed end. The three completed phalange shapes form the fingers, and each finger has a tendon along the top to help move it (I).

The fingernails themselves have to look like they're wedging into the fingers, not just sitting on top (J).

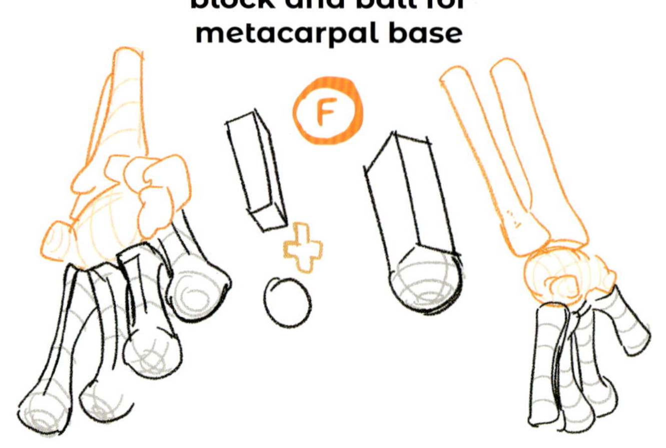

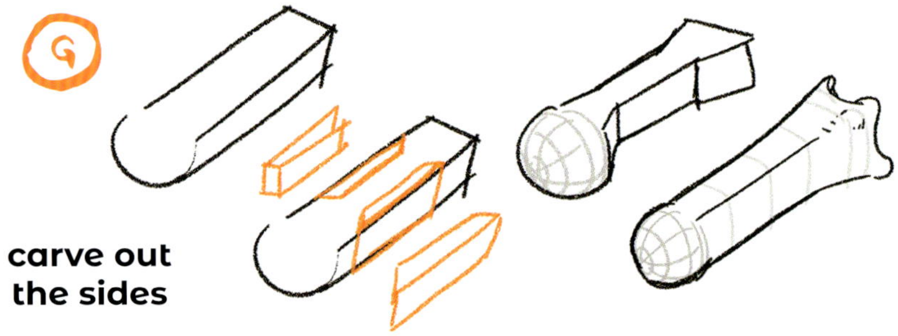

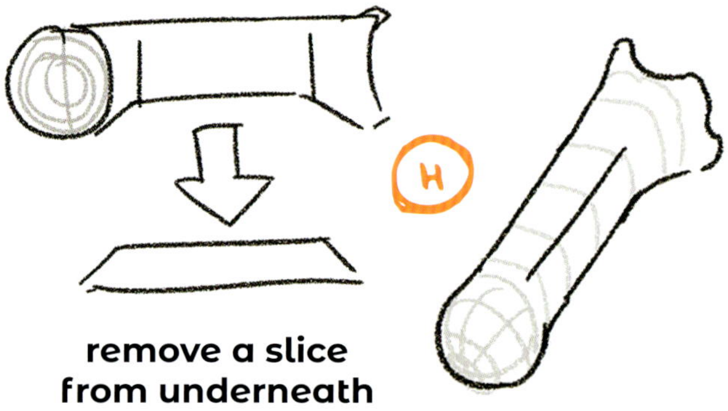

G

carve out the sides

H

remove a slice from underneath

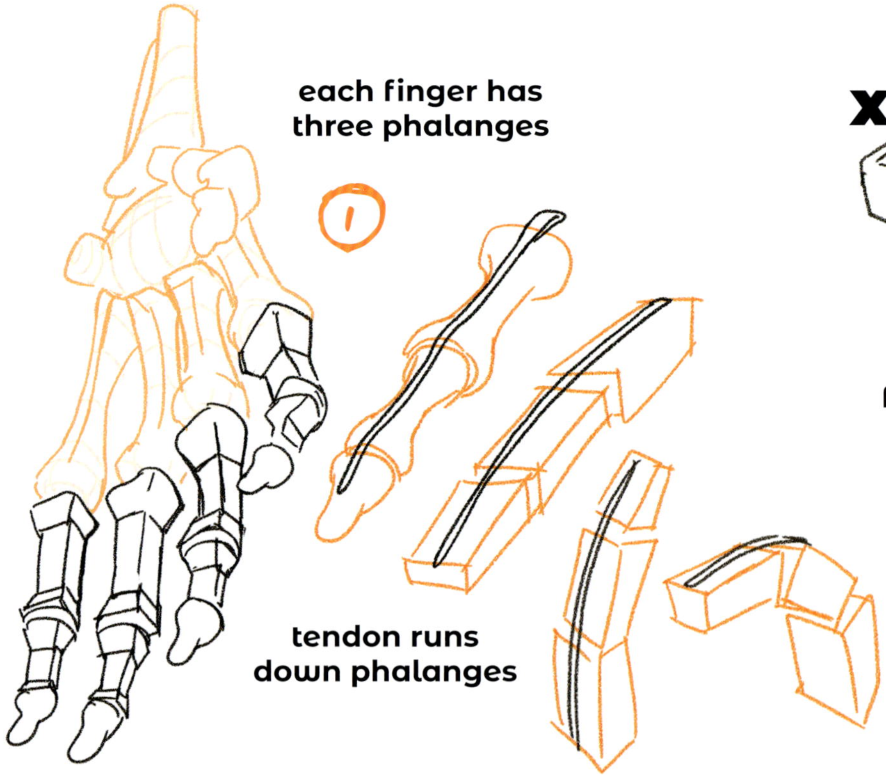

each finger has three phalanges

I

tendon runs down phalanges

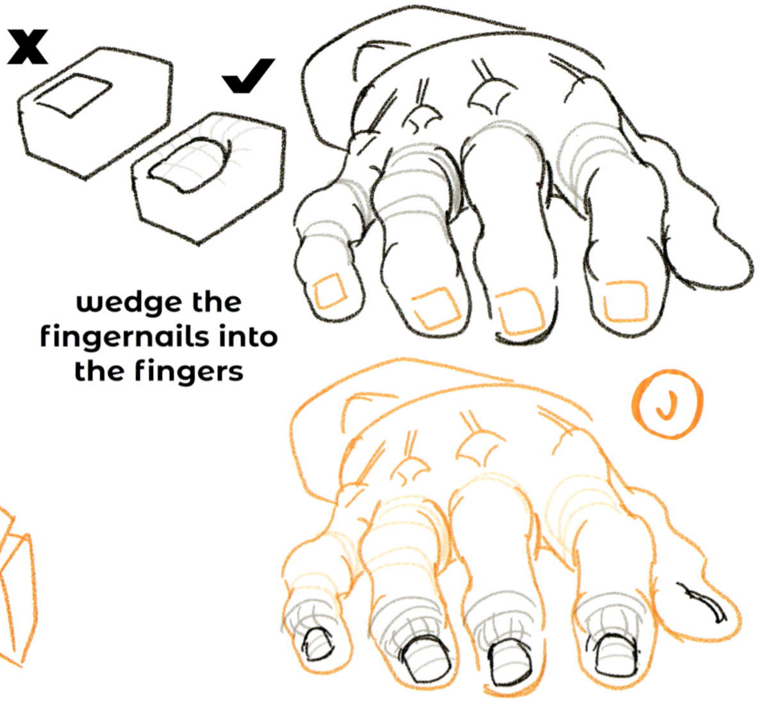

wedge the fingernails into the fingers

J

Between the radius and the ulna, we have connective tissue that stabilizes the bones to prevent them from separating and also provides an attachment point for some of the muscles of the forearm. The hand is really a mass of connective tissue and tendons, with a few small muscles between. Most of the power generated for opening and closing the fingers comes from the lower arm, so really the hand is just bones and their connections covered with some skin and fat.

We have "capsules" that cover the actual joints of the fingers (K), and above those are the tendons of the extensors, particularly the extensor digitorum (literally "finger extender") (L). Above the tendons are all sorts of protective and strengthening tissues, with names like "extensor hood," but we can simplify them into a rubbery tube that sits above (M).

Finally, we have the extensor retinaculum, which is just above the hand, wrapping around like a sweatband. It gives support to all the tendons that run around the wrist and gathers them together (N).

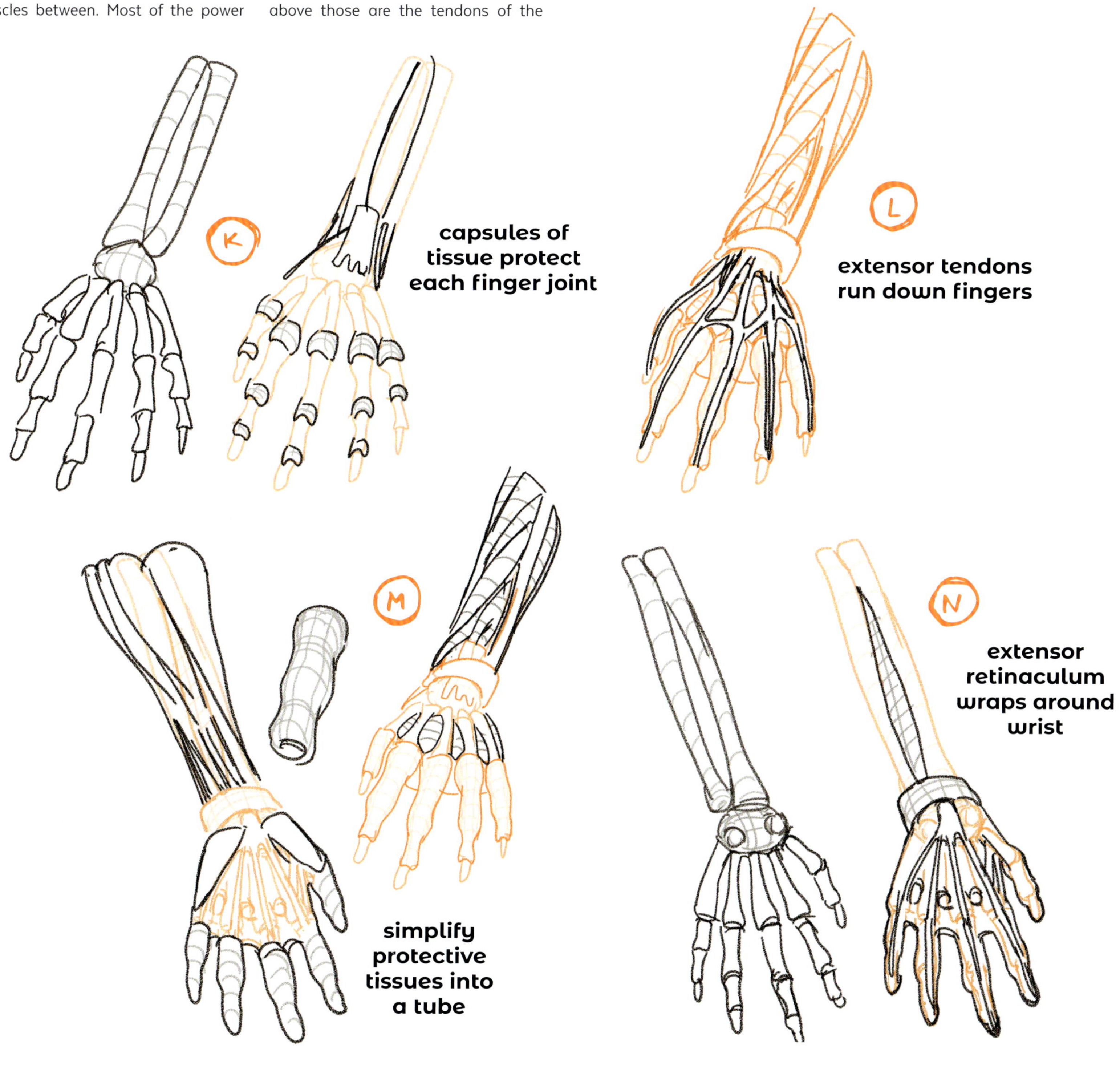

designing the hand

So let's begin designing our simplified mannequin hand, starting with some basic observations. Don't worry about getting all the best anatomy resources – a mirror and some focused attention will give you the real secrets!

First, we can see that the hand's range of motion is limited when raising it up (extension). The extensor muscles can only raise your hands 35–40 degrees. In contrast, our flexors can flex the hand almost 90 degrees voluntarily, and even further with some added pressure (A). The hand itself has a delicate curve that matches the top of the forearm (B).

Note that when we bend our hand forward, it doesn't move down vertically, but usually angles outward slightly (C).

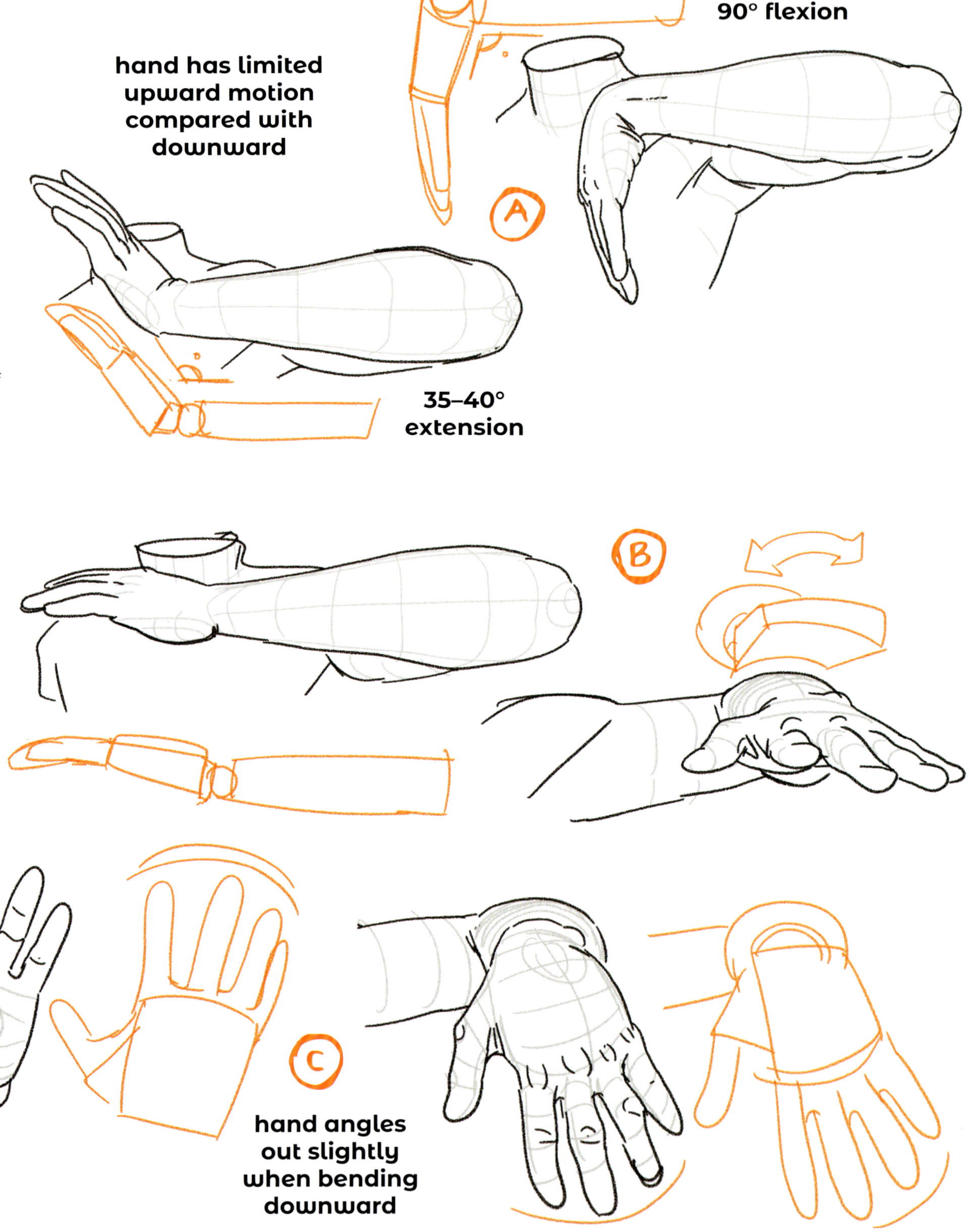

Start the hand design with a block, round off the corners, and give it some curvature. To this, add a triangle on the side for the hinge of the thumb (D), and two small segments for the thumb, representing its base metacarpal and two phalanges (E).

The main challenge isn't the anatomy, but the posing. The forms don't need to be complex, but they do need to be posed well. We all know what a hand looks like in various emotional states!

Add simple fingers with two joints each. We rarely extend our fingers and thumb out straight, so gently curve them inward (F). See how the extensor retinaculum holds the tendons in (G). If we pulled on the hand, the tendons would likely pull away without it.

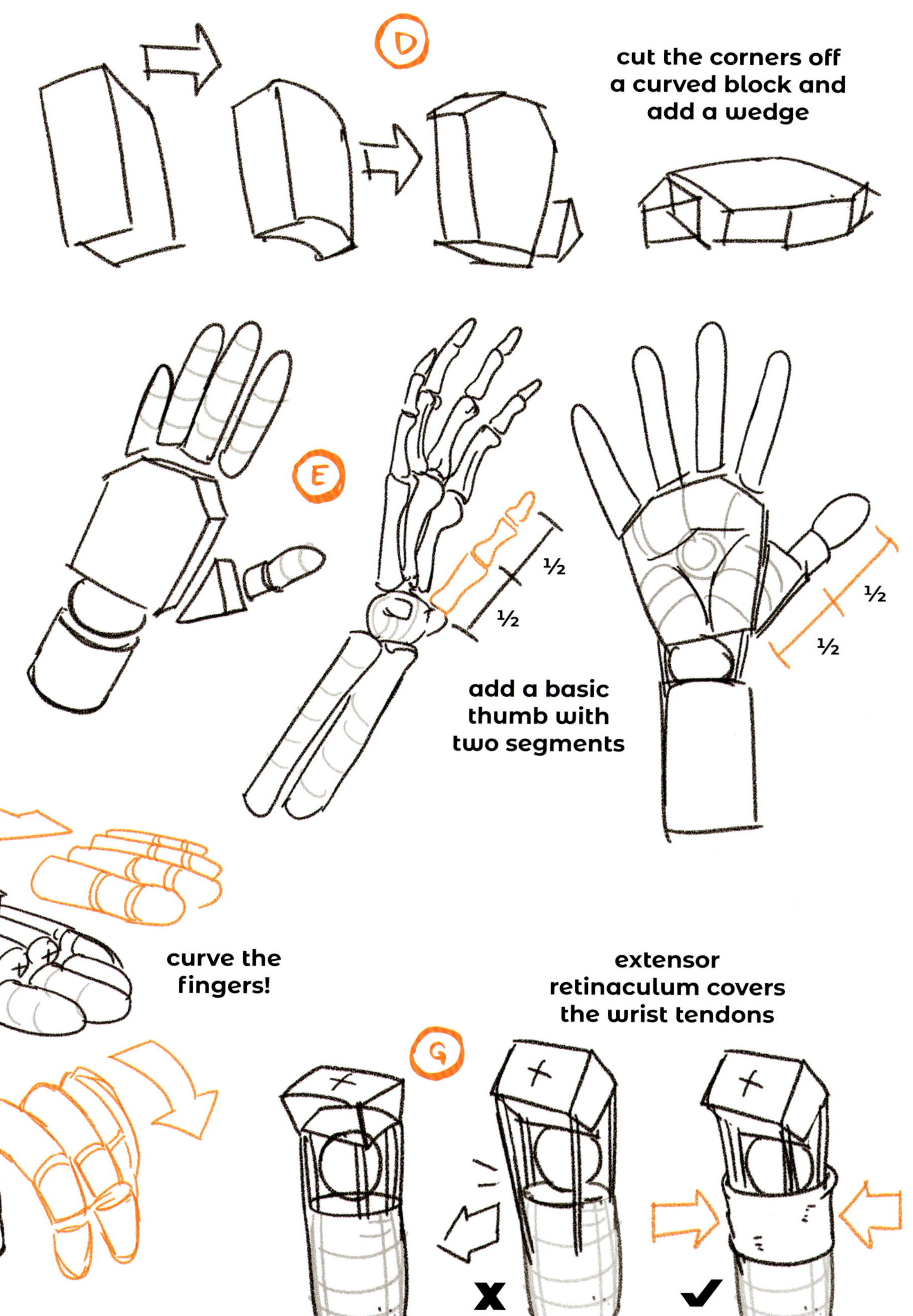

the thumb

Visualize the base of the thumb as a triangle that can swing outward and inward. It has a great range of inward motion for grasping things, but is limited in outward motion (less than 20 degrees) (A). The muscles on the interior of the palm are actually quite small, but are cushioned by thick connective tissue and fat. The general shape of the muscles is shown here (B).

When the thumb is bent inward, don't just bend it over the inner volume of muscle – actually embed it into the mass. It needs to really sink into the form to be believable (C)! Practice drawing the palm of the hand with just a thumb and little finger. Move them around like joysticks and practice overlapping the forms of the hand.

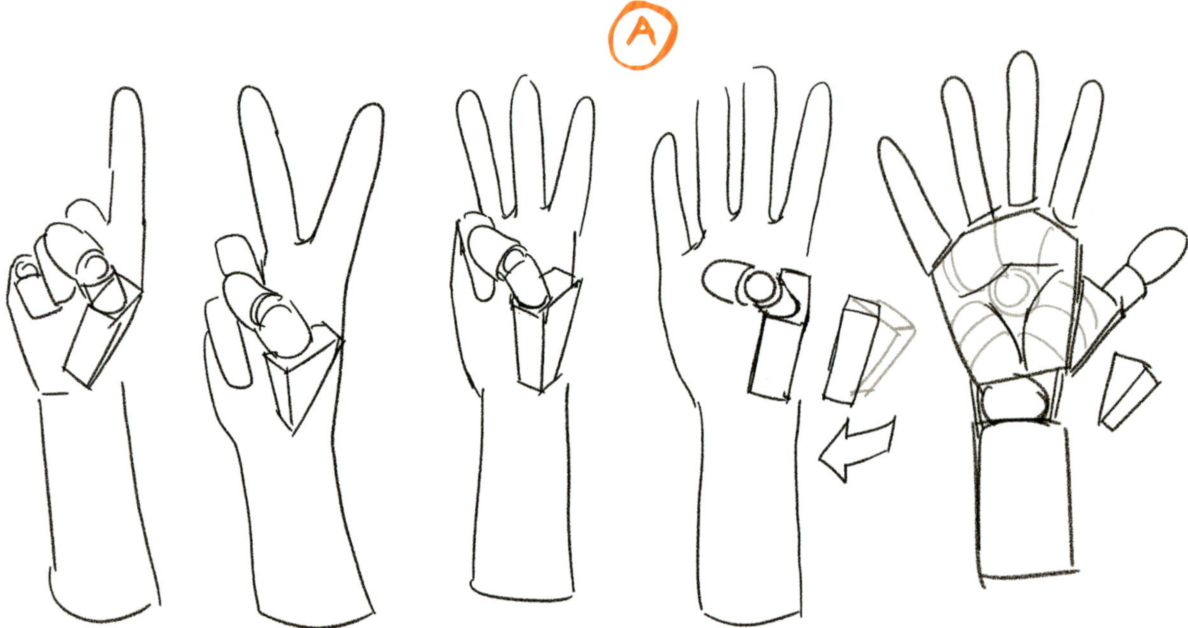

the thumb has limited outward motion

B

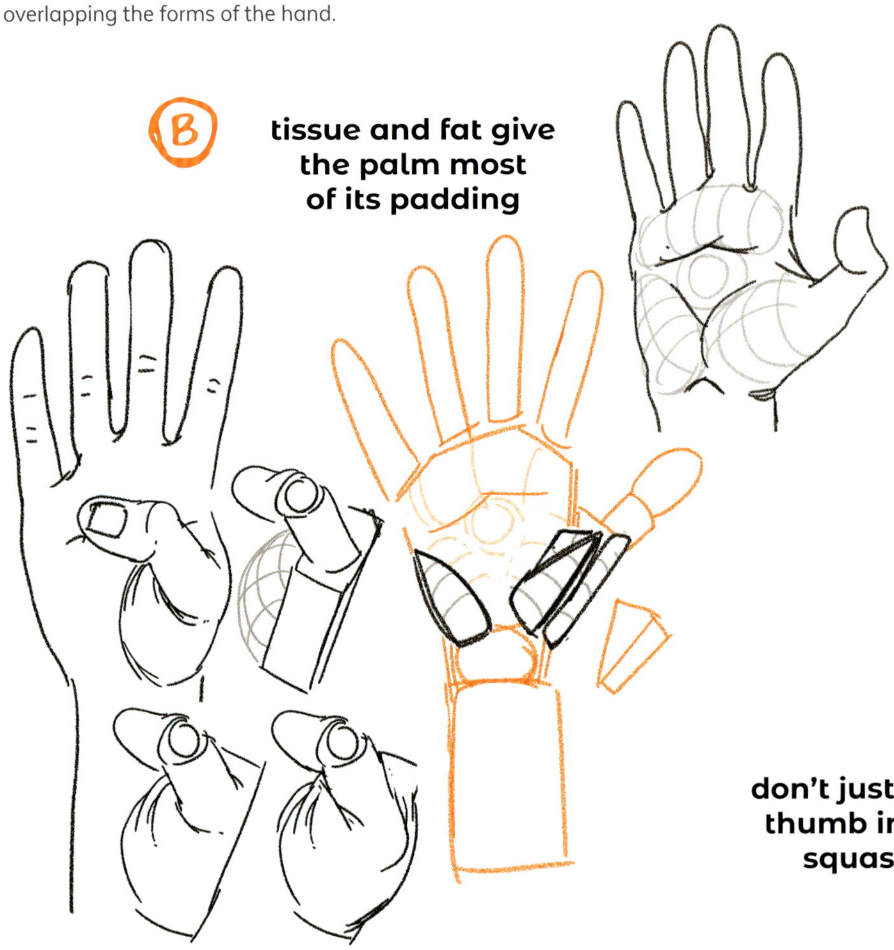

tissue and fat give the palm most of its padding

C

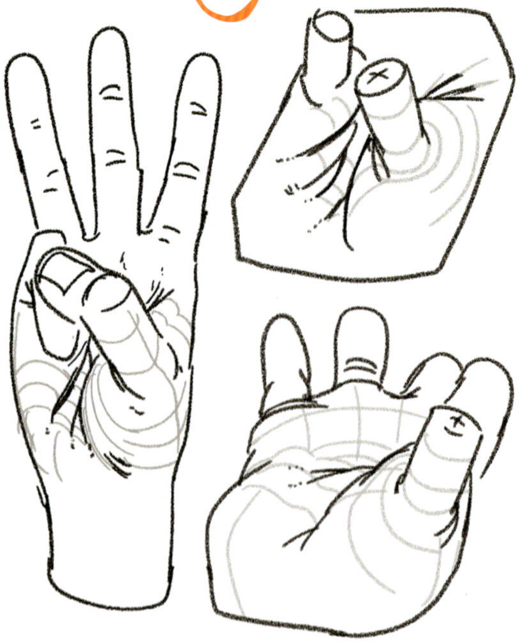

don't just bend the thumb in – really squash it in!

knuckles

To represent the knuckles, you can draw simple diamond shapes on top of the joints where the metacarpals meet the fingers (A). As a quick solution, when you're not interested in drawing details, you can simply draw the finger as a tube with a bulge in the middle to represent the main joint. Making this basic tube more organic helps add realism (B).

Less fat and flesh will make a hand look older and give it character. To draw a really creepy hand, just emphasize the bones even more (C)!

When the hands are extended, don't make the mistake of drawing the forms parallel and flat. Instead, give them a gentle angle inward (D).

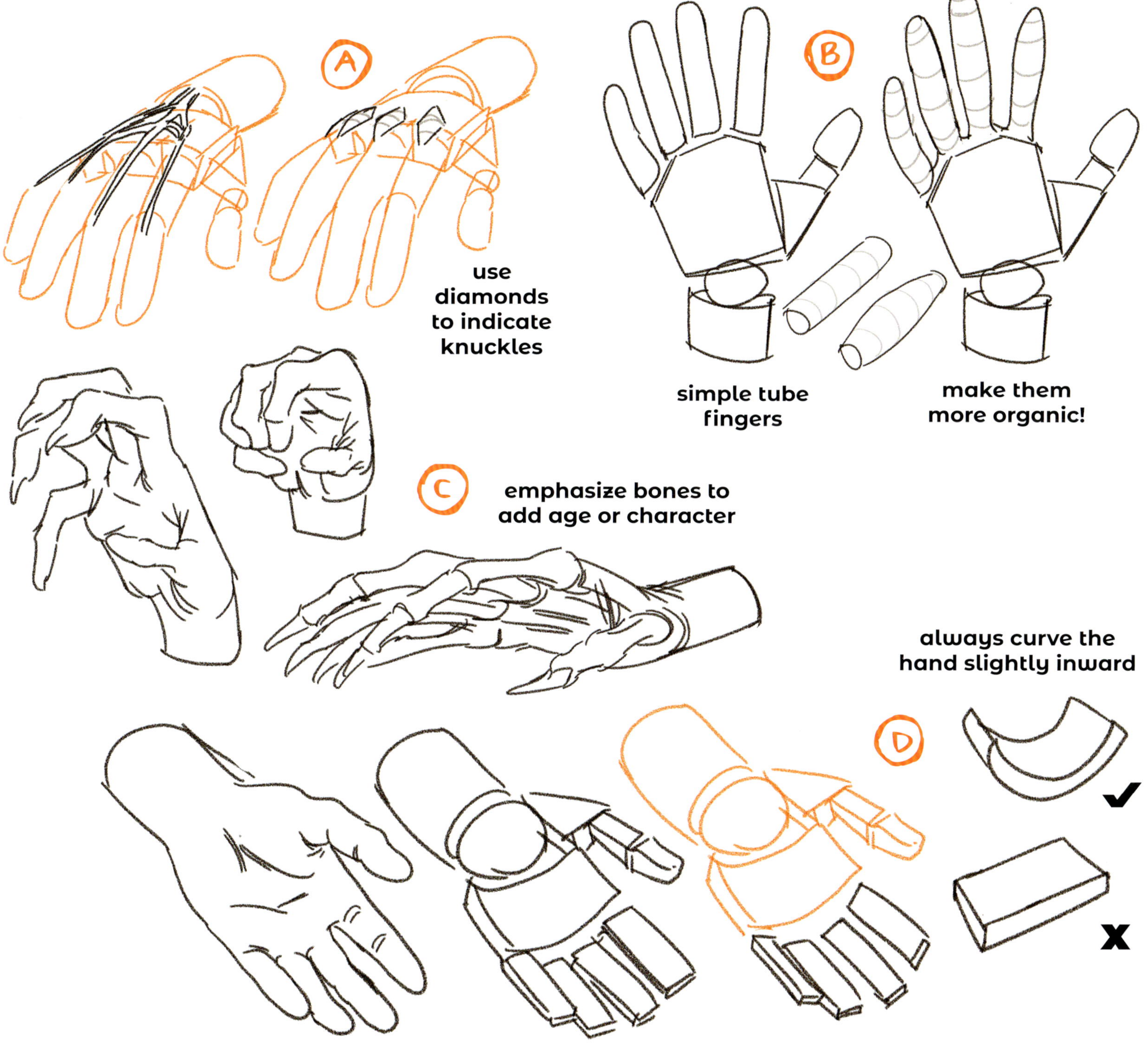

On leaner people, you'll often see the tendons of the flexors (which close the hand) in more active poses. Don't overdo this, though – just adding one or two can add power to your pose (E).

When drawing folds in the skin, remember that they don't originate from a central point like a starfish. Instead, have them clearly overlap each other and choose which line is in front of the other (F).

It's natural to want to draw the loose skin on the knuckles on the top of the hand. Before you do, ask yourself, "Is this appropriate for the pose and model?" Frequently, the skin on top has no clear folds, just some suggested lines. Drawing more folds usually suggests older hands.

When we make a fist, our fingers are almost never parallel (G). You can make a fist with your fingers parallel, but it will look unnatural! The index finger, closest to the thumb, is usually raised higher than the others to make room for the thumb.

In all these examples, we can see one thing that's worth noting: When the fist is clenched, a small bump appears at the side, where the skin bulges (H). This adds realism and tension, so is always worth including.

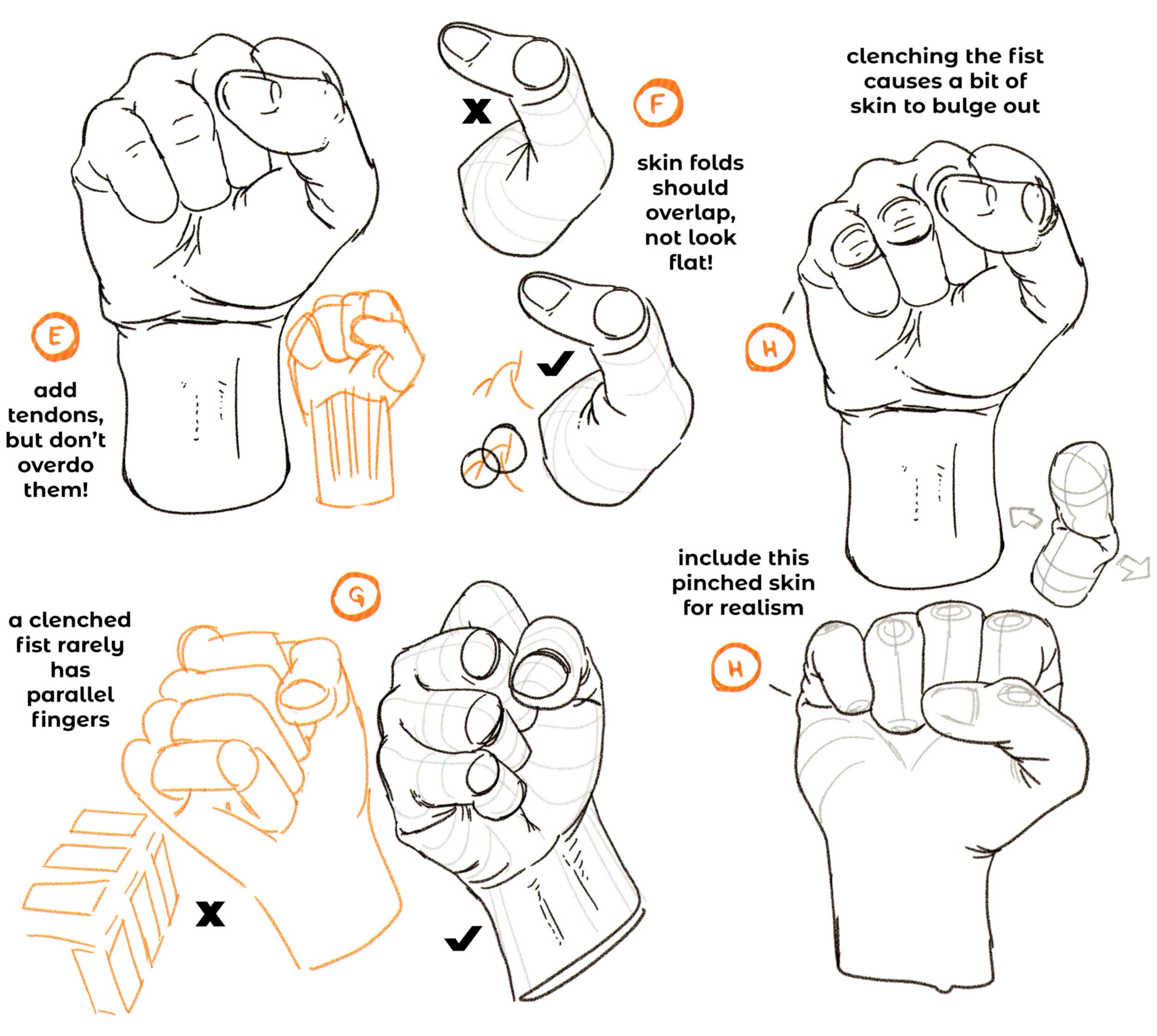

When we extend our fingers in a relaxed way, they form an arc rather than a straight line across (I). We can straighten them with effort, but because our metacarpals are curved, so are our fingers when extended.

The distal phalanges (the end bones of the fingers) have a strange shape. If you pinched a piece of putty and flattened the end, you'd pretty much make that shape. The fingernail sits on top of this small, flattened form (J). Fingernails are surprisingly hard to draw, because they curve and wrap over but are also rounded at the ends. When drawing the knuckles and fingernails, remember: Don't complete shapes (K). This is a golden rule for drawing anything. Just suggesting a shape gives so much more realism than completely outlining it, such as the webbing between the fingers. Whisper the form to the viewer – don't shout it (L).

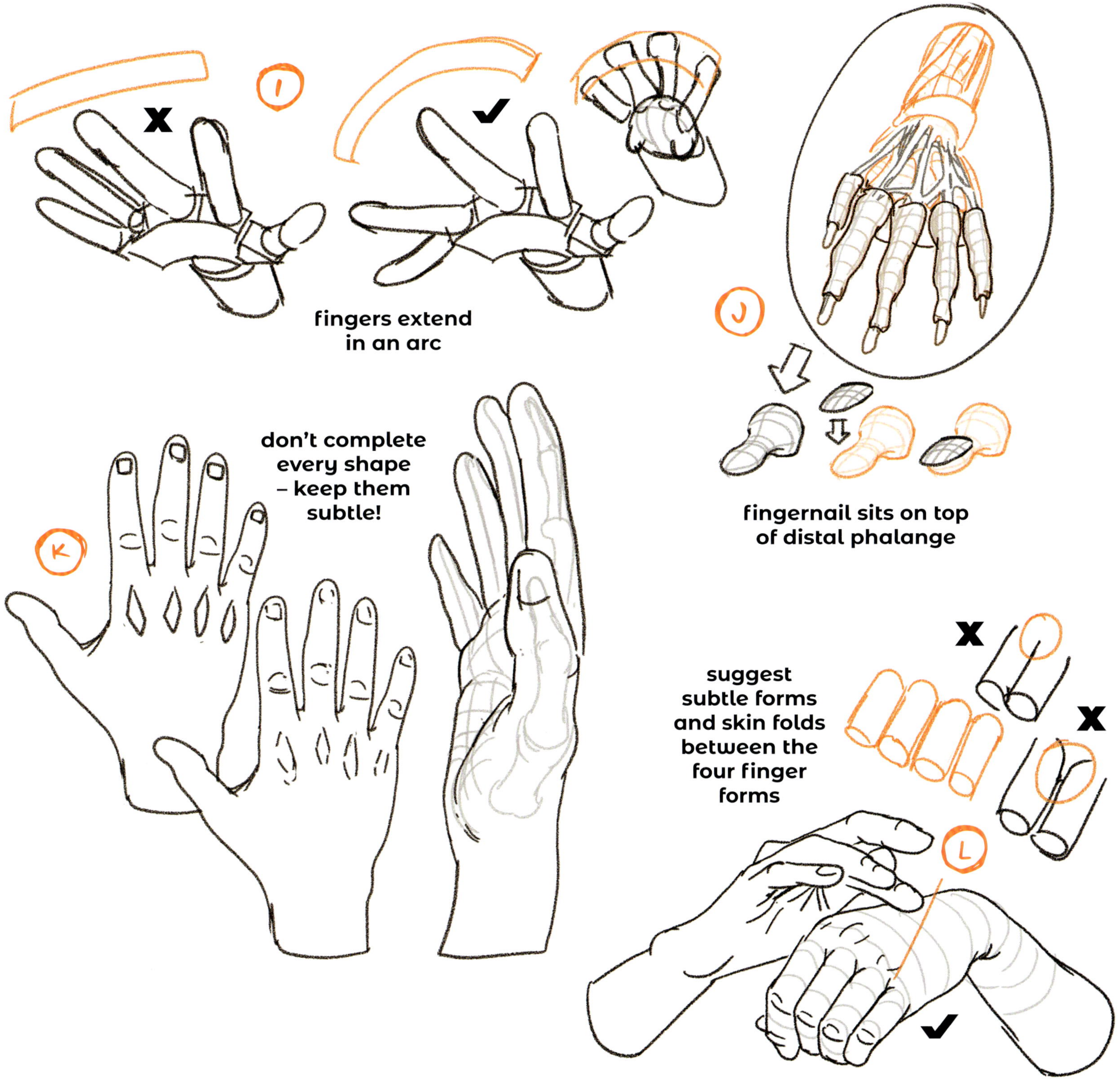

believable hands

When we draw the skin connecting the thumb to the fingers, consider how it will stretch and fold. The form should wrap over itself and have enough excess skin to form creases, but not too many creases (A)! The fingers themselves have webbing between them, but it attaches near the inside of the hand, never near the top side or the middle of the fingers (B).

To practice adding the skin between the fingers, take the box shape of the hand and slice off the top section, so the whole hand is scoop-shaped (C). Then attach the fingers as simple tubes, and add the webbing between them on the inner side of the hand (D).

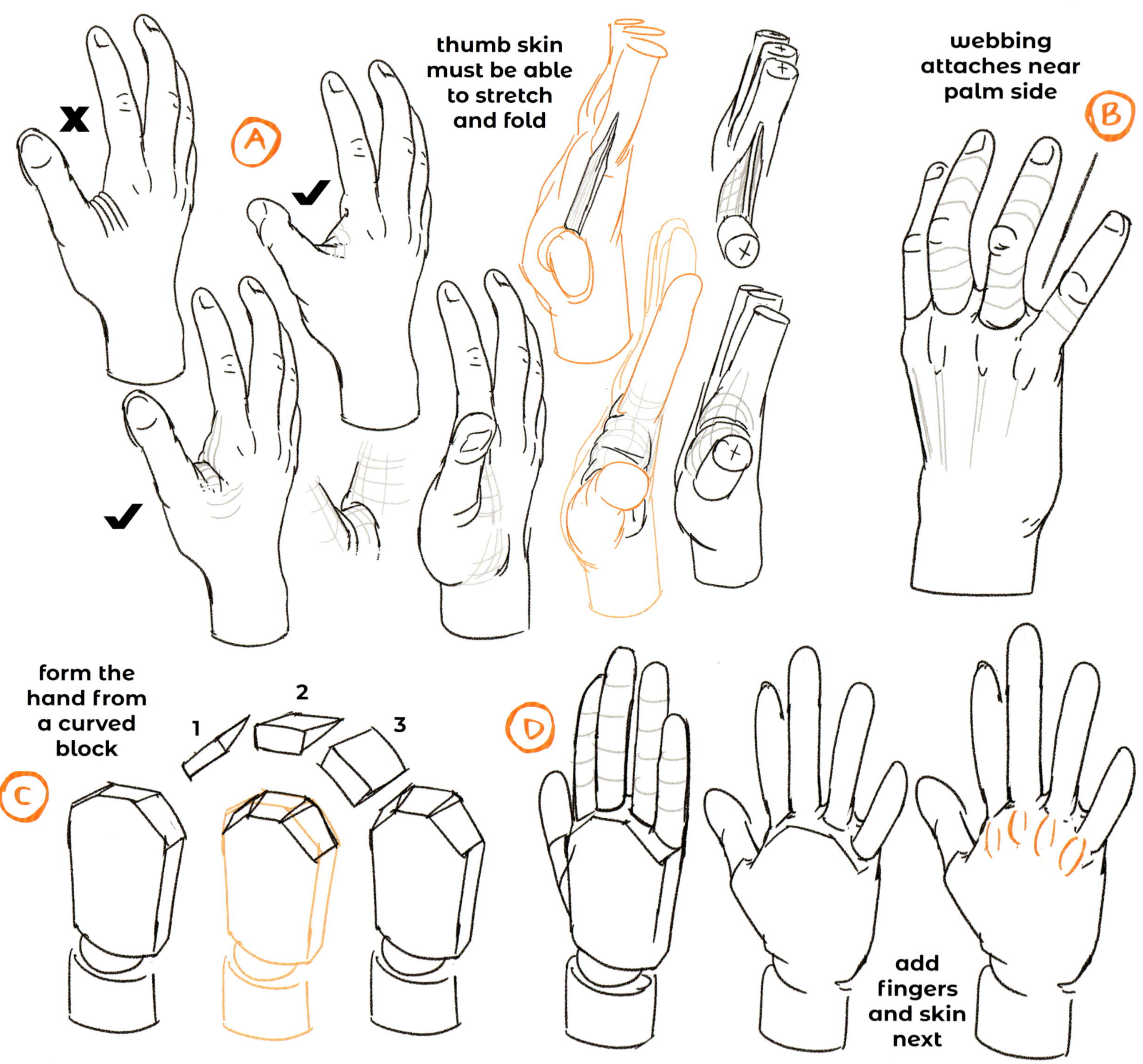

The tips of the fingers aren't equally flattened. The index finger and thumb are flatter than the others (E). When drawing the tendons on the back of the hand, make sure they're not parallel. They converge toward a central point on the back of the hand (F).

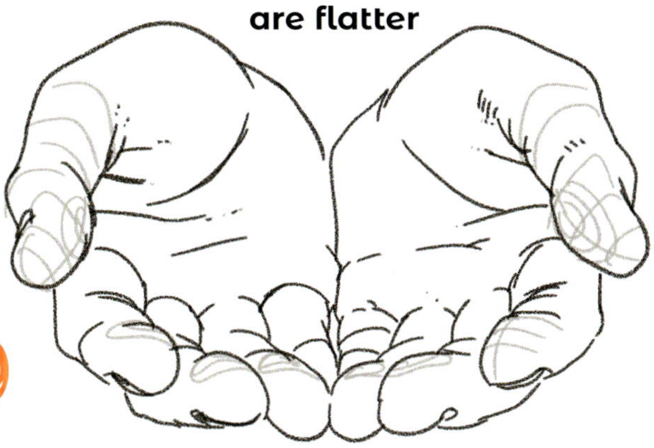

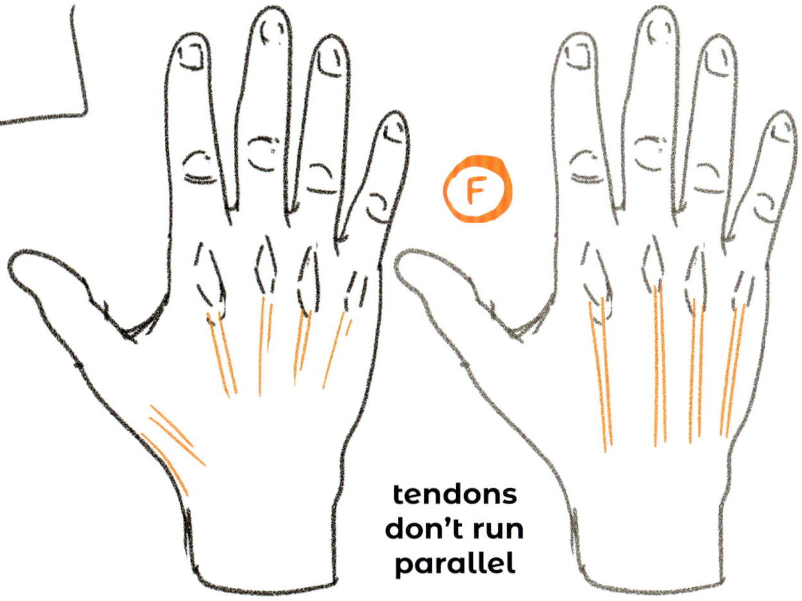

To absolutely guarantee that your hands are more believable and interesting, increase the variety in them: draw fingernails differently, make sure the fingers are angled differently, and try to avoid parallel forms (G). Remember to flatten the fingernails and embed them firmly in the fingers (H).

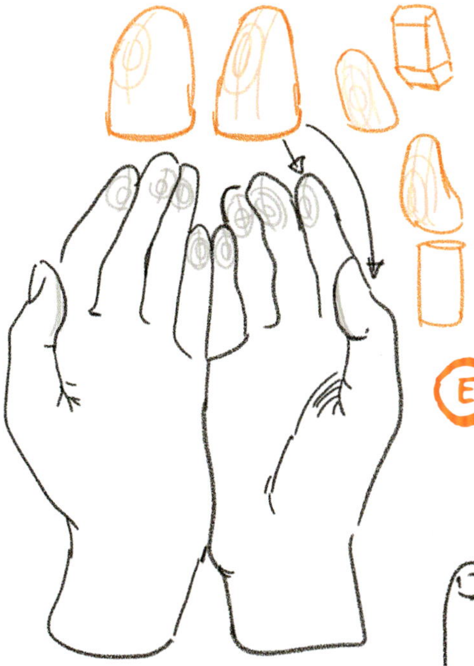

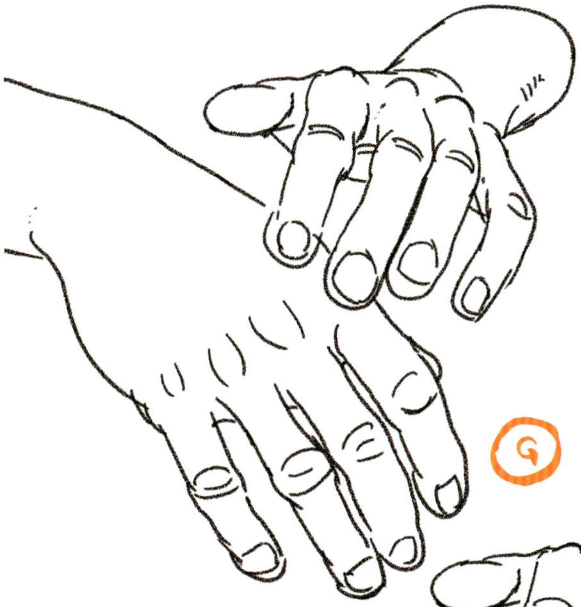

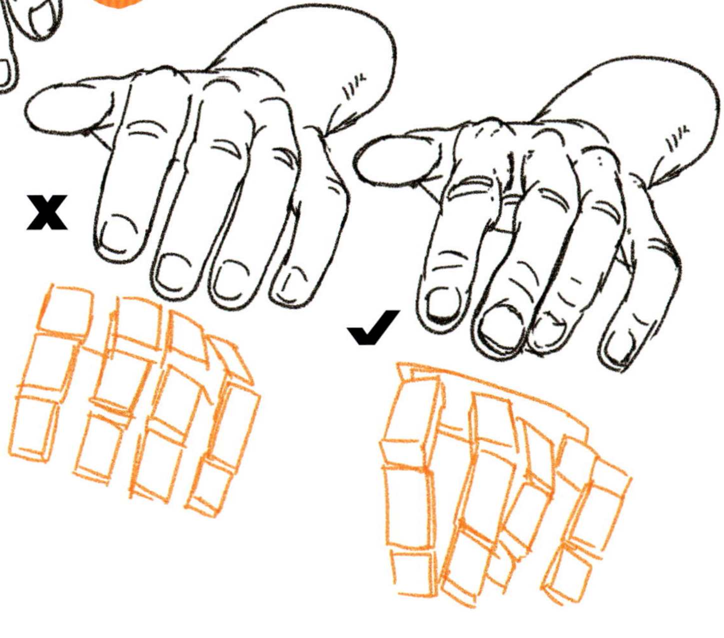

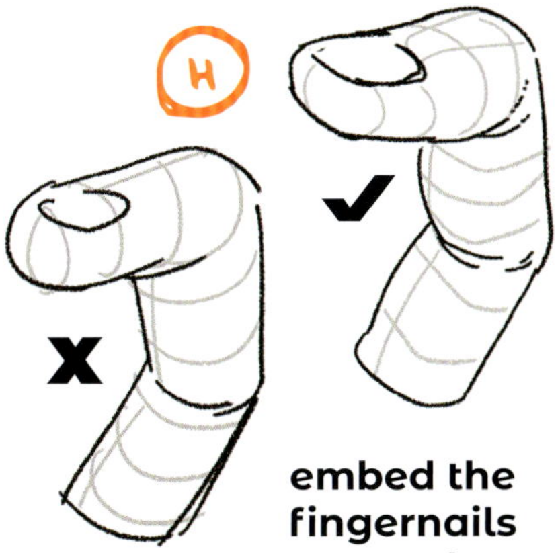

Even though tubes are a quick, easy shorthand for a simple, relaxed finger, it's helpful to visualize the fingers as cuboid forms rather than tubular ones (I). Tubes are difficult to rotate accurately! The marks that suggest the fingers' folds can often ruin a well-drawn silhouette because they look rushed and suggest different rotations for each finger (J). Variety is important, but a few carelessly placed lines can cause a finger to look warped (K)!

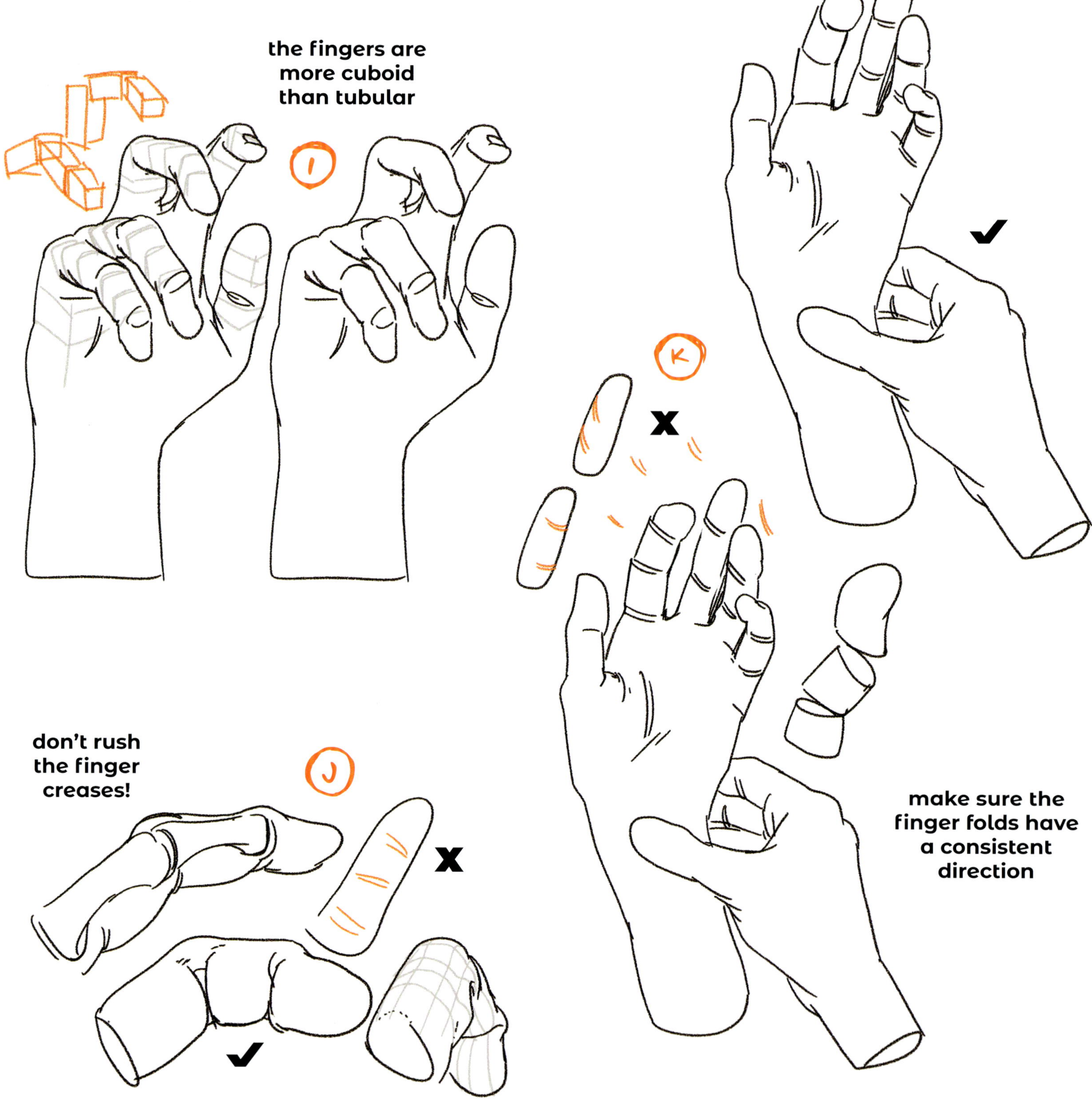

On the back of the wrist, two large tendon groups are often visible. The first is the extensor pollicis longus (or "EPL") (1). Extensor means "extend," pollicis means "of the thumb," and longus means "long." The second group is the extensor pollicis brevis and abductor pollicis brevis (2), but all you really need to know is that they move the thumb around (L).

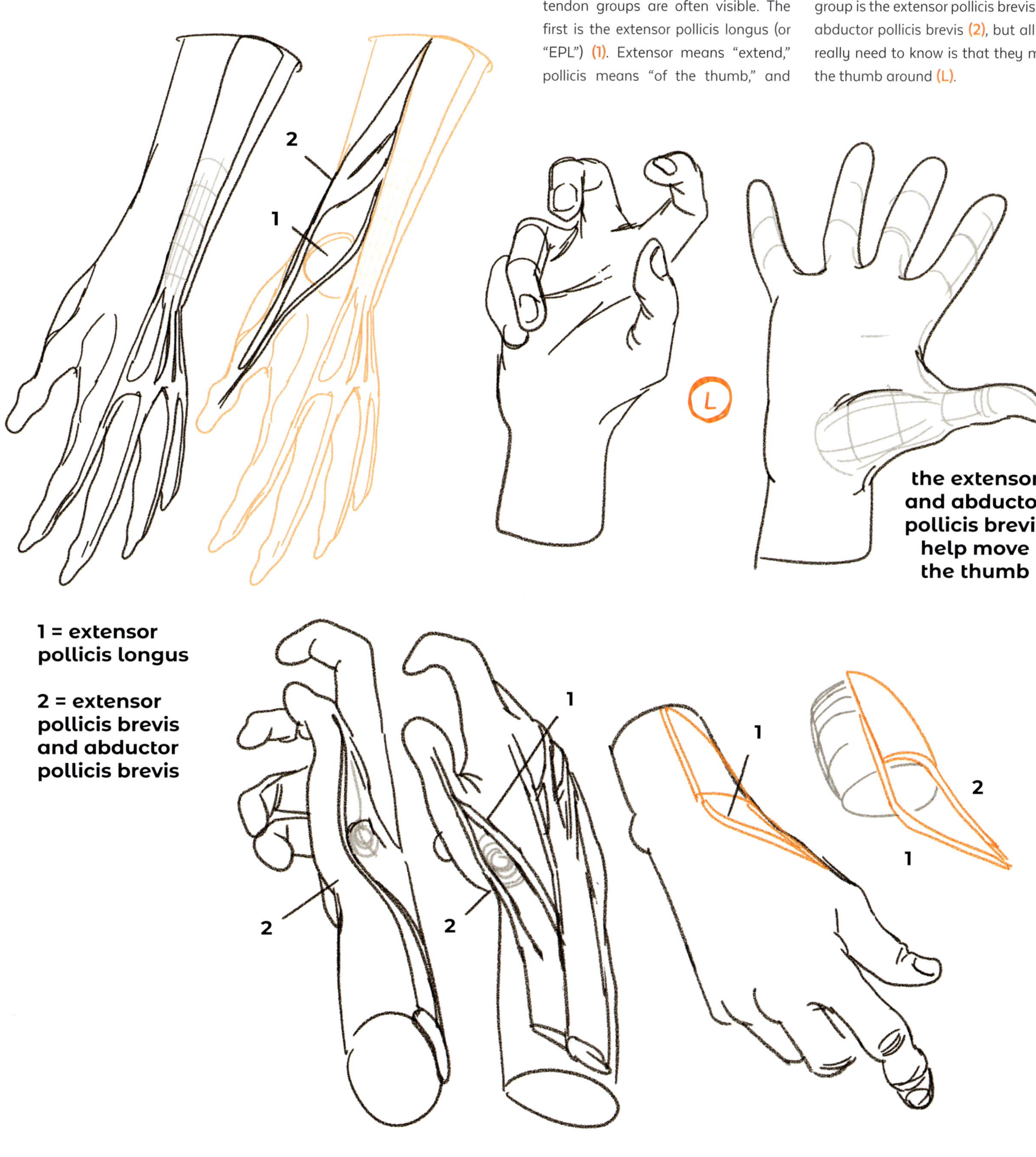

arm summary

We've completed our journey down the arm to the hand, so let's have a run through how we've developed our mannequin arm's level of detail.

We started with flattened cylinders, to which we added epicondyles to form the hinge of the arm (A), with rounded notches to allow movement.

Next we added the deltoids above the ball of the shoulder joint and showed how they attach into the outer (lateral) side of the arm (B). We developed the upper arm into an octagonal shape (C) and ensured it was narrower at the front than the back to show the width of the triceps (D).

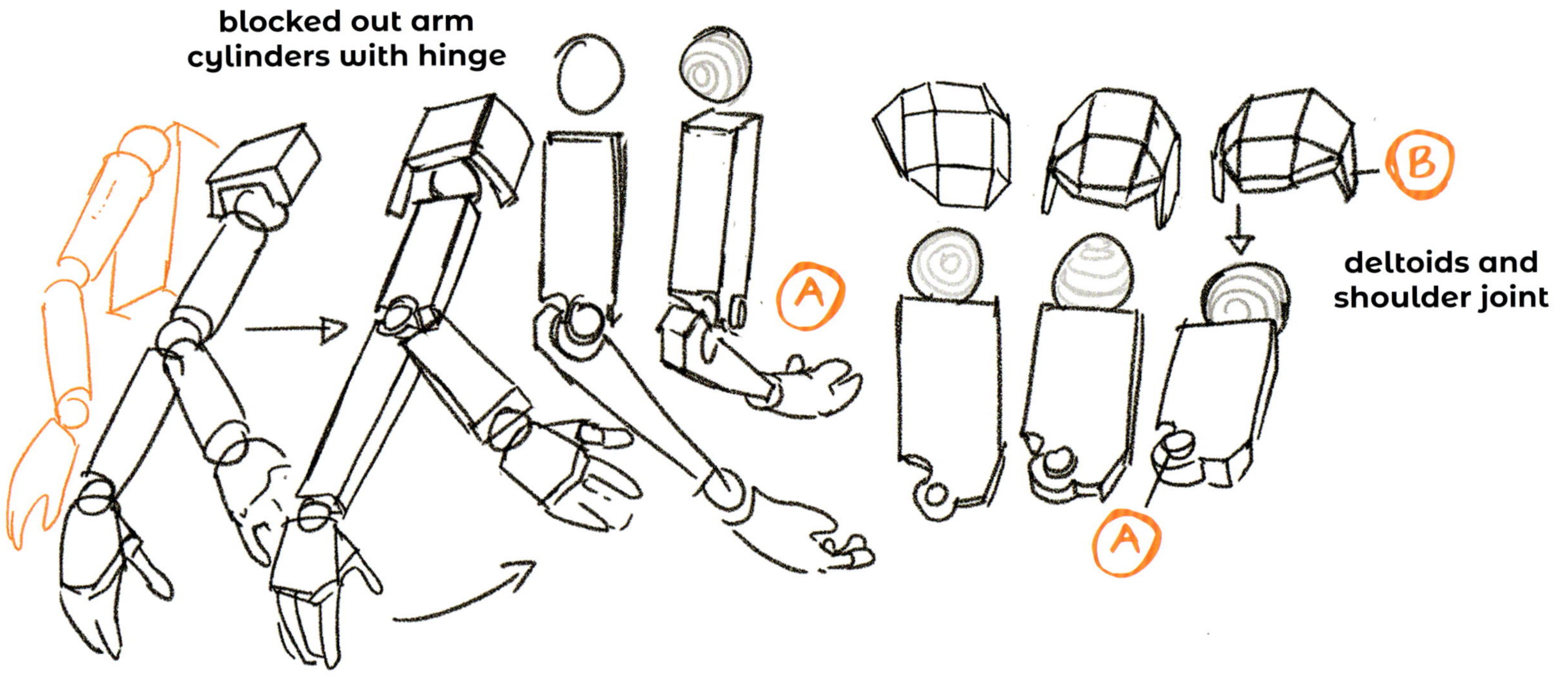

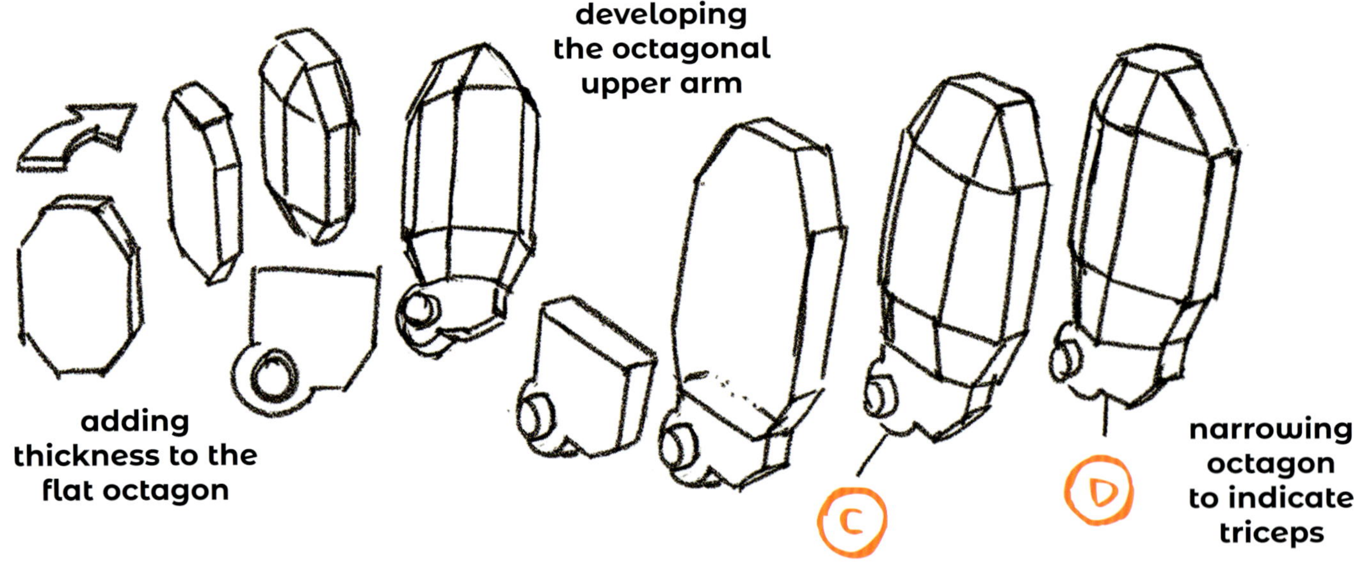

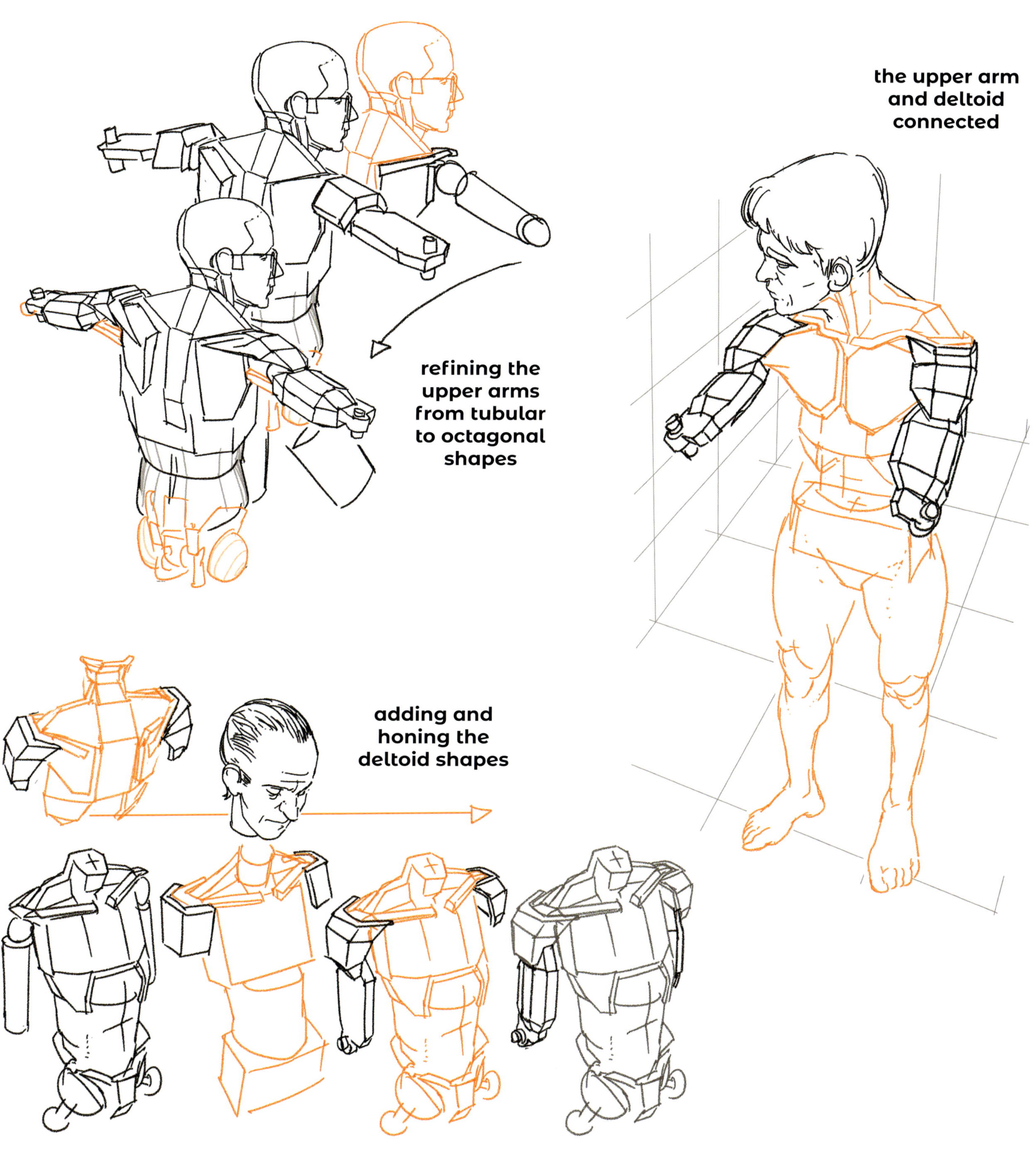
the upper arm
and deltoid
connected
refining the
upper arms
from tubular
to octagonal
shapes
adding and
honing the
deltoid shapes

The lower arm is trickier because it changes shape with supination and pronation. We created two options for it. In option 1, we drew a tapering cylinder with a block for the wrist – a fast option that's still believable if the proportions are correct (E).

In option 2, we drew the bones, then added the three main muscle groups on top: the upper extensors, lower extensors, and flexors. This option is more involved but gives more insight into the arm's workings (F). Either version works well for a mannequin, depending on your preferences (G)!

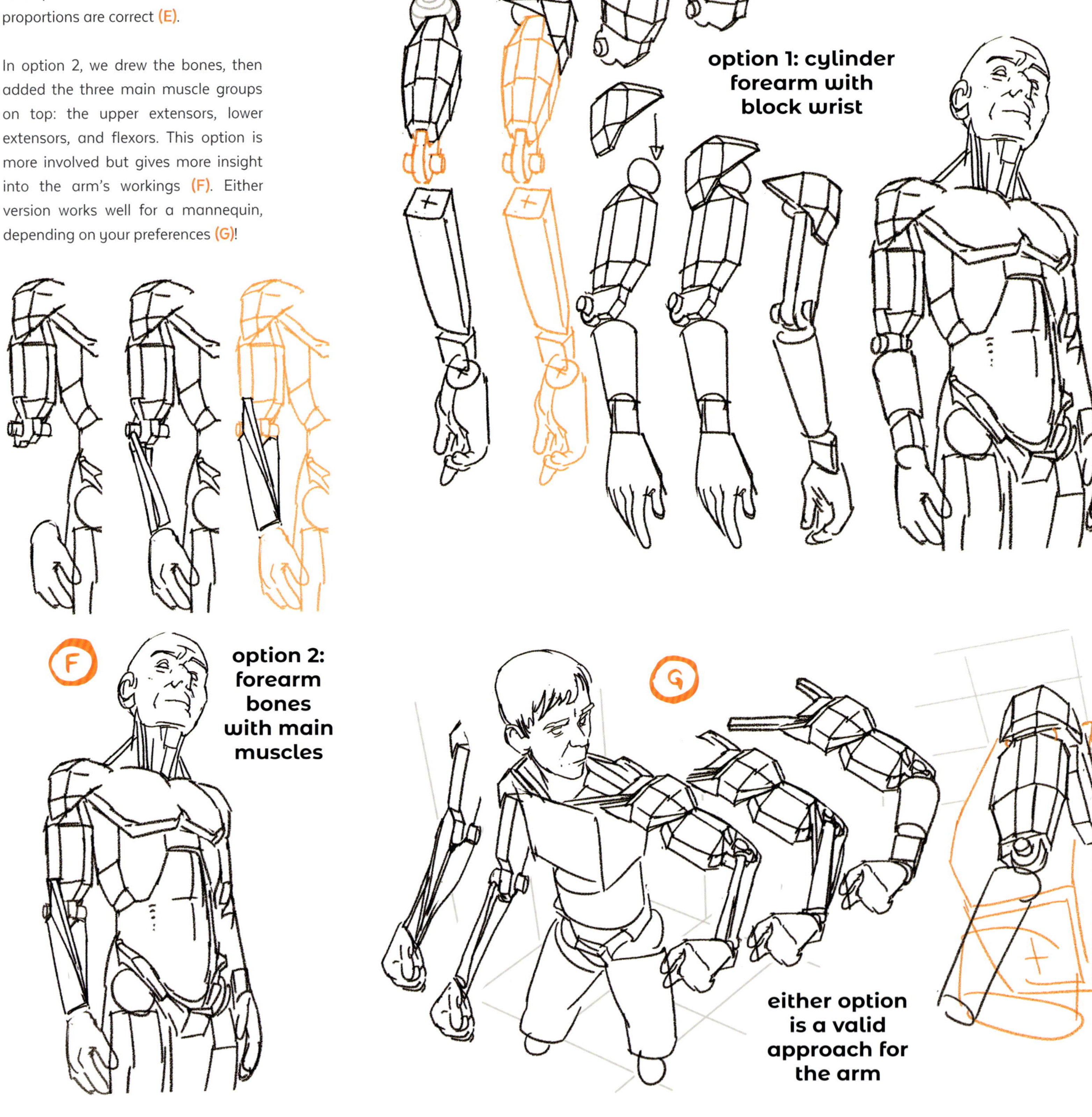

We learned that the lower extensors attach to the outer (lateral) epicondyle **(1)**, the flexors attach to the inner (median) epicondyle **(2)**, and the upper extensors attach to the orange area marked **3**. This is in alignment with the attachment of the deltoids above **(4)**.

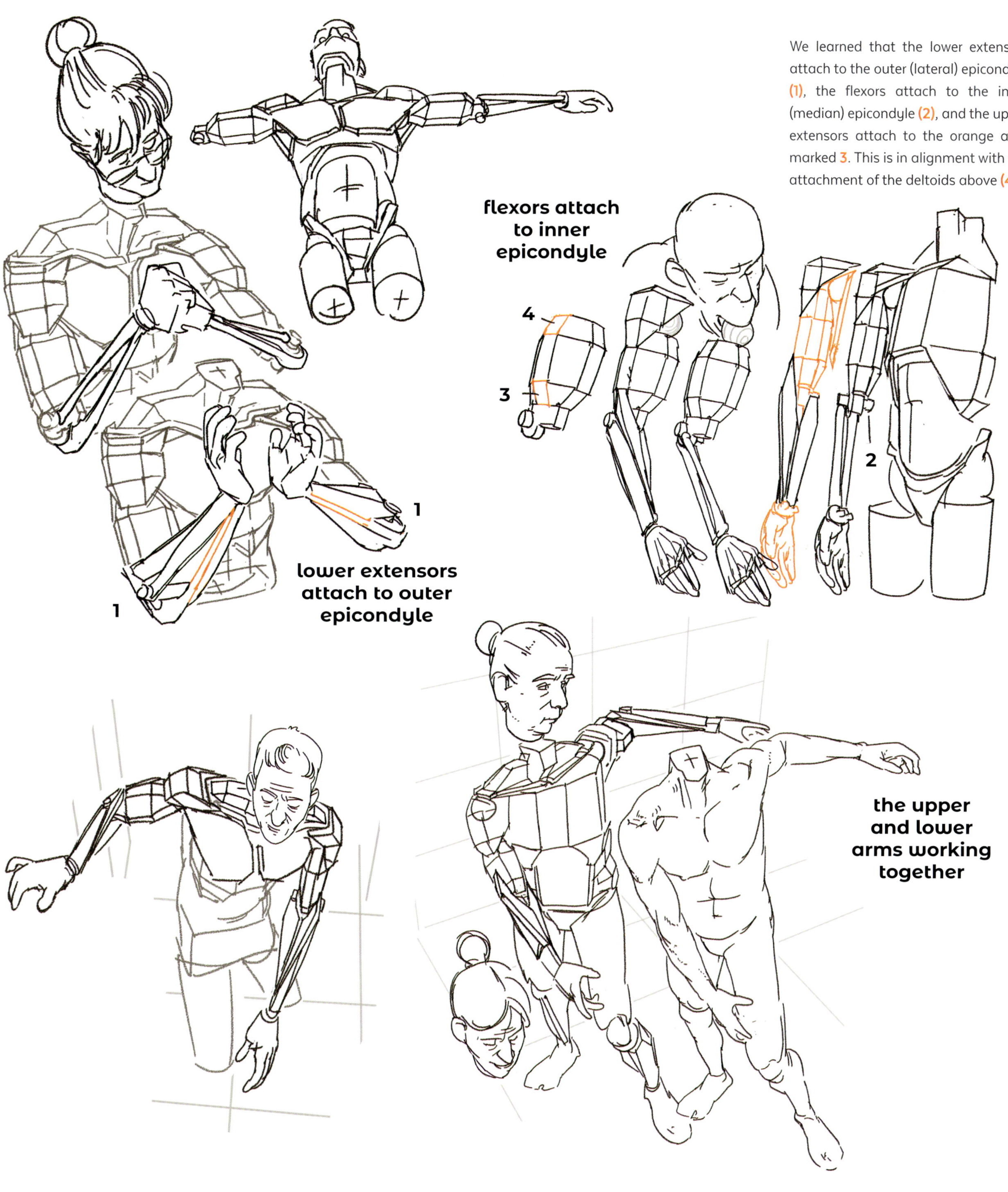

lesson 4:

the core

The core is a large and vital part of the body that's often poorly understood. So much of the body's strength and mobility comes from this flexible area, as we'll discover in this section.

what is the core?

Now let's examine the "core" – the lower part of the torso, roughly comprising the abdomen and mid to lower back. It's usually the least studied part of any student's anatomy knowledge because it has fewer obvious external landmarks. Without a strong understanding of the pelvis, it's virtually impossible to draw. Before we cover the bone, remember: the proportions are what give your drawings form, so focus on those first, and the accuracy of the bones and muscles after **(A)**. The ratio of hips to core to rib cage is powerful.

When drawing the core you'll usually not need to add many interior lines. Most people have few or no obvious core muscles, and look more like **B** than **C**.

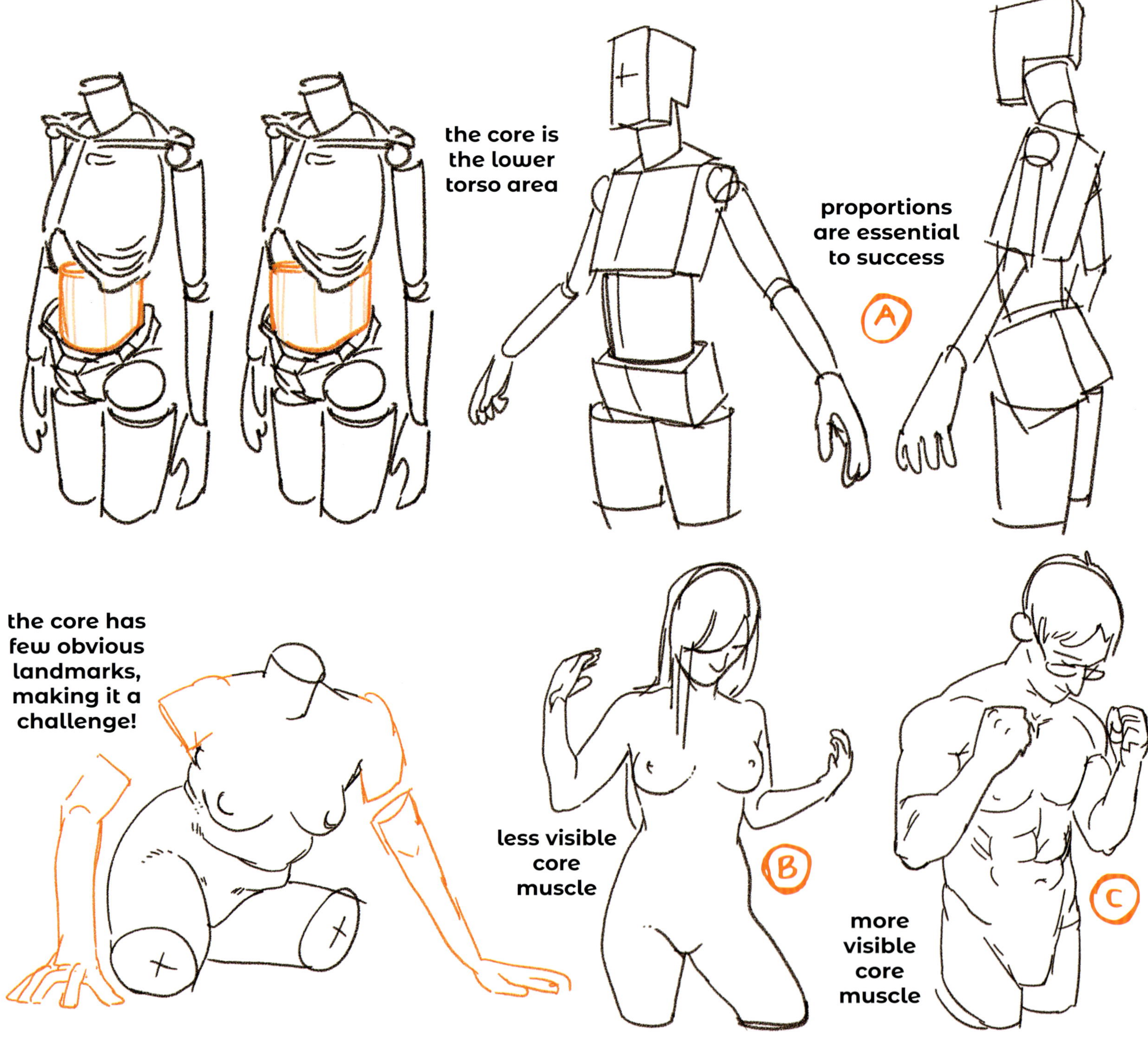

the pelvis

Let's visualize the pelvis as a block. What role does the pelvis need to play? It forms the end of our digestive system, so we need a continuous space within it, with a hole at the bottom for excretion (A). It also needs to provide a stable base for the torso and legs to pull on. The legs and torso must be allowed their maximum range of motion and be able to swing in multiple directions without being impeded. If we attach two tube forms to the bottom of a cuboid, it doesn't allow for much movement because the edges of the forms would prevent it (B). Solution: round off those edges (C)! This allows the legs a wider range of lateral (sideways) movement (D).

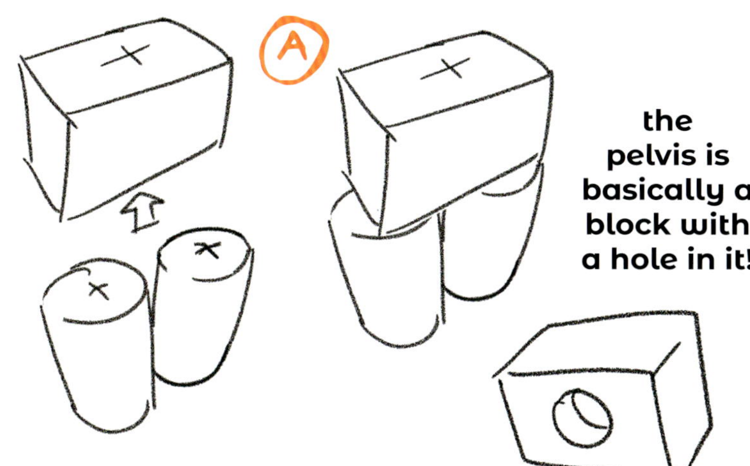

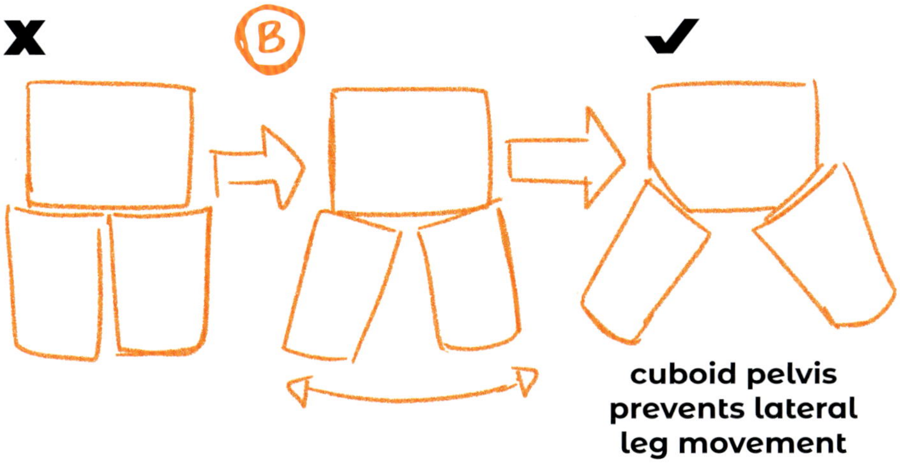

B

cuboid pelvis prevents lateral leg movement

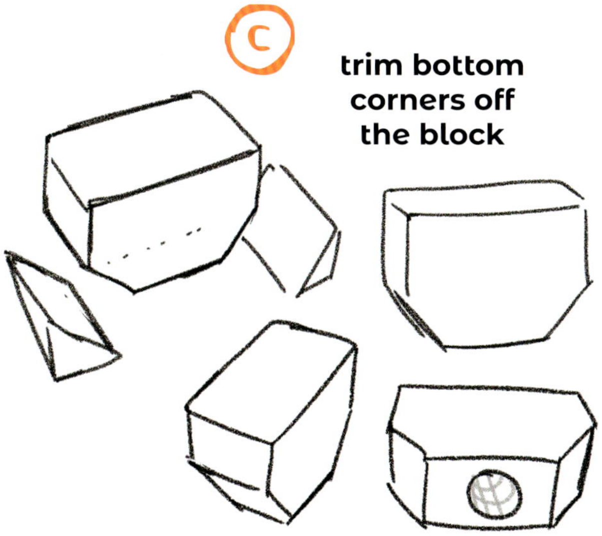

C

trim bottom corners off the block

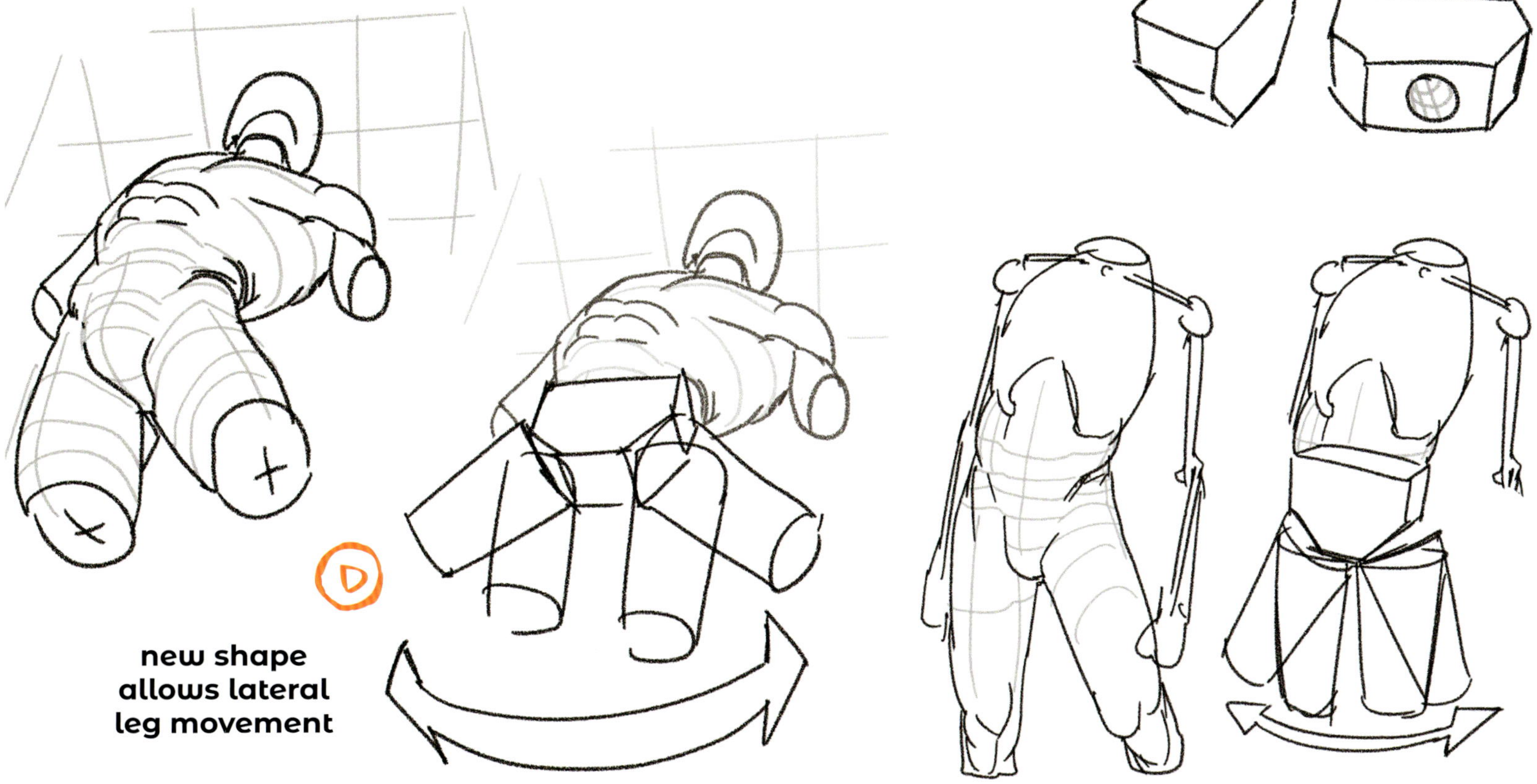

D

new shape allows lateral leg movement

But we need to swing our legs in multiple directions, not just laterally. They must be able to bend forward and backward (E) and even cross over each other (F).

So how can we refine this shape so that it fulfills these needs? We can round it off at the edges, so it's a rounded octagonal shape rather than four-sided (G). In profile view we see that the bottom section wraps below, like underwear, so there are angled sections on the front and back and one totally flat section beneath (H).

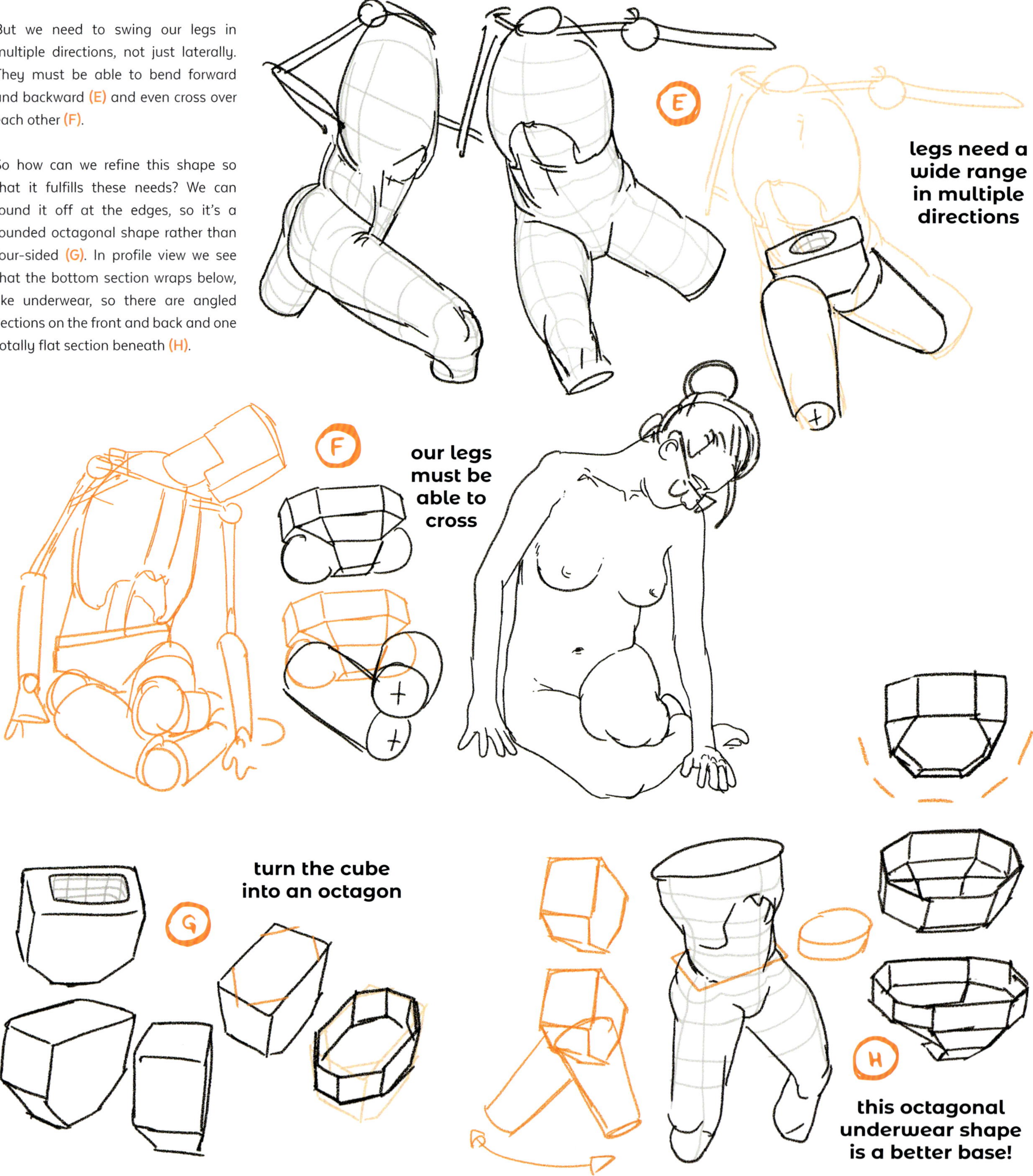

the femurs

Next we need to insert two spheres into the pelvis, representing the ball-and-socket joints of the femurs (A). The femur is the bone of the upper leg, and the largest bone in the body. Just like the arm, the leg has one bone for the upper part (B) and two for the bottom.

Here's an easy way to add these joints (C): Draw the underpants shape in the same orientation as the box (1) and give it some thickness to improve it (2). Add two spheres that hang lower than the bottom of the underpants shape. This allows extra mobility (3).

There is normally an overlap where the front leg covers the rear (from the camera's POV) (D). Occasionally this gap will allow you to see all the way through to the glutes at the back, but that's rare (E).

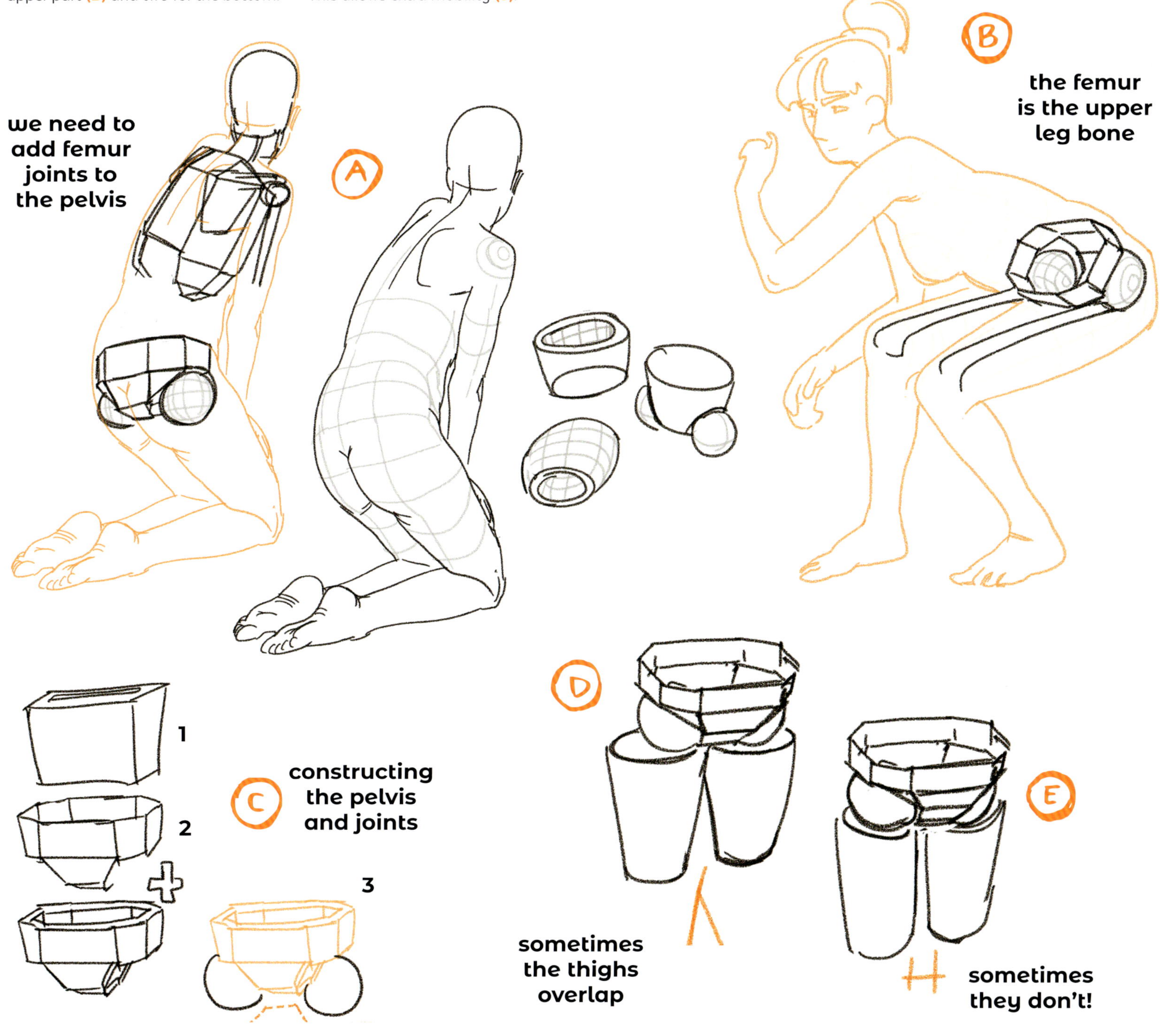

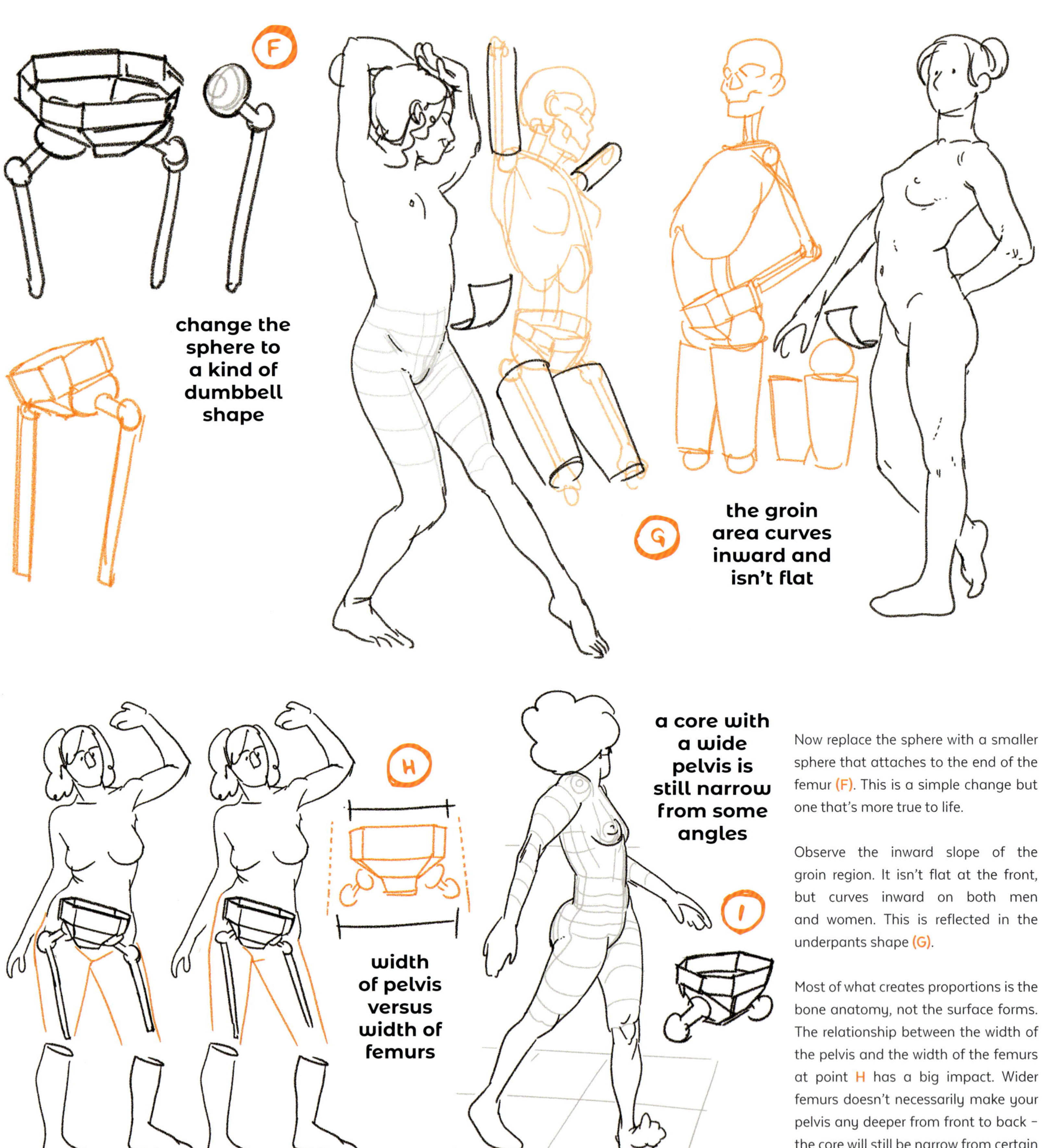

Now replace the sphere with a smaller sphere that attaches to the end of the femur (F). This is a simple change but one that's more true to life.

Observe the inward slope of the groin region. It isn't flat at the front, but curves inward on both men and women. This is reflected in the underpants shape (G).

Most of what creates proportions is the bone anatomy, not the surface forms. The relationship between the width of the pelvis and the width of the femurs at point H has a big impact. Wider femurs doesn't necessarily make your pelvis any deeper from front to back – the core will still be narrow from certain angles (I).

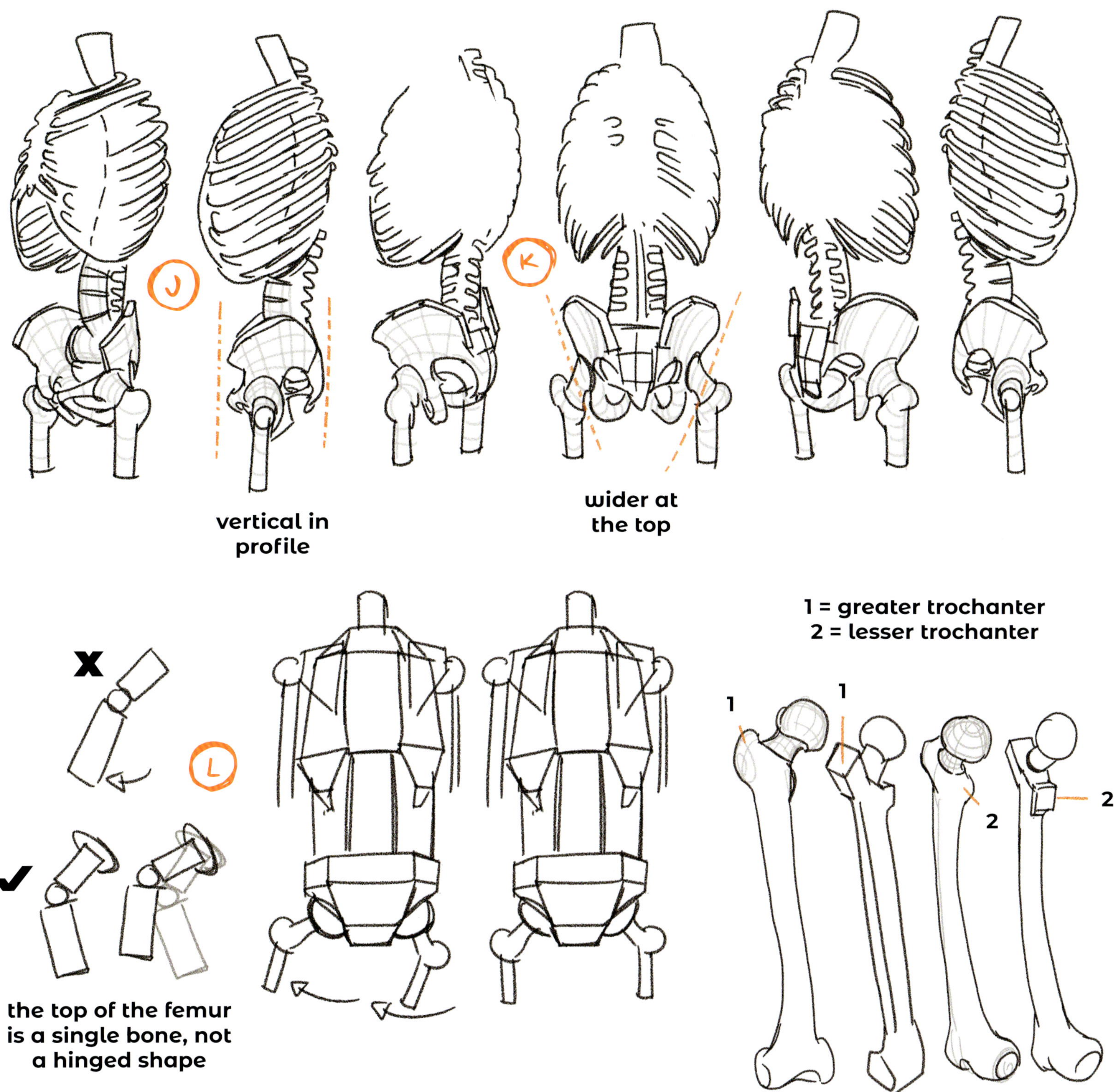

Now we have a basic pelvis model, let's examine the pelvis and spine more closely. Viewed in profile, the front of the pelvis is almost completely vertical when untilted (J). If we ignore the femur, we can see that the pelvis is wider at the top and tapers toward the bottom, like the underpants form we blocked out earlier (K).

The femur is a single bone. Section L is not a joint, but an attachment point – it is immobile. The hinge motion of the leg moves from the ball-and-socket of the pelvis. This mass is known as the "greater trochanter" (1). There's also a "lesser trochanter" below it and inside (2). A trochanter is a bony protuberance where muscles attach.

detailing the pelvis

Here, we see the "wings" of the pelvis clearly. These are part of one large bone called the ilium, which is the largest bone in the pelvis. Instead of asking, "What does this bone look like?" try asking, "What is its role?" There are three answers to this question: It provides an attachment point for the muscles on the sides of the torso, it acts as a bowl to hold the internal organs, and it acts as a container to protect our lower digestive system.

We can simplify it to something like this (A). There's an opening at the back where the two wings of the ilium meet the "sacrum" (B). The sacrum is the triangular piece wedged between them, acting as the connection between the spine and the ilium, and holding the pelvis together. It curves back and down, like a shrimp's tail (C).

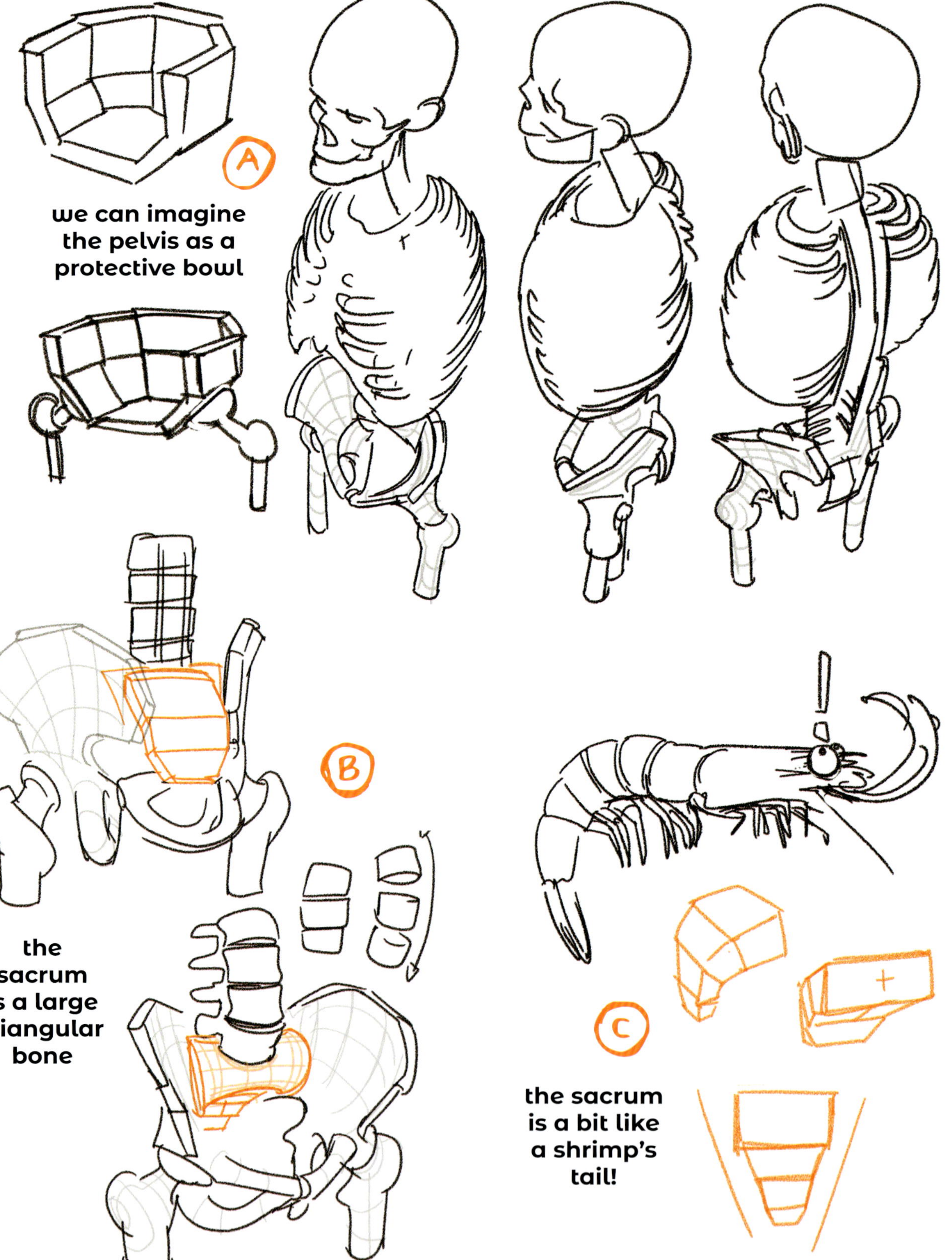

What else can we observe? What are these two forward-facing sections (D)? Those are the pubis (the straight bone) and the ischium (the loop-shaped bone that we'll cover later). The main function of the pubis is to protect the bladder, intestines, and sex organs. The two bones of the pubis provide an important attachment point for the muscles of the leg (E). They are pointed forward, not flattened (F).

The front of the ilium angles backward and the pubis angles forward (G). The visibility of this depends on the tilt of the pelvis, but this "V" shape is what we should generally look for. When viewed from behind, we frequently won't see the pubis (H).

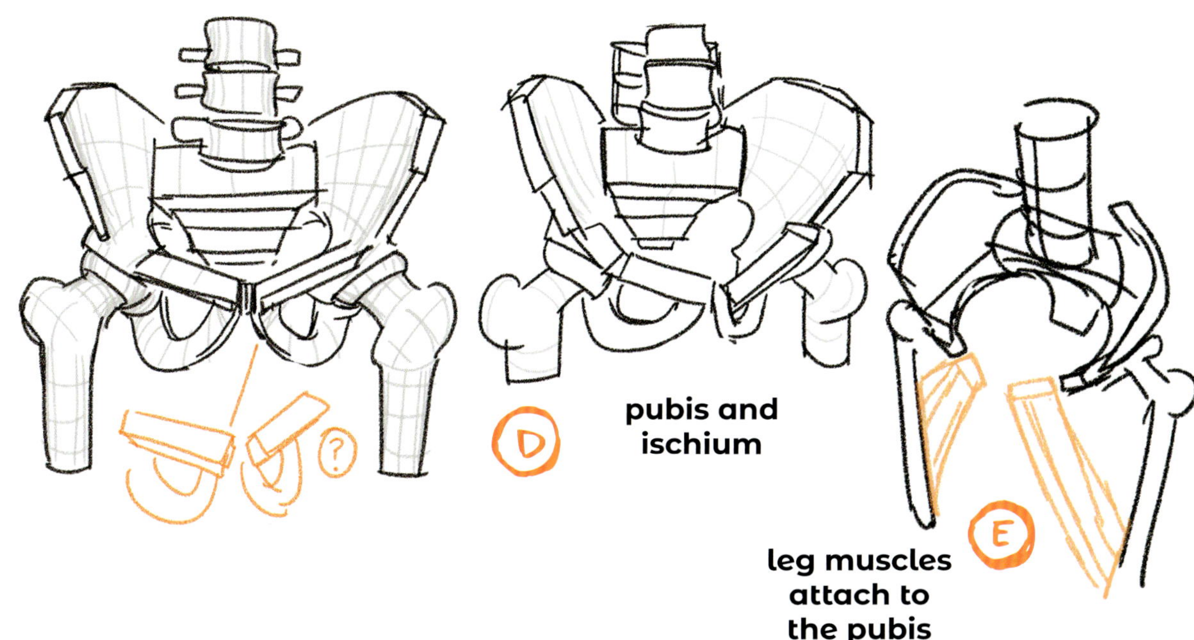

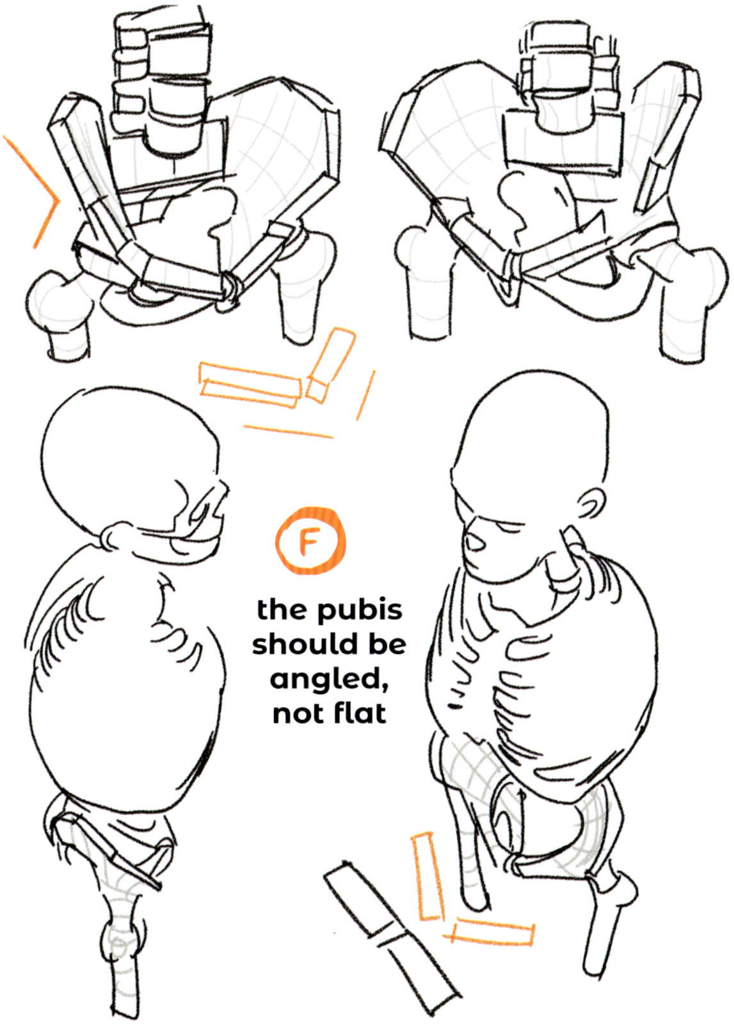

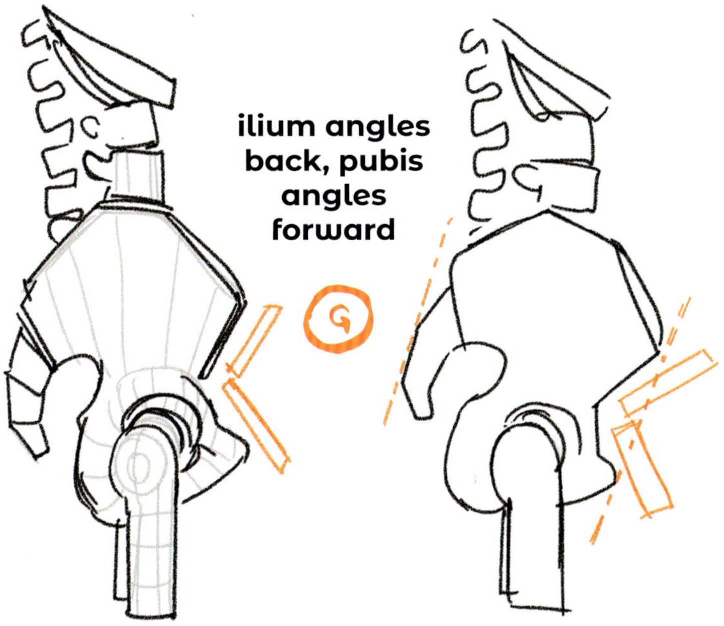

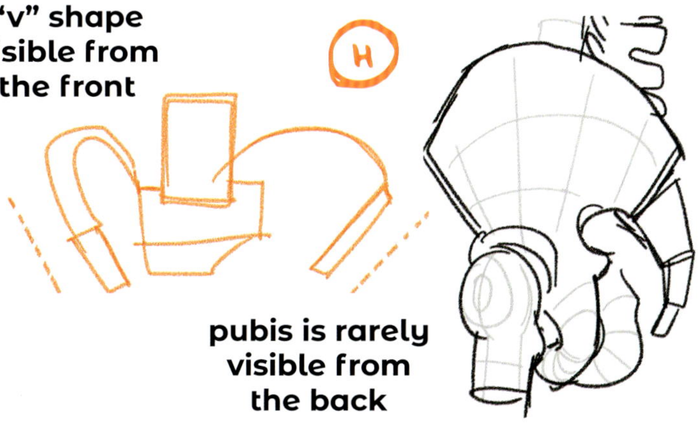

The femur itself points almost exactly straight out to the side, but the socket the ball sits in, the acetabulum, is angled slightly forward (I). This is because we require a greater range of motion moving our legs forward. Think how high you can raise your leg forward compared to behind you (J). Flexing your legs behind you requires the pelvis to tilt.

Think of our locomotion – to walk and crawl requires flexibility to varying degrees (K).

You should also be able to see more of the acetabulum from the front than from the rear (L).

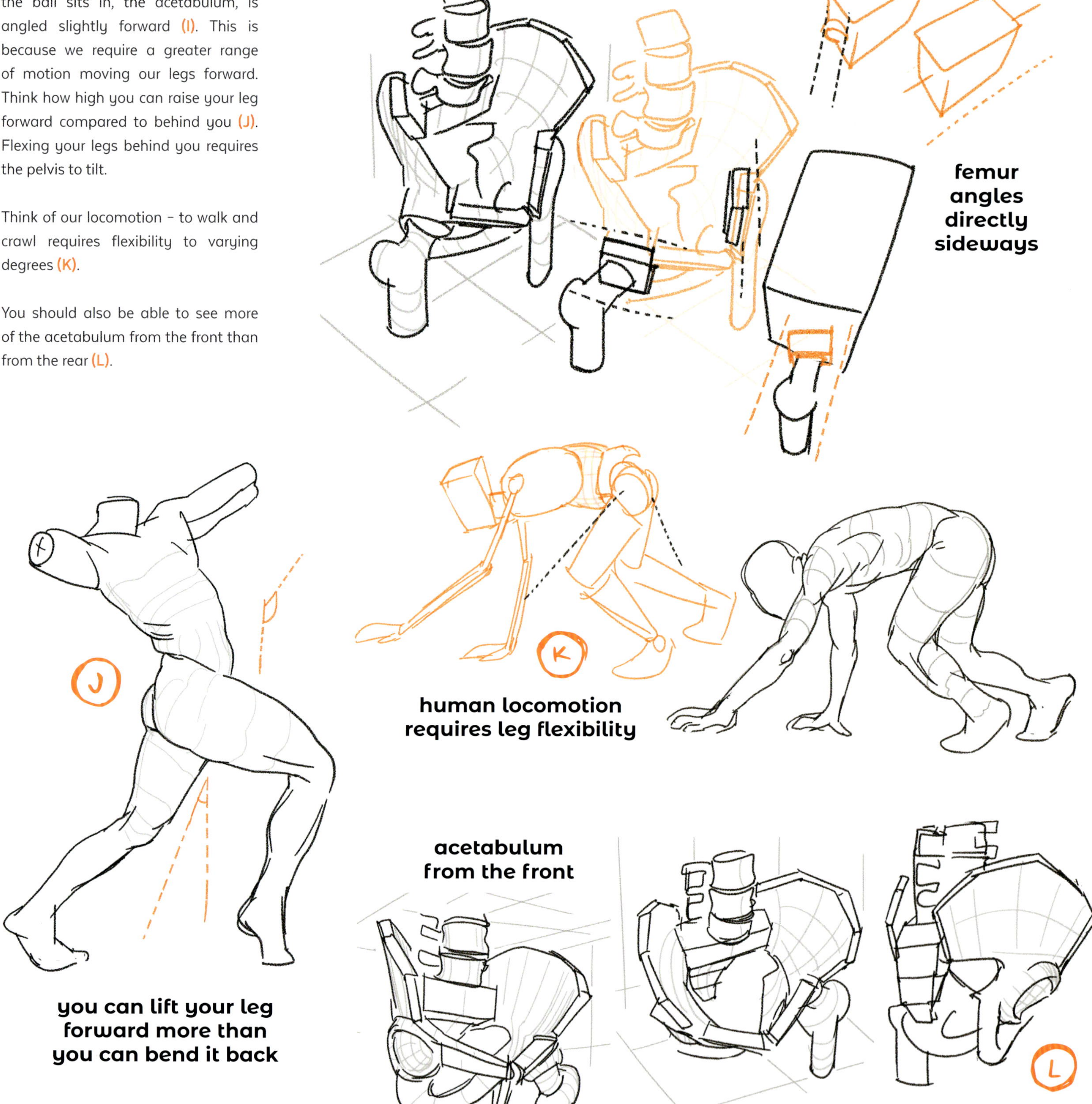

From below we see a lot of the ball-and-socket joints, far more than from above or behind. From angle M we see how clearly angled forward this socket is. From behind we see very little of the head of the femur (N).

The femurs aren't angled 90 degrees. Instead, draw the angle around 45 degrees (O). The head of the femur is covered in cartilage (P).

Note the outward flaring of the ilium (the wings), which is particularly noticeable from behind (Q).

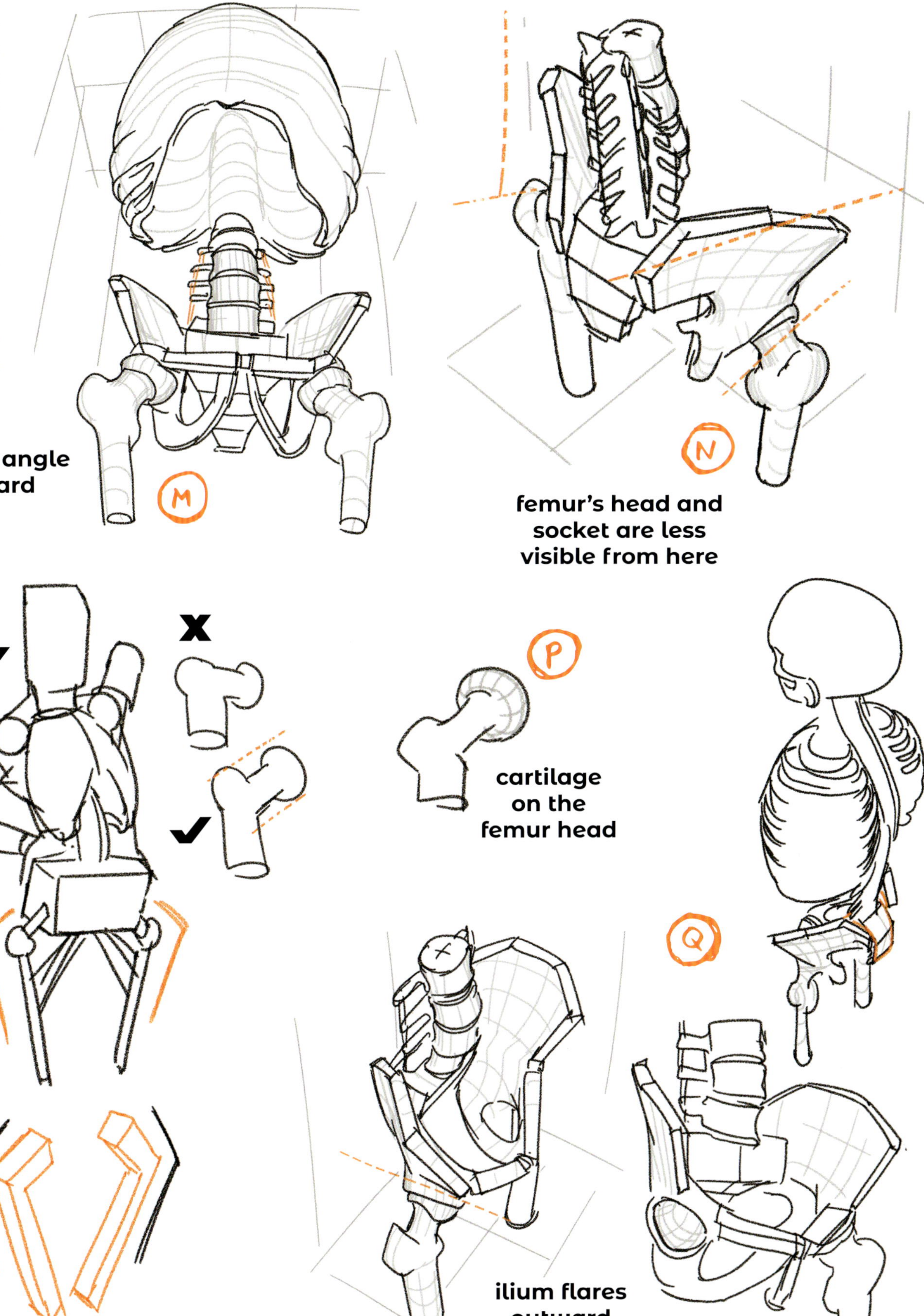

the ischium

The acetabulum (the "socket" of the ball-and-socket joint) is connected to a sort of "loop" hanging off the bottom of the pelvis (A). This is the ischium, mentioned on page 231. To understand what this is, let's consider the role of the pelvis again. The pelvis needs to provide anchor points for the leg muscles to pull on, in order to move the legs forward and back. This is exactly what the two ischia provide (B).

The two ischia are sometimes called the "sit bones" because we can feel them contacting the chair when we sit. Some of the attaching muscles connect these loops to the greater trochanter (C). Now we're starting to understand what these weird bumps at the top of the femur are for! Without the femur being wider than the pelvis, we'd have nothing to pull on if we wanted to move the legs out laterally (D). Nothing in evolution is there for no reason – understand the role and your subject becomes easier to memorize.

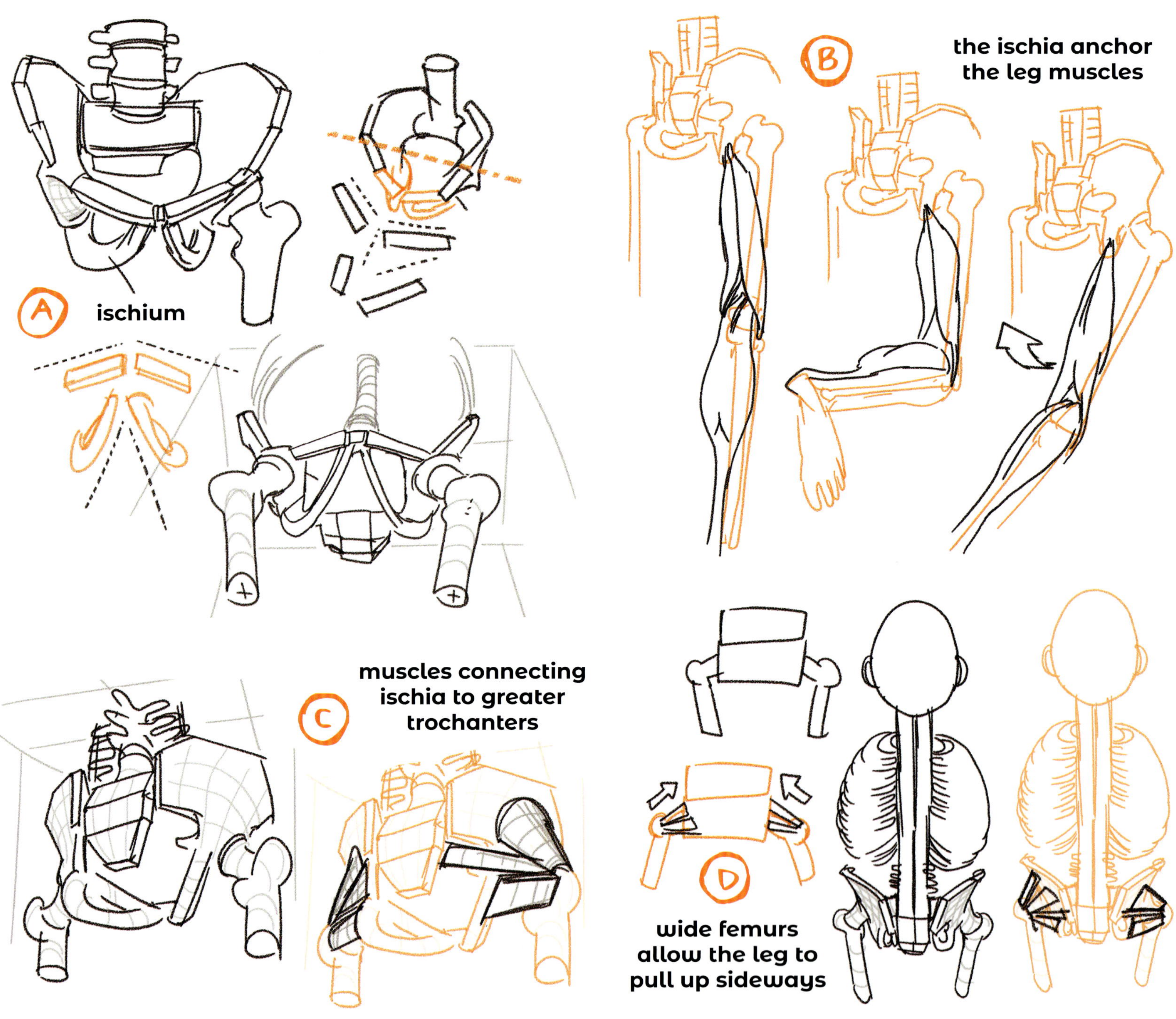

Here are some useful things to know for drawing the pubis and the ischia. The angle of the pubis is relatively flat compared to the more acute angles of the ischia. In E we can see this from below, and in F from above.

This bottom region of the spine is called the lumbar region (G). It's flexible forward and back, but can only bend around 20 degrees to the side (H). Try it yourself! Try to bend to the side without twisting (as twisting increases the range of motion).

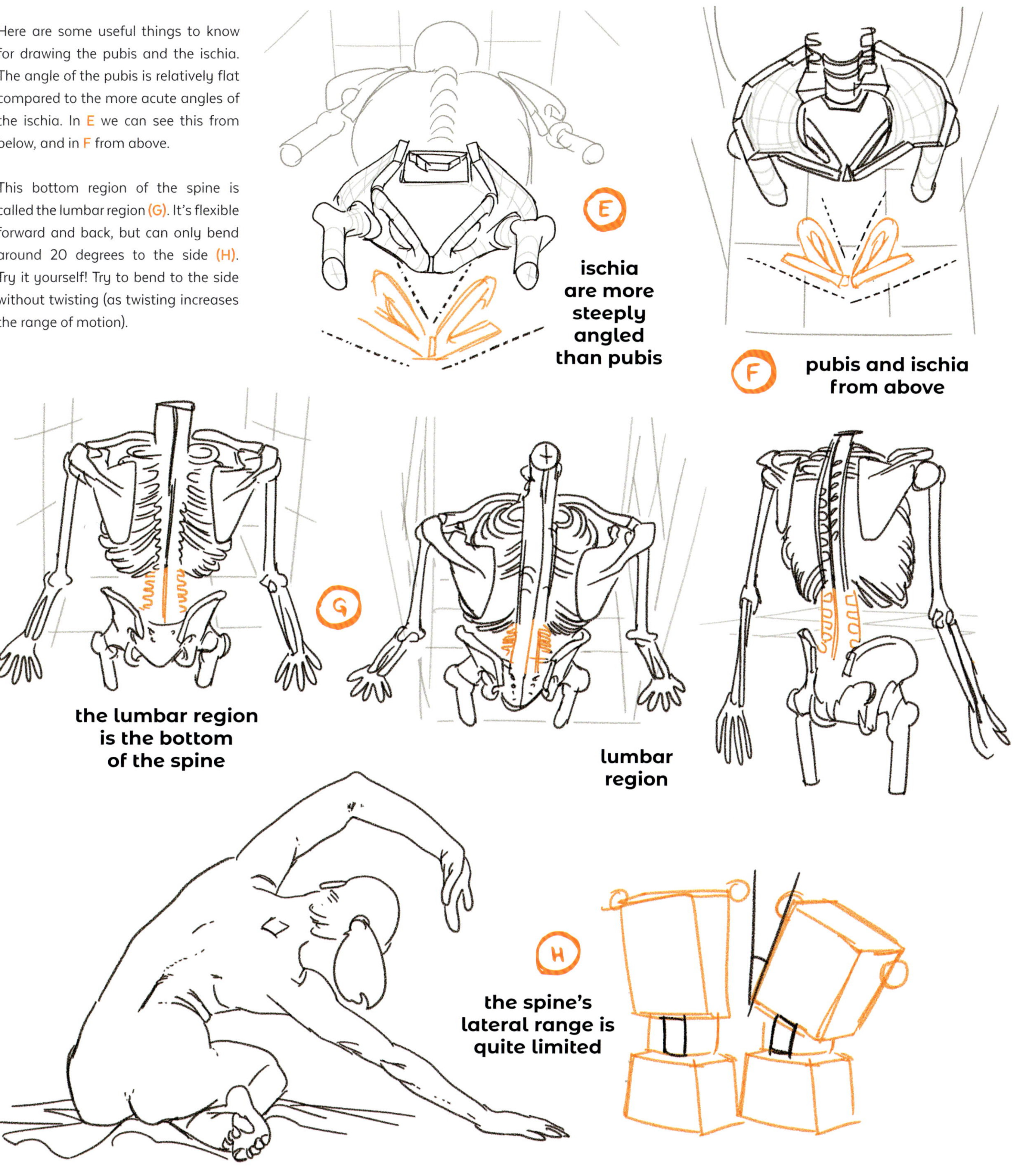

Let's use these observations to improve our pelvis shape further. We left off on page 228 with an underwear shape, with either a ball or more advanced femur shape (I). Starting with our octagonal shape, let's slice off the front section to represent the space above the pubis, leaving a small section at the bottom to represent the pubis (J). We know that the pelvis isn't just an oval or octagon, but flares from back to front, so let's incorporate that flare using three clear angles (K, 1–3).

Add in a space where the sacrum sits, and wedge it in (L). This area isn't just a cutout hole in the wall of the pelvis, but a whole piece with its own depth (M). Keep in mind that we're working toward a final design more like N, which is a simplified pelvis with the spine and femurs inserted, with clear angles to the flared shape.

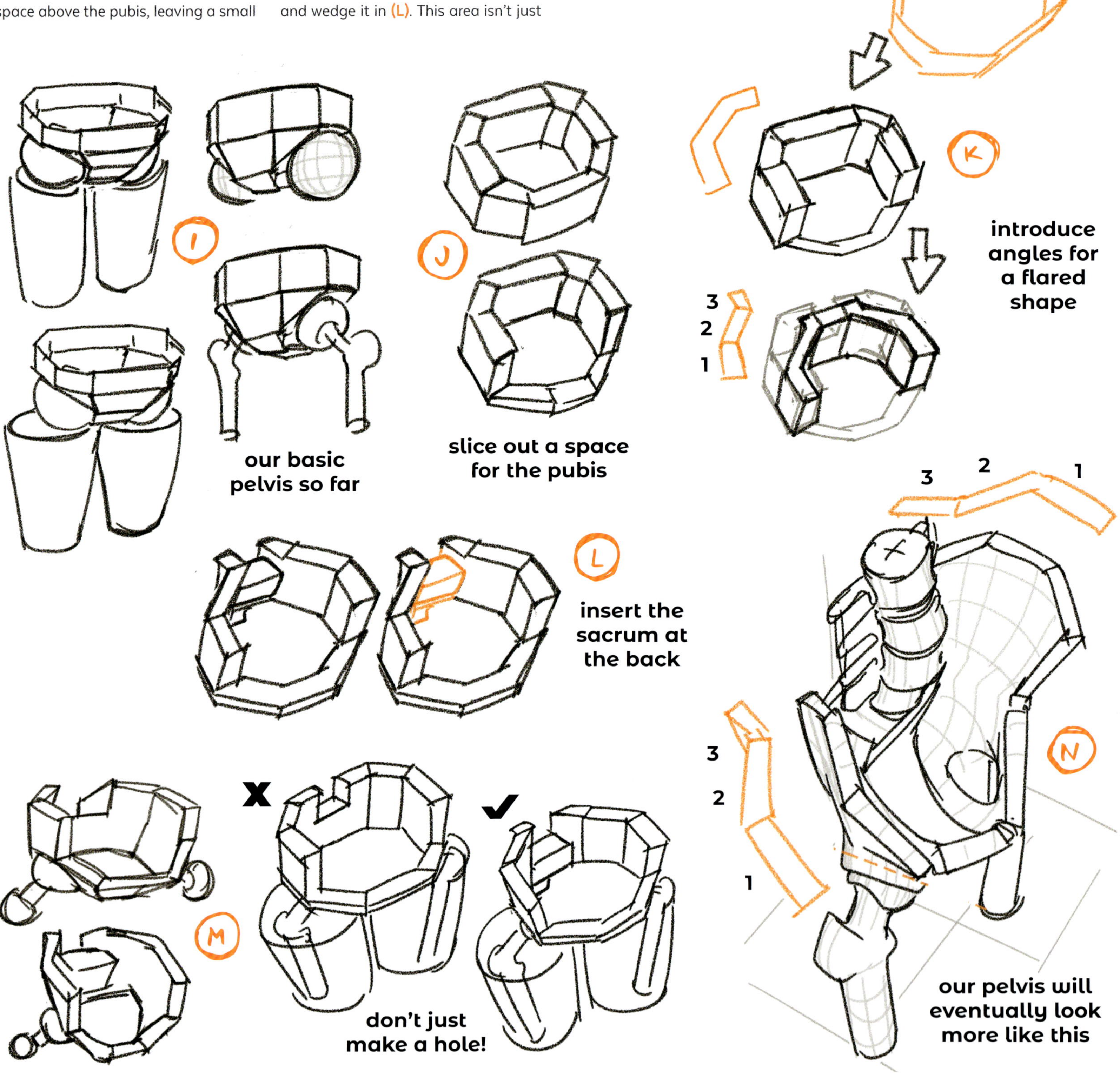

refining the ilium

Remember that there is no one "correct" model! Use what is most useful for you and your current drawing level. Test yourself by rotating your shape through multiple angles. If you can do this easily, you're ready to step up the level of detail.

Now let's angle section 1 downward and lower section 3 on either side of the sacrum. This gives the ilium more of the winglike shape of a real pelvis (A). Slope the walls inward to give the pelvis more of a bowl-shaped structure (B). The two ischium loops attach below, with the acetabulum (the socket) attaching to the sides of the loops (C). The ischia are larger at the back than at the front. In D you can see how far the shape has come from the octagon that we began with!

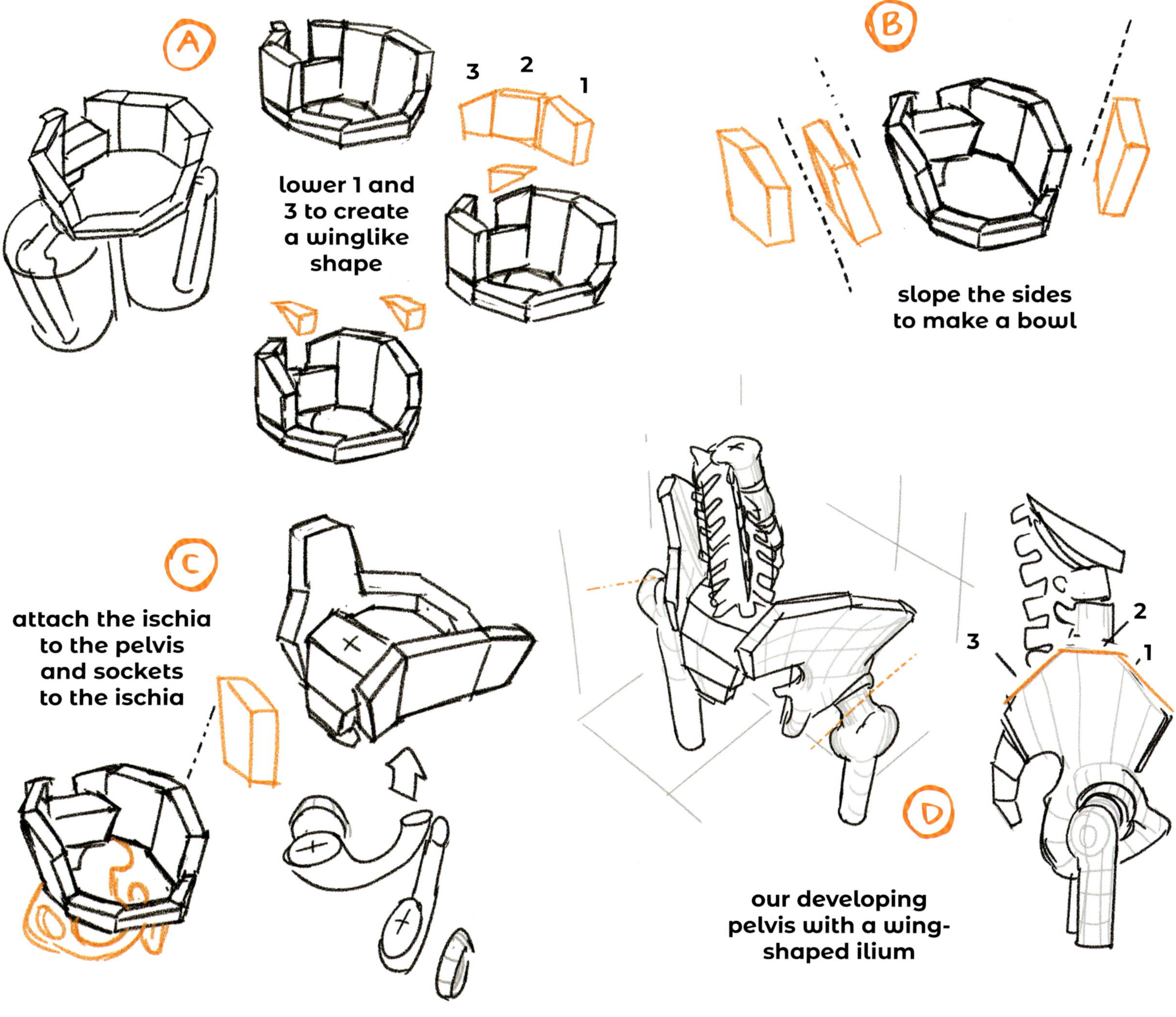

Don't stress about getting the form absolutely perfect. You just need it to be correct enough that the muscles aren't deformed when you draw them on top. Understanding the function behind the design is the most important part!

Some common mistakes include not splaying the ilium enough (E), giving the ilium a C shape rather than an S shape (F), and making the ischia too wide (G).

As with every stage of this book, constantly test yourself. You won't memorize this information by just looking at these drawings. Find photos or go life drawing, and draw the forms beneath. Drawing the silhouette and then "building out" from the skeleton is always a great test of your knowledge (H). The current state of our pelvis should look something like I, but we can streamline this design further.

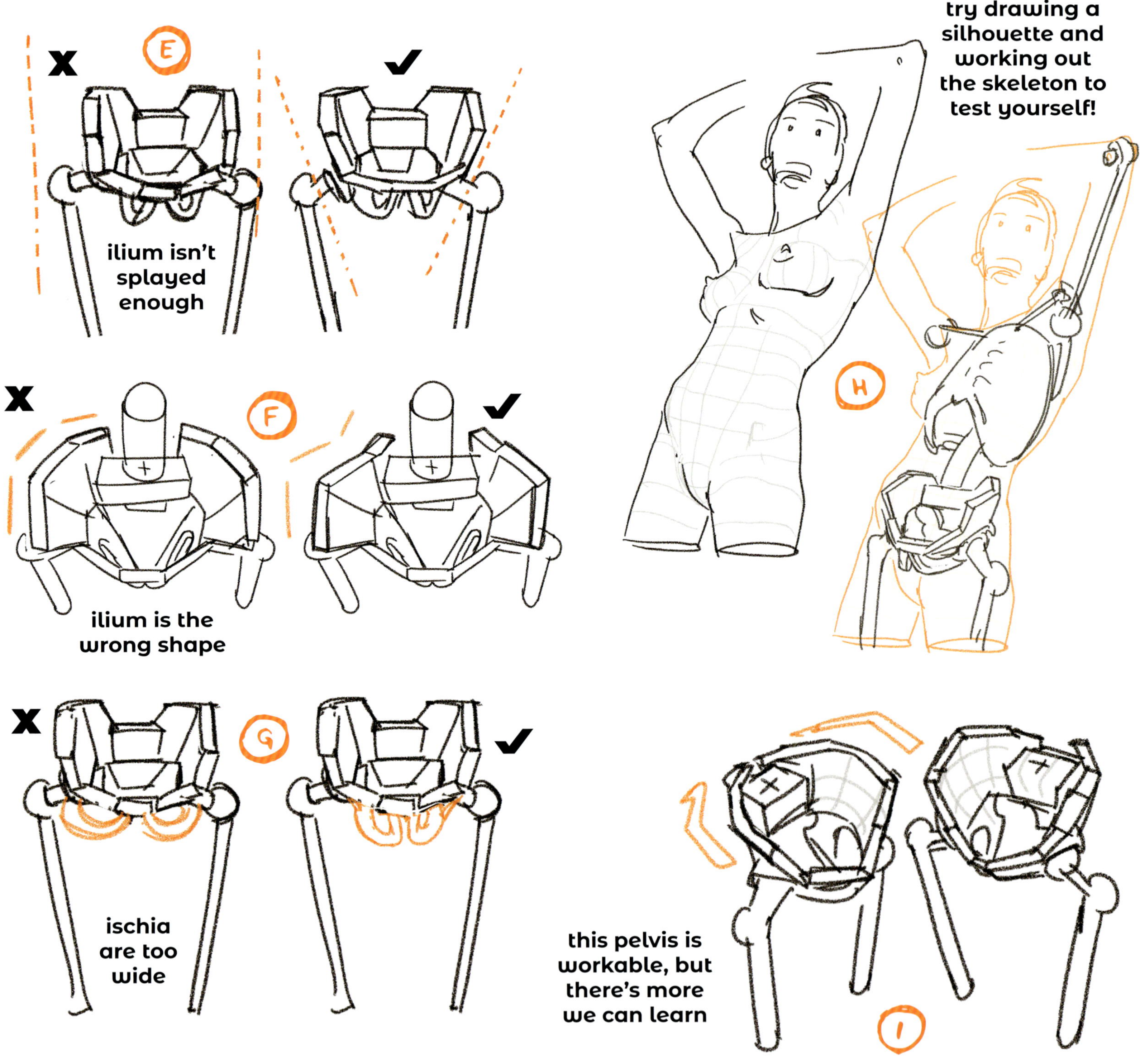

streamlining a pelvis design

Here's a slightly simplified model variation. We want a shorthand for each form. Using a detailed drawing is no better than using a simple one with the same proportions – the silhouette is what's important! Identify the major landmarks and use a shorthand design that shows those. Any level of detail is fine. First, let's review the landmarks. The tips of the iliac crest are called the ASIS, short for "anterior superior iliac spine" (A). Our design will include the ASIS prominently, as well as the sacrum shape at the rear of the pelvis (B). The ASIS is visible on most people (C), particularly when the arms are raised, which lifts the obliques (D).

A

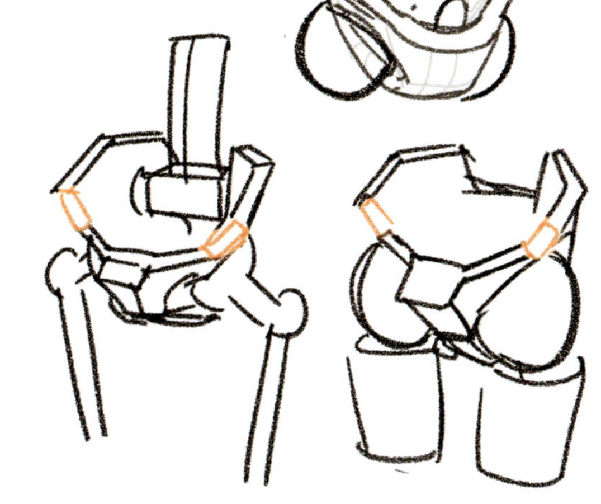

the ASIS (anterior superior iliac spine)

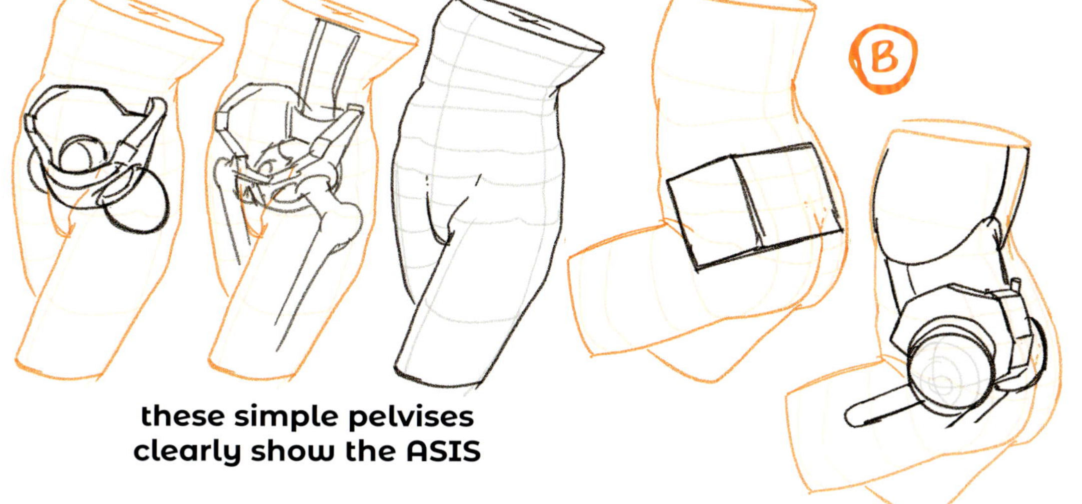

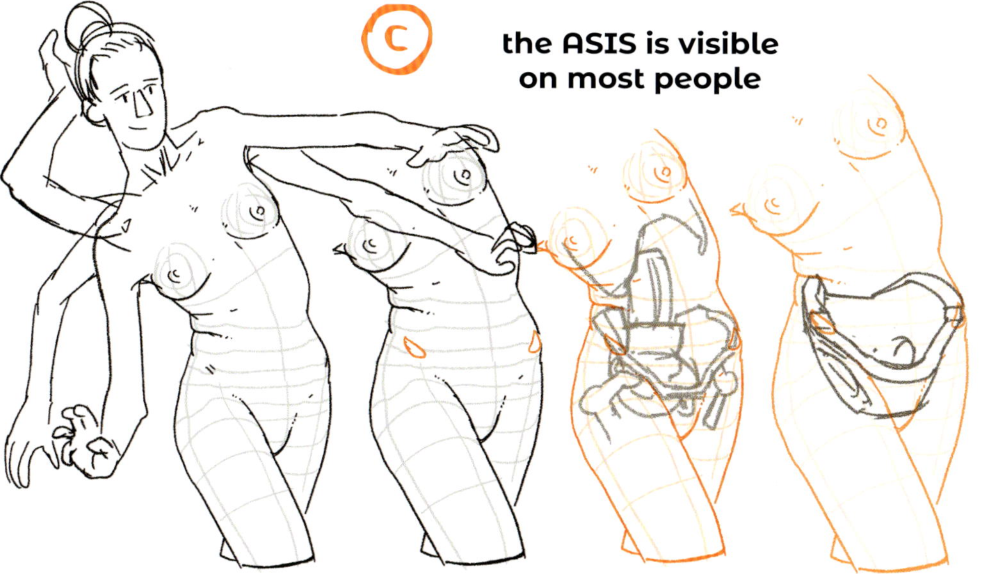

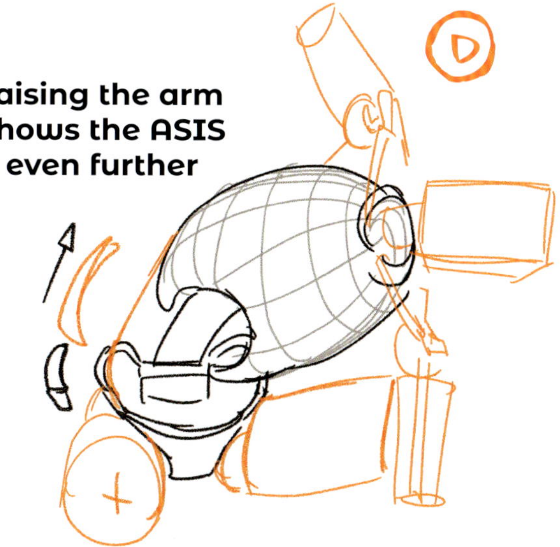

This simplified pelvis is very effective as a base for adding muscles because it incorporates the basic landmarks without adding too much detail.

The important thing to note here is the angle. Notice how the "wings," which represent the ilium, flare both upward and forward (E). This will be important later, when we add the muscles. To this form, we can add the loops of the ischia to create a very practical pelvis shape (F).

Figure H was drawn over the top of G, and it's nicely believable, which is the best test!

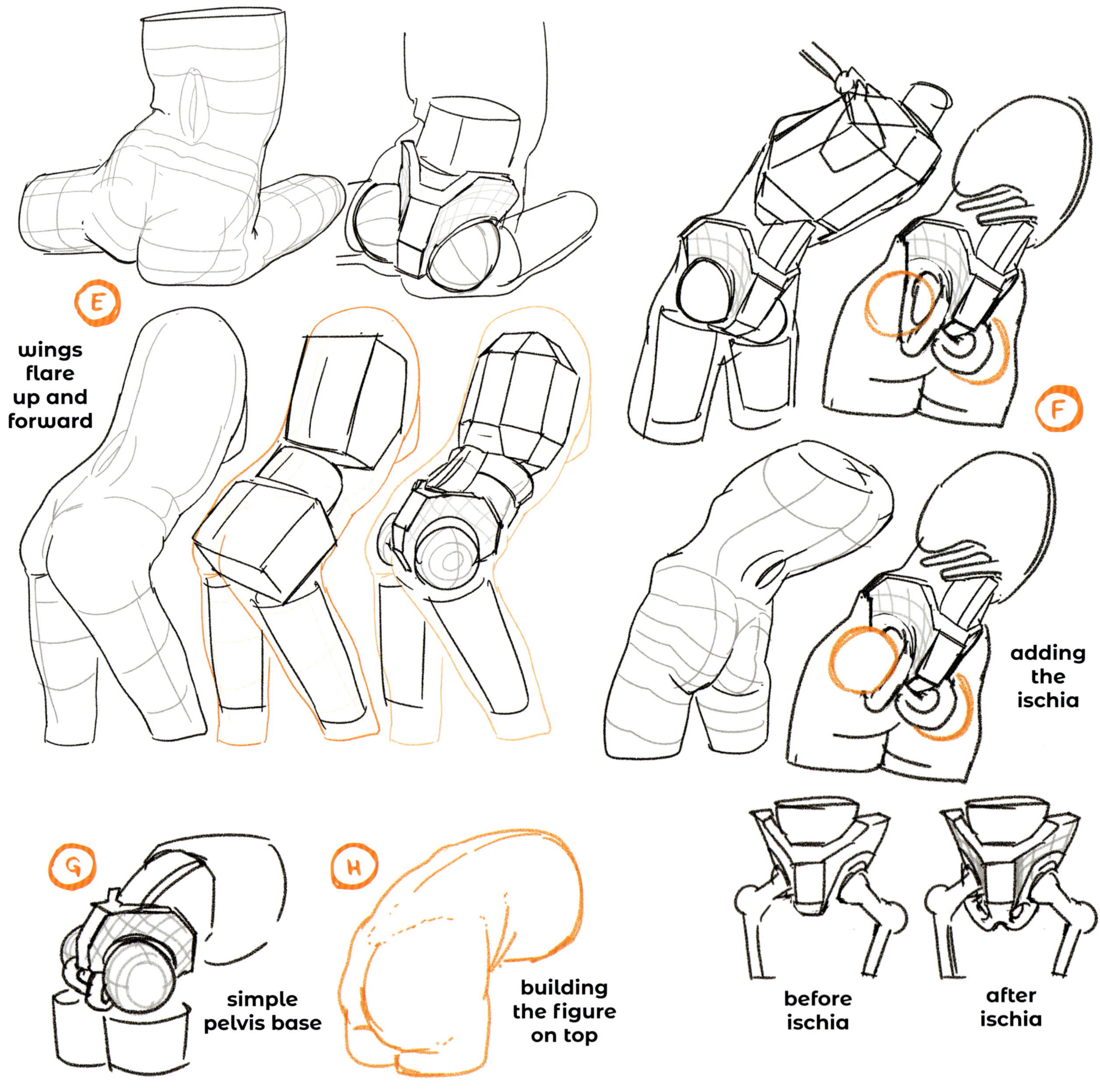

tip: mannequin test

You can add ball joints or real joints to the underpants shape – it doesn't really matter. Try varying the ratio of the spheres' size to the pelvis to create different effects (A). These examples don't include the ischia, but you can add them for extra complexity.

We can now test a pose with our box mannequin, ensuring the proportions and perspective are believable (B). Refine it by adding our more advanced chest and pelvic forms (C). Finally, draw the silhouette and use cross contours to check that the volumes are believable (D). If you're wondering what the lumps on D are, E breaks them down. 1 indicates the obliques sitting on top of the iliac crest (the crest being the top of the "wings"), 2 is the iliac crest itself, and 3 is the muscles of the hip and leg.

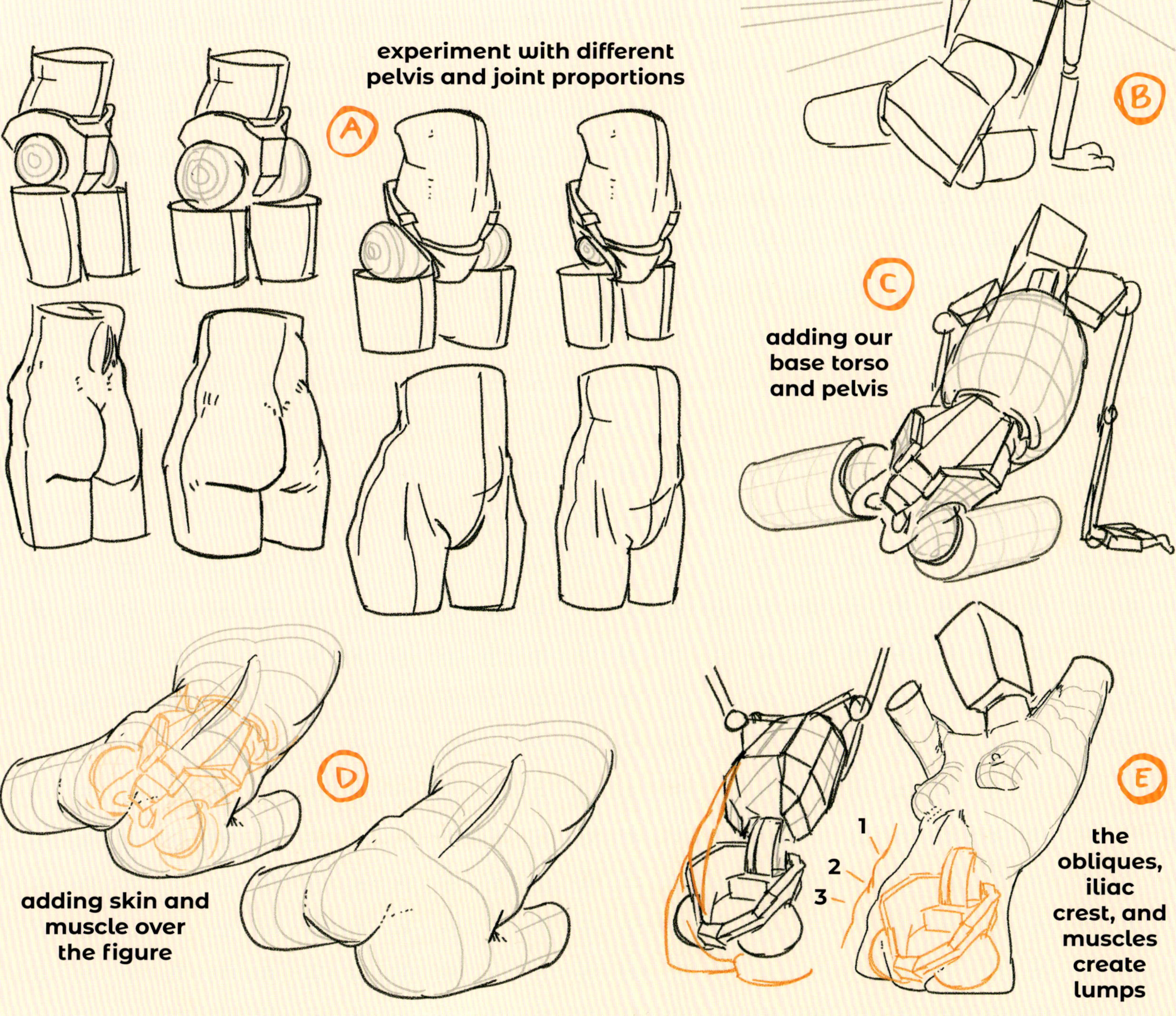

simplified box pelvis

Don't worry if this all seems too complex. It's incredible how believable you can make a complex form like the core look using just a tapered cube form (A). If in doubt, use this as your base model. This shape works so well because the front top corners of the box represent the ASIS (A) while the bottom parts match up with the greater trochanter of the femur (B).

The only problem with the box form is that it creates two top corners at the back, which we don't need (C). Remember that the wings of the ilium have a flared zigzag shape, so they don't form a sharp point. Solution: shave off that corner (D)!

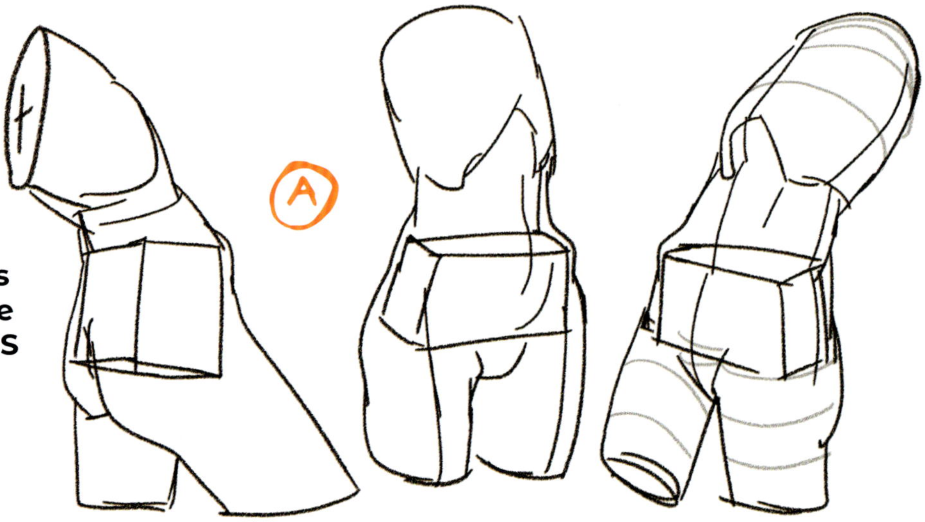

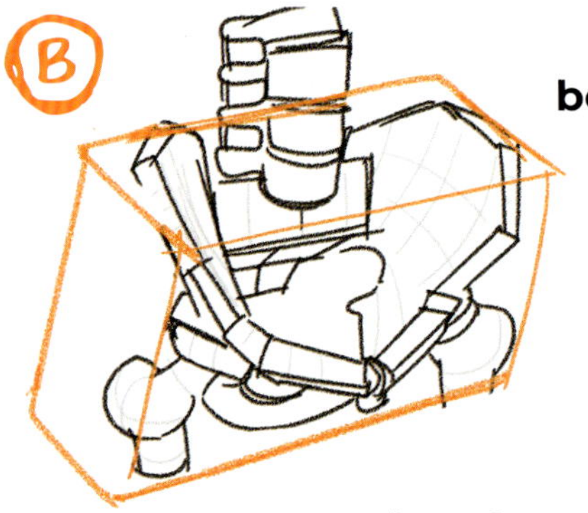

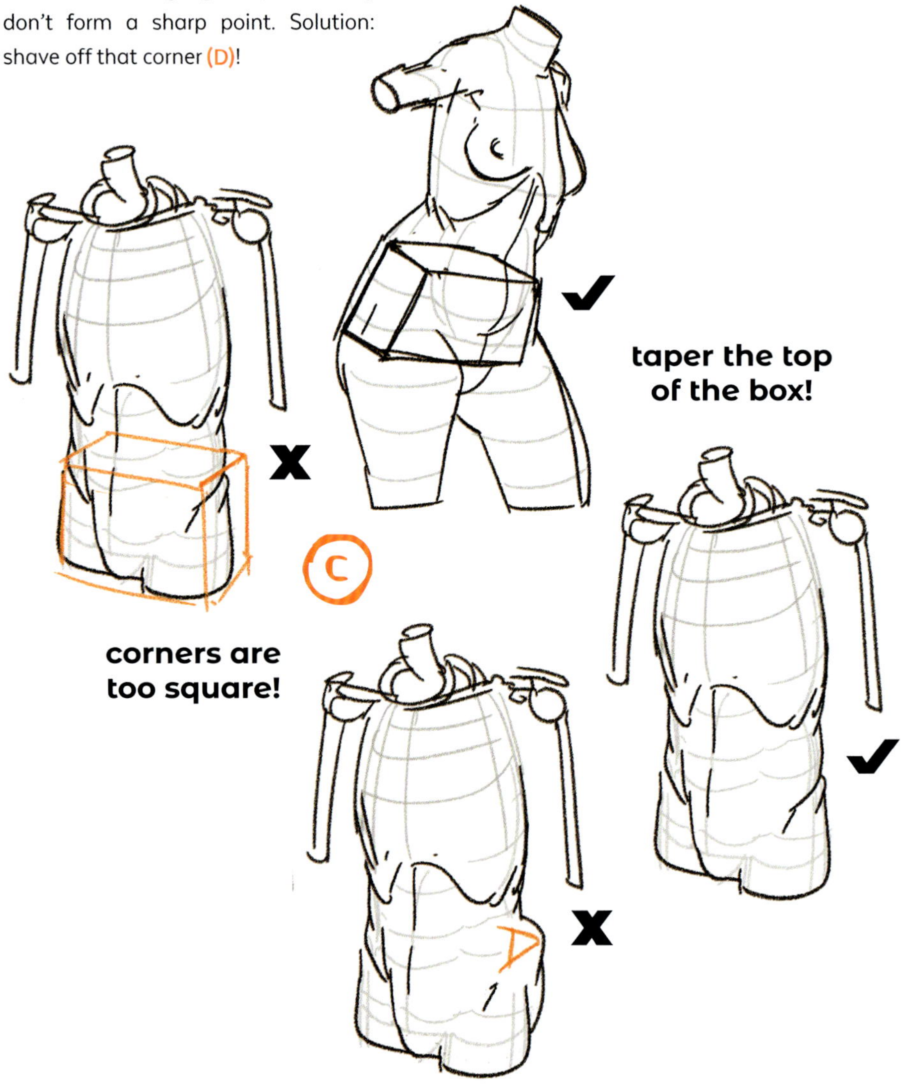

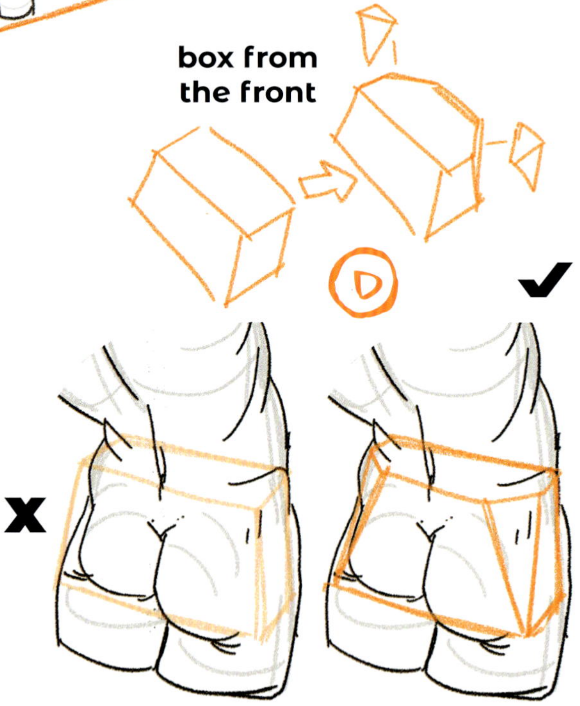

The widest part of the pelvic region is usually the greater trochanter of the femur (E), which makes it easy to place the bottom of our simplified box form. The hips' location and tilt can be trickier. To help place them, draw a line through the ASIS (the tips of the iliac crest), to clarify the tilt and visualize the top of the box form (F).

We've learned that we can shave the back wedges off the box (G). Next, we can add a little more taper to the sides, to take the width of the greater trochanters into account (H). It's common to see the iliac crest drawn quite prominently because artists use it to construct a character's anatomy. However, we never actually see this because it's covered in fat and muscle. For realism, avoid drawing it (I).

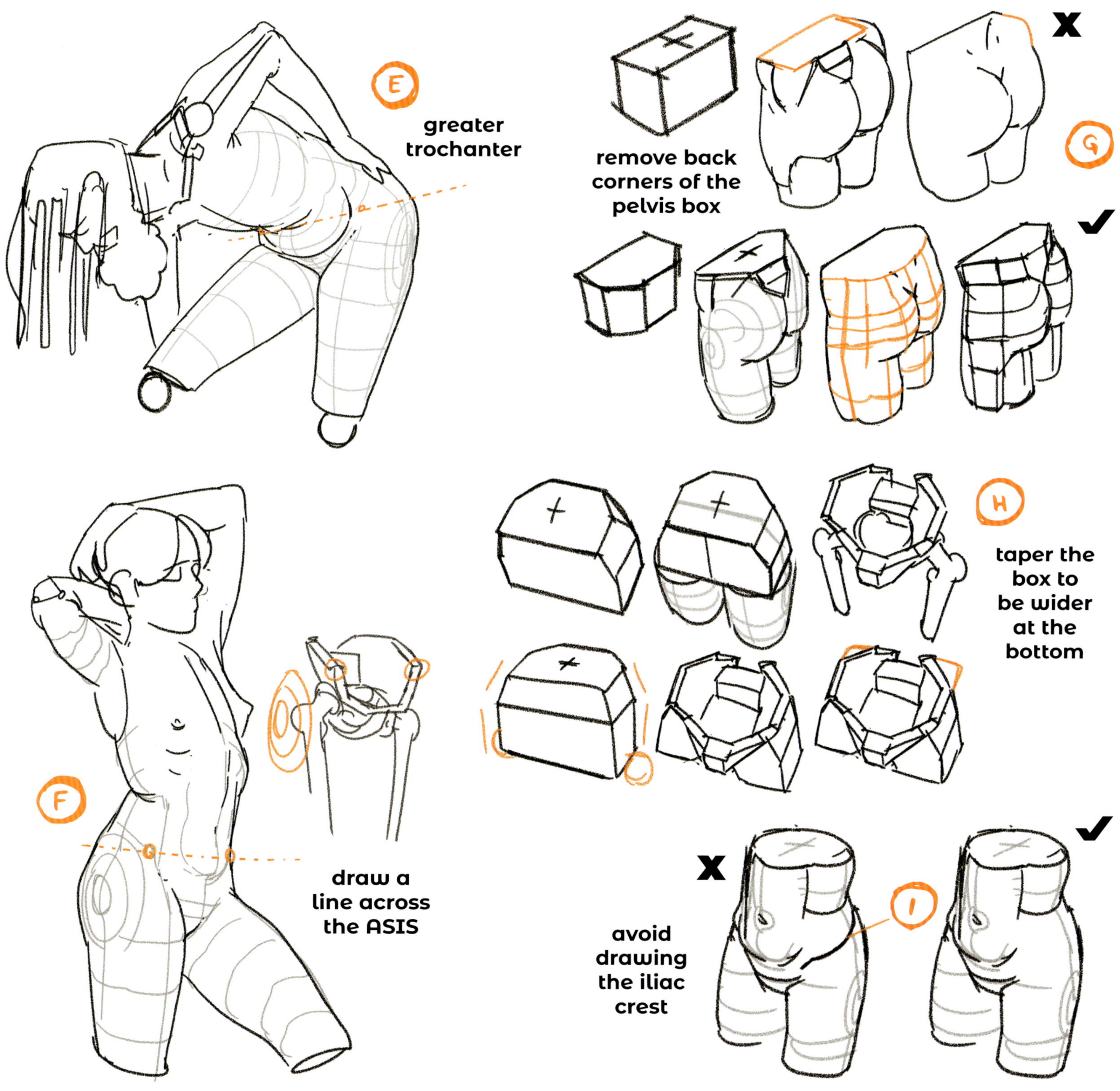

the psoas

People avoid learning the "deep" muscles because you don't see them superficially (from the surface). But if you don't understand how the body moves itself around, you won't be able to visualize the outer forms!

Always remember that muscles can *only pull*. There is no pushing action. This simplifies things for artists, because we only need to ask, "What two parts of the body is this muscle pulling on?"

Focus on how something works, not how it looks. The psoas, for example, is a hidden but major muscle. It attaches mainly to the bottom five vertebrae of the spine (the "lumbar" region) (A), where it can pull our spine forward (B).

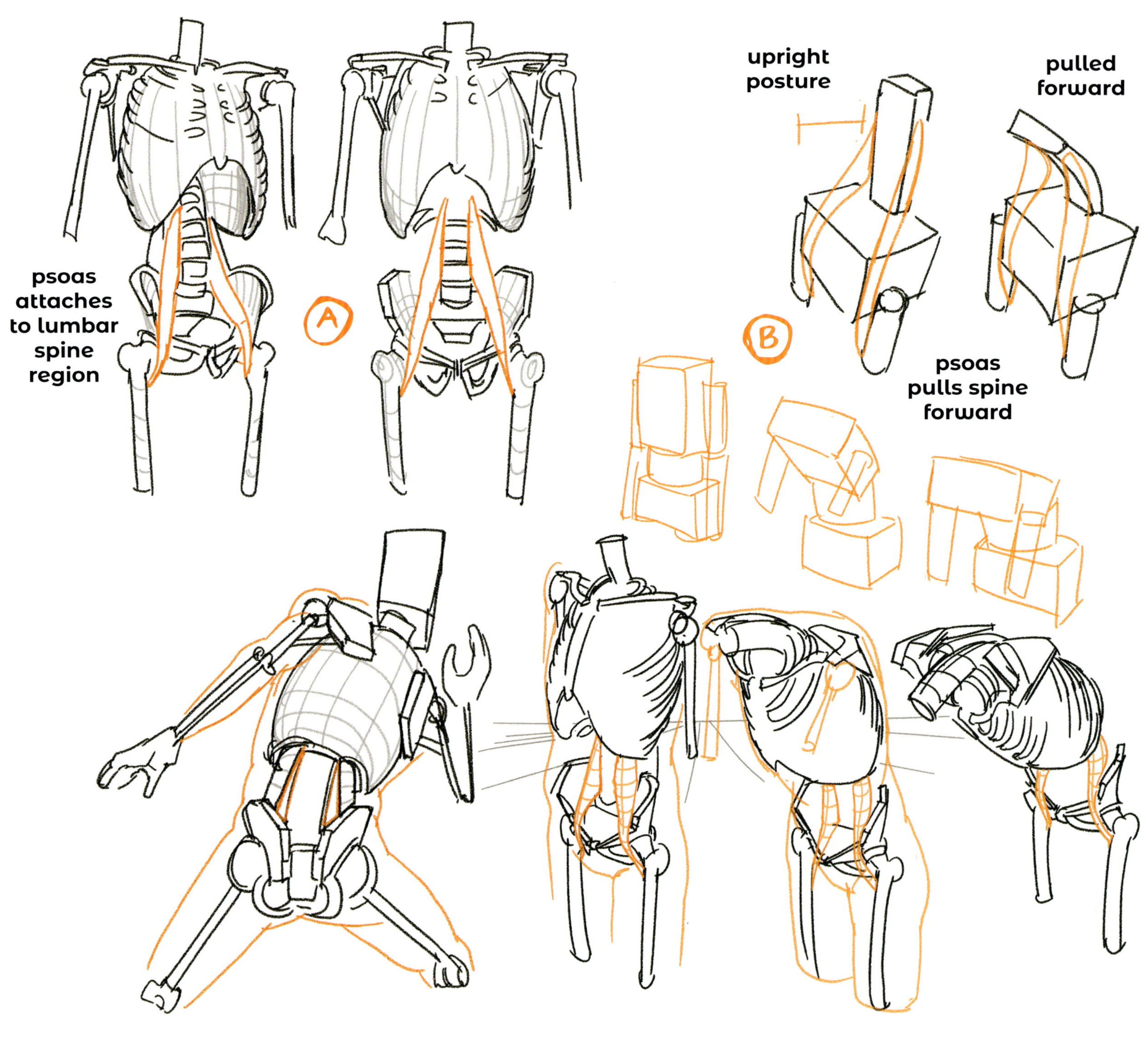

When memorizing muscles, always consider two factors: How far in front or behind are the attachments, and how far out to the sides are the attachments?

For example, the psoas wraps around the front of the pelvis and attaches into the rear of the femur (C). The other end attaches to the sides of the spine, but this attachment is relatively farther back than the attachment to the legs. This suggests that we are probably trying to pull the spine forward (D).

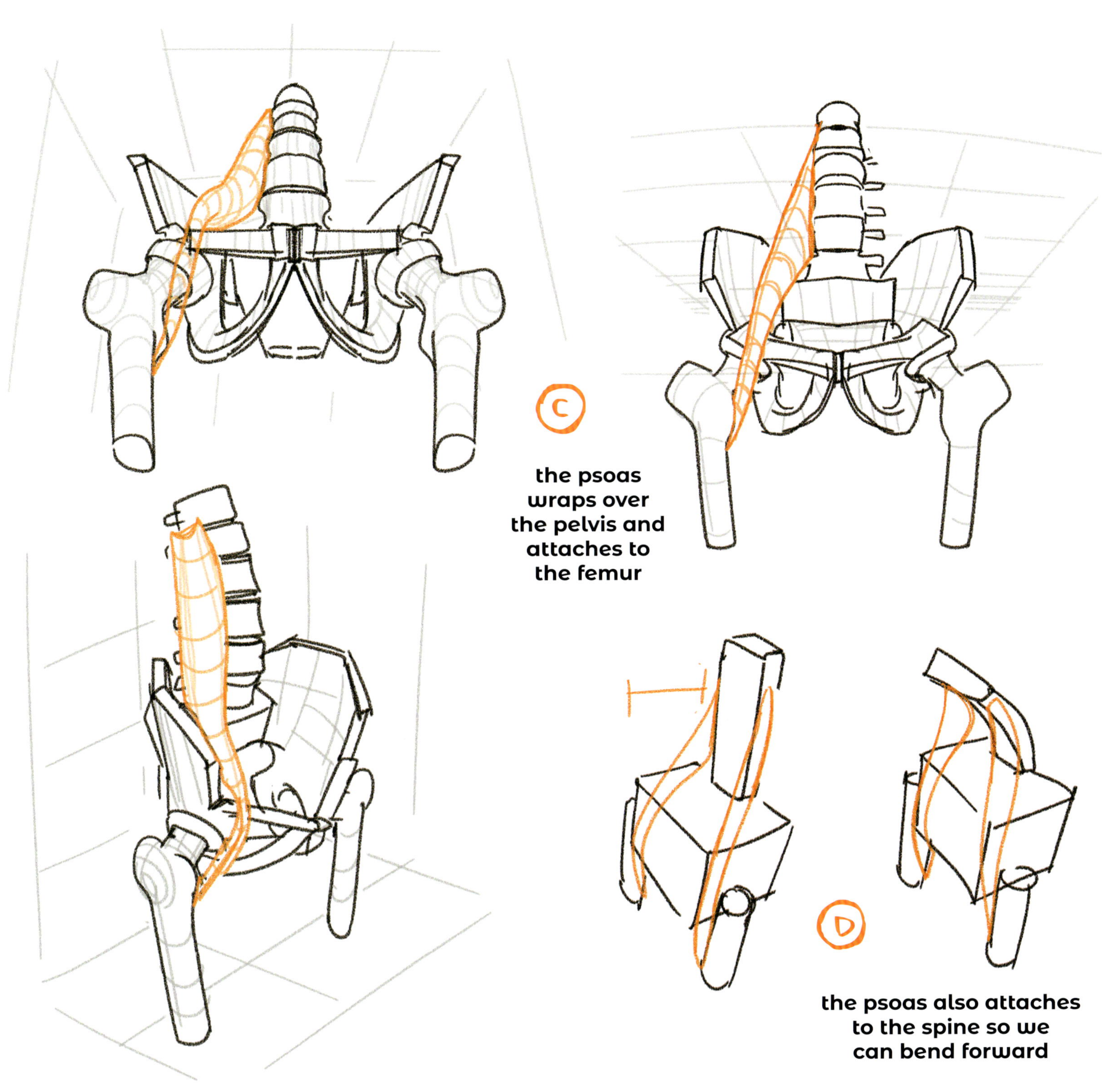

lumbar region

Let's quickly review the lumbar region of the spine (A). It connects the rib cage to the pelvis and consists of five vertebrae. Common mistakes when drawing these vertebrae include drawing them too narrow rather than at their surprising full width (B), and drawing them stacked on top of each other rather than splaying them out in a natural curve (C).

The lateral projections of the vertebrae anchor the quadratus lumborum (or "QL"), a powerful chain of muscles that helps us bend left and right and provides stability to the spine (D).

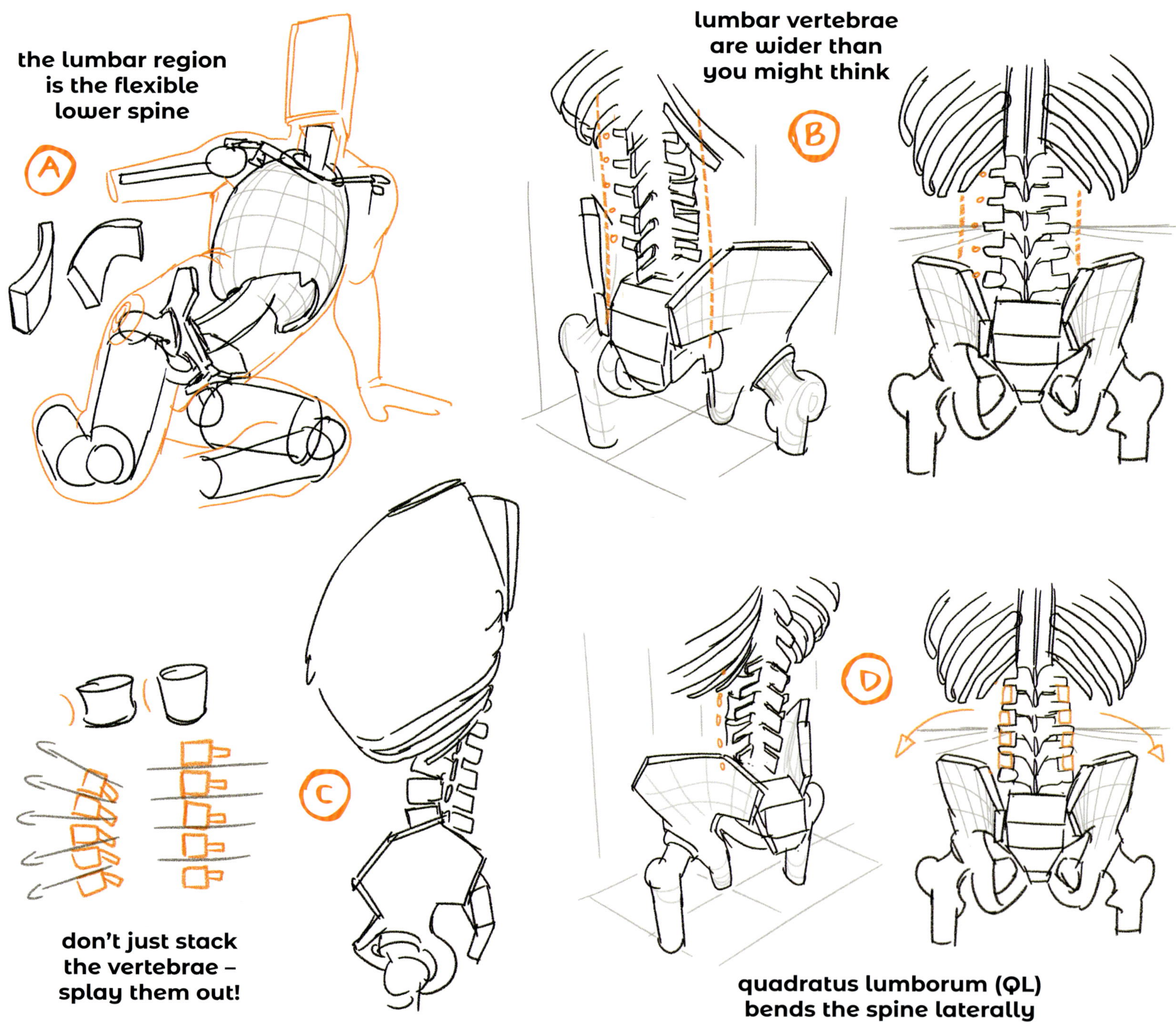

The psoas pulls forward, but also pulls laterally (to the side). However, because of its forward-and-back attachment points, it's not ideal for a lateral role. The QL is better located for this **(E)**. The QL attaches to the back of the ilium (the wings) just above the sacrum (the shrimp-tail) and joins to the sides of the five lumbar vertebrae. Crucially, it also attaches to the bottom rib **(F)**.

If you haven't noticed by now, the lumbar region of the spine is a weak place on the body. There's nothing else joining the two large masses of the body together, and the area has no bone at the front to support it. This is why we tend to suffer lower-back pain – in evolutionary terms, we haven't fully evolved to walk upright!

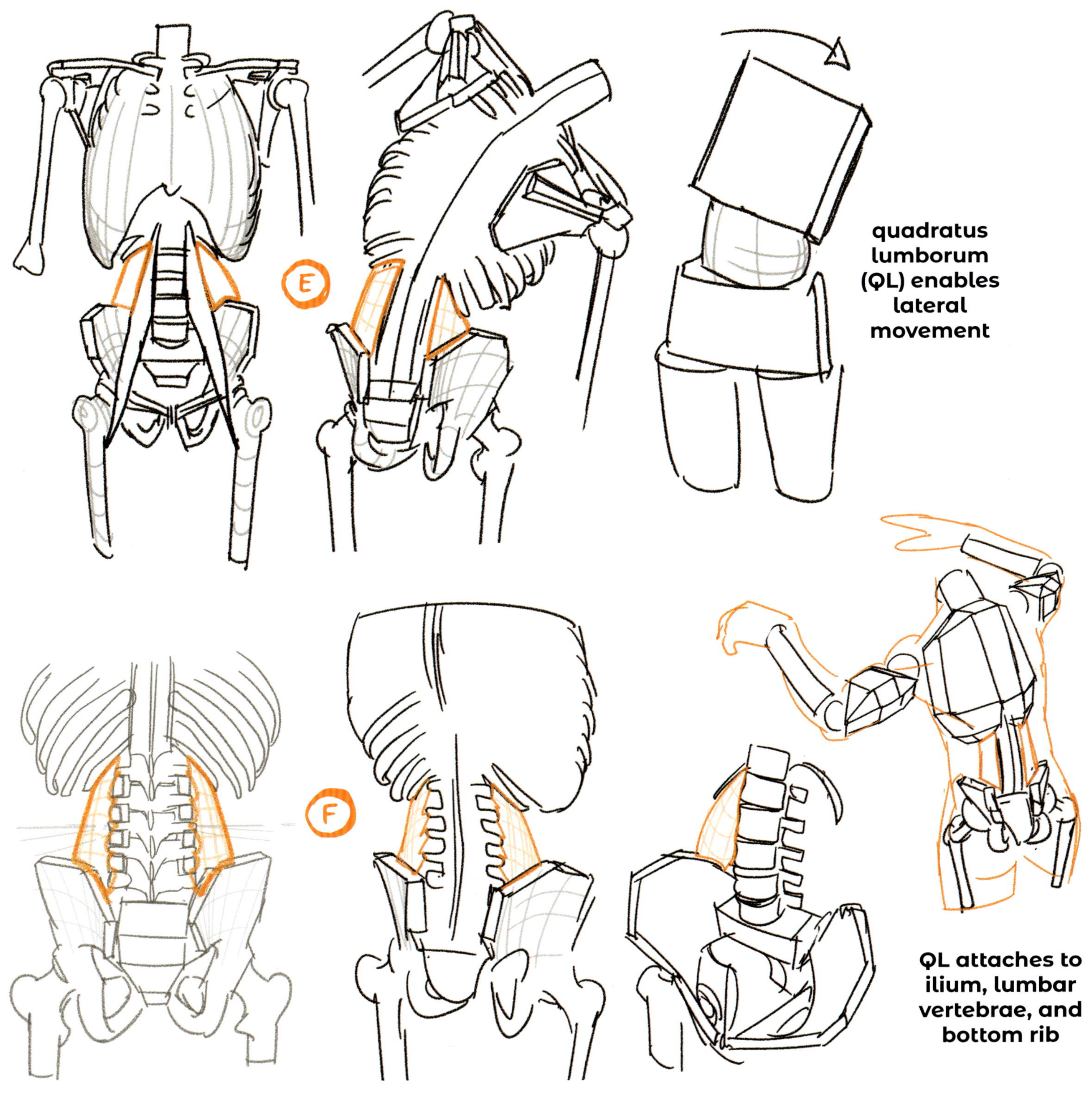

abdominal region

Now let's move on to the nearby transversus abdominis (or "TA"). Often we think of the core as running vertically, but this muscle goes across the body – transversus means "across" and abdominis means "abdomen." The TA holds everything in like a corset (A). It isn't an equal height around the rib cage and it doesn't wrap all the way around (B). Instead, it curves downward and meets the rear edge of the quadratus lumborum ("QL") at the back (C). Note the corset-like shape (D). People with a stronger TA generally have a narrower waist and flatter stomach for this reason.

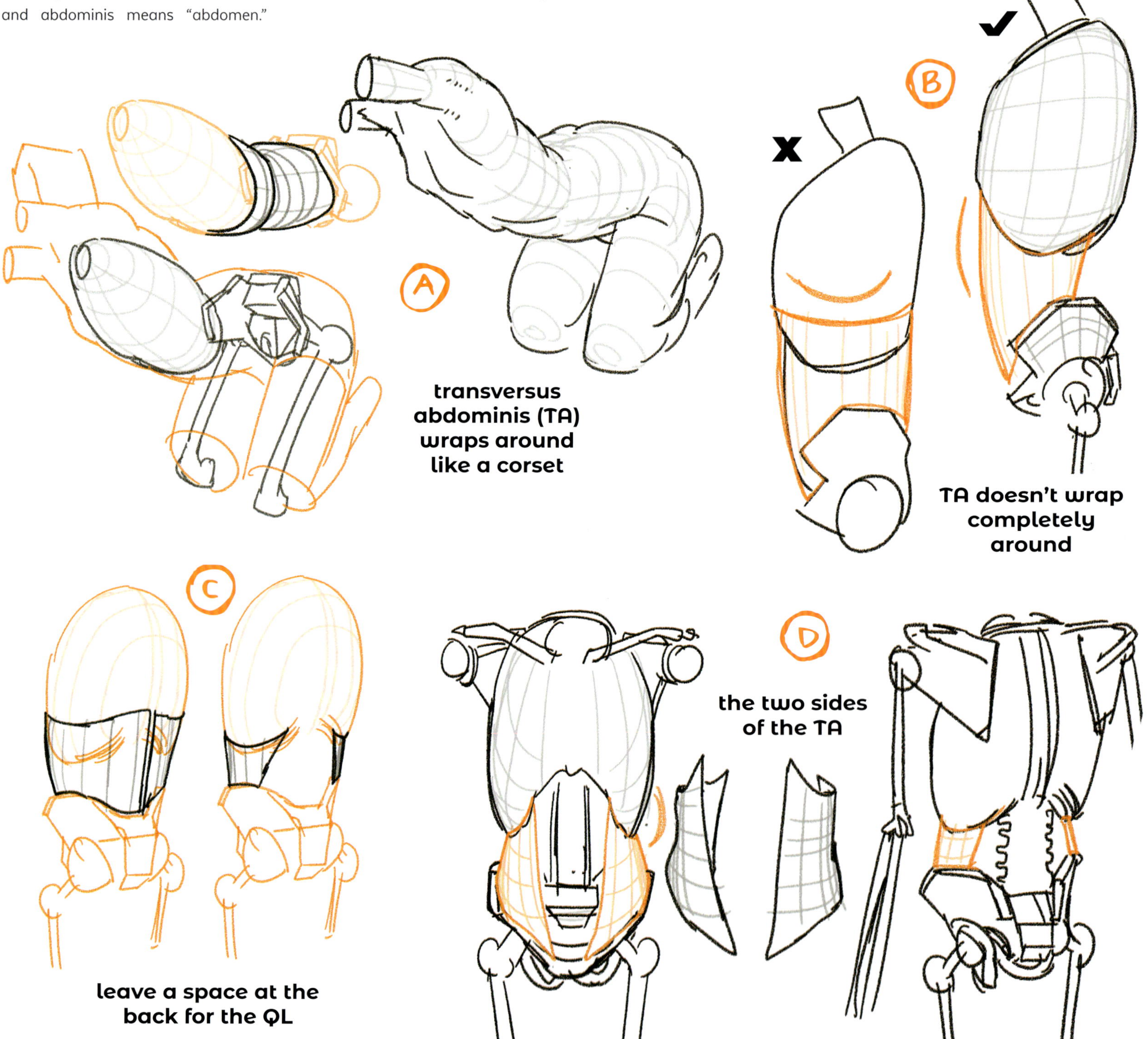

If you're wondering where these abdominal muscles attach, let's go over them now. We have a thick cord called the inguinal ligament (E), which connects the ASIS with the pubis.

This ligament is almost exactly vertical when viewed in profile. It's a good measuring point because most of the time the abdominal muscles extend farther forward than this ligament (F).

Viewed from above in G, the torso will normally show the external oblique muscles at the sides (1, 3). We can also see the rectus abdominis (the "six-pack" or "abs" muscle group) because it attaches to the front of the torso, just above the bottom of the sternum (2).

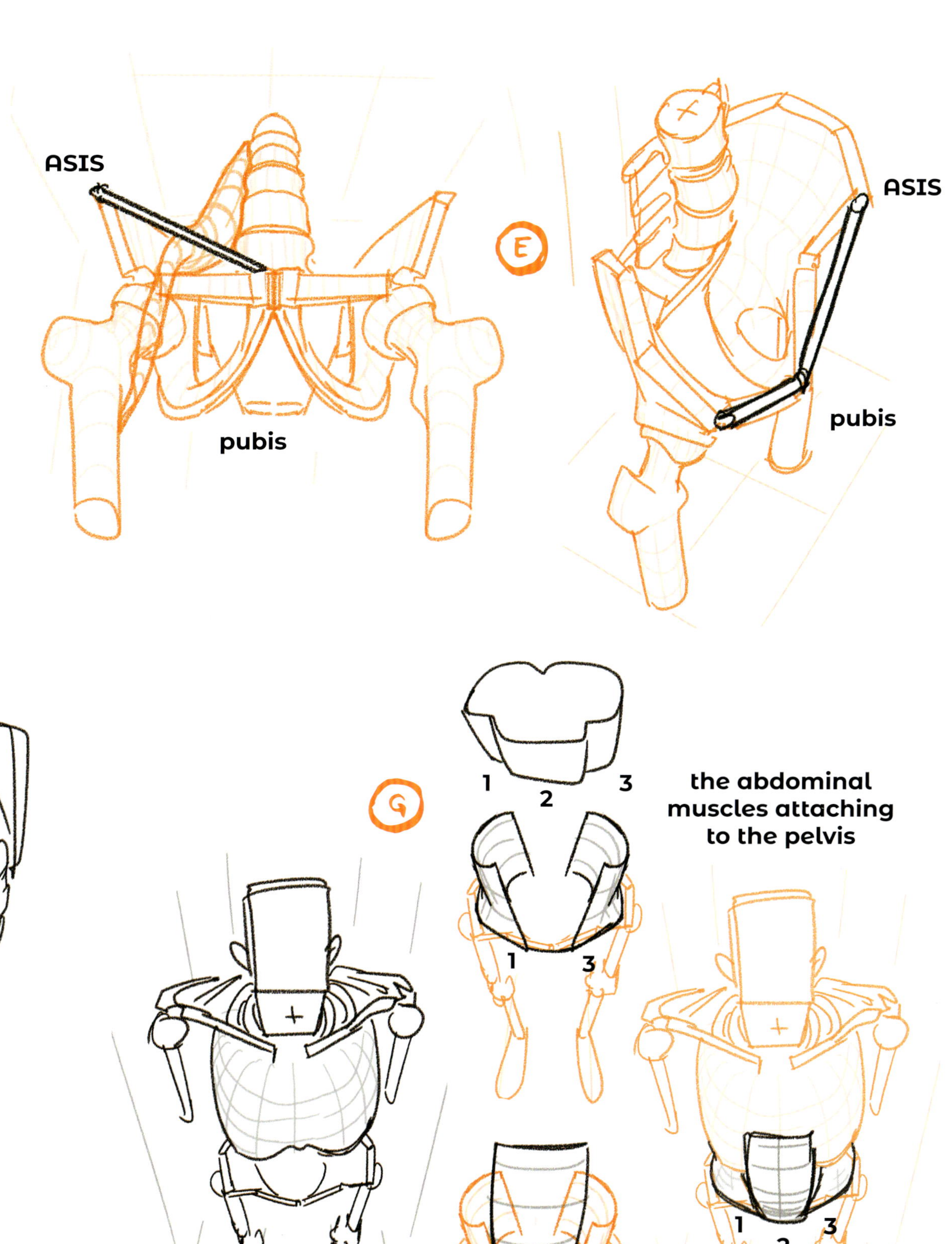

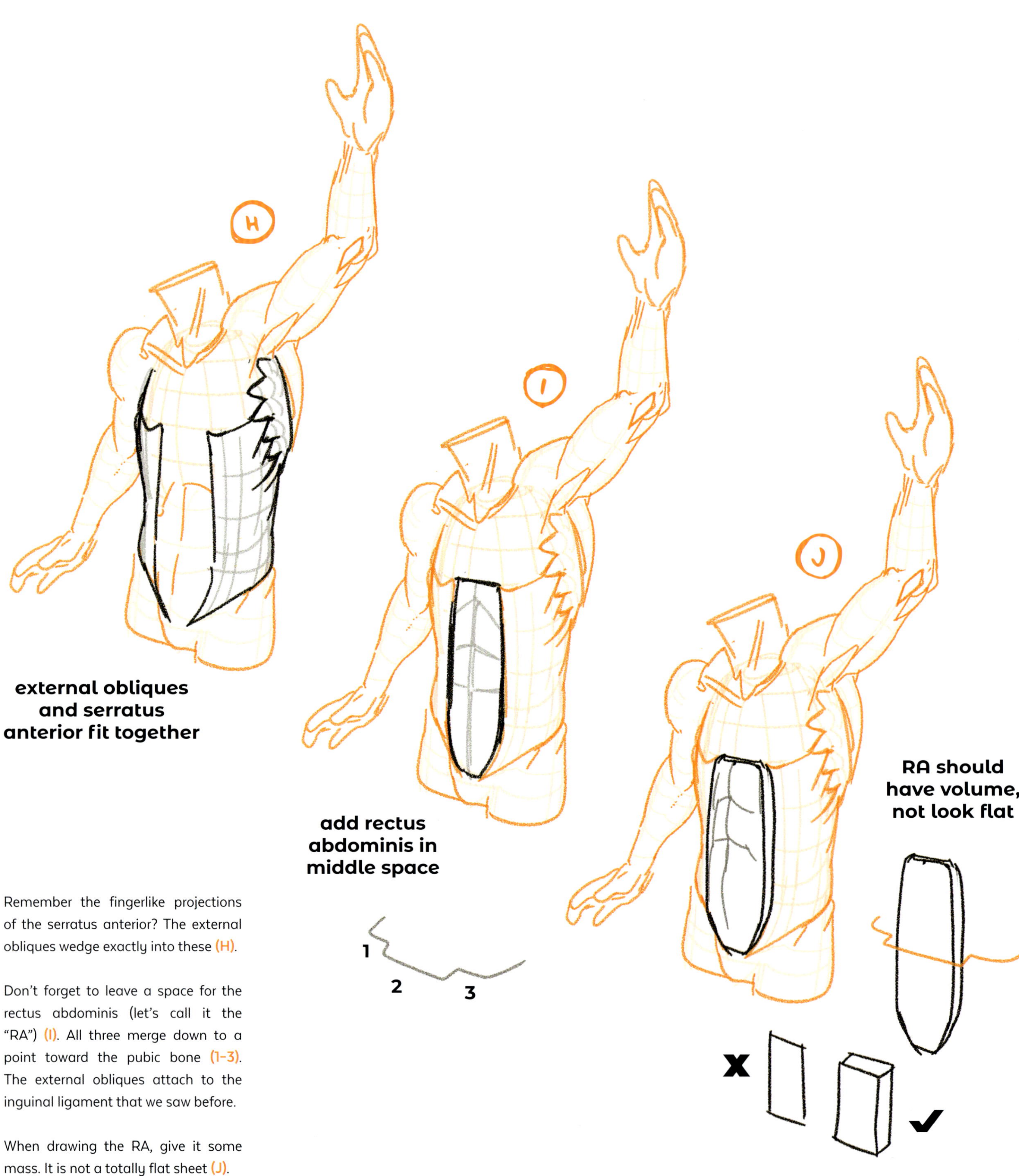

Remember the fingerlike projections of the serratus anterior? The external obliques wedge exactly into these (H).

Don't forget to leave a space for the rectus abdominis (let's call it the "RA") (I). All three merge down to a point toward the pubic bone (1-3). The external obliques attach to the inguinal ligament that we saw before.

When drawing the RA, give it some mass. It is not a totally flat sheet (J).

The more muscular and lean an individual, the more clearly defined the line between the external obliques and the RA will be (K). For most people, there will be almost no distinction between them. When the RA is more developed, the forms bulge out enough that the external obliques are sometimes hidden in a three-quarter view (L). When we twist the core, the ASIS pushes the external obliques upward, causing a bulge (M).

When drawing the core, give it three distinct sides, like our rib cage form. To make it more complicated, add the inward pinch at the middle (N).

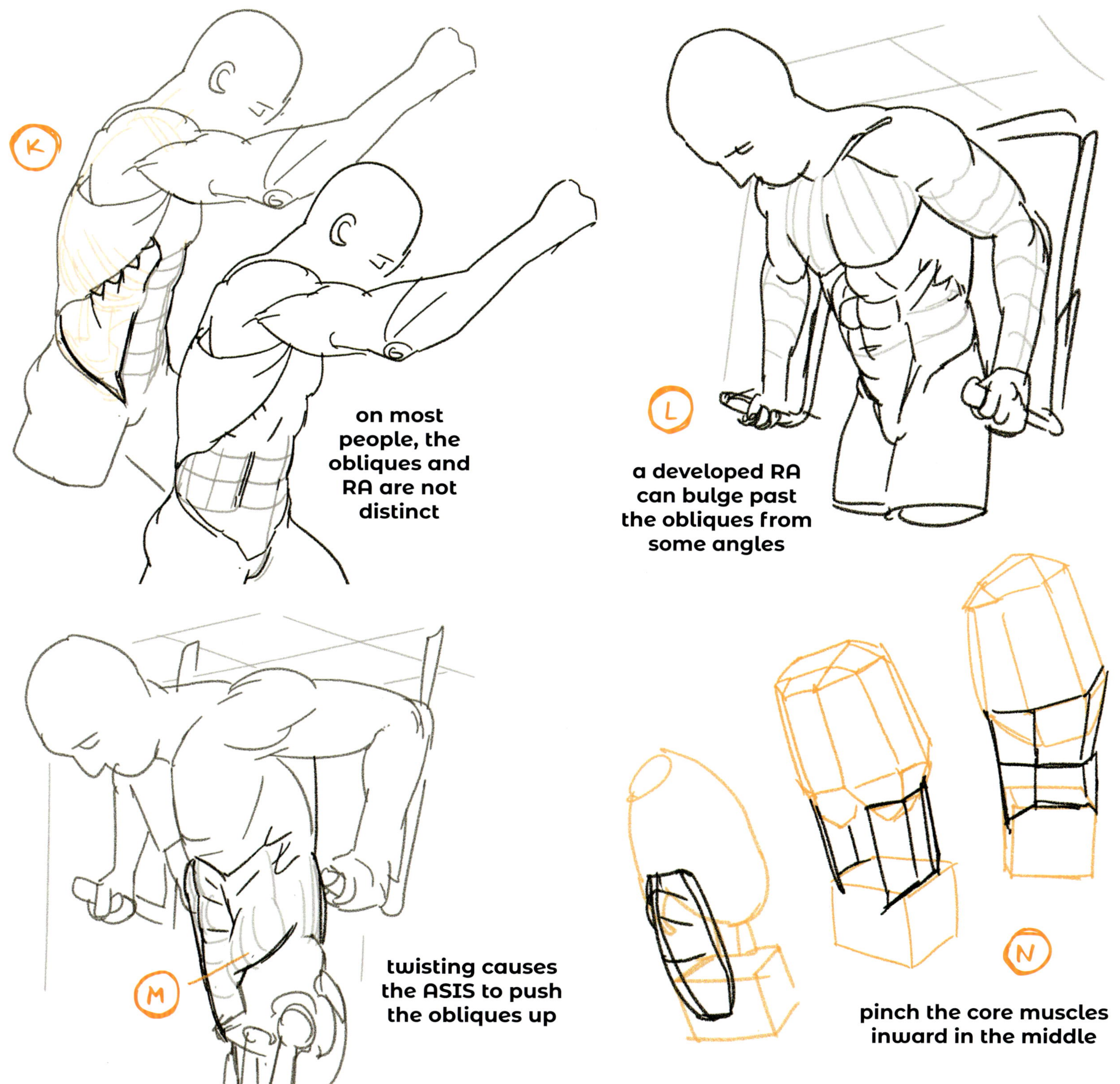

When you draw the figure twisting, the obliques cover not only the side of the body, but the rear of the waist too. They run around the sides to the back. You usually see more of the back than you'd expect in any pose, except from a completely frontal view (O). Note the space (P) where the S-shape of the pelvis allows us to see more of the obliques and gluteal muscles (the "glutes" or buttocks) than you might expect.

Indicating body fat doesn't require adding huge amounts of mass to the figure. The difference can be shown in the depth of the folds – simply draw smaller creases to indicate areas with lower body fat (Q).

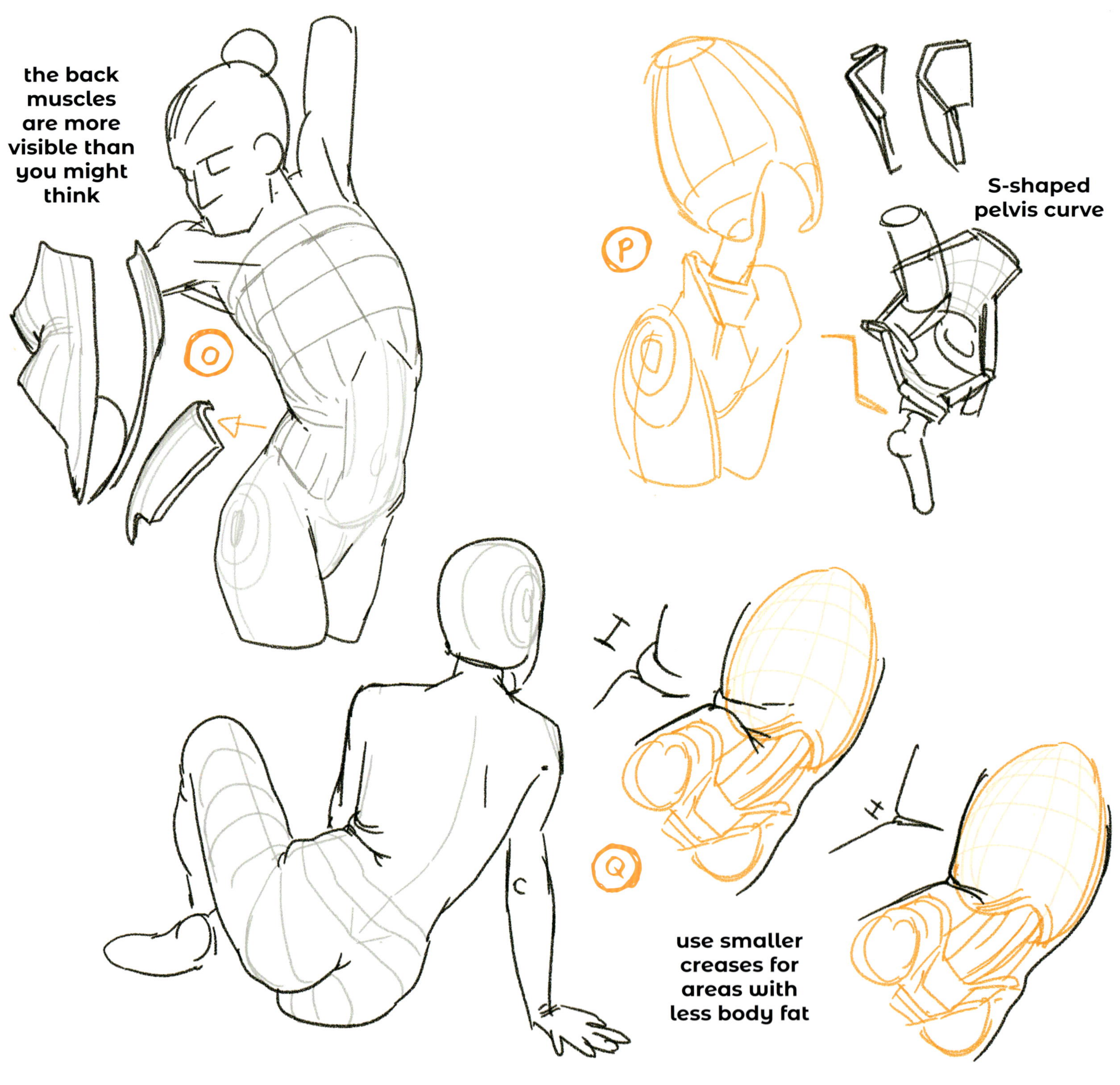

tip: add some twist!

When possible, always include a twist in your poses - this will add variety and believability (A). The two relative points to keep in mind are the ASIS (1) and the bottom corners of the rib cage (2). As these two points move closer together, the muscle in-between has to go somewhere - it bulges outward (B).

twist your figures to make them more real and interesting!

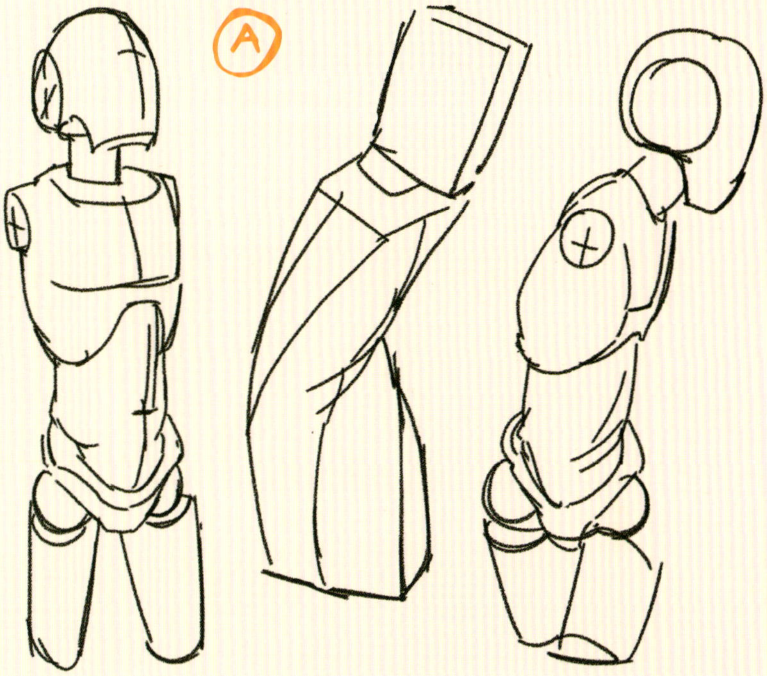

A

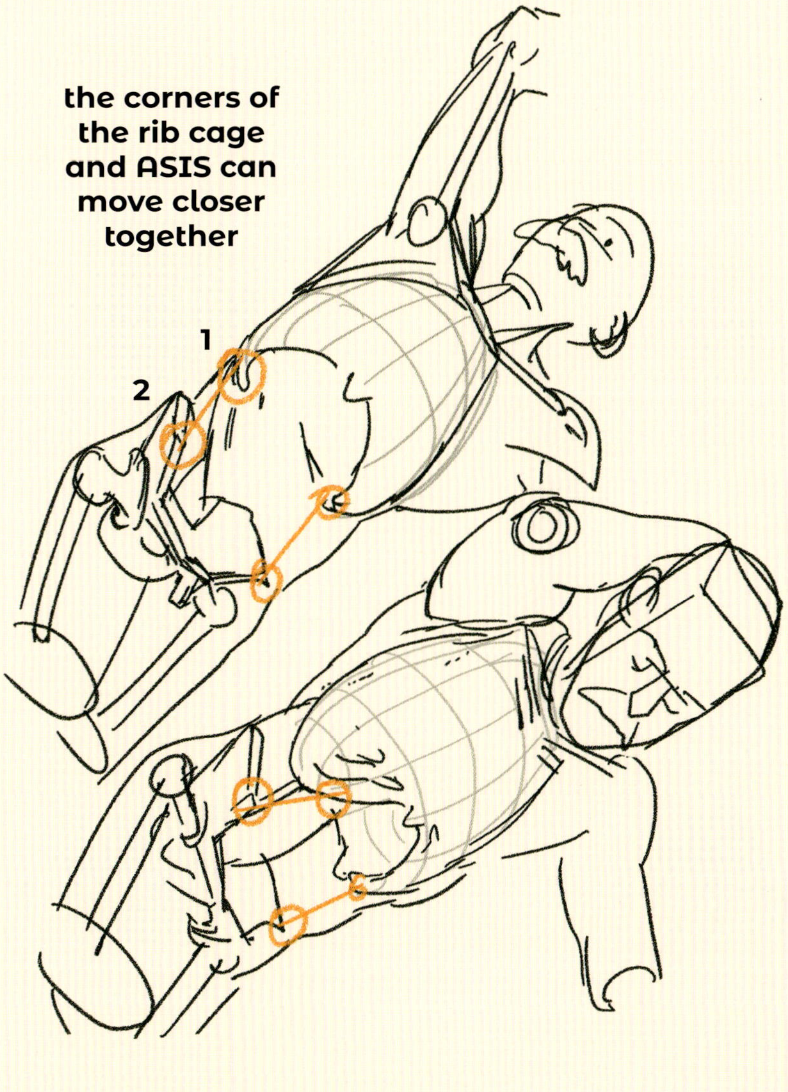

the corners of the rib cage and ASIS can move closer together

1

2

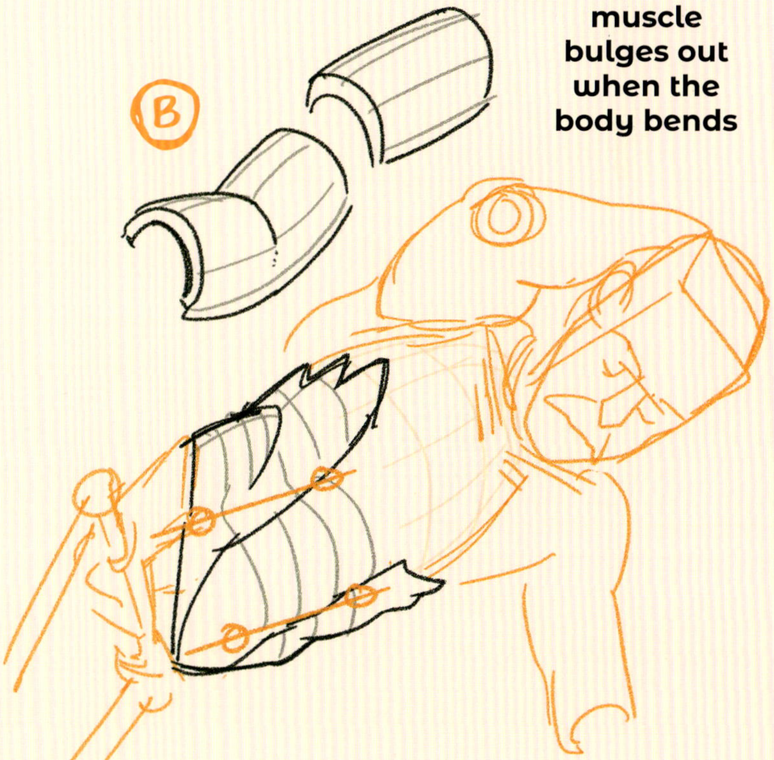

B

muscle bulges out when the body bends

tip: hidden muscles

When drawing the core, as with all muscles, remember not to separate the groups. It's tempting to fall into the habit of drawing flat shorthand symbols instead of how the subject actually appears (A). Remember that what creates form is wedging, as we learned on page 28. Even if the anatomy isn't quite correct, if it "wedges" believably, it will appear more like it is (B). When the rib cage twists, its front corners are buried by the obliques. It is important to show plenty of overlap here. Practice drawing simple forms until you are comfortable with this type of twisting (C).

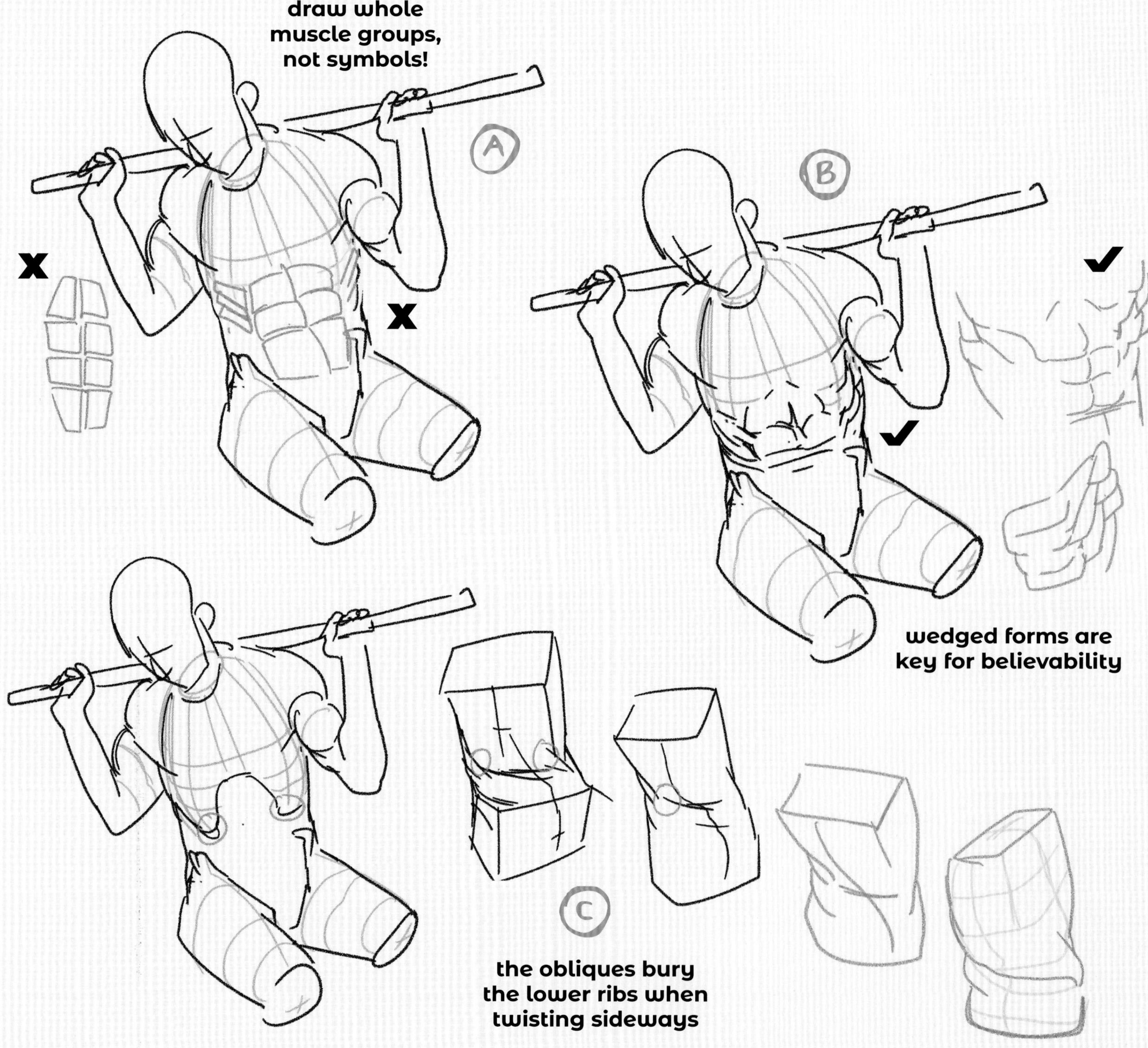

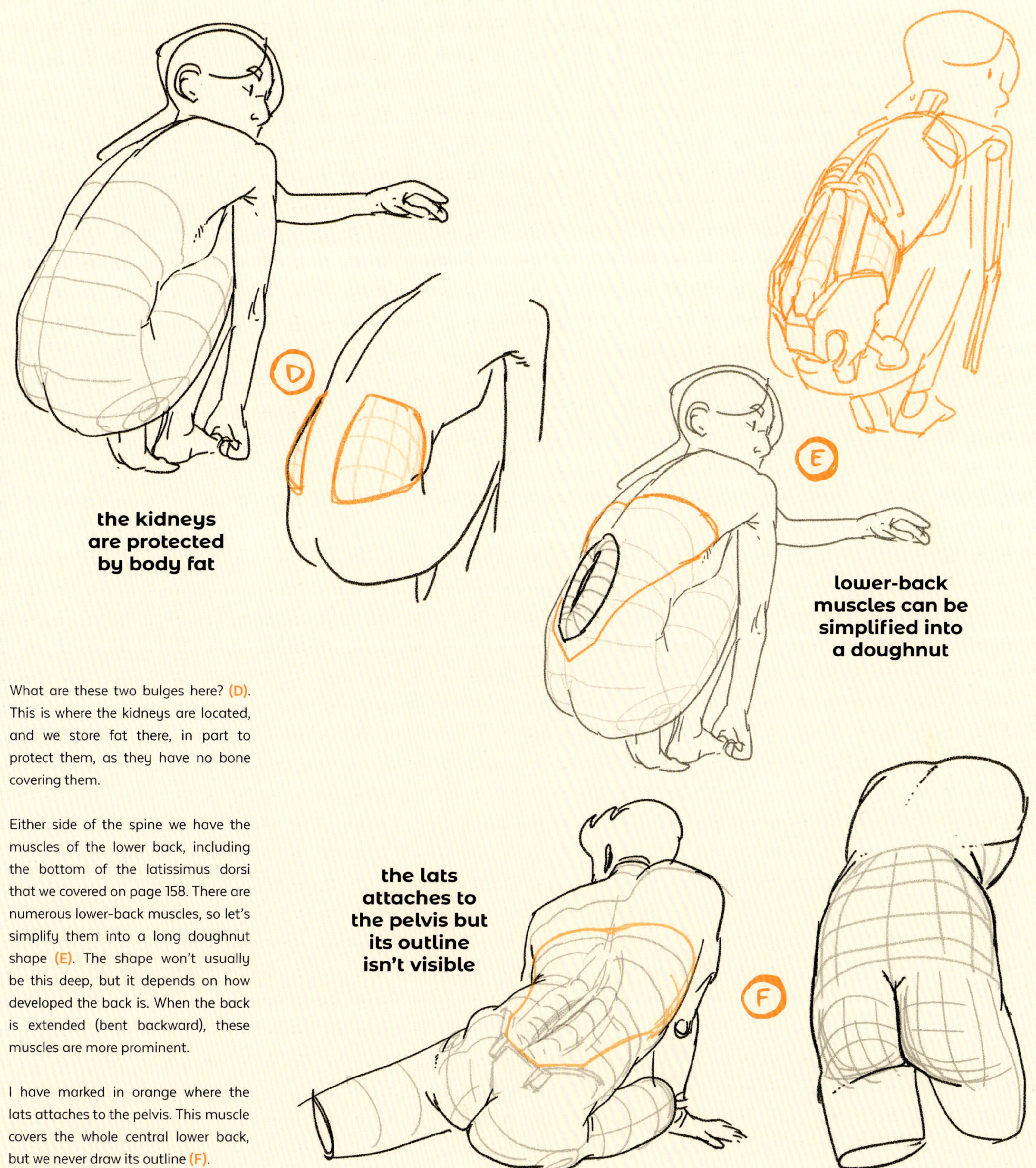

What are these two bulges here? (D). This is where the kidneys are located, and we store fat there, in part to protect them, as they have no bone covering them.

Either side of the spine we have the muscles of the lower back, including the bottom of the latissimus dorsi that we covered on page 158. There are numerous lower-back muscles, so let's simplify them into a long doughnut shape (E). The shape won't usually be this deep, but it depends on how developed the back is. When the back is extended (bent backward), these muscles are more prominent.

I have marked in orange where the lats attaches to the pelvis. This muscle covers the whole central lower back, but we never draw its outline (F).

proportions & gender

So much of our recognition of gender is based upon characteristics such as proportion and musculature. If you see a figure like this (A), it is difficult to define the character's gender because the proportions are mixed.

Key characteristics for women can include wider hips and a smaller rib cage relative to the pelvis. Less essential characteristics would be features like hairstyle, breasts, and genitals, which we don't rely on much for identification in our drawings.

Narrowing the hips makes this figure look more "masculine" (B). Conversely, adding body fat around the waist gives a more feminine appearance (C), as women have a higher body-fat ratio on average.

Above the pubic mound we have a region where stomach fat accumulates (D). You'll often see the bulge and then curve inward, even on very slim people. That rhythm commonly appears like E, with the curve of the rib cage (1), the abdominals (2), and the body fat of the stomach (3).

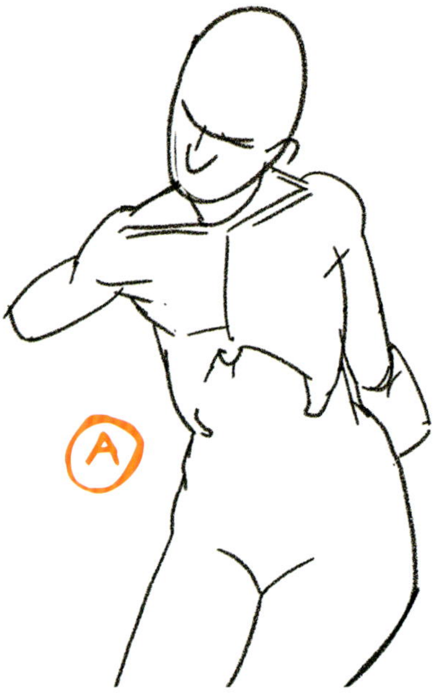

ambiguous proportions

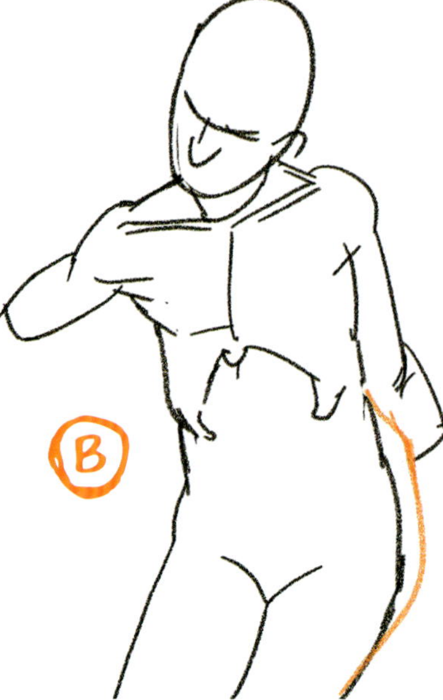

more masculine proportions

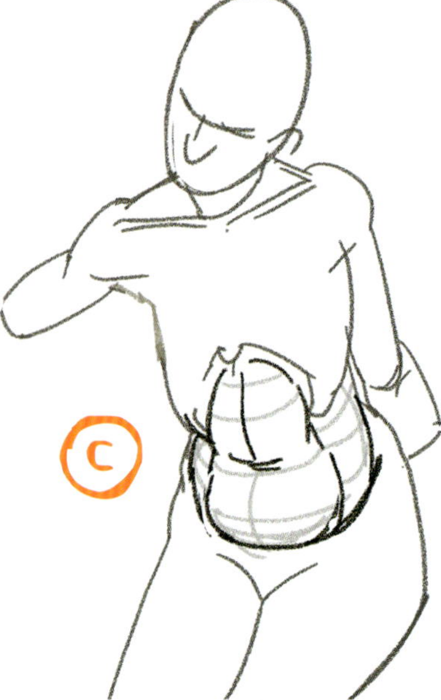

more feminine proportions

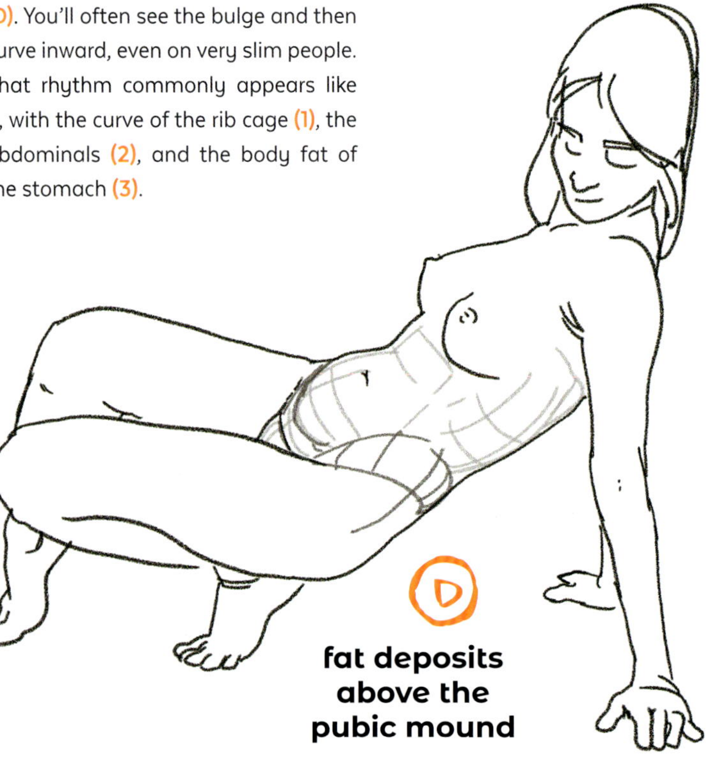

fat deposits above the pubic mound

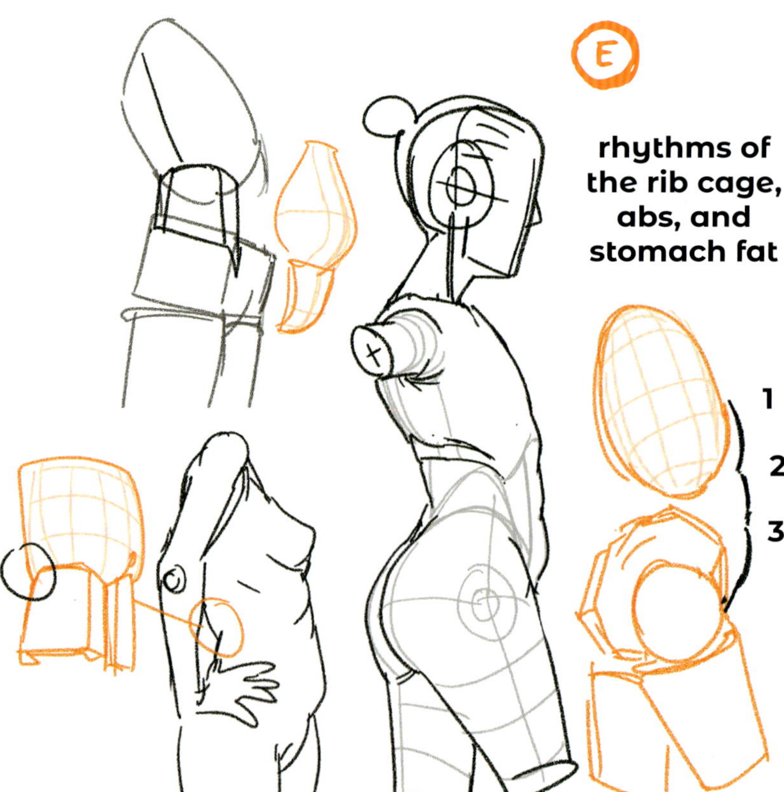

rhythms of the rib cage, abs, and stomach fat

When drawing the core and torso bending, be careful where the folds form. Position F shows a figure bending straight to the side, whereas the folds and taut center line on position G suggest that the rib cage is leaning back.

The obliques tend to hang over the sides of the iliac crest when we bend to the side. Contrary to what you might expect, this is more obvious on people with highly developed muscles than on people who have more body fat (H).

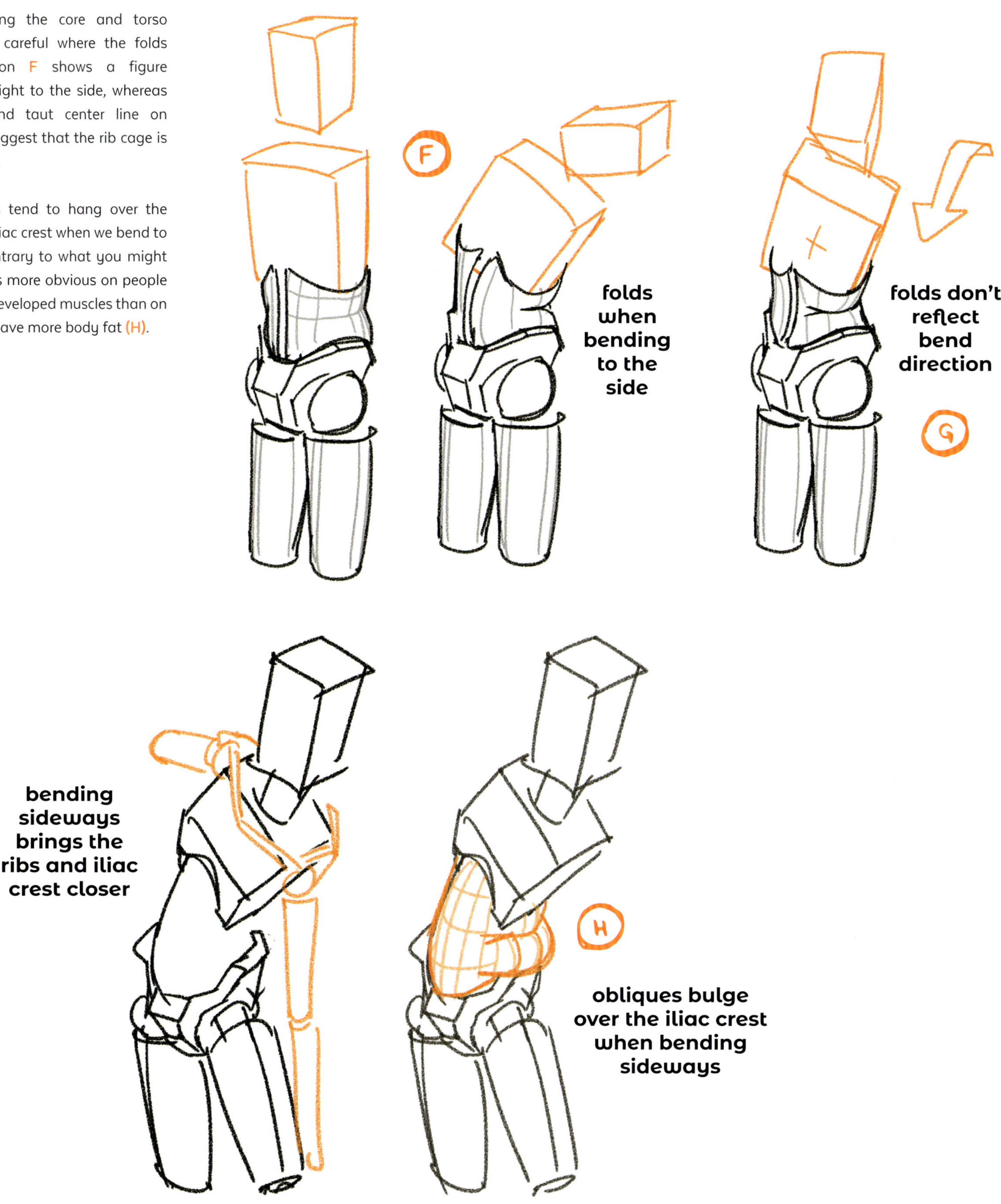

If it helps, you can imagine the obliques and stomach-fat region with the same rhythm as nineties-style high-rise bikini bottoms (I)! Always draw the form of the obliques and waist wrapping around. Frequently, this fat pad will cover the far side of the obliques completely (J). Always be careful when drawing the crease lines of the legs and hips. A crease in a different location (K) or of a different length (L) can suggest a totally different leg angle or body-fat percentage.

imagine a high-rise bikini shape!

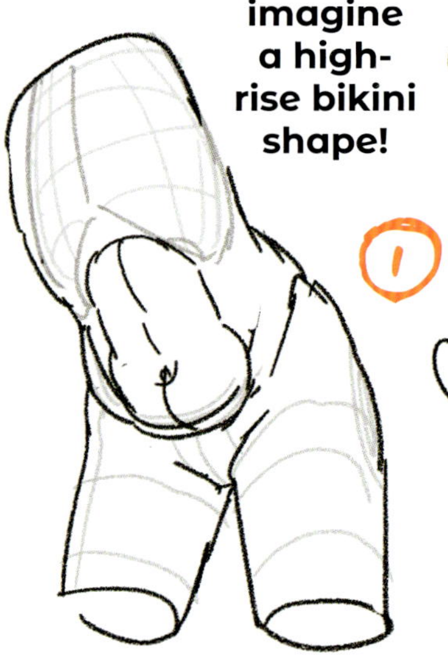

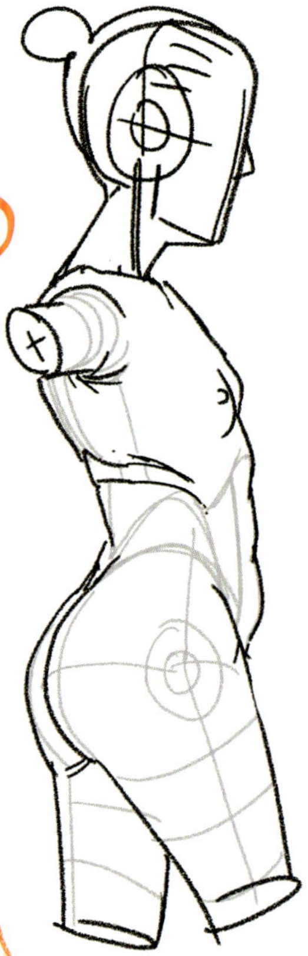

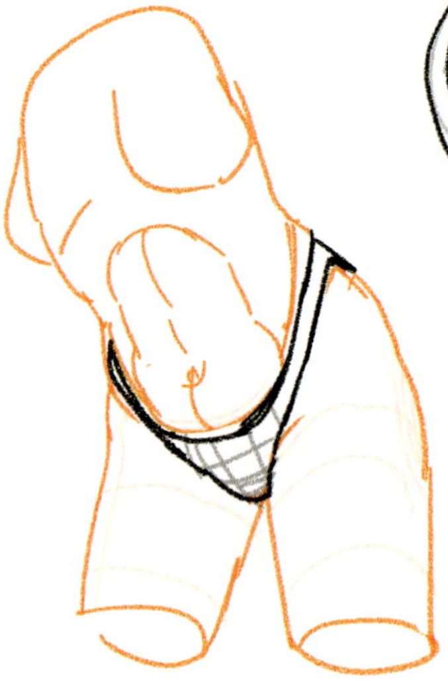

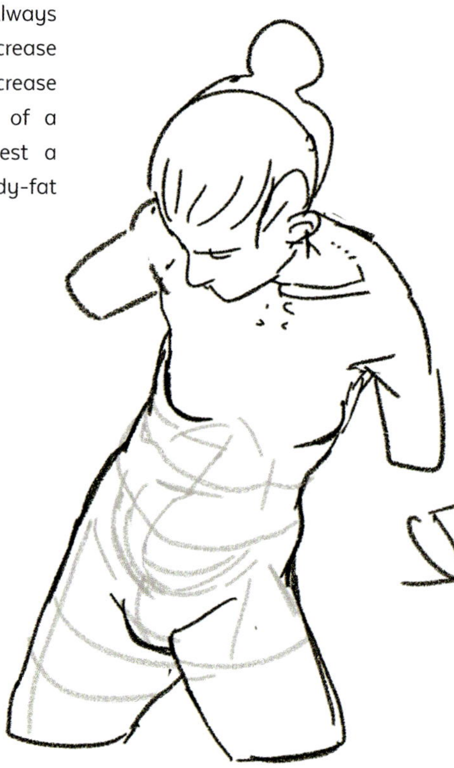

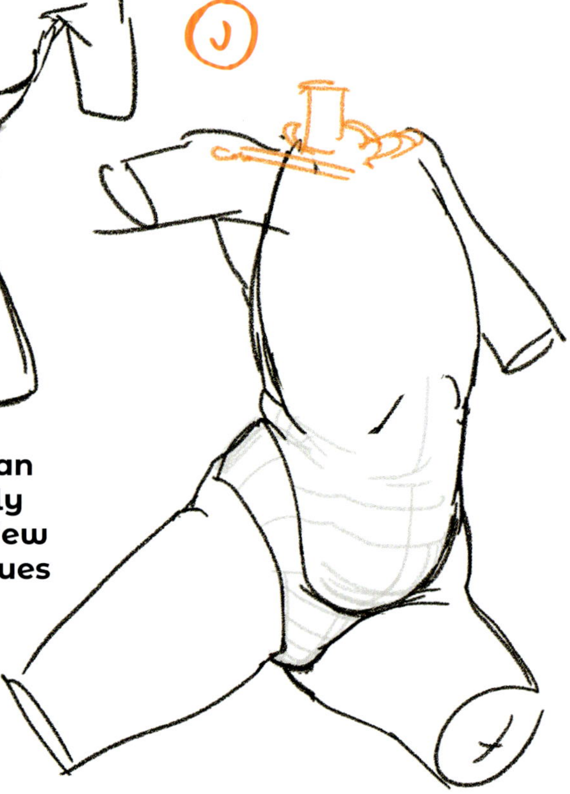

I

J

body fat can completely cover our view of the obliques

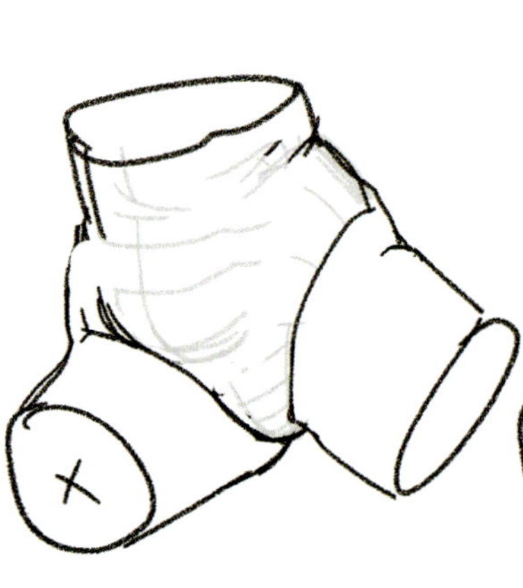

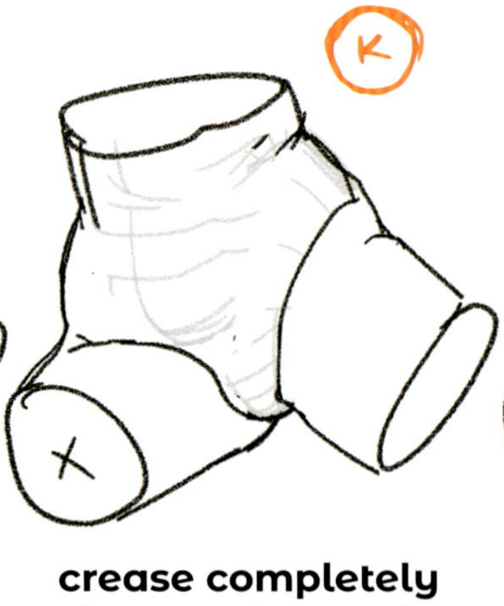

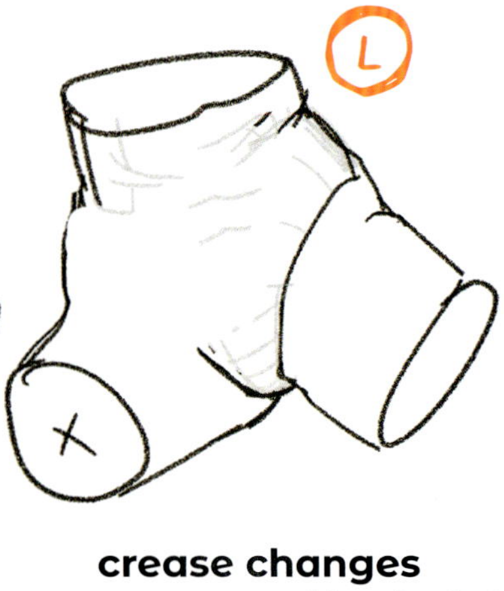

K

L

crease completely changes leg angle

crease changes appearance of body fat

core summary

We've learned that the core is a surprisingly complex, nuanced area of the body, and how a successful core hinges on a good understanding of the rib cage, spine, and pelvis.

We learned about the functions and landmarks of the pelvis, and how to streamline its shape into something more suitable for our mannequin (A).

We explored the muscles and forms that form the core, including the deep muscles that allow us to twist and bend – even if we can't see them from the surface – and the soft tissue and fat that cushion the lower torso (B).

Next, we'll be continuing the journey from the pelvis and tops of the femurs, all the way down the legs to the feet!

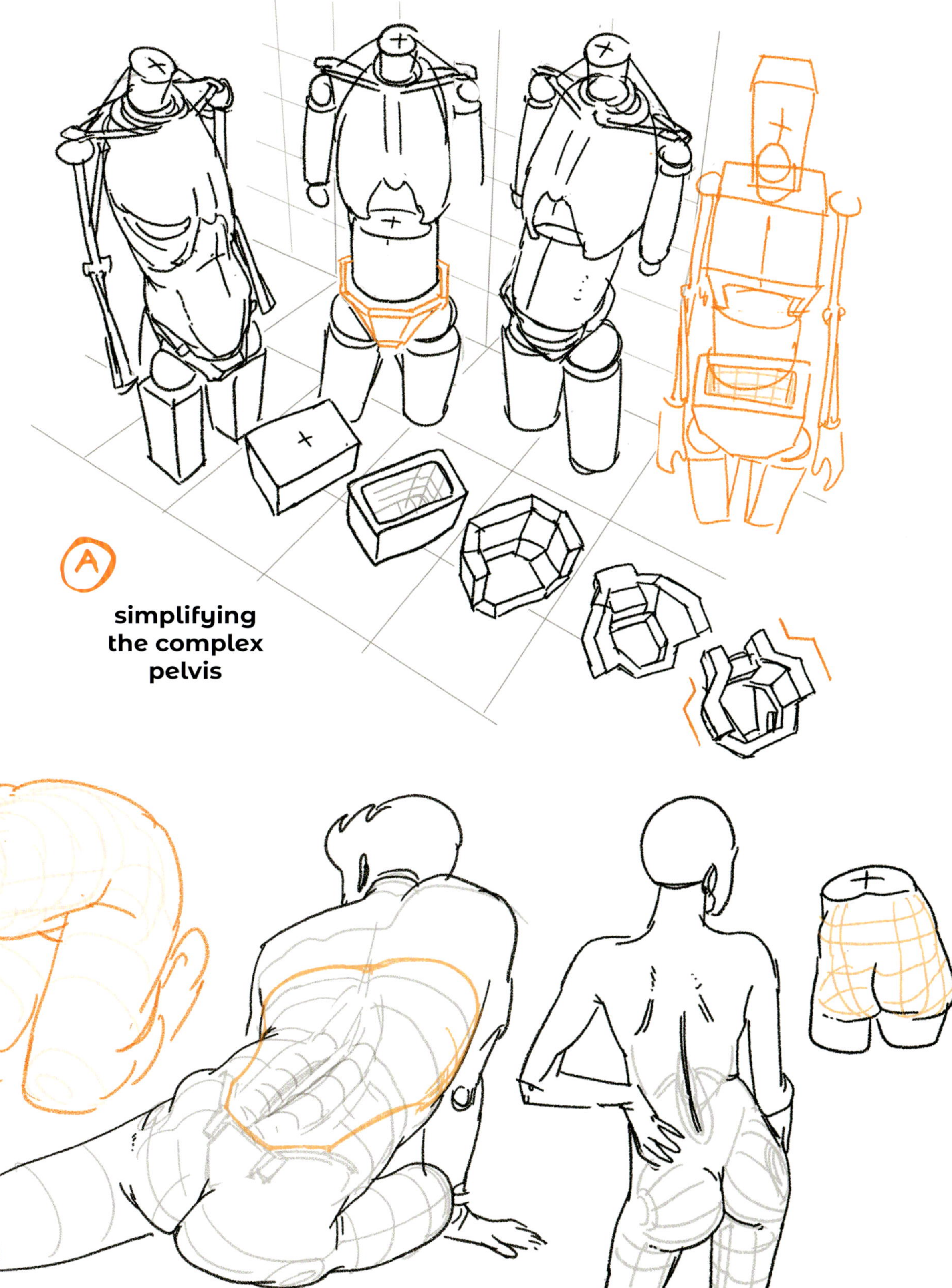

simplifying the complex pelvis

building up layers of muscle and fat to give the core form

lesson 5:

legs & feet

Now let's examine everything below the core, including the bones of the legs and feet, the key muscle groups, and the simplified forms suitable for our box mannequin.

leg bone overview

The number of bones in the legs matches the number of bones in the arms: one for the upper section and two for the lower (A). The upper bone, the femur (1), is extremely strong. The tibia (2) and fibula (3) are the lower two bones. The tibia is weight-bearing while the fibula is thinner and plays a more auxiliary role, just like the ulna and radius of the arm.

When simplifying the leg, draw rectangles rather than cylinders, as this helps you control the XYZ rotation of your shapes.

At the knee end of each section, we see that the shape of the bones flares out (4). Why is this region so large? Why does it bulge out wider than the bones themselves? The answer is that we have many tendons and ligaments attaching the leg bones and muscles together – if this area was smaller, it would be weaker, with less room for attachments (B)! Because of this large amount of connective tissue, the upper and lower legs have very little scope to rotate independently (C).

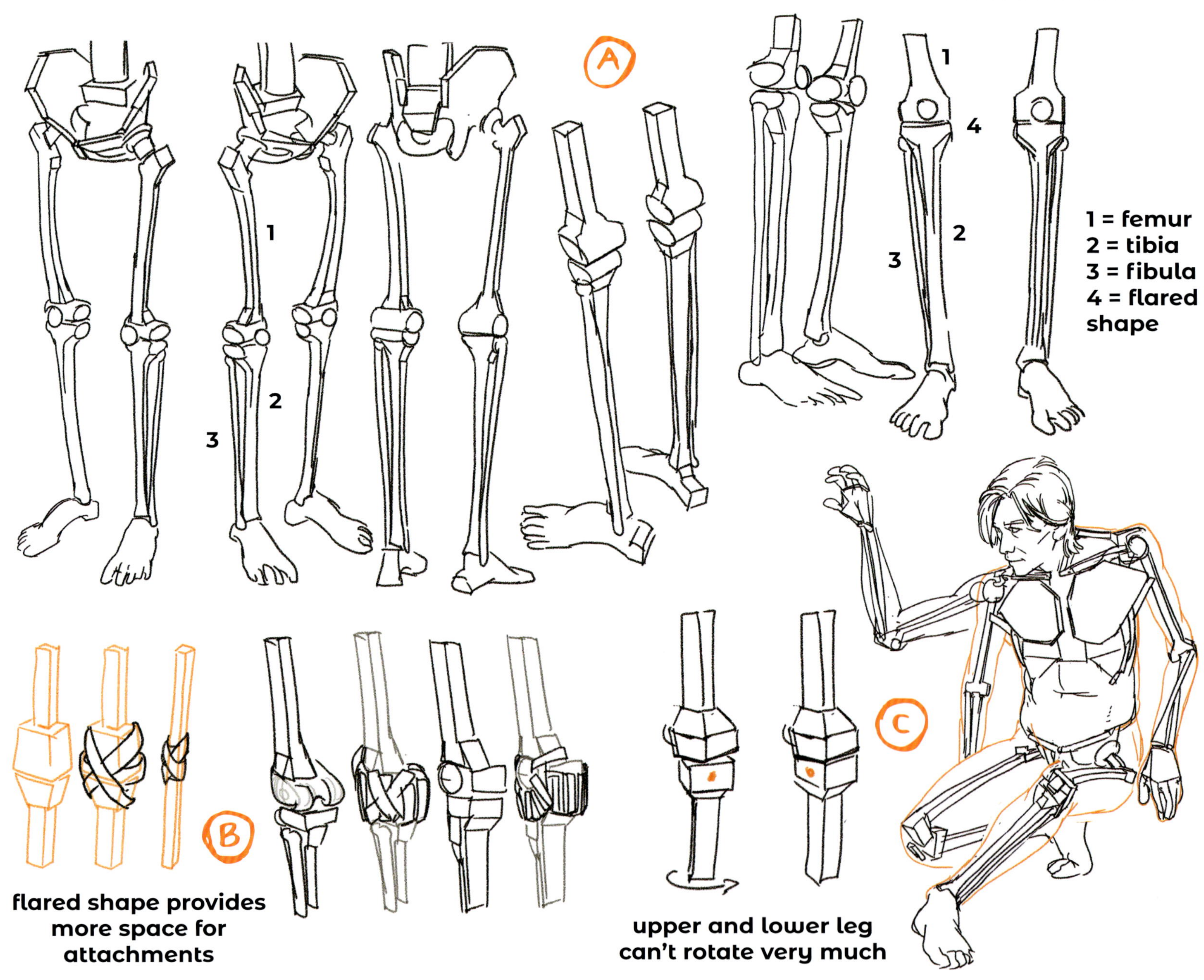

Ensure both the femur and tibia project backward (D). Often we're so focused on the kneecap (patella), that we forget this projection. Draw the upper and lower leg bones as long, thin cuboids with two cylinders meeting at the knee, then flatten the cylinders (E). The hinge of the end of the femur is the shape of a reversed V, with two bumps on the back side, so add this shape next (F). The top of the fibula is farther back than the tibia, and much smaller (G).

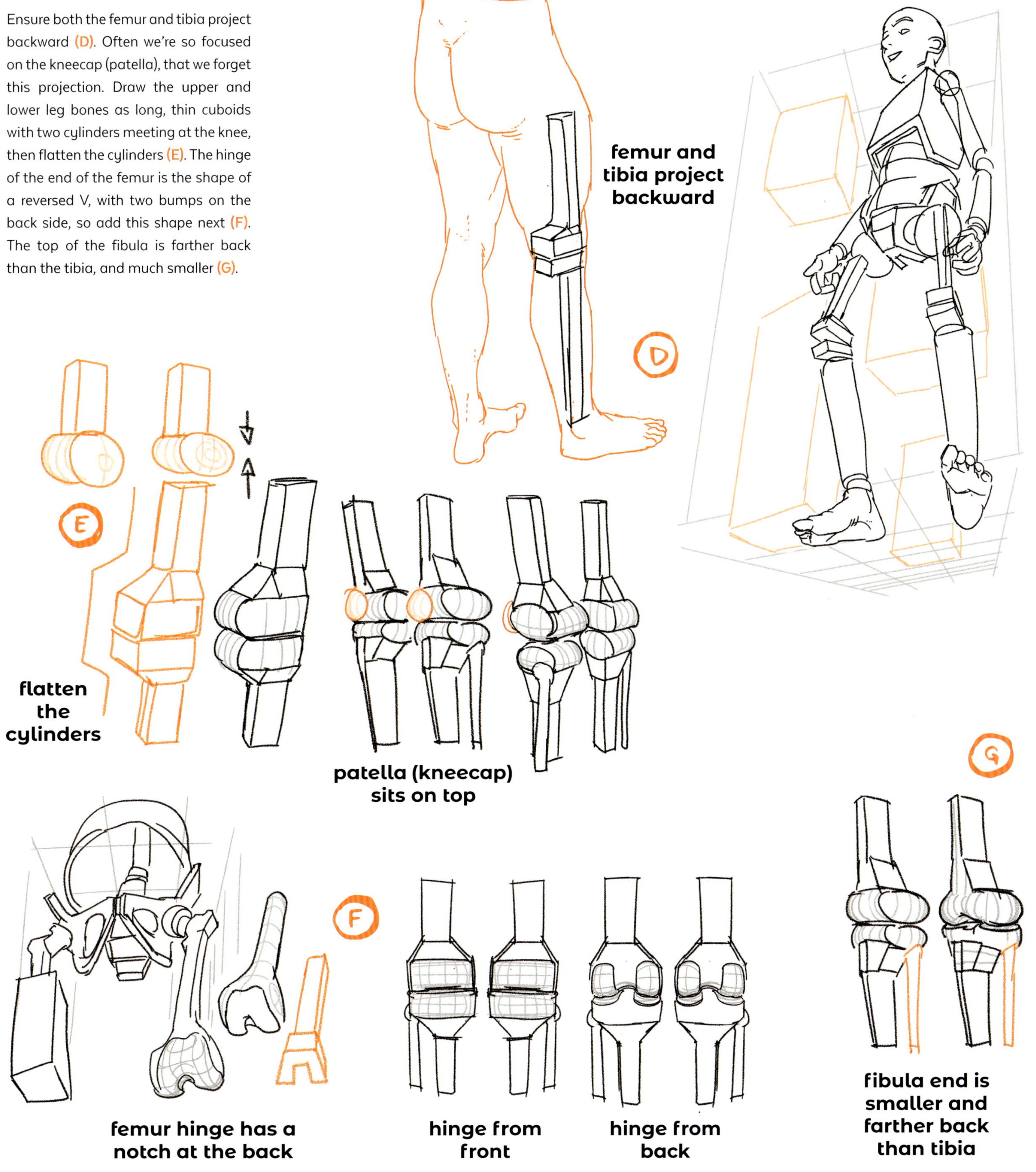

the tibial tuberosity

At the front of the tibia is a bony projection called the tibial tuberosity (A). This is the attachment point for the patellar ligament (B), the ligament that allows the quads to straighten the legs. This lump provides something to attach to and pull on. Note the bulge for the patella, then a step inward, followed by a bump outward at this tuberosity (C).

The simplified structure of the knee resembles D rather than E. Rather than two forms that hinge away from each other at a single point, it consists of an L-shaped upper piece meeting a flatter form below. This whole joint hinges around these points (F).

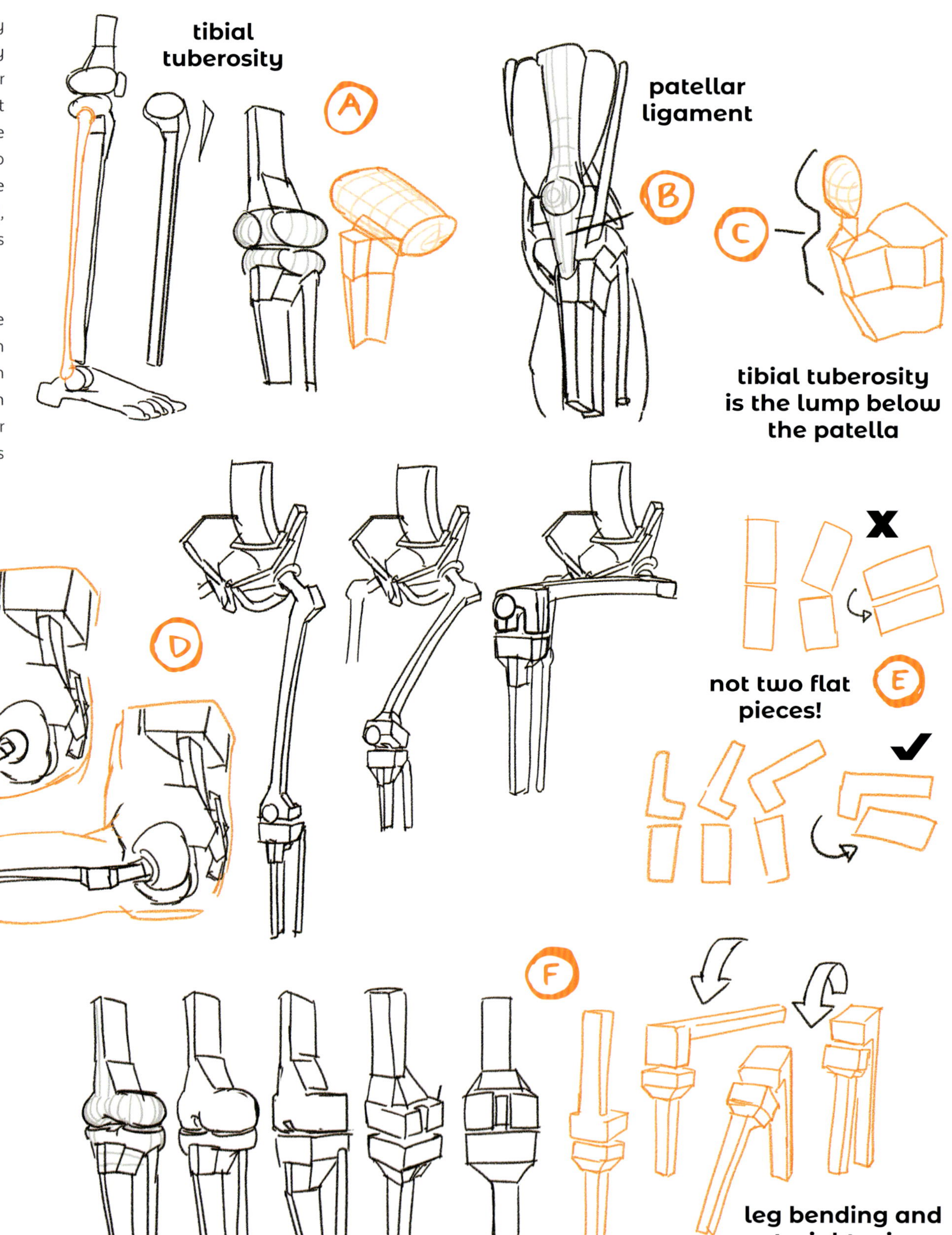

adductors

Adduction is the movement of a body part toward the midline of the body. The adductors muscle group sits on the interior of the leg and performs two major roles. The first function we'll look at is pulling your legs together (A).

To achieve this, the adductors attach to the front of the pelvis (B) and wrap down and around to the back of the femur. At their farthest point from the pelvis they attach to the end of the femur, onto our "block" in the knee area (C). An action like the side splits requires an enormous amount of flexibility because these muscles don't usually deviate too far from their near-vertical positions (D). We can add the adductors by swapping our cylinder leg for a cuboid form, and then attaching a long wedge to the inner side (E).

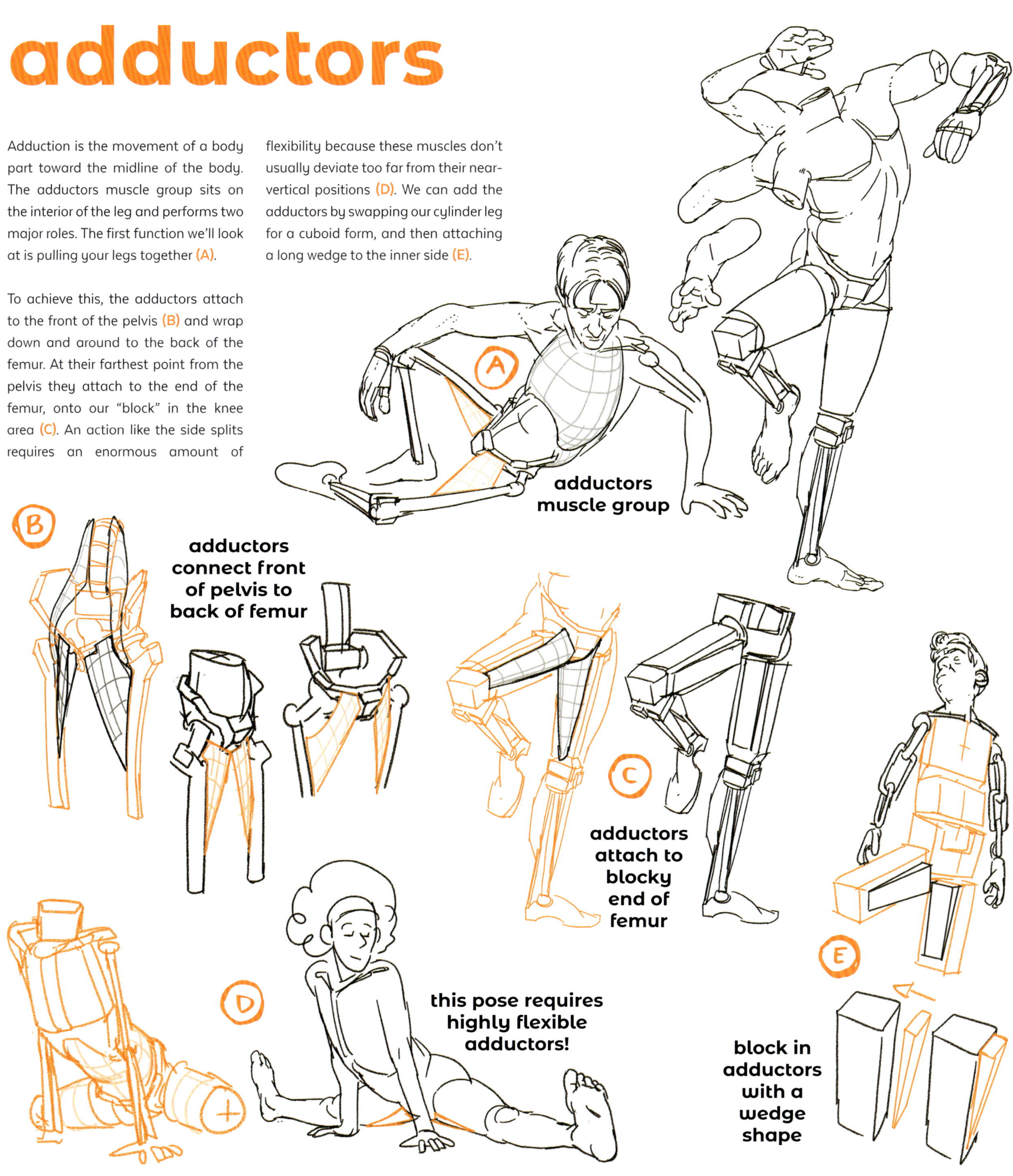

The second role of the adductors is to assist in bringing the legs up and forward (flexion). Because they primarily attach to the rear of the femur, they work together with the psoas (F) and iliacus (G) to assist in flexion of the leg. The psoas, as we learned on page 244, is a long muscle that wraps over the ilium, and the iliacus is a flat muscle that covers in the inside of the wings of the ilium.

When we move our legs out to the side (abduction), our adductors must lengthen (H). When we raise our leg forward (flexion), the action is facilitated by the relative positions of the muscle attachments. Point 1 is farther forward than point 2 on the back of the femur, so the adductors can pull the leg forward.

If we're increasing our mannequin's level of detail, we can simplify the upper leg into a long, flattened octagon with a triangular wedge for the adductors (I).

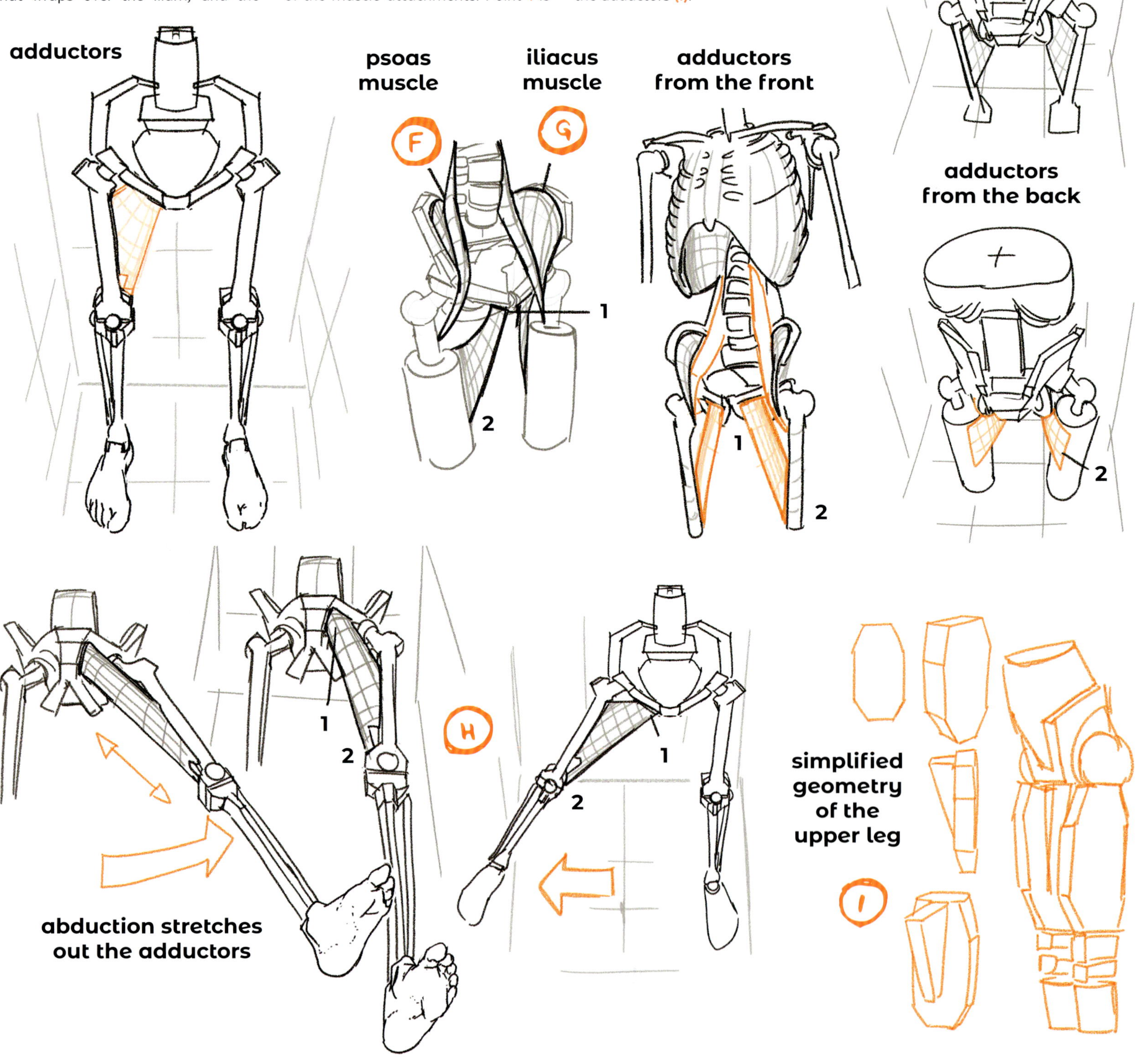

gluteal muscles

The muscle attachments to the top of the femur are similar to those of the shoulder joint (A), almost like the head of a joystick. Muscles radiate out from the greater trochanter (B), the small projection at the top of the femur, like they do to the top of the humerus in the arm. The gluteus minimus is one of three gluteal muscles ("glutes"). It attaches to the front of the greater trochanter, along with some other small muscles that we don't need to know in detail (C). The gluteus medius covers it almost completely and attaches farther out to the side. The gluteus maximus covers that and is even larger (D)!

The gluteus medius is located on the sides, and is thin at the rear of the pelvis. Viewed from above, it hangs closely to the ilium (E). It bulges when the leg is raised to the sides (abduction) (F).

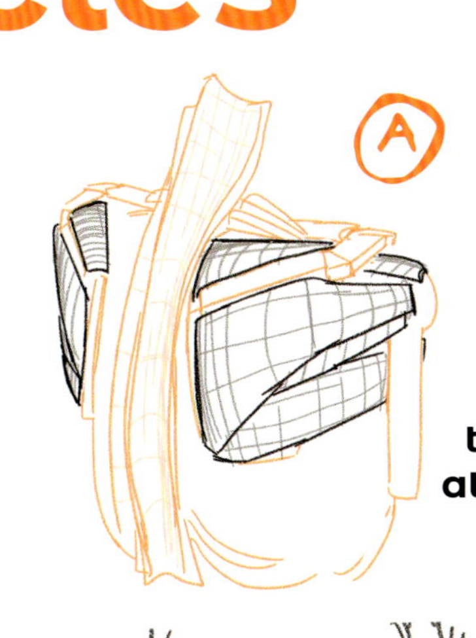
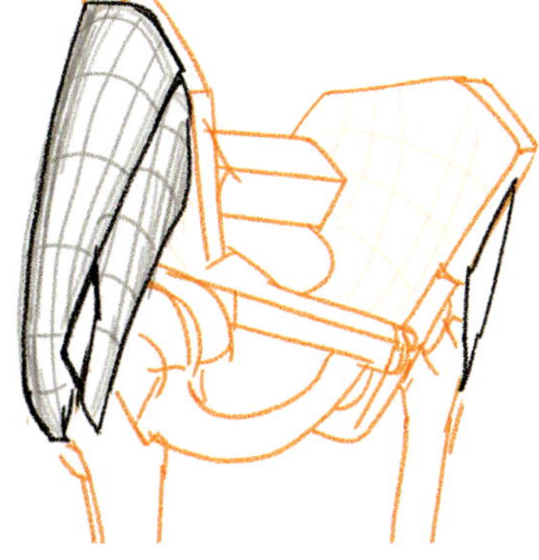

the femur's joints and attachments are similar to the humerus'

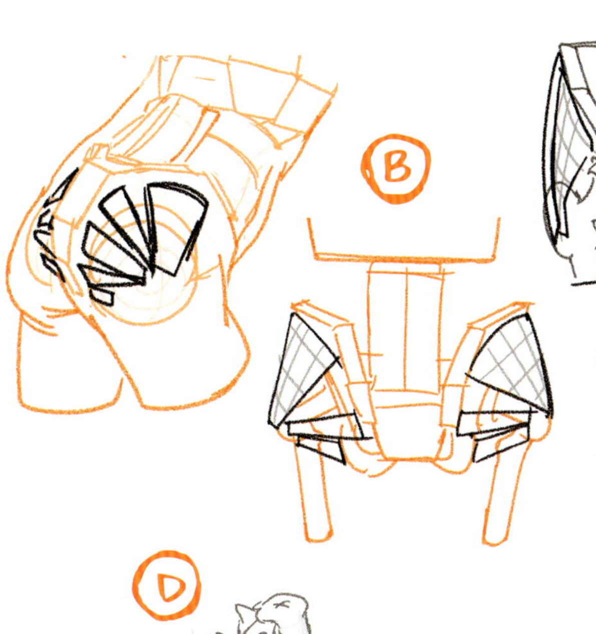

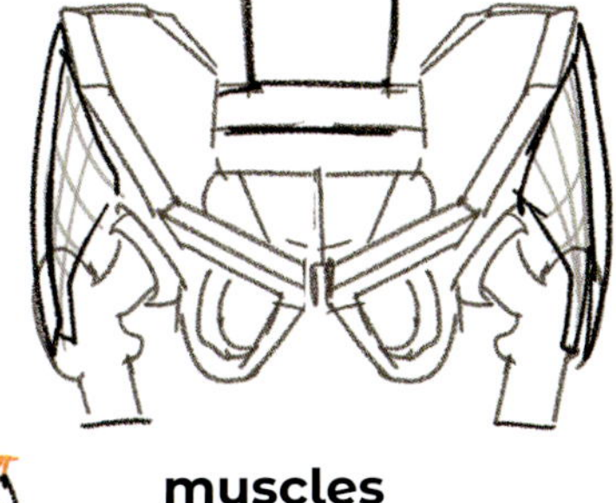

muscles radiate out from the greater trochanter

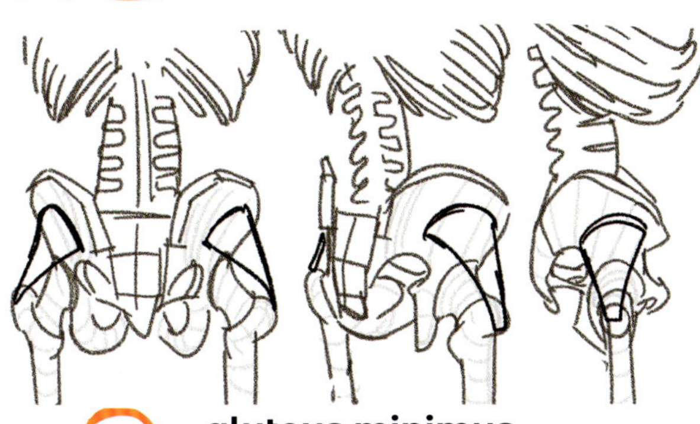

gluteus minimus

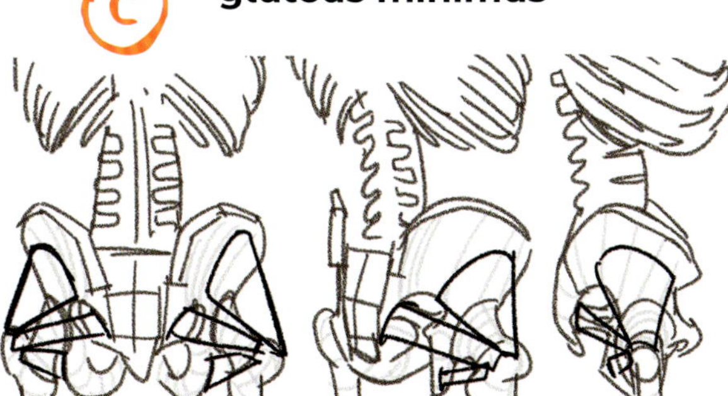

gluteus minimus and nearby smaller muscles

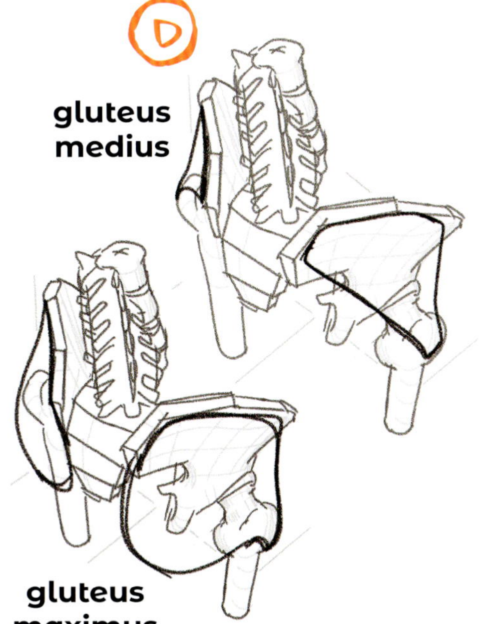

gluteus medius

gluteus maximus

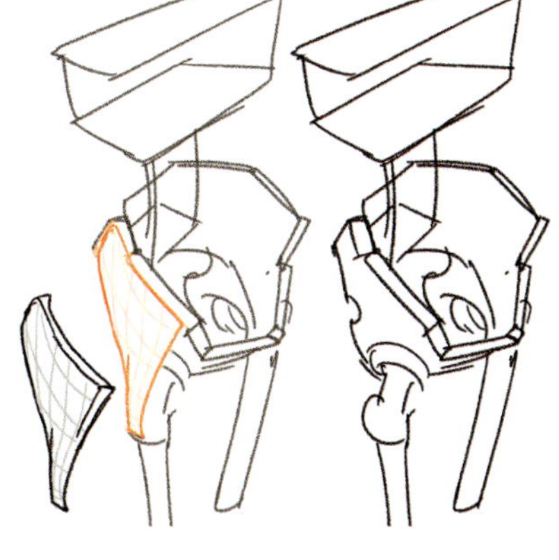
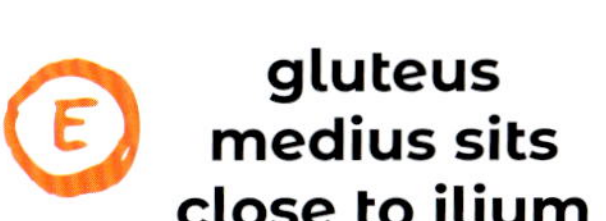

gluteus medius sits close to ilium

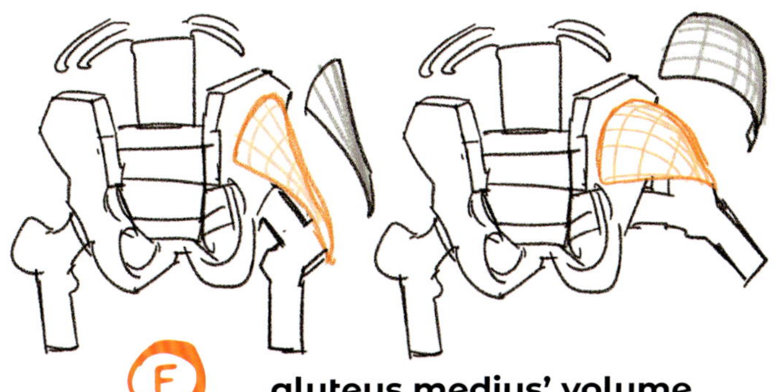

gluteus medius' volume increases with abduction

The gluteus minimus assists in raising the leg due to its slight forward attachment (G). When viewed from the front, there is a space on the pelvis that is filled by the gluteal muscles (H).

The gluteus maximus attaches to the sacrum and rear section of the ilium (I). It runs both outward and down, and ends in two places (J): the outer femur (1) and the iliotibial tract (or "IT band") (2), which we'll cover shortly.

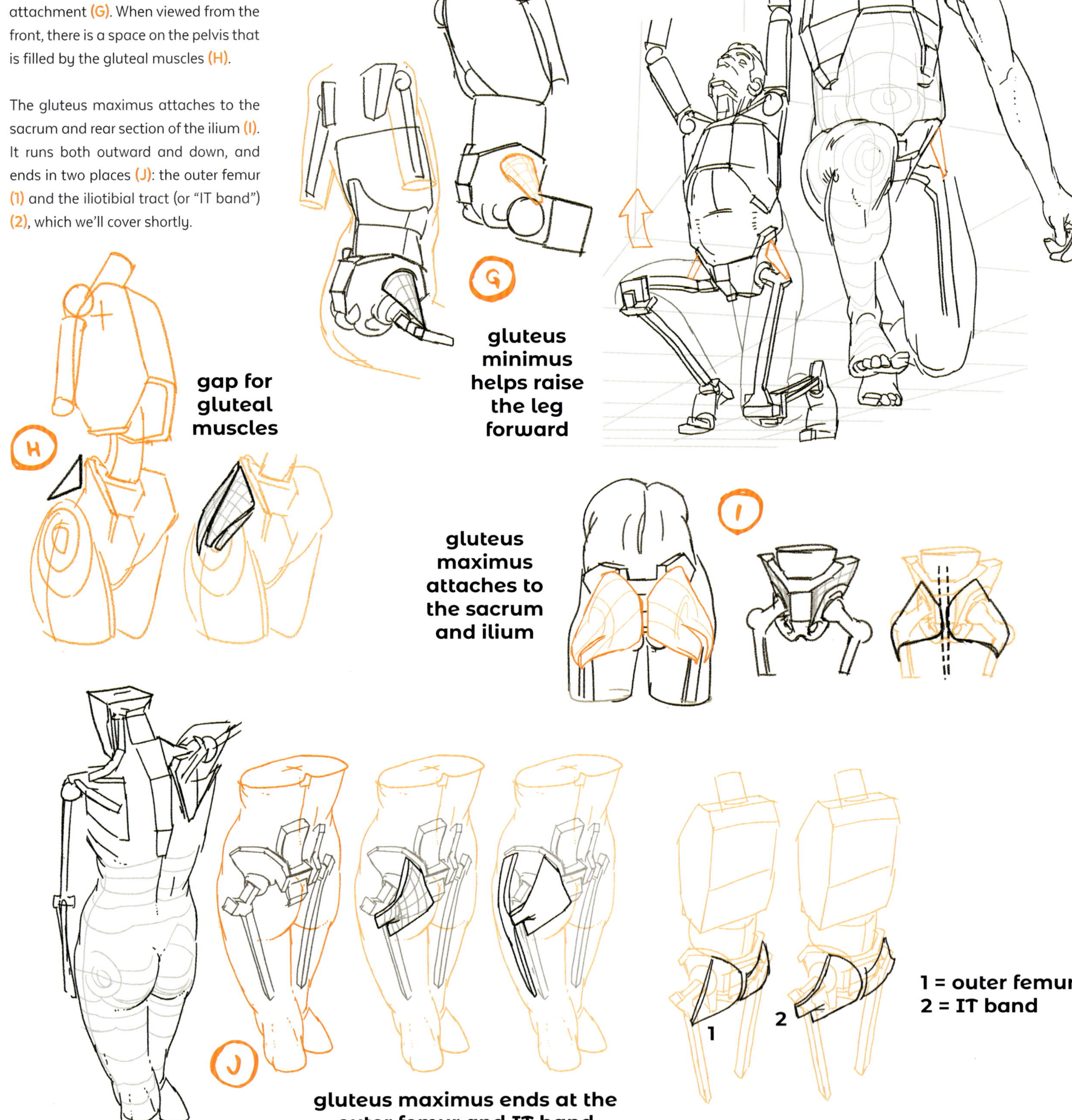

the TFL and IT band

The tensor fasciae latae, or TFL, is a smaller muscle at the front of the thigh that works in tandem with the gluteus maximus to help us walk and balance. The TFL and gluteus maximus are connected by the iliotibial tract, also known as the iliotibial band or IT band, forming a kind of Y shape (A). The TFL attaches to the outer front of the ilium, just behind the ASIS (the tip of the iliac crest) (B). Together, the TFL and gluteus maximus lie on top of the other glutes. The IT band runs down the side of the leg, connecting to the front of the tibia just to the outer side of the patella (C). When the legs are raised, the glutes and TFL will usually form a bulge on the outer leg (D).

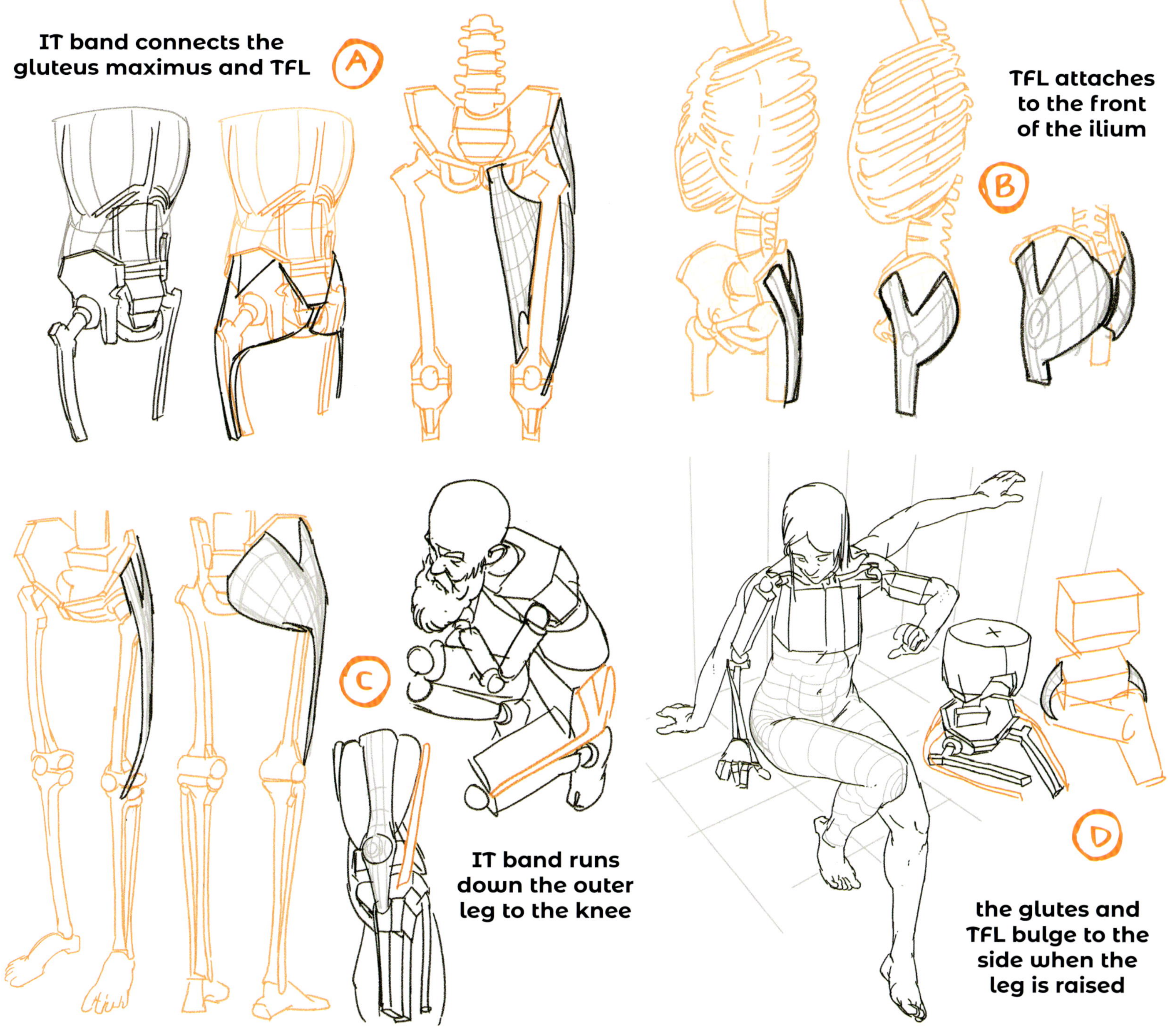

tip: believable glutes

Artists often draw the creases under the gluteal muscles with an upward angle toward the sides (A). However, this is rarely the case, unless we're looking at the figure from above! Instead, note the angling downward from inside to out. The gluteus maximus is higher at the back and lower as it wraps toward the front (B). The glutes are visible from most angles, even between the legs, where they connect with the "scoop" of the pubis (C).

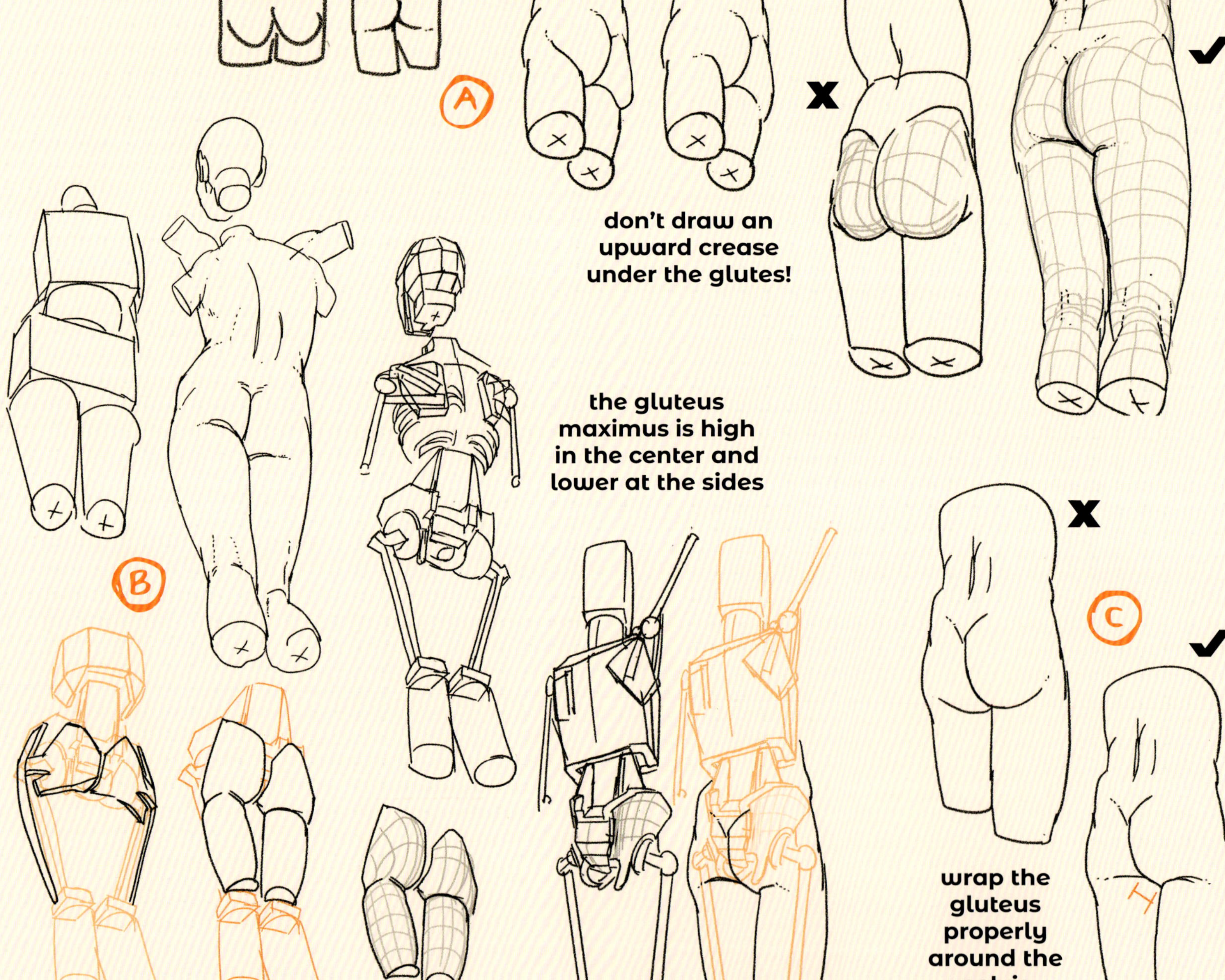

the quads

Let's continue down the leg, simplifying the dome of the patella into a flattened cuboid form (A) for this next stage.

On the front of the upper leg, the quadriceps femoris muscle, or quads, is a group of four muscles that both raise the knee and straighten the leg. We can visualize them as a long, leaf-shaped form wrapping over the cuboid of the femur, with a narrower strip on top (B).

The bottom three muscles of the quads sit on the front-facing surface of the femur and attach at the top near the greater trochanter (C). They pull directly on the patella via the quadriceps tendon (D). The patella is attached to the tibia below via the patellar ligament (E). When the leg bends, the tendon of the quads stretches the most (F), while the patellar ligament is less elastic.

The attachment points for the bottom three quads muscles angle down toward the midline of the body (G). From inside to out, we have the attachments for the vastus medialis muscle (1), the vastus intermedius (2), and the vastus lateralis (3) (meaning "inner," "middle," and "outer").

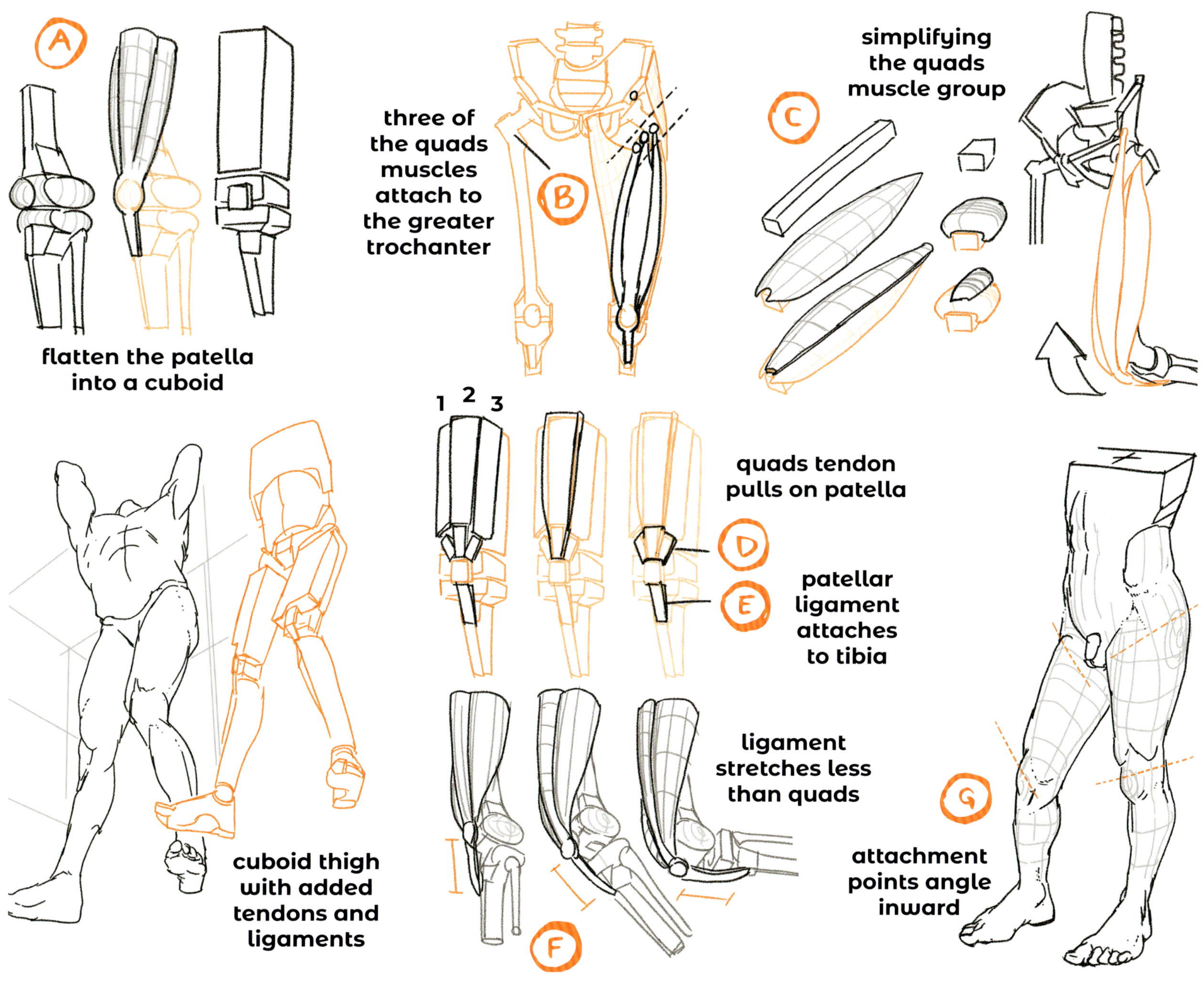

The rectus femoris, the fourth quadriceps muscle, sits on top of the others. Unlike the other three, it attaches to the pelvis directly (H), rather than to the top of the femur. You can group the bottom three into one form for simplicity (I). The rectus femoris assists in raising the leg, so when the leg is raised or tensed you will usually see its form (J).

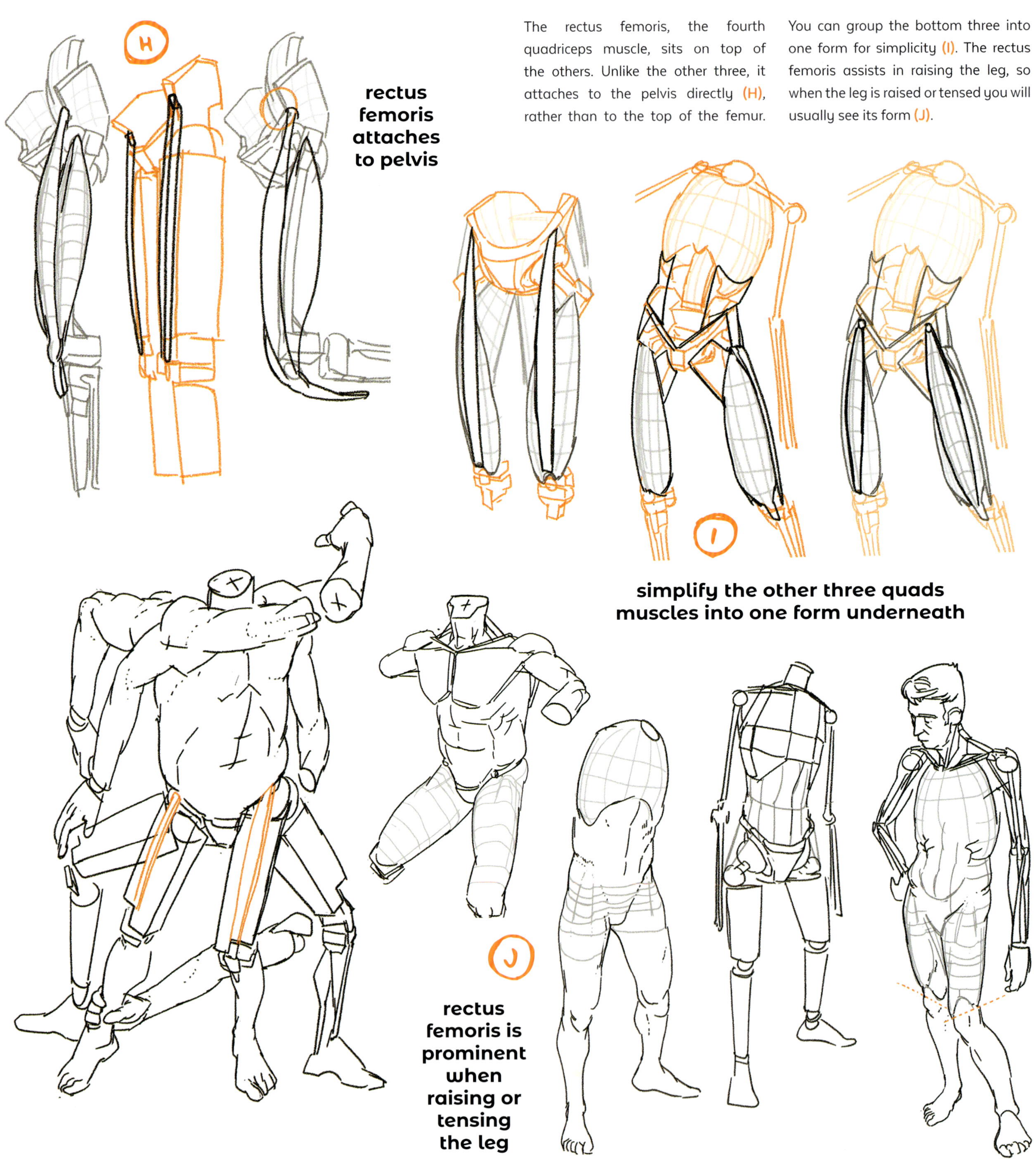

However you draw the leg, add a teardrop shape for the vastus medialis (K), which is the most medial (inner) muscle of the quads. Don't forget to add twist to the forms of the leg!

Not only will we see a teardrop shape, but frequently when the leg is raised we will see a slight depression between the ends of the quads (L). But if the patella is round, why do we see a diamondlike shape here (M)? When the quads pull on the patella, the patellar ligament that connects the kneecap to the tibia is pulled tight, which causes a slight bulge (N).

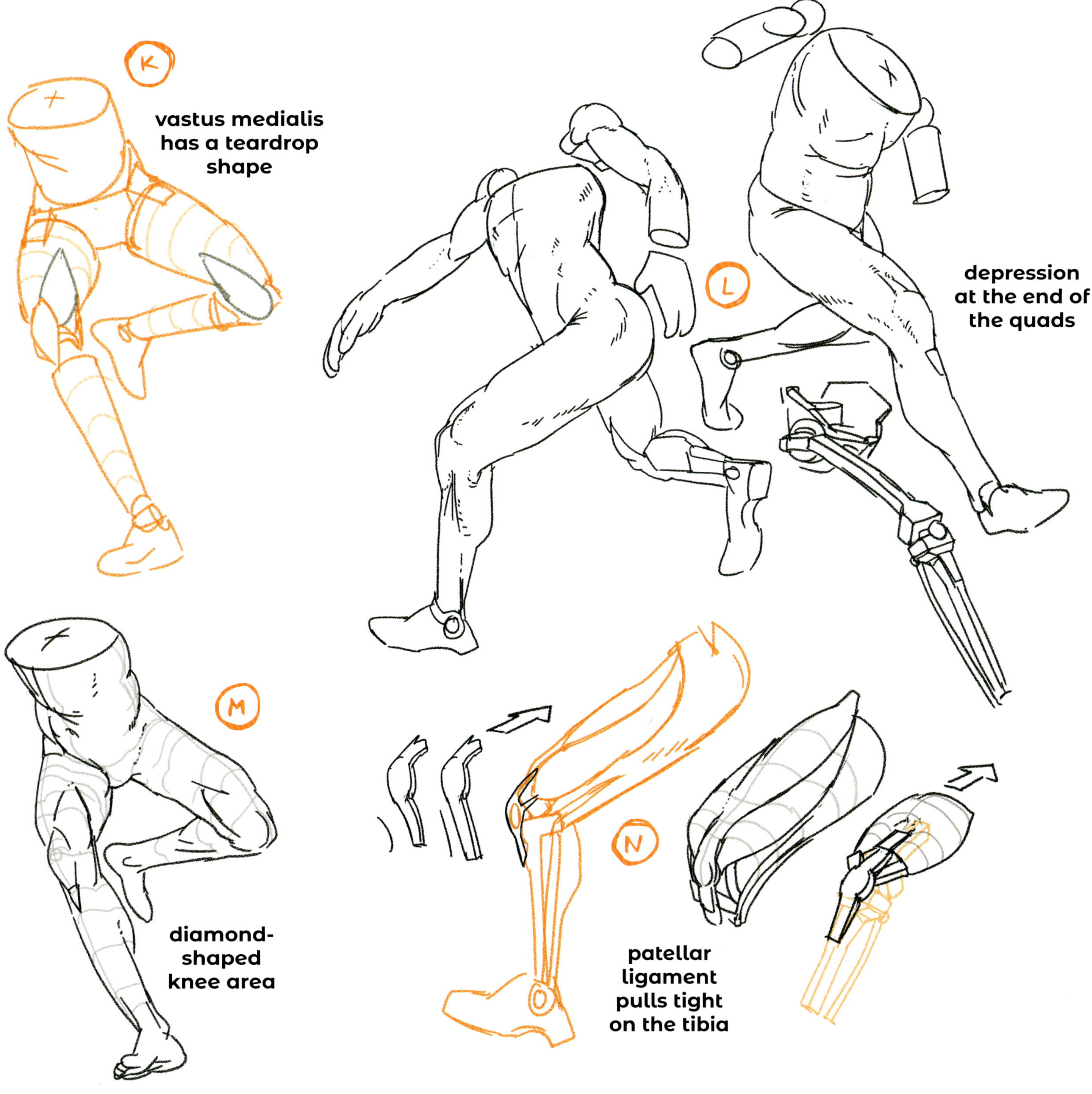

grouping leg muscles

To learn muscles more easily, group them by function. We've already grouped the lower three quads; let's add another group on top of them (A). This group consists of the rectus femoris at the front (1), TFL and IT band on the outer side (2), and sartorius on the inner side (3). They each end at different heights. The top of the sartorius attaches just above the rectus femoris, while the bottom attaches just inside the tibial tuberosity (B). When drawing a raised leg, include a raised area to show where these muscles attach (C).

We can group muscles together because they fulfill a shared function: for example, the bottom three quads muscles straighten the leg, and this second trio raises the leg (D). When the leg is raised, the form of the TFL and IT band is bent. Don't make it a flat shape – imagine how that Y-shaped form would bulge out if forced to bend (E). There should be a small distance between the ASIS and the top of the leg. Note the bulge outward that was just mentioned (F).

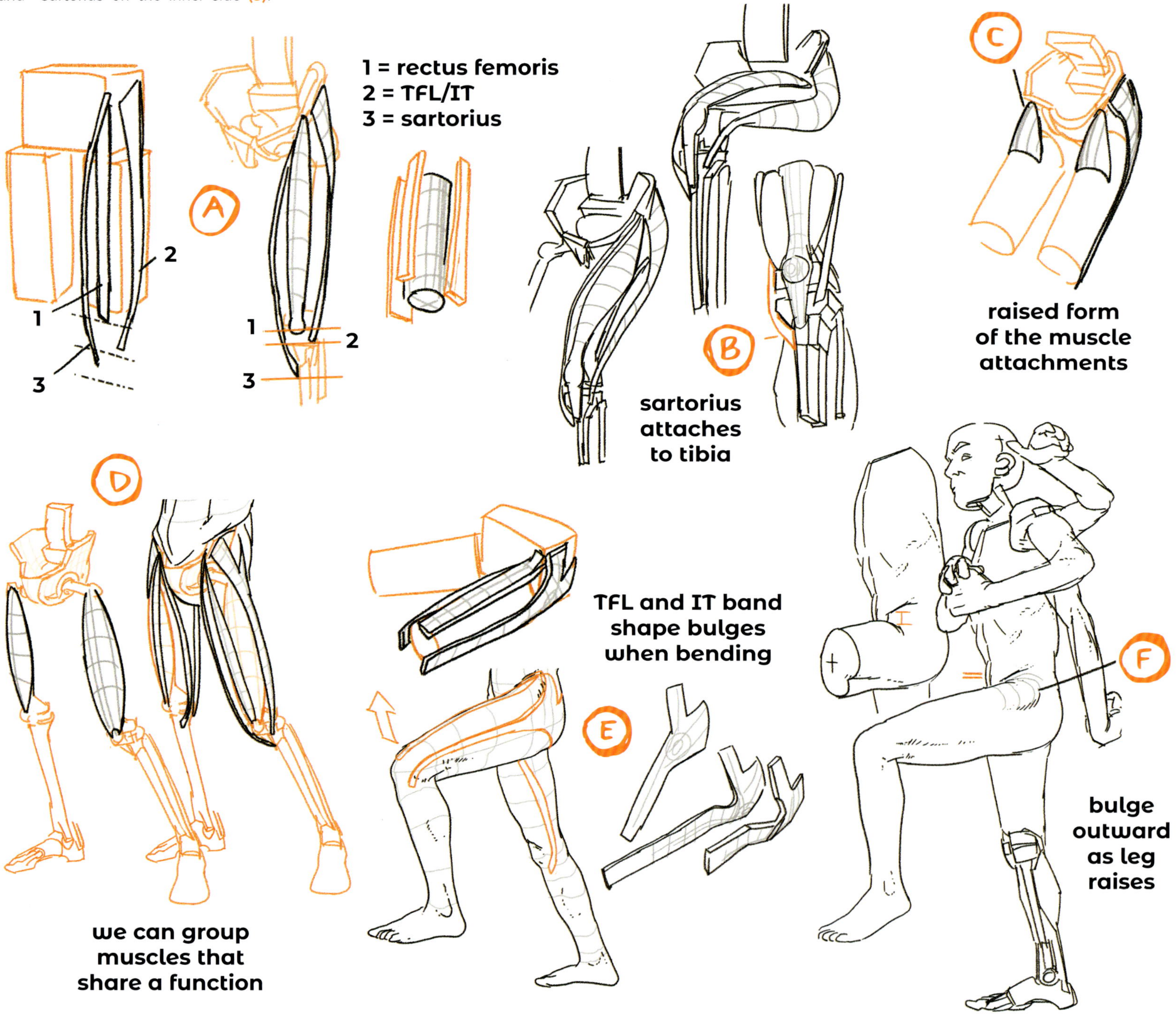

back of the thigh

Let's consider the function of the muscles of the rear upper leg. These muscles are required to bend the leg at the knee, raising the foot behind us (flexion). They must also pull the whole leg back behind us (A).

To achieve these functions, it's more efficient for them to attach to the lower leg at the sides and front rather than at the rear (B).

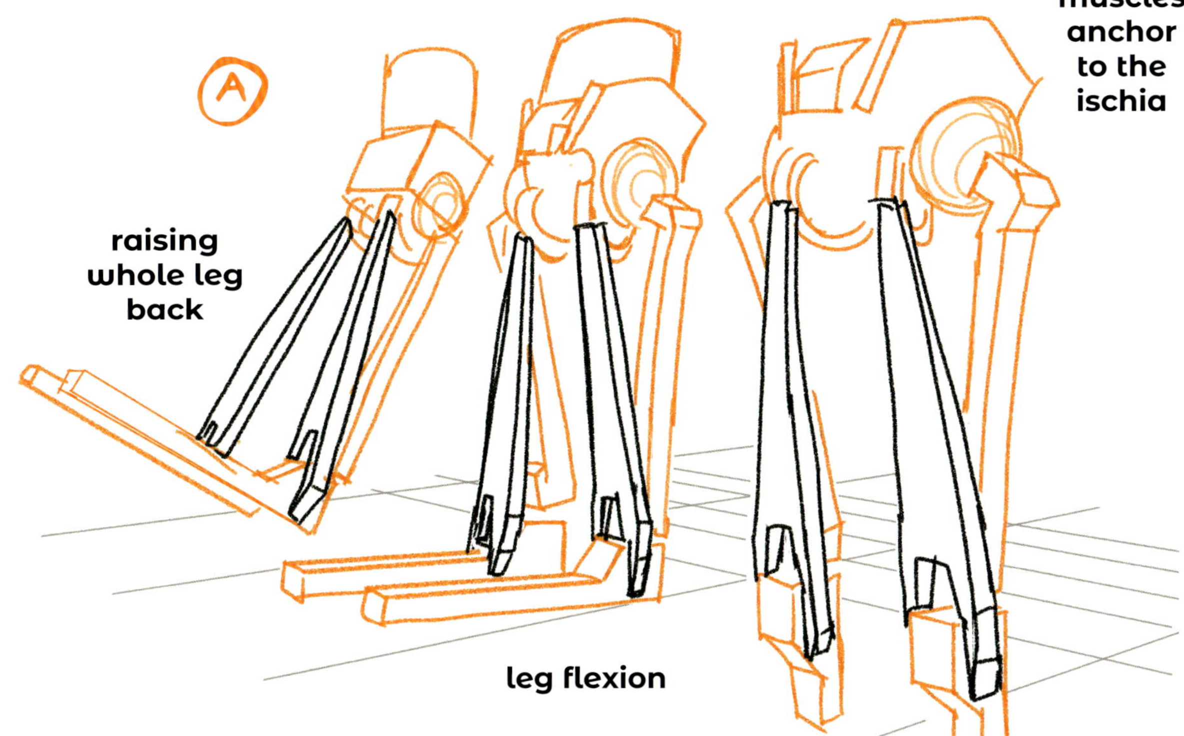

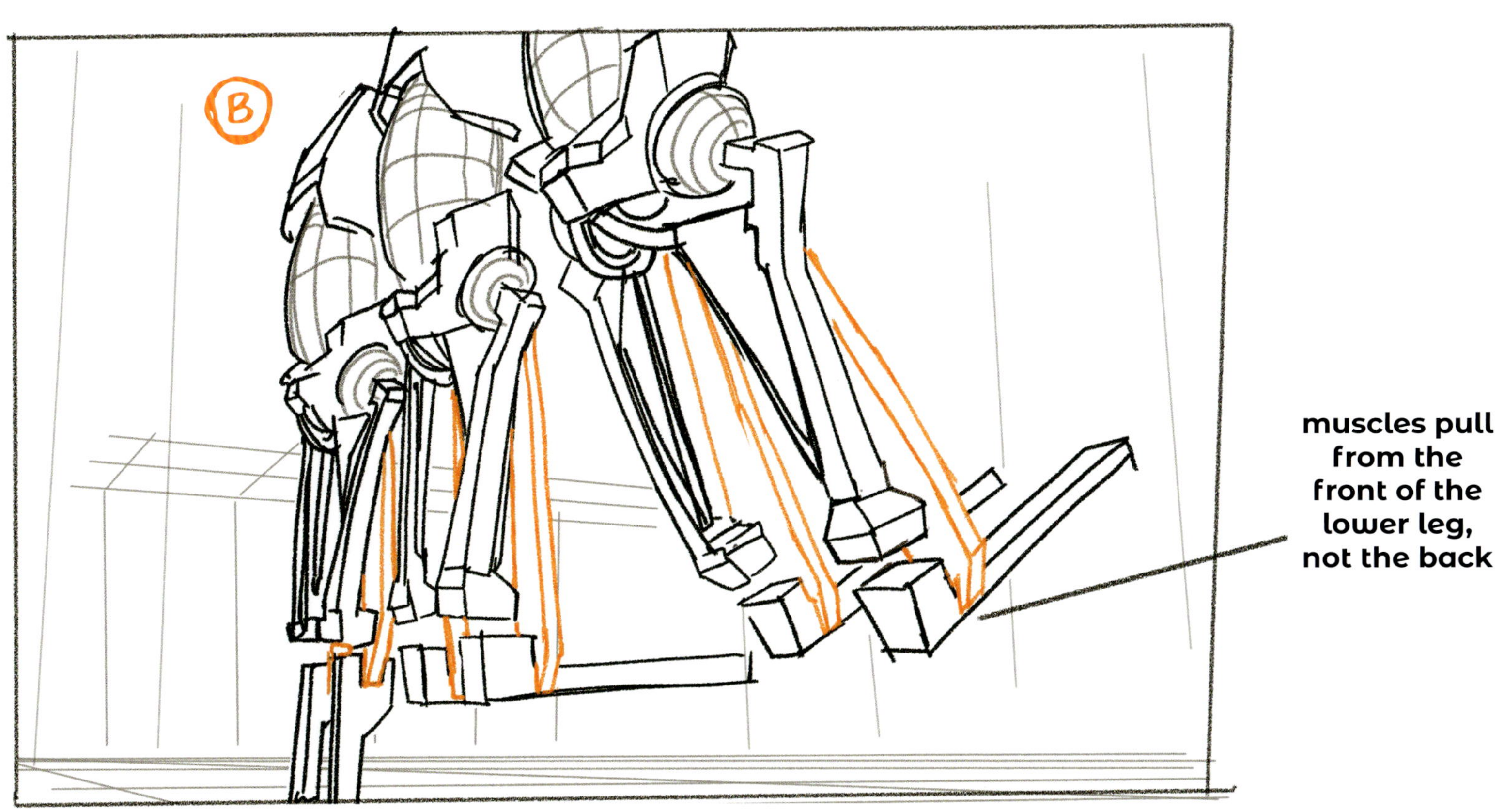

The hamstring muscle group forms the back of the thigh (C). This group attaches to the front of the tibia on the inside of the leg, and to the top of the fibula on the outside (D). Earlier we made a cuboid form for the upper thigh, with a flat wedge on the inside for the adductor muscles. Now let's make that into an octagonal shape, still including the inner wedge for the adductor group (E). If you want to push for a slightly higher level of detail, you can include the greater trochanter of the femur, too (F). Notice how the octagonal thigh shape ends in the flattened cube form for the knee.

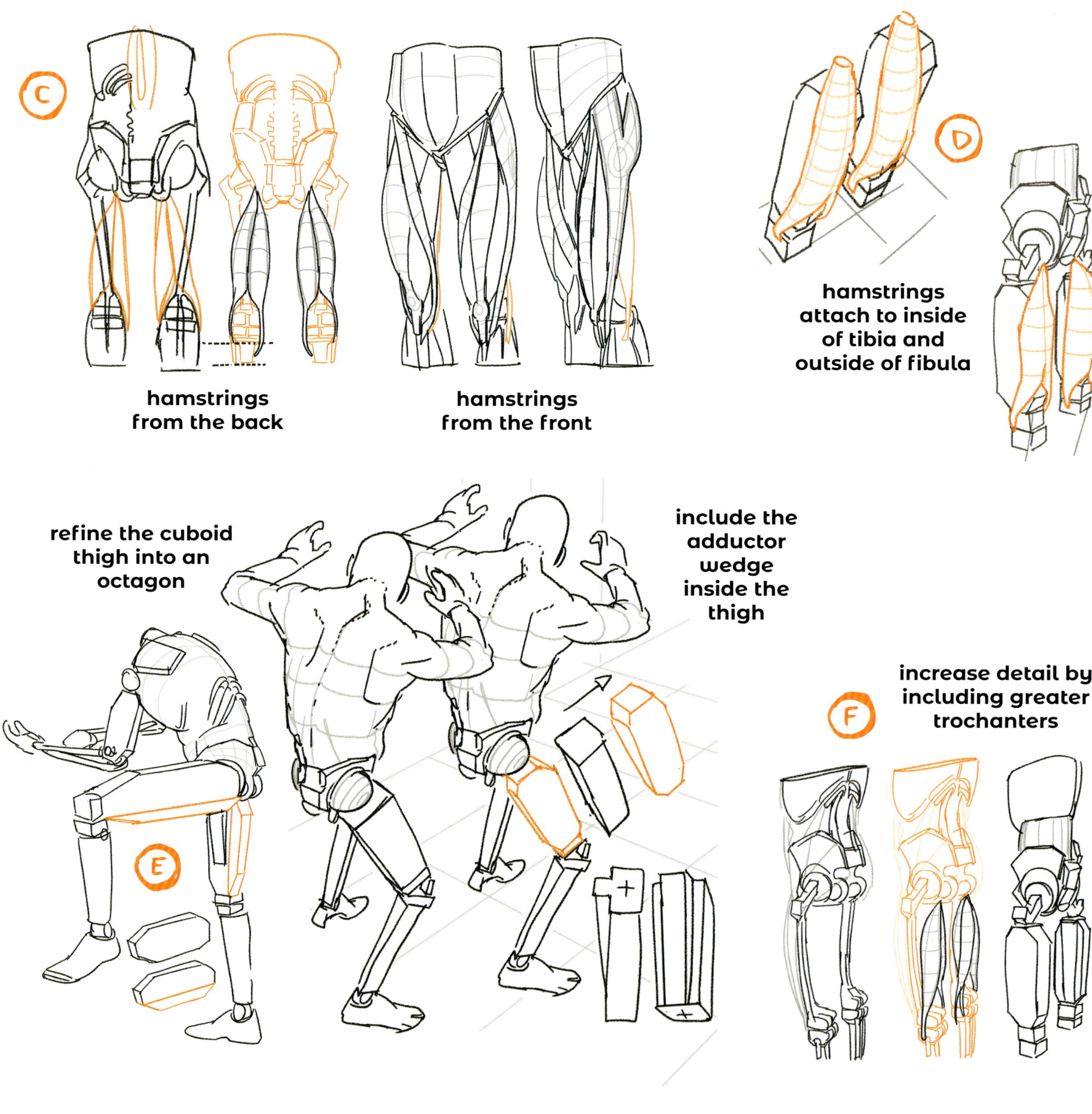

Like we saw with the arm on page 183, there's more than one way to simplify a form! Here's an alternative way to visualize the rear upper-leg muscles (G). Instead of an octagon, this cuboid wraps around the femur, with a wedge on the inside for the adductors, a Y shape on top for the trochanter, and a notch to create a hinge for the knee (H). At this point our mannequin is becoming increasingly detailed, so make sure to simplify if you are struggling to rotate these shapes. A simple form drawn well is far better than a complex form drawn badly (I).

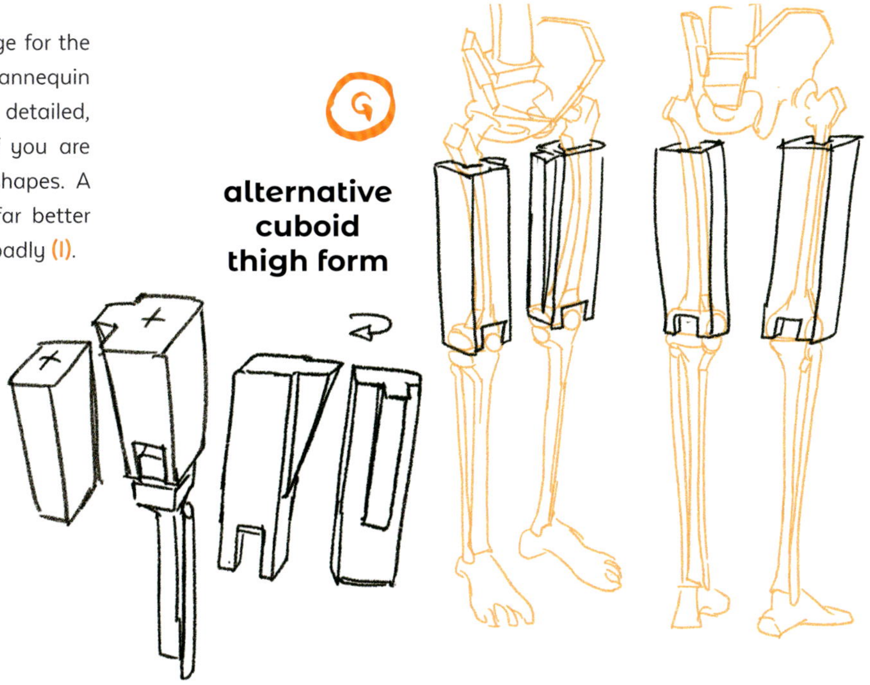

G

alternative cuboid thigh form

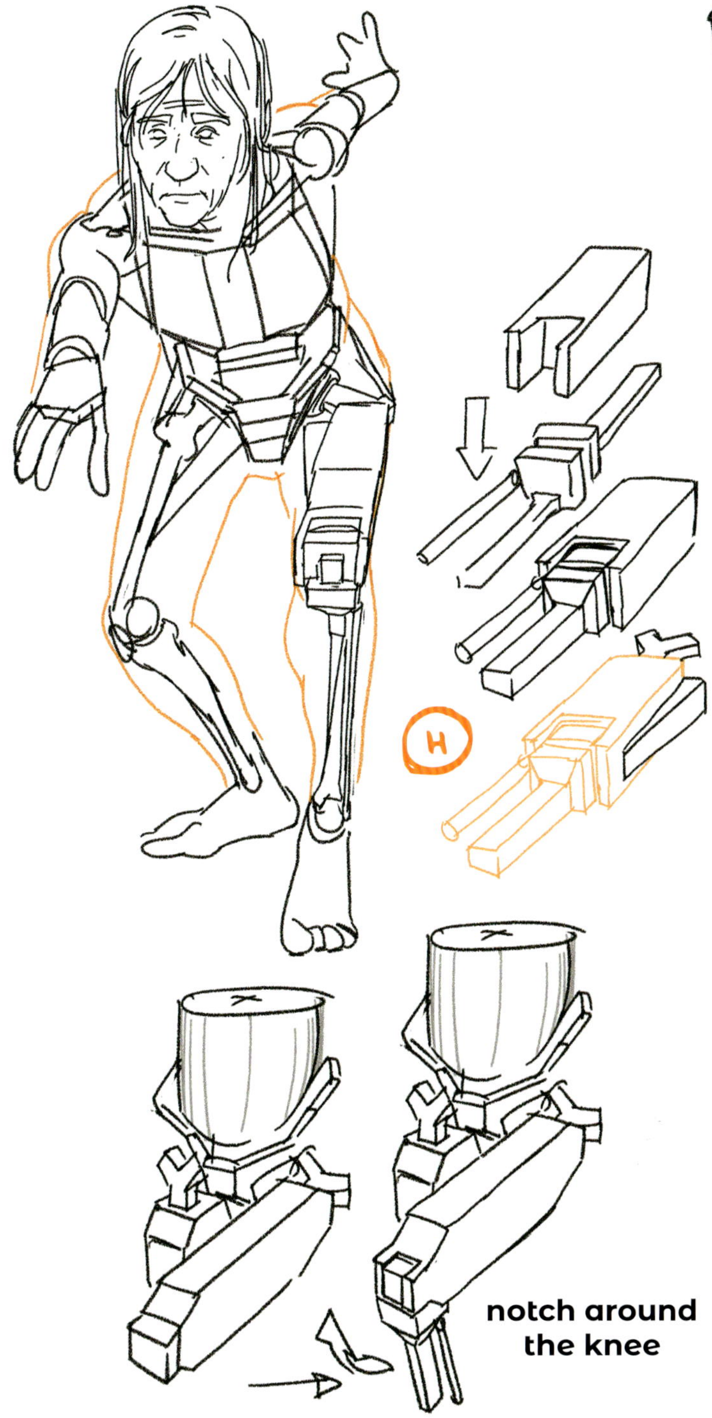

H

notch around the knee

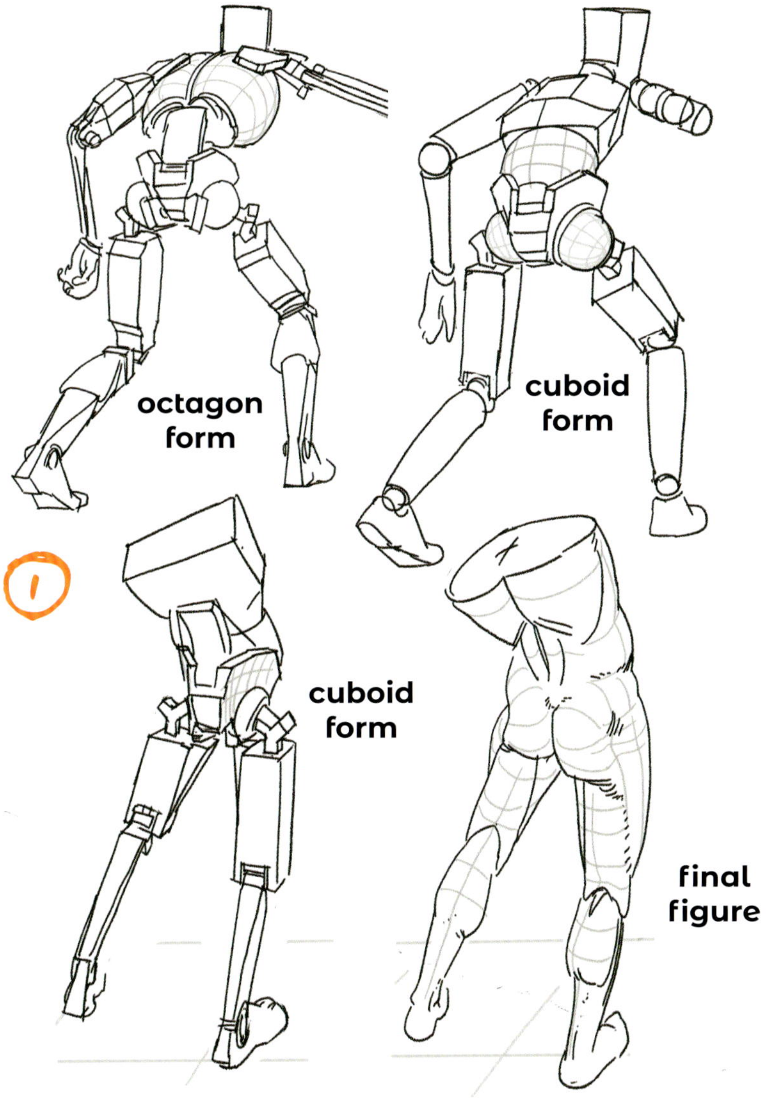

octagon form

cuboid form

I

cuboid form

final figure

When drawing the adductors, give them mass and depth (J). Draw the knee squarer and wider than you think. People often attempt to disguise their lack of knowledge by drawing it smaller, but this just draws attention to problems in the area. The forms should bulge out at the sides. If in doubt, draw the knee squarer and larger (K). When the knee is bent, the crease between the legs won't extend as far forward as you'd think. Give the bones of the legs space to form a cubelike shape at the end, then start the fold further back (L).

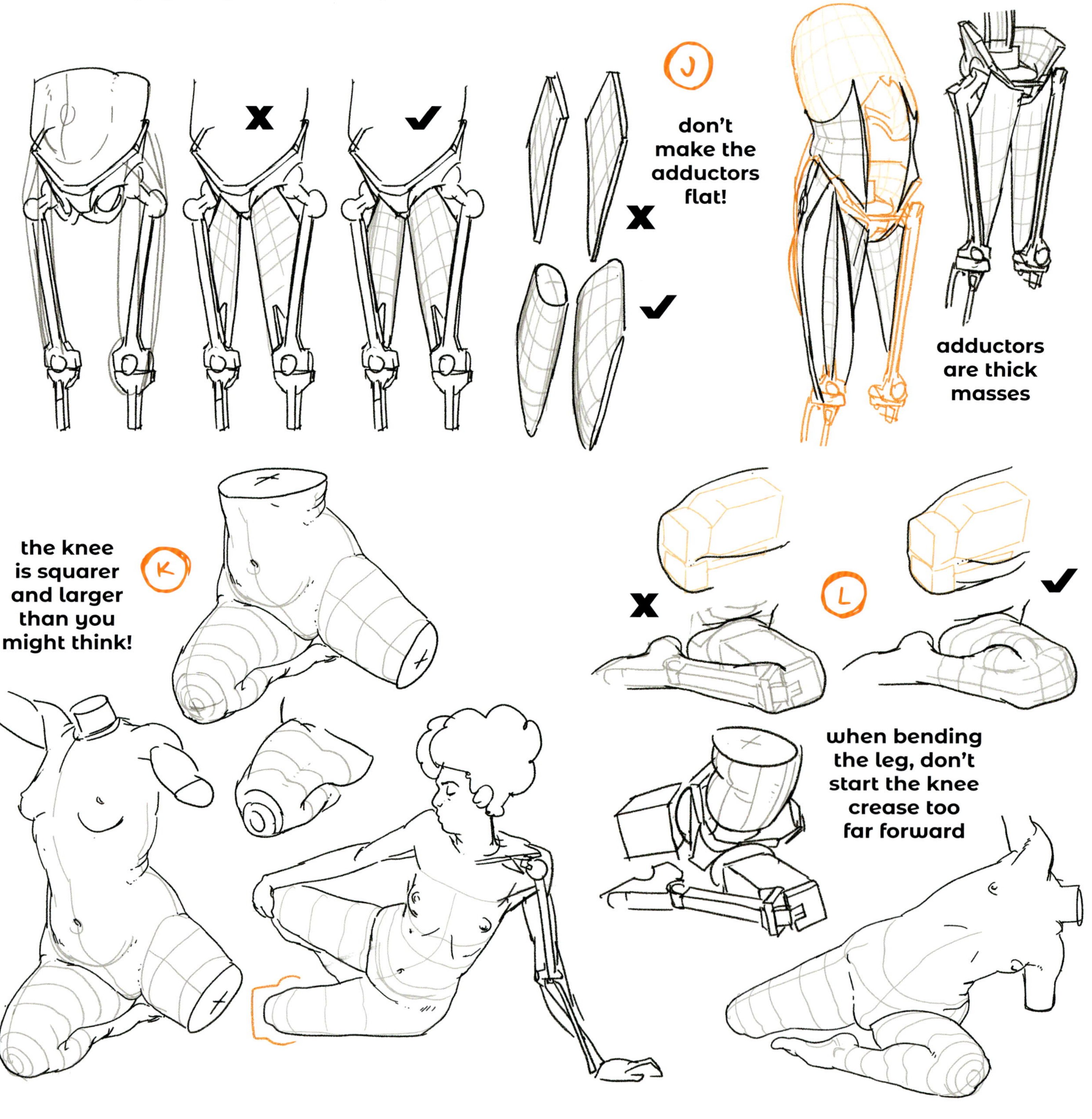

This visible landmark is the step down where the IT band meets the hamstring group (M). The upper leg is wider at the front than at the rear (N). Let's add the IT band to our model (O). Remember that the IT band inserts into the front of the tibia and the hamstring group inserts into the top of the fibula (P). On our model, the IT band attaches to the greater trochanter (Q). Note how this narrow strip doesn't sit directly down the center of the outer thigh, but slightly forward.

Remember that there is no single hard surface model we can use for all poses, because the body is flexible. So, how do we design an effective model? We can rely primarily on hard-surface forms and still include regions of flexibility. The core and the region surrounding the pelvis are two of these particularly flexible areas. If you can draw the hard forms accurately, and you know the muscles' attachment points, then you can design almost any body type.

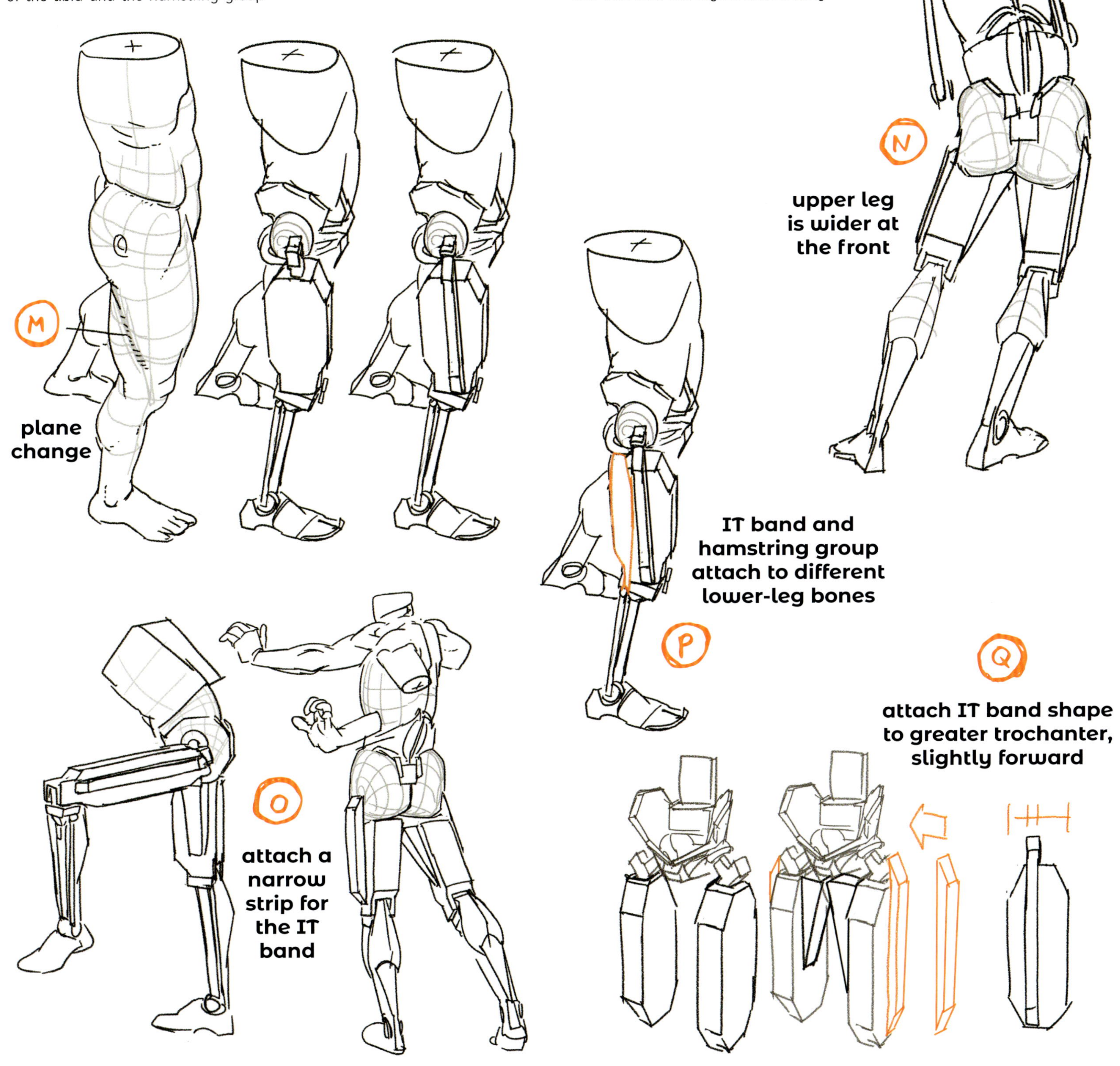

tip: common mistakes

A common mistake is to draw the "arches" of the glutes parallel. Instead, angle them inward (A). Be careful to attach the legs high enough on the pelvis. If we simply draw the pelvis block and then add muscles, the rectus femoris (top quads muscle) will create an unnatural lump! Instead, raise the legs to avoid the appearance of a very long pelvis (B). Note the outward two tiers as we move down the body. The first occurs at the ilium and the second typically happens where the legs widen at the greater trochanters of the femur (C). Also note the general widening as we move from the rear to the front of the pelvic and upper-leg region (D). These major rhythms are important to remember – much more important than memorizing individual muscles.

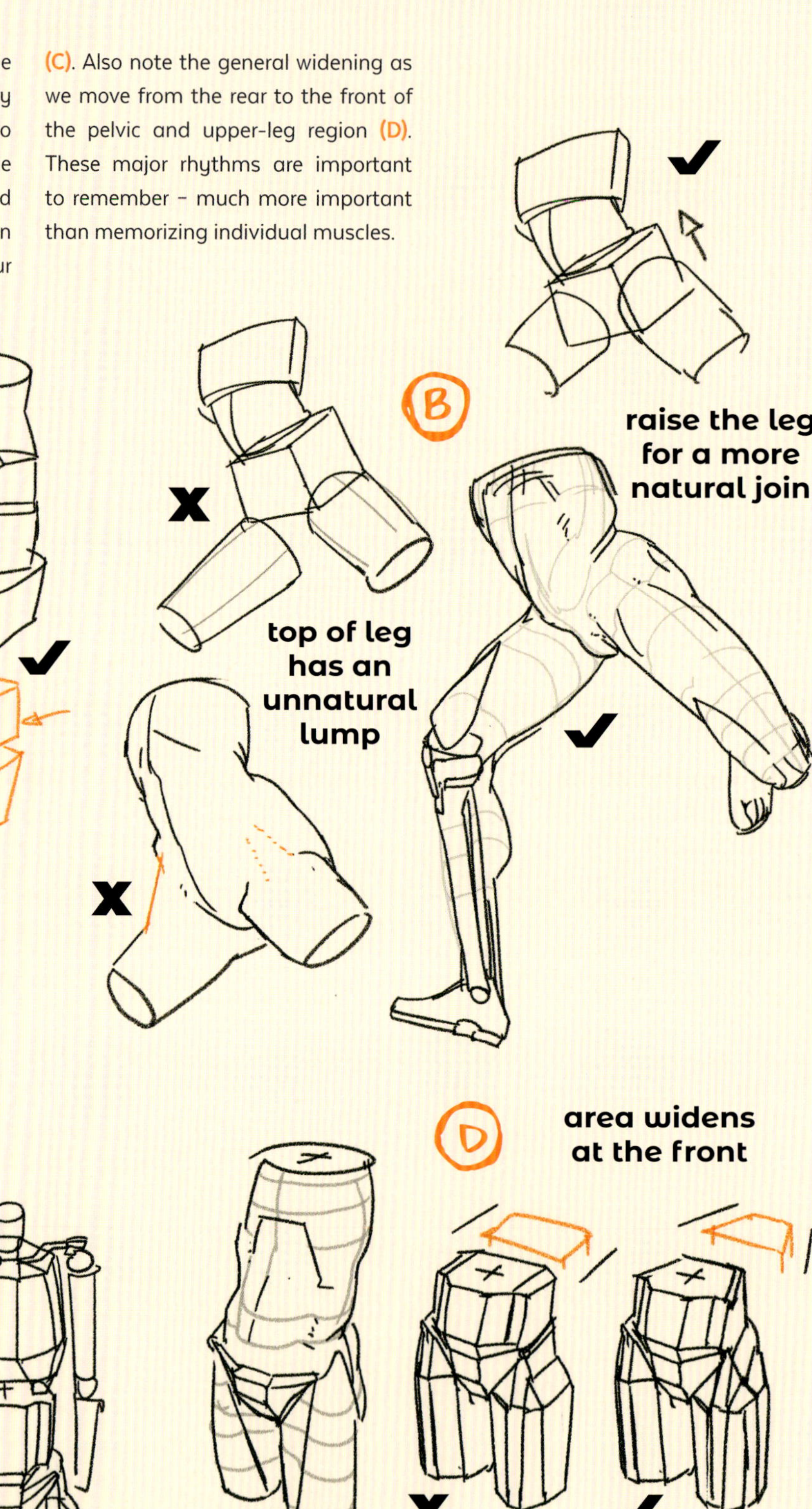

We tend to draw the knee too pointed. We think the interior is shaped like E, with a space between the patella and the ends of the leg bones. In reality, it's more like F, where the patella slides down and occupies that space.

When the leg is bent, the patella isn't located on the top of it. The wide, flat surface we see is the bottom of the femur, covered by the tendons of the quads (G). When we see a pose where the feet are angled outward, remember that the rotation originates at the hip joint, not at the knee. The ankle allows for some rotation, but less than you might assume (H)!

When drawing the folds in the bent leg, keep them subtle. The form is fairly solid, so it won't have multiple lines like fabric (I). Instead, suggest a delicate bulging near the line itself.

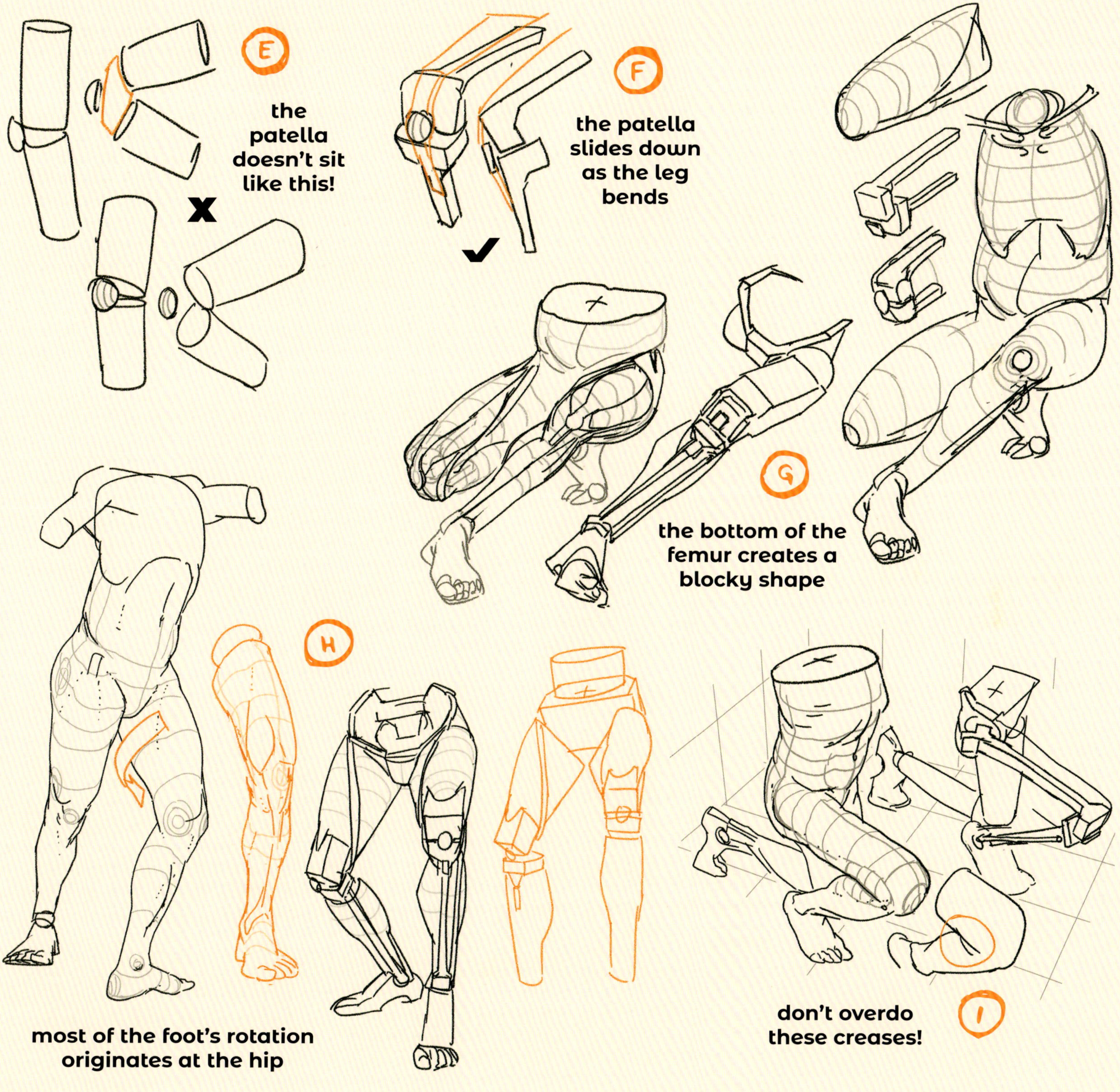

the calves

When we say "the calf," we refer to a group of two muscles - the soleus and gastrocnemius (A). The soleus is mostly hidden below the gastrocnemius. It attaches to the back of the tibia and fibula, and pulls on the Achilles tendon (or "calcaneal tendon"), which causes the foot to push against the ground - useful for jumping and walking (B).

If you look closer at A, you'll see the soleus doesn't attach to the upper leg, but the gastrocnemius does. The gastrocnemius attaches into the bottom of the femur, above the backward projections at the end of the bone. It pulls on the Achilles tendon and also helps raise the lower leg.

The gastrocnemius has three major planes, with a fourth formed by the Achilles tendon (C, 1-4). When the gastrocnemius is placed on top of the soleus, note that we still see the sides of the soleus (D). The hamstring group wraps to the sides of these muscles, which is why they attach centrally (E).

The calves don't cover the whole back of the knee structure, so you'll often see the exposed "block" of the knee when the viewing the leg from behind (F). Viewed from behind, note how the calves taper down (G).

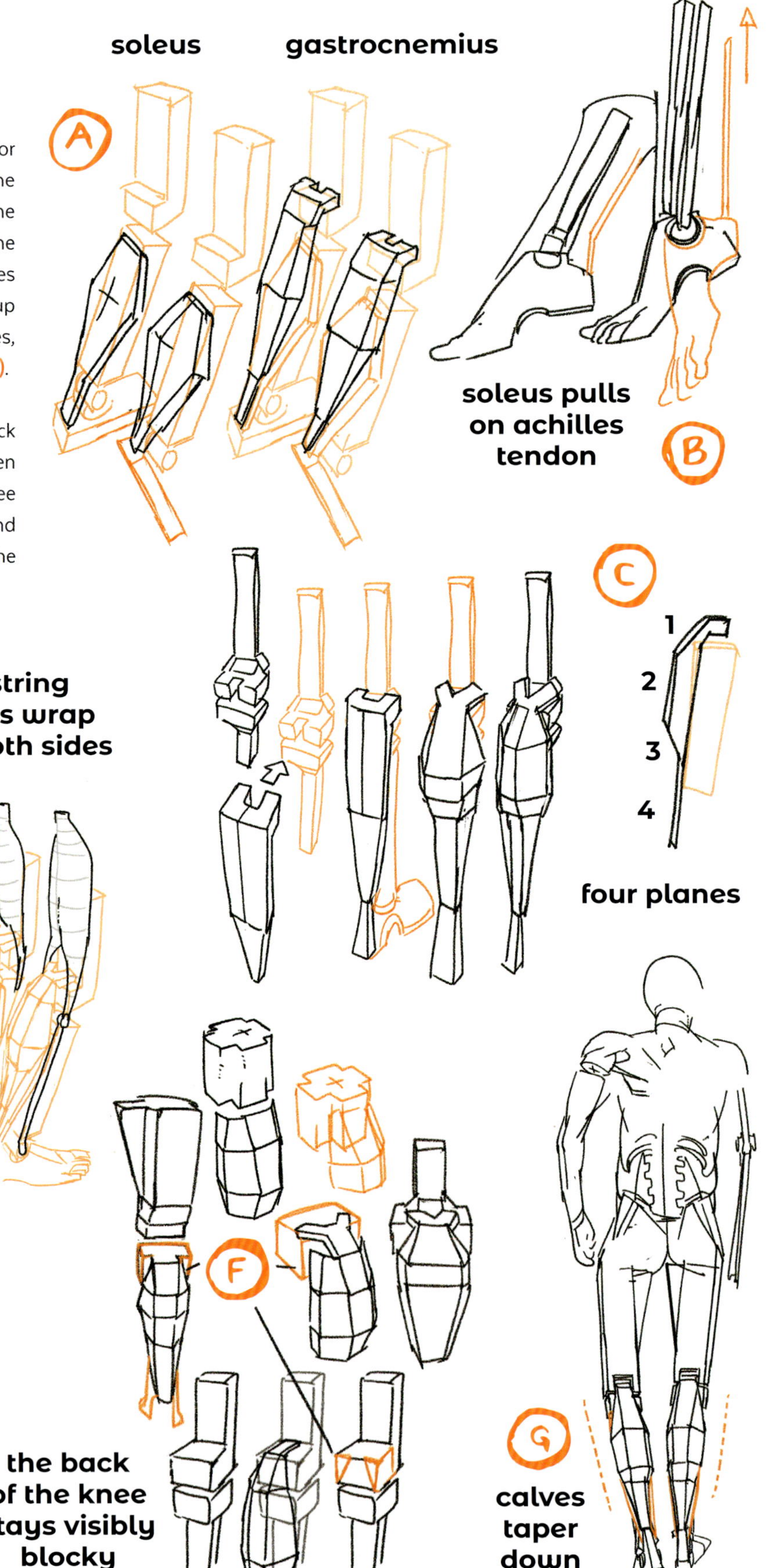

But if we have a space between the hamstrings and the calves, why don't we see a depression like in H? The answer is the popliteal fat pad, one of the fatty tissue areas that cushions the knee area (I). When we straighten our leg, this fat pad bulges out. When the leg is partially bent, the pad is covered by the bulging hamstrings (J). When the leg is nearly fully bent, the forms of the hamstrings visibly bulge out to the sides (K).

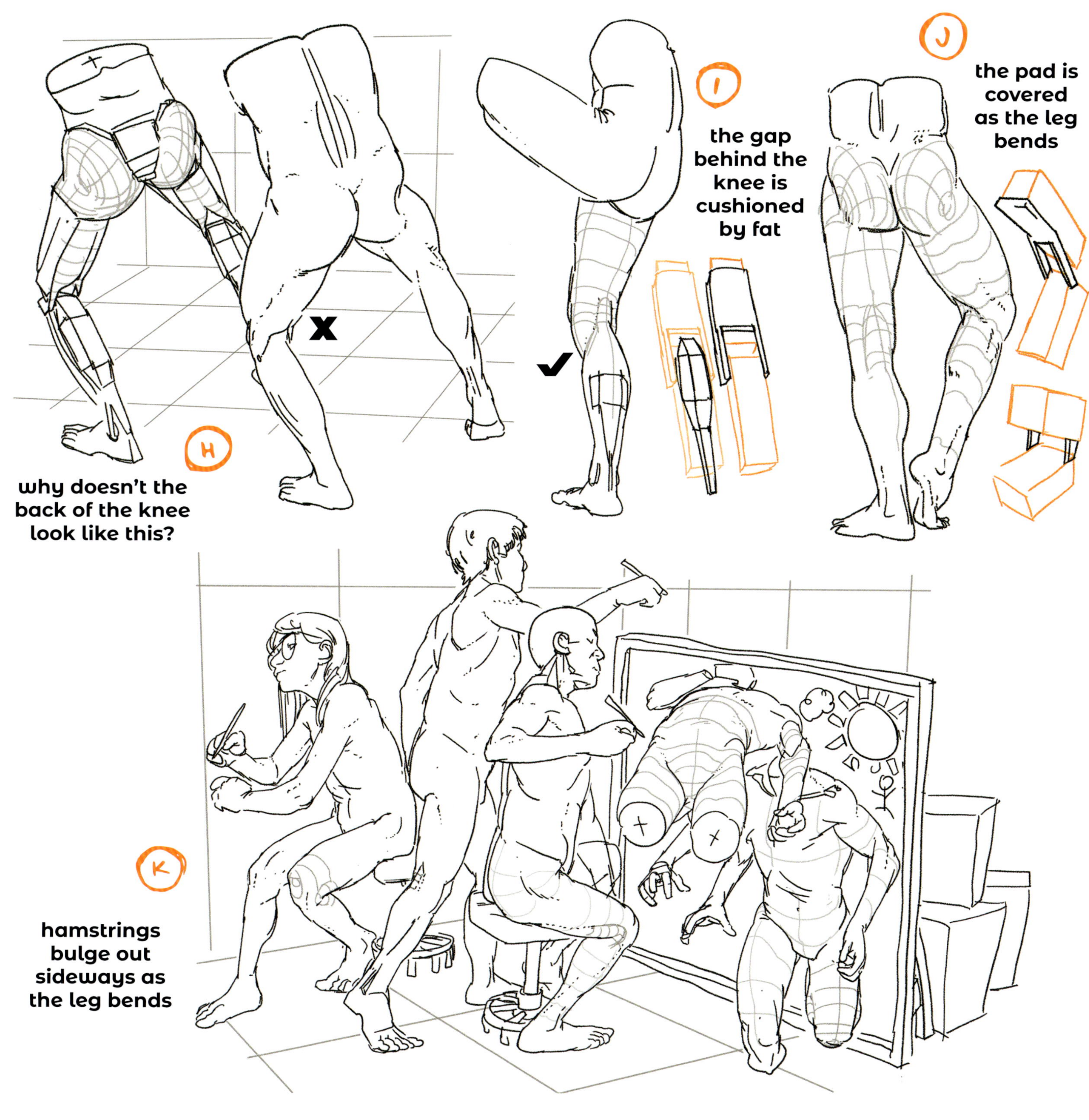

leg extensors

What are these almost parallel marks shown in A? These indicate where the soleus appears beneath the gastrocnemius, with the extensor muscles in front of them.

Just as the arm's extensors attach at the top of the outer bone (the radius), the leg's extensors attach at the top of the outer bone (the fibula). The mass of the extensors causes a bulge that projects forward of the tibia when viewed in profile (B).

But what do the leg's extensors actually do? There are three main things (C): eversion, dorsiflexion, and inversion of the foot. These mean twisting outward, bending back, and twisting inward, respectively.

Note the flow of the muscle from outside in, and how it crosses the front of the shin (D). Also note the exposed section of the tibia, which you can feel on your own legs (E).

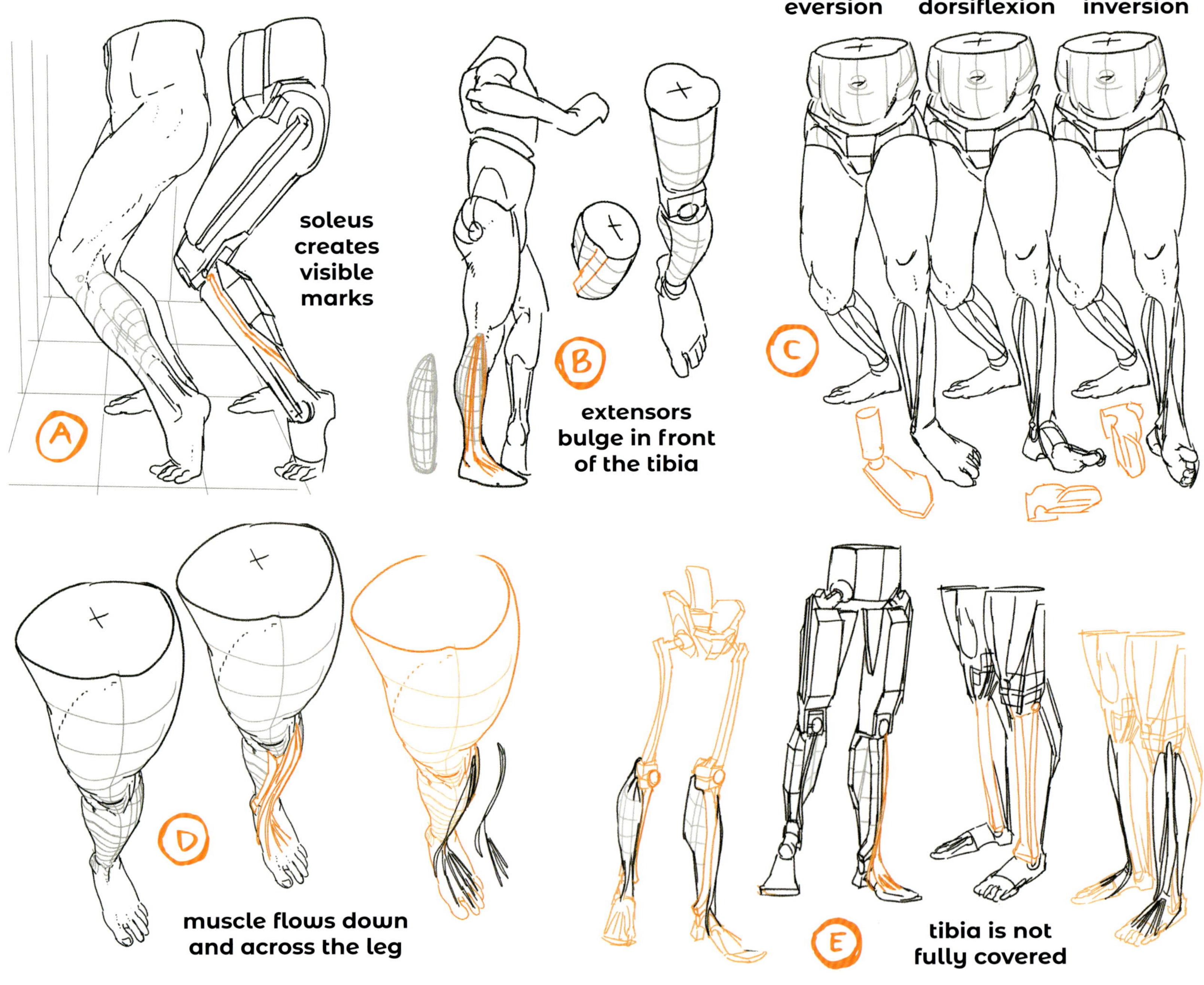

leg forms & landmarks

When viewed from below we can see the cross-sections of the lower leg more easily. The rounded aspect of the outer edges (lateral) is more obvious (A) and the concave shape of the inner side is evident (B). It's always worth exploring your mannequin's forms from angles other than eye-level (C)!

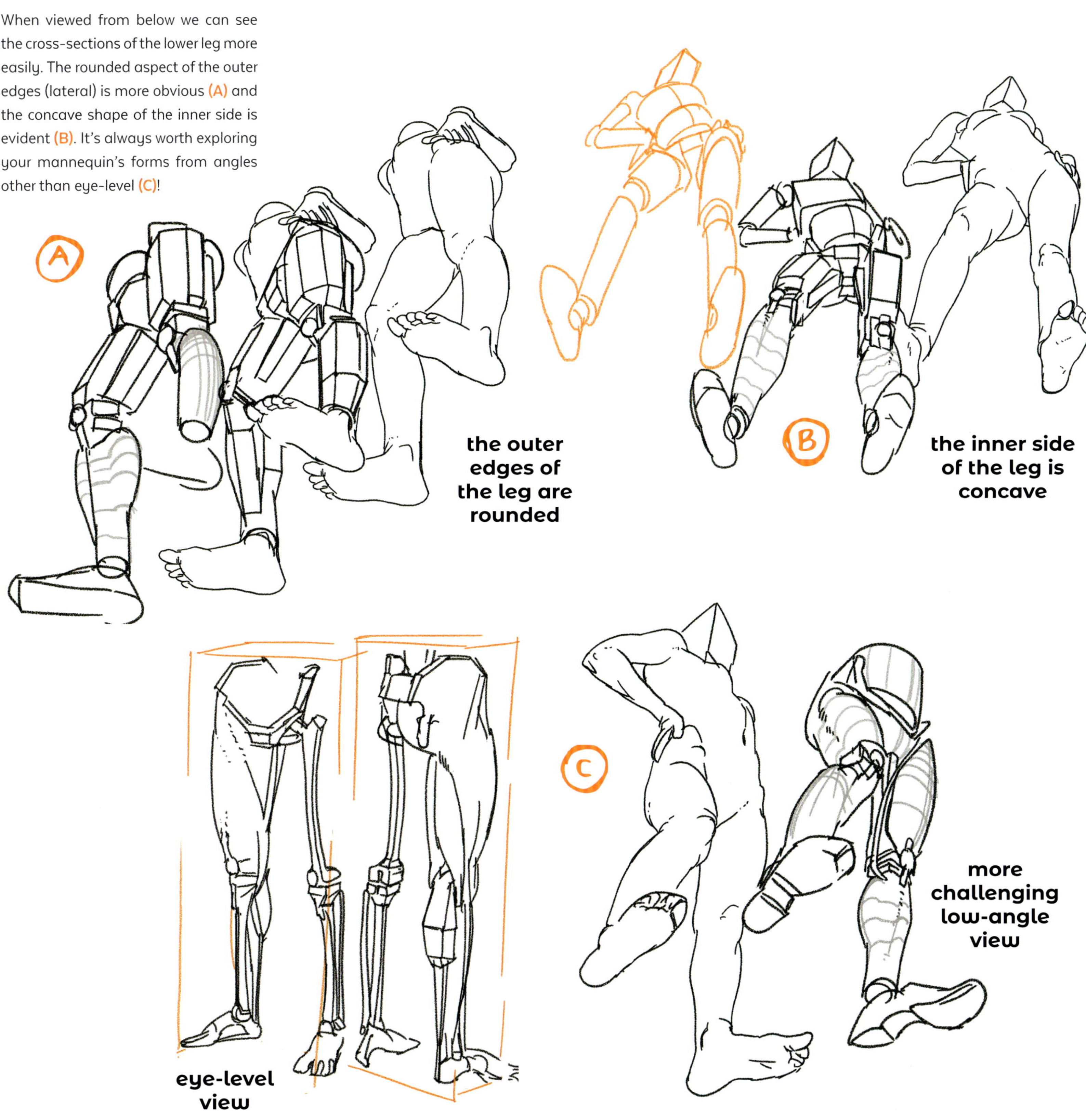

Always search for the obvious landmarks in your figure drawings (D). Some examples are the patella (1), tibial tuberosity (2), exposed inner edge of the tibia (3), the inner (medial) ankle (4), and frequently the top sections of the fibula (5).

The foot is attached to the lower leg by the equivalent of a cylinder (E). The end of the fibula is both farther back and lower than the end of the tibia.

As the lower leg tapers down, its cross-section becomes less like a tube and more like a cross (F). The outer sides of the cross represent the exposed bones of the ankle and the tendons of the extensors. The front side is the forward edges of the tibia and the rear is the Achilles tendon.

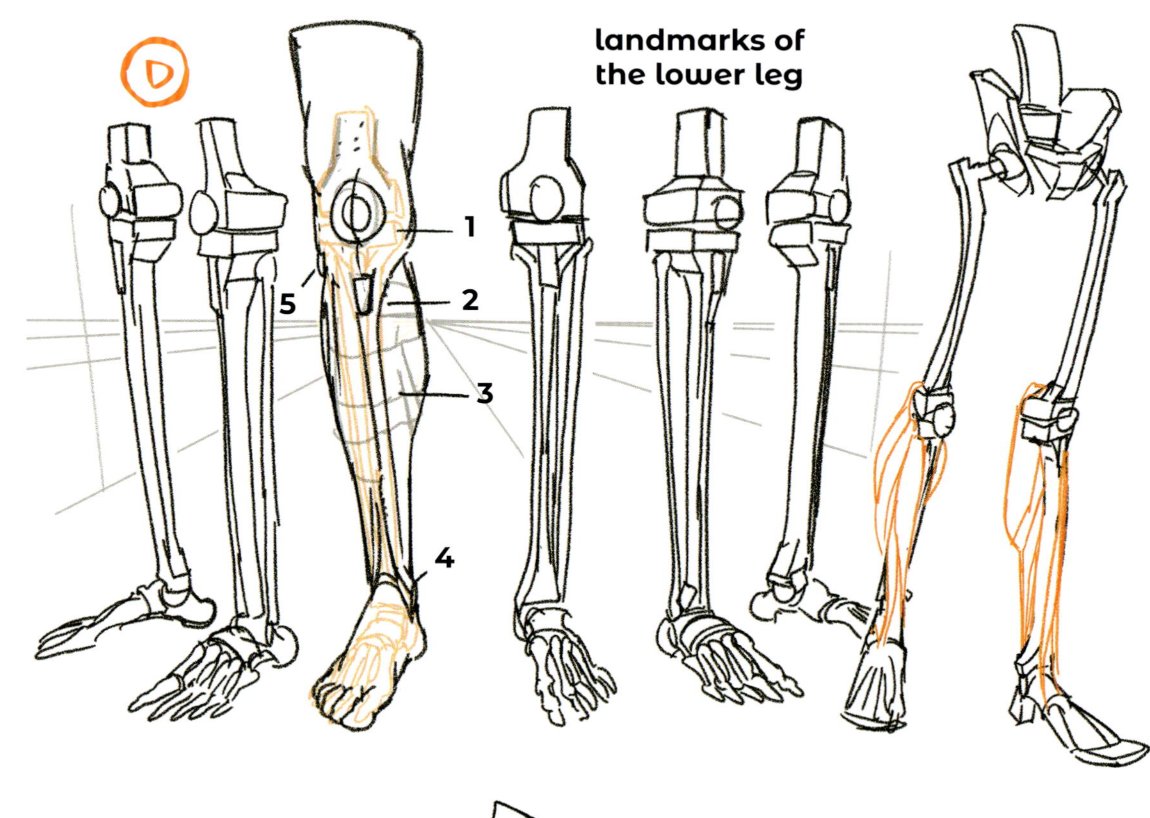

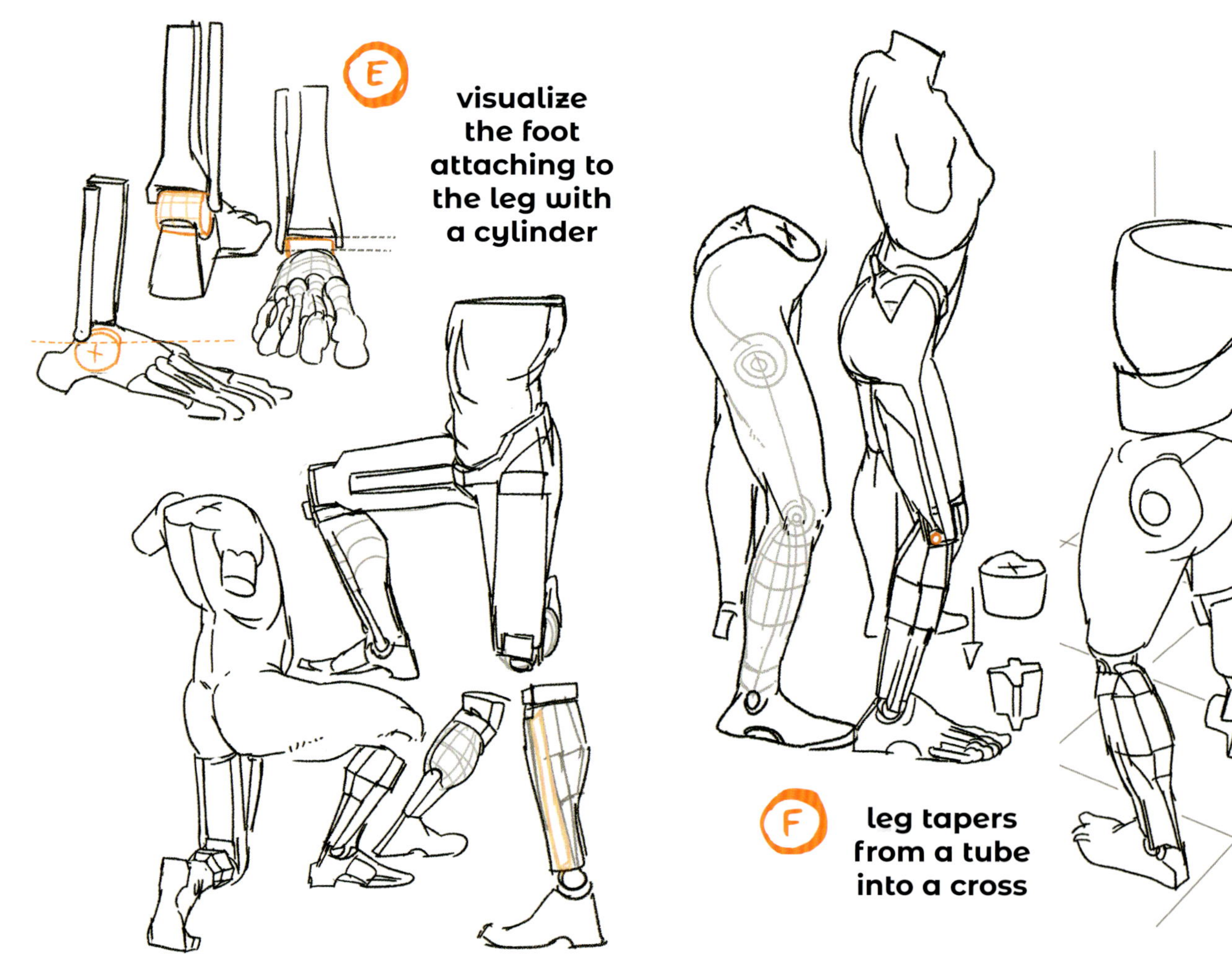

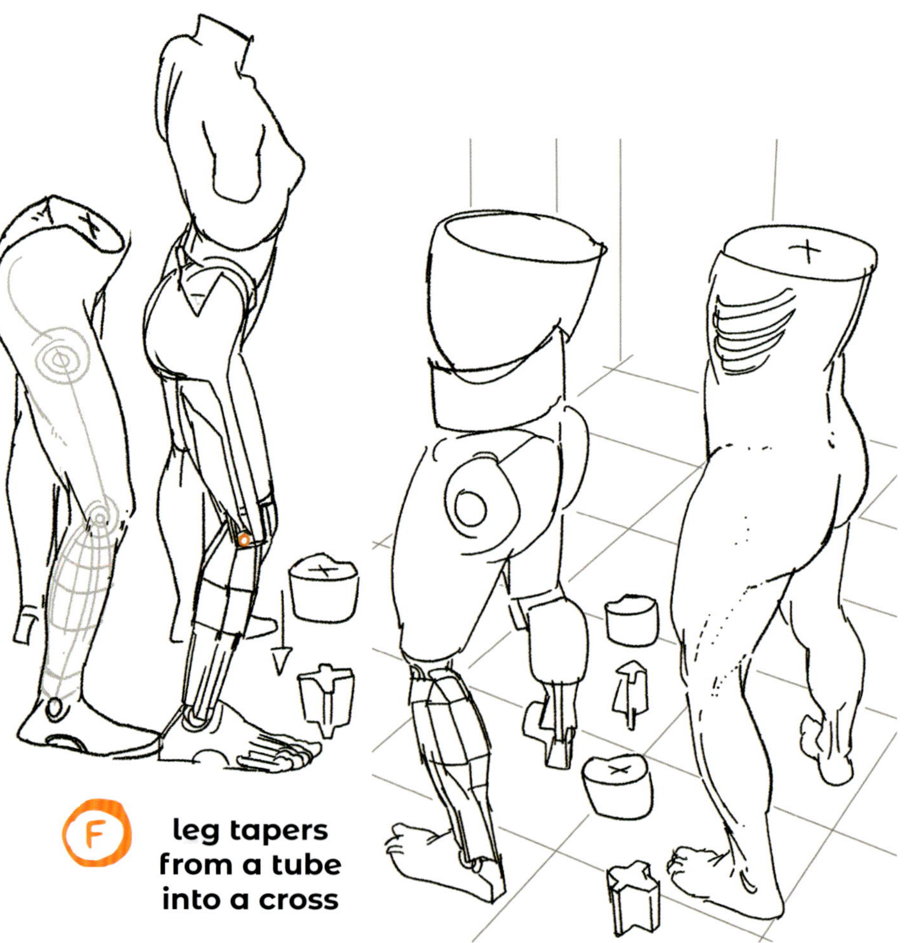

starting the foot

To draw the foot, start with a flat block that is attached to the lower leg with a sphere. Give it some height – the foot is usually taller than you think (A). Shift the whole block backward, so it doesn't hinge from the very rear (B). The ankle joint is a hinge, around which the foot pivots, and this hinge wouldn't work if there was nothing behind this point to act as an anchor.

The bottoms of the tibia and fibula aren't level. The tibia projects down on the inside, and the fibula attaches further down the ankle (C). The feet also naturally spread slightly outward from the center line of the body (D).

A

start with a flat block, then give it height

move the block to make a heel

B

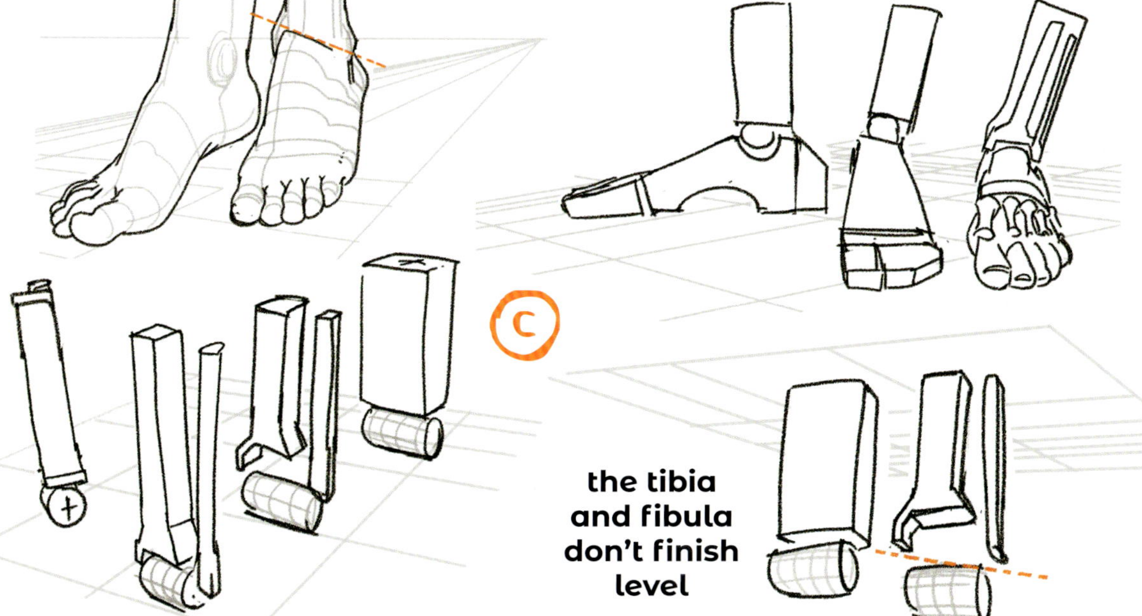

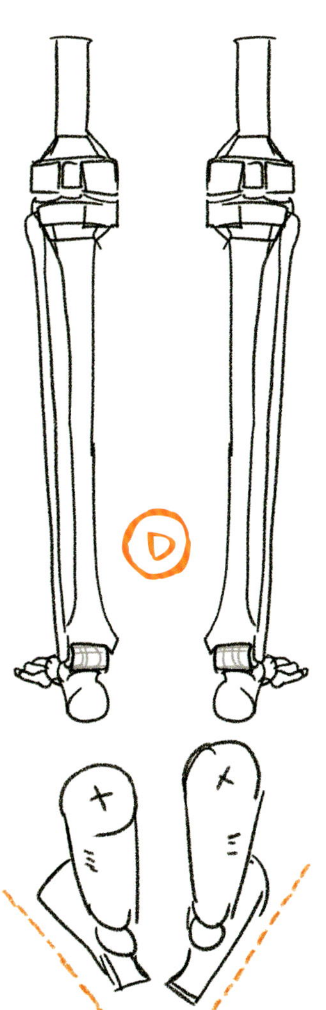

the feet angle slightly outward

Note the outside of the foot isn't straight, but curves delicately (E). The inner section of the ankle is higher than the outer (F). The highest "ridge" on the top of the foot doesn't run down the center, but is located between the big toe and the second toe (G). You can use two cylinders as the basis for each toe, but note that the big toe curls upward at the tip, while the other toes curl down even when raised (H). Be careful not to end your soles too abruptly – round off the edges rather than slicing them flat. The fat pads on the bottom of the foot are thick (I).

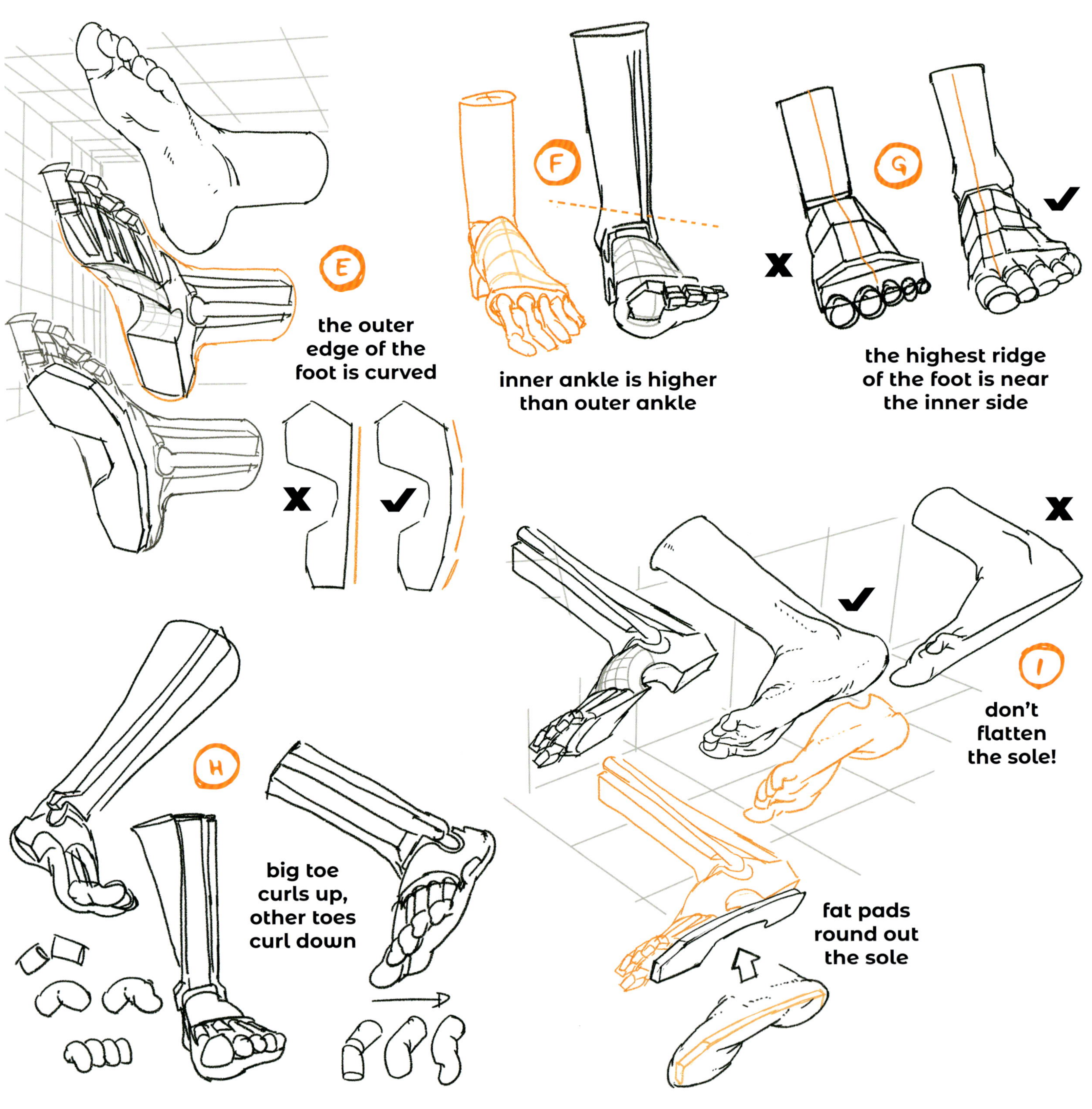

the toes

The toes themselves are wedge-shaped, not rectangular, and the big toe angles in toward the other toes, not running parallel with the foot (A). In fact, all the toes, like the fingers, are angled inward to a degree. They also overlap more as you progress toward the little toe, which is rolled almost completely under, providing the benefit of stability (B). The pad of the front of the foot has a depression in the center, to allow the foot to bend and fold along its length (C). Visualize each toe as two flattened forms, to capture its grasping nature (D).

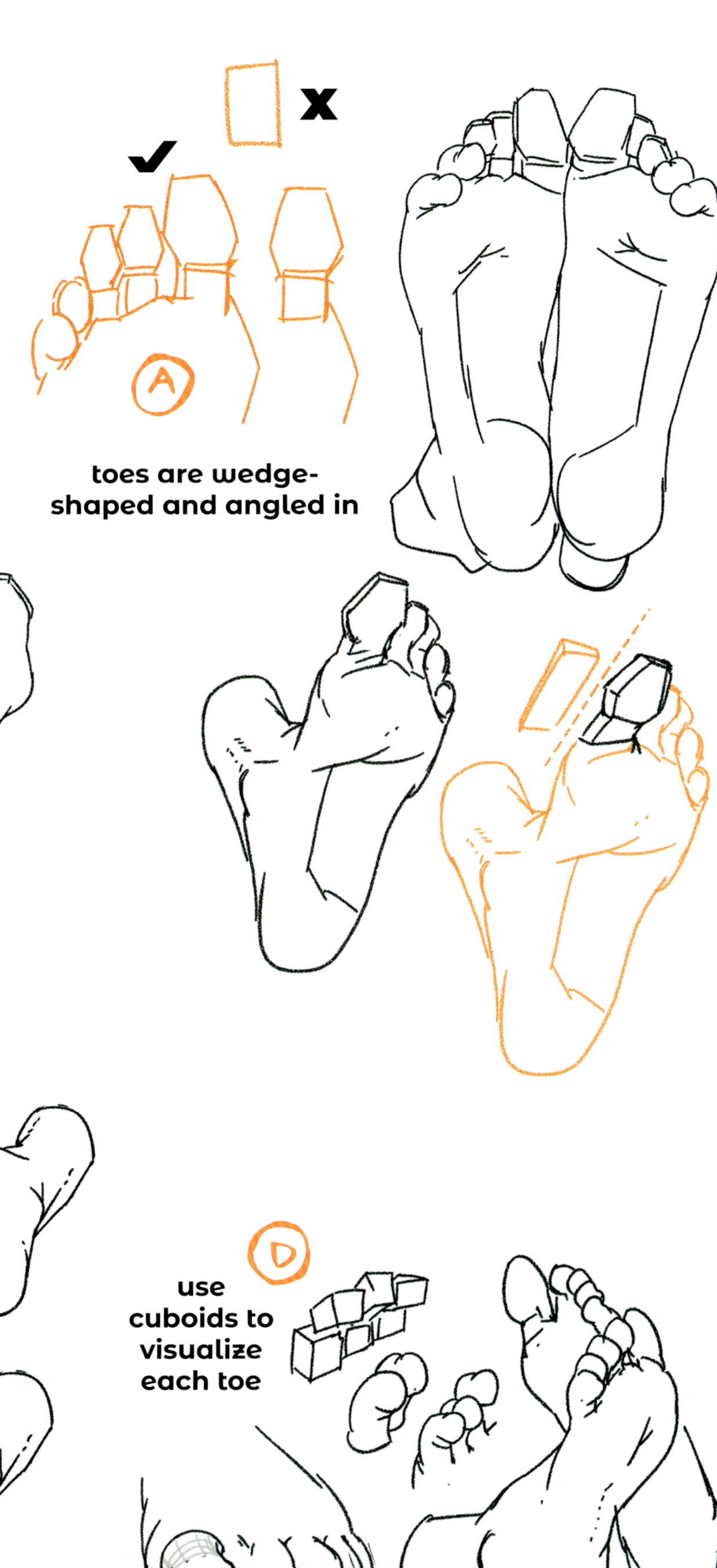

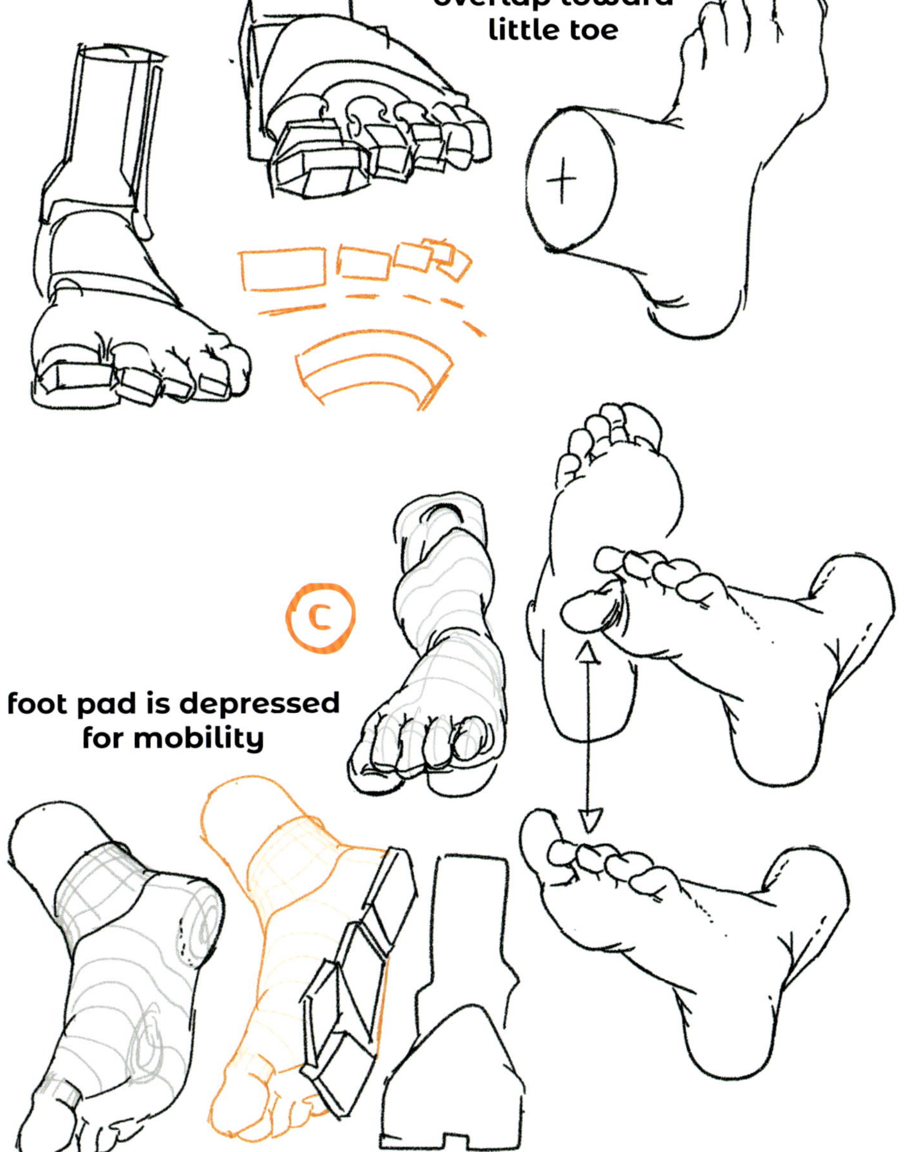

refining the foot

The arch of the foot is higher on the inside than on the outside. The outer edges of many people's feet are in full contact with the ground (A). The arch doesn't just run from front to back, but also from side to side (B). It needs to be strong enough to withstand the force of impact while running and jumping. The ankle region itself flares out, so that the leg transitions into the foot via a kind of wedge (C). The calcaneus (heel bone) is offset – it doesn't run centrally down the foot, but sits more toward the outside (D). The toes fan out and back, rather than being parallel (E).

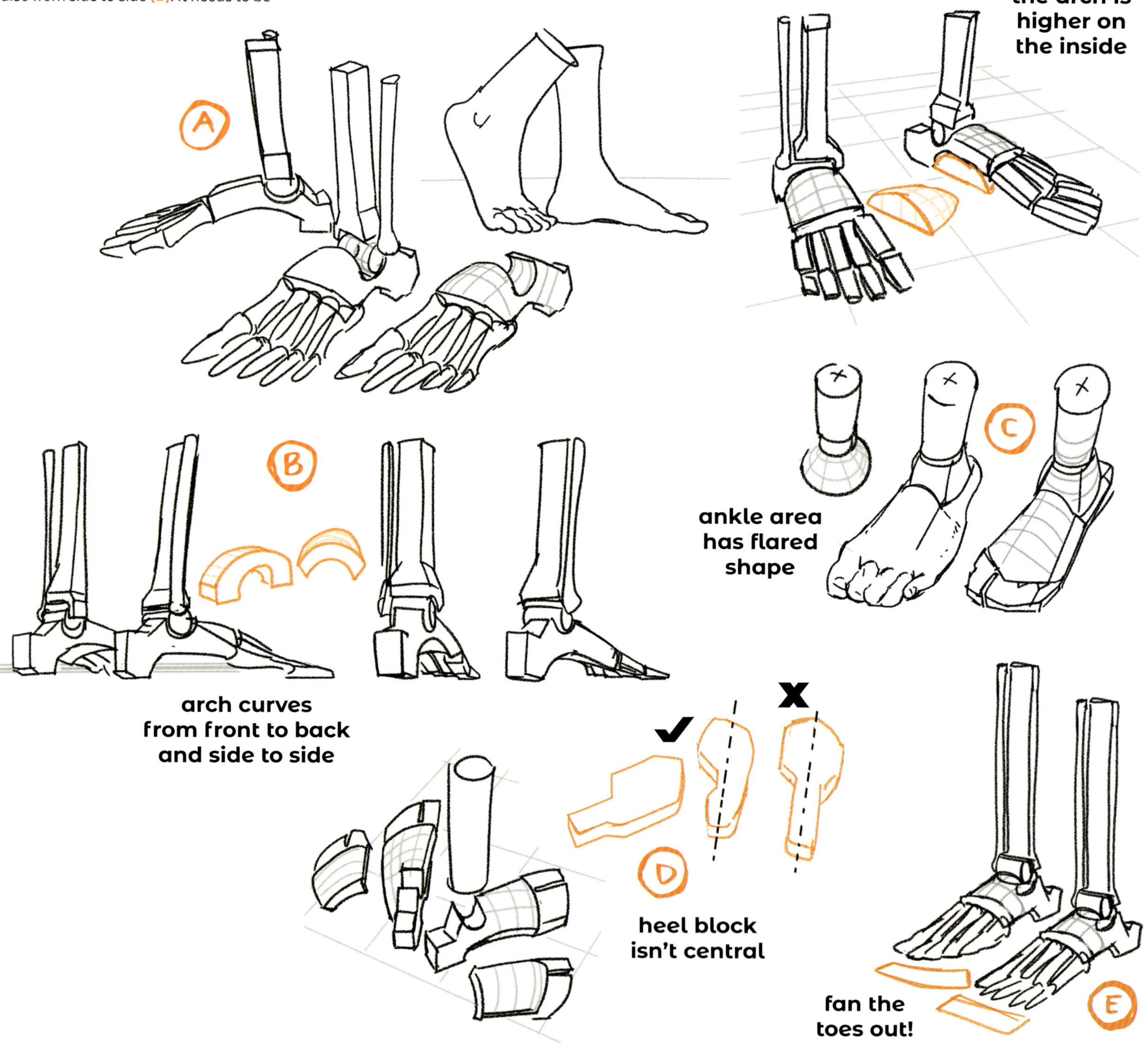

lower body summary

Let's summarize the lower body's various models and levels of detail. With the legs and core particularly, less is more – there won't be many internal lines. Your attention should mostly be focused on the silhouette.

We began with a box form for the pelvis, which developed into an underpants shape based on our observations of the pelvis form (A). We adapted this so that it tapered toward the rear (B), and finally added the two loops of the ischia to the underside (C).

The upper leg began as a cylinder (D), which became a cuboid with the added block form of the knee (E), and finally became an octagonal shape with an inner wedge for the adductors and an outer strip for the IT band (F).

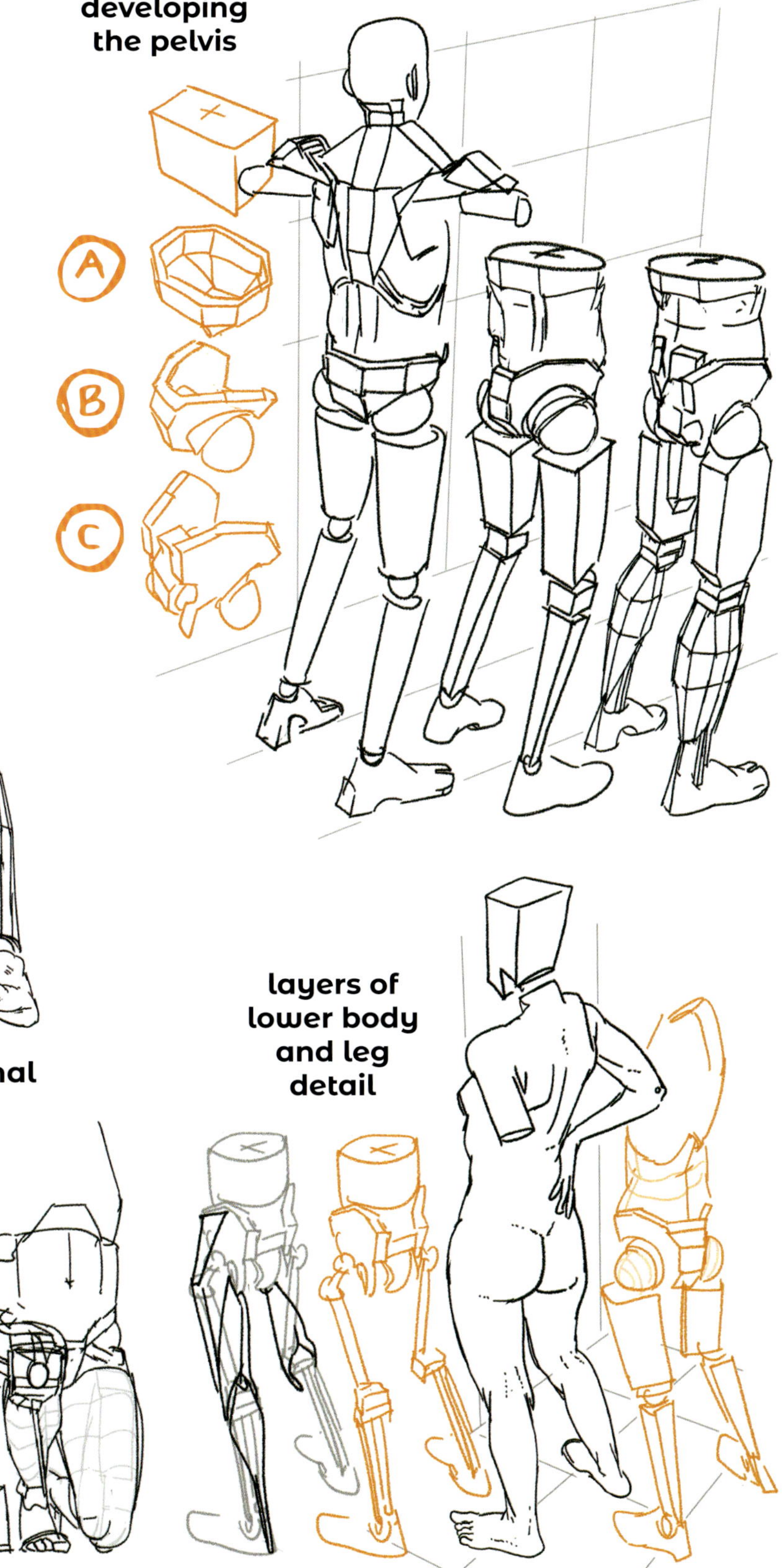

D
cylindrical

E
cuboid

F
octagonal

building up organic surface detail

Here are a few more examples of our mannequin with improved legs and waist. We developed the lower legs to a higher level of detail, but notice how their tapered shape was evident even when they were cylinders (G).

As with every section of this book, we mustn't lost sight of the fact that the goal is a figure drawing, not a mechanical model. The mannequin gives us a framework to build on, but the goal is to draw a figure, not a series of parts. The mannequin is simply a tool to enhance our figures by giving them a strong working foundation (H).

So, draw out your mannequin, and add any extra individual muscles you feel will help you outline the figure. After this, try to describe these forms as economically as possible, using the mannequin as an underdrawing.

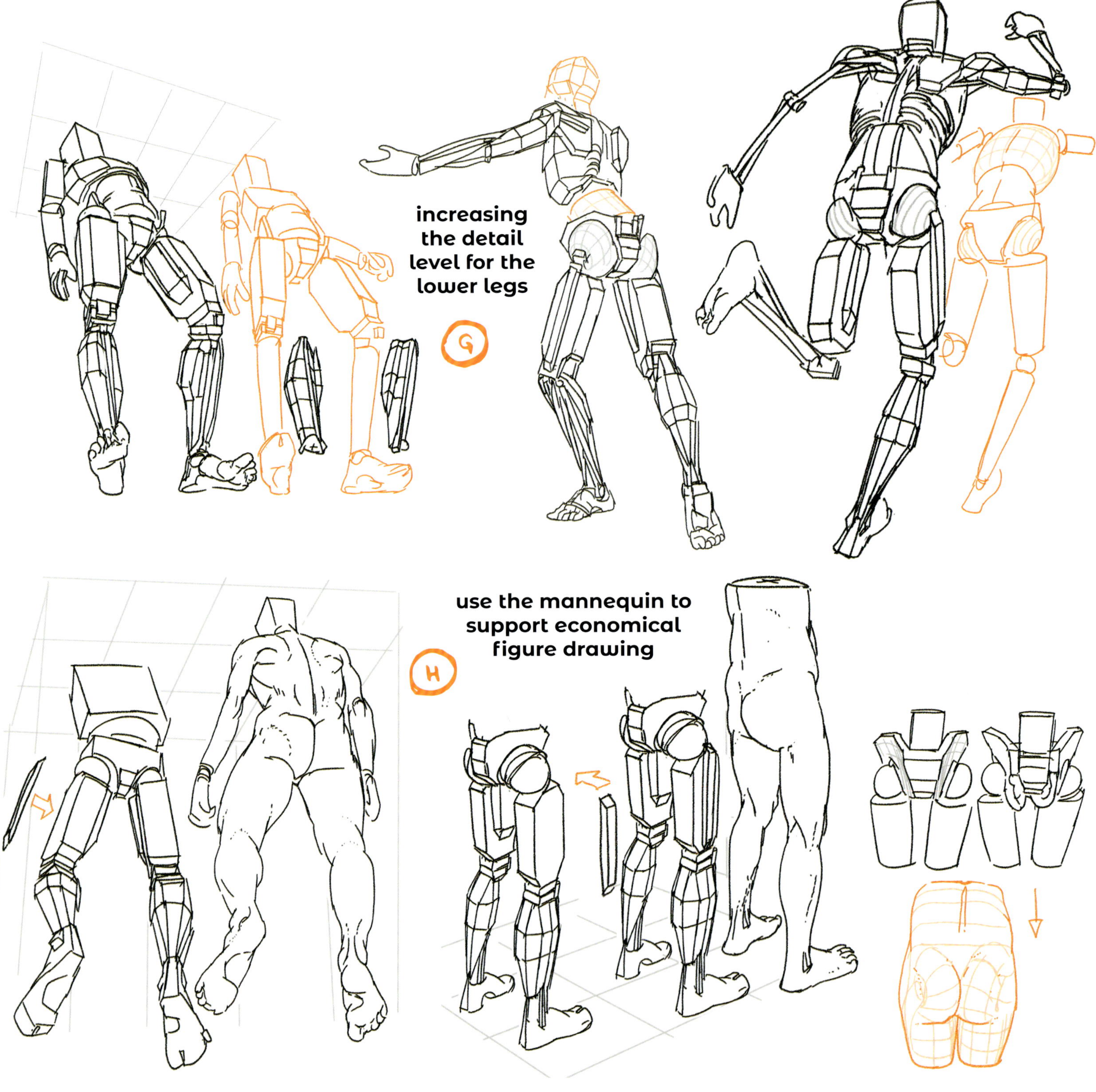

building up an example figure

Now let's see an overview of building up a whole figure. I begin with the box mannequin, then build up to the more advanced mannequin. On top of this, I draw the silhouette, including any muscles in the softer regions like the core and glutes. If I'm unsure about an area, I build up the level of detail to clarify the structure. Finally, I draw the smaller details and clarify any overlaps within the silhouette. Throughout, I keep in mind the subtle details that will elevate the figure, depending on the viewing angle, such as body fat and the thickness of the limbs if they are flexed or twisted.

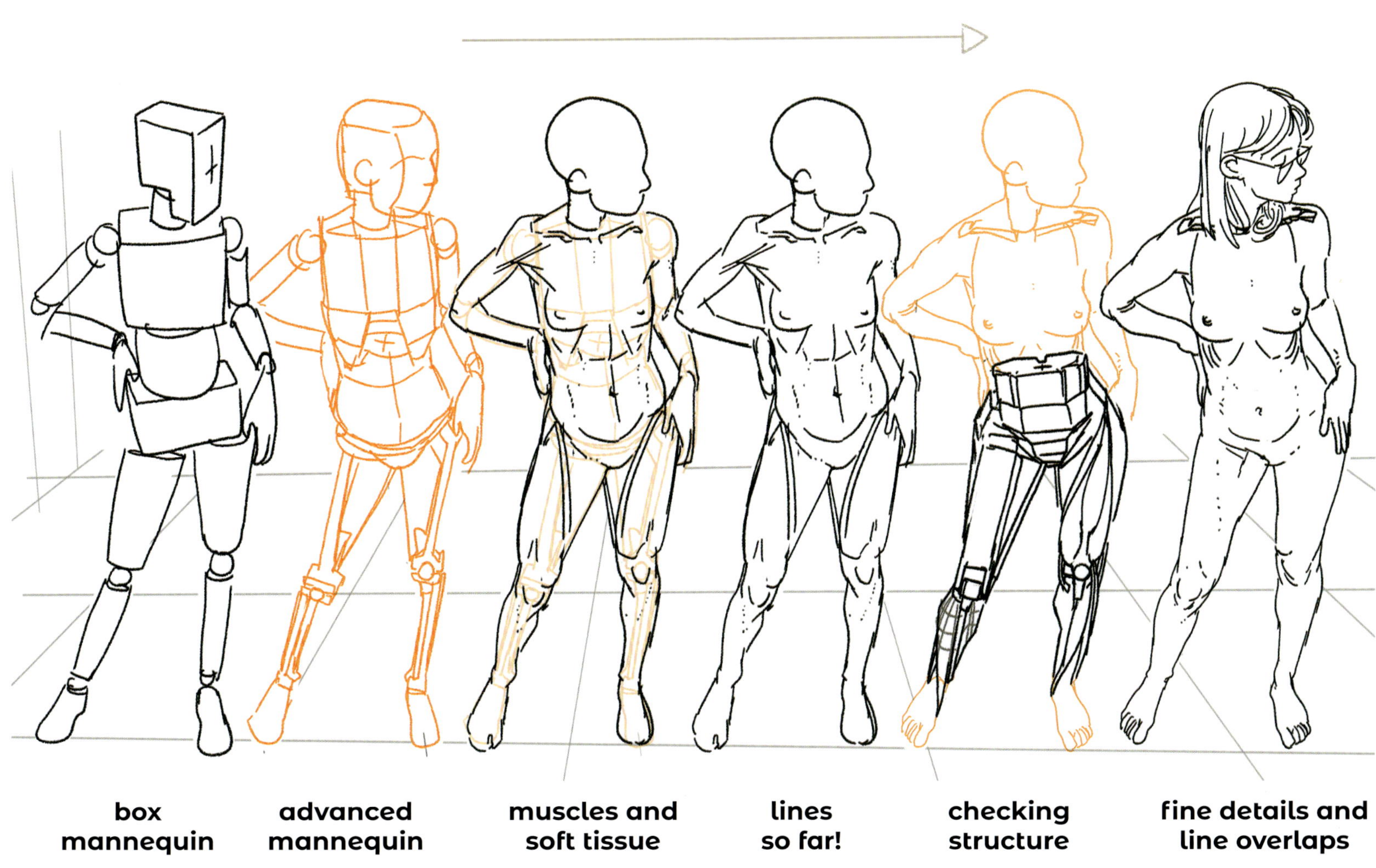

over to you...

Good drawing doesn't require complex methods. You just need to slow down and pay attention to the core skills. The techniques we've covered in this book are simple. However, it's important not to confuse "simple" with "easy." Remembering to practice them and ultimately make them intuitive will take work

As you draw, constantly remind yourself of the techniques we've covered:

- Simplification
- Think in X, Y, and Z
- Overlap lines and forms
- Less is more
- Dare to foreshorten
- Wedging
- Cross contours
- Level of detail

Ask yourself, "Am I looking up or down at this subject?" and "Is this level of detail appropriate for me?" Answers to questions like these are real-time feedback mechanisms. Most people seeing your drawings don't know your objectives or thought processes, and so can't provide much constructive feedback. Even if you have a great teacher, they won't always be around, so remember: The best learning resource is you, the artist. Any time, day or night, you'll be available to give yourself feedback. Learn to provide yourself with positive, helpful critiques.

Imagine being able to honestly reflect on the weaknesses in your work without being overly critical or believing the outcome is linked to your personal worth. If you achieve that, your artistic growth will have no limits.

Finally, remember to enjoy yourself. Anyone can learn critical thinking skills, but to analyze your work without judging yourself too harshly – that's the real challenge! Ultimately, people draw because of the way it makes them feel. Don't lose sight of that sense of playfulness and curiosity.

---

tom fox

instagram.com/tomfoxdraws

tomfoxdraws.com

tiktok.com/@tomfoxdraws

twitter.com/tomfoxdraws

youtube.com/c/tomfoxdraws

glossary

abduction
The action of moving a body part outward, away from the center line of the body.

abductor pollicis brevis
One of the muscles that abducts the thumb and forms its rounded base on the palm.

acetabulum
The round socket in the side of the pelvis, into which the ball of the femur inserts, forming a ball-and-socket joint.

achilles tendon
Also called the "calcaneal tendon." The tendon at the back of the lower leg, connecting the calf muscles to the heel bone and helping to move the foot.

acromion process
A horn-shaped piece of bone that extends from the spine of the scapula and helps connect the scapula to the clavicle.

adduction
The action of moving a body part inward, toward the center line of the body.

alar cartilage
The flexible cartilage forming the lower part of the nose, around the nostrils, consisting of various larger and smaller cartilage pieces.

anterior
Something that is in front of or nearer to the front of a body part.

anterior superior iliac spine
Also called the ASIS. The distinct bony point at the top of the iliac crest of the pelvis.

antihelix
A curved, raised form on the ear. It sits within the helix and often has a "Y" shape.

biceps
The large, two-headed muscle on the front of the upper arm, used for flexing and twisting the lower arm.

brachialis
A muscle that sits on the lower end of the upper arm, below the biceps, and is essential for flexing the lower arm.

brachioradialis
A muscle that sits on the forearm, near the elbow, and helps flex and twist the forearm.

calcaneus
The heel bone - the largest bone in the foot!

carpals
A cluster of small bones that attaches to the end of the lower arm, forming the basis of the hand.

clavicle
Also called the collarbone. A thin bone that sits at the front of the body, between the neck and shoulder, and is one of a pair.

coracoid process
A small, finger-shaped part of the scapula, which helps connect it to the shoulder area.

core
The middle area of the torso, roughly including the abdomen, mid-back, and lower back.

deltoid
A major muscle that wraps around the glenohumeral joint and gives the shoulder its distinctive round shape.

distal
Something that is farthest away from the center or origin of a body part. For example, the distal phalange is the phalange forming the very end of the finger.

dorsiflexion
The action of flexing or bending a body part to point upward - typically referring to the foot.

ear canal
The tubelike inner part of the ear, leading down into the skull.

earlobe
The soft lower part of the outer ear. On some people, it hangs down in a curve, while on others it attaches directly to the side of the head.

epicondyle
A bony projection that can be found on various parts of the body, but in this book is usually referring to the epicondyles of the humerus.

eversion
The action of turning something to face outward, such as turning a foot sideways to face out.

extension
The action of straightening out a limb or body part, as opposed to bending (flexing) it.

extensor
A muscle that helps straighten a limb or body part, such as the extensor digitorum (which extends the finger) or the extensor pollicis brevis and extensor pollicis longus (which extend the lower arm).

femur
The thigh bone - the largest bone in the body!

fibula
The thinner, outer bone of the two lower leg bones.

flexion
The action of bending a limb, as opposed to straightening it (extension).

flexor
A muscle that flexes (bends) a limb or body part.

frontal bone
The large, curved skull bone that forms the forehead, brow ridges, and upper parts of the eye sockets.

gastrocnemius
The large two-headed muscle on the back of the lower leg, forming the distinctive shape of the calf.

glenohumeral joint
The ball-and-socket joint of the shoulder, formed by the humerus fitting into a socket in the scapula.

gluteal muscles
Often nicknamed the "glutes." A group of three muscles (the gluteus minimus, medius, and maximus) that forms the buttock.

hamstring
One of the three muscles at the back of the thigh, running from the ischium down to the knee area.

helix
The firm ridge forming a rim around the top and outer edge of the ear.

humerus
The upper arm bone.

hyoid bone
A small, horseshoe-shaped bone that floats below the lower jaw and gathers the neck muscles together.

iliac crest
The bony ridge running along the top of the ilium (the wing of the pelvis).

iliacus
A flat muscle that covers the inside face of the ilium.

iliotibial tract
Also called the iliotibial band or "IT band." A long, thick band of tissue that runs down the outside of the thigh and supports the knee.

ilium
One of the large, curved hip bones that create the distinctive wings of the pelvis.

inguinal ligament
A groin ligament that runs from the ASIS to the pubis, helping protect the tissues in the lower abdomen.

inversion
The action of turning something to face inward (for example, turning the feet so their soles face inward).

ischium
Sometimes nicknamed the "sit bone." One of the two curved bones (ischia) on the underside of the pelvis. The ischium connects to the pubis to form a loop shape.

lateral
Something that's situated on, near, or toward the side of something else.

latissimus dorsi
Often nicknamed the "lats." A large, flat muscle that attaches to the inner humerus and runs down the back to the pelvis.

levator scapulae
A muscle at the back of the neck that raises the scapulae.

ligament
A band of strong tissue that connects a bone to another bone (similar to a tendon, which connects muscle to bone).

lumbar
Relating to the lower back area, such as the lumbar vertebrae of the spine.

mandible
The lower jaw bone, containing the lower teeth and giving form to the chin and jawline.

masseter
A thick muscle on the side of the mandible, assisting in closing the jaw.

maxilla
A skull bone comprising the upper jaw and most of the mid-face area, including some nasal bones, parts of the lower cheeks, and the upper teeth.

medial
Something that's situated in or near the middle of the body or body part.

metacarpal
One of the five thin bones attached to the carpals, forming the bases of the thumb and fingers within the palm area of the hand.

nasal bone
A bone that forms the bridge of the nose, providing a base for the nasal cartilage.

oblique
One of the muscles on the side and front of the abdomen, such as the external oblique and internal oblique muscles.

occipital bone
The scoop-shaped bone that forms the bottom rear of the skull, with a hole in it for the spine to pass through.

occipitofrontalis
A wide, flat muscle that covers the top of the skull, moving the eyebrows and forehead.

olecranon
The prominent end of the ulna that forms the bony point of the elbow.

patella
Also called the kneecap. A small, rounded bone that sits in front of the knee joint.

phalange
The individual bones forming the segments of the fingers and thumbs, with three phalanges per finger and two per thumb.

pronation
The action of rotating a body part outward, away from the center of the body (for example, turning the hand palm down).

psoas
A deep muscle connecting the lower spine to the femur, helping the body to bend and the leg to lift.

pubis
Also called the pubic bone. One of the pair of bones that forms the very front of the pelvis.

quadratus lumborum
Often called the QL. A deep muscle that connects the lower spine to the ilium, helping the body to bend sideways.

quadriceps femoris
Often nicknamed the "quads." A muscle group of the upper leg, including the vastus medialis, vastus intermedius, vastus lateralis, and rectus femoris.

radius
The shorter of the two bones forming the lower arm, widening toward the hand.

rectus abdominis
Often nicknamed the "abs." A long, flat paired muscle that runs down the front of the abdomen and helps flex the body.

rhomboid
A muscle connected to the scapula in the upper back, where it helps move the shoulder and arm.

sacrum
The large, strong, triangular bone at the base of the spine, forming the back of the pelvis.

sartorius
The long, narrow muscle that runs down the upper leg, from the top of the thigh to the tibia.

scapula
Also called the shoulder blade. A large, wing-shaped bone that sits on the upper back and is one of a pair.

serratus anterior
A muscle that connects the ribs to the scapula in a distinctive series of triangular forms.

soleus
A strong muscle on the back of the lower leg, helping to flex the foot.

spine of the scapula
The prominent bony ridge found on the scapula.

sternocleidomastoid
The thick, diagonal muscle that runs down either side of the neck.

sternum
Also called the breastbone. A long bone at the front of the rib cage, connecting the ribs together in the middle of the chest.

supination
The action of rotating a body part up and in toward the center of the body (e.g. turning the hand palm up).

temporalis
A large, flat muscle on the side of the head, which helps move the mandible.

tendon
A strong band of tissue that connects a muscle to a bone.

tensor fasciae latae
Often called the TFL. A long, thin muscle running down the outside of the thigh, helping to extend the knee.

tibia
Also called the shin bone. The larger of the two lower leg bones, running from the knee to the ankle.

tibial tuberosity
A bony landmark near the top of the tibia, creating a noticeable bump below the kneecap.

tragus
A small, firm cartilaginous form at the front of the ear, joining to the side of the head.

transversus abdominis
Often called the TA. A wide sheet of muscle that wraps around each side of the abdomen, supporting the spine and pelvis.

trapezius
A large, triangular muscle at the top of the back, between the scapulae and running up the back of the neck, where it helps move the head and shoulders.

triceps
The three-headed muscle on the back of the upper arm, where it helps with extension.

trochanter
A rough, bony lump on the femur, to which muscles can attach. The femur has a greater trochanter on the outer side and a lesser trochanter on the inner side.

ulna
The longer of the two bones forming the lower arm, widening toward the elbow.

vertebra
One of the bone segments that forms the spine and surrounds the spinal cord.

zygomatic bone
A facial bone comprising the upper cheek and lower part of the eye socket.

index

A

B

C

D

E

F

G

H

I

J

K

L

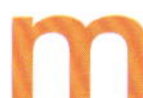

O

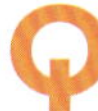

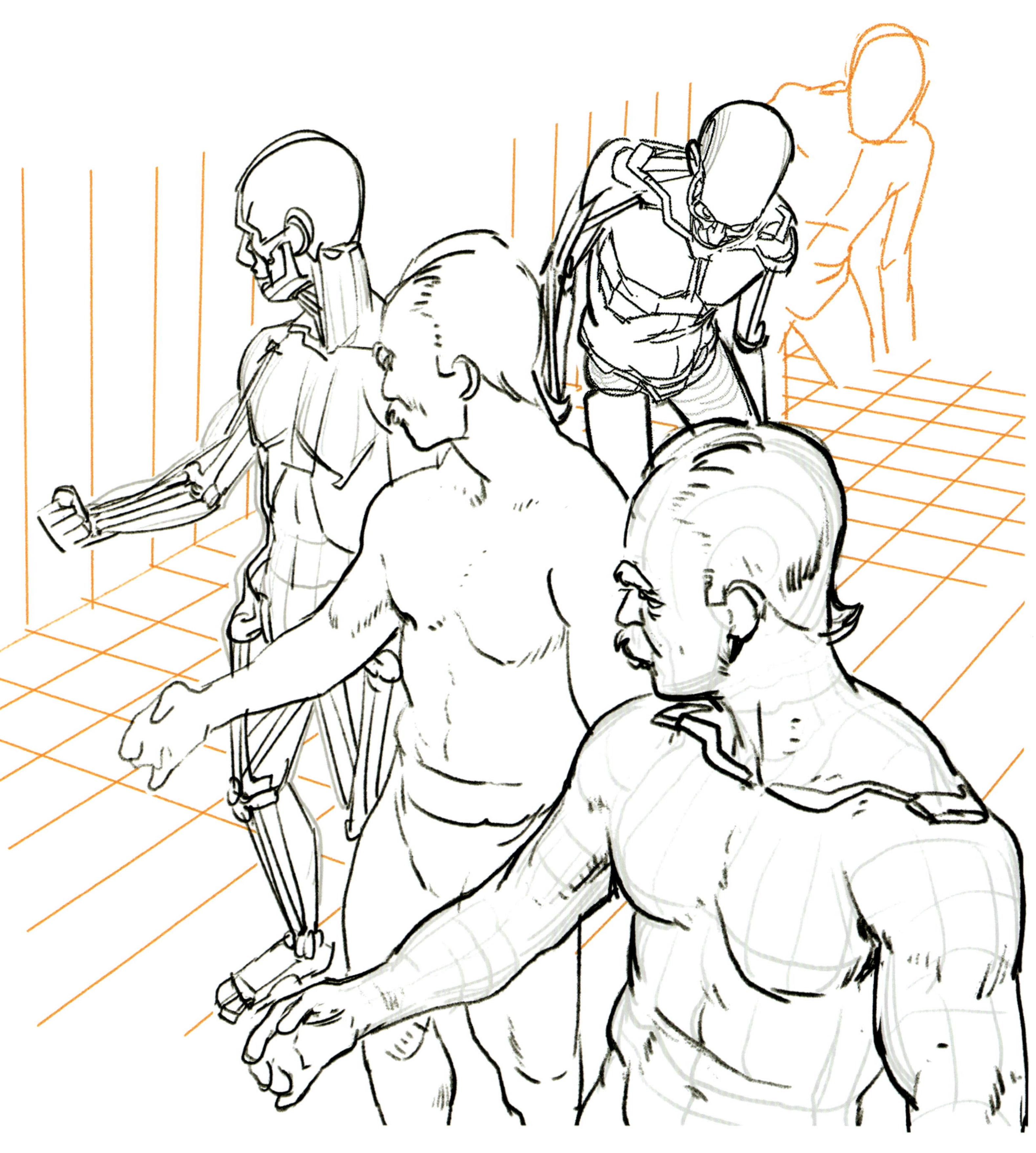

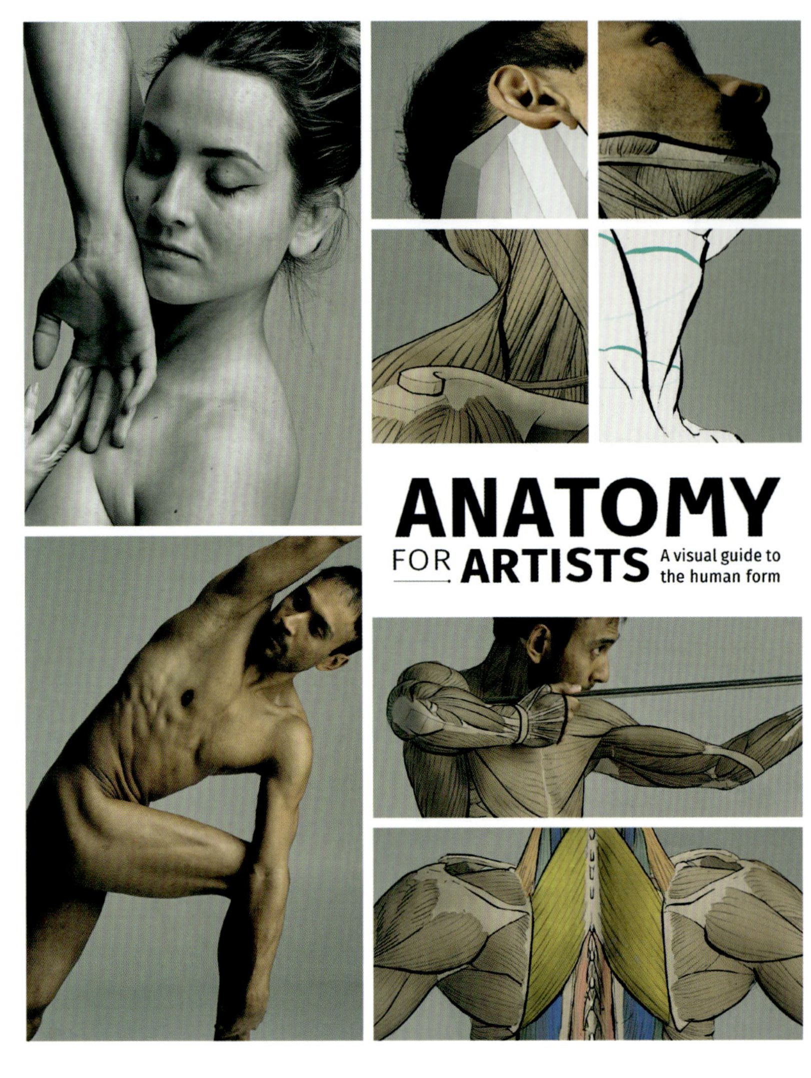

Anatomy for Artists presents an extensive visual reference guide to the human form for artists of all abilities and mediums. Over 240 specially commissioned photographs capture every detail, from muscle definition and bony landmarks to a valuable catalogue of postures and poses. Every photograph is overlaid with musculature, planar, and contour diagrams drawn by figurative fine artist and illustrator Charlie Pickard to deepen your comprehension. The illuminating introduction by expert and teacher Jahirul Amin results in a thorough understanding of the subject and how it relates to your work. Detailed diagrams reveal the inner workings of the joints and muscles, and how their shape and movement affect what you see on the surface, and ultimately in your art.

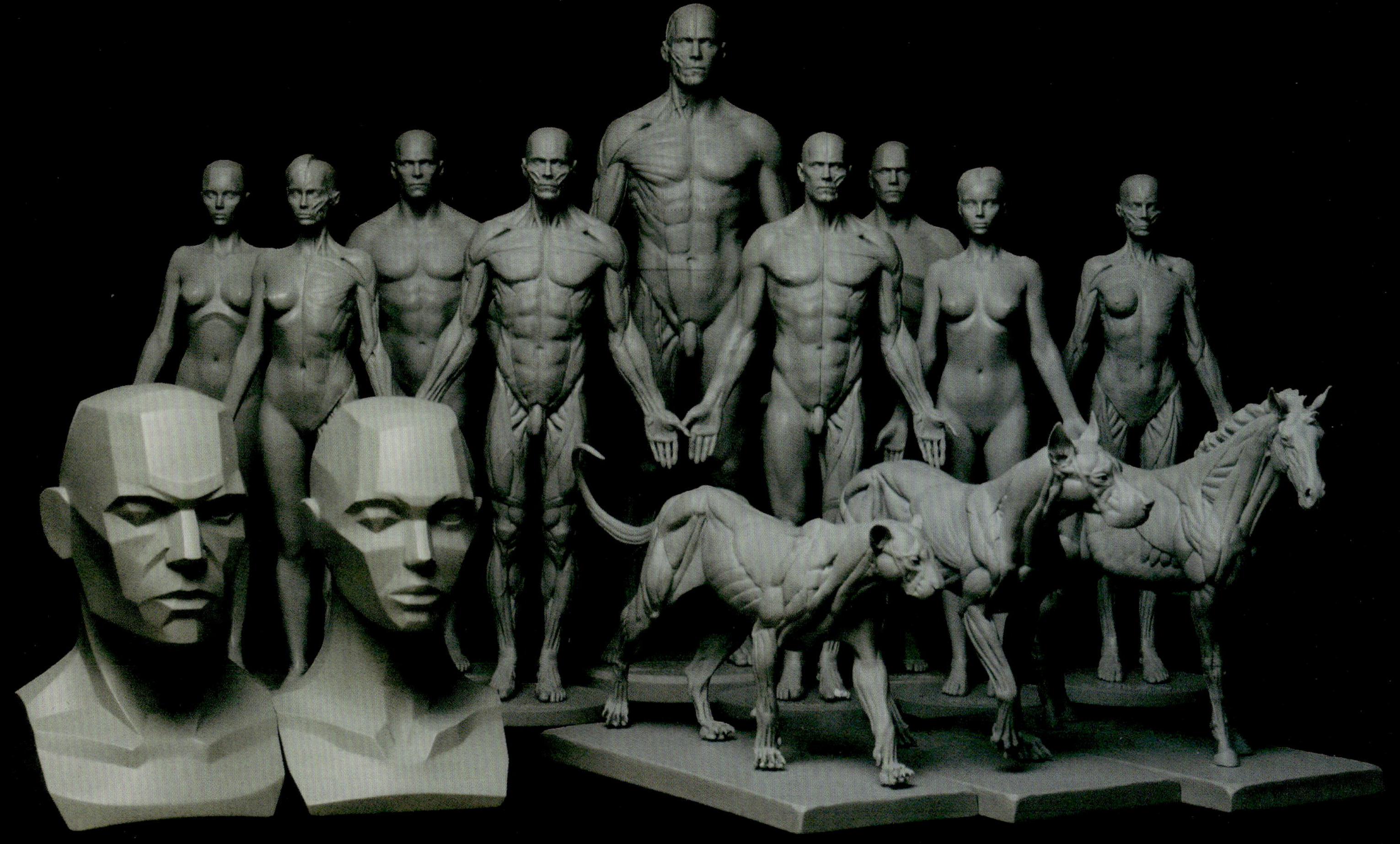

3dtotalPublishing

3dtotal Publishing is a trailblazing, creative publisher specializing in inspirational and educational resources for artists.

Our titles feature top industry professionals from around the globe who share their experience in skillfully written step-by-step tutorials and fascinating, detailed guides. Illustrated throughout with stunning artwork, these best-selling publications offer creative insight, expert advice, and essential motivation. Fans of digital art will enjoy our comprehensive volumes covering Adobe Photoshop, Procreate, and Blender, as well as our superb titles based around character design, including *Fundamentals of Character Design* and *Creating Characters for the Entertainment Industry*. The dedicated, high-quality blend of instruction and inspiration also extends to traditional art. Titles covering a range of techniques, genres, and abilities allow your creativity to flourish while building essential skills.

Well-established within the industry, we now offer over 100 titles and counting, many of which have been translated into multiple languages around the world. With something for every artist, we are proud to say that our books offer the 3dtotal package:

LEARN • CREATE • SHARE

Visit us at 3dtotalpublishing.com

3dtotal Publishing is part of 3dtotal.com, a leading website for CG artists founded by Tom Greenway in 1999.